WEAPONS & WARFARE
OF THE 20TH CENTURY

A COMPREHENSIVE AND HISTORICAL SURVEY OF MODERN MILITARY METHODS AND MACHINES

WEAPONS
&
WARFARE
OF THE 20TH
CENTURY

**Eric Morris • Christopher Chant
Curt Johnson • H. P. Willmott**

derbibooks

cop. a

CONT

ENTS

This edition first published in 1976 in the
United States of America by
Derbibooks and distributed by
Book Sales Inc., 110 Enterprise Avenue, Secaucus, N.J. 07094
© 1975 Octopus Books Limited
ISBN 0 7064 0534 X
Produced by Mandarin Publishers Limited,
22A Westlands Road, Quarry Bay,
Hong Kong
Printed in Hong Kong

INTRODUCTION

The purpose in compiling this book has been to review every major weapon system to have served in the 'modern' or post-industrial period that, broadly, can be said to have begun soon after the demise of Napoleon in 1815. Each main part of the book deals with a significant period – pre-1914, the two world wars, the period between them and the nuclear age since 1945. Within that pattern the principal parts are subdivided into chapters dealing with events relating to one particular arm, usually in the sequence of infantry, artillery, tanks, warships and aircraft. Four authors, each with a special interest in particular aspects of modern warfare, have contributed chapters, thereby helping to build what amounts to a total history of warfare since the Industrial Revolution.

In every period, whatever the political climate or the current state of the technological race, the ordinary foot soldier inevitably occupies a place at the heart of strategic planning. For despite man's perverse and ill-directed genius at producing weapons that kill with ever-greater efficiency, no such weapon can – in the political sense – win a war on its own. In the last analysis it is the unglamorous, often unsung infanteer who must take or hold territory in a manner that no computerized weapon system can rival.

At one time land warfare was controlled by a famous triumvirate – horse, foot and guns. We have briefly looked at the role of the infantry – the 'poor foot' of numberless campaigns. Of the other two arms, the gunner's art was always the more scientifically demanding, calling for a brand of professionalism not generally found in the more debonair outlook of cavalrymen. By the second half of the 19th century, moreover, the horse was beginning to lose its usefulness. As Curt Johnson explains in the chapters focusing on artillery, guns were now in the main too deadly to be stifled by a boot-to-boot cavalry charge. Then the internal combustion engine arrived, and the horse faded still further from view. In 1916 came the tank, and with it a new battlefield equation was set before the generals.

In its short, tempestuous history the tank has found its most potent foe in the artillery piece. Many pundits would argue that it has been a great error to see the tank, as many have done, as the modern extension of horse cavalry rather than as it was originally envisaged, namely as a mobile artillery weapon in a siege environment. Perhaps of all the weapon systems discussed in this book the tank is the most emotive. Its image and shape are menacing, suggesting irresistible powers. From the first it was used as a terror weapon, and today we find that this aspect has assumed a new political relevance, for, irrespective of the might and weight of its nuclear arsenal, a nation's aggressive intent seems now to be measured in direct proportion to the number and quality of its tank divisions.

The combination of the tank and the gun, allied to aircraft, produced in the opening phase of World War II the fearsome realities of Blitzkrieg. If only for a short while, offensive warfare was demonstrated in its ultimate form to that date. In the chapters surrounding this astonishing period Christopher Chant has traced with great skill the growth of military aircraft from the primitive biplanes that shuttled up and down the Western Front, their pilots conforming to their own strange code of chivalry, through to the supersonic combat machines of present times.

The history of war at sea is full of contrasts. H. P. Willmott's account shows how the concept of sea power evolved during the 19th and early 20th centuries to become an indispensable part of large-scale conflicts. In its most concrete form this perhaps reached a peak in World War II when the USA and Britain, though fiercely opposed, succeeded in transporting the necessary men and matériel across the oceans to wage mass war thousands of miles from their metropolitan territories. Their success was crucial to the outcome of the war. By contrast, in the present age we are witnessing a new exercise in the political use of sea power as the Russians seek, by extending their naval presence across the oceans of the world, to exert greater influence over the nations they patrol in this way.

All the weapon systems so far mentioned now face additional challenges from the missile. For almost twenty years the missile's supporters have been proclaiming the end of the gun – even though each successive conflict seems to illustrate the gun's advantages over the missile rather than the reverse. Yet whatever shape the weapons of the future may take, the nature of the human element in war is unlikely to show radical change. In particular, the infantryman's appetite for survival seems undiminished, as does the need of governments for an uninterrupted flow of men – to be deployed variously against conventional forces and guerrilla units and to assist the civil powers, providing a human buffer between state policies and dissident civilians.

In this story of weapons and warfare, a story otherwise dominated by astonishing technological achievements, we have therefore been concerned to emphasize the role of the foot soldier, now better protected than he used to be, and capable on occasion of neutralizing an opponent's armour and air support – but still, as ever, depending for survival on his wits and efficiency as a human being.

ERIC MORRIS

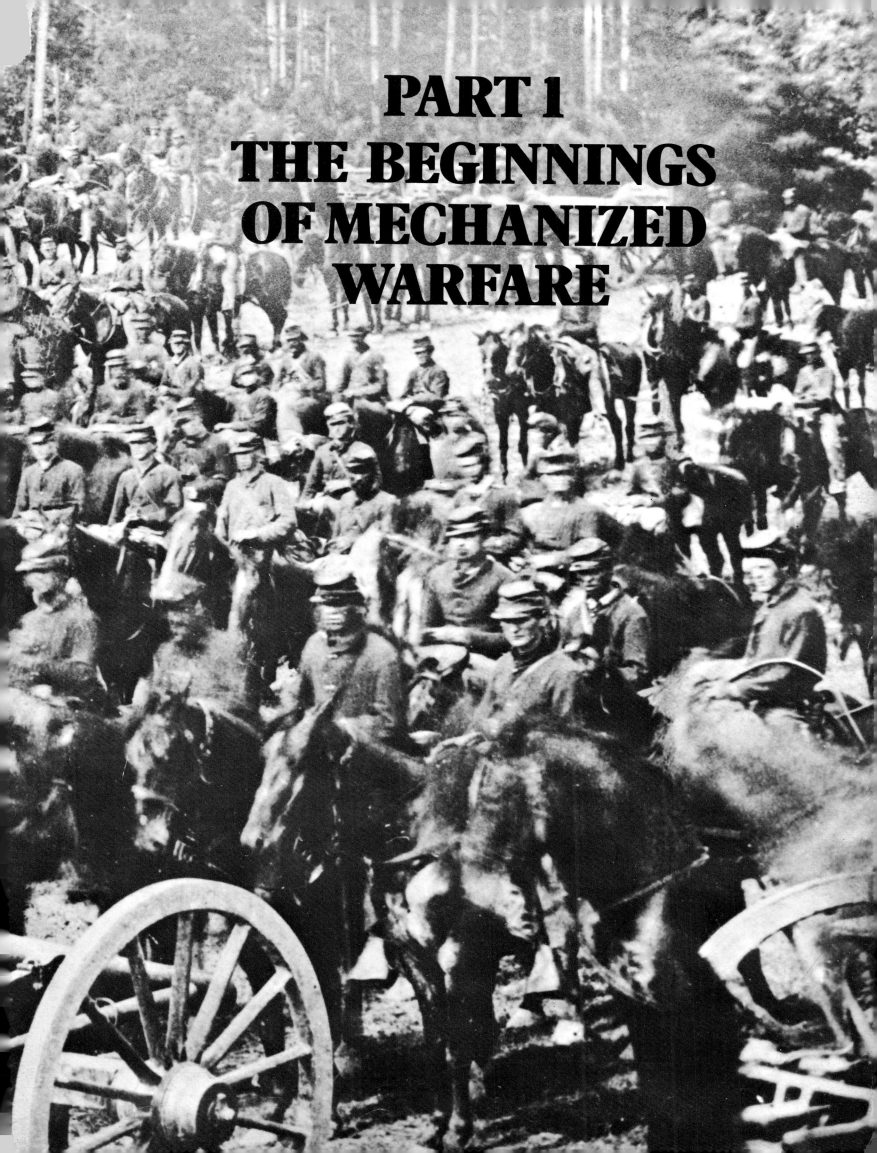

PART 1
THE BEGINNINGS
OF MECHANIZED
WARFARE

1
THE FIGHTING MAN

Age of the musket: the quest for infantry firepower in the 17th and 18th centuries.

The birth of the modern fighting man is usually regarded by military historians as occurring at the time of the Thirty Years' War (1618–48). It was then that Gustavus Adolphus, King of Sweden, created a national standing army of professional fighting men, and co-ordinated their tactics, weapons and organization to forge a powerful military machine. Under Gustavus the three battlefield arms were orchestrated into a symphony of fire and movement: thus the artillery would soften up the opposing army, cavalry would charge and shatter resistance while the infantry, armed with pike and musket, would follow through to complete the destruction of a demoralized enemy. This was also the age that confirmed the eclipse of cavalry as the decisive force. Instead, disciplined companies of infantry became the arbiters of the battlefield, and shock tactics gave way before the tactics of firepower.

For some time to come, however, the musketeers still required pikemen to protect them. In the 17th century the traditional musket, even in the hands of disciplined and competent troops, could produce only an indifferent rate of fire, and a well directed cavalry charge could still on occasion be a major threat. The need for pikemen to defend the musketeers eventually disappeared during the War of the Spanish Succession (1701–14), when socket bayonets were adopted. Once the bayonet was attached to the barrel of the musket (rather than over the muzzle) the infantry could be deployed more boldly, firing as they advanced to contact before closing with the enemy to complete the action with bayonets. Of course, such methods produced heavy casualties – even when seasoned and disciplined troops were available to execute the moves. One consequence was to bring about the demise of citizen armies, who were replaced by long-service professional fighting men.

ABOVE *Gustavus Adolphus, 'Lion of the North', the 17th-century Swedish king considered the father of modern warfare.* OPPOSITE ABOVE *Musket drill demonstrated in an American recruiting poster in the War of Independence (1755–83).* BELOW AND OPPOSITE, BELOW *The progress in the 19th century of the fighting man's chief weapon, from the old flintlock musket, below, and the von Dreyse needle-gun of c. 1840 to the later French Chassepot and the Minié rifle.*

Frederick the Great of Prussia, by iron discipline and a system of constant drill, doubled the rate of fire of his infantry formations. This system became the model for European armies and was exported to North America during the War of Independence (1775–83). A Prussian, Baron von Steuben, became General Washington's drill-master at Valley Forge during the winter of 1777–78, and

there blended the demand for constant drill with a more humane approach to discipline; in so doing he created the foundations of the American military system.

The introduction of the rifle into infantry formations took a long time to complete. This was essentially because the military usefulness of the rifle was not immediately obvious. It was an expensive weapon to construct, took

The foot soldier acquires his own support weapon – the machine gun.

a considerable time to load, and required a marksman to make its possession really worthwhile. Gradually it infiltrated European armies, however. The British and French, who during the Colonial period had encountered the long-barrelled American rifle, could not help but be impressed by its performance. As an example of firepower it was an extremely accurate piece and had a killing range of some 300 yards, more than three times that of the standard-issue musket. But it did require a skilled man to use it; eventually it was employed by the British as a specialist weapon carried by men trained as sharpshooters and skirmishers. Thus Sir John Moore's green-jacketed riflemen led the way in the Peninsula War (1808–14); meanwhile, the bulk of the line infantry still used the simpler and, in their hands, more effective musket.

The tactical organization of the infantry, who became the pivotal force in the armies of the Industrial Revolution, remained virtually unaltered throughout the 19th century. The main change was in infantry weapons, with the gradual substitution of the rifle for the musket, followed by the invention of the percussion-cap and the breech-loading rifle, and finally by the introduction of the infantry's own support weapon – the machine gun.

Attempts to develop an effective breech-loading and repeating infantry weapon date back to the first appearance of small arms on the battlefield. Early failures were undoubtedly caused by over-ambitious schemes that either cost too much or bore no relevance to the technological capabilities of arms manufacturers. Later, in the early years of the 19th century, the stubborn conservatism of military hierarchies also caused a major obstacle to the universal adoption of the rifle. On the eve of the American Civil War (1861–65) the hybrid rifle-musket, which fired a shaped bullet rather than a ball through a rifled barrel,

but was muzzle-loaded, enjoyed supremacy among the inventory of infantry weapons. The British Enfield Model 1853 and the American rifle-musket Model 1855 represent the ultimate development of the muzzle-loader as a military small arm. In the hands of a skilled professional soldier these weapons were lethal at ranges in excess of 800 yards and were capable of firing a maximum of three rounds a minute. They caused massive slaughter in America and ensured victory for the British in their Imperial campaigns, large and small, waged across four continents.

The introduction of accurate and efficient massed firepower at ranges over 500 yards had a number of influences on the fighting man. Artillery was forced back from the immediate encounter zone, and as the gap widened between the gunners and the covering infantry line so their powers were weakened. Guns in future had to be of larger calibre and longer range since any close deployment was suicidal. The American Civil War, at least in conceptual terms, finally established the supremacy of the bullet over the bayonet; and yet, although the infanteer went to ground and sought to be elusive, battle in reality was still resolved only at close quarters, and at fearful cost.

The Civil War saw the development and use of a large number of breech-loading rifles but these were for the most part indifferent weapons. The Sharps Rifle, for example, was ideal for the Plainsman but could not stand up to the rigours of campaign in unpractised hands. It was not until the war was actually over that the United States Government began in earnest to seek a breech-loading rifle as the principal firearm for its infantry and cavalry. They wisely chose the Remington rolling-block breech-loading rifle or Springfield (named after the armoury where it was manufactured), which became not only the standard American military weapon but also a universal

BELOW *The machine gun – a major new weapon for the infantryman, versions entering service from the time of the American Civil War (1861–65). From left to right are Hiram Maxim's first cartridge magazine rifle, forerunner of all his machine guns; a 10-barrelled Gatling gun, and, at the Battle of*

Menin Road Ridge in 1914, a Vickers gun manned by a British crew (one of whom sports a German officer's cap).
OPPOSITE, ABOVE *Machine guns and armourers at Enfield: the guns on display are, from left to right, a Gardner, a Maxim and a Nordenfeldt; all are shown on field mountings.*

rifle serving with armies across the world; it has been estimated that more than a million were in service by the mid-1880s.

The other great infantry weapon to emerge from the American Civil War was the machine gun. The United States Patent Office described the weapon at that time as being capable of 'sustained fire from energy derived from an outside source'. At first the outside source was a manually operated handcrank, and the first recorded use of the machine gun in war was at the Battle of Fair Oaks, Virginia, on 31 May 1862, when Confederate troops deployed a battery of Williams machine guns. However, this and many other derivatives exerted little real influence on the Civil War battlefield because they suffered from inherent draw-backs in design and manufacture; and it was not until Richard Jordan Gatling's creations that the first really effective machine guns appeared on the scene.

The development that allowed the real breakthrough was the self-contained metallic cartridge, which was a cartridge that incorporated a means of ignition, a propellant and a bullet all in a single unit. This gun revolutionized infantry tactics and foreshadowed the demise of horse cavalry since it allowed for rapid fire in long bursts. The Gatling gun, when powered externally, was capable of firing over a sustained period more than 3,000 rounds a minute. Its weakness was in its heavy multi-barrelled arrangement, which imposed severe tactical limitations; these were not fully resolved until Hiram Stevens Maxim, an American inventor living in England, conceived the idea of the first fully automatic gun. Again it was a development in the field of ammunition, in this instance a new propellant in the form of a smokeless powder, which showed the way. For this allowed the principle of short recoil to be used by Maxim for the complete cycling of his single-barrelled gun. The Maxim, manufactured by Vickers, became the standard infantry support weapon from its inception in 1884 up to World War I and beyond. Its influence on the tactics of the fighting man was enormous.

Gatling's self-contained metallic cartridge revolutionizes infantry tactics.

2

THE REBIRTH OF ARMOUR

Carrying the fight to the enemy — armoured chariots and siege vehicles of the Assyrians.

The modern battle tank traces its lineage back to the Western Front of 1916, when it was created to meet the specific needs of that battlefield. But as a concept the tank embraces the same principles of mobility, protection and offensive power that have influenced combat since the beginning of organized warfare.

Many ancient peoples made use of war chariots and armoured horsemen to carry an attack to an enemy at speed, while at the same time equipping their warriors with some degree of protection. The armoured elephants of Hannibal and Kublai Khan were variations of this concept, the chief difference in their case being that they were founded on elephant power, whereas war chariots and most forms of armoured cavalry depended on horse power. The tank, on the other hand, differs from every previous form of cavalry or mobile fighting platform in that it runs on mechanical power.

THIS PAGE *Assyrian engines of war, in the ninth–seventh centuries BC, included the turreted ram (above); as the defenders flung down lighted torches, the Assyrians countered by pouring water onto their machine from a long-armed ladle. Other machines were the war chariot (above right) used for carrying attacks at speed to the enemy, and the long, low ram with front turret (below right).*
OPPOSITE *These pre-1914 cards demonstrate various ways in which cavalry brought mobility and the offensive power of firearm and cold steel to the battlefield – until it was finally rendered obsolete by the rapid-firing weapons of the Industrial Revolution. The cavalrymen shown range chronologically from a Private Gentleman of His Majesty's Own Troop of Guards, 1660 (top left) to a Trooper in the 1st Life Guards Camel Corps, 1884–85 (bottom right).*

Cavalrymen bring improved mobility and offensive power to the battlefield.

The Function of Cavalry

Throughout history cavalry has had to combine the requirements of mobility, protection and offensive power if it was to make a decisive contribution to the battlefield. When employed as part of a balanced military formation its main duties include observing and reporting information about the enemy; screening movements of its own force; pursuing and demoralizing a defeated enemy; maintaining a constant threat to an enemy's rear area; striking suddenly at any weak spots detected; turning an exposed flank, and exploiting a penetration or breakthrough.

Vital as these functions are, they nevertheless represent an essentially secondary role to that of the main force. Almost invariably this has been the infantry, and only on rare occasions in its history has the cavalry been able to achieve superiority over the weapons of the defence and so become an arm of decision. This was the case for a brief period when, for example, the Crusader knights – through the quality of their horsemanship and the protection provided by chain-mail – were able to dominate the battlefield.

But later the introduction of the firearm and its gradual improvement between the 14th and 18th centuries placed increasing limitations on the shock value of cavalry.

In the aftermath of the Napoleonic wars came the further development of the rifle and the bullet and then, for the first time, the foot soldier had an efficient and reliable weapon with a range of 1,000 yards; this sealed the doom of the cavalry charge. At the same time rifled and breech-loading field-pieces worked a revolution in artillery tactics, and the revolver and repeating carbines opened up new vistas for the cavalry and rendered obsolete the charge of lancers.

Defence and Concealment

In the American Civil War (1861–65) cavalry tactics entered a period of transition. The battles of this war were dominated by the weapons of the defence, and the rifle and the earthwork were supreme. By 1863 cavalry tactics on both sides had become concerned primarily with dismounted action – which proved so successful that the mounted charge was rarely used. But the wars that occurred in Europe after 1865 were marked by a complete disregard of the cavalry lessons demonstrated in America. The Austro-Prussian War (1866) saw 60,000 horsemen armed with lance and sabre charging in the face of the breech-loading needle-gun and the Minié rifle. In the Franco-Prussian War, just five years later, an even larger force of 100,000 horsemen, similarly armed, was deployed for battle. Both sides attempted the mass charge. The French cavalry, which had learned nothing since Waterloo, was defeated, while the better-trained and more disciplined Prussians succeeded – though at a terrible cost, since by then the French had developed a machine-gun, the *mitrailleuse*. (It is to Von Bredow's Uhlans that the dubious distinction belongs of providing the last successful

massed boot-to-boot cavalry charge in military history.)

The Boer farmers of South Africa were frontiersmen in the American tradition and at the beginning of the 20th century they taught the British Army a lesson in mobility and firepower which it has never forgotten. The British infantry was constantly outmanoeuvred by the mounted Boer rifleman, while the cavalry, which insisted on retaining the sabre and the lance, proved equally ineffective. It was not until the British commanders created mounted units, organized on a dragoon basis, and deployed them in overwhelming numbers, that the hardy Boer commanders were defeated.

On the Western Front at the beginning of World War I 10 German cavalry divisions numbering more than 70,000 men faced 10 French and one British division across trenches whose construction they had been powerless to prevent – such were the limitations which the weapons of the defence had by now placed on movement. Nevertheless the opening months of the war provided ample opportunity for cavalry exploitation, but once again the generals failed to see that the need was for mounted riflemen and not the European cavalry of the day – which still relied on the sword and the lance in mounted action.

By the spring of 1915 the Western Front had congealed into stagnation. Mobility and manoeuvre, the prime assets of good generalship, had already been displaced by the conflicting demands of static warfare, in which artillery and manpower were most in demand, while the élite regiments of cavalry were relegated to the role of frustrated observers. The quick-firing artillery piece and the machine-gun, together with the trench and barbed wire, had com-

bined together in a grisly yet revolutionary quartet to emphasize what the American Civil War had made clear half a century earlier – and the Russo-Japanese War of 1904–5 had more recently confirmed – namely that through the legacy of the Industrial Revolution warfare had been changed beyond all recognition.

BELOW *In World War* I *the machine gun's deadly effectiveness, combined with the defensive virtues of barbed wire and the trench, brought the battlefield to a standstill.*

OPPOSITE *French cavalry charging at Wörth (6 August 1870) in the Franco-Prussian War; the day of the massed boot-to-boot charge of sabre-armed cavalry was by this date virtually done.*

ABOVE *By the Russo-Japanese War the need for concealment had already produced a new, static kind of warfare. Shown here are Russian artillery trenches and dugouts in a hilltop position defending Port Arthur.*

BELOW *Even in World War I the cavalry of Europe foolishly persisted with the sword and lance. These outmoded heroes are Cossacks at the Battle of Tannenberg on the Eastern Front, 1914.*

3
THE BIG GUNS
1850-1914

The artillery arm changes over from muzzle- to breech-loading weapons.

The decade or so following the Crimean War may be regarded as the gestation period of modern ordnance. It begins with late smooth-bore muzzle-loaders, like the 'Napoleon', in the ascendant, and ends with rifled breech-loaders being adopted by most nations for their field artillery.

Until the mid-19th century ordnance development had been slow if not, at times, barely perceptible. Then suddenly, under the impetus of industrial and scientific progress, startling advances were made. In the Crimean War (1853–56), the belligerents experimented but briefly with rifled artillery; whereas six years later, in the American Civil War (1861–65), half the field artillery employed by the Union Army was rifled.

The Confederate Army, moreover, acquired and used a number of rifled guns with breech-loading mechanisms; the days of the muzzle-loader were numbered. By the Franco-Prussian War (1870–71), the Prussian field artillery was composed wholly of breech-loaders. And within a few years every Western nation followed their lead.

During the Napoleonic Wars, at the turn of the century, there had been a firm balance between each of the three principal arms—infantry, cavalry and artillery. But if any one of the three was a dominant force on the battlefield, then that arm was the artillery, whose powers could be exploited in various ways. For example, one of Napoleon's favourite tactics was to have his batteries unlimber in front of a line of enemy infantry beyond the effective range of their smooth-bore muskets (200 yards or less). Once there, the French batteries would blast a hole in the enemy line using case shot (grape and canister). Then a column of French infantry would pour through the gap to exploit the breakthrough.

After the Napoleonic Wars came the introduction of the rifled musket and the Minié bullet. These innovations gave the infantry a weapon which it could use to great effect against the artillery. The new weapon could kill at 1,000 yards and was accurate at up to 600 yards.

It was clear that field artillery could no longer maintain its former dominant role in the offensive; from now on

ARTILLERY TYPES

This table describes the chief functions of the principal artillery types in use in the mid–19th century. The range figures are those of representative US types in 1861: the gun is a Parrott 10-pounder field rifle at 5 degrees elevation; the howitzer is a Navy Dahlgren 12-pounder rifle at 5 degrees elevation, and the mortar is a 38-inch siege piece.

TYPE	USE	RANGE IN YARDS	TYPE OF FIRE	AMMUNITION
Gun (or cannon)	anti-personnel counter-battery	2,000	'direct' flat trajectory high velocity	canister shot shell spherical case (shrapnel)
Howitzer	anti-personnel against works and matériel	1,770	'searching' mid-trajectory medium velocity	canister shell spherical case incendiary
Mortar	anti-personnel against works and matériel	1,837	'dropping' high trajectory low velocity	shell spherical case incendiary
Gun-howitzer (or licorne)	combines the function of the gun and the howitzer			

rifle fire from enemy infantry could pick off gunners and teams before their guns could be brought into battery at effective range. Indeed, it seemed that it might be the lot of the artillery to assume a secondary defensive role.

What in fact happened, though, was that tactical doctrine did not immediately follow the advances in weaponry. The infantry of most nations continued to use the dense formations of the Napoleonic Wars. This allowed the artillery to play a formidable role with long-range shell fire. Also, until the introduction of good smokeless powder (*c.* 1884), the first salvoes left the field covered in black smoke, which made aimed fire at best haphazard. In this situation the cannon's hitting power at close ranges was greatly valued.

RIGHT *Learning from another nation's conflict: foreign observers of the American Civil War pose with Union officers.* BELOW *Krupp 15-cm breech-loading rifles captured by the Allied Expeditionary Force during the Boxer Rebellion, 1900.*

Long-range infantry firepower vies with the close-range hitting power of the big guns.

SOME ARTILLERY DEFINITIONS

Smooth-bore. The interior of the barrel is smooth. With the exception of grape and canister (which are collections of shot packed respectively in sacks or metal containers), only round projectiles with a diameter smaller than that of the bore may be fired from smooth-bore guns. Because of this windage (space) the projectile 'bounces' down the barrel and emerges from the gun with less velocity and less predictable accuracy than a projectile fired from a rifle.

Rifle. The bore of the gun is machined with spiralling grooves that impart a spin to the projectile, which is usually long and pointed; this method increases accuracy, range and velocity.

Muzzle-loader. A gun loaded from the front of the tube.

Breech-loader. A gun loaded from the rear (breech) of the tube. The charge and projectile (or cartridge) is introduced into the chamber when the breech-block is open. The opening is then sealed behind the charge by means of a sliding-wedge or screw mechanism.

The Crimean War

1854–55: artillery's performance at the Siege of Sebastopol.

The battles of the Crimean War were confused, scrambling affairs sometimes described as 'soldiers' battles', which means, in effect, that the generals were not directing them. In most of these actions the role of artillery was limited, but it did play a central part in the most important event of the war, the epic siege of Sebastopol.

Sebastopol had been the most important Russian naval base and arsenal on the Black Sea since the late 18th century. Its coastal defence system, begun in 1783 and periodically improved, was considered impregnable by the standards of a brick-and-masonry age. In 1837 the Czar had ordered additional defences to be built behind the town, but nothing had been done. So, when war began in 1853, Sebastopol was defenceless on the landward, or southern, side. Eventually in April 1854, Colonel Frants Todleben, an engineer officer, was sent to the base to plan and supervise the building of

BELOW *A scene in the British mortar battery at the Siege of Sebastopol. It shows the gunner at right pouring bursting powder into a hollow spherical shell. Behind him two gunners ram a* propellant charge down the bore of their mortar, while to the rear of the piece a comrade holds his thumb over the vent to stop a premature detonation of the charge.

ABOVE LEFT A Quiet Night in the Batteries, *by William Simpson.*
ABOVE *Gunners at work on mortars behind the British Right*
Attack at Sebastopol; from a painting published in May 1855.

The Allied armies, deterred by Todleben's northern defences, march to the south side of Sebastopol.

ABOVE *Sebastopol from the Malakoff. In the foreground are bomb-proofs in which Russian soldiers sheltered from the Allied bombardment. In the harbour (right centre) may be seen the remains of the pontoon bridge over which the Russian army escaped to the northern side of the harbour.*

BELOW *The interior of the Redan, showing some of the sandbags and gabions (wickerwork cylinders) that were essential parts of Todleben's improvised fortifications. Most of the guns in the Russian works were naval pieces taken from the vessels of the Black Sea Fleet.*

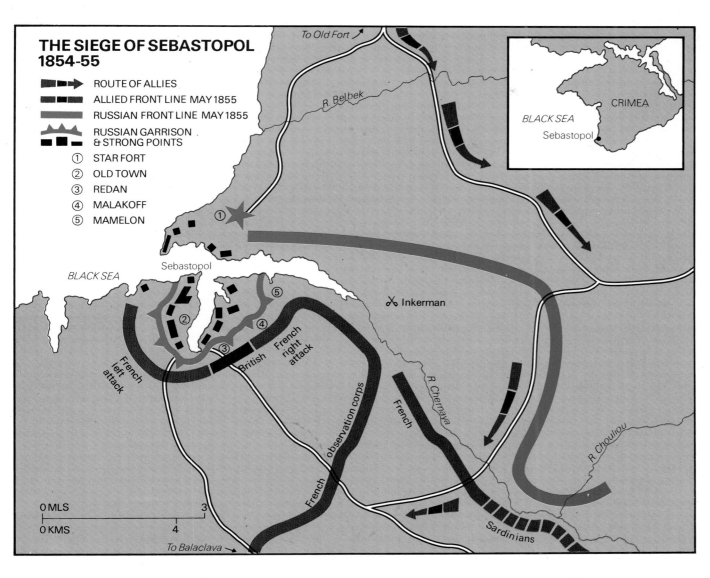

THE SIEGE OF SEBASTOPOL 1854-55

- ➤ ROUTE OF ALLIES
- ▬▬ ALLIED FRONT LINE MAY 1855
- ▬▬ RUSSIAN FRONT LINE MAY 1855
- ▲▲▲ RUSSIAN GARRISON & STRONG POINTS
- ① STAR FORT
- ② OLD TOWN
- ③ REDAN
- ④ MALAKOFF
- ⑤ MAMELON

To Old Fort ➚

R. Belbek

BLACK SEA

Sebastopol

French left attack

French right attack

British

French observation corps

French

R. Chernaya

R. Chouliou

Inkerman

Sardinians

0 MLS   3
0 KMS   4

To Balaclava ➚

BLACK SEA

CRIMEA

Sebastopol

October 1854: 126 Allied guns begin to fire on the town in the greatest artillery bombardment in the history of the world to that time.

land defences. But, because no one anticipated an attack on Sebastopol from behind the town, Todleben took his time. Then, on 13 September, a British and French Allied army began to land at Old Fort some 30 miles away to the north. After defeating Prince Menshikov's Russian army at the Alma on 20 September, the Allies crossed the River Belbek and came within sight of the northern defences of Sebastopol. There they found Todleben's recently constructed Star Fort; considering this too strong to assault, they turned and marched around the town towards the southern defences.

To the south of the harbour, Todleben's works were still very weak. General Cathcart, commanding the British 4th Division, described them as consisting of a martello tower and a 'low park wall not in good repair'. Clearly, Sebastopol could have been taken by storm at that moment, but while the Russians prepared for the worst, the Allied assault was called off. The anticipated cost of an assault, estimated at 500 men, was considered too great. A great opportunity was thus allowed to slip away, and the Allies began formal siege operations.

In the meantime, Todleben had not been idle. He directed every civilian, soldier and sailor that could be found to the task of strengthening the flimsy southern defences. Since he did not have time to construct permanent, brick-and-masonry forts of the type that had been the mainstay of the defensive for centuries,[1] Todleben built

a formidable system of earthen bastions, connecting trenches and supporting batteries. By mid-October, Sebastopol was one of the most formidable fortresses in the world. The older coastal defences mounted 533 guns. Todleben's earthworks mounted 60 guns to the north of the harbour and 145 on the southern defences. There were, altogether, nearly 3,000 heavy guns (including those of the fleet) available for the defences, but most of these were stored because there was simply no place to put them.

The Allies, for their part, had managed rapidly to put together a siege train, and, on 17 October 1854 the Russians felt the first impact of the greatest artillery bombardment in the history of the world to that time. Beginning at dawn 126 Allied guns, most of them sited in three great batteries, began to pound the Russian earthworks.

Formidable as this fire was, the defenders replied with tremendous vigour. Most of the Russian batteries were manned by sailors who fired their guns 'in broadside', that is, all at once, as if they were firing from the gun deck of a man-o'-war. The effect was devastating. At 10.30 am the Russians destroyed one of the magazines of the French batteries firing from Mount Rodolph. Later a caisson was hit. The French commander, finding the fire too hot, 'invited' his gunners to shelter. Not one declined and by

---

[1] The methods of fortifying a town had changed little since the days of Sébastien de Vauban (1633–1707), the French siege-master.

noon the French batteries were silent. After that, the fire of the English batteries became an exercise in futility. The Russians were without doubt the stronger party: they eventually fired 20,000 rounds to the Allies' 9,000. What is more, their works were undamaged.

The October bombardment was but a meagre foretaste of things to come. Other bombardments followed, some of which attained titanic dimensions; one such was the Easter bombardment which began on 8 April 1855 and lasted 11 days.

During each day of the Easter bombardment the Russian works were destroyed, but each night the gallant defenders restored them. Anticipating an assault at any time, the Russian commanders packed their men into dugouts and bombproofs. No assault came, and they lost 6,000 men in the bombardment. Still they persevered, and replied to the Allied bombardment with 88,000 shells from their own batteries.

On 7 June 1855 the French took the Mamelon, an important work close to the main Russian line. Todleben had foreseen that this might happen and, after the Easter bombardment, he had constructed a new work, the Malakoff. Situated behind the Mamelon, the Malakoff commanded the Russian line and the town and, together with a strong work flanking it known as the Redan, held the key to Sebastopol. All the efforts of the Allies were naturally directed towards taking these two works.

The daily bombardments of the Allies increased in intensity, culminating in a tremendous three-day bombardment (5–8 September 1855). The Russians suffered terribly, especially in the last month. Prince Gorchakov, the Russian commander, reported that his casualties were 500–1,000 men per day during that period. The Malakoff was irreparably damaged, and the Redan reduced to a jagged heap. Finally, on 8 September, British and French infantry rushed the two forts. The British were repulsed at the Redan, but the French carried the Malakoff. This determined the fate of Sebastopol. Gorchakov blew up the town and withdrew his men across a pontoon bridge to the northern side of the harbour.

The casualties in the siege of Sebastopol, which had lasted nearly a year, were over 300,000 men. The artillery, crude as it was, had contributed mightily to that toll, especially among the Russians who persisted in massing their men in the trenches during each bombardment. In forts like the Malakoff enormous bomb-proofs had been constructed to shelter the infantry needed to repel attacks, but even these were not sufficient to protect the numbers of men that the Russians crowded into the trenches. And when the Allies gained artillery superiority, as they did during the Easter bombardment, there was little the Russians could do, despite frantic rebuilding, to prevent the steady deterioration of their works. At the end of the siege there were only a few serviceable gun carriages left in Sebastopol, and the forts were formless piles of rubble.

Most of the projectiles thrown into Sebastopol were spherical shot and shell. Shot was solid and was used for battering. A shell consisted of a hollow sphere containing a small bursting charge; it was used against personnel rather than earthworks, where its fragments had little effect. The fuse used with shell was a time fuse, usually ignited by the flash of the propellant powder. Another type of projectile used was red-hot shot. This was shot heated in a furnace prior to firing and carried to the gun with tongs. It was used for its incendiary effect, as were 'carcasses', projectiles which were pierced with holes and fired from howitzers and mortars.

Sebastopol produced few innovations. Some rifled guns – most notably the British 68-pounder oval-bore Lancaster gun – were briefly experimented with, but the results of these tests were unsatisfactory. Otherwise, it is worth noting only that the Russians had some success using cast-iron gun-carriages on a few of their heavy pieces; these were found to make working the guns easier.

Altogether the Allied artillery fired 1,250,000 projectiles into the Russian fortress. The remarkable strength of the Russian earthworks in the face of this storm of shot and shell seems to have been overlooked by most military men of the time. Certainly, the day of the brick fort was past. This was conclusively demonstrated on 16 October 1855, when three French steam-powered floating batteries engaged and demolished the Russian forts at Kinburn on the Bug River after a three-hour bombardment.

LEFT *The Barrack Battery at Sebastopol. Note the rope mantelets at the gun embrasure and around the gun tube; their function was to protect the gunners from small-arms fire.*

The American Civil War

As we mentioned earlier, the Union Army used large numbers of rifled guns during the American Civil War. By 1863 about half the Union Army's field artillery was rifled. Then, however, the ratio dropped, and during the last two years of the war only about one-third of the field artillery was rifled. This happened because, for various reasons, rifling had brought no worthwhile advantage over the Confederate artillery, which was largely equipped with smooth-bores.

One important factor was the nature of the countryside over which the war was fought. There was simply not much point in employing rifles in wooded, half-cultivated areas. Even when rifles could be employed at great ranges, however, the small amount of bursting powder in their shells and the uncertainty of the fuses made them less than fully effective. Also, as soon as the infantry learned to adopt open formations and to advance in rushes using all available cover, long-range fire lost its potency.

At First Bull Run (21 July 1861) two fine batteries of US regular artillery, those of Ricketts and Griffin, equipped with 10 10-pounder Parrott rifles and two 12-pounder howitzers, engaged a Confederate battery of four 6-pounder smooth-bore guns under the command of John G. Imboden. This contest, a classic battle of rifled cannon versus smooth-bores, was conducted at ranges of from 1,000–1,500 yards. The Confederate battery more than held its own despite the disparity in numbers, and this led Imboden to conclude that:

TOP *A Union siege battery near Charleston, South Carolina; the guns shown are Parrott 100-pounder rifles.*
ABOVE *A Confederate Whitworth 12-pounder breech-loading rifle with the breech-block open. It had a range of nearly six miles.*

In open ground, at 1,000 yards, a 6-pounder battery of smooth guns, or, at 1,500 to 1,800 yards, a similar battery of 12-pounder Napoleons, well handled, will in one hour discomfit double the number of the best rifles ever put in the field.

This is not to say that the fire of the rifled batteries had been inaccurate. It was, in fact, so accurate that Imboden confessed that 'hundreds of shells from these fine rifle-guns

US 12-pounder 'Napoleon' gun-howitzer M-1857

The 'Napoleon', destined to be the most-used and most popular field gun of the American Civil War, was designed in 1853 by Louis-Napoleon, the French ruler. It represents the high-point of smooth-bore gun development: in particular it was lighter than its contemporaries of the same calibre and, therefore, easier to handle.

In defence it was an awesome weapon, firing great shot-gun blasts of canister (tin cans filled with large lead balls) up to 400 yards. It also had good range, and could deliver spherical case (shrapnel) and shot to over 1,600 yards. Because rifled small-arms had given the infantry a temporary ascendancy over smooth-bore field artillery, the defensive prowess of the Napoleon—its ability to hit hard at close range—made it well liked by Civil War artillerymen.

The US model was introduced for service in 1857. The Confederates, especially, used large numbers of Napoleons—which in their case were mostly captured pieces. The M-1857 was of bronze, but some Confederate copies were made of cast iron with reinforced breeches. This reinforcement was necessary because of the intrinsic weakness of cast iron as compared to bronze. The M-1857 smooth-bore 12-pounder remained in service with the US Army until the late 1870s.

Ammunition for the Napoleon

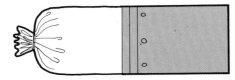

Cartridge bag, made of paper and tied at the head.

Tin case nailed to 'sabot' (wooden base); inside are 27 cast-iron shot.

Shown here is a typical 'fixed' round of canister; this type was used for close-range defensive work.

SPECIFICATIONS

Calibre	4·62 inches
Maximum range	1,619 yards at + 5 degrees
	2,090 yards at + 10 degrees firing shot
Length of bore	63·6 inches
Length of piece	72·6 inches
Weight of tube	1,230 pounds
Weight of carriage	1,128 pounds
Windage (difference between diameter of bore and diameter of projectile)	·01 inch
Powder charge	2 pounds (canister)
	2·5 pounds (shell, case and solid shot)
Weight of projectile	9·52 pounds (shell)
	12·17 pounds (case)
	14·80 pounds (canister)
	12·75 pounds (solid shot)
Muzzle velocity	1,486 fps (solid shot)
	1,495 fps (case)
	1,680 fps (shell)
Rate of fire	2 rpm (aimed)
	4 rpm (canister)
Firing mechanism	friction primer

Implements used by Civil War gunners

Handspikes, used for levering the gun into a firing position.

Rammer, sponge head and stave.

Worm, used to clear obstructions in the barrel.

Gunner's quadrant, for gauging elevation.

Priming wire, for pricking the cartridge bag.

Tangent scale, another method of measuring elevation; each step denoted a given range.

To operate the Napoleon, its crew first manoeuvred the piece into position. On the command 'Load', the No. 1 gunner drove the sponge down the bore, while No. 2 collected a cartridge from No. 5. No. 1 then removed the sponge, and the cartridge was inserted into the bore and seated firmly in the breech with the rammer. Meanwhile the No. 3 gunner had stopped the vent with his thumb (protected by a leather thumbstall) to prevent a premature discharge caused by smouldering combustible material which might have escaped the sponge during swabbing. Next the gunner placed the priming wire in the vent, pricking through the cartridge bag into the powder. The gun's elevation was corrected by means of a sighting device, and the friction tube was attached to one end of the lanyard. On the command 'Fire', the lanyard was pulled, igniting the charge and dispatching the projectile towards its target.

exploded in front of and around my battery on that day . . .'
But, without exception, the high-velocity shells had buried
themselves in the ground before exploding, and no one was
hurt; later, when Imboden viewed the position occupied by
his battery, he remarked that 'the ground looked as though
it had been rooted up by hogs'.

But if the offensive capability of field artillery in the
American Civil War was somewhat dubious, there was no
questioning the potency of a line of guns in defence.
Certainly the infantry feared an encounter with massed
guns more than any other battlefield circumstance.

At Malvern Hill (1 July 1862) the Union chief of
artillery, Colonel Henry J. Hunt, placed nearly 100 guns
hub-to-hub on rising ground with about half a mile of open
ground between them and the Confederate infantry. The
Confederates had 14 brigades of infantry prepared for an
assault. Their artillery, which was to have supported the
infantry, then attempted to deploy. As each battery was
wheeled separately into position, up to 50 Union guns
opened fire. In the inferno that followed, battery after
battery of the Confederate artillery was wrecked.

Late in the afternoon the Confederate infantry emerged
from the woods to attack. Confusion, caused as much by
poor maps as by the broken ground to their front, upset the
rhythm of the attack, and the 14 brigades went in piecemeal,
as the artillery had before them. As each column in succession left the woods and began to climb the slope, every gun
that could be brought to bear, including the siege guns
farther back, opened a deadly fire. Shells alone were enough
to destroy most of the columns, canister being used against
those brave bands of survivors who actually pressed up to
the guns. Nearly half the Confederate casualties at Malvern
Hill were in fact caused by artillery fire–a proportion which
the Confederate General, Harvey Hill, described as 'unprecedented' in the annals of warfare.

During the Civil War massed artillery firing from a
distance was used on several occasions to prepare the way
for an infantry assault. At Gettysburg (1–3 July 1863), for
example, the massed fire of 159 Confederate guns under
Colonel E. P. Alexander was intended to prepare the way
for the famous assault of 15,000 Confederate infantry (now
known as 'Pickett's Charge'). The principal aim of the
Confederate barrage was not to break up or destroy the
infantry formations waiting to receive the attack, but rather
to neutralize or force the withdrawal of the Union guns on
Cemetery Ridge. If this could not be done, it was reckoned
that perhaps the Union guns would exhaust their long-range
ammunition in reply, and much the same object would be
achieved.

But on the Ridge itself the crews of some 80 Union guns,
grouped under the overall command of General Hunt, were
instructed to hold their reply fire for about 20 minutes. This
was done in order to conserve ammunition for the assault
which everyone expected to follow.

Alexander's grand battery fired on the Union line from
1 pm to 2.45 pm on the afternoon of 3 July. A few Union
batteries on the forward slope of Cemetery Ridge (the
objective) were wrecked, but most of the Confederate fire
was long and fell behind the Ridge. On the Union side
Hunt's orders were not completely followed: batteries
along the line of the Union Second Corps were ordered to

reply by General Hancock, the Corps commander. Hunt
made his way towards this part of the line and ordered the
firing to cease, but the guns had by then used up their
long-range ammunition.

When Hancock's batteries stopped Alexander, believing
his fire had silenced the Union guns, gave the signal for the
assault to go in. As the Confederate infantry emerged from
the line of trees and low ridges which had sheltered them,
they were subjected to a devastating artillery fire. This fire
was so effective that the Confederates began to 'drift'
towards the safest point in the enemy lines. This, of course,
was the position occupied by the non-firing Second Corps
artillery, whose area was the only part of the Union line to
be penetrated in the action. Later Hunt was to write that,
had his instructions been followed completely, the assaulting column would have broken up in mid-course. As it was,
no more than 300 of the 15,000 attackers reached the Union
line.

Following the failure of the Confederate assault, there
was pressure in the Union Army for an immediate advance
on the mile-long gap in the Confederate line formerly
occupied by the men of Pickett's assaulting column. At that
point only Alexander's gunners, bravely maintaining their
line, seemed to block the way to a rout of Lee's Army. Even
so, the mere sight of that line of guns was enough to dissuade
even the most sanguine observer. Hunt, who knew too well
what guns could do and had no way of knowing that
Alexander's guns were without ammunition, described
such a move as 'stark madness', and no counter-attack was
made.

In the years leading up to the American Civil War, it had
been generally accepted that in any ship-versus-shore duel
the gunboat would be worsted. This was largely because of
a system of horizontal shell-firing that had been devised in
1822 by a French General, Henri Paixhans (1783–1854).
The exploding Paixhans shell, fired on a flat trajectory, blew

OPPOSITE *Colonel E. P. Alexander, who directed the
Confederate guns at the Battle of Gettysburg.*
ABOVE *James Hope's painting of the Battle of Antietam shows
Union infantry being shelled by Stephen Dill Lee's battery.*
BELOW *A 15-inch Rodman gun photographed in Battery Rodgers
near Hunting Creek on the Potomac River.*

up the old wooden-walled gunboats and made them
obsolete. This was perhaps most graphically illustrated at
the naval Battle of Sinope (1853), when a Russian squadron
shelled and set on fire a Turkish squadron of seven frigates
and five smaller ships.

A further well-established belief of the day was that brick
fortresses – provided their foundations were protected by a
glacis and their defenders adequately armed and pro-
visioned – could resist the attempts of a besieger for months.
The siege of Sebastopol had demonstrated the resilience of
earthworks, too – though most military men remained convinced that proper brickwork forts would have served the
Russians better.

ABOVE *The naval bombardment of Fort Fisher near Wilmington, North Carolina, on 15 January 1865, as painted by Xanthus Russell Smith. At this period, before armour-piercing shot had been developed, steam-driven ironclad warships were able to engage forts with impunity. The monitors of the Union fleet shown here fired on the fort from 1,200 yards and drove the Confederate gunners into their bomb-proofs.*

OPPOSITE *The Great Gun at White Point Battery, Charleston, South Carolina, as depicted by Conrad Wise Chapman in a watercolour dated November 1863.*

LEFT *Battery Marion at Charleston, painted by Chapman in October 1863.*

Devastating power of the new heavy rifled guns.

LEFT *The 'Dictator', a famous heavy mortar that fired 45 rounds during the Siege of Petersburg. It was shunted about on a railway mount.*

In the meantime, the industrialization of war continued apace: most navies converted to steam propulsion, a few ironclads were launched and large-calibre rifled guns appeared. By 1865 all previous thinking on siege and naval bombardment had to be completely revised.

Among the new siege weapons were large smooth-bores cast by Major T. J. Rodman's improved method of cooling the metal from the inside of the bore by a stream of running water. This interior cooling put a permanent compressive strain on the metal surrounding the bore, and Rodman's monster 'columbiads', as they were called, were structurally much sounder (and therefore safer) than previous iron pieces. Rodman's biggest gun was a 20-inch muzzle-loading smooth-bore that fired a solid shot weighing 1,080 pounds.

Major Rodman (1815–71), an American ordnance specialist, also improved muzzle velocity with his invention of a progressive-burning powder, which was much more efficient than ordinary black powder. However, while Rodman's various innovations improved the efficiency and increased the size of smooth-bores, these guns were plainly outclassed as siege weapons by the new large-calibre rifles.

Several types of heavy rifled pieces were used during the Civil War, the most common being those built by Parrott, Brooke, Blakely and Armstrong. The safest were built-up types like the Armstrong 150-pounder. The breech of the Armstrong gun was reinforced by a series of 'hoops' of wrought iron which were shrunk-on over one another and the gun tube. At the other end of the spectrum were the Parrotts, cast-iron pieces with a wrought-iron reinforcing band shrunk-on over the breech. Parrott guns were cheap and easy to make, but they frequently burst. After the naval bombardment of Fort Fisher near Wilmington, North Carolina, during which six Parrotts burst causing 45 casualties in the Union fleet, Admiral Porter pronounced them 'unfit for service, and calculated to kill more of our men than those of the enemy'.

If the new rifles were somewhat unpredictable, they were undeniably effective. No brick-and-masonry fort could stand for long against their fire. The best illustration of this is the brief siege of Fort Pulaski near Savannah, Georgia (10–11 April 1865). Fort Pulaski was a strong brick fort mounting 40 heavy guns either *en barbette* (to fire over the parapet) or enclosed in casemates. It was situated on an island at the mouth of the Savannah River. The nearest firm ground suitable for mounting siege-pieces to bear on the fort was on Tybee Island over a mile away. In the opinion of the Chief Engineer of the US Army, 'The work could not be reduced in a month's firing with any number of guns of manageable calibres.'

However, a Union force under General Quincy A. Gillmore went ahead and emplaced several heavy guns and mortars on Tybee Island; they began bombarding Pulaski at 8.15 am on 10 April. By 1.00 pm, in Gillmore's words: 'It could be seen that the rifled projectiles were surely eating their way into the scarp of the *pan-coupé* and adjacent south face.' By noon the next day two enormous breaches with an aggregate width of 30 feet had been opened in the southeast face, and Union shot was searching the interior of the fort. At 2.00 pm on the 11th, the Confederate garrison surrendered. The two-day bombardment of Fort Pulaski was the first time rifled heavy guns had been used against brickwork forts; more important still, those few hours of shelling had rendered every existing brickwork fort obsolete.

Inevitably, it took some time for this knowledge to penetrate the minds of European strategists. As late as 1870, for example, General von Moltke and the Prussian 'technicians' counselled against besieging French cities protected by concentric rings of brick forts. But when the Prussians did take on French fortresses, their 15-cm guns and howitzers were surprisingly effective, especially the howitzers, which were used to breach 'invisible' scarps (out of sight beyond intervening glacis). This happened, for example, at Strasbourg; in the end, as a result of events in the Franco-Prussian War, all new forts were constructed of concrete and earth.

April 1865: the demolition of Fort Pulaski renders all brickwork forts obsolete.

ABOVE LEFT *The photograph shows breaches forced in the brickwork of Fort Pulaski by General Quincy Gillmore's Union bombardment in April 1865.*
ABOVE *The Union Army's armoured railroad battery on General Grant's City Point Railroad near Petersburg.*
LEFT *A Confederate Armstrong 150-pounder muzzle-loading rifle emplaced at Fort Fisher, near Wilmington.*
BELOW *Gunners at work in a battery of Union field guns in trenches near Petersburg.*

US 3-inch Ordnance Rifle

The 3-inch Ordnance rifle was a lightweight rifled gun manufactured in large numbers during the American Civil War by Rodman and supplied to the field and horse artillery of the Union Army. It was made of wrought iron and was especially noted for its accuracy: one gunner was heard to boast that his 3-inch rifle could 'hit the top of a barrel at a mile'.

A similar rifled gun, the Parrott 10-pounder, had been developed earlier with a calibre of 2·90 inches; in due course the Parrotts were rebored to take ammunition identical to that of the 3-inch gun. The Ordnance rifle was issued to field units from late 1863. It remained in service until the Spanish-American War of 1898.

The aerial view below emphasizes the almost deceptively simple lines of a gun that by repute was deadly accurate at a one-mile range and remained effective at twice that distance. In the side view the nearside wheel is omitted to show more clearly the respective sizes of carriage and gun tube, and how they fitted together. The wooden stock of the carriage served to connect it to the limber and was used to direct the piece. Its lower portion, the trail, rested on the ground when the gun was unlimbered; the ring at the end of the trail, the lunette, received the pintle hook by which the limber was attached. Also shown is the lock chain: fixed to the side of the trail, it was used to keep the wheel from turning.

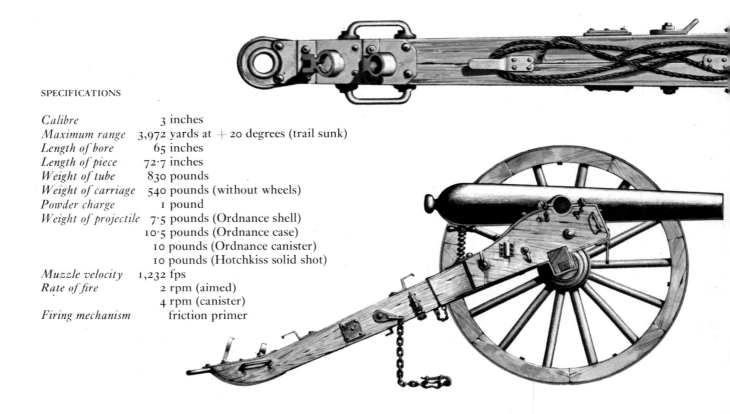

SPECIFICATIONS

Calibre	3 inches
Maximum range	3,972 yards at + 20 degrees (trail sunk)
Length of bore	65 inches
Length of piece	72·7 inches
Weight of tube	830 pounds
Weight of carriage	540 pounds (without wheels)
Powder charge	1 pound
Weight of projectile	7·5 pounds (Ordnance shell)
	10·5 pounds (Ordnance case)
	10 pounds (Ordnance canister)
	10 pounds (Hotchkiss solid shot)
Muzzle velocity	1,232 fps
Rate of fire	2 rpm (aimed)
	4 rpm (canister)
Firing mechanism	friction primer

The Barrel

The gun tube, weighing 830 pounds, rested between two pieces of wood reinforced with iron and known as cheeks (see also the larger view above). The trunnions (G) projecting from the barrel fitted into beds or depressions in the cheeks, and were held secure by iron capsquares.

A   Cascabel
B   Breech
C   Bore
D   Muzzle
E   Body
F   Chase
G   Trunnion
H   Rimbase

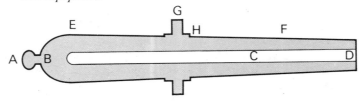

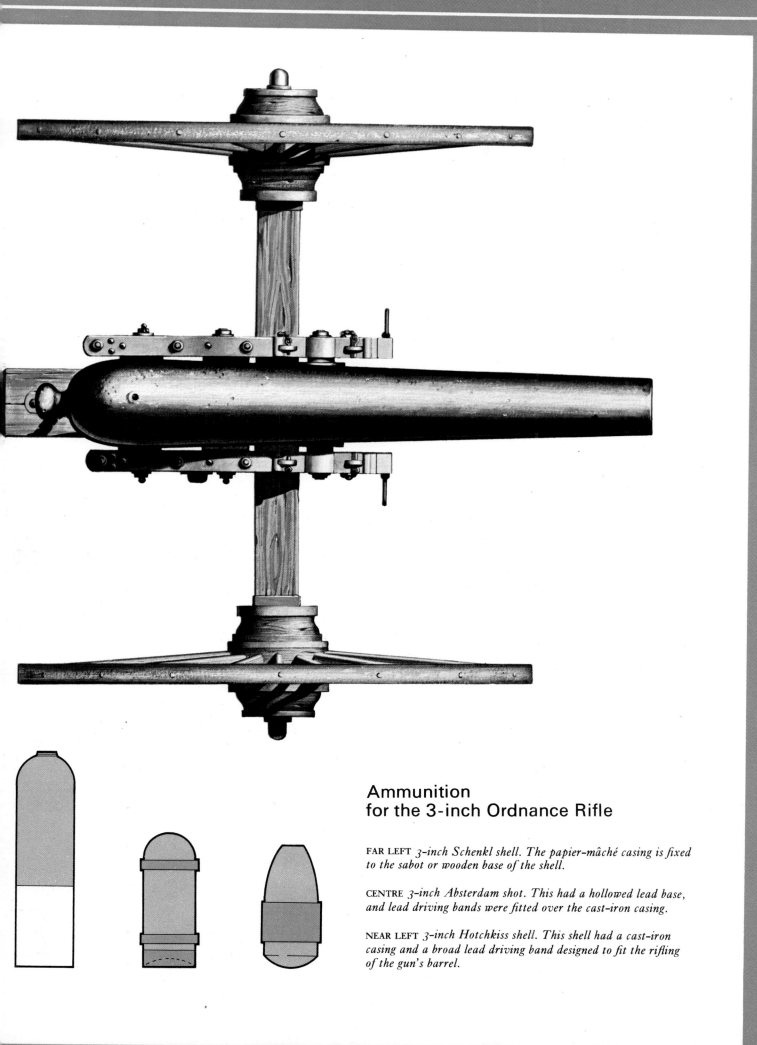

Ammunition
for the 3-inch Ordnance Rifle

FAR LEFT *3-inch Schenkl shell. The papier-mâché casing is fixed to the sabot or wooden base of the shell.*

CENTRE *3-inch Absterdam shot. This had a hollowed lead base, and lead driving bands were fitted over the cast-iron casing.*

NEAR LEFT *3-inch Hotchkiss shell. This shell had a cast-iron casing and a broad lead driving band designed to fit the rifling of the gun's barrel.*

The Prussians at War

In 1866 the Prussian Army entered its war against Austria with a mixture of old and new equipment that indicated a steady, if somewhat hesitant, transition from smooth-bore muzzle-loaders to rifled breech-loaders. Each Prussian army corps had a group of 16 batteries attached to it. Six of the 16 batteries were equipped with old smooth-bore muzzle-loaders, while the other 10 used the new Krupp steel breech-loaders. Of the smooth-bores it was said that, at 1,000 paces: 'The first shot is for the Devil, the second for God, and only the third for the King.' The Krupp rifles were 4- or 6-pounders. Despite its impressive equipment, however, the Prussian field artillery was comparatively in-experienced, having seen only limited action in the Danish War of 1864.

The Austrian artillery was equipped wholly with rifled muzzle-loaders. These guns were inferior to the Krupp breech-loaders in rapidity of fire; in addition, Austrian shells and fuses were often defective. Nevertheless, the Austrians had been taught a lesson by the French in 1859 (the Italian War) and in 1866 they were to prove themselves the better gunners time and again despite their material inferiority.

The problems of the Prussian field artillery in 1866 seem to have had more to do with leadership, tactics and lack of experience than with the guns themselves. While on the march the artillery was relegated to the rear of each column. In battle, those few pieces that were brought into the line (the greater part stayed among the reserves) were deployed here and there in no particular order, but generally as far to the rear as possible. There was no plan to replenish ammuni-tion expended (this could be quite a problem with rapid-firing breech-loaders), and once a battery had fired its complement, it usually left the field. In consequence the Prussian infantry came to despise its artillery, which became more and more of an embarrassment as the campaign went·on.

On the other hand the Austrian artillery fought brilliantly in each engagement, and nowhere more so than in the decisive Battle of Königgrätz (3 July 1866), where it covered the retreat of General von Benedek's army from successive positions. In its comments on this battle, the Prussian *Staff History* noted that 'the well-sustained fire of the powerful line of artillery . . . proved that part, at least, of the hostile army still retained its full power of resistance'.

There could be no mistaking the keen disappointment felt by Prussian artillerists at their dismal showing in 1866. The infantry had achieved glory, but the artillery met abuse at every turn. After the engagement at Bistritz Prince Friedrich Karl, commanding the Prussian First Army, had been heard to remark that his artillery 'was scarcely of more use . . . than it could have been at Berlin'. Clearly, some changes were in order.

By 1870 the artillery was completely equipped with Krupp rifles. Under the demanding eye of Inspector-General Gustav von Hindersin, tactical training reached a high degree of efficiency. A new *Abteilung* (brigade) system was introduced, in which the artillery was placed well to the front in the column of march. Groups of batteries were to go into action at the trot. There was to be no reserve – each battery was to push to the front as rapidly as possible and engage the enemy's guns in combat. The long-range duels of the Austrian War (up to 2,000 paces had been common) were rejected in favour of closer work. No longer were guns permitted to withdraw to replenish ammunition; instead an efficient system of supply was introduced.

The French Army which was to face the Prussians in 1870–71 was notably inferior in artillery. The French gunners were tactically competent, but their guns were mostly old bronze smooth-bores of the Lahitte type that had been rebored to take rifled ammunition. These guns were similar to the Austrian muzzle-loading rifles of 1866; even so, French gunnery was in practice less effective than that of the Austrians. The French, however, were counting on the Chassepot, their superior infantry rifle, and the *mitrailleuse*, a Gatling-like machine gun, to bring them victory.

In the first battles of the Franco-Prussian War the Prussian artillery, imbued with the von Hindersin spirit and eager to overcome the stigma of 1866, dashed into the open with the infantry – sometimes fighting right on the skirmish line. Inevitably, there were heavy casualties. According to Prince Kraft zu Hohenlohe-Ingelfingen, Chassepot fire 'battered' the gunners more than artillery fire, and it was not uncommon for whole batteries to be decimated by small arms fire as they went into action.

The French artillery, although hopelessly outclassed, was still able to play a few tricks on the Prussian zealots. At Gravelotte-St Privat, on 18 August 1870, the French guns duelled with 84 Prussian guns at 2,200 yards. When they found that they were having little effect on the French, the Prussians added more guns and closed to 1,650 yards. Suddenly, the French guns disappeared. A Prussian infantry assault went in; just as quickly, the French guns reappeared and destroyed the infantry. This bold piece of deceit forced the Prussians to close their gun-line to within 1,000 yards of the French position; there they deployed 192 guns and fired on the French guns for two hours before hazarding a further assault by the infantry.

At the Battle of Sedan (1 September 1870), the Prussians caught a large French army in a valley completely sur-rounded by hills. As the King of Prussia, Count von Bismarck, von Moltke and other distinguished persons watched from the heights, the massed fire of the Prussian field guns was turned on the enemy. At first the battle followed the pattern of Malvern Hill (1862). As the French struggled forward seeking a way out of the 'mouse trap', their formations were badly torn by shell fire. Then more and more Prussian guns began to crowd into the gun line. Soon, four-fifths of the Prussian Army's artillery, nearly 600 guns in all, ringed Sedan. More counter-attacks were made. Each met the same fate. One French division sought refuge in the Bois de Garenne: instantly 540 guns were turned on the wood, and, from a distance, it appeared to be consumed in a blanket of flash and smoke. Finally, the French had had enough. Their army, numbering over 100,000 men, surrendered.

It was a traumatic end to the day for the French, whose near-sighted commanders had informed their troops 24 hours previously that the morrow would be spent resting! At the same time the world was served a grim warning as to the present capabilities of massed artillery.

ABOVE *The Montigny* mitrailleuse, *the multi-barrelled machine
gun with which the French had
hoped to surprise and destroy the
Prussians in the War of 1870–71.*
LEFT *Prussian artillery in the
trenches before Strasbourg, 1870.
The gun positions are flanked by
protective gabions – wickerwork
cylinders filled with earth.*

The Small Wars

The period between, roughly, the end of the Franco-Prussian War (1871) and the outbreak of World War I (1914) was one of great upheaval in the realm of ordnance. The reputation of Prussian (or rather, German) arms was at its height, and a cult of imitation swept the West. Soldiers donned the *Pickelhaube* (spiked helmet) in places as far apart as Aldershot in England and Fort Leavenworth, Kansas. What the plain weight of experience had failed to do, the German 'cult' did. The most conservative nations soon adopted rifled breech-loaders for their field artillery, and German arms manufacturers like Krupp enjoyed windfall sales.

The first nation to replace its field artillery was France, which, of course, had had direct experience of Krupp's rifled breech-loaders. The old Lahitte M-1859 rifled cannon-howitzer was supplanted in 1877 by the de Bange 90-mm field gun. The de Bange 'system', really a complete family of guns, had been adopted after intensive competition among French manufacturers. Reffye, Lahitolle, Orly and de Bange had all submitted designs, but de Bange won on

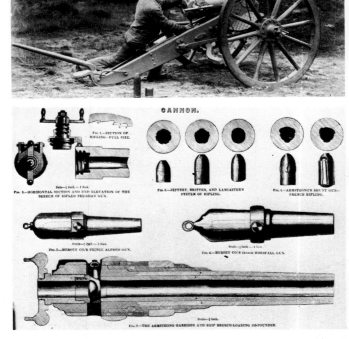

ABOVE *The devastated position of the Austrian Artillery Reserve after the Battle of Königgrätz (Sadowa) on 3 July 1866. During this engagement it was the stubborn fighting withdrawal of the Austrian artillery that saved General von Benedek's army from total destruction at the hands of von Moltke's Prussians.*

OPPOSITE, ABOVE *A Krupp employee works the elevating mechanism of a 2·95-inch field gun L/28.*

OPPOSITE, BELOW *A selection of cannon types and their breeches and rifling systems, as developed for service in the latter part of the 19th century. The largest diagram shows the built-up layers of wrought iron surrounding the breech of an Armstrong 110-pounder.*

ABOVE LEFT *A Krupp 4·13-inch fortress and siege gun L/35 with carriage; chocks were used to help stem the recoil.*

LEFT *The Krupp Works' specially designed heavy-gun transport.*

the merits of his very advanced design for a screw breech with an obturation system utilizing an expansive pad of asbestos, tallow and paraffin plastic[1]. When one of de Bange's guns was fired, the force of the explosion pushed a mushroom-shaped steel head backwards against the asbestos pad, which flattened and sealed the breech against the escape of gases. Since the pad would melt only at very high temperatures, maintenance and wear were kept to a minimum. This very efficient system is the most commonly used today.

In 1860 it had appeared that Great Britain would lead the world in adopting the new rifled breech-loaders. Tests conducted by the Ordnance following the Crimean War had matched Armstrong guns against the unique hexagonal-bore guns of Joseph Whitworth. Whitworth's iron breech-loaders burst frequently (none lasted beyond the tenth round) and took half an hour to load. Armstrong's guns performed well, although the lead coating of the projectiles stripped away during firing. It was decided to convert to Armstrong's pattern, and 12-pounder breech-loaders were ordered for the field artillery. These guns were used in the Second Opium War (1856–60), and although there were few complaints about the guns' performance, it was found that in the heat of action many crews failed to close the breech properly, which led to terrible accidents. Later, in 1863, there were more tests. This time Whitworth submitted a rifled muzzle-loader, and Armstrong's guns were found inferior in every respect to the muzzle-loaders. The conversion to Armstrong guns was halted in 1867, and by 1870 it was decided to revert to muzzle-loaders. The new muzzle-loaders would, however, use Armstrong's three-

[1] The problem of obturation, *i.e.* securing a gas-tight seal in the breech, had preoccupied gunners since the cannon was first introduced to Western armies in the 14th century.

groove system of rifling and fire an improved studded shell called the Woolwich pattern. Not until 1885 did Great Britain finally adopt rifled breech-loaders for her horse and field artillery.

In the United States the 3-inch Ordnance rifles of Civil War fame (see pages 34–35) remained standard until almost 1900–though new 3·2-inch breech-loading rifles were used in the Spanish-American War (1898). In this respect the United States was the most conservative of the Great Powers–a state of mind induced by her more or less isolated position. For her there was simply no compelling reason to modernize or re-equip.

The Russo-Turkish War (1877–78) was in many ways a very modern war. It was the first in which the infantry was uniformly equipped with modern repeating rifles and in which the field artillery of both sides used only breech-loading rifles. The Krupp Works had equipped the artillery park of Sultan Abdul Azeez with 4- and 6-pounder steel breech-loaders, developed after the Battle of Königgrätz (1866), while the Czar had dropped his 'Napoleon' muzzle-loaders after 1870 and re-equipped with Krupp bronze 4- and 9-pounders. Both nations evidently liked what they were buying, for throughout the latter half of the 19th century Russia and Turkey were Krupp's biggest foreign customers.

This was also the first European war in which improvised field-works were commonplace, the Russians being especially skilled in this area. Against them the artillery formed the crack arm of the Sultan's forces.

Despite their modern equipment, artillerymen still preferred in those days to fight their guns on the infantry line. This tendency to close to short range had been observable in all the wars of this era, and may be attributed more to the lack of modern sights and powerful explosive shells than to

other factors. Until these problems were solved, artillerists could not exploit the improved ranges and rapid-firing qualities of their guns to proper effect.

In 1883 the German General Kolmar von der Goltz wrote that 'each new invention and each mechanical improvement seems, somehow, in these days, to find its way into military service'. Ordnance benefited particularly from the great outpouring of scientific ideas, and within a very short time it had been completely transformed.

This rush of scientific activity was on the whole carried out in a humanitarian spirit. Von der Goltz himself believed that science and invention would make wars shorter, perhaps end war altogether; in this he echoed the notion of Robert Southey, the English poet, that 'the chemist and the mechanist will succeed where moralists and divines have failed'. Few foresaw that these developments would make possible the unprecedented carnage of World War I.

Some of the most important of the new developments were:

1 Improved time fuses were devised in France c. 1877.
2 The first good smokeless powder was developed by a Frenchman, Paul Vieille, in 1884; the powder was called 'Poudre B' after General Boulanger. In 1891 the British first produced cordite, a smokeless powder that was stable and retained its potency over a long period of time. Flashless powder (which did nevertheless produce smoke) was developed for night firing during World War I.
3 In 1888 Konrad Haussner developed the revolutionary long-recoil cylinder, which made possible Quick-Firing (QF) guns.
4 By 1896 wire-wound heavy guns were being constructed. These guns were superior by far to the comparatively

1871–1900: the onrush of scientific activity brings improved fuses and powder, and Quick-Firing guns.

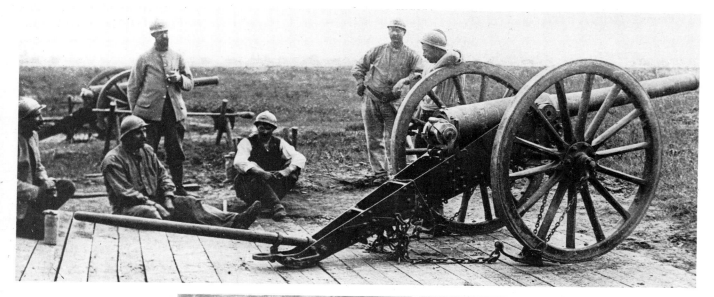

OPPOSITE *A Krupp 28-cm howitzer is towed to its firing position by motor car in two loads; the gun crew accompanies the barrel. In the second pair of photographs, barrel and carriage are joined together. The caterpillars or pattens on the wheels helped to distribute the gun's weight and improved its stability.*

LEFT *Count von Schlieffen, German Chief of Staff 1891–1906, whose master plan for a European war hinged on the invasion of France through Belgium. To deal with the barrier posed by the Belgian forts, Krupp developed their giant 42-cm howitzers.*

ABOVE *A battery of de Bange '90s' in a quiet sector of the Western Front in World War I. Introduced in 1877, de Bange's screw breech design was the most advanced of its day – though obsolescent by the Great War.*

brittle cast or forged guns. Subsequently frettage, a system in which hot steel tubes were shrunk onto one another, became the chief method of constructing guns.

5 The QF field-gun demanded 'fixed' ammunition, and during this period first brass and then steel cartridges were produced. ('Fixed' ammunition employs one cart-ridge-type unit for both charge and projectile, unlike 'bag' ammunition in which the projectile and bag charge are loaded separately.)

The impressive performance of rifled siege guns had rendered every existing brick fort obsolete. European nations sought, therefore, to rebuild their frontier defences using new ideas. The French system, designed by General Séré de Rivière, was begun in 1873. It consisted of fortified localities defended by detached forts. The forts were built of concrete covered with earth, they had cast-steel gun turrets and subterranean magazines and living quarters, and each was meant to be self-sufficient in defence.

The fear of invasion would, in time, lead other nations to construct similar defensive systems. The Germans began a network of forts along the line Thionville-Metz-Strasbourg and then along the Rhine to the Swiss border at Basle. Eventually the Russians and Rumanians began fortress systems, and in 1888 the Belgian engineer Brialmont began the construction of forts at Liège, Namur and other Belgian towns. The Belgian system then complemented and ex-tended the French system northwards.

All this construction was to have an effect on ordnance. The sizes of fortresses and manageable siege guns increased tremendously in the late 19th century. Krupp produced howitzers of 21-cm calibre for the German Foot Artillery. Additionally *die Firma*, as the Krupp Works was also known,

embarked on an ambitious programme of its own for a 42-cm howitzer.

Krupp's first 42-cm type, known as the 'heavy Gamma implement', was demonstrated to the German General Staff in 1911. As it happened, these guns were just what the General Staff thought necessary to deal with Brialmont's forts. Under the German contingency plan for a European war (called the Schlieffen Plan after Count von Schlieffen, Chief of the General Staff, 1891–1906) the German armies were to swing north through a neutral Belgium (thereby avoiding de Rivière's forts) and descend from the north-east onto the flank of the French armies guarding the frontier. The Belgian forts would block the flow of this movement, but it was thought that Krupp's monster 42-cm howitzers would be able to deal with them.

The only problem remaining was that of mobility. The 'Gamma implements' which were first produced had to be transported by rail and required a heavy-duty concrete emplacement before they could be brought into action. While all this was happening, of course, the French armies would be able to redeploy to meet the offensive.

ABOVE *A 3·2-inch breech-loading rifle, standard US field gun in the Spanish-American War and in the Philippines.*
LEFT *The dynamite gun attached to the Rough Riders cavalry regiment, seen in the trenches on San Juan Hill, Cuba, 1888.*
OPPOSITE *A Spanish 12-inch coastal defence gun of the Santa Clara Battery at Vedado, Cuba.*

Krupp solved this problem by creating a lighter 42-cm howitzer which became known as the 'M-implement', or more familiarly as 'Big Bertha'. The new weapon had a shorter barrel than the General Staff's railway gun and was broken down into four loads for road transport. There was, furthermore, no need to construct a special emplacement to bring the gun into action. When the M-implement was fired, its 1,800-pound shell rose almost vertically for three miles and then began to plunge at a very high velocity onto the target some 10,000 yards away. The effect of such a shell may well be imagined.

The Spanish-American War (1898) and the Boer War (1899–1902), although separated in time by barely a year, might well have been decades apart in artillery technique. The US gunners in Cuba used the 3·2-inch breech-loading rifle introduced for service in 1893, and later described by one artilleryman as 'the latest, and the last development of the old non-recoil material, firing unfixed ammunition with black powder charges and unprovided with any kind of laying apparatus for indirect fire'. Against them Spanish sharpshooters firing Mauser magazine rifles forced the

gunners to stay beyond an effective range (2,600 yards at El Pozo, for example) for guns equipped with primitive sights, and American artillery fire was ineffectual. By far the most useful guns in the campaign were machine guns like the Hotchkiss 1-pounder revolving cannon.

In the Boer War the British faced similar problems. Their gunners were well equipped with rapid-fire rifled breech-loaders: field artillery batteries used a 15-pounder, field howitzer batteries a 5-inch howitzer and the Royal Horse Artillery a 12-pounder. These guns were not in the same class as the modern French and German guns of the Boer artillery, but the Boers never fielded more than a handful of guns at any one time. The real problem for the British was the Boer mounted rifleman. Equipped with Mausers, like the Spanish in Cuba, these men were expert shots and adept at picking off gunners from a distance. In their response, however, the British artillerymen were more successful than their US counterparts. They learned the technique of indirect fire and also to utilize every scrap of cover and dip of ground in the sparse veldt. The Boer War was in fact the first war in which indirect fire and firing from concealed positions were extensively used.

One oddity made its début in Cuba during the Spanish-American War. This was the dynamite field gun invented by Captain E. L. Zalinsky, an American engineer. These guns were basically terror weapons, incapable of doing much damage to infantry in open order, since they depended for their effect on the blast of their dynamite and gelatine charge rather than on splinters. The gun used in Cuba was attached to the Rough Riders cavalry regiment and was fired into Santiago from the trenches on San Juan Hill.

In order to fire a material as unstable as dynamite with relative safety, Zalinsky utilized a combustion chamber separate from the firing tube. Approximately 7–9 ounces of smokeless powder were detonated in the combustion chamber, compressing the air in the chamber. The compressed air was then conducted into the firing tube behind the shell casing, forcing it along the barrel. The gun had a range of 2,600–3,600 yards depending on the amount of combustion powder used: it was not much used in the war because of its short range and inaccuracy.

The Boer War was also notable for freak guns. Prominent among them were the 'home-made' guns used to help defend the towns of Mafeking and Kimberley. The 'Wolf', a 4·5-inch howitzer used at Mafeking, had a barrel made from a drainpipe. 'Long Cecil', the Kimberley gun, was more conventional but was made in the factory of a mining company by men who had never made a gun before.

Immediately following the Spanish-American War, United States troops became involved in putting down the insurrection of Emilio Aguinaldo in the Philippines. This difficult guerrilla war, fought largely in paddy and bamboo jungle, cost the US Army more men than the Spanish-American War. A few guns were available but not much ammunition. Even so, the field guns were next to useless against the *insurrectos*, who took care to construct wide-ranging systems of slit trenches whenever they decided to defend a locality. One US artilleryman, commenting on the difficulty of shelling the rudimentary works of the Filipinos, repeated the old adage that 'you cannot shoot an enemy out of a position'. The plain fact was that the modern shrapnel shell, so recently invented, was proving to be useless against troops clever enough to conceal themselves; nor could field guns designed for low-trajectory work fire their HE with any real effect against trenches constructed with proper care.

Artillery in the Boer War (1899–1902), the Spanish-American War (1898) and in the Philippines Insurrection (1899–1902).

Light guns fight
with the infantry
in the Philippines.

OPPOSITE, TOP *American 1·65-inch infantry cannon used in a forward position during the Philippines Insurrection.*
OPPOSITE, BELOW *A Royal Artillery gun crew in the Boer War prepares to fire.*
BELOW *A 'home-made' artillery piece, marshalled for the defence of Mafeking, 1899.*
BELOW RIGHT *A British howitzer battery on the road in South Africa; the gun shown is a 5-inch field howitzer, a type introduced in 1896.*

In the Russo-Japanese War (1904–5) indirect fire was the norm. Improved panoramic sights, goniometers (for measuring angles), aerial observation (by balloon) and the extensive use of field telephones, especially by the Japanese, allowed batteries to fire on targets they could not see but which were within their range. Since a gun's field of fire was now equal to the frontage of an army corps, flag and telephone could mass the fire of an entire corps' guns.

An artillerist's view of actions in the Boer War.

At the beginning of the war the Russian field artillery received a new long-recoil type Quick-Firing field gun – the M-1903 Putilov 76·2-mm. This gun, an improvement on a similar 1900 model, was very modern; even so it was heavier and less mobile than the comparable Japanese gun. (The older M-1900 76·2-mm gun had, incidentally, an interesting and unique feature – a recoil system made of India rubber to avoid freezing in the severe Manchurian winter.)

The standard Japanese field gun was designated the 7-cm (actual calibre 7·5-cm) M-31 (1898). This gun did not have a modern recoil system and its overall performance was unsatisfactory; nevertheless its light weight was a distinct advantage in the trackless wastes of Manchuria. Its replacement, the Type 38 (1905) 75-mm gun, was not produced in time to see action in the war, but incorporated design features that the Japanese felt essential after their experiences with the Type 31. It had a hydraulic buffer system, improved sights and increased velocity. The Type 38 remained in service until World War II. It is interesting

1904—05: the Japanese gunners grow skilled in the arts of camouflage and concealment.

also to note here that the Japanese had used French 4-pounders up to the time of the Franco-Prussian War, and Krupp rifles thereafter. The first field guns manufactured in Japan were 4-pounder muzzle-loaders produced at the Osaka arsenal in 1872.

One of the more modern aspects of the Russo-Japanese War was the need for batteries to conceal their positions from enemy observers. The Japanese brought the art of camouflage to a high state during the war, using trees and netting to hide their guns and even watering trails along which guns were to be moved so that their movement would not raise tell-tale clouds of dust.

The six-month siege of Port Arthur by the Japanese was a turning-point in the war. General Velichko, the man who planned the Port Arthur defences, was a highly competent

ABOVE *Japanese artillery officers observe the effect of the fire of their mountain guns during the Russo-Japanese War.*
BELOW *Breech-loading rifles in a Russian fort overlooking the harbour of Port Arthur.*
OPPOSITE. *In the upper picture a Japanese field gun is manhandled into position under fire. Below is a heavy gun at Port Arthur, 1905. Note the obsolescent barbette carriage and observation tower at left—equipment typical of that supplied to imperial outposts at the turn of the century.*

engineer with advanced ideas. While he did not totally reject the ideas of Brialmont and de Rivière, he did not accept their contention that all the guns in a perimeter defence must be in the forts. The forts that Velichko designed for Port Arthur contained a few heavy guns, but most of the guns were outside the forts in batteries. This

A turning-point in the war: Japanese howitzers bombard the Russian fleet at anchor in Port Arthur harbour.

meant that the attacker would have to divide his fire, also that there would be no 'dead' ground which might allow his infantry to slip through the perimeter unmolested by artillery fire.

The Japanese attacked Velichko's forts using the heaviest ordnance and most up-to-date fire-direction and ranging equipment then available. Before this siege 15-cm guns and howitzers, such as the Prussians had used against Paris in 1871, had been the largest pieces normally found in siege trains. At Port Arthur the Japanese used howitzers up to 28-cm in calibre.

The Japanese artillery command post was sophisticated even by later standards. A camera obscura was used to study the Russian fortifications in the manner of a periscope, and telephone lines relayed the orders of the chief of artillery to each battery. Even when the artillery commander left his concrete command post, he was followed by a man playing out telephone cable so that he should be in instantaneous communication with his batteries at any time.

Despite their thorough organization, the initial effect of the Japanese bombardment was less than decisive. Eventually, however, a crucial Russian fortress (203-Metre Hill) was taken with heavy infantry losses. That was the moment of breakthrough. For when the Japanese then emplaced 28-cm howitzers on 203-Metre Hill and bombarded the Russian Pacific fleet in the harbour 4,000 yards away, only one vessel, the *Sebastopol* (ironically enough), escaped scuttling or sinking. It was the beginning of the end; within a few weeks the survivors in the Russian garrison surrendered.

4

SEA POWER

The limited offensive power of early fighting ships, driven by oars and armed with rams and crude cannon.

Sea power is the means by which a nation contests, secures and maintains a command of the sea sufficient to allow it to transport economic and military resources at will whilst denying such facilities to an enemy. This power is built on several distinct foundations, e.g. bases, dockyards, ordnance factories and the merchant marine; but in many people's minds sea power is identified more particularly with the warship.

Yet if the warship has a certain symbolic value, this is clearly a secondary function. What, then, are the primary or 'real' tasks of the warship? What strategic and tactical aims does it fulfil?

Essentially, the strategic and tactical concepts of every nation are determined by the most powerful weapon of destruction in existence at any given time; and the nature of the weapon itself is dictated by the level of technical sophistication at that time. Warships, which are a compromise between armament, defence, the power that drives them and the material they are made of, reflect the technological situation at any given moment. They are, moreover, built either directly around the most powerful weapon of destruction or in support of the ship that carries it.

In 1815 the only type of fighting ship was one built around a crude and inaccurate cannon. Armed with broadsides of smooth-bore muzzle-loading cannon and moved by wind and tide, the wooden sailing ship had, from the latter part of the 16th century onwards, largely taken over from the galley (and its immediate successor, the galleass) as the principal naval unit.

The galley had dominated the waters of the Mediterranean for centuries. It was light yet strong and possessed powers of independent movement – achieved through its banks of oars – but little offensive power. Its ram was not a particularly effective weapon and there was but a fine distinction – measurable in terms of a few yards – between ramming and being rammed. Sea fighting was little more than an extension of land warfare. The main weapon was the boarding party with 'fire support' from arrows, lime, flame and stone. At this stage the skill of the mariner was subordinate to the command of the soldier. The galley remained dominant until the cannon ceased to be a small, weak, anti-personnel weapon fit for use only against boarders and had developed into a heavy ordnance piece capable of inflicting serious damage on a ship.

Increasing weights of gun and shot could not be countered by the galley. Heavier gun carriages necessitated stronger decks; heavier shot needed thicker sides for defence; but

RIGHT *Reconstruction of a Phoenician war galley of the 7th century* BC.
BELOW RIGHT *Egyptian relief showing a naval encounter at the time of Rameses II (13th century* BC*). Of necessity, the combatants fought hand-to-hand or at very close range with spears and bows.*
BELOW *An English galleass of the 16th century. This early type of gunned fighting ship carried too few guns and was superseded by the sailing ship.*

DIAGRAMMATIC SECTION
AMIDSHIPS.

16th century: the naval gun acquires a more effective platform – the sailing ship.

the accumulation of weight would have robbed the galley of its two great advantages: speed and mobility. Unsuccessful attempts were made to incorporate guns on a galley (the galleass) but no satisfactory solution appeared until the power of independent movement – via the oars – was sacrificed in the cause of improved offensive power.

The gun demanded and obtained its own platform – the sailing ship. This type of vessel, unlike the short-ranged galley, possessed the power of virtually unlimited sea endurance. The sailing ship flourished along Europe's Atlantic seaboard where waters were rough and where the galley could not be as effective as it was in the generally calmer Mediterranean. Thus it was the northern European countries, particularly England, that largely pioneered the development of the gun-carrying sailing ship. Voyages of discovery and the acquisition of overseas empires accelerated the process and other European states followed this lead.

Even so, for much of the 16th century the galley/galleass and the sailing ship existed side by side. Indeed the galley survived almost until the 19th century in the calm and well-charted waters of the Black and Baltic Seas – though these were now backwaters, the balance of naval power having shifted elsewhere. In much the same way that many machines achieve the peak of their power just before their replacement by superior devices, the galley and the galleass reached their zenith at the Battle of Lepanto in 1571 – only 17 years before the gunned sailing ships of England and Spain fought their historic duel around the coasts of the British Isles.

Between 1588 and 1815 the development of the fighting ship was very slow. There was continual evolution as keel construction changed and ships grew in size and displacement, in complement, and in the number and size of their guns. Yet, fundamentally, Nelson's ships were little

ABOVE *Galleys and galleasses in conflict at the peak of their development, in the Battle of Lepanto, 1571.*
OPPOSITE *A new era dawns in naval warfare as the gunned sailing ships of England and Spain meet in their famous battle of 1588. The scene depicts the fighting off Gravelines, with the English fire-ships going into action.*
LEFT *HMS* Victory, *Admiral Nelson's flagship; her design was little different from Drake's 16th-century warships.*
BELOW *A 24-pounder cannon retrieved from the Swedish warship* Vasa, *which sank in 1628.*

different from those of Drake, and the Englishmen who opposed the Armada could have manned the *Victory* with little difficulty; the skills of seamanship and gunnery had not changed. Since, too, knowledge of ship construction was universally the same, there was a marked similarity between the ships of different nations. However, within 50 years of Waterloo, the harmony of two and a half centuries of evolution was swept aside by the impact of the Industrial Revolution.

In the vanguard of change were the French. An impressive run of defeats had made them willing, indeed anxious, to consider new methods of construction and fighting that

ABOVE *The launching in 1814 of the American double-keeled steam warship* Demologos. *The advent at this time of steam propulsion was the first of many technological changes.*
RIGHT *The* Napoleon, *laid down in 1850; this was the first battleship designed with auxiliary screw power.*
OPPOSITE *The British tug* Monkey (1821), *the first steam ship in the Royal Navy.*

1812–25: the fighting navies of Europe and the USA experiment with steam propulsion.

would challenge Britain's supremacy. All the nations followed France's lead – even Britain, though she tended to do so with reluctance, being loath to abandon systems that had served her well. As a result of this new surge of activity, the similarities in design that had existed collapsed as the paths of the nations gradually divided. Working with new materials and with new concepts on the very fringes of knowledge, designers now had no common pool of experience or guidance on which to draw. The results were individualistic, often bizarre, and occasionally disastrous.

The first technological change came in the field of propulsion. The steam engine was developed virtually simultaneously in Britain, France and the United States at the time of the French Revolutionary and Napoleonic Wars. Passenger-carrying steam ships seem to have been in use in the first decade of the 19th century and probably the first cargo-carrying steamer plied the Mississippi in 1811. During the War of 1812 the Americans, spurred by defeat and the pressures of a naval blockade, planned a double-keeled steam ship called the *Demologos* to contest the Royal Navy's command of the seas; but peace was signed before anything came of it. In 1815 the British carried out unsuccessful experiments with a converted ship, the *Congo*, but failed to pursue the work after early reverses. The first application of steam to the fighting navies came in a much humbler form and followed the lead of the merchant fleets, which used tugs to take ocean-going ships to sea against prevailing winds. The first steam ships in the Royal Navy were the tugs *Monkey* (1821), *Comet* (1822) and *Sprightly* (1823).

It was quickly realized that auxiliary steam propulsion would be of great value even in ocean-going ships, since it would avoid the problems of being becalmed and would also give some tactical as well as strategic mobility. But, initially, attempts to fit warships with steam power were unsuccessful, for at this time the paddle provided the method of movement and the placing amidships of paddles and engines led to a considerable reduction in gun power; independent movement had been regained – but at too great a price in offensive power. Eventually the screw propeller solved this problem: it was carried beneath the waterline and, unlike the paddle, was largely invulnerable to gunfire; moreover, the engines had to be carried lower

LEFT La Gloire *(1858); a new type of ship, designed in France, its wooden hull was protected by iron.*

in a screw ship than in a paddlewheeler, and so they had little adverse effect on gun space.

However, it took a long time for screw propulsion to gain widespread acceptance and it was not until 1850 that the first battleship designed with auxiliary screw power was laid down. In a sense this ship, the *Napoleon*, started the first technological naval race as France and Great Britain sought to out-build and out-convert one another. By 1858 there were 76 ships with auxiliary screw power, evenly divided between the two countries, but already the advantage lay slightly with the French who had, in 1855, announced a programme that totalled 40 battleships, 30 corvettes and 60 other craft. The British, on the other hand, had no long-term programme and were responding to events rather than imposing their will upon them.

A new threat was posed by increasing offensive power. Shells had been used with devastating effect by the Russians against the Turkish fleet in November 1853 at the Battle of Sinope, an encounter that showed the vulnerability of wooden ships to explosive and incendiary shells.

The immediate answer to the shell was provided by the French. On 17 October 1855, during an attack on the fortress of Kinburn, the French used three naval batteries, those of the *Devastation*, the *Tonnante* and the *Lave*, with their main battle line. These craft had auxiliary steam power

PREVIOUS PAGES *Steam leading sail. The 'Fighting Temeraire' is towed to her last berth, 1838; from the painting by Turner. Inset is the* Great Britain, *Brunel's revolutionary steamship.* BELOW *The* Dévastation; *a predecessor of* La Gloire, *she served in Crimea with armour plating added to the hull.* ABOVE RIGHT *HMS* Warrior, *the world's first iron-built warship.*

and carried 16 guns that fired 56-pounder shells. But, most important of all, each ship had 4·5 inches of iron plating covering the basic 18 inches of wood that protected the ships. Between them the French ships took 134 hits but suffered no appreciable damage.

Armour seemed to offer an effective answer to the shell. But shells, too, were undergoing revolutionary changes, as were the methods used to fire them. Soon after the Crimean War it was appreciated that the cylinder made a more efficient projectile shape than the long-established sphere, and the cylinder was then generally adopted. This, coupled with the rifling of gun barrels – to impart spin and hence a better-controlled flight – promised greater accuracy as well as improved penetrative powers. In addition, improved breech mechanisms were appearing which made it likely that most guns would in time be breech-loaded.

In 1858 the French, after some hesitation, laid down at Toulon a new type of ship, a wooden-hulled but iron-protected frigate – *La Gloire*[1]. Three further ships were ordered, one of which was to have an iron hull. But the French were outbuilt by the British. As early as 1845, possibly influenced by Brunel's revolutionary steamship, the *Great Britain*,[2] the Admiralty had countenanced iron frigates, but had been prevented from taking such a step by outraged public reaction. Since that time, engines and boilers had improved and grown larger, so increasing the strain on the wooden parts of ships. The promise – or threat – of still bigger guns and the new onus of armour were burdens that wood could no longer take; by now it had reached the limit of its strength. Finally, on 29 December 1860, the *Warrior*, the world's first iron war ship, was launched and with her came a new era of ship construction.

---

[1] Although she had about twice the displacement of a battleship, she was classified as a frigate because her guns were laid out on a single deck.

[2] Brunel's remarkable ship was the first ocean-going ship to be built of iron, to have a clipper bow, screw propulsion and a balanced rudder – an impressive collection of 'firsts'.

Warships of Iron

The *Warrior*, a frigate displacing over 9,200 tons, carried an armament of 26 68-pounder, 14 110-pounder and 4 70-pounder guns. Unlike *La Gloire*, which was armoured over the complete length of her waterline, the *Warrior* was unarmoured at bow and stern; her belt, 4·5 inches of wrought iron backed by 18 inches of teak, extended only over 56 per cent of her length. The ends were sealed by 4·5-inch bulkheads which thereby produced a citadel within which most of the guns were sited. The French, on the other hand, correctly appreciated that in future *all* guns would have to be behind armour; the *Magenta* and the *Solferino*, the only two-deck broadside ironclads ever built, carried all their 34 16-cm and 16 19-cm guns within the citadel.

The *Warrior* and the early French ships shared a common disability: though very strong defensively, they lacked the firepower to sink another ironclad warship. Rifling did not substantially aid that firepower, and the first breech-loaders anyway left much to be desired. Indeed, the *Warrior*'s 68-pounder muzzle-loading guns showed themselves to be superior to the others, which were all breech-loaders, with the result that the ship was subsequently re-armed solely with 68-pounders. Nevertheless, not even these guns could inflict damage on a scale that was likely to be decisive. To overcome the power of the defence, heavier and more powerful guns were needed.

The French attempted to solve this problem by the suppression of the broadside. The latter was, in fact, an inefficient method of arranging guns since it meant that the field of fire was mainly restricted to one at 90° to the ship's direction of travel. The broadside was suppressed in favour of fewer but heavier guns capable of firing through wide arcs. All of these 'pivotal' guns were positioned behind armour in what became known as a 'central battery'. The British followed and developed the French idea until the first years of the 1870s, by which time this type of arrangement was passing into obsolescence.

The era of the central-battery ship coincided with the meteoric rise of the 'ram ship'; but this, like a meteor, faded from the scene almost as rapidly as it had arrived. In 1866, at the Battle of Lissa, the Austrian battleship *Ferdinand Max* had rammed and sunk the Italian battleship *Re d'Italia*. That the Italian ship had been previously crippled by gunfire and, furthermore, that this was the only occasion when a ship was successfully rammed in the course of a battle that abounded in such attempts, were

factors brushed aside at the time as being of no account; and so the ram became established as a powerful offensive weapon. In the late 1860s ram ships were built by most navies, though it quickly became apparent that rams were much over-estimated. The chances of ramming a ship that still had full power of manoeuvre and adequate sea room were small, and the increasing power of artillery suggested that a ram ship would be unable to close to effective range, without herself being crippled.

Nevertheless, in the course of its short life, the ram ship helped to produce a successor to the central-battery idea. Ram ships carried little in the way of gun power, and what they had was generally sited over the bows. From this alternative pattern it was next recognized that all-round fire was desirable, and the *Hotspur*, laid down in 1868, incorporated a turret. A moving turntable trained a single gun through four loopholes cut in fixed armour.

It seems that the turret was first patented in 1859 by Captain Cowper Coles, RN. His idea had sprung from an armoured raft that he had designed in 1855 as a result of combat experience in the Crimea. There he had constructed an armed raft that drew only 20 inches of water and was used for inshore bombardment. The turret could be incorporated in such craft, and in river gunboats, because in their design little store was set by seakeeping qualities. Designers of ocean-going craft had, on the other hand, to allow for the fact that the weight of a turret tended to reduce freeboard – the area between waterline and deck – to the detriment of seaworthiness. But this did not prevent Coles from designing a ship of 9,200 tons with 10 cupolas – the dome-shaped structures protecting the guns – and 20 breech-loaders. Not surprisingly the idea was rejected, but in 1861 the Admiralty carried out tests on turrets.

The turret showed unanticipated powers of resistance – and this was confirmed in the fight between the USS *Monitor* and the CSS *Merrimack* in Hampton Roads on 9 March 1862. The 10-gunned *Merrimack*'s easy successes gained against wooden Union ships (including the first successful ramming of a ship, the *Cumberland*, in modern times) were not repeated when the Confederate vessel engaged the 2-gunned, turreted *Monitor*. A six-hour engagement did no serious damage to either ship but the *Monitor*'s performance proved the obvious desirability of turrets; it was equally obvious that ships such as the *Monitor*, whose deck was only a few inches above the water, were

BELOW *The US double-turretted warship* Terror; *this was a retrograde design, being made of wood.*

The search for greater firepower brings the suppression of the broadside in favour of central-battery and turret armaments; the brief life of the ram ship.

TOP *A view of the historic six-hour engagement between* Monitor *and the Confederate ship* Merrimac; *this battle established the virtues of the turreted fighting ship.*
ABOVE *The raft* Lady Nancy, *carrying a 32-pounder gun into shallow waters at Taganrog, Crimea. In the foreground is a whaler mounting a Congreve rocket launcher.*
LEFT *The* Monitor, *a turreted steel-clad warship that fought on the Federal side in the American Civil War.*

not capable of anything but the most limited operations. Indeed, the *Monitor* was lost in the first gale she encountered in December 1862.

The first British turret ships were coastal defence craft, then in 1868 the launching took place of the first ocean-going ship with turrets, the *Monarch*. Able to make nearly 15 knots under steam and sail, the 8,300-ton *Monarch* carried four 12-inch guns in two central turrets. She was followed by the *Captain*, which carried the tallest and heaviest masts in the Royal Navy. She also had a very low freeboard of 8·5 feet which was further reduced as excess weight was worked into her during construction. The *Captain* soon foundered, in a gale that she should have survived. Her loss, on 6–7 September 1870, resulted in a temporary set-back for the turret but hastened the passing of masts and rigging. After the *Captain* only three British battleships

carried a full rig, and steam emerged from being the auxiliary to become the only means of propulsion.

The 1860s was thus a confused era of shipbuilding with several different types of armament vying with each other for acceptance. But by the early years of the next decade the issues of steam and sail, turret, central battery and broadside had been largely resolved. In the 1870s the major developments centred around the monster gun. In 1872 the Italians laid down the *Duilio*, a battleship to be armed with four 12-inch 38-ton guns. During construction she was altered to take first 15-inch 50-ton guns and then 17·7-inch 100-ton guns. The continual modification of the initial design caused the Italians a variety of problems: ultimately the ship was so weakly armoured that she could not have engaged any comparable ship with much hope of survival. Her huge guns were also so slow to work that the chances of hitting an enemy were rather slim. Nevertheless the *Duilio* was widely acclaimed and her effect was immediate. Other nations had to increase the size of their guns and the armour protection afforded their ships. The *Inflexible*, the British response, carried up to 24 inches of compound armour (iron backed by teak and steel) in her central areas while her waterline bulkheads were up to 22 inches thick. She also incorporated an armoured deck below the waterline and was extensively sub-divided in order to control flooding.

The era of the monster gun was, however, fairly short. The destructive potential of a 110-ton gun was formidable – on paper. In reality it was less impressive. Not only were the guns extremely slow to fire (the *Inflexible*, with one round every two minutes, was comparatively fast), they were also very inaccurate. As early as 1871, attention was drawn to the poor shooting of British ships: in one trial a

advantage without having to close to ranges at which even the monster guns, with their erratic record, would find it impossible to miss.

In the 1880s several major developments in gunnery took place, as a result of which, after extensive trials and many errors, the breech-loading gun was generally adopted in favour of the muzzle-loader. The new breech-loaders were lighter than earlier versions had been, and this prompted two design changes in the ships that carried them. Firstly, high freeboard was regained, and with it came immediate benefits in terms of speed and seaworthiness. Secondly, more guns could now be carried per ship, and battleships began to assume the design usually associated with modern warships in general and with

carefully laid gun on HMS *Hotspur* missed the target (another battleship) at 200 yards' range in a flat calm, both target and firer being stationary.

One further problem arose at this time, that of whether the ships could take the strain caused by the prolonged firing of their own guns. There was obviously a need for ships with smaller and more numerous guns that would put down a heavy volume of fire rather than a few very heavy shots. From such a volume of fire, it was reckoned, there should be enough punishing hits to secure a lasting

OPPOSITE, ABOVE *HMS* Sultan, *a central-battery armoured ship, seen offshore during a trial run.*
OPPOSITE, BELOW *Gunpowder in the late 19th century: the rail-mounted Nordenfeldt 6-inch breech-loading rifle is seen with a close-up of the Eastman breech-loading system.*

ABOVE *A Krupp gun mounted on a naval carriage; to the rear of the piece is the lifting tackle used to hoist ammunition up to the breech.*
BELOW LEFT *The Italian battleship* Duilio, *whose main guns were increased during her construction from 12 to 17·7 inches.*

battleships in particular : this incorporated a main armament in turrets fore and aft, with the intermediate and secondary armaments placed amidships between the heavy guns. The *Collingwood*, launched in 1882 but not completed for another four and a half years, was the first British ship to adopt this general design – though her heavy guns were in unprotected barbettes and not turrets. The *Collingwood* was also the first British ship to carry her secondary and tertiary armaments grouped in batteries. By the time she entered service, a third development, the introduction of the Quick-Firing (QF) gun, was in the pipeline. The *Nile* and the *Trafalgar*, both laid down in 1886, were the first

British ships to carry a QF secondary armament and within a short space of time even the heavy guns were capable of rapid fire.

The QF gun met a pressing need for the navies of the world. It provided a means of countering the first development to challenge the monopoly of the gun – the torpedo, and its delivery system, the torpedo boat.

Until the 1870s the word 'torpedo' described any underwater weapon; thereafter, as the search for such weapons intensified, the word came to embrace all weapons with the power of independent movement. They were thus distinguished from weapons that were either moored or moved by tide and current.

The idea of striking at a ship at its most vulnerable part – below the waterline – by means of an explosive charge may be traced back to the latter part of the 16th century, but it was not until the beginning of the 19th century that the prototype of the modern mine was developed. Robert Fulton, an American, invented an explosive charge contained in a metal case for action against ships; the charge was detonated by clockwork. The first major breakthrough in mine development came in 1843 when Samuel Colt, the inventor of the revolver, devised a 'controlled' mine that was detonated by an electric current operated from an observation post ashore. A similar though separate develop-

ment was made in Kiel at about the same time and weapons of this type were used in the defence of the harbour against the Danish fleet in the war of 1848.

Subsequently contact mines, designed to explode when in collision with a ship, came into being. A small gunpowder charge was detonated when the tubes protruding from the sides of the mine were broken by collision with their target. This brought sulphuric acid into contact with potassium chlorate and sugar which in turn generated enough heat and flame to set off the main charge.

Mines were extensively used by the Russians during the Crimean War but they caused no losses; the first ship lost to a mine was the USS *Cairo* in the Battle of Yazoo River on 12 December 1862. Mines were improved when a more efficient method of detonation was found, and a means of safely laying the mine to a prescribed depth. The British solved the latter problem by laying the mine with a sinker (or anchor) which dropped it to the seabed. The mine was automatically released once the laying ship was clear and then rose on a cable towards the surface. When it reached the level at which it was to operate, water pressure activated a hydrostat which in turn worked a brake on the cable. At that point the mine was armed and ready for action.

By the end of the 19th century the mine had developed into a formidable weapon. In the course of the Russo–Japanese War of 1904–5 – the first war in which it was used on an extensive scale – the Russians lost a battleship, a cruiser, two destroyers and two smaller craft to mines while the Japanese lost, to the same weapon, two battleships (their only battleship casualties), four cruisers, two destroyers, a torpedo boat and a minelayer. The war clearly showed the dangers facing any navy that tried to blockade an enemy coast. Although it could be laid with equal facility in the open sea or offensively in the enemy's home waters, the mine was seen, ideally, as a defensive weapon that protected a coastline and its harbours.

The 'locomotive' torpedo, sometimes called the 'fish' or 'Whitehead' torpedo, was developed in Fiume, Austria (later Trieste, Italy) in 1866. The men responsible were Captain Luppis of the Austrian Navy and Robert Whitehead, a Scottish engineer who collaborated with him and who later introduced an improved model. Not unnaturally, the first prototypes were erratic and poor performers: this was partly because they lacked adequate means of steering and depth-keeping. Measuring some 14 feet by 14 inches and weighing 300 pounds (of which only 18 pounds was warhead), these early torpedoes had a maximum range of

OPPOSITE *The British ocean-going turret ship* Captain, *whose design was dangerously encumbered by the tallest and heaviest masts in the Royal Navy.*
TOP *HMS* Collingwood, *the first British warship to carry her main armament fore and aft (in barbettes, later ships had turrets); her secondary and tertiary guns were grouped amidships.*
ABOVE *HMS* Devastation, *a double-screw armour-plated turret ship built in 1871.*

about 370 yards at 6 knots. At this low speed avoiding action was not difficult and an attacker had to come virtually alongside his intended victim to be sure of a hit. But the range of the 'locomotive' torpedo was not as poor as those of its immediate rivals – the 'spar' and 'towed' torpedoes.

The 'spar' was an explosive charge carried on the end of a pole over the bows of a very fast attacker. It was detonated either by ramming it into the side of a victim or by lowering it under the keel and then activating the charge by pulling a string. It was by the former method that a Confederate hand-cranked submerged craft sank the Union sloop *Housatonic* on the night of 17 February 1864 – the first time a surface warship was sunk by an underwater craft (which was itself destroyed in the attempt).

The 'towed' torpedo was pulled by a very fast craft at

an angle to its course across the bows or stern of the intended target. The latter, fouling the wire that held the torpedo, then in theory pulled the weapon onto itself. But, in reality, the 'towed' torpedo needed liberal assistance on the part of the victim if it was to be successful.

The 'locomotive' torpedo at least had the advantages over its rivals that it was capable of improvement and did not demand suicidal tendencies on the part of the user. It also outlived one further challenge, that of the 'Brennan' torpedo. This was a wire-guided torpedo developed in Australia in the 1880s. However, the mass of wire needed for long-range work was dangerous on board a ship, and so the 'Brennan' was used mainly from the shore.

The problems encountered by Whitehead's improved locomotive torpedo in maintaining a steady course and a set depth were gradually overcome. Contra-rotating propellers helped to steady a torpedo on its course, but it was not until the invention of the gyroscope in the mid-1890s that accuracy could be guaranteed; the horizontal rudder, developed in 1877, went some way to solve the problem of depth-keeping. But even without these refinements the torpedo was able to claim its first victim. On the night of 25–26 January 1878 the Russian ships *Tchesma* and *Sulina* sank the 2,000-ton Turkish guardship *Intikbah* in Batum

While submarine pioneers struggle to solve their problems, the proponents of torpedo warfare rely on surface craft to launch their weapon.

harbour – though they had to close to less than 80 yards.

But, in general, the growing size and range of torpedoes made it possible to attack with greater safety. By the beginning of the 1890s the torpedo had a 300-pound warhead and a range of over 1,000 yards at 30 knots, and it was possible to launch the weapon from below the waterline of a moving ship.

The development of the torpedo gave a much-needed boost to the morale of submarine pioneers, for, unlike its predecessors, it did not entail immediate danger to the attacker. Furthermore, the submarine, by attacking under water, would avoid the heavy fire that any surface ship would have to face in view of the torpedo's restricted range. However, the technical limitations of the day kept the submarine as still merely an ideal. The same horizontal

rudder that aided the development of the torpedo substantially helped to control the dive of a submarine but there was no safe and reliable means of propulsion, either on the surface or submerged. Steam propulsion was not suitable to a vessel that had to dive (though *Le Plongeur*, a French craft built in 1863, was able to travel considerable distances underwater with her fires banked and using the head of steam that had been built up). Neither at the time was there any means of accurate underwater navigation, nor had any really suitable material been found for building submarines. Thus the proponents of torpedo warfare were forced in the early years to use surface craft as the means of launching the new weapon.

The first torpedo boats were built in the mid-1870s by France and Russia; both countries appreciated the potential

ABOVE *British seamen fit an electro-contact mine aboard* HMS Vernon.
RIGHT HMS Majestic, *laid down in 1893, was first in a new class of battleships using Harvey steel armour and the wire-wound 12-inch gun.*

for threatening British naval supremacy with the new weapon and its launching craft. The first torpedo boats were small and not particularly seaworthy, consisting of little more than boilers and engines encased in a lightweight hull. Everything was sacrificed to high speed. The ships had a limited range and no accommodation and their crews soon proved unable to cope with their tasks in poor weather conditions. It was quickly seen that such craft could not operate offensively on the high seas.

An alternative did exist, however. This was to take the torpedo boats with the fleet on-board other, larger ships. Thus for a while small, 20-ton torpedo craft were carried to the scene of an action, there to engage the enemy. (How then to recover them, in the face of the enemy, seems to have been an unresolved problem.) The Royal Navy built

one such carrier, the *Vulcan*: launched in 1889, she carried six small torpedo boats; but by then it was already clear that she and her like could never be more than a short-term expedient. The real solution lay in heavier, more seaworthy torpedo boats that were greater in both speed and range.

So the torpedo boat began to increase in size. The first Russian versions, which appeared in 1877, were only 75 feet × 10 feet – allegedly small enough to be moved between the Baltic and Black Seas by rail. But in the same year the British built a 90-foot ship capable of 19 knots – a speed that earned her the name *Lightning*.

As these new ships emerged from the dockyards, there arose a need for a ship to counter them. After initial experiments with heavier but underpowered 'catchers', it was clear that some form of totally new craft was needed.

The introduction of steel armour brings great savings in weight with no loss of defensive power.

The Arrival of Steel

Between 1890 and 1914 there was a period of relative stability in ship design. Many important changes and developments took place but mainly these were evolutionary rather than revolutionary in character. This period also marked an end to the era of rapid advances that had produced ships of widely differing characteristics and power and prevented the building up of homogeneous squadrons.

The new continuity that was being achieved was most marked in the battleship. In December 1893 the British laid down the first of the *Majestics*, a new class. The basic design of this class was to be followed until 1900, by which time 29 ships had been laid down. The *Majestics* benefited from the introduction of Harvey steel armour and the new wire-wound 12-inch gun: considerable savings in weight were thereby effected for no loss of power. The compound armour of earlier classes was halved with no loss to the defence; turrets enclosed the new guns whilst 6-inch casements defended the 6-inch armament. Throughout the citadel, armour was a uniform 9 inches thick, with a 14-inch bulkhead forward. A 2·5-inch curved protective deck ran from the citadel to the extremities. This basic design was improved upon by successors though the essentials were retained. Thus the later *Canopus* class ships were fitted with improved Krupp steel armour and the new water-tube boilers, which gave them a 2-knot advantage over the *Majestics*. And the *Formidable* class, laid down in 1898, incorporated the new 12-inch 40-calibre gun, which fired a smaller shell than the older 35-calibre weapon of the *Majestics* but had a much higher muzzle velocity and greater powers of penetration.

The first major British departure from the *Majestic* type of layout came with the *King Edward VII* class. This was brought about as a result of pressure exerted by overseas designs. On ships of similar displacement, the British found the ships of other nations carried greater armament. Whereas the *Majestic* class carried four 12-inch and 12 6-inch guns in the main armament (with 16 12-pounder and 12 3-pounder guns for anti-torpedo boat work), the USS *Oregon*, laid down two years before the first *Majestic*, carried an intermediate gun in the main armament. She carried four 13-inch, eight 8-inch and four 6-inch guns,

1905: the *Dreadnought*, using only big guns in the main armament, inspires fundamental changes in battleship design.

while the later *Kentucky* had four 13-inch, four 8-inch and 14 5-inch guns in the main armament. Italian ships also carried three types of gun in the main armament, but with them a more important factor was their high speed. Seeking to take advantage of their country's central position in the Mediterranean – and very conscious of the exposed nature of her long coasts – the Italians placed great store by the strategic and tactical mobility conferred by very high speed. (It was a policy which they were to continue until World War II). The *Sardegna* of 1893 and the *Vittorio Emanuele* of 1907 could make over 20 knots – though this was obtained at the expense of armour protection.

The *King Edward VII* class brought the British into line with these more powerful ships. They carried four 12-inch, four 9·2-inch and 10 6-inch guns in the main armament; however, this arrangement was heavily attacked. Its opponents felt that there were too many types and too few guns, and that the 6-inch guns could have been suppressed in favour of more 9·2-inch guns. The latter was much more powerful than the 6-inch and only a little slower in its rate of fire. With the *Lord Nelson* class, laid down in 1905, this alternative arrangement was tried. The two ships of this class carried four 12-inch and 10 9·2-inch guns and were the last British ships to carry a mixed primary armament. Even before these ships were laid down it was suggested within the Admiralty that the main armament should be 12 12-inch guns, but the idea was rejected.

That same year (1905) the concept of a uniform heavy armament was accepted independently in the USA and Britain. This happened for two reasons. Firstly, the effectiveness of light and medium weapons was increasingly questioned; only the heaviest guns seemed likely to inflict damage upon a well-defended battleship. Thus there was an inducement to arm battleships with the heaviest guns available. Secondly, a uniform heavy armament simplified the problems of fire control. Uniformity of guns ensured a uniform flight time for shells firing to the same range. It was now possible to carry out salvo firing in order to estimate range – correction being made after observers had noted the fall of shot.

This procedure had become essential because the development of the torpedo had brought an end to close-range actions. At the turn of the century the accepted battle range was still about 1,000 yards, for although by that time the torpedo had grown in size and speed, it had not greatly improved in range and accuracy. But by 1905 the 18-inch torpedo had a range of 4,000 yards at 19 knots or a speed of 33 knots over 1,000 yards. Accuracy had been improved and new methods of propulsion had been developed. There was obviously a need for ships to be able to fight at longer ranges.

The result was the *Dreadnought*, a ship whose name became a universal description for ships of her type. With her armament of 10 12-inch guns, she completely outclassed

1905–14: thirteen nations enter the race to build their own squadrons of dreadnoughts, as the new type became known.

any other battleship; the fighting value of every other mixed-armament battleship, either built or being built, was drastically reduced. It was seen that henceforward the first nation to acquire its own squadrons of dreadnoughts would be very powerfully placed to secure command of the sea. In the subsequent race to build up dreadnought fleets, the British had the priceless advantage of being first in the field, which gave them a one-year lead over other nations. In addition they possessed superior building facilities, but

OPPOSITE *The US battleship* Kentucky, *carrying four 13-inch, four 8-inch and 14 5-inch guns in her main armament.*
ABOVE *The USS* Michigan *(1909); one of the first American dreadnoughts, her guns were arranged in the superimposed, all-centre-line style that originated in the USA and was widely copied.*
BELOW *Japanese picquet boats in the Russo-Japanese War, rigged for dropping mines off Port Arthur.*

this did not prevent serious challenges from emerging – particularly from Germany.

Between 1905 and 1914 nine nations built and commissioned dreadnoughts and four other nations programmed this type of ship. During that time considerable improvements were made and the ships' dimensions and gun power were continually increased. The *Dreadnought*, on a 17,900-ton displacement, carried five twin turrets; but broadside fire was limited to eight guns because two turrets were carried *en echelon*. This system of mounting guns was followed by the Germans, the French and the Japanese; other nations, not among the first to lay down dreadnoughts, followed the American system of all-centre-line guns. But few followed the superimposed arrangement that the Americans introduced into their first dreadnoughts, the *South Carolina* and the *Michigan*. In these ships the Americans developed the classically simple outline of

TOP *HMS* Queen Elizabeth *(1915), armed with 15-inch guns; battleships of this class were the first to dispense with coal in favour of oil power.*
ABOVE HMS Invincible, *first of the battlecruisers introduced to act as a fast battle squadron.*

OPPOSITE, TOP *HMS* Orion *(1909), one of the Royal Navy's first super-dreadnoughts; she was the first British battleship to adopt the superimposed, all-centre-line gun arrangement.*
ABOVE *HMS* Tiger, *Britain's last coal-burning capital ship.*
BELOW *A Russian light cruiser in the defence of Port Arthur.*

battleship that was later adopted by all nations.

This arrangement made possible much smaller dimensions: the *Michigan* was nearly 40 feet smaller than the *Dreadnought* and displaced only 16,000 tons, but she had the same broadside. She also had one turret fewer, which was also a great saving given that speed of construction was governed not by shipbuilding facilities but by ordnance capacity. The British did not lay down an all-centre-line/superimposed battleship until the *Orion* of November 1909. This ship also marked the first increase in gun size carried out by the British.

While most navies adopted the 12-inch gun for their first dreadnoughts, the Germans chose the slightly inferior 11-inch gun. In 1908 they came into line and this in part prompted the British to adopt, in 1909, the 13·5-inch gun. The same process was followed by all navies: the Japanese, after one class of 12-inch guns, moved up to 14-inch guns with the *Fuso*, which was laid down in March 1912; and the French increased to a 13·4-inch gun after producing only the *Paris* class.

The Americans worked on the number of guns rather than their size. They built five entire classes carrying 12-inch guns before the 14-inch gun was adopted in the *New York* class of 1911. In that time, too, the length of US dreadnoughts had grown from the 452 feet 9 inches of the *South Carolina* to the 562 feet of the *Wyoming*. The latter, a 26,000-ton ship, was able, moreover, to carry 12 12-inch guns.

During this period turret arrangements also changed. Before 1914 the British never broke faith with the twin turret, whereas in 1909 the Russians and Italians incorporated the triple turret in their first dreadnoughts. This lead was followed by Austria–Hungary in 1910 and by the Americans in the *Oklahoma* class, laid down in 1912. In 1913 the French projected the *Normandie* class, whose

ships were to have carried 12 13·4-inch guns in three quadruple turrets; but the ships were never completed.

The seeming disadvantage of the British in terms of numbers of guns per turret was offset by a superior number of ships and by the greater size of those ships. The last and most important change before World War I was the adoption of the 15-inch gun in the *Queen Elizabeth* class, whose ships also had the distinction of being the first battleships to dispense with coal in favour of oil. In many ways these ships were classics of their time, for they were faster and more heavily armed than any other battleship in the world – and as well protected. Yet such power was obtained only at a price. The 25,800 tons of the previous class had increased to over 29,000 tons, whilst engine capacity had almost trebled. In 1911 the *Iron Duke* class made 21 knots with 29,000 horsepower; the new battleships, specially designed to be a fast squadron of 25 knots, needed 75,000 hp to achieve their best speed of 24 knots.

Earlier, while the *Dreadnought* was being programmed, three ships of a new type were laid down. These were battlecruisers, which had the armament of a battleship and the speed and protection of a cruiser. They were intended to act as a fast battle-squadron that could scout for and support the battleships as well as hunt down enemy commerce-raiders (fighting ships which attacked merchantmen). Only the Germans and Japanese followed with their own battlecruisers.

Initially the battlecruiser was smaller and less powerful than the battleship. The *Invincible*, the first of the type, displaced 17,250 tons and carried eight 12-inch guns, six of which could be fired on the broadside. Armour was very thin with only a 6-inch belt and 7 inches of armour over the turrets and barbettes. She was designed for 25 knots but proved capable of over 28 knots. This speed, however, could not disguise the fact that she could not

HMS Dreadnought (1906)

This design, using all big guns in the main armament revolution-ized the appearance of battleships; after her, battleships in service were divided into categories of pre- and post-dreadnought. The diagram (opposite, top) shows the *Dread-nought*'s gun layout: five twin turrets, two mounted *en echelon*, carried her twelve 12-inch guns.

SPECIFICATIONS

Displacement	17,900 tons
Length	527 feet
Beam	82 feet
Draught	26 feet 6 inches
Armament	10 12-inch guns
	27 12-pounders
	5 18-inch torpedo tubes
Main armour	11-4 inch belt
Engines	23,000 hp; turbines
Speed	21 knots

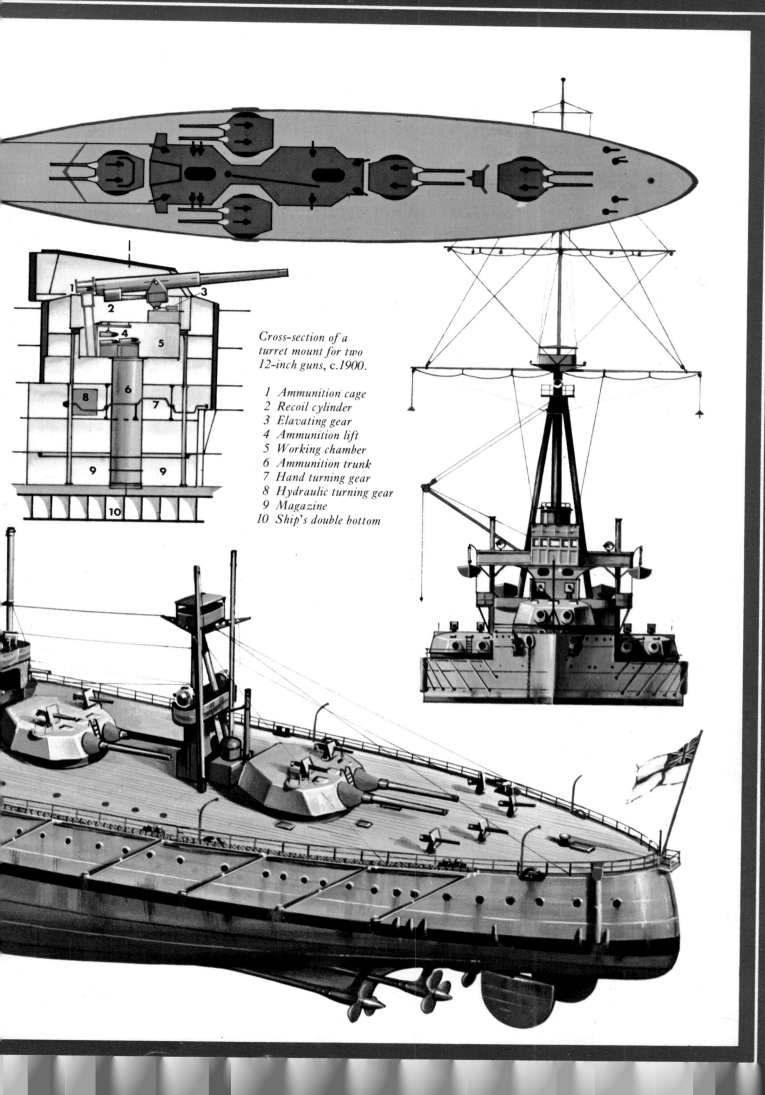

Cross-section of a
turret mount for two
12-inch guns, c.1900.

1 Ammunition cage
2 Recoil cylinder
3 Elevating gear
4 Ammunition lift
5 Working chamber
6 Ammunition trunk
7 Hand turning gear
8 Hydraulic turning gear
9 Magazine
10 Ship's double bottom

1907: turbines enter service in destroyers, and are soon adopted for all classes.

take punishment of the kind she was able to inflict. German battlecruisers, on the other hand, were far better equipped defensively. The *Von der Tann*, Germany's first battle-cruiser, had a 9·75-inch belt, and all her eight 11-inch guns could be trained on either broadside. The battle-cruisers were subject to exactly the same increases in size and power as the battleships, but the demand for higher speed was often the critical factor.

By this time the torpedo had increased significantly in power, and the destroyer had shown a corresponding increase in size. In terms of passive defence against the improved torpedo, anti-torpedo nets were needed and also armoured double-bottomed keels with the outer bottom sub-divided longitudinally and transversely. In the 1890s the French introduced a partially successful semi-circular bulkhead, whilst the Russians tried armoured bulkheads backed by bunkers. Extensive sub-division was worked into all heavy ships after 1905.

But while it was desirable to contain damage, it was obviously more important to avoid it in the first place if possible. High speed was one counter but better still was an increased anti-torpedo-boat armament that would keep the attacker outside effective range. At the turn of the century the 12-pounder gun was quite adequate to deal with the small craft then in existence. The battlecruiser *Invincible* was given 4-inch guns but for many years the British resisted logic and refused to adopt a heavier weapon in spite of the diminishing effectiveness of this weapon. The Japanese were better prepared, clearly as a result of their war experiences; initially, the 6-inch gun was their main secondary weapon, but this was later followed by the handier 5·5-inch gun. The Americans introduced the 5-inch gun into their second dreadnought programme, and the Germans had their 5·9-inch gun.

Like other types of ship the torpedo boat and the destroyer also grew in size and performance during this period. From 1908 onwards the Royal Navy, the emphasis of its tactical doctrine now placed on defence, discontinued building the relatively lightweight torpedo boats and concentrated on building destroyers capable of defending the battle line. The Germans, on the other hand, were wedded to an offensive concept and built destroyers that lacked the heavy-gun armament of the British ships but carried a greater torpedo armament. German destroyers, initially called large torpedo boats, were built for the first time in 1899 and carried three 4-pounder guns and three 18-inch tubes. One of the chief characteristics of German destroyers was their high forecastles, which made them very seaworthy and gave a good speed in bad weather. The early British destroyers were turtle-decked, and this meant that their speed quickly fell away in rough conditions. When the high forecastle was introduced in 1903 in the *River* class, the increase in weight caused speed to be reduced to 26 knots from the very high speeds that had been obtained with the steam turbines of the *Viper*. Launched in 1899, the latter had been designed for 31 knots but at trials she made 36·8 knots. Unfortunately she was subsequently wrecked and another destroyer with turbines, the *Cobra*, was also lost: these two losses checked the introduction of the turbine into widespread service for several years.

The first class to be given turbines was the *Tribal*: launched between 1907 and 1909, these were also the first

BELOW LEFT *A newcomer to naval duties was the airship, used for reconnaissance and bombing duties. Shown here is the Zeppelin L-1, which was delivered to the German Navy in 1912.*
BOTTOM LEFT *The two-man Goubet submarine; should the electric motor fail, it could be propelled by hand.*
OPPOSITE *The first aerial torpedo launch, made one week before the Great War began by a Short floatplane of the Royal Naval Air Service.*
BELOW *The British A-3; her periscope is aft of the hatch.*

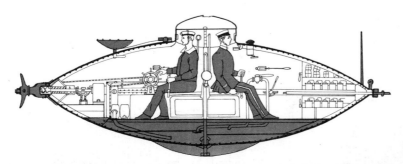

ships to burn oil instead of coal. The first ships of the class were given three 12-pounder guns but the later ships carried two 4-inch 25-pounder guns. British ships lacked uniformity, however, for the builders were allowed great freedom within certain limits. It was not until the *Basilisk* (1909) and *Acorn* (1911) classes that standardization was achieved.

German destroyers showed greater uniformity: partly this was because only three dockyards built destroyers. Turbines were first incorporated in the *S-125* (launched in May 1904) and used in every class after 1909. The Germans did not abandon coal until quite late in the day: ships of the *U-25* class, the first of which was launched in January 1914, were the first to carry oil and no coal. The Americans were moving at approximately the same pace. After an initial class of 16 ships, no destroyers were built

between 1902 and 1909 but thereafter the *Smith* class was given turbines and the subsequent *Pauldings* were oil-burners. These craft were well-gunned but a little slow by European standards.

By the outbreak of war in 1914 the destroyer was only one of three means of delivering torpedoes. The latest method was achieved just one week before Britain declared war on Germany. At Calshot, on 28 July, an especially lightened Short aircraft of the Royal Naval Air Service launched a 14-inch 800-pound torpedo from the air. Even though the torpedo was small compared to those carried by destroyers, it was still a remarkable performance in view of the fact that the first controlled flight did not take place until 1903.

The aircraft that launched this torpedo was a seaplane, just one of four types of flying device competing for the limited funds available for air research and development at the time. The seaplane's immediate rival was the land-based wheeled aircraft. The balance between them was close. The seaplane had a slower rate of climb, inferior mobility and a lower ceiling than the other, but it could carry a radio and it could be recovered at sea. Both types had a very limited endurance and small bomb loads, which made them inferior to airships.

There were two types of airship – the non-rigid and the rigid (or Zeppelin). Of the latter, more formidable type, the German version was superior in quality to those of other nations. In 1909 the Zeppelin LZ-5 was accepted by the German Army after a 24-hour endurance flight, during which time she cruised 820 miles. This provoked British imitation in the form of Naval Airship No. 1, which failed to live up to her nickname, the 'Mayfly'. Then in 1912 the German Navy took delivery of its first Zeppelin, the L-1. This craft had a 47-knot speed and a lifting capacity of 9·25 tons. Within a year the L-3 had proved its endurance

1914: three means now exist to deliver torpedoes – by destroyer, by aircraft (including airships) and by submarine.

capabilities; this craft, moreover, could carry a bomb load of 1,000 pounds.

The non-rigid airship lacked the very long range and the relatively heavy payload of the rigid type but it was much smaller and needed only one-third of the crew carried by a Zeppelin. The chief weaknesses of the rigid airship were that very large numbers of men were needed to man and service the craft, and also that moving them into and from their mooring sheds in blustery conditions proved to be a dangerous exercise. When war broke out, Britain had seven airships of different types compared to Germany's single Zeppelin.

The final means of delivering the torpedo was the submarine, which had been developed at the turn of the century. The previously insoluble problems that had thwarted submarine development – the lack of a suitable building material, a safe method of propulsion and an accurate method of navigation – had been overcome. Steel, light yet strong, proved the ideal material; the invention of the internal combustion engine provided a means of surface propulsion whilst the development of the accumulator battery gave a means of underwater movement. Finally, the gyrocompass promised to overcome the problem of accurate navigation when submerged; the first submarine to have such a compass carried it on the outside of the hull where it was observed through glass.

By 1900 six navies had 10 submarines between them. The French had been the pioneers of the new craft and they had had no small success with it, but the decisive breakthrough came in the United States. An American submarine, the *Holland*, named after its Irish inventor, became the prototype for most of the world's navies (only the

Germans and French remained aloof). The *Holland* displaced 105 tons and had a surface speed of 8·5 knots. Her hull was divided into three compartments which housed the engine, control and torpedo rooms. Under the latter two were tank and battery space. She carried a single bow tube. The British, who for years had tried to discourage the development of such craft, secured the plans and built their own submarine, the *A-1*. This was superior to the *Holland* in that it incorporated a periscope and a conning tower, both of which the *Holland* lacked.

The British and French quickly pulled ahead of other nations in the number of submarines they had in commission. In 1914 Britain had 75 and France 67, but many of these were old and their strength in modern, long-range submarines was no greater than that of Germany, which had only 30 U-boats (Unterseeboote). Germany started building submarines in 1906 and from the start incorporated double-hulls and twin-screws in all boats. Unlike the British, who had started with petrol engines, the Germans initially installed heavy oil engines until 1908, when they introduced diesel engines. After their first major programme of 1907, the Germans concentrated on large 'overseas' boats. The *U-19*, completed in 1913, had a 4,000-mile range and a diving depth of 275 feet.

Most submarines carried torpedoes within the hull, either in the beam or fore and aft. The French *Daphne* class and the Russian *Lake* and *Volk* classes seem to have broken this general rule. Although some mystery surrounds the Russian ships, those of the *Volk* class are alleged to have had eight torpedoes in external dropping gear; The *Lake* class seems to have been exceptional in that naphtha apparently was used to provide the submarines' source of power when on the surface.

Before World War I the development of the submarine not only outpaced that of possible antidotes to it but also any systematic consideration of how submarines might best be used. For political and humanitarian reasons, nations were unwilling to accept the idea that submarines would be used primarily against commerce. It was generally assumed that this form of war would be conducted by cruisers.

Traditionally, cruisers had fulfilled two roles: on the one hand they scouted for the battle fleet and on the other they protected or preyed on commerce. Because iron came, first of all, to battleships, the cruiser then suffered an eclipse from which it did not emerge for many years. In those early years, not surprisingly, the wooden cruiser could neither run away from nor stand up to the iron battleship. Later, when iron and then steel were used in the construction of cruisers, there was no agreement over what constituted a

Submarines: the American *Holland* becomes the prototype for most of the world's navies.

OPPOSITE ABOVE *The* Dupuy de Lôme *(1888), a French commerce raider capable, at 20 knots, of evading battleships and, with a 4-inch belt, of standing up to most cruisers.*
OPPOSITE, BELOW *HMS* Iris, *one of the first steel cruisers, laid down in 1878. Her 18·6-knot speed ensured that she was faster than the battle fleet she was designed to scout for.*
LEFT *HMS* Inconstant, *the first iron cruiser.*
BELOW *The French cruiser* Jeanne d'Arc, *built following the* Dupuy de Lôme's *success.*

proper balance between high speed, long range and gun-power. As a result the cruiser, in the period between 1870 and 1890, went through the same sort of uncertain phase as had befallen the early iron battleships – a phase marked by continued experimentation at the expense of continuity and uniformity.

The first iron cruiser was the British *Inconstant*, which was almost as large as contemporary battleships. Her high cost and expensive upkeep would have ensured smaller successors had it not been for developments overseas. In 1870 the Russians laid down the first armoured cruiser, the *General Admiral*. She carried an armoured belt on the waterline but no protection for her four 8-inch and two 6-inch guns. The British answer to this theoretically very strong ship was the *Shannon*, a cruiser that was built to double as a battleship on foreign stations. In place of a waterline belt the *Shannon* had a protective deck: this arrangement became generally adopted in cruisers and was also used by the Americans in their dreadnought *Oklahoma*, laid down in 1912. The protective deck was a curved steel deck; although only a few inches deep, its purpose was to deflect a hit upwards and away from vital machinery. Where the protective deck met the sides of the ship, it was below the waterline, but its apex was above the line.

Until the 1890s, there was a broad diversity in the size, gun power, armour and speed of protected cruisers. Some ships, such as the *Iris* and the *Mercury* – the first steel cruisers, laid down in 1878 – gave priority to speed. Making 18·6 knots, they were more than 4 knots faster than the battle fleet for which they were to scout. Within five years, however, cruisers of roughly the same displacement as these ships (3,730 tons) were demonstrating great fighting power as well as high speed. The Japanese *Takachiko*, built in Britain, carried two 10·3-inch and six 5·9-inch guns and had a 3-inch protective deck. She could make 18·5 knots and had a 9,000-mile range at 13 knots. Her displacement was only 3,650 tons.

At the end of the 1880s two developments led to increases in the size and cost of cruisers. Firstly, the introduction of Quick-Firing guns aided the process, for it meant that large, well-armed cruisers could not take on the older battleships

with every hope of success. Secondly, there emerged the French *Guerre de course* school – firmly committed to the idea that raids on commercial shipping were the surest means of bringing Britain to her knees. This led the British to construct protector ships that were larger than the raiders produced by the French. To make their policy work the French, in 1888, ordered the *Dupuy de Lôme*. Displacing 6,300 tons, she carried two 7·6-inch and six 6·4-inch guns, all of which were carried in turrets with wide arcs of fire. Her 20 knots made her faster than contemporary battleships though a little slow compared to cruisers; but her 4-inch belt and turrets meant that she was much better protected.

The British responded with a baffling variety of ships, the greatest of which were the *Powerful* and the *Terrible* and the *Diadem* class. The former two ships carried two 9·2-inch and 16 6-inch guns in the main armament and had 6 inches of deck armour. Their high speed of 22 knots made them extremely powerful commerce-protectors with a great range; but, being almost as big as the latest battleships, they were expensive to maintain. The *Diadems* were smaller and carried a uniform 6-inch armament.

These ships were the last of the protected cruisers, for the development of Krupp steel now enabled belt armour to be carried without any loss of speed or other fighting qualities. Belt armour had the advantage that it tried to keep out shells rather than confine their damage once they had penetrated a ship. The armoured cruiser, as the next type was called, was largely an Anglo–Japanese enterprise. The Japanese were particularly interested in armoured cruisers for they were aware of the need to build up their fleet for the impending struggle with Russia, but lacked the finances to afford many battleships. Armoured cruisers, able to sustain even the heaviest hits, afforded a cheap means of acquiring powerful ships capable of taking on the older of the Russian battleships.

The tasks of armoured cruisers in war were not particularly well defined, nor were they for their principal successors, the battlecruisers. Armoured cruisers were really too slow to be the fast supporting wing of the battle fleet and too slow to be good in a scouting role. Their replacement for most purposes by the battlecruiser did not

WORLD WAR I

The Balance of Power at Sea, August 1914

By the time the nations went to war in 1914 several trends were discernible. The British had more ships than their enemies but they were not necessarily better ships. The various types of ship differed in both role and quality from nation to nation. In many respects, too, especially in the air and beneath the waves, all nations were unprepared for the war that was to follow. At its outbreak the strengths of the navies were as follows:

CATEGORY	BRITAIN	FRANCE	RUSSIA	JAPAN	ITALY	USA
Battleships	20	4	2	2	3	10
Battlecruisers	9	—	—	2	—	—
Pre-dreadnoughts	40	21	11	16	10	23
Heavy cruisers	47	19	8	12	5	21
Light cruisers	61	6	5	13	5	11
Destroyers	225	81	106	47	33	50
Submarines	75	67	36	18	14	39

CATEGORY	GERMANY	AUSTRIA–HUNGARY	TURKEY
Battleships	14	3	—
Battlecruisers	5	—	—
Pre-dreadnoughts	24	12	3
Heavy cruisers	27	3	—
Light cruisers	23	4	2
Destroyers	152	18	8
Submarines	30	11	—

OPPOSITE *The Japanese first-class cruiser* Nisshin, *at Port Said in 1917.* BELOW *HMS* Nottingham, *a Birmingham class light cruiser.*

entail the complete disappearance of cruisers. The battle-cruiser was invaluable for certain tasks, but for reconnaissance another type was needed: this gap was filled by the light cruiser.

The first of the light cruisers was the German *Bremen*, which displaced 3,250 tons and carried 10 4·1-inch guns at a top speed of 23 knots. Subsequent improvements in speed led to the *Karlsruhe*, which was half as big again as the *Bremen* and made 29 knots. The British, on the other hand, placed greater store on defence and firepower. By the outbreak of war the British light cruiser had crept up to 5,400 tons and carried eight 6-inch guns.

5

PRINCES OF THE SKY

Pioneers and visionaries dream of flying – though some fear the consequences.

For as long as man has dreamed of flying, there have been prophets of the purposes, both evil and good, to which the new art would be put. On the one hand there were men such as William Cowper (1731–1800), who wrote: 'I would . . . make it death for a man to be convicted of flying . . . Historians would load my memory with reproaches of phlegm, and stupidity, and oppression; but in the mean time, the world would go on quietly, and if it enjoyed less liberty, it would at least be more secure.'

On the other hand there were both practical and visionary men, among them Sir George Cayley (1773–1857), the pioneer of flying, and the poet Alfred, Lord Tennyson (1809–92). In 1816 Cayley wrote: 'An uninterrupted navi-

OPPOSITE *The hot-air balloon, designed by the Montgolfier brothers, in which Jean-Francois Pilâtre de Rozier, a 29-year-old French physician, made the first free (untethered) balloon flight by man, in November 1783; as crew he carried the Marquis d'Arlandes, who was an enthusiastic passenger but disliked the essential work of stoking the brazier.*
ABOVE *Inflating a balloon; from William Martin's* Parlour Book: or Familiar Conversations on Science and the Arts.
ABOVE RIGHT *A pioneer balloon in flight, from* Illustrations of Natural Philosophy, *published in 1850.*
RIGHT *A 'Montgolfiere' on the reverse of a medal struck to commemorate the work of the ballooning brothers.*

gable ocean, that comes to the threshold of every man's door, ought not to be neglected as a source of human gratification and advantage.' Tennyson, though he feared that aerial warfare would be inevitable, was on the whole optimistic:

> For I dipt into the future, far as human eye could see,
> Saw the Vision of the world, and all the wonder that would be;
> Saw the heavens fill with commerce, argosies of magic sails,
> Pilots of the purple twilight, dropping down with costly bales . . .
>
> (From *Locksley Hall*)

The warnings and exhortations of such men were, however, of little point until some means of flying had been invented. There had been many attempts to produce a flying machine since the days of Leonardo da Vinci (1452-1519), and a few even before his time, some laughable in their simplicity, others commendable for the courage they demanded of their authors. But they all fell foul of one particular obstacle: until the end of the 19th century, there was no power source capable of making the aeroplane a practical possibility. Men such as Cayley, quoted above, had investigated the problems of flight from the theoretical point of view and had produced flying machines that might conceivably have been capable of sustained flight had an engine been available; but this was not to be until the invention in 1885 of the first practical petrol engines, built independently by Karl Benz and Gottlieb Daimler.

Until then, the only successful aerial machines had been balloons. The first effective balloon was that invented by the Montgolfier brothers in France in 1783, its lift being provided from the hot air produced by a fire lit under the balloon.

The leaders of the French Revolution, which began in 1789, were avidly interested in any invention that might further their cause, and in the early years of the revolution set up a military balloon school. This institution had the honour of supplying the world with its first military airmen, whose observations from a balloon at the Battle of Fleurus in 1794 were instrumental in securing a French victory. Napoleon Bonaparte was not impressed by the potentialities of the balloon as a military weapon, however, and closed the balloon school.

Thereafter the balloon went into decline as a military vehicle for about the next fifty years. There were occasional attempts to revive interest in it, but the next time any use was made of balloons was in 1849, when the Austrians tried unsuccessfully to drop bombs from unmanned balloons on the besieged city of Venice. After a further pause the French once more turned to the use of balloons: in 1870, during the siege of Paris by the Prussians, several prominent Frenchmen and a considerable amount of mail were dispatched from the city by balloon.

Interest in military ballooning had also caught on in other countries. During the American Civil War of 1861–65 balloons were used sporadically by both sides to obtain information of the other's battlefield movements; but it was mainly the Unionist side, with its greater industrial capacity and inventiveness, that profited from the venture. The US Signal Corps established a balloon school in 1892 and attempts were made to use an observation balloon at the Battle of San Juan Hill in the Spanish-American War of 1898. The British, spurred on by the energetic Colonel Robert Baden-Powell, had by then established balloon companies in the Royal Engineers, and one of these accompanied the expeditions to Bechuanaland and Suakin, Sudan, in 1884–85, and later saw more extensive service in the Boer War (1899–1902).

Back in Europe, the last component needed to make powered and sustained heavier-than-air flight a real possibility had by then been invented – the internal combustion engine. In its early forms, as developed independently by Benz and Daimler, the internal combustion engine was heavy, of low power and totally unreliable. But the basic idea was there, and design improvements swiftly followed. If the engine could next be coupled to some sort of lifting surface, the aeroplane would be ready to fly. In the meantime, other important developments had taken place.

As early as 1809 Sir George Cayley, the pioneer of aeronautics, had summed up the complexities of flight in a sentence: 'The whole problem is confined within these limits, *viz.* to make a surface support a given weight by the application of power to the resistance of air.' In other words, the surface (the wings) must support the given weight (machine, pilot and load) by providing lift. This can only be done by making air flow round the airfoil section of the wing, normally by moving the wing forward through the air. In this forward motion the resistance of air (drag) must be overcome by the application of power (engine, or, in the days before sufficiently powerful engines had been developed, gravity).

The first truly successful heavier-than-air craft, the gliders of Otto Lilienthal, depended on gravity for their motion because at the time (1891–96) the internal combustion engine was still not sufficiently developed to allow its use in a heavier-than-air craft.

But while heavier-than-air machines were still not possible, lighter-than-air craft had been able to profit by the invention of the petrol engine. Through a long and somewhat bizarre chain of experiments, the spherical balloon had been turned into an elongated cigar-shaped object, normally held in shape by an external beam, on which the pilot and

OPPOSITE *A military balloon in service as a French observation post at the Siege of Mayence, 1794.*
TOP *Sir George Cayley (1773–1857), many of whose designs anticipated the Wright brothers by almost a century.*
ABOVE *During the Siege of Paris in 1870 balloons were used to airlift men and mail by night to destinations beyond the Prussian lines. After numerous balloons had fallen short and been captured a French engineer, Dupuy de Lôme, developed a balloon with steering powers that was driven by a propeller turned by four men. Shown above is his Mark 2, which required eight men to work the propeller.*

the machine's cumbersome motor were located. This was the dirigible, an airship that could be flown in approximately the direction desired by the pilot if the weather were not too inclement. Power was still so low and controls so rudimentary that chance played a very important part in the progress of the early dirigibles. Among the pioneers in this field were the French-built versions of Santos-Dumont and Lebaudy.

In Germany, Count Ferdinand von Zeppelin had gone a stage further. Rather than adapt the balloon, with all its attendant problems of maintaining the shape of the gas envelope, Zeppelin decided that the true future of the airship lay in a rigid framework containing gasbags for lift. Thus even if the pressure of the air fluctuated, or the gasbags began to leak, the outside shape of the ship would not be altered and the engines could still propel it and the controls direct it along its course.

The development of a successful rigid airship was finally achieved by von Zeppelin in 1900 after considerable personal sacrifice, and the Zeppelin type of airship was later adopted by the German armed forces as a reconnaissance machine. Compared with early aircraft, it had excellent range, was relatively reliable and made a good observation platform. The design philosophy of the Zeppelin was fixed virtually at the birth of the concept, and any improvements that were made were the result of better materials and more powerful engines, rather than of any radically improved design.

But while von Zeppelin was working with all his heart and resources on his airship designs, on the far side of the Atlantic the Wright brothers of Dayton, Ohio, were feeling their way carefully towards the world's first successful heavier-than-air, powered aircraft. Inspired and helped by Octave Chanute, doyen of American air enthusiasts, Orville and Wilbur Wright progressed from simple tethered gliders, on which they could check their control system, to free-flying gliders, and from there to their first powered machine, driven by an engine of their own design and construction. On 17 December 1903, at Kittyhawk, North Carolina, Orville Wright piloted the Flyer, as the brothers called their machine, for a flight of 12 seconds. It was the world's first powered, sustained and controlled heavier-than-air flight. Initial reports of the Wrights' success were greeted with scepticism, and the brothers worked on in obscurity for the next two years, perfecting what was in all ways a practical flying machine. This was the Flyer III, capable of reaching almost 40 mph and of staying in the air for nearly 40 minutes.

Realizing the importance of their invention, the Wrights on three occasions offered it to the United States Government, but each time they were rebuffed on the grounds that the Government had no interest in a machine that did not exist. This strange state of confusion had arisen partly because, shrewd businessmen that they were, the Wrights had not been prepared to let anyone see their creation until the patents covering it had been granted; and so the Government had thought that the brothers were asking for financial aid to build the machine. Disgusted with the replies they had received from their own government, in 1905 the brothers then offered their machine to the British Government. But despite an enthusiastic letter from Colonel J. E. Capper, Superintendent of the Government Balloon Factory at Farnborough (which was later to become the Royal Aircraft Factory and the present Royal Aircraft Establish-

1903: Orville Wright keeps his Flyer aloft for 12 seconds – the world's first powered, sustained and controlled heavier-than-air flight.

ment), who had visited the Wrights and seen photographs of their machine flying, the British Government also turned down their offer. The French Government, too, declined an opportunity to support them. Dejected by these rebuffs, the Wrights gave up all flying and experimentation for the next two years.

Although the general attitude shown towards the Wright brothers was one of scepticism, some informed members of the European aeronautical fraternity were prepared to give credence to the Americans' claims to have flown. The news in effect spurred the Europeans in their own attempts to produce a flying machine. There had already been numerous experiments, many of them initially encouraged by Lilienthal's successes, but the wonderful assortment of machines produced by Karl Jatho in Germany, by Robert Esnault-Pelterie, Ferdinand Ferber, Ernest Archdeacon and the Voisin brothers in France, by Samuel Cody and John Dunne in Great Britain, and by Jacob Ellehammer in Denmark were no more than tentative stepping stones – and not all of them in the right direction.

It was not until 12 November 1906, nearly three years after the Wrights' achievement at Kittyhawk, that the first European success was recorded. This took place when Alberto Santos-Dumont, a diminutive and dapper Brazilian domiciled in France, made the first sustained flight in Europe in his 14-*bis*. Given that the machine was virtually a powered box-kite with no controls worth speaking of, this pioneering effort could hardly be called true, controlled flight; certainly the attempts to better Santos-Dumont's record (722 feet in 21 seconds) continued at a great rate.

Early in 1907, the 'pusher' biplane configuration (in which the engine is mounted behind the wing in order to 'push' the aircraft) was finalized in the Voisin-Delagrange biplane; but the aircraft itself was not successful when tested. That was in February and March, and it was not until 9 November that the first European flight of over a minute took place. On that occasion Henry Farman, an Englishman resident in France, flew a circular course of

about 1,000 yards in his Voisin-Farman I pusher. At about the same time, too, Louis Blériot introduced the tractor monoplane layout to the world.

Prompted by the claims made by European aviators, the Wright brothers decided in 1908 to enter the lists once

again. Wilbur Wright came to Europe, and Orville attempted once again to interest the US Government in the Flyer.

Wilbur Wright's visit to Europe proved devastating. His complete and absolute mastery over his aircraft, not to mention the staggering performances he put up compared with his European rivals, astounded the European flying world. His best flights lasted for periods of around 2½ hours, whereas the best of the European pilots had still to break the 30-minute barrier. Léon Delagrange put it perfectly: 'Well, we have been beaten. We just do not exist!'

Wilbur's astounding performances had the considerable benefit of encouraging European aviators to greater things. And here they had one distinct advantage – the rotary engine. This has a crankshaft fixed to the aircraft, and it is around this crankshaft that the cylinders revolve, with the propeller bolted to them. It was a particularly practical type of engine with an excellent power-to-weight ratio in comparison with its water-cooled inline counterparts. Moreover, the intense rivalry of the European aeronautical scene ensured that progress was kept going.

While Wilbur Wright was in France, Orville had been showing off the new Flyer A to the American military authorities at Fort Meyer near Washington. During the course of one of his demonstration flights, on 17 September 1908, the Flyer crashed and Orville's passenger, Lieutenant Thomas Selfridge, was killed – the first man to die in a powered aircraft accident.

The practitioners of early aviation were divided into two

OPPOSITE, ABOVE Otto Lilienthal flies one of the gliders which he developed in the 1890s and which were the first truly successful heavier-than-air craft. The next problem for the heavier-than-air school was to produce an engine that would give them powered flight.
OPPOSITE, BELOW In 1901 Alberto Santos-Dumont, a dashing Brazilian living in France, made a startling aerial tour of the Eiffel Tower in a dirigible of his own design powered by a petrol engine. He made a round trip from St Cloud in under 30 minutes.
RIGHT AND BELOW Wilbur Wright photographed in 1903 and at the controls of a Flyer in 1905.

schools: those who believed that the aeroplane should be inherently stable and those who did not. The first school believed that the aeroplane should be all but capable of flying itself, so that the pilot was nothing more than a chauffeur, merely pointing the machine in the direction he wished to go. Most of the Europeans belonged to this school. The other school believed that the relationship between pilot and aeroplane should be more in the nature of that between rider and horse, the two working together; it followed that the aeroplane should be unstable, so that the pilot had to fly it the whole time, and thus learn complete mastery of his craft. The chief adherents of this latter school were the Wrights. But with the increasing dominance in the flying world of European ideas, the chauffeur school prevailed. That it did so was to have considerable repercussions in World War I.

In those early days of flying, there were two ways of controlling the movement of aircraft in roll – by wing-warping and by ailerons. Given the flimsy structures then necessary for weight reasons, most early aviators favoured wing-warping, whereby lateral movement of the control column pulled wires which twisted the trailing edges of the wings up or down to deflect the airflow and cause the plane to roll. Others, notably Léon Levavasseur, favoured a more rigid wing with the outer rear portion of each hinged to a spar and moved by wires. This was first seen on the Antoinette IV in October 1908, and was accepted universally from about the middle of World War I.

The aeroplane was now a practical machine, and though performances were still low and gave little margin for error the more adventurous spirits turned their attentions to what could be done with the new machine in war. As it was still not capable of carrying much of a load, clearly the most important contribution it could make would be in the realm of reconnaissance, to keep the generals informed of what the enemy was doing. But the thought of doing merely this did not satisfy all those adventurous spirits. They foresaw a more active role for the new machine in war: attacking ships

Controversy: should aircraft be inherently stable and fly themselves, as the 'chauffeur' school maintained, or unstable and in constant need of piloting – the view championed by the Wright brothers?

Aircraft in war: the generals favour restricting them to reconnaissance work.

at sea, bombing railway junctions and even attacking the enemy's troops with machine-gun fire or small bombs. But the governments who would have to find the money, and the generals who would have to use them, were against aircraft being attached to their armies for any purpose other than as observation machines; even then the authorities were mostly sceptical of how useful aircraft might be. Since the end of World War I, much criticism has been levelled at these politicians and military men who were so loath to divert even a small amount of their armaments budgets to military aviation. But it should be pointed out in their favour that they were being asked to invest money in a new and completely untried weapon of war, one that even its adherents were compelled to admit was not reliable. Aircraft were

ABOVE *French pioneer Louis Blériot arrives at Dover after making the first-ever cross-Channel flight, on 25 July 1909.*

BELOW *Henry Farman's No. 1 bis* pusher biplane; *the engine is mounted behind the wing and 'pushes' the aircraft forward.*

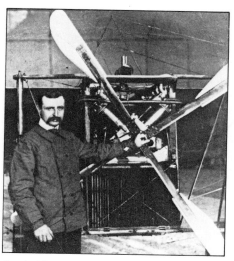

Louis Blériot with his tractor monoplane; a front-mounted engine 'pulled' the aircraft.

The Antoinette Monobloc, a French-built design that favoured the monoplane layout and a more rigid wing structure than had formerly been used.

Early rigid-wing monoplanes make their mark; Blériot flies the English Channel.

still in their infant, experimental stages, and to standardize one type would have been foolish, whereas the supply problems caused by squadrons equipped with several different types could only provoke constant headaches. It is hard to see what else the European nations could have done, except perhaps to have laid better contingency plans for increased production in the event of the aeroplane finally proving itself.

Though depressed and bitter about what they considered to be military reactionism, air enthusiasts determined to go their own way and so demonstrate that the military were wrong. In the United States, Eugene Ely took off in his standard Curtiss biplane from an 83-foot platform built on the bows of the American cruiser *Birmingham* to be the first man ever to take off from a ship. That was on 14 November 1910. On 18 January 1911, Ely flew out to sea and landed on another cruiser, *Pennsylvania*, and then took off and returned to shore. Later that year, on 30 June, Glenn Curtiss himself, the great designer-pilot, became the first man to carry out bombing runs when he attacked the buoyed outline of a battleship on Lake Keuka with dummy bombs.

Shortly after this, radio was used for the first time in an aeroplane: on 27 August the Canadian James McCurdy sent and received messages in his Curtiss biplane over New York State. Possibly the aeroplane's greatest contribution to the Allied victory in World War I was made by artillery observation machines, and in this field radio was all-important. But the Horton set used by McCurdy was bulky, heavy and short-ranged, and much work had still to be done to make radio the practical possibility it later became.

Earlier in the year, on 26 January, Glenn Curtiss had introduced the world's first practical seaplane, and thus laid the foundations for the type of aeroplane that was to play so important a part in both world wars against the submarine.

In Germany, meanwhile, the Zeppelin had at last reached maturity, first as a passenger machine and then as a military one. This stimulated other, more slothful Europeans into thinking about what might happen in the event of another war, and the political leaders of what were to become the Allies began to take a more active interest in the aeroplane as a war-weapon, as witness the French *Concours Militaire* in October and November 1911 and the first substantial allocation of money for aircraft in Great Britain.

Several firsts in military flying have been mentioned above, and to these must be added the first live bomb test, made by a US Army Wright biplane in January 1911. This was also the year in which the machine gun first made its appearance in an aircraft, and though it is impossible to say who first took such a weapon aloft, the best mounting was that on the 1911 two-seater Nieuport.

The year 1912 was marked, in aeronautical circles, by the beginnings of a major military interest in aviation. Principally for military reasons of strength and reliability, a ban was somewhat abruptly imposed on monoplanes after a couple of accidents. This was a retrograde step, not least because no thorough investigation into the causes of the accidents was carried out. The effect of the ban was to hamper the development of monoplane aircraft in favour of structurally stronger biplanes built with trussed wing planforms. Now, too, the pusher type was at last beginning to go

ABOVE *A brace of Zeppelins, the rigid airships that the Germans were transforming into sophisticated military machines; below is a Zeppelin shed at Friedrichshafen.*

out of fashion, to be replaced by the tractor biplane, which had a higher performance. The best example of this type to emerge in 1912 was the Royal Aircraft Factory's BS-1, designed by Geoffrey de Havilland. Another innovation of 1912 was the monocoque fuselage, which instead of having longerons braced internally in all three dimensions by wire, has an unbraced shell-like outer covering of wood or metal, which takes all the loads. The best example of this type of fuselage was in the Monocoque Deperdussin, which raised the world speed record to over 100 mph for the first time.

The growing importance of flying achieved almost universal recognition. In Great Britain, for example, a Royal Flying Corps was established in April 1912 and the first Military Aeroplane Competition was held on Salisbury Plain in August that year. The Farnborough-designed BE-2, clearly the best aeroplane at the competition, was not allowed to compete because it had been designed at a government establishment. However, it flew *hors concours* and was judged the best machine present. Another step forward in British military aviation was the first successful

RIGHT *The Sopwith Batboat, a hybrid floatplane/flying boat type; the crew sat in the float-like hull.*
CENTRE LEFT *Lieutenant Eugene Ely, the first man to take off from a ship (the USS* Birmingham*), here takes off from the US cruiser* Pennsylvania, *on which he had landed earlier the same day, 18 January 1911.*
CENTRE RIGHT *An American Curtiss seaplane during naval manoeuvres off the Massachusetts coast.*
BELOW *The British Army Aeroplane No. 1 developed by Samuel Cody; by 1912 the military was showing a major interest in aviation, and in April of that year a Royal Flying Corps was established.*

1911–12: machine guns are mounted in aircraft for the first time; Britain holds a Military Aeroplane Competition.

1913: the Russians unveil the world's first four-engined aircraft, later to become the Ilya Muromets bomber.

artillery spotting mission, flown by a BE-1 over Salisbury Plain. In France, too, the growth of the Zeppelin menace had led to the expansion of the national air force, particularly in terms of bombing aircraft; and in the massive manoeuvres, held in September near Poitou, aircraft were widely used. Finally, in this summary of events in 1912, the first parachute descent from an aircraft was made on 1 March in the USA by Captain Albert Berry.

The year 1913, the last full year before World War I, was a great one for flying. It will be remembered most of all as the year in which aerobatics was invented. The first man to loop the loop was a Russian, Lieutenant Nesterov, who did so on 20 August at Kiev. But the man who developed aero-

were used by the Italians in Libya. The Italian Army had received its first aircraft in 1910, and used them during the manoeuvres of August 1911. Here the four aeroplanes allocated to each army had proved entirely inadequate because of their low serviceability. The Italians were the first, in fact, to learn the lessons that Britain, France and Germany were to be taught the hard way in 1914 and 1915: above all they learnt of the need for a plentiful supply of reserve aircraft, for trained observers so that the pilot could concentrate on his flying, and for adequately trained ground crew.

The Italian Army also used small airships. These started operations in Libya together with a few aircraft on 23 October 1911. The Italians were so short of aircraft that

batics more than any other was Adolphe Pégoud, a Frenchman. He perfected Nesterov's loop, and also many other manoeuvres, including inverted flight. All these seemed merely sensational at the time, but they were to be essential in the war that was looming ahead. While the French continued to break records (pushing the speed record up to 127 mph, the distance record to 635 miles and the altitude record to 20,079 feet), the British were beginning to produce the world's first true fighting planes: the Farnborough FE-2a fighter and the Vickers Destroyer. Other outstanding aircraft were also produced: the inherently stable BE-2, modified from de Havilland's design by T. E. Busk, and the Sopwith Tabloid, a small two-seater so manoeuvrable and possessed of such a performance, especially in climbing, that the monoplane was more or less abandoned in Britain.

The other outstanding aeroplane of the year was the improved Deperdussin, which pushed up the speed record to 127 mph. This was also the year when the world's first four-engined aircraft appeared – the Russian Sikorsky Bolshoi, later developed as the huge Ilya Muromets bomber. The Bolshoi, with a span of over 90 feet, could carry eight people for up to two hours – quite a performance for the time.

Initially 1914 was a quiet year for aviation, and energies were devoted more to production than to innovation. The Ilya Muromets took the limelight from the Bolshoi when, on 11 February, it flew with 16 people on board; later it was ordered into production for the Imperial Russian Air Force.

This is an appropriate moment to look back to the first operations undertaken in war by aeroplanes. Contrary to general opinion, these did not take place in World War I but in the Turko-Italian War of 1911–12, when aircraft

they eagerly welcomed the arrival of two flights sent out by a Turin sporting magazine.

In terms of its influence on operations in World War I, the Libyan campaign immediately established the need for aerial photography, from which better maps could be made, and for air-to-ground radio so that artillery fire could be corrected. It also saw the first use of air-dropped bombs (4·4-pounders dropped by the pilot after he had pulled out the pin) and the first protest against bombing atrocities, by the Turks who claimed that a hospital had been hit.

Had they troubled to do so, the military leaders of Great Britain, France and Germany could have learnt much more about air warfare from the Libyan campaign, particularly about the tactical reconnaissance operations that aircraft could be expected to undertake. Instead, their gaze was directed inward, their thoughts all too bound up with the holocaust that they were about to unleash on themselves.

OPPOSITE, LEFT *Dawn of the bomber; a Short Wright biplane of 1910 is shown, equipped with bomb release gear.*
OPPOSITE, RIGHT *A Sopwith Tabloid, a small and highly manoeuvrable two-seater introduced in the year before the war.*
BELOW *The giant Russian bomber Ilya Mouromets; in February 1914 this four-engined machine flew with 16 people on board.*
BOTTOM *The BE-2a, a staple aircraft in Britain's air strength in the period immediately before the outbreak of war.*

The Italians use recce aircraft in Libya to deliver hand-dropped bombs.

CHRONOLOGIES OF THE GREAT WAR

The War at Sea

The symbol □ denotes activity over an extended period of time

1914

JUNE

28   Archduke Franz Ferdinand of Austria-Hungary assassinated at Sarajevo.

JULY

1   Naval wing of Royal Flying Corps (RFC) becomes Royal Naval Air Service (RNAS).

28   Austria-Hungary declares war on Serbia.

AUGUST

1   Germany declares war on Russia.

2   Germany declares war on France and invades Belgium.

4   Britain declares war on Germany.

4-9   Escape of German ships *Goeben* and *Breslau* to Constantinople.

6   Austria Hungary declares war on Russia.

10   France declares war on Austria-Hungary.

12   Britain declares war on Austria-Hungary.

12   Start of transportation of British Expeditionary Force to France.

15   First submarine sunk: *U-15* rammed by HMS *Birmingham*.

23   Japan declares war on Germany.

26   German signals book recovered by Russians from *Magdeburg*.

28   Battle of Heligoland Bight.

SEPTEMBER

□   ANZ forces occupy Samoa, New Guinea, Solomons and Bismarck Arch.

26   HM armoured cruisers *Cressy*, *Aboukir* and *Hogue* sunk by *U-9*.

OCTOBER

□   Japanese forces occupy Marshalls, Palau, Marianas and Carolines.

17   U-boat penetrates into Scapa Flow; Grand Fleet withdraws to Loch Swilly.

20   First merchant ship, the *Glitra*, sunk by U-boat (in this case by a boarding party from U-boat).

27   HMS *Audacious*, battleship, lost on a mine outside Loch Swilly.

28-9   Sortie by *Goeben* to attack Russian Black Sea ports.

31   Russia declares war on Turkey.

NOVEMBER

1   Allied declaration of war on Turkey. Battle of Coronel.

2-6   Abortive British invasion at Tanga (East Africa).

3   First naval attack on Turkish forts at the Dardanelles; first German cruiser attack on English east coast.

6   British landings in Mesopotamia.

7   Capitulation of German fortress of Tsingtao to Japanese forces.

9   German cruiser *Emden* destroyed by *HMAS Sydney* after a two-month cruise during which she sank or captured 25 ships.

DECEMBER

8   Battle of Falkland Islands.

13   Turkish battleship *Messudieh* sunk by submarine *B-11*.

15   Abortive RN air attack on Cuxhaven base.

1915

JANUARY

25   Battle of Dogger Bank.

FEBRUARY

15   First naval assault at Dardanelles.

18   Opening of first submarine campaign against Allied commerce.

MARCH

18   Allied naval attack at Dardanelles flounders in minefield.

APRIL

□   Initiation of Otranto blockade by French Navy.

25   Landings on Gallipoli; Russian attacks on the Bosphorus.

MAY

7   Liner *Lusitania* sunk off Ireland by *U-20*.

23   Italy declares war on Austria-Hungary.

25   *U-21*, after entering Mediterranean from Germany, sinks HMS *Triumph* off Dardanelles.

JULY

10   German cruiser *Königsberg* sunk by monitors *Severn* and *Mersey* in Rufiji Delta, East Africa.

SEPTEMBER

1   First submarine campaign around British waters called off following sinking of the *Arabic*; U-boats concentrate in Mediterranean where few American ships are operating.

14   Bulgaria declares war on Serbia.

15-16   Britain and France declare war on Bulgaria.

OCTOBER

16   Allied declaration of war on Bulgaria.

22   Withdrawal of German heavy units from the Baltic following sinking of *Prinz Adalbert* by British submarine *E-8*.

DECEMBER

1   Start of landings at Valona by Italians. Throughout the year there are continuous Russian attempts to sever the Zonguldak–Constantinople coal trade.

1916

JANUARY

□   Depth charges distributed to British warships.

8   Last sortie of the *Goeben* in the Black Sea.

9   Evacuation of the Dardanelles completed.

FEBRUARY

1   First British merchant ship lost to air attack.

21   Submarine offensive renewed.

MARCH

24   The *Sussex* sunk – an end to the submarine offensive.

APRIL–MAY

□   Laying of Dover mine barrage off Nieuport and the Scheldt in attempt to restrict passage of U-boats through Channel.

APRIL

18   Russian combined operation takes Trabzon, on Black Sea.

MAY–JUNE

31-1   Battle of Jutland.

JUNE

□   German surface reinforcements sent to the Channel.

AUGUST

19   Abortive sortie by German fleet in North Sea. Leads to withdrawal of fleet submarines to prepare for renewed commerce war.

27   Italy declares war on Germany. Rumania declares war on Austria-Hungary.

28   Germany declares war on Rumania, followed on 30th by Turkey and on 1 September by Bulgaria.

OCTOBER

□   Renewed submarine offensive against commerce.

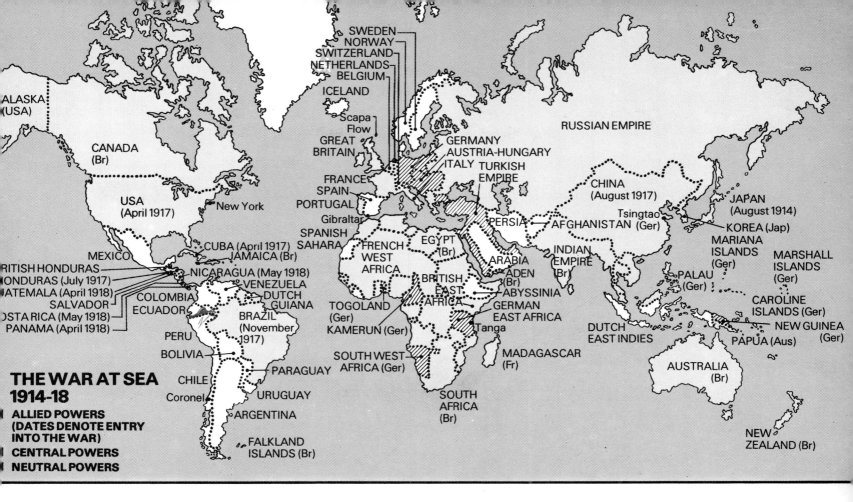

THE WAR AT SEA 1914-18

- ALLIED POWERS (DATES DENOTE ENTRY INTO THE WAR)
- CENTRAL POWERS
- NEUTRAL POWERS

NOVEMBER
9-10 Seven German destroyers lost in single attack on Baltiski Port.

1917

JANUARY
☐ Introduction of convoys on French coal-trade route (from south-coast ports of England to France) following 40% losses in December.

FEBRUARY
1 Germans launch unrestricted submarine warfare against commerce.

MARCH
12 Start of first Russian revolution. Provisional Government under Prince Lvov.

APRIL
6 USA declares war on Germany.
20 Last major German surface sortie in the Channel.
26 British Admiralty authorizes ocean-going convoys.
☐ Allies lose 430 ships (843,549 tons) during this month; merchant ship-to-submarine exchange-rate reaches 167:1.

MAY
4 First US destroyers arrive in Ireland.
10 First inward convoy from Gibraltar sails; regular Gibraltar convoys established in July.
24 First eastbound convoy leaves Hampton Road, Virginia.

AUGUST-JANUARY
☐ U-boat losses exceed replacement for first time (46:42).

AUGUST
☐ Outward convoys formed in attempt to combat heavy losses.

OCTOBER
12-17 German amphibious assault on Riga, the Russian's Baltic bridge head.
13 U-boat strength reaches 70 at sea.

NOVEMBER
☐ Convoys extended right into UK ports and not dispersed in Channel. Convoys introduced into Mediterranean. Arrival of US battle squadron at Scapa Flow.
7 Second Russian Revolution.
17 Last capital ship engagement between German and British forces.
21 Merchant ship losses reach lowest point since February.

DECEMBER
7 USA declares war on Austria-Hungary.
15 Russia and Germany agree armistice terms; Treaty of Brest–Litovsk takes Russia out of war in March 1918.
19 Start of deep mining and illumination of Dover barrage; German submarines forced to make 6-day passage around Scotland.

1918

JANUARY-NOVEMBER
☐ Shipbuilding exceeds losses by 1·75 m tons (4 m:2·25 m).

APRIL
1 Formation of RAF: Navy loses control of its air wing.
22-3 Zeebrugge raid.
23-4 Last sortie of German fleet.

MAY
☐ Exchange rate of merchantmen to submarines reaches lowest point (10:1).

JUNE
☐ Start of laying of North Sea barrage – 75% ready by November.
19 Austrian dreadnought *Szent Istvan* sunk by Italian *MB-21* off Pola.

SEPTEMBER
26 Bulgaria sues for armistice.
☐ Merchant shipping losses total 99.

OCTOBER
17–19 Belgian Army clears its coast of German naval bases.
27 Austria-Hungary sues for armistice.
29 Start of Kiel mutiny.
30 Armistice concluded with Turkey.
31 Revolution in Vienna and Budapest.
☐ Only 25 Allied merchantmen lost.

NOVEMBER
9 Revolution in Berlin.
10 Flight of Kaiser.
11 Armistice concluded with Germany.
21 Surrender of German fleet; internment of fleet in Scapa Flow.

1919

JANUARY
18 Assembly of Paris Peace Conference.

JUNE
21 German naval units scuttle themselves in Scapa Flow.
28 Germany signs Treaty of Versailles.

JULY
Blockade of Germany lifted.

The War on Land and in the Air

The symbol □ denotes activity over an extended period of time

1914

JUNE
28   Archduke Franz Ferdinand of Austria-Hungary assassinated at Sarajevo.

JULY
1   Naval wing of Royal Flying Corps (RFC) becomes Royal Naval Air Service (RNAS).
18   US Congress authorizes formation of Aviation Section in US Signal Corps.
28   Austria-Hungary declares war on Serbia.

AUGUST
1   Germany declares war on Russia.
3   Germany declares war on France and invades Belgium.
4   Britain declares war on Germany. Liège forts surrender after bombardment by Krupp 42-cm 'Berthas'.
6   Austria-Hungary declares war on Russia.
10   France declares war on Austria-Hungary.
11   RFC personnel begin to arrive in France.
12   Britain declares war on Austria-Hungary.
13   Advance guard of British Expeditionary Force (BEF) arrives in France.
14   French offensive opens in Lorraine.
19   RFC becomes operational: reconnaissance flights begin over France.
20   Fall of Brussels.
22   RFC reconnaissance reports movement of General Kluck's First German Army against BEF.
20–25 Main German force sweeps back Allies at Battles of Mons, the Sambre and the Ardennes.
23   Japan declares war on Germany.
25   Namur forts surrender after bombardment by 'Berthas' and 30.5-cm 'Emmas'. First aerial victory: three machines of No. 2 Squadron down a German aircraft.
26–31 Russians crushed at Tannenberg on Eastern Front.

SEPTEMBER
2   General Kluck's army reaches the Marne, 25 miles east of Paris.
5–10 First Battle of the Marne. Germans withdraw to a line Noyon-Verdun.
15–18 First Battle of the Aisne. Armies swing northwards to coast in 'Race to the Sea'.
16   Formation of Canadian Aviation Corps.

OCTOBER
21   Russia declares war on Turkey.

OCTOBER–NOVEMBER
□   Heavy fighting in Flanders. BEF denies Channel ports to German army in first Battle Ypres.

NOVEMBER
1   Other Allies declare war on Turkey.

DECEMBER
21   First air-raid on Britain.
□   Germans dig in along Western Front establishing static trench warfare from North Sea, near Nieuport, to Swiss border, near Belfort.

1915

JANUARY–JUNE
19–20 First Zeppelin raid on Britain; King's Lynn bombed.
23   RFC reconnaissance detects Turkish forces moving towards Suez Canal.
□   Allied offensives on Western Front beaten back.

FEBRUARY
15   First naval assault at Dardanelles.
18   Opening of first submarine campaign against Allied commerce.
24   British Admiralty Landships Committee set up to examine means of ending trench stalemate.

MARCH
3   National Advisory Committee for Aeronautics established by US Congress.
10   Battle of Neuve Chapelle. First great artillery barrage of war fired as preparation for British attack.
22   Surrender to Russians of Przemsyl, Bohemian fortress, after bombardment and siege lasting 194 days.

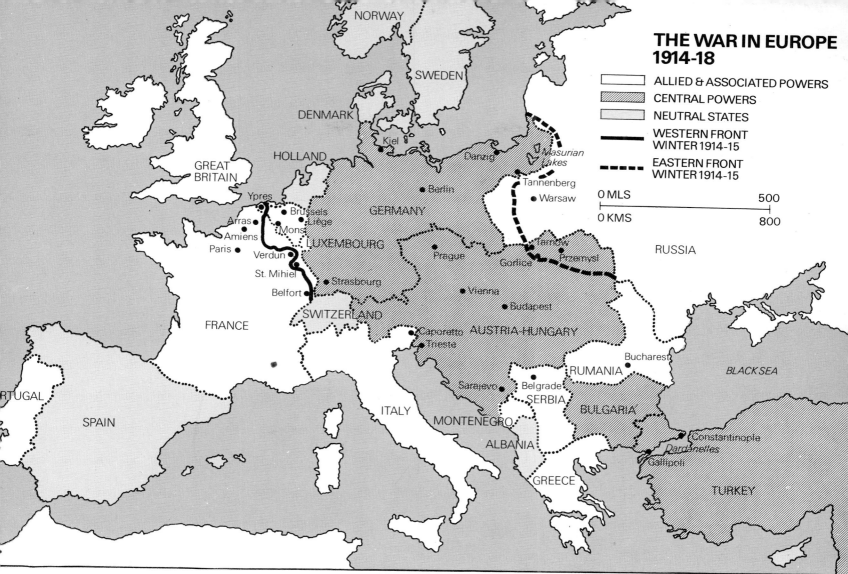

THE WAR IN EUROPE 1914-18

☐	ALLIED & ASSOCIATED POWERS
▨	CENTRAL POWERS
░	NEUTRAL STATES
▬	WESTERN FRONT WINTER 1914-15
▬ ▬	EASTERN FRONT WINTER 1914-15

0 MLS   500

0 KMS   800

APRIL

22   First use of gas, by Germans at Second Battle of Ypres.

25   Allied landings begin at Gallipoli.

☐   German build-up on Eastern Front.

MAY

2   Austro-German armies break through at Gorlice-Tarnow.

23   Italy declares war on Austria-Hungary.

31   First Zeppelin raid on London.

JUNE

7   Zeppelin destroyed in air by Flight Sub-Lieutenant R.A.J. Warneford.

30   British War Office defines its requirements for an armoured cross-country vehicle able to negotiate a trench 10 feet wide.

JUNE–SEPTEMBER

☐   Russians retreat to a line south of Riga.

AUGUST

12   Short seaplane makes first successful aerial torpedo attack, on Turkish merchant vessel in Dardanelles.

19   Colonel H. M. Trenchard takes command of RFC in France.

SEPTEMBER

14   Bulgaria declares war on Serbia.

15–16   Britain and France declare war on Bulgaria.

22   Successful trials in England of 'Little Willie' – first prototype tank.

☐   Allies renew offensive on Western Front, until November, with scant success.

DECEMBER

17   General Haig assumes command of BEF.

1916

JANUARY

9   Evacuation of Gallipoli peninsula completed after disastrous eight-month campaign.

29   First official trials of 'Big Willie' or 'Mother', second prototype tank.

FEBRUARY

12   British Tank Supply Committee orders 100 Mark I tanks.

21   Battle of Verdun begins with intensive four-hour bombardment; air combat becomes increasingly common, notably Fokker Eindekkers against Nieuport Bébés; battle lasts until December.

MARCH

☐   Recruiting begins for 'Heavy Section' of British Machine Gun Corps.

MAY

17   Air Board formed in Britain to co-ordinate RFC and RNAS procurement.

JUNE

24   Seven-day artillery bombardment begins in preparation for British assault on the Somme.

JULY

1   Battle of the Somme begins. British infantry suffer 60,000 casualties on first day. Despite heavy losses RFC gains air superiority over battle area.

13   British horse cavalry used en masse for last time in Europe – mown down by German fire on Somme front.

☐   New Russian offensive under General Brusilov weakens resources of Central Powers, notably at Verdun and on Italian Front; offensive lasts until September.

AUGUST

25   Italy declares war on Germany. Rumania declares war on Austria-Hungary.

28   Germany declares war on Rumania, followed on 30th by Turkey and on 1 September by Bulgaria.

SEPTEMBER

2–3   First German airship shot down over Britain, by Lieutenant W. Leafe-Robinson.

15   British tanks deployed in action for first time in final phase of Battle of the Somme.

SEPTEMBER–NOVEMBER

☐   Tanks make minor sorties at Thiepval, Flers, Le Sars and Beaumont Hamel.

OCTOBER

28   Death of Oswald Boelcke, father of true air combat, in an accident.

NOVEMBER

28   First German bomber raid on London.

1917

FEBRUARY

1   Germans launch unrestricted submarine warfare against commerce.

FEBRUARY–APRIL

☐   Germans withdraw on Western Front behind heavily defended zone – the Hindenburg Line.

MARCH

12   Russian Revolution begins.

APRIL
6   USA declares war on Germany.
9–15 Battle of Arras. British attack in preparation for Nivelle offensive.
16–20 Nivelle Offensive. Disastrous attack by 1.2 million French troops supported by 7,000 guns. French deploy tanks for first time at Battle of Chemin des Dames.

APRIL–NOVEMBER
☐   Tanks, though poorly deployed at Arras, Buillacourt, Messines and Passchendaele, influence morale on both sides.

MAY
7   First night air-raid on London.
20   First U-boat (U–26) sunk by an aircraft (British flying-boat).
25   First major daylight air-raid on Britain, by 21 Gothas.

JUNE
2   US Army Signal Corps Aviation Section becomes Airplane Division.
7   Battle of Messines. British attack after 17-day bombardment consuming 3.5 million shells.
13   First major Gotha raid on London kills 162, injures 426.
☐   Advance guard of First Division of American Expeditionary Force (AEF) arrives in France.

JULY
11   Cabinet committee established to consider needs for air defence of Britain.
27   British Tank Corps established by Royal warrant.

JULY–NOVEMBER
☐   Third Battle of Ypres (Passchendaele). Preliminary bombardment of 4.3 million shells; altogether 107,000 tons of shells fired in greatest artillery concentration in British history.

AUGUST
2   First successful deck landing, by a Sopworth Pup on HMS *Furious*.
22   Last daylight air-raid of the war on Britain.

SEPTEMBER
1   General von Hutier's Riga offensive begins after short intensive bombardment planned by Colonel Bruchmüller.
2   First major night air-raid on Britain.

OCTOBER
11   RFC forms its 41st Wing, to bomb strategic targets in Germany.

OCTOBER–NOVEMBER
☐   Battle of Caporetto. Germans and Austrians use 'Hutier' tactics to break through; Italians suffer disastrous defeat.

NOVEMBER
7   Second Russian Revolution. Bolsheviks under Lenin and Trotsky seize power.
20   British Mark IV tanks breach Hindenburg Line in Battle of Cambrai

DECEMBER
7   USA declares war on Austria-Hungary
15   Russia and Germany agree armistice terms.

1918

JANUARY
2   Air Ministry formed in Britain.

MARCH
19   First operational sorties by American aircraft in France.
21   Ludendorff opens spring offensives on Western Front using Hutier tactics First phase ends 5 April.
23   Paris Gun opens fire; on 29th, Good Friday, shell collapses vault of Church of St Gervais, near Hôtel de Ville, killing 88 worshippers. Shelling continues intermittently until 7 August
26   First appearance, at Colincourt, of medium Whippet tanks.

APRIL
1   Royal Air Force formed by amalgamating RFC and RNAS.
9–17 Ludendorff's second offensive (Luys)
12   Last effective Zeppelin raid on Britain

21 Death of Manfred von Richthofen, greatest air ace of World War I, over the Somme. He was accredited with 80 victories.

24 First tank v tank action, at Villers-Bretonneux. British Mark IV meets German A7V.

MAY

19–20 Last effective air-raid on Britain.

27 Ludendorff's third offensive (Aisne) begins. Reaches the Marne on 30th. US divisions appear in strength in Allied line.

28 Battle of Cantigny. First American offensive of war.

30 Battles of Château-Thierry and Belleau Wood fought by American troops.

31 Renault FT light tanks deployed in battle for first time.

JUNE

8 Formation of Independent Air Force under Major-General Trenchard for strategic bombing of Germany.

9–13 Ludendorff's fourth offensive (Noyon-Montdidier). Assault by Hutier's 18th Army disrupted by Allied counter-preparation bombardment.

12 First bombing mission flown by US aircraft in France.

JULY

4 British Mark Vs make successful début spearheading counter-offensive at Hamel.

5–19 Ludendorff's fifth offensive (Champagne-Meuse). Allied counter-preparation bombardment again breaks up German stormtrooper formations.

18 Allied counter-offensive begins on Aisne-Marne Front.

26 Death of Edward Mannock, greatest British air ace of World War I, killed by ground fire. He was accredited with 73 victories.

AUGUST

8 'Black Day' of German Army. Allies advance seven miles in nine hours behind spearhead of 400 heavy and medium tanks in Battle of Amiens.

21 Second phase of Amiens offensive by Allies.

28 John D. Ryan appointed US Assistant Secretary for War, with responsibility for Bureau of Aircraft Production and for Division of Military Aeronautics.

SEPTEMBER

5 Formation of Royal Canadian Naval Air Service.

12–16 American ground and combined air-ground assaults drive Germans out of St Mihiel salient.

26 Americans begin Meuse-Argonne offensive.

27 British storm Hindenburg Line.

28 Allied offensive opens in Flanders.

OCTOBER

6 First German request for armistice.

14 Handley-Page bomber drops first giant (1,650-pound) bomb.

26 Major-General Trenchard becomes Commander-in-Chief of Inter-Allies Independent Air Force.

27 Ludendorff resigns. Austria-Hungary sues for armistice.

29 Mutiny at Kiel of German High Seas Fleet.

31 Revolution in Vienna and Budapest.

NOVEMBER

9 Revolution in Berlin.

10 Flight of the Kaiser.

11 Armistice concluded with Germany.

PREVIOUS PAGES *Trouble in the mud at Ypres in 1917. A water cart is bogged down, one of the horses and a cart wheel having gone over the edge of the brushwood track.*

OPPOSITE *Rolls Royce armoured cars in Palestine, where both petrol-driven vehicles and horse cavalry had the freedom to fight a war of movement.*

BELOW *A British RNAS Seabrook armoured car of 1915; these 10-ton vehicles carried a crew of six and were armed with a 3-pounder gun and four Vickers machine guns.*

PART 2
WORLD WAR I

6

THE INCREDIBLE SIEGE

Machine guns on the Western Front sap the infantryman's offensive spirit.

It was the tragedy of the Great War that the preceding century had witnessed the absence of major conflict in Europe; for this meant that tactics and strategy had become increasingly less relevant and out of tune with parallel developments in weapons, and especially in defensive firepower. The American Civil War, the Franco-Prussian and Russo-Japanese Wars all pointed significantly to the tremendous improvements made in firepower from small arms through automatic weapons to heavy artillery. Against such a concentration of fire, infantry advanced at their peril. But such lessons went largely unheeded by General Staffs who had been trained in the more romantic campaigns of Imperial conquests. In the Boer War the lines of British infantry, taught in the classic mould of Waterloo, with the bayonet still seen as their major weapon, suffered cruelly at the hands of Boer marksmen. The latter, making clever use of cover and equipped with smokeless powder, completely outclassed the staid tactics of the Imperial infantry. There were some reforms after this highly unsatisfactory war and the infantry in particular concentrated on the need to improve the standard of their musketry. Thus in 1914 the British Expeditionary Force had probably the highest standards in this field of military skill of all the major combatants in the Great War. It was, however, a dangerous asset, for in the event the BEF, conditioned to the doctrines of the advance, were destroyed by the overwhelming numbers and firepower of their opponents.

In the early years of this century armies were re-organized almost beyond recognition. To co-ordinate the movements of large conscript armies (by 1914 the French and German armies each numbered more than a million men, and the Russians even more), the field telephone and telegraph were widely used, and technical and service formations such as engineers and signallers, quartermasters and ordnance units were needed in ever greater numbers as adjuncts to the fighting arms. The railways also played an important part, and mobilization, especially in countries such as France and Germany, was organized around the timetables of railways radiating out from the principal towns and mobilization centres to the threatened frontiers. From these advanced positions the horse still provided the essential means of transporting men and supplies to the battlefield, though even before 1914 the motor car and lorry were increasingly used to speed up movement and communication.

The Great War has often been called the machine-gun war, for this weapon within a very short while came to dominate the battlefield. Throughout the history and development of automatic weapons, new situations have stimulated design, and the large standing armies of Europe furnished both the impetus and the ready market for this particular weapon of mass destruction. Each nation had its own machine gun and the majority of them were designed and developed in the United States by men such as Hugo Borchardt, Benjamin Hotchkiss, Colonel Isaac Lewis and later John Browning and his brothers. The weapons they invented all had the same basic characteristics: they fired bullets of the same calibre as a rifle at a rate of at least 250 rounds per minute. Although such weapons as yet could not maintain a fire over any sustained period of time, nevertheless short bursts of about twenty seconds aimed at knee height, across open ground in a scythe-like motion, made exposure by advancing infantry invariably hazardous and on occasion suicidal.

In 1914 the infantry soldier had become the common denominator of the modern battlefield. The Continental system of military service brought thousands of citizens into uniform as conscripts, and it was the average man's reactions to the stringencies of military service as well as his ability to handle new weapons that set the pace for modern armies. The ordinary soldier of the day was imbued with the spirit of the offensive. This tactical doctrine as a recipe for suicide reached its zenith in France in what was known as *l'offensive à l'outrance*. The French soldier was, moreover, indoctrinated with the belief that he was racially superior to the German and that his offensive spirit would overcome the Germans' strength in numbers. But high morale is not bullet-proof and the French infantry of 1914, uniformed in red breeches (for the sake of morale), endured frightful losses. The German High Command was a little more realistic, but they too had complete faith in the offensive and saw any tendency towards caution and defensive tactics as defeatism. In turn their ranks of field grey, even though they advanced in open order, provided a lucrative harvest for both the rapid fire of French field artillery and the accurate musketry of the British Expeditionary Force.

Even after a year of combat, by which time the war of movement had died before a trench system of fortifications which stretched from the sea to the Swiss frontier, the generals could still not see the error of their ways. The new

British Commander-in-Chief, General Haig, as late as the autumn of 1915 was to assert that the machine gun was 'a much over-rated weapon'. It was left to the politicians to be more sanguine and realistic. Thus Lloyd George, then Minister of Munitions, told the British Parliament in his blunt way that 80% of British casualties had been caused, in his estimation, by machine-gun fire. It is reasonable to assume that the other armies suffered on a similar scale.

RIGHT *Bringing up barbed wire for a night working party.*
BELOW *Five Germans in a shell hole at Ypres; one is sentry, another acts as observer. All carry long-handled grenades.*
BOTTOM *Trench scene on the Somme, 1916. Exhausted soldiers sleep, and a sentry mans the fire step.*

7

TRIAL BY BARRAGE

The big guns of the
warring nations – a
summary of equipment
and tactics.

In the years leading up to 1914 few Allied strategists accurately foresaw how increased firepower would influence the course of the next war. The French and the British prepared for a war of movement in which the decisive actions would be fought along classical lines and the enemy defeated after a short campaign. In such a war heavy artillery and machine guns (seen as static or defensive weapons) would not be important factors, and the French and British general staffs reduced the number of such weapons in their tables of organization.

The Germans, as it turned out, planned more wisely. They placed their faith in the weight of fire available to each division and army corps. They did not go along with the idea, then current in France, that the hypothetical battlefield of the future would be dominated by light Quick-Firers like the '75'; they had, moreover, the foresight to integrate numbers of light howitzers with their divisional artillery, and they also provided heavy howitzers at corps level.

Broadly, by 1914 the tactical doctrine of the major fighting nations may be summarized as follows:

OPPOSITE *British artillerymen on the Western Front realign the massive wheels of a 4·7-inch naval gun.*
RIGHT *The efficient Russian 76·2-mm field gun M-1903.*

1 ALLIES

France. French tactical use of artillery in 1914 was centred entirely on the M-1897 Puteaux 75-mm field-gun. The '75', although a superior direct-fire weapon, was tactically obsolete in 1914 because its low-trajectory fire was ineffective against infantry or artillery sheltering behind rudimentary field works or in convolutions of the terrain. In such situations the howitzer, with its mid-angle trajectory, was at its best, but for various reasons the French were woefully deficient in howitzers.

In the event of the French meeting an enemy in the open, a group of three 4-gun batteries (amounting to one-third of the '75s' attached to each division) would act as

IMPROVEMENT OF FIELD GUNS 1815–1919

CATEGORY	TYPE OF GUN	DATE	PERFORMANCE
1 Muzzle velocity	Early rifled guns	1863–70	1,090 feet per second
	Later rifled guns	1870–93	1,466 feet per second
	Early Quick-Firers	*c.* 1900	1,696 feet per second
	Later Quick-Firers	1914–18	1,770 feet per second
2 Range with shrapnel	Smooth-bores	1815–50	1,257 yards
	Early rifled guns	1863–70	2,004 yards
	Later rifled guns	1870–93	4,120 yards
	Early Quick-Firers	*c.* 1900	6,160 yards
	Later Quick-Firers	1914–18	6,500 yards
3 Range with shell	Smooth-bores	1815–50	1,670 yards
	Early rifled guns	1863–70	3,965 yards
	Later rifled guns	1870–93	6,168 yards
	Early Quick-Firers	*c.* 1900	7,340 yards
	Later Quick-Firers	1914–18	8,500 yards
	With streamline shell	1918–19	12,~30 yards

A study in contrasts – tactical doctrines of the Allies.

'infantry batteries', firing on the objectives of the *poilus* (as the French infantrymen were known). The rest of the divisional artillery engaged the enemy's guns.

The French exaggerated the counter-battery potential of the '75' and, again, visions of batteries going into action at a smart trot, fighting in the open from 'semi-concealed' positions and engaging and defeating opportunity targets danced in the minds of senior officers. It was as if the next war would duplicate the conditions of 1870. This time, though, the French saw themselves wielding the stick, and in the aura of confidence surrounding 'notre glorieux "soixante-quinze"' ('our glorious "75"'), the gun's limitations went unnoticed and some of the technical improvements of the previous decade – such as telephone communication between groups of batteries – were ignored.

Great Britain. British tactical use of artillery and organization closely resembled German practice (see below), but

the British howitzers were obsolete in 1914 and, besides, were often supplied with defective ammunition. Also, the British were deficient in weight of metal and numbers of guns at army corps level. Standard British field-pieces included the 3·3-inch 18-pounder and the 4·5-inch howitzer. Heavy fire was provided by the 5-inch 60-pounder, which in 1914 had a range of 10,500 yards.

Russia. The artillery was the crack arm of the Czar's Army. The Putilov 76·2-mm field-gun was comparable to anything the Germans or Austrians could field, but the Russians were without a good field or heavy howitzer. Numbers of elderly Krupp howitzers and 155-mm 'long'

BELOW *British 9·2-inch heavy howitzers are seen in battery on the Western Front; in the foreground a supply of shells is lined up on a ramp. To the rear of the battery passes an ammunition column whose function is to feed the lighter guns closer to the front line.*

OPPOSITE *A German 77-mm field-gun crew dashes forward under fire at the Marne; from a painting by Albert Reich. Inset is General von Emmich, whose Army of the Meuse invaded Belgium with two 42-cm Berthas, pride of the Krupp Works.*
ABOVE *A Big Bertha and crew; despite their awesome size, the supremacy of these super-guns was limited to the first weeks of the war.*

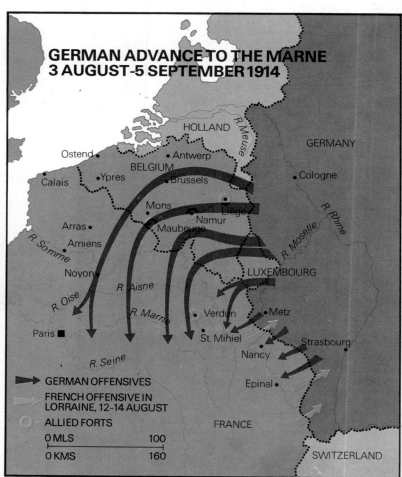

**GERMAN ADVANCE TO THE MARNE
3 AUGUST–5 SEPTEMBER 1914**

HOLLAND

R. Meuse

GERMANY

Ostend

Antwerp

Calais

Ypres

BELGIUM

Brussels

Cologne

Mons

Liège

R. Rhine

Arras

Namur

Maubeuge

R. Somme

Amiens

R. Moselle

LUXEMBOURG

Noyon

R. Oise

R. Aisne

R. Marne

Verdun

Metz

Paris

St. Mihiel

Strasbourg

R. Seine

Nancy

Epinal

➤ GERMAN OFFENSIVES
FRENCH OFFENSIVE IN
LORRAINE, 12–14 AUGUST
ALLIED FORTS

FRANCE

0 MLS   100

0 KMS   160

SWITZERLAND

von EMMICH

The Germans produce a versatile range of guns, and develop the techniques of indirect fire.

guns were available, but these guns were not up to 1914 standards. A Russian copy of the Schneider 155-mm howitzer was produced but not in quantity, and the Czar's artillery, caught in the middle of a modernization pro-gramme, never was able to recover from its handicap in this category.

2 CENTRAL POWERS

Germany. The Germans not only had a reliable field-gun in the much-reworked Krupp 77-mm M-1906, they also recognized the inherent limitations of field guns, and so they provided three batteries of light 105-mm howitzers for every nine of field guns at division level. Backing these were heavier 155-mm howitzers at corps level. In addition there was an extraordinary number of heavier howitzers and field mortars (all of which were remarkably mobile) in the heavy batteries of the Foot Artillery.

The Germans made extensive use of indirect fire in their pre-war manoeuvres and were rarely seen in the open, preferring to fight from carefully chosen, fully concealed positions. The *Abteilung* system (effectively a three-battery group) was still in use, and, as in 1870, artillery took precedence over infantry in positioning.

The first great artillery event of the war was not announced

OPPOSITE, ABOVE *The two upper pictures demonstrate the loading and firing of 'Granny', one of the British Admiralty's 15-inch heavy howitzers. Painted on the side of the gun are the names of actions in which it had fought to that time . . . Aubers Ridge, Festubert, Loos, Ypres.*
OPPOSITE, BELOW *To compensate for the inherent limitations of field guns, which could only give direct, low-trajectory fire, the Germans entered the war with plentiful stocks of howitzers; this example is a 105-mm light howitzer 98/09.*
BELOW *German gunners on winter watch in the Vosges Mountains; the gun is a 150-mm heavy field howitzer 13.*
BOTTOM *A German 77-mm field gun C 96 n/A firing in the Champagne sector of the Western Front.*

Mystery of the Big Berthas: how effective were these elephantine so-called 'secret weapons'?

Army of the Meuse under General von Emmich swung through neutral Belgium with the object of enveloping the Allied left flank. On 3 August 1914 the German army entered Belgian territory, and by 4 August the Germans faced their first serious obstacle, the Brialmont forts at Liège. German infantry failed to take the forts but filtered through the 'dead spaces' in the perimeter and captured the town of Liège four miles beyond. However, the forts had to be taken before the invasion could proceed.

There were two Berthas with von Emmich's army. By 12 August the laborious task of emplacing them had been completed, and early that evening they began the systematic reduction of each fort. According to the Belgian commander, General Léman, the guns' shells tore holes in the ground large enough to 'put a three-storey house in'. The morale of the defenders cracked under the terrible bombardment. The forts were wrecked one by one. The concrete was penetrated time and again, steel gun turrets were blown topsy-turvy and the survivors of each garrison emerged dumbly amid the rubble and smoke.

After reducing the eastern perimeter, the Berthas were shifted into the town itself and began to pound the western forts. General Léman was pulled dazed from the ruins of Fort Loncin after a shell penetrated its concrete and blew

by the drum-fire of the '75s' but rather by the earth-shaking roar of Krupp's monster 42-cm Berthas bombarding the Belgian forts. So much nonsense has been written about this event that it sometimes becomes difficult to sift fact from fancy, or, worse yet, to separate the truth from the 'big lie'. There can be no doubt that the propaganda mills were churning at a great rate after the bombardment; oddly enough, too, the story they told suited everyone's purpose. Certainly, the reputation of the Big Berthas seems to rest solely on their performance against the Belgian forts, for when the same guns were used against Ypres in April 1915, and later against Verdun, they produced nothing more than a great deal of noise and much German disappointment.

The generally accepted account of the bombardment is that, in accordance with the Schlieffen Plan, the German

up the magazine. By 16 August the Belgians had had enough, and the last forts surrendered. The two Berthas had caused the surrender of each fort—some through devastating bombardment and others through intimidation.

From Liège the Berthas moved to Namur where they were joined by a two-gun battery of Austro-Hungarian 30·5-cm 'Schlanke (slim) Emmas'. The Brialmont forts at Namur surrendered after a four-day bombardment (21–25 August 1914) by the four howitzers. After Namur the forts at Maubeuge were subjected to the same treatment.

If we accept this version of events, two Berthas and four Emmas (a second Emma battery was present at Maubeuge) battered a path for the German Army through three obsolete but quite formidable fortress systems. In this context the German 'secret weapon' (as its propagandists

French 75-mm Puteaux Field Gun M-1897

The '75' was the first modern Quick-Firing field gun. Its appearance in 1897 heralded a revolution in the design and capabilities of artillery. The 'secret' of the 75-mm gun and the mechanism that set it apart from all previous guns was its long recoil cylinder – a device which absorbed the energy of the recoil and returned the gun to battery smoothly and efficiently without disturbing the position of the gun's carriage. This removed the need to re-lay the gun after each shot (a time-consuming operation) and made possible a high rate of fire.

The '75' was the invention of Commandant de Port of the Ateliers de Puteaux. By 1898 the first guns were in service. Subsequently the gun went on campaign in China, Morocco and the Balkan Wars. During World War I the '75' was the standard field gun of France and the American Expeditionary Force; many were still in service in World War II.

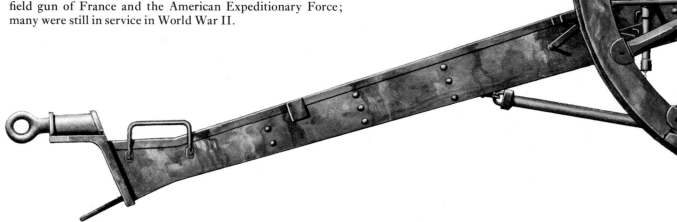

Operation of the Nordenfeldt eccentric screw breech block

The mechanism was opened by grasping the handle and turning the breech block 120 degrees to the left. This circular displacement uncovered the bore. A cartridge was inserted into the breech, and a reverse motion closed the breech block. These very simple motions could be performed by a skilled crew in a few seconds. Obturation, *i.e.* the sealing of the breech to prevent the escape of gases, was performed by the metallic cartridge case.

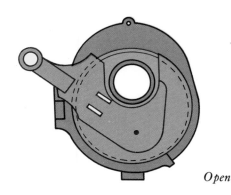

Open

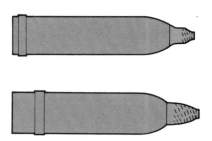

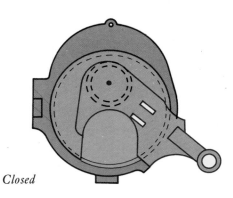

Closed

LEFT *Two shell types fired by the '75'. The upper diagram features the 12-pound HE (high explosive) shell which was filled with melanite. In the lower picture is the heavier 16-pound shrapnel shell.*

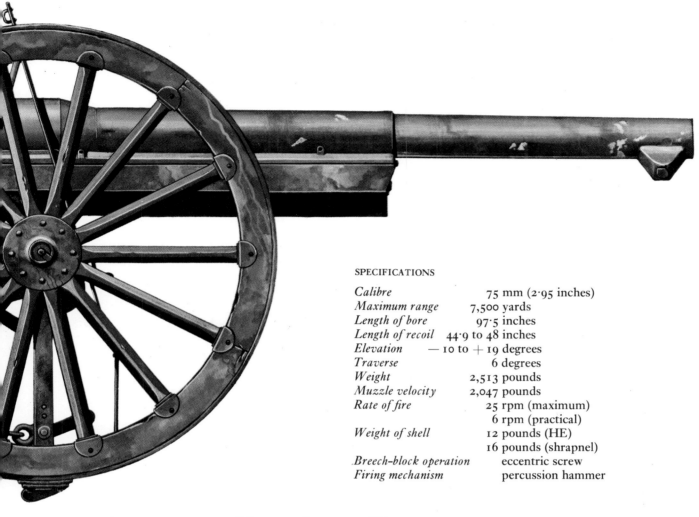

SPECIFICATIONS

Calibre	75 mm (2·95 inches)
Maximum range	7,500 yards
Length of bore	97·5 inches
Length of recoil	44·9 to 48 inches
Elevation	− 10 to + 19 degrees
Traverse	6 degrees
Weight	2,513 pounds
Muzzle velocity	2,047 pounds
Rate of fire	25 rpm (maximum)
	6 rpm (practical)
Weight of shell	12 pounds (HE)
	16 pounds (shrapnel)
Breech-block operation	eccentric screw
Firing mechanism	percussion hammer

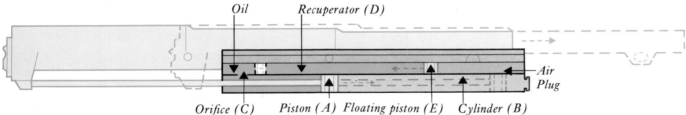

Operation of the long-recoil cylinder

When the gun is fired, the piston (A) is drawn through a cylinder (B) filled with oil. The action of the piston compresses the oil and forces it through a small orifice (C) into another cylinder, the recuperator (D), which is filled with compressed air beyond the floating piston (E). The energy of the recoil then further compresses the air in the recuperator until, the recoil force being dissipated, the compressed air 'spring' forces the oil back into the recoil cylinder and returns the gun to battery.

The long-recoil cylinder was the invention of Konrad Haussner, a Krupp engineer, but it was rejected by Krupp and the German authorities as 'impracticable for use in the field'. There can be no doubt that the French worked directly from Haussner's patent in designing their long-recoil cylinder for the '75'.

LEFT *The caisson or ammunition chest in which shells for the '75' were towed to the firing position.*

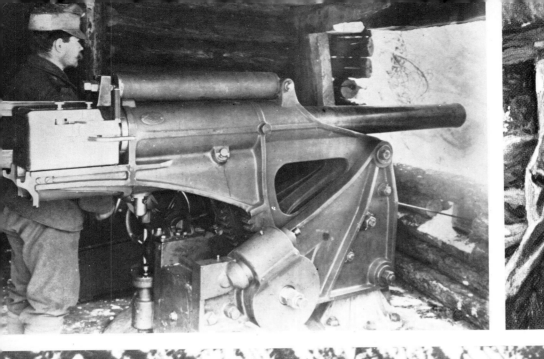

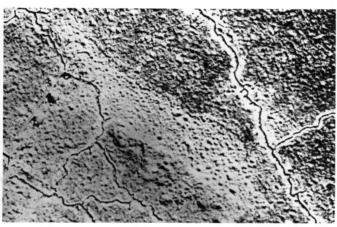

OPPOSITE, ABOVE LEFT *In the mountains of the Tyrol an Austrian 75-mm cannon on a heavy pedestal mount guards the pass.*

OPPOSITE, ABOVE RIGHT *In a trench on the Western Front a German artillery officer uses a stereoscopic telescope to observe the effect of his battery's fire.*

OPPOSITE, BELOW *A British 8-inch heavy howitzer in action near Messines. The gun has just been fired and is in partial recoil, running back on to chocks placed behind the wheels.*

TOP *One of the monsters that failed to win the war – an Italian gun abandoned to the Germans during the retreat to the Tagliamento in November 1917.*

ABOVE *An aerial photograph of shell-pocked terrain on the Western Front. In some sectors the ground was so savaged that it has only recently become cultivable.*

called it) was a great success. Meanwhile, too, the Allies could claim that the gallant resistance of the tiny Belgian Army in the face of these 'terror weapons' (their term for the Berthas) gained precious time for the French and the British Expeditionary Force to complete their mobilization and deployment; this in turn helped to produce victory at the First Battle of the Marne.

On the other hand, it becomes difficult to suppress doubts about the veracity of official German and Belgian accounts after reading Lt-Col Karl Justrow's narrative in *Die Dicke Berta und der Krieg*. According to Justrow, who was in a position to know, those tremendous holes Léman spoke of were not caused by the Berthas but, rather, were the result of dynamiting by German engineers after the surrender. One begins in fact to suspect that the photographers were assembled *after* the dynamiting so that more impressive pictures could be taken of the Berthas' 'devastations'.

In addition, there is testimony here and there in German reports that the bombardment produced, in the words of one account, 'a *superficial* picture of indescribable devastation, with heaps of earth and debris everywhere' (my italics). This, coupled with the comparatively slight losses of the Belgian garrisons, seems to point to the fact that the Belgians simply lost their nerve and surrendered to a lot of noise, smoke and dust. Finally, there is the unquestionable failure of the Berthas after the Belgian campaign. It seems, for example, that in the operations against Verdun Bertha's shells could not penetrate concrete and shattered upon striking the steel turrets of the forts. But whichever version of the Belgian campaign one believes, there is no doubt that the Berthas made a lasting contribution to the folklore of war – even if their period of supremacy was limited to a few days in August 1914.

The German invasion was brought to a halt little more than 20 miles from Paris in the mammoth First Battle of the Marne (5–10 September 1914). French armies under Marshal Joffre and General Galliéni checked the advance of General von Gronau's right-flank forces on 6 September, and by 8 September the Germans had begun to retreat to the Aisne. The French 75-mm guns, operating in the open for the last time until the 1916 breakthrough battles, seemed to be everywhere. They savaged the German infantry advance with rapid fire *rafales* – storms of shells that could blanket and obliterate an infantry column in seconds. On some occasions, as happened for instance at the Grand Couronné de Nancy, the fire of the '75s' alone was sufficient to break up major German attacks.

The German artillery, on the other hand, fired very effectively from concealment. It soon became apparent too that, despite its effectiveness against infantry in the open, the '75' was failing in the counter-battery role. Losses in the '75' batteries were very high, not least because of the inanely rough-and-ready tactics of the French gunners, who on countless occasions exposed themselves needlessly to German fire. Moreover, the German heavy howitzers never failed to capitalize on their advantage in range over the heaviest French guns. Victory at the Marne was bought not so much by the '75s' as by a tremendous sacrifice of lives. French losses in August–September 1914 totalled 329,000 men, fully one-sixth of their total for the war.

After the Marne the war on the Western Front degenerated into a stalemate. Both sides rapidly constructed parallel lines of trenches from Nieuport on the English Channel to the Swiss frontier 450 miles away. For the first time in history armies fought a war in which there were no flanks; victory could be gained only by costly frontal attacks or by exhausting the enemy's ability or will to make war. On the Eastern Front a similar situation prevailed following the early German victories at Tannenberg and the Masurian Lakes. Later on, new fronts were established in northern Italy and the Balkans.

The Germans were well prepared for this new form of warfare. In addition to their large stocks of machine guns and heavy artillery, they possessed 2,000 trench mortars, or Minenwerfer. The trench mortar was not new – great numbers of them had been used in the American Civil War and at Port Arthur; but only the Germans had acted in time to provide large stocks for their infantry.

Types of Barrage Fire in World War I

1: ROLLING BARRAGE

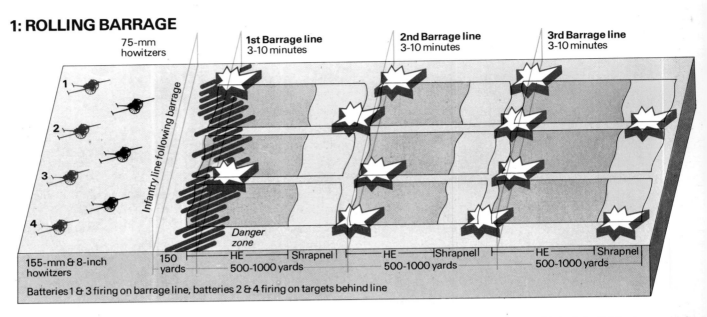

75-mm howitzers

1st Barrage line 3-10 minutes
2nd Barrage line 3-10 minutes
3rd Barrage line 3-10 minutes

Infantry line following barrage

Danger zone

155-mm & 8-inch howitzers

150 yards | HE 500-1000 yards | Shrapnel | HE 500-1000 yards | Shrapnel | HE 500-1000 yards | Shrapnel

Batteries 1 & 3 firing on barrage line, batteries 2 & 4 firing on targets behind line

The rolling barrage was first used in 1915 in an attempt to break the trench warfare stalemate. The barrage was indiscriminate, each battery firing down a 'lane' (roughly 200 yards of front per battery) to a predetermined barrage line. This barrage line–the 'danger zone'–was always about 150 yards ahead of the infantry advance. Once this line had been pounded for 3–10 minutes (the time it took the infantry to advance 100 yards), the fire was lifted to the next barrage line and then on to the next. The 'jumps' the barrage made were usually 500–1,000 yards deep. Thus the infantry was expected to advance unmolested behind a curtain of high explosive and shrapnel. Heavier guns and howitzers would fire to barrage lines or concentrate on points deeper in enemy-held territory.

In any rolling barrage about one-third of the field guns would fire shrapnel ahead of the HE (shell) barrage line. The divisional artillery would add heavy shrapnel shells but for the most part in their engagements they fired HE.

Rolling barrages were found to be generally ineffective–the enemy simply waited in his bomb-proofs until the barrage line had passed. Besides, they presented tremendous logistical problems for the gunners. It was calculated, for example, that for each 2,500 yards of infantry advance at least one day of artillery preparation was needed; thus the theoretical rate of advance was rarely sustained. By 1918 the advocates of surprise attack had won the day, and some attacks were then made with no artillery preparation whatsoever.

2: BOX BARRAGE

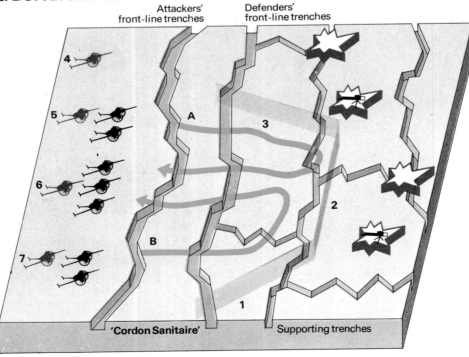

Attackers' front-line trenches

Defenders' front-line trenches

'Cordon Sanitaire'

Supporting trenches

Sequence of fire

1: 75-mm shrapnel barrage
2,3: 75-mm shell barrage, to form 'Cordon Sanitaire'
4,5,6,7: 155-mm shell barrage to neutralize communications trenches and machine-gun emplacements

A,B: Routes of raiding parties

The box barrage was developed late in World War I for use in conjunction with trench raids and infiltration tactics. First, a random preparation was fired. Then, as shown here, the artillery constructed a box or 'cordon sanitaire' with HE and shrapnel around the sector of the enemy's trenches to be raided. The heavier guns and howitzers fired beyond the box at vital points in the enemy's trench network and at machine-gun nests–areas from which the raiding party might be attacked.

3: PROTECTIVE BARRAGE

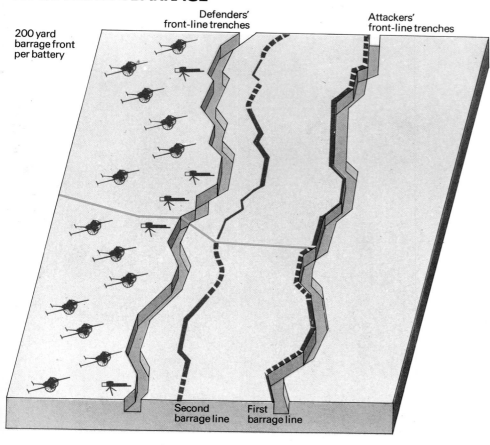

200 yard barrage front per battery

Defenders' front-line trenches

Attackers' front-line trenches

Second barrage line

First barrage line

The protective barrage was a technique used throughout 1917, but which almost invariably failed. The idea was to break up attacking lines and destroy the attacker's morale by bringing a sudden, overwhelming concentration of fire to bear on his jump-off point just as his attack began. Lines of approach and attack were plotted and each battery was allotted 200–250 yards of the enemy's front to saturate with a brief but rapid concentration of fire. Later, the barrage line was moved to a point only 150 yards from the trench line to be defended. When it was found that even this was inadequate, because the enemy's forward elements were slipping through with minimal casualties, concentrations just forward of critical points were tried, but, again, there was no diminution of the enemy's ability to drive his attack home. By 1917 this technique was being abandoned in favour of the counter-preparation technique.

4: COUNTER-PREPARATION BARRAGE

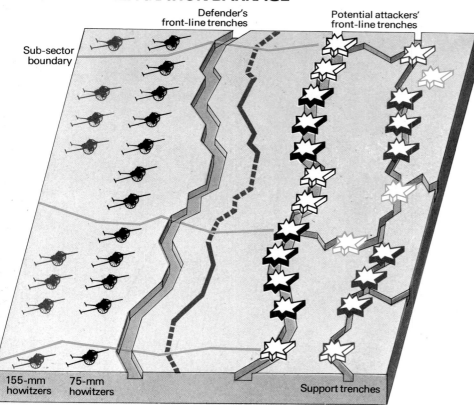

Sub-sector boundary

Defender's front-line trenches

Potential attackers' front-line trenches

155-mm howitzers

75-mm howitzers

Support trenches

The counter-preparation barrage, like the protective barrage, was intended to break up a hostile attacking formation and destroy the morale of the attacker. Some aspects of the protective barrage were retained, but the counter-preparation barrage differed basically in that it was begun the moment an attack was *anticipated or thought probable*. At that moment a saturation fire would be poured onto all possible assembly points, lines of approach and other critical areas of the enemy's line. The fire of each battery, including those of divisional and corps artillery, was predetermined from observation of the enemy's lines.

TYPES OF GERMAN TRENCH MORTAR IN WORLD WAR I

TYPE	CALIBRE	WEIGHT (POUNDS)	RANGE (YARDS)
Early light rifle	3 inches	220	1,150
Improved light rifle	3 inches	312	1,420
Medium	170 mm (6·7 inches)	1,100	1,100
Smooth-bore Minenwerfer	180 mm (7 inches)	1,000	550
Flugelminenwerfer	240 mm (9·45 inches)	3,000	1,700
'Albrecht'	–	3,500	2,200
Heavy rifled muzzle-loader	245 mm (9·8 inches)	1,362	600 (with light Drake projectile) 1,000 (with heavy shell)

The value of the trench mortar lay in the fact that it provided the infantry with its own portable artillery. It was light in weight, compact, of simple design and easy to manufacture in quantity. Its high-angle fire made it an ideal weapon with which to bombard trenches.

The German trench mortars came in a variety of calibres, ranging from 3-inch to 9·8-inch. The larger types were complex, crew-served weapons. The Allies, outpaced to begin with, launched their trench-mortar programme with a copy of the German model, but by late 1915 the excellent British-designed Newton-Stokes trench mortar was in use at the front.

The range of the trench mortar was short, but in situations where the opposing lines were often no more than 100 yards apart, this was no handicap. The early shells 'tumbled' in their high trajectory and were easily spotted by alert soldiers. This led to the introduction of rifled Minenwerfer and the use of elongated or 'streamlined' shells. These new elongated projectiles in turn prompted the adoption of percussion fuses. The earlier 'billiard-ball' shells had been fitted with time fuses or a very hazardous 'all-ways' percussion fuse.

Late in the war, when the Germans had perfected infiltration tactics, stormtroopers used Minenwerfer to batter strongpoints. Eight thousand Minenwerfer were used in the German spring offensives of 1918, and much of the latter's early success must be attributed to the skilled use of Minenwerfer by attacking parties.

Not all the tactical surprises of the war sprang from the German camp, however. The Allies managed, for example, to produce a deadly trench mortar-type weapon that the Germans never could quite understand or copy. This was the Livens toxic gas projector. For all the secrecy surrounding it, the Livens projector was really a very simple apparatus. Steel tubes with metal base-plates were sunk into the ground in multiple units of 25. A propellant charge was placed at the bottom of each tube, and a drum of poison gas 25-inches long and 8-inches in diameter inserted in each. Then the charges were fired all at once by means of an electric generator. A barrage of drums fired from a bank of such tubes could easily overwhelm a German position. The Livens projector was a great improvement over other modes of gas delivery. The silence of the projector ensured surprise, and the great capacity of the drum gave it a fearsome power, dramatically amplified when a bank was fired simultaneously.

There were basically two schools of thought on how to break the trench-warfare stalemate. One school maintained that the enemy could be worn down and physically defeated in a war of attrition. On the battlefield this policy was translated into long, steady artillery bombardments which 'walked' to and fro over the trenches of the enemy, sometimes lasting for days and weeks on end. The intention was once the enemy's fortified zone had been sufficiently prepared, for the infantry to advance into the wasteland created by the artillery, effect a breakthrough into open country beyond and restore a war of movement. The chief advocates of the war of attrition were to be found among the Allied High Command.

The other school favoured sudden, overwhelming artillery barrages of comparatively short duration (hours rather than days) followed by infantry attacks against the defender while they were still stunned. These tactics were first used by the Germans on the Eastern Front in 1915 and came to characterize most German offensives.

Of the two systems, that developed by the Germans was the more successful. Surprise, an important element in the German system, had always been a decisive factor in warfare. But whereas the Allies assumed that trench warfare had removed surprise from the soldier's 'bag of tricks', the Germans felt that surprise and her handmaiden, confusion, could be achieved by clever artillery tactics. In addition the simplicity and economy of the German tactics were recommendations in themselves.

The 'hurricane' bombardment, as it became known, was first applied at Dunajec, Galicia on 14 May 1915. There the Germans effected a breakthrough along 26 miles of the Russian lines. After Dunajec the German and Austrian

ABOVE *On the Isonzo Front men of the Austrian 16th Corps demonstrate the loading of their 220-mm Minenwerfer; an officer indicates polite interest.*
BELOW LEFT *A cross-section of the Allied Livens gas*

projector, usually fired in deadly banks of 25.
BELOW RIGHT *Cutaway view of a German terror weapon – the gas shell delivered by the 170-mm medium Minenwerfer, which had a range of 1,100 yards.*

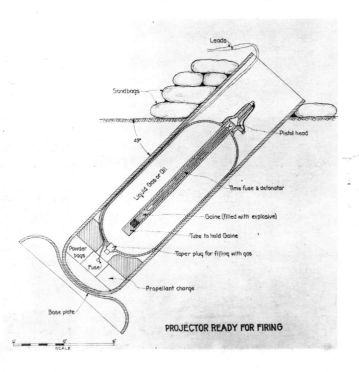

PROJECTOR READY FOR FIRING

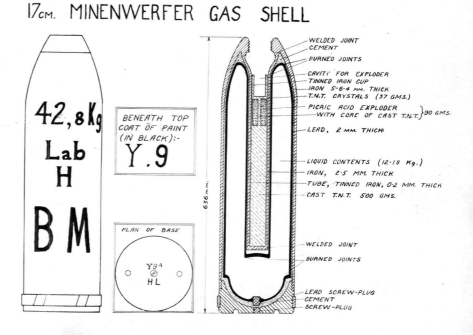

17CM. MINENWERFER GAS SHELL

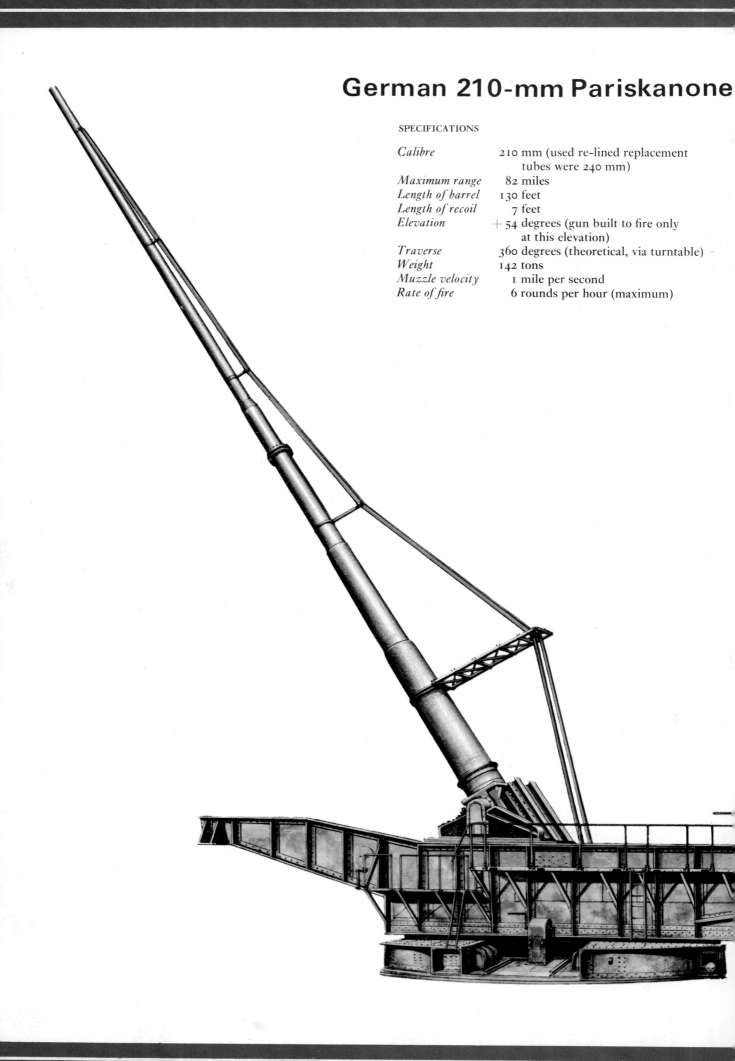

German 210-mm Pariskanone

SPECIFICATIONS

Calibre	210 mm (used re-lined replacement tubes were 240 mm)
Maximum range	82 miles
Length of barrel	130 feet
Length of recoil	7 feet
Elevation	+ 54 degrees (gun built to fire only at this elevation)
Traverse	360 degrees (theoretical, via turntable)
Weight	142 tons
Muzzle velocity	1 mile per second
Rate of fire	6 rounds per hour (maximum)

The 'Paris Gun', erroneously called 'Big Bertha' by Allied soldiers, may be the best-known and most mysterious gun of all time. There are few who do not know the story of the bombardment of Paris at a distance of 79 miles from a point 10 miles behind the German lines in the St Gobain Wood near Laon. On the other hand, there are few who know anything about the gun which achieved such an incredible feat.

The Paris Gun was designed by a team of Krupp engineers led by Professor Rausenberger. It (there were three mountings and several barrels) was first used to bombard Paris on 23 March 1918, opening fire at 7.20 am. The bombardment continued intermittently until 7 August 1918. Altogether 203 shells were fired and the majority hit the city. Allied efforts at detecting the guns succeeded in determining their general location despite elaborate efforts to conceal them. Aerial bombardment and long-range shelling of the St Gobain Wood by French railway guns were of no avail, however. Eventually the mountings (but no barrels – they were never found) fell into Allied hands and the shelling of Paris was halted.

The shelling had no noticeable effect on either the French war effort or the people of Paris. To be sure, there was profound shock and horror at the casualties – especially those caused when a shell collapsed the vault of the Church of St Gervais, near the Hôtel de Ville, on Good Friday, 29 March 1918 – but otherwise life went on more or less as usual.

As for the true purpose of the Paris Gun, we shall probably never know. Some speculated that the Germans used it as a terror weapon, hoping to break the morale of the French people. Others felt that its function was to cause people to flee Paris and in doing so disrupt the roads and railways.

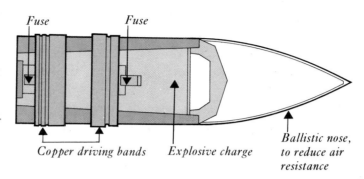

Fuse   *Fuse*

Copper driving bands   *Explosive charge*   *Ballistic nose, to reduce air resistance*

Shell of the Paris Gun

This was a 210-mm HE shell with copper driving bands. The life of each inner gun tube was thought to be 60 rounds, so 60 numbered shells, each a little larger in calibre than the one preceding it (No. 60 was 222 mm), were provided for each barrel and fired in sequence. The weight of the propellant also varied with each shot.

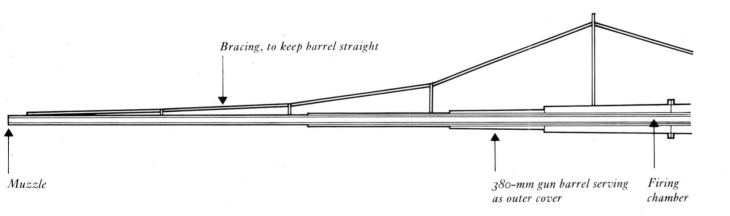

Bracing, to keep barrel straight

Muzzle

380-mm gun barrel serving as outer cover   *Firing chamber*

Barrel of the Paris Gun

Note that the barrel is braced by a suspension system. This was necessary because of the great length and weight of the barrel, which vibrated for two minutes after each firing. (Many long-barrelled, large-calibre guns have a barely perceptible 'droop' in the barrel: this straightens out momentarily on firing.)

armies used similar tactics time and again to break stable fronts in Serbia, Russia and Italy.

The first Allied attempts at breaking through were conceived as 'limited objective attacks' – though in reality they were limited not only in terms of objective but also in matériel, for the Allies were still inferior in heavy guns; during 1915–16, too, there was a severe shortage of shells. As a result, many of the artillery bombardments were suppressed by German counter-battery fire. Still, there were gains: but they were measured in hundreds of yards and hundreds of thousands of casualties.

By 1917 the Allies had secured industrial supremacy. The guns along their fronts were massed in two or more lines, and expenditure of ammunition reached colossal proportions. Yet numbers alone were not enough. The Germans countered by dispersing their infantry and creating in-depth defences. When Allied soldiers advanced they were additionally impeded by having to cross large shell-torn zones created by their own artillery.

In the meantime, on the Eastern Front, the Russians had adopted the German idea of the surprise bombardment and used it with devastating effect in the six-hour artillery preparation for Brusilov's offensive (4 June 1916). This bombardment completely broke the morale of the Austro-Hungarian 7th Army. The subsequent breakthrough caused the transfer of 45 German and Austrian divisions from the Verdun sector and materially affected the course of the war.

The first use of the surprise bombardment on the Western Front was at Verdun on 21 February 1916. Here, although the bombardment was a success – the German gunners completely shattered the French defences – the main attack was not. The German infantry went forward in driblets, tentatively probing the French lines. The French, given time to recover, held. Thereafter, Verdun became a classic battle of attrition.

A sophisticated variant of the surprise bombardment was introduced in September 1917 in the artillery preparation for General Oscar von Hutier's Riga offensive. At Riga, von Hutier coupled his new infiltration tactics for the infantry with clever artillery tactics devised by his artillery commander, Colonel Bruchmüller. Bruchmüller used every gun and Minenwerfer available in a brief but intensive bombardment. Gas shells were fired on an unprecedented scale. Some guns fired on strongpoints, while others fired a rambling barrage which shifted to and fro over the Russian lines. When it was time for von Hutier's stormtroopers to go in, almost all the guns switched to a rolling barrage to cover their advance. The Russians were routed and Riga was taken at comparatively slight cost. Later, when Russia withdrew from the war, the Germans quickly shifted their

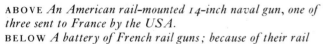

Rail guns add new
flexibility to long-
range artillery work.

ABOVE *An American rail-mounted 14-inch naval gun, one of three sent to France by the USA.*
BELOW *A battery of French rail guns; because of their rail mounting these guns acquired unprecedented mobility.*

eastern armies to the Western Front, hoping to use the additional manpower to win the war before the arrival of the American Expeditionary Force.

The spring offensives of 1918, directed by General Ludendorff, used the Hutier-Bruchmüller tactics throughout. These offensives came within an ace of succeeding, but the appearance and rapid impact of the Americans, together with the Allies' artillery superiority, spoiled them in mid-course. By 1918 the Allies had perfected the technique of the counter-preparation bombardment and many German attacks were broken up before they began.

Railway Guns

Railway artillery had been introduced during the American Civil War and was used extensively in World War I. Such guns could be used only in certain specific situations. They were ideal for coastal defence or on static fronts where the existing rail system was adequate enough to allow them to be used where they were most needed.

The French had the most advanced railway-gun programme before the war, and during the war they converted many ex-naval and coastal guns to railway mounts. The country's excellent rail system allowed them to use these guns for support fire, raking the enemy's lines of communications, and in long-range counter-battery work. The presence of a supplementary, mobile artillery arm was especially valued among the French, who were generally weak in heavy guns.

Among the few guns which the United States sent to Europe were three 14-inch battleship guns on special armoured railway mounts. These guns were manned by Navy personnel and fired 782 projectiles during the last days of the war. They are credited with destroying a German supply depot at Laon and with cutting the Metz-Sedan railway at several points.

Thus, railway guns made an important contribution to the Allied war effort. Within the next few decades, however, the potential of aerial bombardment would relegate the monster railway and coastal-defence guns to obscurity.

Mountain Artillery

In 1914 all the Continental Powers had batteries of mountain guns. These were usually light guns or howitzers which were easily dismantled into six to eight pack-loads for transport by mules over rough terrain. A good crew could have its guns assembled and ready to fire within two minutes of halting its animals.

These mountain batteries not only served in mountainous areas like Galicia or the Italian Front, they were also useful as accompanying artillery for infantry on the offensive. At Verdun in 1916 German field artillery fired at maximum range to prepare the way for the infantry assault. In such situations, the infantry usually went forward without direct support until the field artillery batteries could move forward to new positions. At Verdun, however, batteries of the German Alpine Corps advanced with the infantry and

provided close fire support. The idea of accompanying artillery then caught on, and during 1917 the Germans used numbers of *Nahkampfbatterien* (close-combat batteries) with a great variety of equipment, mostly captured field guns.

Because they were usually with the forward elements, these infantry gun batteries inevitably ran foul of the Allied tank effort. The Germans countered by mounting the M-1906 77-mm field gun on low wheels and providing it with AP shells equipped with delay fuses that allowed the shell to burst within the tank.

Later, when von Hutier's infiltration tactics had gained wide acceptance, German shock troopers attacked with a full arsenal of artillery firepower including the various Minenwerfer types, and mountain and accompanying guns. Ludendorff, however, seems to have disliked the idea of accompanying batteries and discouraged their use in the great 1918 spring offensives.

LEFT *German mountain guns in use as infantry accompanying weapons.*
BELOW *A gun crew demonstrates how the accompanying guns were moved about in support of an infantry advance.*

Anti-Aircraft Guns

Perhaps the first purpose-built anti-aircraft gun was a single 1-inch 'balloon gun' used by the Germans in the Siege of Paris in 1870. It is not recorded that this contraption ever brought down one of Léon Gambetta's balloons, but there was a lot of speculation in artillery literature before World War I concerning the merits of firing on balloons and Zeppelins with shrapnel. Shooting at balloons was not as easy as the textbooks made it out to be, and aircraft would prove to be an even tougher proposition.

Nevertheless, anti-aircraft guns became common during World War I. Usually, a field gun was coupled with a specially designed mount allowing a high angle of fire or a pedestal or pit mount allowing both high-angle fire and all-round traverse. Various mechanical devices were introduced to allow the gunners to calculate the target's speed, height and direction and correlate this with the fire of the gun. None of these mechanical 'predictors' was very successful, and commanders resorted to area defences and anti-aircraft barrages. An area defence relied on siting

ABOVE *In Salonika, a French 75-mm field gun M-1897 is seen on a special anti-aircraft mount.*
BELOW *On the Italian Front, a British 13-pounder AA gun is mounted on a Peerless truck.*
OPPOSITE *American soldiers examine a captured German AA gun in Oudenarde, November 1918.*

batteries of anti-aircraft guns behind the front in such a manner that when aircraft were detected by sound-ranging equipment, the gun crews were alerted and could then concentrate their fire on the aircraft. Groups of machine guns were sited 1–2,000 yards behind the front line to prevent low-level strafing and observation. Two thousand yards behind the machine guns was a line of regular anti-aircraft batteries sited 4–7,000 yards apart. These guns were to protect the reserve areas. Finally, the rear areas were surrounded by further batteries of anti-aircraft guns.

A different method was used to protect cities or vital points far behind the lines. In this system batteries were sited along the lines of approach commonly used by aircraft. The anti-aircraft batteries protecting Paris, for example, were sited along the rivers and rail lines leading to the city. Since aircraft navigational devices were still quite crude, pilots used natural or man-made features of the terrain as their principal means of guidance, and this brought them in range of the guns. However, the system could only be called partly successful: on average one aircraft was brought down for every 3,000 shells fired!

Artillerists develop area defence and barrage tactics, but reap small reward.

8

TANKS ON THE WESTERN FRONT

The internal combustion engine goes to war.

In this gigantic siege war of the 20th century, a 20th-century solution was needed to break the stalemate that had taken hold in the trenches. When it came it was based, appropriately, upon the device which came to dominate the first half of the century as the queen of inventions – the internal combustion engine, created in 1885 by Gottlieb Daimler and Karl Benz.

Motor vehicles had already appeared on the battlefield: in World War I the lorry and the bus were used to transport men and supplies; and, following the earlier lead of the French firm of Charron-Girardot et Voigt, which in 1904 had developed the first production armoured car, the British Admiralty brought in armoured cars to defend its air squadrons based at Dunkirk. At first the latter were ordinary motor cars fitted with sheets of mild steel boiler plate. Later the firms of Rolls Royce, Wolseley and Lanchester developed custom-built armoured cars, but by the time these machines were ready the opportunities for their

THIS PAGE *Lt-Col Ernest Swinton, who in 1914 thought of converting artillery tractors, below, into fighting vehicles.*

ABOVE *An early type of armoured car was the Maxim-armed Rolls Royce model of 1914. Although these were useful behind the lines on the Western Front, they were a failure as mechanized cavalry because they were soon bogged down in the shell-torn landscape. Elsewhere, for example in the flat open spaces of Palestine, where they could manoeuvre more freely, they enjoyed a correspondingly greater success. Weighing 3·5 tons, they had 8-mm armour and carried a crew of three.*

BELOW *This was the first production armoured car. It was developed in 1904 by the French firm of Charron-Girardot et Voigt, weighed 3 tons and mounted a fully rotating turret with a machine-gun. On the side of the car channels were provided for crossing ditches. The Charron was sold to Russia and was used by the French in Morocco. Armoured cars were first employed in battle in the Turko-Italian War (1912).*

Swinton's and Churchill's efforts result in the building of the first prototype tank – 'Little Willie'.

use as a new form of mechanized cavalry had been lost – for they were essentially road-bound and could not deploy across the artillery-made bogs that soon appeared along the Western Front.

One of the official British war correspondents, or 'Eye witnesses', as they were called, was Lt-Col Ernest Swinton. In October 1914 he had seen an American invention, the Holt caterpillar tractor, being used to pull heavy artillery behind the lines. He was struck with the idea of arming and armouring these vehicles as an antidote to the barbed wire and the machine-guns of the Germans. Swinton was an engineer by profession, and he had also written the official British military history of the Russo-Japanese War in Manchuria, which in 1904 had produced the first war of trench stalemate in the 20th century. Convinced that he had found the answer to the problems of the Western Front, he presented his ideas in a paper to GHQ in France; there it received a brutal rebuff from generals who were not only ignorant of modern technology but were also totally committed to the gospel which proclaimed the sanctity of personal combat. Swinton sent a copy of his paper to his good friend and mentor, Lt-Col Maurice Hankey, at that time Secretary to the Committee of Imperial Defence in London. Hankey was impressed with Swinton's ideas, reproduced them in the form of a Cabinet Memorandum and tried at the same time to lobby support in Whitehall. In this period of the war all questions connected with British fighting motor vehicles were regarded as the province of the Royal Navy, and so Hankey's memorandum was circulated through the various channels of the Admiralty. In January 1915 the paper reached the desk of Winston Churchill, then First Lord of the Admiralty; he, suitably impressed with the idea, enlisted the support of the Prime

Minister, Lord Asquith. Two Holt tractors were evaluated by a small select body of experts, which in turn reported favourably, and Churchill created the Admiralty Landships Committee to examine the concept in greater depth and detail. One lasting result, incidentally, of the Admiralty's involvement in these early stages is that certain naval terms then came into use which persisted, various parts of the tank being referred to as the hull, turret, deck, sponson, barbette, superstructure, bow, etc.

Meanwhile Swinton, now back in France, but shortly to return to London, made one more attempt to interest the High Command in his idea for an armoured fighting vehicle. He submitted a new paper entitled *The Armoured Machine Gun Destroyer* and this time he received a more sympathetic response from GHQ; they passed it on to the Inventions Committee, which had been established at the War Office to examine new ideas. In June 1915 Swinton was back in London (as Secretary to the Dardanelles Committee) and there he learned for the first time of the progress of the Admiralty Landships Committee. An engineering company called Fosters, of Lincoln, which built heavy artillery tractors, had by this time produced a prototype vehicle. This was in due course commonly called 'Little Willie'.

However, the Admiralty Committee was by now in deep trouble; it had run foul of the new Ministry of Munitions under Lloyd George, who felt that it was poaching in the Ministry's domain, and dissension was rife. The Prime Minister next ordered the two factions to combine, and a new organization was set up entitled the Experiments Committee, in which the original Admiralty personnel apparently retained a controlling interest. In September 1915 a design team consisting of Fosters, William Tritton and Lt W. G. Wilson overcame certain problems with the tracks which had beset the original prototype and a new machine, known as 'Big Willie', was built. It was at this point that the word 'tank' was coined by Swinton. For reasons of security, the hull and chassis for the experimental vehicle had been constructed in different shops and the hull had been referred to as a water-carrier or water-tank, for use in Mesopotamia. Swinton later recalled this in the autumn of 1915 when everyone concerned was trying to think of a name for the new vehicle; he suggested the adoption of the word 'tank', which has since come into use in almost every language in the world.

After the failure of the Dardanelles Expedition Churchill, as its creator, was ousted from the Cabinet and in a fit of pique returned to his first profession, soldiering, and soon found himself as second-in-command of a Guards battalion on the Western Front. He still regarded the tank as his brain-child and bombarded GHQ with papers on how the new weapon might be used. A final field demonstration was held in England, to which Haig, the British commander, undoubtedly prompted by Churchill, sent an engineering officer on his staff, Major Hugh Elles, as official observer. The final demonstration was a great success and Lloyd George ordered his ministry to put the tank into quantity production.

The first British model, designated the Mark I (of which 150 were to be built) was produced in two types: a 'male', weighing 31 tons and mounting two 6-pounder naval cannon and four machine-guns; and a 'female', weighing 30 tons and armed with six machine-guns. At a maximum speed of 3·7 mph these tanks, fitted with wrap-round tracks which completely embraced the hull, could traverse obstacles 4½ feet high and negotiate a trench 11½ feet wide. They were remarkable machines but suffered from a host of teething troubles and their first designers felt that they needed more time before the tanks could be considered ready for combat. But they were denied this luxury for, in the later summer of 1916, Haig and his armies found

OPPOSITE *A 10-ton Holt tractor of 1914; these vehicles inspired development of the first tanks.*
RIGHT *Two American-built machines that also preceded the tank: the 1915 Jeffrey armoured car, above, and the Caterpillar.*
BELOW *The Killen Strait tractor, an experimental vehicle fitted with a 'torpedo' wire-cutting device.*

British Mark IV (Male) Tank 1917

The Mark IV was the first tank to be used en masse and was the key vehicle at Cambrai (see also pages 30–31). It kept the rhomboidal shape of its predecessors but had thicker armour (up to 12 mm), a shorter and handier 6-pounder gun, and was the first to carry the excellent Lewis machine-gun.

The front view (left) shows the observation ports for the driver and the commander, the 6-pounder and Lewis gun mounted in each side sponson, the unditching beam chained on top, and the extended track 'grousers' which improved the vehicle's running performance over difficult terrain.

The 28-ton 'male' was 26 feet 5 inches long, 12 feet 9 inches wide and 8 feet 2 inches high. It had a trench-crossing capacity of 10 feet and a maximum speed of 3·7 mph. Its crew of 8 was armed with two 6-pounder (57-mm) guns and four Lewis machine-guns.

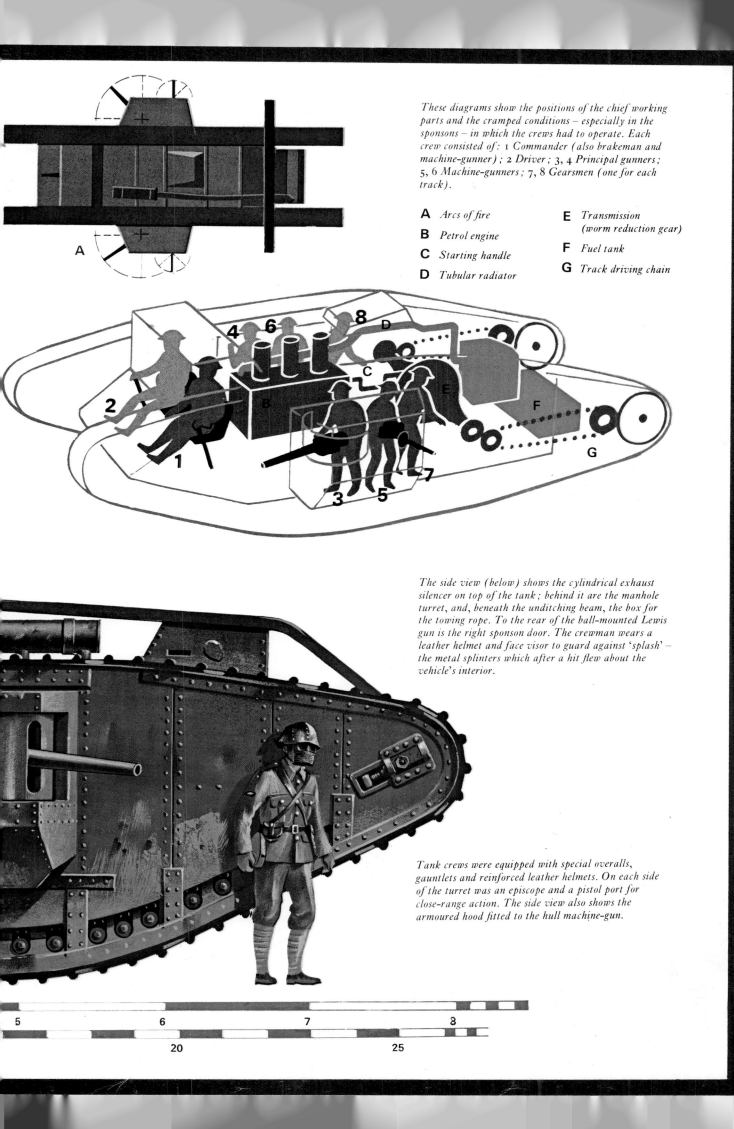

These diagrams show the positions of the chief working parts and the cramped conditions – especially in the sponsons – in which the crews had to operate. Each crew consisted of: 1 Commander (also brakeman and machine-gunner); 2 Driver; 3, 4 Principal gunners; 5, 6 Machine-gunners; 7, 8 Gearsmen (one for each track).

A Arcs of fire
B Petrol engine
C Starting handle
D Tubular radiator
E Transmission (worm reduction gear)
F Fuel tank
G Track driving chain

The side view (below) shows the cylindrical exhaust silencer on top of the tank; behind it are the manhole turret, and, beneath the unditching beam, the box for the towing rope. To the rear of the ball-mounted Lewis gun is the right sponson door. The crewman wears a leather helmet and face visor to guard against 'splash' – the metal splinters which after a hit flew about the vehicle's interior.

Tank crews were equipped with special overalls, gauntlets and reinforced leather helmets. On each side of the turret was an episcope and a pistol port for close-range action. The side view also shows the armoured hood fitted to the hull machine-gun.

themselves in a desperate plight. In order to draw German pressure away from the French at Verdun he had been forced prematurely to commit the new and raw divisions of Kitchener's army to an offensive along the Somme Valley. The first phase of the great offensive had stalled on the wire of the German trenches and Haig next called for tanks to be committed to the battle at the earliest opportunity.

The first tanks did not leave the factories in England until July and it was August before 50 tanks could be shipped out to France. A new organization had been created to man and fight the tanks which, for security purposes, was called the 'heavy' section of the Machine Gun Corps. The initial establishment was 184 officers and 1,600 men and their tanks were divided into six companies of four sections; there were three 'male' and three 'female' tanks to each section.

The main defect of the Mark I tank – besides its mechanical unreliability – was the tremendous strain it placed on the eight-man crew. The noise inside the hull was so great that conversation was impossible and the driver had to communicate his orders to the gearsman by banging a hammer on the engine cover to a set code. It was impossible to stand upright in the tank and the temperature inside after some 30 minutes rose to well over 100°F. In action crews

start-lines to spearhead the assault by Rawlinson's Fourth Army in the final phase of the Battle of the Somme. Even then surprise, in the strategic sense, was lacking, since Rawlinson heralded the advance by a pre-battle bombardment of 1,250 guns (one gun for every three yards of front) which lasted three days. Only 36 tanks then crossed the start-lines and many more were quickly disabled in the cauldron of no man's land. Nevertheless, where the tanks either alone or in groups, broke through the German defences their impact was immediate and a new dimension in terror warfare had been created.

Few tanks were in any fit condition to engage in combat after the first day but Haig and many of his commanders felt that the new weapon system had earned a second and bigger chance. He requested that 1,000 tanks be produced for the following year and on 8 October 1916 supported the establishment of a separate Tank Corps. Elles, who had been with the tanks from the beginning, was confirmed as commander of the new organization, and as his chief staff officer he was given the brilliant if temperamental Major J. F. C. Fuller, a man who brought genuinely original ideas to the tactical side of tank warfare. Together Elles and Fuller formed a unique and successful partnership which created out of an amorphous collection of men and machines a

drank up to a gallon of water per day per man. After some hours they would emerge sick and often mildy delirious from the hot fume-filled hulls. Very few of these tank men had seen action on the Western Front and they were drawn from all branches of the arms and services. Nevertheless the demands of strategy dictated that inexperienced men, who hardly had had enough time to get to know one another or their machines, were committed to battle in tanks which themselves had not been tested under battle conditions. The generals were only too well aware of the folly of going against the time-honoured principle that a brand new weapon, particularly one like the tank which represented a revolutionary design in warfare, needs a small battlefield trial; but to have done so would have destroyed the all-important advantage of surprise.

On 15 September 1916, 49 tanks rumbled towards their

coherent fighting force. Volunteers flocked to join the new corps, men of skill and enthusiasm many of whom had experienced combat as soldiers on the Western Front and who therefore readily understood the vital role that tanks could play. The tanks, also, were new: there had been a considerable improvement in tank technology and design and in the spring of 1917 the Mark IV appeared in France a better armoured and mechanically more reliable tank than the Mark I had been on its début.

At first tanks were used in driblets and with little effect. In 1917, at the Battles of Arras, Buillacourt, Messines and Passchendaele, the tanks were wastefully deployed in pairs behind the usual artillery bombardment. But despite their misuse the presence of the tanks raised Allied and lowered German morale. The German High Command, for its part, had completely dismissed the tank as a viable

THIS PAGE *The first British tank to appear was 'Little Willie' (left). Next came 'Big Willie' or 'Mother' (top); the rear wheels acted as a steering 'tail'. From this design the first Mark 1 tanks were produced. 'Male' versions had 6-pounder guns in the sponsons, while the 'female' version (centre) carried machine-guns clad in armoured jackets. Note also the anti-grenade netting on the 'female'. the long-barrelled 6-pounder gun, seen on the outskirts of Arras, 1916.*
OPPOSITE *A British Mark II tank with experimental tracked vehicle fitted with a 'torpedo' wire-cutter.*

weapon system. The Germans saw it primarily as a terror weapon, which could be countered by the high morale of their own troops and the skill of specially trained artillery batteries. (There were a number of Holt tractors in Germany and the Army did develop a wooden mock-up on a chassis but at this stage did not proceed any further.)

The French, led in this respect by Colonel J. E. Estienne, were if anything even more enthusiastic than the British – although their development of the tank proceeded along entirely different lines; there is, moreover, no evidence of any collusion between the two Allies. By the spring of 1916 the French companies of St Chamond and Schneider had developed what were really two versions of an assault gun: they were called *artillerie d'assaut* and were in effect nothing more than the excellent French 75-mm cannon mounted forward on a Holt chassis and enclosed in an armoured box. The French had more teething troubles with their tank than the British but would not be rushed into premature employment in battle; eventually they appeared in April 1917 at the Battle of Chemin des Dames.

It was still later – November 1917 and the Battle of Cambrai – before Elles and Fuller were allowed to deploy tanks en masse and in tune with the tactical doctrine which they had evolved. The Allied situation by this time was grave: the French armies were recovering from wide-scale mutinies, the Italians had suffered a major reverse at Caporetto and the Russian Front in the East had collapsed. Politically the Allied cause was in desperate need of a victory; the only bright star on the horizon was the entry of the United States into the war (in April 1917) but at that time all she had to offer was a vast reserve of untrained manpower.

Originally Fuller had conceived Cambrai as a tank raid in a sector where the terrain had not been ploughed into a bog by the artillery. The Allied search for a military victory of major dimensions, fortified by the enthusiasm of General Byng and the Third Army, transformed the operation into one in which the tanks would aim to secure a rupture of the German front through which the Cavalry Corps – with 40,000 horsemen – could exploit and perhaps lead the way to a crushing victory. It is the paradox of Cambrai that while in many ways it was one of the most ineptly conceived battles in British military history, it also contained, at least in the plan for the initial assault, a daring, meticulously thought-out and superbly executed tactical experiment which changed the nature of war.

The initial problem was that of breaching the formidable defences of the Hindenburg Line, which had three lines of mutually supporting trenches, ample artillery fire support and avenues of barbed wire. The operational plan devised by Fuller was accepted by all but one of the assault divisions (the 51st Highlanders). There was to be no long pre-battle bombardment, which had so often in the past robbed offensives of any strategic surprise. The artillery instead was to open fire with a hurricane bombardment as the tanks moved forward, and aircraft were to be used to supplement the guns by strafing the forward gun positions

French specialists in armour favoured artillerie d'assaut, *in effect self-propelled 75-mm guns mounted in armoured boxes. Two types were put into production, the 23-ton St Chamond seen opposite at the factory stage and above on manoeuvres, and the 14·6-ton Schneider, above.*

and the German lines of communications. The tanks operated in groups of three and each tank carried a fascine weighing $1\frac{1}{4}$ tons which it dropped in the trench; four platoons of infantry advancing in close column (rather than the traditional method of extended line) moved forward in support of each group of tanks.

Everyone was reasonably optimistic about the plans for the advance and breakthrough of the German front; there were doubts, however, about the plans for the exploitation phase. Haig's chief intelligence officer, Brigadier-General

20 November 1917: tanks force a major breakthrough at the Battle of Cambrai.

John Charteris, succinctly summed up the situation when he wrote in his diary: 'We shall be alright at first, afterwards is in the lap of the God of Battle'. This was so because there were no reserves either of infantry or tanks available to exploit success, and everything depended upon the performance of the four divisions of cavalry in both the timing of their move through the ruptured front and in their ability to exploit the ground beyond.

Except for the comparative failure of the 51st Highland Division, everything went according to plan on 20 November 1917. A solid phalanx of 476 tanks crawled forward across no man's land and penetrated the bloody chaos caused by the initial artillery bombardment. Behind the fighting tanks and their jubilant infantry moved a new phenomenon on the battlefield, a mechanized army of radio tanks, wire-pulling tanks and supply tanks ready to support the spearhead formations.

By the end of the first day, and at a cost of fewer than 4,000 casualties, a breach six miles wide and 4,000 yards deep had been achieved; the church bells pealed out the news of a victory in England that night. If the battle had been terminated at that point and kept within Fuller's original concept of a tank raid then indeed it would have been a great victory. But the commanders demanded exploitation. The cavalry had already failed once to break through and so the infantry and a few surviving tanks[1] were ordered to widen the breach and make it yet more secure for the horsemen. Resilient German defences blocked the advance and the last British reserves were exchanged for extra ground that was measured in yards. Ludendorff, the German commander, counter-attacked the salient on 30 November and in places the British fell back to beyond their original start-line. But at least the tanks were not blamed for the subsequent disasters, and

[1] Only 100 tanks were fit for combat duty after the first day at Cambrai.

indeed at Gouzeaucourt they gained fresh laurels when the German advance was reversed by a timely tank counter-attack – which to some extent proved that tanks could hold as well as capture ground.

The battle of Cambrai was the first major demonstration of tank power. It showed that tanks, operating en masse but with surprise and on firm ground could, when adequately supported by infantry and artillery, achieve rapid and complete command over the strongest dug-in defences. But there remained the unresolved problem of exploitation. Some writers have criticized Fuller and Elles for not keeping back more tanks to ensure an adequate reserve for the days following the initial attack. But such criticisms lack validity because if fewer tanks had been used on the first day the dimensions of the rupture would have been that much smaller, so leaving the reserves an even greater task. In any case the Mark IV, though an excellent tank, was not suited to the role of exploitation; it was slow, too heavy, and it lacked the necessary endurance. Since horse cavalry had proved even more unsuited to the task there grew up a demand for a lighter, faster tank which could meet the needs and rigours of exploitation. The French had already developed such a vehicle in the excellent Renault FT, the first tank to be built with a revolving turret, but there is no evidence to suggest that the British were interested in either acquiring or copying it for their own needs.

By the spring of 1918 ever-increasing numbers of the United States Army had arrived in France. At first the Americans had expressed little interest in the tank: although they had a number of prototypes under development there was little urgency to build a battle tank for the Army. However, Cambrai completely changed American thinking. The US Army began to demand its own tanks but then found that American industry could not produce anything suitable in time; consequently the American tank corps was equipped with British and French tanks.

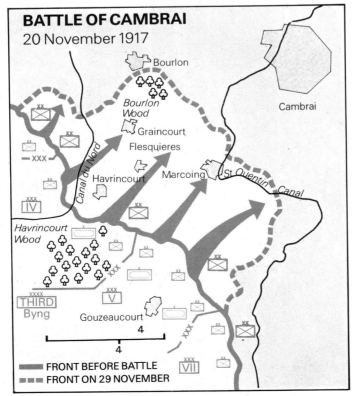

BATTLE OF CAMBRAI
20 November 1917

Bourlon
Bourlon Wood
Cambrai
Graincourt
Flesquieres
Havrincourt
Marcoing
St Quentin Canal
Canal du Nord
Havrincourt Wood
THIRD Byng
Gouzeaucourt
IV
V
VII

4
4

━━━ FRONT BEFORE BATTLE
▪▪▪ FRONT ON 29 NOVEMBER

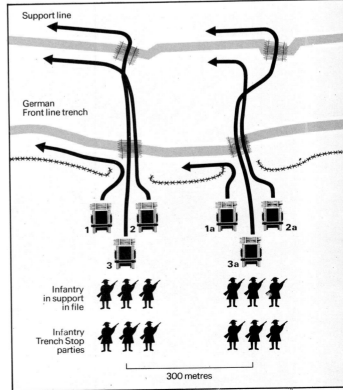

Support line

German Front line trench

1   2   1a   2a
3   3a

Infantry in support in file

Infantry Trench Stop parties

300 metres

America joins the war; her newly formed tank corps takes the field.

OPPOSITE *At Cambrai the Allies used Mark IV tanks loaded with fascines to bridge the trenches of the Hindenburg Line in the sequence shown. Behind the armour came the infantry, moving in close column rather than in the traditional method of extended line.*

TOP *French Renault FT tanks armed with the short cannon.*
ABOVE *British mobile artillery, consisting of a 60-pounder gun that could be moved about the battlefield on tracks, its wheels having been taken off and chained to the hull sides; its offensive potential was never fully realized.*

In the meantime the German Army, not surprisingly, was also feeling the strain and pressure of almost four years of incessant warfare. Her associates were faltering and the Allied naval blockade of her ports was causing widespread deprivation to the German population. Submarine warfare had failed either to starve Britain into submission or to halt the arrival of American troops. Ludendorff, gathering together the last of his reserves, planned to launch a major offensive against the British (whom he considered the most vulnerable of the Allies) and thereby win peace. Tanks were not to figure in any real scale in this offensive, there being only a handful of clumsy 30-ton land fortresses available (called the A7V). The Germans were to rely for their mobility on new tactics which had been devised for the infantry – from which the concept of Blitzkrieg, or lightning war, was eventually to evolve. These were infiltration tactics, sometimes known as Hutier tactics after the German general who had first used them (on the Eastern Front at Riga in 1917). The tactics introduced a new type of infantryman, the 'stormtrooper': armed with the newly developed Bergmann submachine-gun, he moved at speed through the enemy's lines, bypassing strongpoints which were dealt with by the main body of the infantry following on behind.

In March 1918 Allied armies reeled back under the shock of the first German hammer-blows. Such tanks as were deployed in the defence were used in penny packets as mobile pillboxes. These posed little problem to the Germans but elsewhere tanks came together in fighting groups and made a major contribution to stemming the momentum of the German advance. Behind the front line the Allied commanders carefully husbanded resources and prepared for the moment when the German advance lost its main thrust and they could counter-attack. Two new tanks had been built by the British, the medium 'Whippet' and the Mark V, the latter being a major improvement on earlier models since it required only one man to drive the tank – instead of as many as four, as had been the case with

Marks I–IV. At Hamel, 60 Mark Vs led a counter-attack by the Australians under General Monash (who also had some American infantry companies in the operation) and inflicted a resounding defeat on the Germans. This operation saw the most decisive use of tanks to date, success being achieved through the precise co-ordination of infantry and tanks in the assault.

LEFT *Col J. E. Estienne, leader of the
pro-armour school in France.*
OPPOSITE AND BELOW *The photograph
opposite well illustrates the roles in which
early tanks were most effective, i.e. as
obstacle-crossing, wire-crushing weapons
of terror. Faced by such monsters, which
its own General Staff was reluctant to
copy, the German propaganda machine
struck back with encouraging material
(below) showing how vulnerable tanks
were to the Kaiser's flamethrowers.*
RIGHT *A British observation post at
Cambrai, stationed on a broken-down
Mark IV tank. (The initials WC stand
for Wire Cutter.)*

4 July 1918: the
Allies counter-attack
at Hamel, led by 60
Mark V tanks.

In July 1918 it became obvious that the German advance had been held, and as the troops consolidated along the new defence perimeter the three Allied leaders, Foch (who now was commander-in-chief of all Allied forces), Haig and General John J. Pershing of the American Expeditionary Force, met to plan the counter-blows. German morale was on the point of collapse and this the Allied commanders intended to exploit in a series of strong, carefully spaced offensives: the French were to attack along the Aisne and Marne, the British at Amiens and the American Corps in

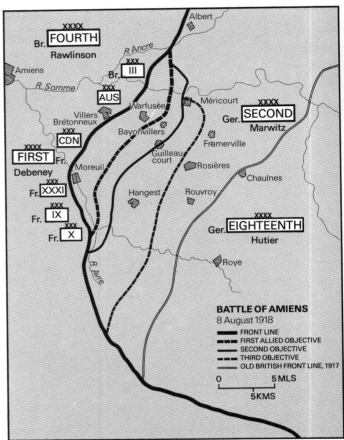

BATTLE OF AMIENS
8 August 1918
FRONT LINE
FIRST ALLIED OBJECTIVE
SECOND OBJECTIVE
THIRD OBJECTIVE
OLD BRITISH FRONT LINE, 1917

0   5 MLS

5 KMS

THIS PAGE *British Mark V tanks, successors to the Mark IV, had a raised cupola at the rear for improved visibility, and needed only one driver, i.e. no gearsmen. Weighing 29 tons and having a maximum speed of 4·6 miles and a range of 45 miles, they performed well in the 1918 campaigns. Those above are being assembled at the Birmingham works of the Metropolitan Carriage and Wagon Company.*
OPPOSITE *German tank production in World War I was limited to 20 of these cumbersome A7V 'land fortresses'.*

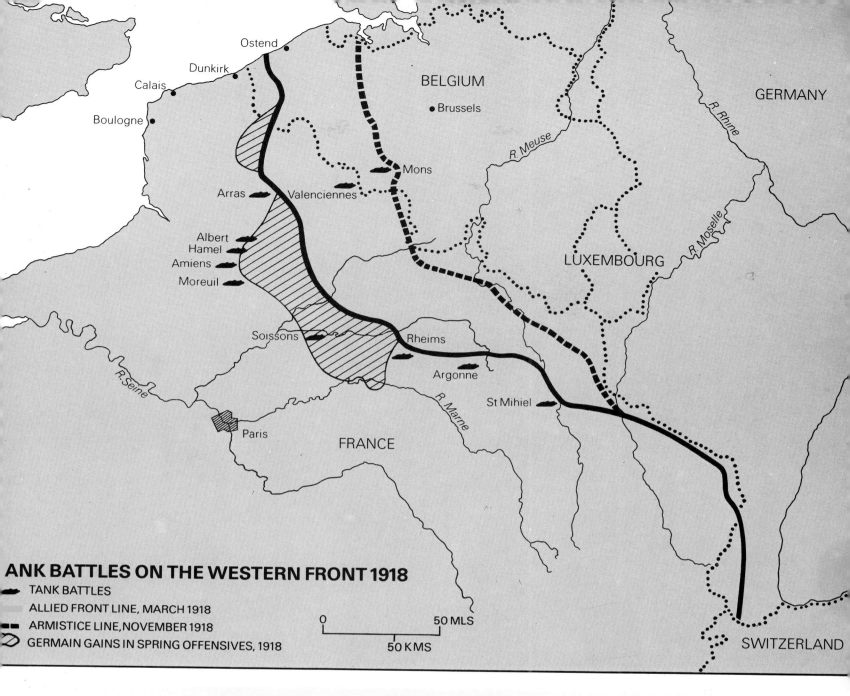

ANK BATTLES ON THE WESTERN FRONT 1918

- TANK BATTLES
- ALLIED FRONT LINE, MARCH 1918
- - - ARMISTICE LINE, NOVEMBER 1918
- GERMAIN GAINS IN SPRING OFFENSIVES, 1918

0   50 MLS

50 KMS

the St Mihiel salient south of Verdun. At Amiens Rawlinson, now a convert to armour, followed the precedent set by Monash and deployed the smallest practicable force of infantry with the largest practicable force of tanks. On the morning of 8 August 1918, 400 Allied tanks spearheaded the assault of eight divisions of infantry. The Germans were caught completely by surprise and a major rupture of their front occurred. By early afternoon the third Allied objective was taken (see map), which also meant that Rawlinson's Fourth Army had advanced more than seven miles in less than nine hours. For exploitation the British had massed a mixed force of Medium A Whippets, horse cavalry and armoured cars. The cavalry and tanks failed to achieve any meaningful co-operation but the armoured cars, towed by heavy tanks across the front and then 'unleashed' beyond the third line, caused havoc among the retreating and disorganized Germans. After 10 August the battle lost much of its momentum, most of the tanks had become

casualties[2] and the infantry, by now so heavily dependent on tanks, would not advance without their support.

In the event the Germans credited the British with a victory and for that reason 8 August is referred to as the 'Black Day' in the annals of the German Army. Ludendorff believed that the Germans lost the war on that day; morale was irretrievably broken and although he was still able to stabilize the front and contain Allied advances, the heart had gone out of his soldiers and staff officers alike. Very few Germans were in fact killed by tank fire: its lurching hull, poor field of fire and restricted vision did not make for a stable gun platform; but as a morale-breaker it was superb.

Throughout August and September Foch launched major offensives along the whole front and the tanks played their part in maintaining the momentum of the Allied advance. The final phase of the war saw the German

[2] 145 tanks were available on 9 August, 63 on the 10th and 38 on the 11th.

Army trading space for time in front of the British, using river and canal lines and holding doggedly to the rugged terrain of the Argonne against the Americans.

In the early autumn the Americans, in a series of brilliant offensives spearheaded by tanks, cleared the Argonne while the British broke out into the more open country beyond Le Cateau. The Germans fell back skilfully and never really lost their cohesion, and in this way they were undoubtedly aided by the comparative ineffectiveness at this stage of the Allied tanks. Now these mechanically unreliable machines had to operate ever farther from their base repair shops, and they broke down more and more frequently. The cavalry could do little since it was still compromised by the machine-gun and by rearguard German artillery. Nevertheless tactical improvisation with the tank abounded during the closing stages of the war. Night attacks were attempted and co-operation with aircraft, which had already played a major part in the success of previous operations, reached new heights. A number of tank-versus-tank encounters occurred right up to the last days of the war and, ominously enough, the British Tank Corps began to acknowledge that the Germans, despite their still more limited experience, were proving to be very effective in their handling of the new vehicles.

Tank units experiment with night attacks and ways of co-operating with aircraft.

LEFT *A captured British tank in the main street of Armentières, repainted in German markings.*
BELOW *American-manned Mark Vs in action in 1918.*

Numbers of Fighting Tanks
WORLD WAR 1

CATEGORY	BRITAIN	FRANCE	GERMANY
Heavy tanks	1,970	—	20
Medium (Whippet) and *artillerie d'assaut* (St Chamond, Schneider)	240	800	—
Light tanks (Renault FT)	—	3,500	—

9

BLOCKADE: THE WAR AT SEA

The Germans, their battle fleet trapped in the North Sea, entrust their naval offensive to submarines.

The war began at a time when the battleship had passed the peak of its powers. Some 10 years earlier armour and gunnery had been nearly absolute, the torpedo little more than a nuisance. During the Russo–Japanese War mines had accounted for many units whilst torpedoes had failed to live up to expectations. But subsequent improvements, combined with the proven power of mines, prompted the British to revise their traditional policy of closely blockading an enemy coast. In the summer of 1914 an interim policy of observational blockade across the lower part of the North Sea was discarded in favour of a more distant blockade of Germany based on Scapa Flow and Dover. It was clear evidence of the fear instilled by underwater weapons that such changes had to be made.

At sea the Great War was largely deadlocked: British guns and German underwater weapons cancelled each other out with little apparent advantage to either side. Britain's overwhelming superiority in surface ships was to some extent neutralized by the Germans' refusal to risk battle and by their defensive minefields laid in the southern North Sea. Until Germany's heavy ships were eliminated, British light forces could not penetrate deep into Heligoland Bight to clear the minefields and lay new ones that would confine German units to their harbours; nor could major surface units be moved to other theatres as long as the German Navy remained intact. The Germans were prepared to risk action but only after mines and torpedoes had taken such a toll of British ships that such actions had a reasonable chance of success; in fact this never happened. Instead the Germans adopted a more passive policy, allowing the presence of their fleet to tie down its British counterpart while the active prosecution of the war was left in the hands of the submariners.

Britain's greatest single advantage over Germany and Austria-Hungary during World War I lay in her geographical position. By holding Dover, Scapa Flow, Gibraltar and Suez, she effectively controlled German and Austrian communications with the outside world. From 4 August 1914 Britain imposed an economic blockade of the Central Powers that increased in severity with each year of the war and was a major factor in bringing about victory. It was not, however, fully effective until the entry, in 1917, of the USA into the war – an event which enabled the Allies completely to disregard the rights of neutrals. Up to that time Britain had had to be careful not to offend neutrals, particularly the USA, and this had allowed some loopholes in the blockade. To close them the British had tried to restrict neutral trade with Germany and even to buy cargoes outright in order to stop them finishing up in enemy hands. Such actions had been of dubious legality and had caused offence; but on every occasion when difficulties arose with the Americans, the Germans had turned opinion against themselves by their practice of conducting restricted submarine campaigns against commercial shipping moving into Britain. The campaigns were introduced as a retaliatory measure against the British blockade of Germany. Because of them neutral nations, including America, suffered losses for which, not unnaturally, Germany was blamed; the best-known single incident was probably the sinking of the *Lusitania*, in which 128 American citizens lost their lives.

From the beginning the British impose on the Central Powers an economic blockade of growing severity.

BELOW *The sinking of HMS* Audacious, *lost on a mine outside Loch Swilly on 27 October 1914.*
ABOVE AND RIGHT *Two German torpedo successes. Above, the flotilla leader HMS* Scott, *a destroyer, is hit by a German submarine in the North Sea, 15 August 1918. In the lower picture an Allied steamship is struck by a torpedo from the German submarine U-35.*

The initial successes of the U-boats, despite the restrictions placed on them, led to mounting pressure in Germany in support of an *un*restricted campaign, which after the bloodily indecisive battles before Verdun and on the Somme, seemed to offer Germany her best hope of victory. At the time the German Naval Staff estimated that, unrestricted, the U-boats could sink 600,000 tons of shipping result of political pressure on the Admiralty. After disastrous losses on the cross-Channel coal trade in the last months of 1916, the French insisted that the British adopt a convoy system on that route. Convoys were started and losses fell drastically in the first quarter of 1917. Encouraged, the British became more positive: they saw how few oceangoing ships left the United Kingdom each week (about 130)

every month. This was a rate of loss far beyond the Allies' replacement capacity and would be sufficient to scare off neutral trade with Britain. Even if the USA entered the war, the Germans believed that the campaign would bring Britain to her knees before American help could become effective.

During the earlier restricted campaigns Allied countermeasures proved of little use. Until 1916 there was no means of detecting a submerged submarine; nor was there a satisfactory anti-submarine weapon. The Allies ceaselessly patrolled the sea lanes in anticipation of action but the submarines easily evaded the patrols and waited for the single, unescorted merchantmen that were certain to sail past sooner or later. Only a defensively armed merchant ship stood much chance of escaping the submarines: successful evasions sometimes occurred because submarines preferred to try and stop ships and sink them by gunfire or explosives rather than deplete their limited number of torpedoes.

Three factors helped to contain the number of U-boat sinkings during the restricted campaigns. These were, firstly, the limited number of U-boats at sea; secondly, the limited nature of their armament and endurance, and, thirdly, political considerations.

Once the political restrictions were lifted, the German submarines were able to sink nearly 2,000,000 tons of shipping in the three months after 1 February 1917. British counter-measures continued to have little success until the introduction of convoys – a decision taken in April as a

and realized how relatively easy it would be to provide escorts for them. The convoy system was soon applied to both inward and outward sailings and gradually, through its extension, the submarine menace was controlled – even though it was never beaten. Other contributory factors were Britain's severe food rationing programme, her strict allocation of cargo spaces and her ruthless concentration of shipping on the North Atlantic route. Losses were thereby reduced to a level that could be covered by American ship construction.

During the war the Germans sank 12,850,814 tons of shipping, of which 7,750,000 tons were British; but despite this huge total they failed to sink sufficient numbers of ships escorted in convoys. Of the 16,070 ships that sailed in ocean convoys only 96 were lost, and only 161 out of the 67,888 ships that sailed in coastal convoys. Losses among stragglers and ships sailing independently were heavier but not enough to give Germany victory. On the other hand submarine losses were fairly severe: nearly half the submarines commissioned during the war – 178 out of 373 – were sunk, though only for a short time did their losses exceed their rate of replacement. The reason why the unrestricted campaign failed was not because of the losses taken by the U-boats, but because they failed to maintain the rate of sinkings that was achieved for a brief period between February and April 1917.

Improvements in design and the discovery of new techniques were naturally accelerated by the war. Some develop-

Specialized ship designs of World War I include mine-laying submarines and Q-ships.

OPPOSITE *German U-boats in Kiel Harbour in October 1918; later that month the German fleet mutinied.*
ABOVE *HMS* Kempenfelt, *a Marksman class destroyer, with the destroyers* Mounsey *and* Rob Roy.
RIGHT *The non-rigid British Naval Airship C-23A escorting an outward-bound convoy off the coast of Cornwall in December 1917. The convoy system, introduced in June that year, brought a dramatic cut in losses to U-boats and helped to save Britain from the spectre of starvation.*
from the spectre of starvation. Out of some 95,000 ships sailing in convoy, only 393 were lost.
BELOW *The map shows how the Allies used mines to deny the German fleet access to the Channel; to the north there was a blockade based on Scapa Flow.*

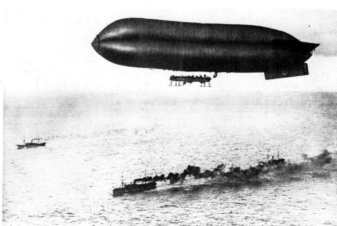

FOLKESTONE – CAP GRIS NEZ BARRAGE, 1918

+ + MINES
⚓ LIGHTSHIPS
〰 SHOALS

NORTH SEA

North Foreland

Ramsgate

GREAT BRITAIN

Goodwin Sands

Deal

Dover

South Foreland   Net mines

Folkestone   Deep mines

Mines at 30 feet

Mines at 40, 60 & 70 feet   The Varne

Mines at 40 & 60 feet

Dungeness   Calais

The Ridge   Cap Gris Nez

Mines at 40, 60, 80 & 100 feet

FRANCE

Boulogne

0 MLS   20

0 KMS   30

ments were quite strange. There was a seaplane carrier with auxiliary sails; and torpedo craft equipped with spiked tracks so that they could scale nets and booms. Submarines were built with 12-inch guns that could be fired when awash and there were fleet submarines whose steam engines gave a surface speed of 25 knots but which took 30 minutes to dive. Other exotic ideas included experiments with pink camouflage paint and patrol craft with similar stems and sterns.

But the oddities were outnumbered by more serious and important developments. The war encouraged numerous increases in the size of ships and also specialized designs. By 1916 the British had plans for a 36,000-ton battlecruiser and had built ships with 18-inch guns. The *Renown* class battle-cruiser reached 30 knots and destroyers were approaching 40 knots. Submarines grew in size so that by the summer of 1916 they could operate out of Germany as far as the east coast of the United States. Mine-laying submarines made their début in 1915, and purpose-built minesweepers and minelayers increased in numbers and importance. Monitors and armed merchant cruisers proliferated, as did patrol-boats and Q-ships (armed merchantmen used as submarine decoys), but the most important developments for the future took place in the air and beneath the surface of the sea.

As early as 1915 the British developed two counters to the submarine: one was a means of destruction and the other a

method of detection. A passive listening device, called the hydrophone, provided the first means of detecting a submerged submarine. But its value was limited because the ship carrying the hydrophone had to be stopped before it could pick up the sound of the submarine's propellers, and several ships were needed to work together before an accurate position could be calculated. Unfortunately, no other method of detection was available during the war, although in mid-1917 the British carried out trials with an active search device known as Asdic; this, however, did not come into service before the end of the war.

The depth-charge brought the first really effective method of destroying a submerged U-boat other than by ramming. It consisted of a heavy high-explosive charge designed to go off at a depth of between 40 and 80 feet by means of a hydrostatically controlled detonator. It entered service in January 1916 and it made its first kill on 26 March when *U-68* was sunk by the Q-ship *Farnborough*. On 6 July *UC-7* gained the dubious distinction of being the first victim of a successful combination of hydrophones and depth-charges. These methods of detection and destruction became increasingly effective after the introduction of convoys. In their hunt for merchantmen, submarines could no longer rely on picking off helpless independent ships but had to attack the escorted ships – a process that naturally exposed them to counter-attack from the new weapons.

Perhaps the most remarkable fact about the convoy system was that, of the ships lost, only five were sunk when aircraft were present – despite the latter's very limited offensive power. During the war aircraft registered many 'firsts'. Japanese seaplanes achieved the first sinking of a warship from air attack when a small German minelayer was sunk at Tsingtao in 1914; and seaplanes from the *Ark Royal* spotted for naval gunfire at the Dardanelles for the first time on 1 March 1915. On 12 August aerial torpedoes claimed their first victim – a grounded ship – and three days later, again at the Dardanelles, sank ships with sea room. In the Baltic, the Germans carried out the first successful bombing of a

Naval aircraft and the evolution of the carrier.
TOP *Lieutenant C. R. Samson makes the first take-off from the deck of a British warship (HMS* Africa*) in January 1912.*
OPPOSITE, ABOVE *A Short Folder seaplane being lifted out of the hold of HMS* Ark Royal.
ABOVE AND OPPOSITE, BELOW *An aerial view of the aircraft carrier HMS* Furious *and the scene as a Sopwith Pup lands on the after flight deck. Note the Pup's skid undercarriage and the vertical arrester wires fixed to the deck.*

Early carriers are beset by problems of landing and take-off, not effectively solved until the post-war introduction of the island structure.

ABOVE *Survivors take to the water and pack the side of the doomed German cruiser* Blücher, *which sank at the Battle of Dogger Bank, 25 January 1915.*

battleship on 27 April 1916 – a Russian pre-dreadnought being heavily damaged. In the spring of 1917 both the Russians and Germans started aerial mining.

The successful use of aircraft prompted two developments – the search for a vessel capable of operating aircraft and the mounting of anti-aircraft guns in heavy ships. Although France was the first nation to commission a (seaplane) carrier, with the *Le Foudre* in 1913, it was the Royal Navy that quickly seized the lead in this field and carried out much of the early experimentation. The planes did not fly off the deck of the first British seaplane carrier, the *Ark Royal* – a converted collier – but were winched out of the ship onto the sea, where they took off. The system then operated in reverse when the aircraft returned from its mission. This clumsy and long-winded process proved a major deficiency with the slow-moving *Ark Royal*, since she could not load and unload seaplanes and at the same time keep up with the fleet and so carry out her reconnaissance role. Fast cross-Channel steamers were converted to carriers on the outbreak of war, but it was from an ex-Cunarder, the *Campania*, that the next major breakthrough occurred,

when in August 1915 an aircraft with wheeled floats took off from her forward deck.

The true function of the seaplane and the carrier was reconnaissance. By 1917 the task of air defence had been handed over to aircraft that were carried on the cruisers and capital ships of the Grand Fleet. These aircraft were wheeled and had a considerably superior performance to the seaplane, but, unlike the latter, they could not be recovered. The concept of an aircraft taking off from and landing on a flight-deck took a long time to be accepted. The first experiment in deck landing was carried out on 2 August 1917. An attempt to repeat the performance three days later cost the pilot his life. In order to try to avoid such accidents, the British built two different types of flight-decks into ships. To the *Furious*, on whose fore-deck the previous experiments had taken place, a separate landing-deck was added behind the funnel. This proved unsatisfactory because the turbulence from the funnels made landings unreasonably hazardous. Next the *Argus*, then under construction, was given a continuous free deck clear of any obstruction, but unfortunately the ship was completed too late to see action. For the duration of World War I landings on the surface of the sea, from where the planes were winched aboard, remained the only means of recovery.

Nevertheless, with the *Argus* the British had evolved the

prototype aircraft carrier. There were still major problems to overcome but the basic concept had been settled. After the war the fitting of catapults (which had begun in 1912 in the US Navy), the evolution of arrester gear and the location of bridge and funnels were problems that were met and overcome by the navies of the Great Powers. That of the location of bridge and funnels was possibly the most serious, and various attempts were made to clear smoke and fumes away from the flight-deck through side vents. It was not until the British developed the island structure, offset to starboard, that the matter could be resolved. This arrangement was generally followed in other navies though the Japanese did build carriers with port-side islands.

The first carrier with an island structure was the *Eagle*, which entered service in the Royal Navy in 1923. Soon, however, the Royal Navy went into a period of relative decline. It had lost control over its air arm in 1918 and a series of stringent post-war budgets deprived it of money for research and development in the field of aviation. In the meantime other navies were more favoured. In December 1922 the Japanese completed the first purpose-built carrier, the *Hosho*. The implications were clear; and, indeed, from about that time the Japanese and American navies overtook Britain and left her behind in the development of aircraft carriers.

Surface Actions

Throughout the war, and in every theatre, there were regular clashes between the light forces of the various navies. Throughout the war, too, all combatants tried to use their submarines to reduce the forces opposed to them, though in no theatre did the latter policy enjoy lasting success.

Little, in fact, happened in the course of the war at sea to alter the fundamental *status quo*. The supremacy of the British Grand Fleet was rarely disturbed even by its chief opponent, the German High Seas Fleet, which remained largely bottled up in its home waters for the duration of the war. Indeed, so daunting was the destructive power of the heavy ships on either side that in no theatre was an inferior fleet prepared consistently to challenge a superior one. Nor were the superior navies ever in a position to compel the enemy to come out and give battle.

Even when navies did meet on the open sea, the theoretical likelihood of a battle being decisive was small: given that one of the parties was inferior and would therefore wish to break off contact quickly, there was little the other could do – lacking the present-day indispensables of radar, a good communications system and adequate night-fighting equipment – to press home its advantage. Only in the Anglo-

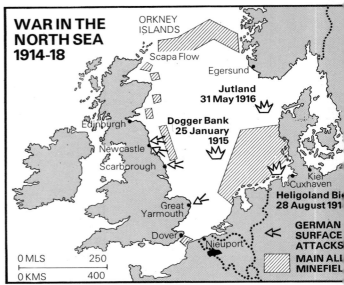

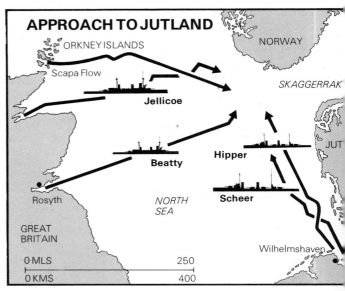

ABOVE *At the Battle of the Falkland Islands, on 8 December 1914, HMS* Inflexible *stands by while survivors from the German cruiser* Gneisenau *are rescued from the icy waters; 190 men out of the ship's complement of 764 were saved. This photograph was taken from the battlecruiser HMS* Invincible, *which also took part in the rescue operation.*

German struggle did any major conflicts occur – and for the most part these were not willingly sought by the Germans. In the whole course of the war, no more than two battles were fought to the bitter end, and both of these happened in non-European waters.

The first battle of the war was a dashing action fought in August 1914 by British battlecruisers and light forces against German light forces engaged in mine warfare in the Heligoland Bight. It was a confused battle fought among shifting fog banks, a battle noted for its astonishingly bad staff work, and one which had little material effect but a profound influence on morale. In numerical terms the British sank three light cruisers – the *Köln, Mainz* and *Ariadne* – and one destroyer at no cost to their own fleet. More important, however, was the fact that the battle, fought on Germany's doorstep, confirmed the Royal Navy in its sense of ascendancy over the German fleet. Fortunately for the Royal Navy, its confidence was not unduly shaken in the following month when three of its armoured cruisers – the *Aboukir, Cressy* and *Hogue* – were lost to a single submarine, the *U-9.*

The two decisive actions mentioned above were fought in November and December 1914 off the coasts of South America. In the first, Admiral von Spee's German cruiser squadron, fleeing from superior forces in the Far East, met and annihilated an inferior force of hastily commissioned British cruisers at the Battle of Coronel off the coast of Chile, the British losing two armoured cruisers and one armed merchant cruiser.

In the following month the German squadron was caught, in its turn, by a superior British force that had been assembled and dispatched at great speed to the South Atlantic by the British Admiralty. It included two battlecruisers, the *Inflexible* and *Invincible*, which were supported by two armoured and two light cruisers and one armed merchant cruiser. Von Spee was caught off the Falkland Islands and the *Scharnhorst* and *Gneisenau* were sunk, together with two

light cruisers, the *Nürnberg* and *Leipzig*. Another light cruiser, the *Dresden*, escaped but was later caught and scuttled by her crew to avoid capture.

On 24 January 1915 the first conflict between heavy units in European waters took place at the Battle of Dogger Bank. The Germans, attempting an attack on Britain's east coast (their third in the war) were intercepted by a superior British force of five battlecruisers. During the action the Germans lost an armoured cruiser, the *Blücher*, but three battlecruisers escaped, mainly because of the poor signalling of the British flagship. In the euphoria of victory this point was largely ignored, as was, in British circles at least, the need for anti-flash protection to guard the magazines from exploding after a hit. The Germans, on the other hand, saw the value of such protection, with the result that the balance of losses was reversed in the next engagement.

This action was the Battle of Jutland. Although on the day it proved something of a non-event, Jutland stands as a crucial encounter in that, on 31 May 1916, for the first and only time in the war, the world's major contending navies came, if briefly, in range of each other.

The battle came about as a result of wireless interceptions made by the British, the history of which goes back to the sinking of the *Magdeburg* in August 1914 and the acquisition by the British of the German ship's code-books, which gave

Jutland — the war's
only clash of the
main battle fleets.

The Battle of Jutland, 31 May—1 June 1916

At Jutland – the only time the main battle fleets fought each other in the entire war – the British hoped to use their naval might to score a crushing victory. Such were the risks, however, that Admiral Jellicoe, the British commander, was, as Churchill put it, 'the only man on either side who could lose the war in an afternoon'. But, as the tables show, Jellicoe would have had to have lost calamitously for the balance of naval power to be reversed. In reality Jellicoe was cautious and the losses, though heavy, were roughly proportionate to those suffered in the other principal surface actions of the war.

1 THE BALANCE OF FORCES			2 LOSSES	
CATEGORY	BRITISH GRAND FLEET	GERMAN HIGH SEAS FLEET	BRITISH	GERMAN
Battleships	28	16	—	—
Battlecruisers	9	5	3	1
Pre-dreadnoughts	—	6	—	1
Armoured cruisers	8	—	3	—
Light cruisers	26	11	—	4
Destroyers	78	61	8	4
Seaplane carriers	1	—	—	—
Totals	150	99	14	10

ABOVE *The British battleships* Royal Oak *and* Hercules *at Jutland, their guns trained to starboard. A notable difference between the two is that one is making smoke and is coal-powered while the other, being oil-powered, has a clear funnel.*
BELOW *The battlecruiser HMS* Indefatigable *going into the Battle of Jutland.*

them more than a headstart in subsequent intelligence work. However, nearly two years later, contact on a telling scale with the German High Seas Fleet still eluded the British. Then wireless messages were received which suggested that a major German fleet movement was in progress. The Grand Fleet put to sea and on the next day Admiral Beatty's advance screen of battlecruisers came up against the decoy battlecruisers of Admiral Hipper. The Germans in fact planned to lure part of the main British fleet to oppose Hipper and then to strike with the superior weight of the High Seas Fleet, which for the present was tailing Hipper some 50 miles to the south.

The battlecruisers fought an initial action and the British lost heavily: the magazines of the *Indefatigable* and *Queen Mary* exploded, and the *Lion* was narrowly saved from a similar end, her magazines being flooded just in time. After having made contact with Admiral Scheer's main fleet, Beatty led the enemy northwards with the result that there followed two brief engagements between the main fleets, in which the Germans suffered a severe battering but managed to escape under cover of night and regain their ports in safety.

The battle was a great disappointment to the British, whose superiority in numbers, gun power and tactics had seemed likely to bring success; but failures in communication, and a general inability to appreciate the enemy's intentions, combined to deny Britain a decisive victory. Although their losses were greater than the Germans', the British retained a secure command over the surface of the world's oceans; thereafter the Germans confined their efforts to a few sorties of little significance until the surrender of November 1918.

Britain fails to win decisively at Jutland, but retains command of the oceans.

OPPOSITE, TOP LEFT *The magazines of the* Indefatigable *explode after one of her 12-inch turrets was hit by a heavy German shell; the ship broke in half and sank in about 15 seconds with the loss of 1,025 officers and men.*
ABOVE LEFT *The British airship NS-8 flies above ships of the surrendered German fleet on 21 November 1918.*
LEFT *After scuttling their ship at Scapa Flow, some of the crew of the German cruiser* Nürnberg *wait to be taken aboard HMS* Revenge.
BELOW *The* Seydlitz *after the Battle of Jutland.*

10

THE FIRST WARPLANES

Observer aircraft patrol the Western Front in the first months of the war.

World War I spread to most of the nations of Europe in the last days of July and the first days of August 1914. Few men at first saw how different this war was to be compared with earlier European wars, and the general consensus was that it would be a short, sharp war. Consequently, little or nothing had been done to prepare for a long conflict.

This is particularly evident in the use of 'air power' in the early months of the war. There were about 390 aircraft available to the combatants in the Western theatre of operations at the outbreak of hostilities (136 French, 48 British and 24 Belgian against about 180 German machines); but these were a hotch-potch of different designs that could hardly be grouped into homogeneous squadrons. The British were in the worst position, flying a motley of BE-2 variants, Avro 504s, Sopwith Tabloids and Bristol Scouts, plus a few French-designed machines. The French were slightly better off, being equipped with Morane-Saulniers of various types, Caudron G-IIIs, and a number of large Voisins which were pressed into service as rudimentary bombers. The Germans were equipped with a large quantity of Taube types and Albatros B-Is and B-IIs. The Taube design had a large dove-like monoplane wing, and had been designed in Austria-Hungary by Igo Etrich. It was built in Germany by a variety of manufacturers in the early stages of the war.

With some notable exceptions, such as the Sopwith Tabloid and the Morane-Saulnier Type-N, most of these machines had a maximum speed of about 75 mph and an endurance of some three hours. Armament was officially forbidden by most authorities, and it was only the most enterprising of pilots who took a pistol or carbine with them. Moreover, as a result of the almost total lack of government preparation in the last years of peace, these aircraft were intrinsically civilian types and little able to undertake military tasks – the most important of which was to observe the enemy's movements. Thus, for example, in what was probably the best flying machine of all, the British BE-2b, the pilot sat in the rear cockpit while the observer found himself in the forward one between the wings and surrounded by a mass of rigging wires, from which point he could achieve very little, so limited was his view. In the German Taube, the observer again sat in the forward cockpit, not this time surrounded by a Gordian knot of rigging wires, but right over the broad-chord wing, which again severely hampered his chances of making a successful reconnaissance.

The best types for reconnaissance in the early months of the war were the French Morane-Saulnier parasols and the pusher Farmans. The Morane-Saulnier Type-L clearly reflected that firm's design preferences: the wing wa

OPPOSITE *A Bristol Scout, one of Britain's early reconnaissance types.* LEFT *The Avro 504, another British machine, here seen in peacetime colours. Best known today for its work as a trainer, the 504 was originally built in 1914 for reconnaissance and bombing work; its role was later extended to cover anti-airship and night-fighter duties.* BELOW AND BOTTOM *The bird-like wings of the Etrich Taube (Dove), a reconnaissance machine designed in Austria-Hungary and built for widespread service by a variety of German manufacturers.*

The airmen defy official policy and arm their planes with machine guns, also with steel darts, grappling hooks and other home-made weapons.

mounted above the fuselage on a framework of struts, supported by bracing wires. The crew, sitting underneath the wing, had an almost uninterrupted downward view. A different philosophy was apparent in such designs as the Farman MF-7 and 11. Here the design was based on the pusher principle, with the engine mounted behind the wings and driving a pusher propeller. The tail structure was mounted on booms stretching back from the wings outside the disc swept by the propeller. Naturally enough, little in the way of slipstreaming could be achieved with such a design, and performance was lower than in tractor designs. But, more importantly perhaps in those early days, the crew was accommodated in a shoe-like nacelle perched on the leading edge of the wing. This afforded both the pilot and the observer an excellent view both forward and downward.

It was with such equipment that the airmen of World War I started their eventful careers; not surprisingly, the fear of mechanical failure on the part of their own aircraft was a far more dominant factor than any fear of enemy action. Even though many pilots ignored official policy and attempted to arm their aircraft, they were almost universally unsuccessful in providing themselves with effective armament. The first months of the war were marked by an amazing assortment of supposedly lethal gadgets fitted to aircraft: there were guns firing off at 45° to the line of flight

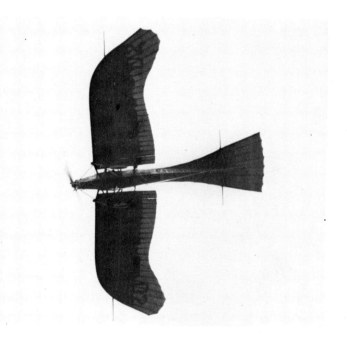

in order to clear the propeller (which made sighting all but impossible); boxes of steel darts; some crews even carried grappling hooks or bricks fixed on the end of a length of line, with which they tried to break off enemy propellers. More important strategically were the French attempts to bomb

Primitive bombing raids are launched over Germany and the Western Front — and hard lessons are learned.

German production centres in the south with their Breguets, and the Germans' efforts to use their Zeppelins over the Western Front. The Germans soon learnt, however, that small arms or light artillery fire was more than sufficient to cripple their very expensive airships: the target presented to the French gunners was large and, with all its hydrogen-filled gasbags, highly inflammable. Thereafter the Zeppelins were used for reconnaissance over the sea or over Russia, where defences were not so strong, and for bombing England by night, when defensive fire would be less accurate.

ABOVE *A rigging class held at the Crystal Palace for Probationary Flight Officers of the Royal Naval Air Service, introduced in July 1914. On the blackboard is a Farman biplane.*
BELOW *A French Morane-Saulnier Type-L; its crew, seated under the single parasol wing, had an almost uninterrupted downward view, greatly facilitating reconnaissance work.*
RIGHT *The pilot of a DH-2 single-seat pusher fighter aims his Lewis gun along the aircraft's line of travel. This type was introduced as a short-term answer to the 'Fokker scourge', while the Allies developed their own interrupter gear, enabling pilots to fire through the propeller blades.*

The War on Land

Probably the most important single contribution made by aircraft in 1914 was the news brought by the crew of a British machine that the German right flank, which was intended to sweep round the west side of Paris early in September, had in fact veered more to the south and would now pass to the east of the French capital. This opened the eyes of the Allied High Command to the possibility of a counterstroke from Paris as the German flank moved past. The result was the Battle of the Marne, Germany's first serious setback in World War I, a setback that halted her victorious advance and sent her hurrying back north in the 'Race to the Sea'. (This in turn gave rise to the continuous front and the stagnant war that produced such hideous casualty figures.)

As yet there were no true fighting aircraft. The machines described above were merely short-term expedients. The problem which held up further development is simple to describe: the machines with the highest performances, and therefore the best chance of catching an opponent and forcing him down, were the tractor-engined biplane scouts such as the Bristol Scout or Avro 504. But because they had a propeller in front of the pilot, it was impossible to mount a machine gun on the fuselage in such a way that it could fire forward through the disc swept by the propeller. Alternative measures were adopted, such as guns mounted to fire off at an angle from the line of flight, but they had little success.

A machine was then produced that can be considered as the world's first true fighting aeroplane. This was the Vickers FB-5, nicknamed the 'Gunbus', which had been designed from the outset for aerial combat on the guiding principle that if it was worth getting one's own air reconnaissance, it

was also worth preventing the other side getting theirs. The Vickers FB-5 was a conventional two-seat pusher biplane, in which the pilot sat in the rear seat and the gunner/observer in the front seat, from which he commanded an excellent field of fire and observation. Armament was a single ·303-inch Lewis gun. This gun, which became one of the most successful aircraft guns of World War I,

was an air-cooled light machine gun fed from a 47-round drum (later a 97-round drum was used). The chief fault of the FB-5 (the initials stood for Fighting Biplane) was that it was a pusher, with all that basic type's failings in terms of performance (speed 70 mph and ceiling 9,000 feet). The type began to arrive in France in February 1915.

The Vickers FB-5 was clearly not the answer. Fighting aircraft have always needed to have a higher performance than their quarry. The next step in the evolution of the fighter aeroplane was crucial but also, paradoxically, quite false. Early in 1914, Raymond Saulnier of the Morane-Saulnier company had seen where the true answer to air combat lay: this was in the production of an armament that fired along the line of sight and line of flight of pilot and aeroplane. But the propeller of any tractor type would be in the way, so how was he to overcome this problem? Clearly it was necessary to halt the stream of bullets from the machine gun while one of the propeller blades was in the line of fire; this could be done, Saulnier saw, by synchronizing the action of the machine gun with the movement of the propeller. Saulnier designed an interrupter gear that would achieve this, but the uncertain quality of French machine-gun ammunition was such that rounds might 'hang fire' and then fire the bullet when the next blade was in the line of fire. To mitigate the effects of such stray rounds on the wooden propeller blade, Saulnier fitted wedge-shaped steel deflectors to the rear of each blade, along the line of fire. The problem of the ammunition appeared impossible however, and Saulnier abandoned his experiments. At much the same time as Saulnier was at work on the Allied side, a German designer, Franz Schneider, was conducting similar experiments with machine-gun interrupter gears for the LVG company.

In the spring of 1915, the French pre-war stunt pilot and aviation pioneer Roland Garros was serving with the French Air Force. Disgruntled by his lack of success in shooting down German reconnaissance machines, Garros persuaded Saulnier to let him use the Type-L parasol monoplane fitted with the deflectors only, the interrupter gear having been removed. The results were startling. In less than three weeks Garros had disposed of five German reconnaissance machines. But then on 10 April he was forced down behind the German lines and captured, together with his machine.

The Germans at once realized the significance of the deflectors and decided to develop an efficient system for their own aircraft. A young Dutch designer working in Germany, Anthony Fokker, was called in and told to produce a proper interrupter gear. Fokker promptly handed over all the information on Saulnier's device to his technical staff and told them to set to work. A few days later the result was ready for testing and proved entirely successful. Fokker persuaded the German authorities to allow him to test the new interrupter in one of his own aircraft, an M-5K monoplane, and, when the air tests proved equally successful, to order fighter aircraft using this device from him. The result was the Fokker E-I monoplane, the world's first true single-seat fighter. In all ways an indifferent machine, indeed a dangerous one, the E-I nearly always prevailed by virtue of its superior armament— a synchronized 7·92-mm Parabellum machine gun. Later E-types had two or even three Spandau machine guns,

February 1915: the Vickers 'Gunbus', the world's first aircraft designed for combat, arrives in France.

LEFT *A British BE-2 stands outside the sheds; more than 3,200 BE-2s were built in several versions, and the type remained in active service until the Armistice.*
BELOW *The Fokker Eindekker, first with the interrupter gear enabling the pilot to fire through the propeller.*
BOTTOM *The Morane-Saulnier Type-N, a fast fighting scout whose designation was changed to Military Type V; capable of 102 mph at 6,500 feet, it served from 1914-16.*

though the fitting of three guns adversely affected the plane's performance.

In the hands of pilots such as Oswald Boelcke and Max Immelmann, the Fokker proved itself master of the skies over the Western Front, so much so that the period from autumn 1915 to spring 1916 is now known in aviation history as the time of the 'Fokker scourge', and machines such as the BE-2 as 'Fokker fodder'. The Allies had nothing to match the German fighter, and design work continued feverishly to find a counter.

Lacking an interrupter gear of their own, the French and British had to find other, short-term solutions while development went on. The first answer was the French Nieuport 11 or 'Bébé'. This was a compact, high-performance sesquiplane armed with a Lewis gun on the upper wing which fired over the propeller. (A sesquiplane is a biplane with the lower wing very much smaller in area than the upper wing.) Considerably faster, more manoeuvrable and stronger than the Fokker, the Nieuport 11 began the eclipse of the German type.

The Nieuport was soon joined in this task by Britain's answer, the Airco de Havilland (DH) 2. This was introduced in the spring of 1916 and was issued to No. 24 Squadron, which thus became the first British squadron to be equipped throughout with single-seat fighters. The DH-2 was a small pusher biplane with the Lewis gun mounted in the nose. The gun was at first movable, but most pilots found it better to fix the gun along the line of flight and aim the whole aircraft at the opposition. With the large-scale arrival of DH-2s in France the Fokker was totally outclassed and the Allies enjoyed a period of complete air supremacy. The other major fighting aeroplane of the day was the Royal Aircraft Factory's FE-2b, a big and sturdy two-seat pusher biplane that was used for escort, bombing and reconnaissance missions.

While the development of fighter aircraft had been progressing, the main burden of air operations rested on the shoulders of the crews of the various types of reconnaissance and artillery-spotting machines shuttling up and down the front. It was the protection or destruction of these all-important types that was the *raison d'être* of the new fighters. The requirements of their job made the recce planes large, stable and slow, and therefore difficult to defend against more nimble fighters.

The British were still using large numbers of the inherently stable BE-2s, but a new type, the RE-8, began to enter service in the second half of 1916. The RE-8 acquired an unenviable and not altogether justified reputation as a tricky aircraft to fly, but fulfilled its tasks excellently in the last two years of the war. It had a top speed of 102 mph, an endurance of $4\frac{1}{4}$ hours and an armament of one fixed ·303-inch Vickers machine gun, firing through the disc swept by the propeller with the aid of the newly developed British interrupter gear, and one (later two) Lewis guns for the observer. Another mainstay of the Royal Flying Corps and Royal Naval Air Service was the Sopwith 1½-Strutter, a delightful machine to fly and one that was capable of fulfilling the fighter, bomber and reconnaissance roles. It was the first British aircraft to be designed with provision for an interrupter gear. Capable of 106 mph, it could climb to 15,000 feet, had an endurance of $4\frac{1}{2}$ hours and could carry up to 130 pounds of bombs.

In the French Air Force, reconnaissance was still carried out by the types that had been in service since the early days of the war – Farmans, Caudrons, and Morane-Saulnier Types LA and P. The last type was introduced in 1915 and had a speed of 97 mph, a ceiling of 12,000 feet, an

Fokker perfects his interrupter gear, permitting forward fire through the propeller; the Allies hasten to develop a similar device.

1916: aircraft begin contact patrol work, their task being to pinpoint the positions of the infantry in the heat of an offensive.

endurance of $2\frac{1}{2}$ hours and an armament of one fixed Vickers machine gun and one flexible Lewis gun. These were by 1916 established as the main Allied machine guns.

The Germans, on the other hand, had decided early in the war that their reconnaissance aircraft should be more capable of defending themselves without a fighter escort than were the Allied machines. The result was a series of startlingly efficient biplanes. Albatros, a firm that was later to become famous for its shark-like fighters, introduced the C-III in 1916. This was not very fast (87 mph), but it had good range, adequate armament and it was very sturdy. The type was supplanted later in 1916 by the C-VII: this had a 200-hp instead of a 160-hp engine, which raised the top speed to 106 mph and made the aircraft much liked by its crews.

The year 1917 saw the introduction of some of the best German reconnaissance machines of the war. Albatros developed the C-X and C-XII, strong and fast machines that were built in substantial numbers. In that year also came the widespread entry into service of the DFW C-V, developed late in 1916 from the earlier C-IV. The C-V was powered by the 200-hp Benz BzIV inline engine and had a top speed of 97 mph. With a ceiling of 16,400 feet and an endurance of $3\frac{1}{2}$ hours, it was one of Germany's best all-round aircraft, capable of undertaking reconnaissance, photographic, artillery-spotting and infantry contact-patrol work.

Infantry contact patrols were started in 1916 because commanders had been finding it impossible to establish where exactly their front-line troops had got to in offensives. Aircraft were thus sent out to find the markers which their troops had been ordered to lay out. The LVG C-V,

OPPOSITE, ABOVE *The Sopwith 1½-Strutter, a versatile machine that in wartime was a mainstay of the RNAS.*

OPPOSITE, BELOW LEFT *The Nieuport 17, the French successor to the Bébé and a fighting partner of the Sopwith Pup.*

OPPOSITE, BELOW RIGHT *The Albatros D-I, a powerful German fighter armed with two forward-firing Spandau machine guns at a time when most of its opponents carried only a single gun.*

LEFT *The observer of an FE-2b demonstrates the manoeuvrability of his Lewis gun.*

BELOW *The Nieuport XI (Bébé), the fast and strong fighter that in 1916 began to restore Allied fortunes, shattered earlier in the 'Fokker scourge'.*

BOTTOM *The pioneering Vickers FB-5. 'Gunbus'; the observer/gunner, armed with a Lewis machine gun, sat in the front seat where he commanded an excellent field of fire.*

1917: The Germans introduce high-performance recce types capable of outdistancing Allied fighters.

designed by the same man as the DFW C-V, had a generally similar performance, and was one of the biggest two-seaters to see service with the Germans in World War I, having a span of 42 feet 7¾ inches. The Rumpler C-IV and C-VII both appeared in 1917 and did excellent work for the Germans. These were basically similar to other German reconnaissance types, but in addition they both had a very good high-altitude performance, which made them relatively immune from the attentions of Allied fighters.

In 1917, too, came the introduction of the best all-round aeroplane of the war, the Bristol F-2 Fighter. A very strong handy design, with the fuselage suspended between the

Germany enjoys the benefits of greater firepower with its two-gunned Albatros fighters.

OPPOSITE *The French Spad S-7, a strong fighter that entered service in September 1916 with a 150-hp engine; one year later an improved model was introduced with a 175-hp engine.*
BELOW *The famous Sopwith Pup, a superb single-seat fighter capable of 111 mph on its 80-hp Le Rhône engine.*
BOTTOM *The Sopwith Triplane, produced for the RNAS; the design was chosen because it improved on the Pup's rate of climb and manoeuvrability.*
OVERLEAF *The mysteries of an aerial dogfight, high over the Western Front, as recorded by N. C. Arnold.*

wings, the Bristol Fighter had an inauspicious entry into service because its pilots tried to adopt normal two-seater defensive tactics. But once they recognized the machine's potential for offensive work, with the observer covering the tail, the F-2A and its better development, the F-2B, became the war's best two-seater.

While this advance in two-seaters was taking place, the balance of air supremacy was again shifting to the Germans. The Allies had capped their defeat of the Fokker mono-

plane in early 1916 by introducing during the summer the Sopwith Pup fighter. This was essentially a single-seat scaled-down version of the 1½-Strutter, and is generally recognized as the most perfect flying machine of World War I; with an engine of only 80-hp it was capable of 111 mph and had a ceiling of 17,500 feet, at which altitude it was still highly manoeuvrable. But armament remained unchanged at one Vickers machine gun. In the Allied squadrons the Pup was complemented by the Nieuport

German supremacy did not last long, however. In spring 1917 the first of the Royal Aircraft Factory's new fighter, the SE-5, arrived in France, followed in early summer by its up-engined development, the SE-5a. The latter was powered by a 200-hp Wolseley Viper engine in its definitive version, compared with the SE5's 150-hp Hispano-Suiza. Both were armed with a synchronized Vickers machine gun in the fuselage and a Lewis gun firing over the propeller arc on the upper wing. The SE-5a had a top speed of 138 mph

The Allies hit back with the SE-5 and the agile Sopwith Camel, armed with twin synchronized machine guns.

company's successor to the Bébé, the Nieuport 17. This had a single synchronized Vickers machine gun and a performance very similar to the Pup's, but with a 110-hp rotary engine. The rotary engine was now in its heyday, still being powerful enough to cope with the latest designs, but light and compact, thus giving the aeroplane extreme manoeuvrability.

Of a different design philosophy was the French Spad S-7 fighter. This was a heavier and more powerful machine, still armed only with a single machine gun, but capable of 119 mph and a ceiling of 18,000 feet on the 175 hp of its Hispano-Suiza inline engine. Though lacking the rotary-engined fighters' agility and responsiveness, the Spad was immensely strong and an excellent gun platform. Deliveries began in August 1916.

The Germans, however, had gone a step further in the evolution of the fighter when they introduced the Albatros D-I and II fighters in the autumn and winter of 1916. Powered by a 160-hp Mercedes engine, the D-II had a speed of 109 mph at a ceiling of 17,060 feet. But whereas Allied fighters still had only one gun, the Albatros had two, which gave it a distinct advantage in firepower. The Germans followed up this advantage quickly, introducing the Albatros D-III in the spring of 1917. This was an updated D-II, with wings of greater span supported by V-shaped interplane struts instead of the earlier models' parallel struts. With the arrival of the D-III German supremacy was complete, and the immediate result was 'Bloody April' 1917 – when Allied types, mostly British, were shot down in droves.

and a ceiling of 19,500 feet, with an excellent rate of climb as well, but like the Spad its chief qualities lay in its ruggedness and steadiness as a gun platform. The SE-5a held its own against all opposition to the end of the war.

At about the same time that the first SE-5a's were reaching the squadrons, another new British fighter was making its appearance. This was the redoubtable Sopwith F-1 Camel, the war's most successful fighter (in terms of aircraft destroyed). The Camel was designed as a successor to the Pup. Although it had a slightly greater span than its predecessor, the Camel had a shorter fuselage. In the forward seven feet of this were crammed the pilot, fuel, guns and ammunition, and a 100- to 170-hp rotary engine. With most of the aeroplane's weight close to the centre of gravity, the Camel had phenomenal agility, though it took an experienced pilot to make the most of it. Moreover, its twin synchronized Vickers machine guns were a match for the twin Spandaus of the latest German fighters. With a 130-hp Clerget rotary, top speed was 115 mph and ceiling 19,000 feet.

Earlier in the year, in an effort to improve the pilot's view and increase the rate of climb – without losing any of the Pup's manoeuvrability – the Sopwith company had produced the Sopwith Triplane for the RNAS. This featured three narrow-chord staggered wings braced only by two plank-type interplane struts. The machine had a short and spectacular career until it was replaced by the Camel. Its most important contribution to the war in the air was to spark off a considerable number of German designs for triplane fighters.

Just as the Camel had succeeded the Pup, in the French Air Force the Spad S-13 succeeded the Spad S-7 in the early summer of 1917. Armed with two machine guns and equipped with a more powerful 235-hp Hispano-Suiza inline engine, the Spad S-13 also had aerodynamic refinements intended to improve manoeuvrability. Like the SE-5a, it had a top speed of 138 mph, but it had a better ceiling (21,800 feet) and proved capable of taking on the latest German fighters up to the end of the war.

Spurred on by these Allied successes, the Germans also continued to improve their fighters. The Albatros works produced another version of their basic fighter design in the summer of 1917. This was the D-V, powered by a 180-hp Mercedes inline. Basically similar to the D-III, the D-V was not much of an improvement on the earlier type, having a speed of 116 mph and a ceiling of 20,500 feet. Essentially, the problem was that the design had reached its development limit; what was needed was another design.

The first new design to be produced in any quantity was the Fokker Dr-I. This was a diminutive triplane inspired by the Sopwith Triplane. It was slow (103 mph) compared with contemporary Allied designs, but its ceiling and rate of climb were good and its manoeuvrability excellent. In the hands of skilled pilots it performed usefully, but it was not the answer to Allied superiority.

The right answer was not in fact found until 1918, when the Fokker D-VII made its appearance. This design entered service in April 1918. It was powered by a 185-hp BMW inline engine and had a top speed of 124 mph and a ceiling of 22,900 feet. But though its performance was only about the same as that of Allied fighters, its handling qualities at altitude, and its ability to 'hang' on its propeller, made it a formidable fighter. Fokker's last fighter of the war, the D-VIII, is also worthy of note. This was a parasol-winged

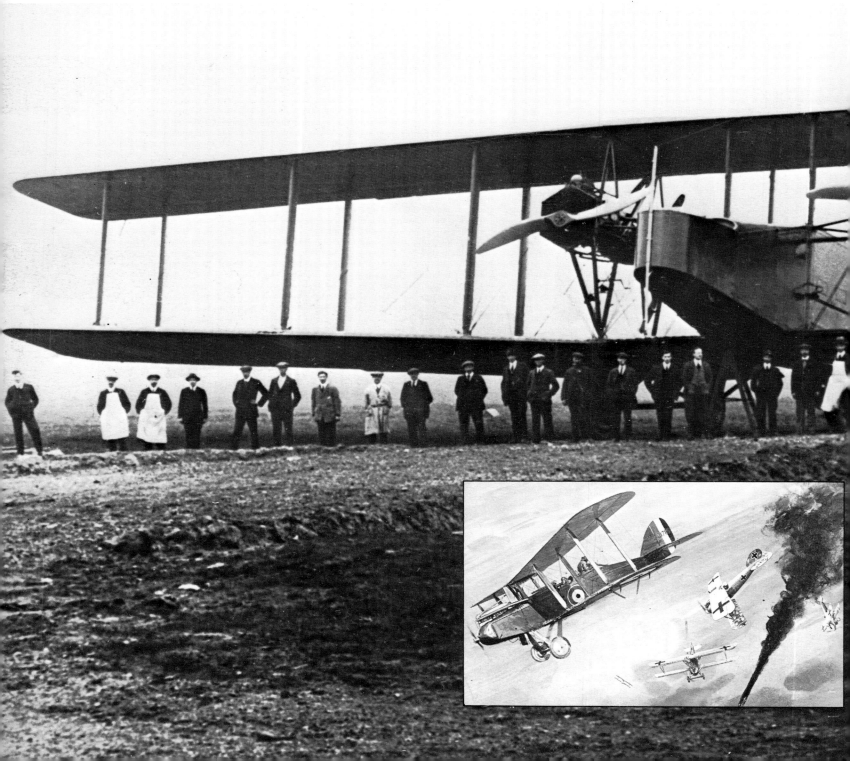

machine, powered by a rotary and not very fast, but agile with good rates of climb and dive. Only a few were completed before the end of the war.

In the Allied camp, a new generation of fighters would have entered the lists in large numbers if the war had continued into 1919, and some of these should be mentioned. Sopwith had just introduced two good designs, the Snipe fighter, a faster development of the Camel, and the Dolphin escort and ground-attack fighter. Another manufacturer, Martin & Handasyde, was about to commence large-scale delivery of the fastest Allied fighter to appear during the war, the F-4 Buzzard, which was powered by a 300-hp Hispano-Suiza inline and had a top speed of 145 mph. The French were about to introduce the latest of the Nieuport line, which was the first of that company's fighters not to be powered with an inline engine. This was the Nieuport 29, a lumpy and not very attractive design

that nevertheless emerged a fast and rugged performer.

Although the fighters were best-known to the public, and made the greatest advances in performance, there were other types of aircraft operating over the front that proved the real work-horses of the war. Whereas the early years from 1914 had seen little distinction in types other than into fighter and reconnaissance/bomber categories, in 1917 and 1918 the non-fighter types rapidly multiplied.

The British produced a pure bomber type, the Airco

Allied fighters that would have entered the war had it lasted into 1919.

BELOW *Thirty-four men, well spaced, emphasize the Handley Page V/1500's massive 126-foot span; only six of these four-engined bombers, capable of bombing Berlin from bases in Britain, were completed before the Armistice.*
BOTTOM LEFT *An aerial combat scene featuring a DH-9 light bomber and an Albatros D-V.*
BOTTOM RIGHT *A Handley Page 0/100 heavy bomber; maximum bomb load was 2,000 pounds—five times that of the DH-4.*

Royal Aircraft Factory SE-5a

The Scout Experimental (SE) 5a was the Royal Aircraft Factory's best design of the World War I period, and was bettered in results as a fighter only by the superlative Sopwith Camel. In design philosophy, the two standard fighters of the 1917–18 period were poles apart. The SE-5a (derived from the lower-powered SE-5) was a very robust, powerful machine, and enjoyed its combat success as a result of its speed, strength and stability as a gun platform rather than because of its agility.

The type was flown by most of Britain's top aces. As can be seen from the specifications, the SE-5a was powered by a variety of engines, the best of which was probably the Wolseley Viper. Deliveries of the SE-5a began in June 1917, and a total of 5,205 machines of the SE-5/5a family were built. Plans for the Curtiss company to build another 1,000 in the United States were cancelled after the war.

The SE-5a illustrated is fitted with a Wolseley Viper engine. Note the long exhaust (there was another on the port side) necessary to prevent the fumes adversely affecting the pilot.

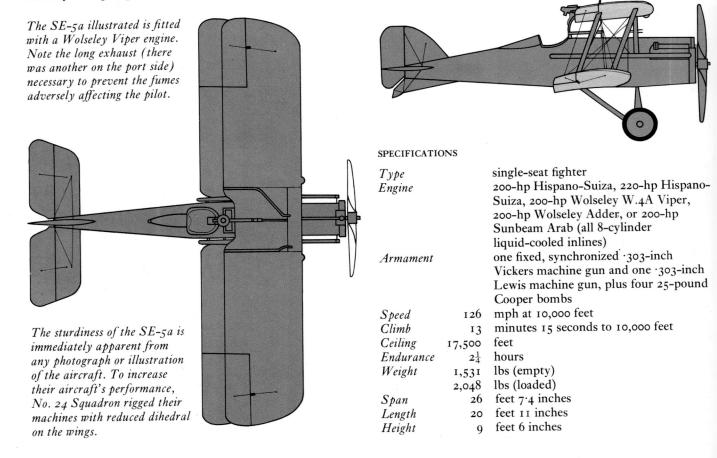

The sturdiness of the SE-5a is immediately apparent from any photograph or illustration of the aircraft. To increase their aircraft's performance, No. 24 Squadron rigged their machines with reduced dihedral on the wings.

SPECIFICATIONS

Type		single-seat fighter
Engine		200-hp Hispano-Suiza, 220-hp Hispano-Suiza, 200-hp Wolseley W.4A Viper, 200-hp Wolseley Adder, or 200-hp Sunbeam Arab (all 8-cylinder liquid-cooled inlines)
Armament		one fixed, synchronized ·303-inch Vickers machine gun and one ·303-inch Lewis machine gun, plus four 25-pound Cooper bombs
Speed	126	mph at 10,000 feet
Climb	13	minutes 15 seconds to 10,000 feet
Ceiling	17,500	feet
Endurance	$2\frac{1}{4}$	hours
Weight	1,531	lbs (empty)
	2,048	lbs (loaded)
Span	26	feet 7·4 inches
Length	20	feet 11 inches
Height	9	feet 6 inches

Sopwith Camel

In terms of enemy aircraft destroyed (1,294), the Sopwith Camel was the most successful fighter of World War I, its only rival for the title of the best fighter of the war being the Fokker D-VII. Unlike the contemporary SE-5a, the Camel (developed from the Pup) was designed with extreme manoeuvrability in mind: the positioning of most of the heavy items of equipment (engine, fuel, guns, ammunition and pilot) in the front seven feet of the fuselage ensured this, although it took an experienced pilot to get the best out of the Camel. The F.1 Camel entered service in the middle of 1917, and was soon joined by a shipboard version, the 2F.1, which had a single Vickers gun and a Lewis gun on the top wing. A total of 5,490 Camels was built.

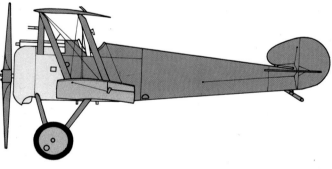

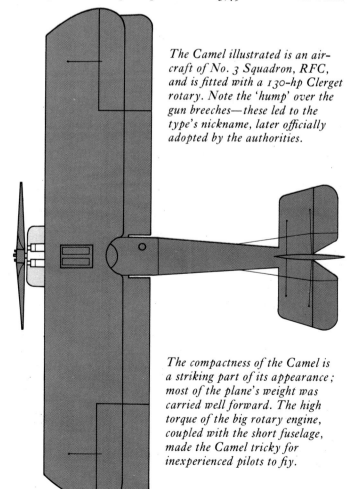

The Camel illustrated is an aircraft of No. 3 Squadron, RFC, and is fitted with a 130-hp Clerget rotary. Note the 'hump' over the gun breeches—these led to the type's nickname, later officially adopted by the authorities.

SPECIFICATIONS

Type		single-seat fighter
Engine		110-hp Clerget 9Z, 130-hp Clerget 9B, 140-hp Clerget 9Bf, 110-hp Le Rhône, 100-hp Gnome Monosoupape, 150-hp Bentley BR1, or 170-hp Le Rhône 9R (all 9-cylinder rotaries)
Armament		two fixed, synchronized ·303-inch Vickers machine guns (or two ·303-inch Lewis machine guns on the night fighter version)
Speed	104½	mph at 10,000 feet
Climb	11	minutes 45 seconds to 10,000 feet
Ceiling	19,000	feet
Endurance	2½	hours
Weight	962	lbs (empty)
	1,482	lbs (loaded)
Span	28	feet
Length	18	feet 9 inches
Height	8	feet 6 inches

The compactness of the Camel is a striking part of its appearance; most of the plane's weight was carried well forward. The high torque of the big rotary engine, coupled with the short fuselage, made the Camel tricky for inexperienced pilots to fly.

DH-4, which made its appearance in 1917. Essentially a light bomber, it was followed in 1918 by a development of it, the DH-9. The former was one of the best aircraft of the war, serving in large numbers with the British and Americans. With the 375-hp Rolls Royce Eagle inline, the DH-4 had a top speed of 143 mph, a ceiling of 22,000 feet and a range of 435 miles. Its defensive armament included up to four machine guns, and its offensive load comprised 460 pounds of bombs. The performance figures would have been extremely creditable in a fighter. The DH-9 was intended as an improvement on the DH-4, but its engine power was considerably less and performance suffered

comprised three to five Lewis guns and an offensive load was carried of up to 2,000 pounds of bombs or a single 1,650-pounder. In 1918 Handley-Page introduced an improved version of the o/100, the o/400. This was powered by two Rolls-Royce Eagles of 360-hp each, and had a speed of 97½ mph and a range of 750 miles. Defensive armament included up to five Lewis guns, and the offensive load was again up to 2,000 pounds of bombs. The largest British bomber of the war was the Handley-Page V/1500. Only six had been built by the time of the Armistice. Power was provided by four Rolls-Royce Eagles developing 375 hp each. This gave the bomber a speed of 97 mph and

accordingly. It did, however, possess the one major advantage, compared with the DH-4, of having the two crew members placed back-to-back, rather than separated in different parts of the fuselage.

The role of these light bombers was not spectacular, but they were of considerable importance in keeping up a continual harassment of the German rear areas. Their raids helped to slow down the rate at which German matériel reached the front, and they also forced the German fighter squadrons to take to the air and thus meet Allied fighting machines roving on the east of the lines. Moreover, aircraft such as the DH-4 were capable of giving a good account of themselves in an air battle. Such types were to be greatly valued – they harassed, bombed, fought, and also acted as reconnaissance machines. The larger bombers, as described in the next paragraph, were not so successful, however. Air theorists had vastly overestimated the effect, both on morale and on buildings, that small raids by heavy bombers would make. It was not until the advent of the great bomber fleets in 1944, and the A-bomb in 1945, that the idea of strategic bombing achieved real, practical success.

The first British version of what was intended to a strategic bomber was the Handley-Page o/100, which entered service in September 1916. Powered by two Rolls-Royce Eagle inlines of 250-hp each, the o/100 had a speed of 85 mph and a range of 700 miles. Defensive armament

FOKKER TRIPLANE.

ABOVE *Two Fokker types that made an impact in the latter stages of the war: the Dr-I triplane, an agile machine inspired by the Sopwith Triplane, and the excellent D-VII.*

water-cooled radial of 260 hp, the 2A-2 had a top speed of 115 mph and a ceiling of 20,500 feet. It was a very strong machine, and agile for its size. Its defensive armament of one fixed Vickers and two flexible Lewis guns enabled it to give a very good account of itself in combat.

France had been attached to the idea of bombing far sooner than the British, and by 1918 she had a large number of bomber squadrons. The types most commonly used in these squadrons were the Breguet 14 and the Voisin Types 6 to 10. The Voisin types had been in service since 1916. The Type 10 was powered by a 300-hp Renault inline driving a pusher propeller, and had a top speed of 84 mph

OPPOSITE *The Breguet 14, a French bomber capable of carrying up to 520 pounds of bombs.*
TOP *The Junkers CL-I, a German armoured trench-fighter of all-metal construction that arrived in 1918 and would have made an even greater impact had hostilities continued into 1919.*
ABOVE *The French Salmson 2A-2, a heavy reconnaissance type that also served in large numbers with the AEF.*

a range of 1,200 miles. Armament was up to five Lewis guns and 7,500 pounds of bombs.

Another British type classification was that of the trench fighter, designed for ground-attack use. This was an armoured machine built to operate at low level against the German trench lines. Such fighters flew along the line of the German trenches, immune from ground fire (it was hoped) because of their armour plating, strafing the infantry in their dug-in positions. The intention behind them was twofold, firstly to kill a significant number of the opposing infantry, and secondly to reduce the efficiency of the rest by keeping them constantly on the alert. The type was developed too late to make any great impression, however. The first trench fighter was a modified Camel, but a definitive version was the Sopwith TF-2 Salamander. This had a large amount of ammunition for the twin Vickers, and 650 pounds of armour plating. Top speed, with a Bentley BR-2 rotary, was 125 mph.

In the French camp, one of the best aircraft of the war was produced in 1918. This was the Salmson 2A-2, a reconnaissance type. Powered by a Salmson-Canton Unné

and a range of 310 miles. Bomb load was up to 600 pounds. The Breguet 14 was a far superior machine, and appeared in two versions, the 14A-2 and the 14B-2. The former was a two-seater reconnaissance machine, and the latter a bomber. Powered by a 300-hp Renault inline, the Breguet 14B-2 was a large tractor biplane capable of 121 mph, a ceiling of 19,000 feet and a range of 330 miles. Armament comprised one fixed Vickers and two or three flexible Lewis guns, plus up to 520 pounds of bombs.

Finally, on the Allied side, mention should be made of several outstanding Italian aircraft. The best of these was the Ansaldo SVA-5 strategic reconnaissance machine. This purposeful-looking tractor biplane first appeared in the autumn of 1917. Powered by an SPA-6A inline, it had an excellent top speed of 143 mph and an endurance of four hours. Ceiling was slightly under 20,000 feet. In the field of bombing, the firm of Caproni made a significant impression, producing a large number of types between 1915 and the end of the war. Most notable of these were the Ca-32, 33, 40, 41, 42, 43, 44, 45, 46 and 47. The Ca-42 was a triplane with twin booms holding the empennage (the early term for the tail unit). Power was provided by three Fiat, Isotta-Fraschini or American Liberty inlines of 270-hp each. Armament was up to four Revelli machine guns and 3,910 pounds of bombs. Speed was 87 mph and endurance 8 hours.

The chief American contribution to the technical side of the air war lay in the field of engines. A large range of

ABOVE *A Bristol F-2B, the war's best two-seat fighter. Armed with one fixed, forward-firing Vickers machine gun and one or two free-firing Lewis guns, it entered service in 1917.*
RIGHT *In* Closing Up, *by G. Davis, the outgunned British pilots form a pack prior to breaking off contact with the enemy.*

Liberty inlines was designed which, if the war had lasted into 1919, would have powered numerous types of Allied aircraft. The USA's own aircraft industry produced no worthwhile combat types of indigenous design during the war with the exception of the Curtiss America series of flying boats. The best of the series was probably the H-12 Large America. This was powered by two 275-hp Rolls-Royce Eagle inlines, and had a top speed of 93 mph and an endurance of 6 hours. It was used on anti-submarine patrols, and had a defensive armament of four Lewis guns and an offensive load of 460 pounds of bombs.

By 1918 the Germans had produced a considerable number of aircraft types designed for bombing or ground attack. The standard German bombers from 1917 onwards were the Gotha G-IV and G-V. These were large tractor biplanes, and from the spring of 1917 onwards the former took over from the Zeppelins the task of bombing Great Britain. Power was provided by two 260-hp Mercedes inlines, and although speed was not spectacular at 87 mph, ceiling and range, at 21,320 feet and 305 miles, were more impressive. The G-IV carried a bomb load of 1,100 pounds and was protected by two flexible Parabellum machine guns. However, in 1917-18 Germany produced some true giants. The most successful of these was the Zeppelin-Staaken R-VI. This had a wingspan of 138 feet $5\frac{3}{8}$ inches

(larger than the span of the Boeing B-17 Flying Fortress) and was powered by four 260-hp Mercedes inlines. Top speed was not good at 81 mph, but its endurance capability of 10 hours and bomb load of nearly 4,000 pounds were considerable.

In the field of ground-attack aircraft, Germany produced some most interesting designs. One of the earliest of these was the Halberstadt CL-II, a two-seat tractor-engined biplane that appeared in 1917 during the summer, and was soon supplemented by the improved CL-IV. Armament was three machine guns, and the type proved very effective in the German offensives of autumn 1917 and spring 1918.

One of the early pioneers of all-metal construction for aircraft was Dr Hugo Junkers, whose armoured J-I ground-attack machine appeared in the early summer of 1917. The J-I was a large two-seat tractor biplane with thick-section cantilever wings. Though heavy on the controls, the type was popular for the strength and protection of the metal construction. Its 200-hp Benz inline engine was not really enough for its considerable weight and size, and top speed was only 96 mph. But the armament of two fixed and one flexible machine gun was good. Better than the J-I, however, was the Junkers CL-I of 1918. This was developed from the all-metal D-I fighter, and was in effect a scaled-up version that took a crew of two.

How they flew

HM Government issues hints on aircraft handling and battle tactics to novice pilots.

Even at the very end of World War I, the art of flying was still understood only imperfectly. This lack of thorough knowledge, combined with the exigency of the training given to most novice pilots before their hasty dispatch to the sorely-pressed front, meant that many pilots lacked basic piloting and tactical skills. To remind them of what they had learned or to teach them some new development, therefore, the authorities from time to time commissioned drawings of aircraft handling and tactical factors for issue to the squadrons. These were also sent to training establishments.

Although there were a few great pilots on both sides who knew almost instinctively what to do in any given situation, in handling and in tactics, the majority of pilots desperately needed any information or hints they could get to cope with such eventualities. Illustrated are four lessons in handling and air safety. They describe the techniques of looping what to do in the event of engine failure and when land-

relegated to training.

However complete a pilot's training, though, the most dangerous episode in his operational career was always his first few days in combat. Here he tried to put the theory of his training into the practice of real combat, probably against more experienced opponents. It was in this phase of metamorphosis from total novice to experienced pilot that the care and hints of his co-pilots were of great use to the new man. Other pilots could give him hints on the ground, draw off a dangerous adversary in the air and perhaps set up a 'kill' for him. But most important was the disabusing of a novice of any erroneous ideas he might have–such as the utility of aerobatics in combat. Aerobatics rely heavily on relatively slow speeds combined with a long, predictable movement. Combat flying demands just the opposite–high speeds and a lack of predictability. There could be little more easy to shoot down than an aircraft at the top of a loop, hanging almost motionless in the air.

The CO of the British 34 Squadron wrote out a series of notes for his pilots. Their tone is informal but the elementary level of his advice betrays the lack of ex-

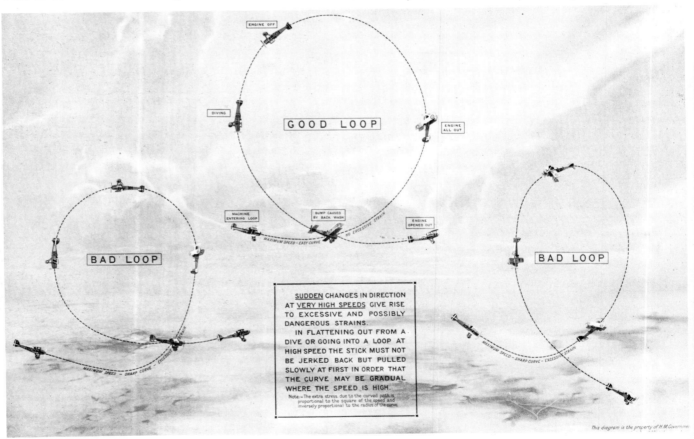

ing in hazy conditions, and a tactical lesson to be applied in combat.

The lessons were clearly useful (they were updated and expanded in scope in World War II, both by the Air Ministry and by individual squadrons or commanders). But what was really needed was a combination of two factors: a more systematic and energetic approach to the investigation of the problems of flight; and a more intensive and prolonged training programme for novice pilots, leading on to a course in operational aspects of flying with good instructors, rather than instructors who were for some reason or other unsuited for the front and therefore

perience among fighting pilots. For example: 'With the engine off the thing to avoid is gliding too slowly. At 65 mph or below, when gliding, the machine suddenly loses speed.' And: 'The machine gives very little indication of losing its speed until it suddenly shows an uncontrollable tendency to dive which cannot be corrected in time if you are near the ground.' Necessary words in the circumstances – but how much better if they had been rendered superfluous by a longer and more comprehensive training scheme. Such was the turnover in pilots, however, that any lengthier training schedule could well have jeopardized the outcome of the war.

IN CASE OF ENGINE FAILURE
DON'T TURN BACK — PUT HER NOSE
DOWN AT ONCE AND MAKE SOME
SORT OF A LANDING AHEAD.

1ST POSITION.
MACHINE CLIMBING
ENGINE FAILING.

2ND POSITION.
PILOT DECIDES TO TURN BACK
AND ENDEAVOURING NOT TO
LOSE HEIGHT STALLS MACHINE.

3RD POSITION
MACHINE OUT OF CONTROL
SPIN COMMENCING.

4TH POSITION.
SPINNING NOSE DIVE.

5TH POSITION.
CRASH.

This diagram is the property of H.M. Government
and is intended for Official use only.

How to loop, land
after engine failure
and in the dark, and
how to stay clear of
enemy gunners.

OPPOSITE 'Good and Bad
Looping': sharp curves at
high speeds can put excessive
strains on an aircraft; the good
loop is begun gradually, when
speed is greatest.
ABOVE 'Getting Off – Engine
Failure': an RE-8 wrongly
tries to turn back – with
disastrous results.
RIGHT 'Night Flying through
Mist or Haze': beware using
flares that create too much
dazzle and obscure the ground.
BELOW 'Outmanoeuvred':
how to prevent a hostile two-
seater from bringing its rear
gun to bear on your attacking
aircraft.

IF A LANDING MUST BE MADE
THROUGH MIST OR HAZE, IT IS
BETTER NOT TO USE THE FLARES.
EVEN A THIN AND RELATIVELY
TRANSPARENT MIST WILL APPEAR
A DAZZLING WHITE OPAQUE SHEET,
WHEN BRIGHTLY ILLUMINATED FROM
THE NEAR SIDE. – UNDER SUCH
CONDITIONS IT IS QUITE IMPOSSIBLE
TO SEE THE GROUND.

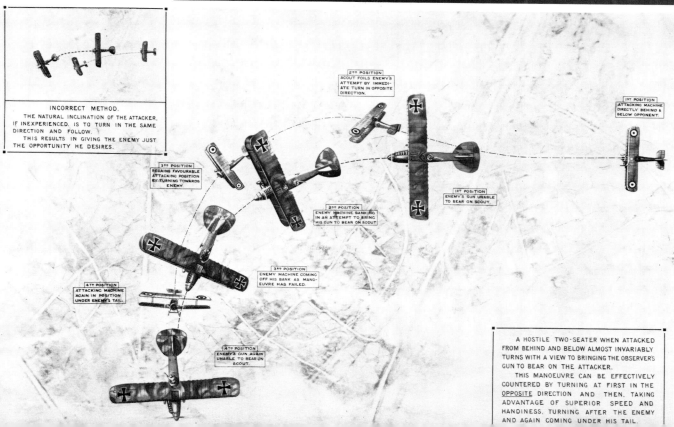

INCORRECT METHOD.
THE NATURAL INCLINATION OF THE ATTACKER,
IF INEXPERIENCED, IS TO TURN IN THE SAME
DIRECTION AND FOLLOW.
THIS RESULTS IN GIVING THE ENEMY JUST
THE OPPORTUNITY HE DESIRES.

1ST POSITION
ATTACKING MACHINE
DIRECTLY BEHIND &
BELOW OPPONENT.

1ST POSITION
ENEMY'S GUN UNABLE
TO BEAR ON SCOUT.

2ND POSITION.
SCOUT FOILS ENEMY'S
ATTEMPT BY IMMEDI-
ATE TURN IN OPPOSITE
DIRECTION.

2ND POSITION
ENEMY MACHINE BANKING
IN AN ATTEMPT TO BRING
HIS GUN TO BEAR ON SCOUT.

3RD POSITION
REGAINS FAVOURABLE
ATTACKING POSITION
BY TURNING TOWARDS
ENEMY.

3RD POSITION.
ENEMY MACHINE COMING
OFF HIS BANK AS MANO-
EUVRE HAS FAILED.

4TH POSITION.
ATTACKING MACHINE
AGAIN IN POSITION
UNDER ENEMY'S TAIL.

4TH POSITION
ENEMY'S GUN AGAIN
UNABLE TO BEAR ON
SCOUT.

A HOSTILE TWO-SEATER WHEN ATTACKED
FROM BEHIND AND BELOW ALMOST INVARIABLY
TURNS WITH A VIEW TO BRINGING THE OBSERVER'S
GUN TO BEAR ON THE ATTACKER.
THIS MANOEUVRE CAN BE EFFECTIVELY
COUNTERED BY TURNING AT FIRST IN THE
OPPOSITE DIRECTION AND THEN, TAKING
ADVANTAGE OF SUPERIOR SPEED AND
HANDINESS, TURNING AFTER THE ENEMY
AND AGAIN COMING UNDER HIS TAIL.

Staaken R.VI

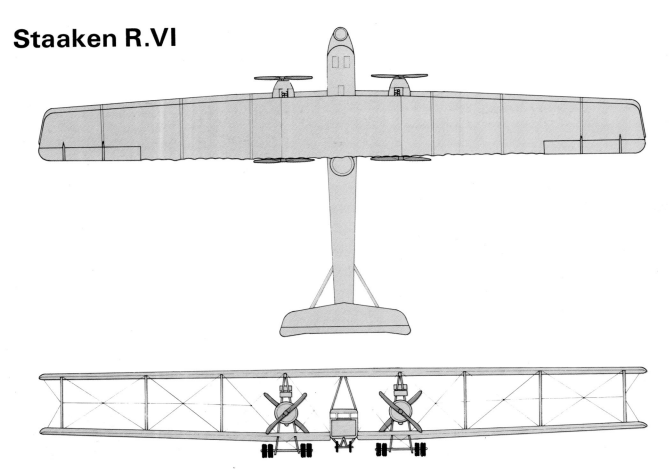

The enormous size of the R.VI is easily gauged when one remembers that each of the four propellors was some 14 feet in diameter. The aircraft illustrated is R.27/16 (Schul), which was accepted by the German air force in October 1917, and taken onto the strength of Rfa 501 on 23 January 1918. (Rfa stands for Riesenflugzeugabteilung or Giant Aeroplane Squadron.) It crashed-landed in Belgium on 7/8 March 1918.

SPECIFICATIONS

Type		seven-seater giant bomber
Engines		four Mercedes D.IVa 6-cylinder
		water-cooled inlines, 260-hp each
Armament		three or four .303-inch Lewis guns,
		plus up to 4,400 lbs of bombs
Speed	81	mph at sea level
Climb	55	minutes to 9,840 feet
Ceiling	12,470	feet
Endurance	8–12	hours
Weight	16,934	lbs (empty)
	25,269	lbs (loaded)
Span	138	feet $5\frac{1}{2}$ inches
Length	72	feet 6 inches
Height	20	feet 8 inches

Amongst the most remarkable and ambitious aircraft designed in Germany during World War I were the various 'R' machines and projects, the R standing for *Riesenflugzeug* or Giant Aeroplane. Nor was the appellation Giant untrue – the R.VI was the largest aircraft operated by the Germans against Great Britain in both world wars, and its structure marked an important step forward in the design of such large aircraft.

The Zeppelin works at Staaken entered the field of giant aircraft construction in 1914, and their first design, the V.G.O. I, first flew in April 1915. The culmination of four years of wartime work was reached in the R.VI, of which 18 were built. Basically, the fuselage and wings of the R.VI were fairly orthodox by the standards of the time, the construction being mostly of wood, with fabric covering. The tailplane, however, had an unusually large amount of aluminium embodied in its structure. The tricycle undercarriage, although simple in design, had no less than 18 wheels. Although the maximum bomb-load was 4,400 lbs, this could be carried over very short ranges only, and the normal load for a long-range raid, such as night missions over London, was in the order of 2,200 lbs. The R.VI was capable of dropping Germany's largest bomb of the war, a 2,205-pounder.

The first of the new machines to be delivered was the R.25/16, in June 1917, the second machine, R.26/16, following in July. Zeppelin-Staaken built only six R.VIs, the remaining twelve being built under licence (three by Schutte-Lanz or Schul, six by Aviatik, and three by Albatros).

The first R plane raid on Great Britain was made on the night of 28/29 September 1917, and in all 28 missions against British targets were flown, the last being on 19/20 May 1918. In the course of all the combat missions flown, 11 R.VIs were lost, although only three of these were attributable to direct enemy action, the rest being caused by operational accidents. No less than three R.VIs crashed on landing in fog on the night of 9/10 May 1918.

Most successful of the R.VIs was probably the Staaken-built R.39/16, dropping 57,000 lbs of bombs in 20 missions. R.39 also dropped the only three 2,205-pounders to be dropped on Great Britain during the war, but was shot down by the Poles on 4 August 1919 near Ratibor. The aircraft was being used to fly currency from Germany to the hard-pressed and short-lived independent republic of the Ukraine at the time.

Naval Aircraft

The aircraft used in the early days of World War I for operations over the sea were of simple design and were intended merely to scout for signs of enemy activity. For this both landplanes and floatplanes were employed, and of the latter type the Sopwith Schneider and Baby were typical. Single-seat tractor biplanes, they were little more than landplanes adapted for sea use with the addition of twin floats. The British continued to use them throughout the war for scouting and anti-Zeppelin operations.

Far more importance was attached to the floatplane by the Central Powers. In Germany the main producers of floatplanes were Friedrichshafen and Hansa-Brandenburg, who also supplied most of Austria-Hungary's machines. Friedrichshafen's most successful floatplane was the FF-33, which first appeared in 1915 and was built in a bewildering number of variants for patrol and escort duties. The FF-33l, of autumn 1916, was powered by a 150-hp Benz inline. Apart from its twin floats, it was a perfectly conventional tractor biplane and had a speed of 85 mph, an endurance of 6 hours and an armament of one fixed and one flexible machine gun.

Hansa-Brandenburg produced several very striking floatplane fighter and patrol aircraft under the design leadership of Ernst Heinkel. First came the KDW, whose biplane wings were braced with a star-shaped set of interplane struts. The type was mounted on twin floats and had a top speed of 107 mph with its 160-hp Maybach inline engine, and was armed with two fixed machine guns. The type was introduced in mid-1916 and was replaced a year later by the W-12 two-seater floatplane. Powered by a 150-hp Benz inline, the W-12 had a top speed of 100 mph and was armed with three machine guns. Heinkel's best design was the W-29, which appeared in mid-1918. This was a twin-seat twin-float monoplane, which could achieve 109 mph on the 150 hp of its Benz inline.

Most other countries in World War I opted for the flying-

ABOVE *A Sopwith 1½-Strutter takes off from a platform mounted over a gun turret on board the battlecruiser HMS* New Zealand *: this technique was first used successfully in April 1918.*
BELOW LEFT *The fore flight deck of the British carrier HMS* Furious *; the hinged palisades acted as a windbreak and protected the aircraft.*
BELOW *A Short seaplane is prepared for flight.*

Ship-borne aircraft are seen to hold the key to naval warfare; experiments with landing and take-off platforms.

boat configuration for their seaplanes. In Austria-Hungary the most common type was the Lohner Type-L patrol and reconnaissance machine, which entered service in 1915. It was a pusher type, with the engine mounted between the wings, the lower of which rested on the hull. Speed via the 160-hp Austro-Daimler engine was 65 mph, but endurance was 4 hours and up to 440 pounds of bombs could be carried – as well as a single machine gun.

Italy adopted the same sort of configuration as the Lohner on her Macchi floatplanes. One of these, the M-5, was a single-seat fighter that had the quite remarkable top speed of 117 mph on the 160 hp of its Isotta-Fraschini inline. Armament was two machine guns.

France also followed this configuration, and the FBA Type-H became the most widely built flying boat in the war. The Italian-built Type-H was powered by a 180-hp Isotta-Fraschini, which gave it a top speed of 87 mph. It carried one machine gun and a small bomb load.

Mention has already been made of the Curtiss flying boats, and from these were developed the best flying boats of the war, the British Porte-Felixstowe F-2A and F-3. The main failing of the Curtiss boats was the poor design of their hulls, and so the new aircraft's designer, Squadron Commander J. C. Porte of the Royal Naval Air Service, worked out a new hull shape and fitted more powerful engines. The result was a handsome-looking and very efficient and formidable anti-submarine and patrol boat. The F-2A was powered by two Rolls-Royce Eagles of 345

hp each, which gave it a speed of 95 mph and endurance of 6 hours; it was armed with seven Lewis guns and 460 pounds of bombs. The type entered service in 1917.

Most important of all in the long term, however, was the introduction of ship-borne aircraft. We have already seen that the first experiments were undertaken by the Americans, but the first landing on a moving ship was made by a British pilot in a Sopwith Pup on 2 August 1917. The British developed flying-off platforms on the turrets of capital ships and cruisers, but as there was no way of landing the reconnaissance aircraft back on the ship, the pilot had to ditch, which almost inevitably meant the loss of his machine. The British therefore began to conduct experiments with aircraft-carriers, the first of which, HMS *Furious*, made possible the historic landing mentioned earlier. Thereafter much ingenuity was devoted to producing aircraft that could land on the early carriers on skids which reduced their landing runs. By the end of the war the *Furious* had been converted from its early form with a taking-off platform in the bows and a landing-on platform in the stern to a single full-length flying-deck, from which ordinary wheeled aircraft could operate.

From now on, carrier-borne aircraft using bombs and torpedoes would become the arbiters of the war at sea. The first aeroplane to be designed specifically for carrier operations was the Fairey Campania floatplane, and with the introduction of torpedo planes such as the Sopwith Cuckoo, the era of the battleship was about to end.

PART 3
THE INTER-WAR
YEARS

11

NEW ROLES FOR ARMOUR

Legacies of World War I: Fuller's Plan 1919 and France's stockpile of 3,000 tanks.

In many of its later aspects World War I had evolved as a tank war – even though the cease-fire came before the true potential of the tank could be properly demonstrated. Had Fuller, for instance, been able to implement his famous Plan 1919 (see diagram) then Western Europe would have witnessed the deployment of tanks and aircraft on an unprecedented scale, and many of the questions left unanswered concerning the strategic potential of these new weapon systems would have been resolved. Instead these issues were destined to provide the forum for debate, speculation and eventually bitter controversy.

France had ended the war with the largest army and the biggest stockpile of tanks and she now led the field in tank tactics and deployment. However, the little Renault FT, which provided the bulk of France's 3,000 tanks, was suited only to an infantry-supporting role. In due course this great quantity of light tanks, coupled with problems of economic retrenchment, meant that French armoured doctrine was held back for more than a decade; the Renault FT, though an efficient tank in itself, became in effect a millstone to further progress.

In Britain Fuller launched the first salvo in the great debate with Plan 1919; thereafter he acted as the driving force in the tank lobby while the Royal Tank Corps (constituted in 1923 as a permanent body with four battalions) provided the battleground over which the arguments raged. In the beginning the military hierarchy gave little support to Fuller and his ideas on the strategic role of armour. The prevailing attitude towards peace, added to conditions of economic strain and the traumatic influence of the Great War, were factors hardly conducive to the promulgation of new doctrines. In 1924 the Tank Corps received its first post-war tank, the Vickers Medium Mark I. Armed with a cannon and a machine-gun in a fully revolving turret and with respectable endurance capabilities, it was the first tank which was able to translate Fuller's theories into practice.

These new plans for armoured warfare had begun to attract a lot of attention and one of the first to support them was Basil Liddell-Hart, a one-time career officer who in 1924 was forced into early retirement because of ill health.

In 1920 Liddell-Hart had rewritten the official infantry manuals in the light of the tactics used by the Germans in the spring offensive of 1918. After studying Fuller's ideas for an independent role for the tank he became convinced that the new infantry manuals were in fact better suited to the tank. In 1925 Liddell-Hart was appointed Military Correspondent of the London *Daily Telegraph*, and with Fuller's influence by that time on the wane he used this medium to continue the battle against an ambivalent General Staff. He also made profitable use of his many contacts within the War Office and generally acted as a pamphleteer, disseminating the ideas of others through his newspaper articles, and later through his books. He differed from Fuller in that he was far more involved in expounding the strategic potential of the tank, and unfortunately many of the tactical problems in his doctrine were often glossed over. Nevertheless this doctrine took shape and substance as the concept of the 'Indirect Approach', in which he evolved a method of attack which was designed to turn 'opportunism into a system'.

Looking ahead:
Liddell Hart's 'moving
torrent' theory,
using tanks to overrun
and paralyse the
enemy's HQ and
supply system.

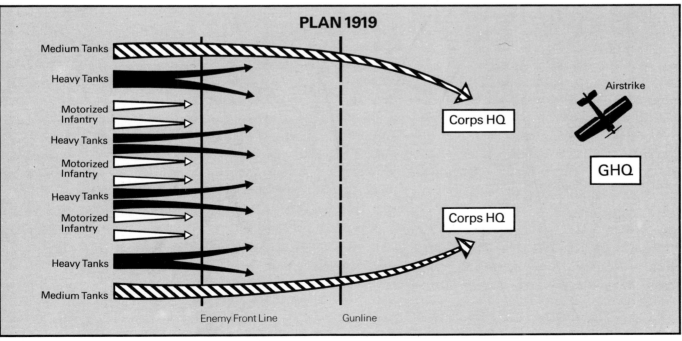

PLAN 1919

Medium Tanks

Heavy Tanks

Motorized Infantry

Heavy Tanks

Motorized Infantry

Heavy Tanks

Motorized Infantry

Heavy Tanks

Medium Tanks

Corps HQ

Corps HQ

Airstrike

GHQ

Enemy Front Line   Gunline

OPPOSITE *Colonel, later Major-General, J. F. C. Fuller, who at the end of the war led British thinking in the use of armour.* ABOVE *Fuller's Plan 1919 with which he planned to crush the enemy had the war continued beyond the turn of the year.* TOP *The Medium D tank that Fuller envisaged as his spearhead; in the event it never went into production. Designed for a speed of 27 mph, the Medium D's low profile announced a new generation of fast and manoeuvrable tanks.*

Liddell-Hart envisaged a moving torrent of tanks which would attack a fortified front along the line of least expectation, sapping, crumbling and eventually overwhelming strongpoints before pouring through to achieve strategic exploitation behind the enemy's lines. The object was to paralyse the 'brain' or central nervous system of the opposing forces (headquarters, supply dumps, etc.); this, Liddell-

Germany acquires tanks through a secret deal with the Soviet Union; the rise of Heinz Guderian.

Hart thought, could be achieved through the persistent pace and momentum of the advance. He saw infantry and artillery as providing support to the armour; when suitably mounted in their own vehicles the former would also be able to keep in touch with the advance. Additional artillery was to come from tactical air forces capable of providing instant and telling fire support to an army on the move.

The imaginative and highly persuasive writings of both Liddell-Hart and Fuller within a few years attracted new disciples to the 'cause', among them men of high calibre and vision like Hobart, Lindsay and Broad. But against this rising tide of reform was ranged the full weight of the stolid military hierarchy. This powerful body, although reluctant to concede ground, eventually in 1927 sanctioned the creation of an 'experimental brigade' to test the new theories (see diagram). Demonstrations were held on Salisbury Plain and witnessed by official observers from the United States and Europe; these proved an obvious success and the overseas observers returned home suitably impressed. However, the ravages of unemployment and the frightening financial disasters occurring all over the world prevented the much-needed reformation in the doctrine and deployment of tanks from being fully implemented. In 1929 Colonel Broad completed his official report on British tank experiments and the pamphlet, entitled *Mechanized and Armoured Formations*, was given a restricted circulation. But its contents leaked to the Press and, more ominously, were reproduced in their entirety in Germany, where they came into the hands of that country's leading exponent of tank warfare, Colonel Heinz Guderian.

The German Army of the Weimar Republic was restricted to 100,000 men and was denied the use of tanks, aircraft and heavy artillery under the Treaty of Versailles, signed in June 1919. This gave the Germans a small but distinct advantage in that they were not saddled with a great deal of obsolete equipment, as was the case with their former enemies. But the terms of the treaty also meant that any interest the Germans showed in new weapons had to be taken in a clandestine manner. The dire impact on morale of events in 1918 had provided a lesson which the new German Army, a small but élite force, was determined to benefit from, and in the early 1920s the Army set about acquiring its own tanks. In Sweden the Bofors Company built small quantities of a German tank, the LK II, under licence; but greater progress was made as a result of a secret agreement made with the Soviet Union. This marriage of mutual advantage resulted in the establishment of a tank school in Kazan, deep inside the Tartar Republic and beyond the scrutiny of the complacent Western powers. At first the Swedish-built tank was shipped into Russia and assembled at Kazan but in 1930 the Russians purchased the British Carden Loyd light tank from which was developed the Pzkw I (Panzerkampfwagen I).

Guderian had in the meantime become the leading expert on armour and mechanization in Germany, and by the time that Hitler finally emerged as the German leader after the 1933 putsch, he was in command of a motorized battalion and now in a position to experiment with the theories he had read about and evolved by himself with the help of dummy tanks and guns[1]. There was opposition from within the High Command to these new ideas but it never reached the same proportions as in Britain and France. Hitler attended one of Guderian's demonstrations and was immediately impressed with the potential which the tank offered. The Army was expanded and a significant

---

[1] Guderian was not a tank theorist of long standing. His ideas on mobility and mechanization first took root when he was a staff officer with the Army Transport Service. Remarkably, he did not see his first tank until 1929, when he visited Sweden.

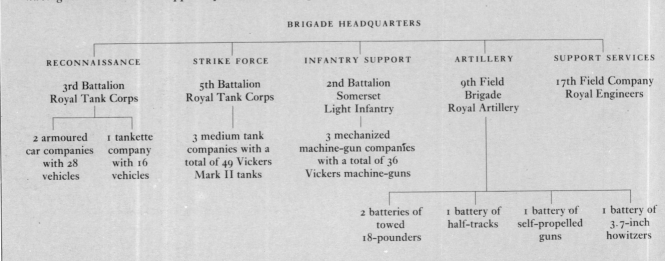

THE EXPERIMENTAL MECHANIZED FORCE 1927

The Force, assembled for demonstrations on Salisbury Plain, England, incorporated all the units of the different arms that had been mechanized by that date and were available for inclusion. It contained every important element of armoured formations of the future – with the exception of specialized vehicles for crossing gaps and clearing minefields. Although at little more than brigade strength, the Force was entirely self-sufficient, even to the extent of having its own RAF air support squadrons. Its composition is shown below:

BRIGADE HEADQUARTERS

RECONNAISSANCE	STRIKE FORCE	INFANTRY SUPPORT	ARTILLERY	SUPPORT SERVICES
3rd Battalion Royal Tank Corps	5th Battalion Royal Tank Corps	2nd Battalion Somerset Light Infantry	9th Field Brigade Royal Artillery	17th Field Company Royal Engineers
2 armoured car companies with 28 vehicles — 1 tankette company with 16 vehicles	3 medium tank companies with a total of 49 Vickers Mark II tanks	3 mechanized machine-gun companies with a total of 36 Vickers machine-guns		
		2 batteries of towed 18-pounders	1 battery of half-tracks — 1 battery of self-propelled guns — 1 battery of 3.7-inch howitzers	

Vickers Medium 1927

Production of the Vickers Medium tank began in 1923, and some 160 Marks I and II were built. In shape the Vickers Medium stands between the lozenge of World War I and the low profile of the modern battle tank. It was the first tank in the British Army to have all-round traverse and geared elevation for the gun.

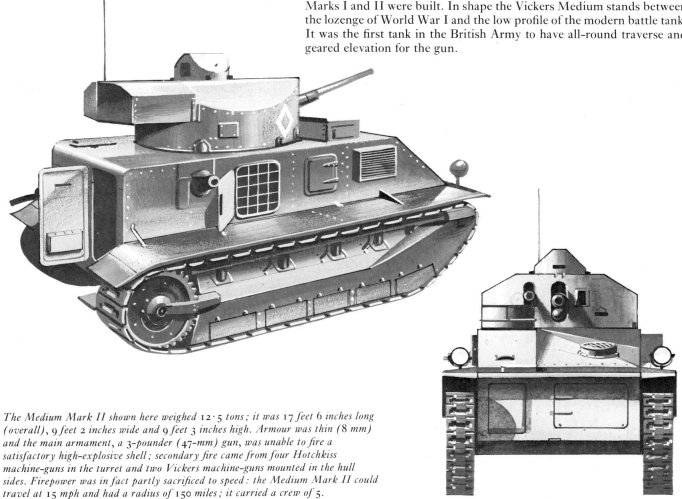

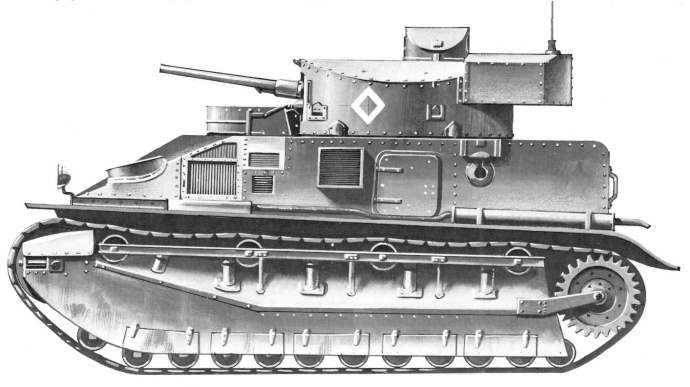

The Medium Mark II shown here weighed 12·5 tons; it was 17 feet 6 inches long (overall), 9 feet 2 inches wide and 9 feet 3 inches high. Armour was thin (8 mm) and the main armament, a 3-pounder (47-mm) gun, was unable to fire a satisfactory high-explosive shell; secondary fire came from four Hotchkiss machine-guns in the turret and two Vickers machine-guns mounted in the hull sides. Firepower was in fact partly sacrificed to speed: the Medium Mark II could travel at 15 mph and had a radius of 150 miles; it carried a crew of 5.

By 1935 Russia possesses the world's largest mechanized force; Britain and France are slower to exploit the tank's potential.

proportion of the new effort was devoted to creating new armoured, or Panzer, divisions; by 1935 three Panzer divisions were in existence and more were planned.

In the United States the National Defence Act of 1920 eliminated the wartime tank corps and merged tanks with infantry; the budget for tanks that year was 500 dollars. Many good officers and men deserted a lost cause and tank doctrine as such sank into oblivion. Not surprisingly the US Army, now sheltering behind illusions of geography and perpetual peace, was little interested in the work of Walter Christie, an American who designed revolutionary suspensions for tanks. Nevertheless a few experimental vehicles using the new suspension were developed: one of these, the M-1931 (or T-3), was years ahead of its time – but it was the Russians, not the Americans, who saw it.

The Russians purchased two of these tanks and from them developed their BT series and eventually the famous T-34. By the early 1930s the Russians had developed a powerful mechanized army which was masterminded by their leading tank expert, Marshal Tukhachevski. A Military Academy of Mechanization and Motorization was established and although Hitler abandoned the Kazan school the Russians continued to develop new tank designs

Meanwhile in both Britain and France the tank was still low on the list of priorities. The French relied for their salvation on the fortification of the Maginot Line and the British were chiefly gripped by an exaggerated faith in the power of the bomber – although they had in principle accepted mechanization as a substitute for horse cavalry. Britain had four major vehicle types: the tankette for machine-gun and mortar, the light tank (Vickers Mark IV) for reconnaissance, the cruiser tank (A-9 and A-10) for cavalry exploitation, and the infantry tank for close infantry co-operation. An armoured division was established in 1937 and was equipped with the cruiser and light tanks. These machines, however, emphasized mobility rather than mobility plus firepower, which severely restricted their capabilities. Their introduction reflected the current thinking of Elles, then Master-General of Ordnance. He had earlier been convinced that the anti-tank gun was superior to the tank and so had opposed any development of heavier armour along the lines the Germans had taken. But by 1930 he had begun to relent a little and in that year had ordered a new heavy infantry tank from Vickers (the firm which alone had survived the rigours of the inter-war years and now had a monopoly). Working to a strict budget

LEFT Mark I Panzers parade before Hitler on his birthday in 1937.
OPPOSITE, TOP The M-1931 tank designed by an American, Walter Christie. Although it made little impression in his own country, Christie's tank with its revolutionary suspension was taken up by the Russians, who bought two and from them developed their BT series, leading eventually to the famous T-34.
OPPOSITE, BELOW Russian BT-7-2 tanks at the Kiev manoeuvres of 1935.

of their own. By 1935 the Soviet Union possessed the largest mechanized force the world had seen, but the Stalin purges which followed decimated the ranks of 'progressive' officers. The old cavalry diehards now filled the vacuum left by Tukhachevski, the mechanized corps were disbanded and the tank was relegated to the subordinate task of co-operating with the rifle divisions.

Vickers produced the Infantry Tank Mark I: this had heavy armour protection but in other respects, with only a two-man crew and a machine-gun for the main armament, it was quite inadequate for combat. Nevertheless it went into quantity production and a battalion of the Royal Tank Corps took it to France in 1939. It was closely followed by the Mark II, better known as the Matilda; this

German firepower increases in the 1930s with the Panzers Marks III and IV.

was a bigger tank which possessed the same degree of protection and was armed with the excellent 2-pounder (or 40-mm) cannon.

Guderian's Panzers did not make the same mistakes as the British; even so, their main tank, still the Panzer Mark I, was more suited to training than to combat. But new tanks were planned and at least the armoured divisions contained infantry and support formations capable of operating at the speed of the tanks. As early as 1935 Guderian had seen the need for a medium tank armed with a 75-mm gun and shortly afterwards work began on the Mark IV tank, the last German tank to be developed before the war. In the meantime the Mark II, armed with a 20-mm gun, and the Mark III, which had a short-barrelled 50-mm gun, began to appear in the armoured divisions in increasing numbers.

The British, on the other hand, were totally committed

BELOW *The Russian T-26 light tank, adapted from the Vickers 6-tonner. The horizontal tubing is a wireless aerial; troops also used it as a handrail.*

ABOVE *The A-10 cruiser tank, one of the main British types developed in the 1930s; it was a cavalry tank, built to exploit breakthroughs in enemy lines.*
LEFT *French armour was relatively strong at the outbreak of World War II. One of the best types was the Somua, a fast 20-ton vehicle armed with one 47-mm gun and one machine gun.*
BELOW *The British Mark I infantry tank, predecessor of the famous 'Matilda'.*
OPPOSITE, BELOW *The Spanish Civil War (1935–39) was a major proving ground for Russian and German armour. Here rebel troops examine a captured Russian T-26C tank.*

186

BELOW *In mid-1939 the Russians gained invaluable battlefield experience in a border war in Manchuria against the Japanese. At that time a new hero of the armoured divisions emerged –* G. K. Zhukov, later the saviour of Moscow. In the photograph Soviet infantrymen advance with tank cover at Khalkhin Gol, where Zhukov won his first significant victory.*

Theories on armour crystallize; Guderian publishes *Achtung Panzer*.

ABOVE AND OPPOSITE *On the one side in* 1939 *stood the brave squadrons of Polish horse cavalry, descendants of the celebrated square-capped lancers of Napoleon's day. On the other were the German dive-bombers which rapidly claimed command of the air and so could give virtually unrestricted support to their Panzer divisions spearheading*

1 September 1939:
the Polish cavalry
blunt their lances
against Hitler's tanks.

Germans learned much about tactical air support.

The Russians, however, learned still more in Manchuria during a series of border clashes with Japan. There, in August 1939, a little-known tank general called Zhukov inflicted a major defeat on the Japanese at Khalkhin Gol in what was to become a blueprint operation for his great victories over the Germans at Stalingrad and Kursk.

On the eve of World War II none of the main protagonists had cause to feel completely satisfied with the quality of its tank formations. The French had belatedly entered the race and had 3,000 modern tanks deployed for war. Of these, the Somua was one of the best tanks in Europe. In terms of doctrine, however, French ideas were sadly backward: the bulk of the armour was still tied to the apron strings of the infantry while the three light mechanized divisions (each with 220 tanks and a brigade of infantry) inherited the tactics of the old French light cavalry and were deployed as a screen to the main body of the armies as, on the brink of war, they advanced into Belgium.

Even the Panzers, the élite of the Wehrmacht, were still a long way from Guderian's concept of a balanced armoured force: the infantry and support elements still lacked their armoured half-tracks and the supply units were road-bound. There were six Panzer divisions and four light divisions, making a total of 3,195 tanks, and it was they that spearheaded the advance of 44 divisions into Poland on 1 September 1939. The Luftwaffe easily achieved total air superiority and the ill-equipped Polish Army reeled back before the full onslaught of Blitzkrieg. The Poles had few tanks or anti-tank guns and though their massed brigades of horse cavalry charged the German tanks with suicidal bravery there was little they could do to prevent the invasion and swift overrunning of their country.

12
ARTILLERY: THE GREAT DEBATE

Artillerists in the West fall into complacency after World War I, disinclined to look at new ideas.

Dr Vannevar Bush, the brilliant scientist who directed the US Office of Scientific Research and Development during World War II, once wrote that 'there is something about the word ordnance that produces stodginess in its adherents . . . this is not a matter of this country alone; it seems to be a general affliction'. Although it is partly understandable in a peacetime situation, at no time was the 'stodginess', or conservatism, of the artillerist more evident than during the inter-war years.

A dangerous complacency appeared in the wake of World War I. To most observers, especially the French, the defence had triumphed decisively. Against this view the lessons inherent in the successes of the early tanks, the possibilities to be derived from coupling Bruchmüller's use of artillery with von Hutier's infiltration tactics, indeed any comprehension of a war of movement such as had just taken place in the Middle East and during the final Allied offensive, seemed beyond the capabilities of the general staffs of most nations. Ordnance development ground to a halt.

In Germany, however, there was no drag on development.

Even during the Weimar period, when the country's armed strength was limited by the Treaty of Versailles, there were those who planned for the day when Germany should once again assume her place as a major power. Much ordnance development during these years was of the 'black' variety, which is to say it was private and unsolicited by the army authorities.

These clandestine programmes surfaced and bore fruit after Hitler came to power in 1933. In due course the great munitions makers like Krupp and Rheinmetall functioned as easily under Hitler as they had under the Hohenzollerns; they even enjoyed a favoured position in German industry as the firms that were to bear the great brunt of German re-armament.

At that time the Germans had to rebuild their artillery from almost nothing. The Treaty of Versailles had stripped away most of Germany's World War I stock of guns on the pretext of denying her a war-making capability. What this in effect did was to remove the 'tail' of previous develop-ment – a large inventory of outdated guns which would otherwise have inevitably postponed new development.

Germany and Russia
hasten to build up
stocks of new guns;
revelations of the
Spanish Civil War.

As an example of how rapidly the German arms makers developed radically new guns we need only cite the story of the 88-mm anti-aircraft/anti-tank (AA/AT) gun Flak 18. Work on this versatile gun was officially begun in 1933– though there is evidence of co-operative 'black' development during the 1920s between the firms of Krupp in Germany and Bofors in Sweden[1]. By 1934 the first models of the '88' were delivered to the Wehrmacht, and when the gun was fully unveiled in the Spanish Civil War (1936–39), its capabilities astounded the military world. It was in this way that Germany entered World War II with a completely new range of artillery weapons, thoroughly modern and quite superior to that of any prospective rival.

Another nation steadily renewing her artillery was the Soviet Union. The Soviets opted for simple design, mobility and performance in their new family of guns; this policy helped them to rebuild at speed, and when, in June 1941, the storm of Operation Barbarossa broke on their western border, they were well on their way towards com-

[1] Bofors' projects during this period also included building LK II tanks under licence for the Germans.

OPPOSITE *A half-ton shell, delivered by trolley, is rammed into the breech during an American drill session.*
ABOVE *Manoeuvres with guns of 19th-century vintage (French '75s') at Fort Meyer, Virginia, in 1929.*
BELOW *German '88s'; these dual-purpose anti-tank/anti-aircraft weapons first tested in the Spanish Civil War here fire at Russian tanks on the Eastern Front; from a painting by Preuss.*
BOTTOM *Even after the invasion of Russia armies still relied on equipment developed several years earlier; an example is this German 37-mm Pak 35/36 anti-tank gun.*

pleting the process. Two main factors drove the Russians along in their re-equipment programme. One was the relative absence of modern medium and heavy artillery in the Czarist stockpile inherited by the revolutionary regime. The second was the growing likelihood of war with Hitler.

In the West, few artillerists questioned the uses of their guns, but one group that did was the Westervelt Board, a US study group which met in 1919. The Westervelt Board concluded that the light field guns which formed the bulk of any nation's artillery park were not especially useful. It recommended the replacement of the M-1897 75-mm guns of the US Army by a 105-mm gun-howitzer. The latter would combine the low-trajectory capability of the field gun with the ability of the howitzer to fire mid-angle 'searching' shots. By 1939 every Western nation but France had replaced field guns with gun-howitzers.

Anti-tank weapons represented a comparatively new field. As late as 1922, US artillery manuals described anti-tank guns as 'guns detached from batteries and pushed forward for individual use against tanks'. However, anti-tank gun development was not regarded as a top-priority matter and little real progress was made. Nevertheless, one project – the German Gerlich gun – deserves a closer look.

On 6 April 1942 a British newspaper correspondent covering the North African campaign filed a story on a new, 'particularly revolutionary' German anti-tank gun. The Allies had captured a diminutive, sleek-looking gun with a barrel that tapered from 28-mm at the breech to 21-mm at the muzzle. The revolutionary aspects of this gun were its coned-bore design and the tremendous muzzle velocity (over 4,000 fps) imparted to the tungsten-carbide projectile it fired. This gun was among the first produced which utilized the Gerlich-pattern barrel. Its super-high-velocity

projectile was capable of penetrating the armour of any tank in the world.

The story of the Gerlich gun begins in Weimar Germany. A Kiel engineer, Max Gerlich, had been tinkering with the application to field guns of the coned-bore principle, which had been used in hunting rifles for several decades. By 1933 Gerlich had perfected his gun. The extraordinarily high muzzle velocity was produced as the shell was forced down the barrel of the gun. The shell itself had a core of diamond-hard tungsten carbide. Around this core were a series of rings or flanges of a light alloy. The flanges conformed to the breech calibre, and, when the gun was fired, they were squeezed down into grooves behind them and around the core. This squeezing-down of the projectile as it travelled down the barrel concentrated an exceptionally long explosive impulse on the ever-decreasing base area of the shell. The result was a muzzle velocity much greater than that produced with conventional weapons.

The Germans, characteristically, disguised the development of their experimental Gerlich guns by putting about rumours of a high-velocity shell which they styled the 'Hagar Ultra Shell'. Strangely though, from the point of view of national security, Gerlich himself had travelled abroad on séveral earlier occasions to try and sell his invention to other nations. It seems, however, that only the German War Office was interested in his progressive ideas. The first production models of Gerlich's gun were built by Krupp in 1941, when it was designated as the 2·8-cm Schwere (heavy) Panzerbüchse 41.

With the exception of the experimental Gerlich gun development in Germany, most nations seemed content with what they had in the way of anti-tank guns during the 1930s. The day of the gun-armour race had not yet dawned,

and light anti-tank guns like the French Hotchkiss 25-mm gun were perfectly adequate against under-armoured early tanks – even though the latter's performance was laughable by World War II standards. The advocates of armour were not standing still, however, and where they had the ear of an attentive government, as in Germany and Russia, they were teaming up with designers to produce radical new tanks – heavier, faster and more powerful than many men imagined possible.

The result of these revolutionary developments in tank design and doctrine, combined with the staunch conservatism of the artillerists, produced some ghastly consequences less than a decade later. Many British anti-tank gunners in Libya, for example, were subjected to the unnerving and often fatal spectacle of German Mark III tanks stopping 600 yards from their emplacements (200 yards beyond the effective range of their 2-pounder AT guns) and pounding them with armour-piercing machine-gun fire which easily penetrated their gun shields.

Even the Germans, who led the world in anti-tank gun development during the 1930s, were not unsurpassable. They too were thrown into confusion when they encountered the first Russian T-34 tanks in 1941. These superb vehicles were the product of inter-war Russian tank design, and the Germans in effect never entirely recovered from the set-backs they experienced during the Russian winter of 1941.

The Spanish Civil War (1936–39) proved to be a sig-

OPPOSITE *The Gerlich gun: its tapering bore squeezed the projectile, imparting a much greater muzzle velocity.*
BELOW *Knocked-out Polish anti-tank guns, suddenly overwhelmed by the ferocity of the German onslaught levelled at them by land and from the air in September 1939.*

nificant rehearsal ground for World War II. The Soviet Union, supporting the Republic, and the Fascist powers of Germany and Italy, supporting Franco's Nationalists, all sent men and equipment to Spain. Hitler's Kondor Legion arrived with the latest products of Germany's rearmament programme, including light tanks, Stuka dive-bombers and the '88'. German weapons and tactical doctrine received a thorough test, and a few valuable lessons were learned. It was found, for example, that the map-firing stressed by artillery instructors was often best forgotten in real conditions; in combat it was the forward observer who became the key figure in directing a battery's fire. The Kondor Legion was also able to try out its new radio equipment, which added flexibility and increased the effectiveness of its guns. Previously, the time taken to lay the miles of telephone wire connecting the various field and gun commanders and the FOOs (forward observations officers) had been time wasted. Yet another lesson pointed to the ineffectiveness of counter-battery fire without aerial observation. Again, to be really successful, the Kondor Legion's commanders saw that in any future war there would have to be wireless communication between the guns and aircraft.

In the course of the Spanish Civil War anti-tank guns were used extensively for the first time. Here the light inter-war models proved adequate against the assortment of light tanks and armoured cars fielded by the belligerents. But no unified anti-tank doctrine was formulated, and stopping tanks was still a matter of luck more than anything else. Thus, when World War II began, none of the Great Powers had developed a clear-cut plan for dealing with masses of tanks; this was a near-disastrous flaw from which both sides were to suffer in the armoured conflicts to come.

The development of tanks in the 1930s outstrips that of guns capable of providing an adequate counter.

13

THE NAVIES REBUILD

Britain is ousted as the leading naval power by Japan and the USA.

By the end of World War I the bonds that had linked Britain, Japan and the United States were being loosened. The defeat of Germany and the destruction of her Navy in Scapa Flow did not lead to a general reduction of naval strengths. Instead, conflicting ambitions grew more and more apparent and, in the resulting atmosphere of suspicion and distrust, erstwhile allies began to look at each other as future enemies.

Although Britain was impoverished by the war, Japan and the United States emerged from it with greatly increased industrial power. Both, moreover, nurtured interests and ambitions in the western Pacific which the war had done nothing to reconcile; and by 1918 both nations had embarked on warship construction programmes whose products seemed destined to be used against each other at some unspecified date.

Earlier, in 1915, the Japanese had announced their '8–8' programme of 16 battleships and battlecruisers. These ships were to have a life expectancy of only eight years; in other words, they were scheduled to expire long before they were worn out. But if the Japanese then chose to build new ships at the end of the eight-year period without scrapping those already in existence, they could, within a decade, build a fleet so strong that it would completely dominate the Far East.

The USA, on the other hand, was determined to have a navy 'second to none', and to achieve this she had, in August 1916, ordered 10 battleships. Although only three had been laid down by the end of 1919, these at least kept pace with the Japanese in terms of armament: each now had the 16-inch gun.

Britain, meanwhile, sought equality with the other leading naval powers but was really in no position to maintain parity. Although after the war she had a numerical superiority, it was founded on 11 old capital ships, armed with 12-inch guns, that were in fact worn out, obsolete and in need of immediate replacement if she was to retain her relative position. Given her impoverished state, Britain could ill afford a massive building programme. However, developments in the Pacific forced her hand. In 1921 she laid down four 48,000-ton battlecruisers and programmed battleships with 18-inch guns – a move designed to counter Japan's proposed *Class 13* battlecruisers that were to have a 13-inch armour belt, 30 knots and eight 18-inch guns.

By 1921 the capital ships being built and projected would have cost the Great Powers over £250 million, and costs were rising. The USA, anxious to avoid a heavy programme

Inter-war treaties limited both the numbers and size of warships, and those nations that kept within the limits had to renovate their older ships and devise fresh concepts for their new ones. Thus, in an effort to save weight, British ships like the Rodney *(below), carried all their main armament forward in triple turrets, while the* Warspite *(right), emerged in 1937 totally transformed from her 1915 appearance.*

How the arms
limitation treaties
affected warship
design.

ABOVE *The Japanese battleship* Kongo.

ABOVE RIGHT *HMS* Argonaut, *a Dido class cruiser equipped with high-angle guns.*

RIGHT *The US battleship* Washington, *an inter-war design which incorporated nine 16-inch guns.*

OPPOSITE, TOP RIGHT *The German battleship* Bismarck, *laid down in 1936, puts to sea in 1941 on what was to be her last voyage.*

of construction, found herself in the fortunate (if paradoxical) position of being able, through her ability to outbuild her rivals if the need arose, to force the other nations into agreeing to limit their armaments. The British were willing enough to limit theirs, but the Japanese were less keen. Not only were the Japanese programmes nearer completion than those of the other nations, their statesmen also disliked the limit proposed for their navy and suspected, quite correctly, that there were racialist undercurrents in the common Anglo–American policy.

However, despite Japanese reservations, the Washington Treaty of 1921 fixed a balance between the fleets of the world and placed limits on the sizes of ships. With certain exceptions no capital ships were then laid down before 1931, by which time the Depression had emptied the world's treasuries and so delayed any new construction for a while. At the 1930 London Conference, new building was put back until after January 1937 – although France and Italy were each allowed two new ships. The Great Powers, meanwhile, were confined to refitting and rebuilding their existing ships.

The rebuilding programmes of the various navies followed roughly similar lines. Increasing concern about aerial and torpedo attack dictated a thickening of deck armour, increased bulges, augmented anti-aircraft defences and the fitting of aircraft and hangars into capital ships. The Japanese, with a smaller number of ships, rebuilt more extensively than did the Western navies. The *Nagato* was the most powerful ship in the world when she was completed in 1920. She was refitted in 1924 and rebuilt between 1934 and 1936. During the refit her distinctive pagoda bridge was given more platforms and her forward funnel was trunked; in the rebuilding phase, triple bottoms and increased bulges added to her passive defence whilst deck armour was doubled and turret protection increased by 50 per cent. The pagoda was extensively rebuilt and enlarged and the anti-aircraft armament was increased. The range of elevation of her 16-inch guns was raised to 43°. Tonnage increased by 6,300 tons but speed did not fall away because she was re-boilered and re-engined and changed over to oil. The rebuilding of all the big Japanese ships conformed to this basic pattern.

With the exception of the *California* and *Maryland* classes, the American ships were all rebuilt. Most of them lost their distinctive cage masts: in their place tripod superstructures were built up, and anti-aircraft defences were increased and the ships re-engined to burn oil. The British were less thorough. Many of the fast *Queen Elizabeth* class were ultimately rebuilt, but none of the *Revenge* ships was substantially altered[1]. Those British ships that were rebuilt failed to hold their speed as the American and Japanese ships had done; although their armour was thickened, little could disguise their all-round inferiority to their contemporaries. At the time the battlecruiser *Hood* was Britain's, and the world's, greatest warship; but despite this, and perhaps because of it, no major refit was completed before World War II. Her side armour was by then obsolete, and her deck armour was anyway minimal. Her graceful lines and fine profile did not make up for her lack of protection.

Italian and French ships contained several novel features. They were, by Pacific standards, under-protected. But whereas the Italian *Vittorio Veneto* was very well armed

with nine (3 × 3) 15-inch guns, the French *Dunkerque* and *Strasbourg* carried only 13-inch guns. There were eight of these, and they were all carried forward of the bridge, in the same manner as the *Nelson* class. The French ships could make 30 knots but the graceful, lightweight *Vittorio Veneto* could reach 35 knots.

The ending, in 1937, of the limitations on capital ship building led the nations once more to go their separate ways. The British, pressed by the deteriorating European situation, adopted the 14-inch gun for their new 33,000-ton battleships, which were laid down in 1937. Initially they were to carry 12 guns in three turrets, two forward and one aft, but the need for increased armour caused the superimposed forward turret to be reduced to a twin. In 1936 the Germans – who formerly had observed the limitations of the Versailles Treaty – laid down the *Bismarck* and *Tirpitz*. These ships followed the gun arrangement of the last German class to be laid down some 20 years before – eight 15-inch guns in four twin turrets. The Americans, on the other hand, combined the 16-inch gun with the triple turret; the new *Washington* class carried nine 16-inch guns. These very impressive ships displaced 35,000 tons,[2] carried 20 5-inch dual-purpose (DP) guns[3] and an 18-inch armour belt.

But even the Americans were dwarfed by Japan's new ships. Depending on quality to offset their inferiority in numbers, the Japanese built the *Yamato* and *Musashi*. Both ships were completed after the raid on Pearl Harbor (December 1941). They displaced 64,000 tons, made 27 knots and carried nine (3 × 3) 18·1-inch guns that could fire a 3,200-pound shell nearly 25 miles. The main belt was over 16 inches thick and turret-face armour exceeded 25 inches. Deck protection was up to 9 inches. Only 53 per cent of the waterline was covered by the belt but protection was augmented by having 1,147 watertight compartments. These two battleships, the only ones to be completed out of a class of four, were intended to be the last word in

---

[1] In fact by 3 September 1939 only *Warspite* had been rebuilt; *Barham* was barely altered; *Malaya* had a hangar added; the *Valiant* was commissioned in October 1939, and the *Queen Elizabeth* in July 1940.
[2] The 35,000-ton figure is the one given in the US Navy lists, but it seems that this is a deliberate understatement. It is hard to see how ships with these characteristics could displace so little when other nations were exceeding 35,000 tons for ships of lesser power.
[3] Dual-purpose guns could be used in two capacities – anti-ship and anti-aircraft.

Mid-1930s: the carrier race begins; specialized aircraft are built for naval duties.

battleship design, exceeding as they would any American ship capable of using the Panama Canal. Unfortunately for the Japanese, by the time they were built they were obsolescent; the balance of power had shifted to the carrier and its aircraft.

Until 1939 the Royal Navy retained a numerical superiority in aircraft carriers over any other navy. This failed to disguise, however, the obsolescence of her carrier aircraft and their small numbers as compared to the American and Japanese navies. And although the carriers themselves were numerous, they were small in carrying capacity. HMS *Eagle* (22,600 tons) carried a maximum of 21 aircraft, and the *Courageous*, despite having been programmed for 52 aircraft, could handle only 33. Such figures seem especially low beside their Japanese and American counterparts. The *Kaga* may be taken as representative of Japanese carriers: she, like many of the earlier carriers, was a converted capital ship; she displaced 27,000 tons and carried 60 aircraft. A refit between 1934 and 1935 added another 11,000 tons and space for 30 more aircraft. Meanwhile the Americans had the *Lexington* (36,000 tons), which carried 72 aircraft – and later was able to carry 90.

When building restarted in the mid-1930s, the same pattern was repeated. Although the 22,000-ton British carrier *Ark Royal* could handle 60 aircraft, the Japanese *Hiryu* (only 16,000 tons), could carry 13 more and the USS *Enterprise* (20,000 tons) operated 80. Unfortunately for the British, further ground was lost with their next carriers, the *Illustrious* class. The first of this class carried only 36 aircraft on 23,000 tons. On the other hand, British carriers were more heavily armoured than those of other nations. American carriers were protected only along the waterline and over machinery spaces; the *Illustrious* had heavy flight-deck protection (3 inches) and the magazines and hangars were protected by 4·5 inches of armour. However, in view of the weakness of Britain's carrier

aircraft, the carriers needed this protection.

Until the entry of the monoplane into service, Britain's inferiority in the air was not too marked either in terms of quality or quantity; but Japan and the USA had meanwhile pressed ahead in the theory and practice of carrier operations. The two Pacific powers were conscious that aircraft would be very important in the future and might play an independent role in the next war; whereas the British saw the aircraft as a support for the battleship and not as a possible threat to its superiority. Furthermore, the Japanese and Americans were conscious of the need for specialized aircraft, and recognized the need for dive-bombers, torpedo-bombers and fighters. The British tried to make their aircraft double up on duties, with the result that their performance was substantially inferior to those of the other powers.

From 1936 onwards the Royal Navy's difficulties increased: while other navies were equipped with monoplanes her own partner, the Royal Air Force, took most of Britain's modern aircraft. In 1939 the Royal Navy had only one type of monoplane in service. This was the Skua, a multi-role aircraft unable to discharge any single task well. The recce aircraft was the Osprey, a two-seater biplane introduced in 1932. Land-based aircraft were similarly inferior to contemporaries and the shortage of aircraft was crippling. In 1939 the Royal Navy had 300 aircraft; by comparison, in 1941 – when they went to war – the Americans had over 5,000 and the Japanese over 3,200.

Perhaps it was inevitable that once the Washington Treaty had limited their battlefleets the nations should attempt to outbuild one another in cruisers, which, though limited by the Treaty in terms of displacement (10,000 tons) and gun power (8-inch guns), were not for the time being limited in numbers built.

The Japanese and Americans both built up to and beyond Treaty limitations. The former began with the *Kako* class, laid down in 1922. These ships mounted

A loophole in the Washington Treaty encourages the mass construction of cruisers; Germany designs the pocket battleship.

ABOVE *The American carrier* Lexington; *built to handle 72 aircraft, her capacity was later increased to 90.*
OPPOSITE *Two carrier profiles. Above is HMS* Illustrious, *below is the Japanese ship* Shokaku, *heavily armed against attack from the air.*

7·9-inch guns in single turrets (these were doubled in a refit in 1939). Then, with the *Ashigara* class, the Japanese exceeded Treaty limits from the outset. The four ships of this class displaced 10,900 tons (after a 1940 refit over 13,000 tons) and carried 10 7·9-inch and six 4·7-inch guns. Twelve torpedo tubes and two aircraft completed an impressive offensive capability. The ships could make over 35 knots and had up to 5 inches of deck armour and a 4-inch belt.

The Americans built roughly similar craft. In the *Pensacola* class 10 8-inch guns were fitted in twin and triple turrets; later the *Northampton* class carried weight-saving triple turrets which gave these 9,000-ton cruisers nine 8-inch guns. When the Japanese moved to smaller guns for their cruisers the Americans immediately followed. The *Mogami*, laid down in 1931, carried 15 (5 × 3) 6·1-inch and eight 5-inch DP guns; but this proved to be to the detriment of stability and she was subsequently given a main armament of 10 8-inch guns. The *Brooklyn* carried the same number of 6-inch weapons. However, the Americans did not follow the *Tone* class. These unique Japanese cruisers carried all their armament forward and operated five aircraft from a clear flying-off deck aft.

The British, on the other hand, were reluctant to build cruisers with 8-inch guns simply because that was the maximum size that could be laid down. However, afraid of becoming completely inferior in gun power, they were eventually prompted to build some maximum-size cruisers. The *County* class cruisers all carried eight 8-inch guns; but the *York* class had six 8-inch guns and subsequent cruisers, with the exception of the *Dido* class, carried 6-inch guns. The British, with both European and Pacific commitments in mind, opted for numbers rather than for having a few very powerful ships.

German shipbuilding policy in the late 1920s indicated a preference for powerful commerce-raiders. The *Leipzig* and the *Köln* class carried powerful 5·9-inch armaments within the 6,000-ton limit imposed in 1919 by the Treaty of Versailles. In the 1930s the British responded with the *Leander* class, which had eight 6-inch guns, and the *Southampton* and *Belfast* classes. The latter carried 12 6-inch guns and had an armour belt theoretically capable of standing up to 8-inch gun fire.

Protection was never a priority of Italian design. Speed, though, was a permanent fetish, and the Washington Treaty cruisers were no exception. The *Trento* had a top speed of over 36 knots and the *Zara* made 34 knots – about the same speed as Italy's latest battleship.

In 1929 the first of a new type of cruiser was laid down by Germany. Under the Treaty of Versailles Germany could replace ships over 20 years old but capital ships were not to exceed 10,000 tons. The new cruiser, the *Deutschland*, was called a pocket battleship and was in the capital ship class, but she was designed for commerce-raiding. The three ships of this class exceeded their limitation figure by 1,700 tons despite weight-saving devices. Triple turrets carried six 11-inch guns, which were capable of a broadside of 4,020 pounds at 30,000 yards. Her diesel engines produced 27 knots, which meant she could outrun all but

New submarines and light surface craft emerge; among the latter are destroyers, sloops and corvettes.

a few ships and outshoot any Washington Treaty cruiser. Her 3,280-ton fuel capacity gave her a 10,000-mile radius at 20 knots.

In light surface craft the needs of Britain differed substantially from those of Japan and the USA. The Japanese and Americans were more interested in fleet destroyers than in the destroyer escorts, sloops and corvettes which were of great importance to the British. After 1937 British construction was increasingly slanted towards sloops and corvettes (and after 1940 towards frigates, which were enlarged oceanic corvettes); all these types were smaller, cheaper and quicker to build than destroyers. Although sloops and corvettes were slower than destroyers this was no great disadvantage because the performance of Asdic fell away at speeds above 20 knots. Furthermore, these ships were more manoeuvrable and had smaller turning circles than destroyers – important considerations when hunting submarines. Their anti-aircraft and anti-submarine capabilities were in fact superior to those of destroyers, for the latter were designed with emphasis on speed, gunnery and torpedo armament.

Most of Britain's destroyer construction was to a standard 1,300-ton displacement until 1935. But because the Americans and Japanese were building much larger and more powerful ships, the British were forced to follow suit. The result was the *Tribal* class: these ships displaced 1,900 tons and doubled the main and AA armaments of previous classes – though at a corresponding cost to the torpedo armament. Unfortunately the *Tribals* were too expensive to be repeated and subsequent classes were smaller and had something like the old balance of armament. The *J* and *K* classes were unique because their longitudinal construction and a reduction in the number of boilers meant that they had single funnels; the *L* class was the first to have dual-purpose guns.

At the outbreak of the Pacific War, the US Navy had 171 destroyers in service of which 100 had been built after 1932. The remainder were World War I vintage and of the 'flush-deck' variety, 50 of which were sold to Britain in 1940. The modern destroyers conformed to a basic 5-inch gun and torpedo-tube armament; these were carried centre-line. The most important single factor about these destroyers was that, beginning with the *Gridley* class, American destroyers, which already had a very long range of 9,000 miles at 15 knots, were able to refuel at sea. From the mid-1930s the Americans were breaking away from a land-based fleet in favour of a navy supported by a fleet train.

Japanese destroyers were, not unnaturally, very similar to their US contemporaries. Those built after World War I carried 4·7-inch guns (the same 47-pounder weapon carried in the British *V* and *W* classes). Later the larger destroyers carried a 5-inch gun but the *Type B* destroyers, though they displaced 2,700 tons, carried 3·9-inch guns. This very powerful gun had a high rate of fire and outranged the contemporary American 5-inch weapon.

Japanese submarine construction fell into three categories. In the 1920s Japan built short-ranged craft with a 20-day endurance and a maximum range of about 10,000 miles. During the 1930s longer-ranged craft were built. The *KD-6A* and *KD-6B* classes had a 45-day range with a 14,000-mile radius of action; this was subsequently increased with the *J-2* and the *J-3* class, which could operate for two months. The *A-1* type, laid down in 1938, had a 90-day range. During the inter-war period, too, some very long-range submarines were built. A 2,430-ton

OPPOSITE, FAR RIGHT *The German cruiser* Köln, *designed to fall within the 6,000-ton limit imposed on German shipbuilding by the Treaty of Versailles. She carried powerful 5·9-inch guns in the main armament.*
ABOVE *The German commerce raider* Deutschland; *laid down in 1929, she was the first of a new type referred to as 'pocket battleships'; her main armament consisted of six 11-inch guns. She is seen here at Gibraltar in 1937.*
BELOW *A Japanese J-class submarine, built in the 1930s for long-range duties in the Pacific.*

submarine with a 20,000-mile range was completed under the 1919 Programme, but she was not successful. The development of the *M* class by the Royal Navy prompted the Japanese to build a similar type of craft, i.e. one of long range that could carry a seaplane. The *J-1* class carried a seaplane and had a range of 25,000 miles. Throughout the 1930s there were various Japanese yards building seaplane-carrying submarines, but with the passing of time their popularity was eroded; an important factor was that the aircraft could only be used at a cost of imperilling the parent vessel. This did not stop the construction, during World War II, of the super *STo* class. These were the largest conventionally powered submarines ever built; displacement exceeded 6,500 tons and their range was 37,000 miles. They carried three seaplanes and were intended for a raid against the Panama Canal – which never in fact took place.

In virtually every aspect of her equipment, the Imperial Japanese Navy was very powerful at the outbreak of World War II. Her naval aviation and carrier force, though smaller than that of the Americans, was of extremely high quality and had combat experience; the lighter craft were also formidable though, alas for the Japanese, deficient in numbers. But, irrespective of ranges, speeds and gun armament, the most impressive aspect of Japanese destroyers, cruisers and submarines (and their aircraft) was their torpedo armament. In 1933 the *Type 33* torpedo entered service: this was the famous Long Lance, a weapon infinitely superior to anything the British and Americans possessed. Driven by oxygen and leaving no track, it had a 25-mile range at 36 knots and a 49-knot speed over $13\frac{1}{2}$ miles. British and American torpedoes, by comparison, could make 46 knots over $2\frac{1}{2}$ miles or 30 knots over 6·25 miles; their warheads were not more than 320 kilograms against the 500-kg warhead carried by the Japanese weapon.

Japan builds giant seaplane-carrying submarines, and in the Long Lance has the best torpedo of all the naval powers.

WORLD WAR II

The Balance of Power at Sea, 1939–41

Germany, France and Britain were at war from September 1939; Italy entered the war the following year. In June 1941 the Soviet Union was invaded by Germany and in December the war was extended into the Pacific following Japanese attacks on Pearl Harbor and on European possessions in the Far East.

CATEGORY	GERMANY	FRANCE	BRITAIN	ITALY	USSR	JAPAN	USA
Battleships	2*	6	12	6	3	10	17
Battlecruisers	2	—	3	—	—	—	—
Seaplane carriers	—	1	2	1	—	3	—
Aircraft carriers	—	1	7	—	—	10	7
Heavy cruisers	4*	7	15	7	1	18	18
Light cruisers	5	12	47	12	9	18	19
Destroyers	17	70	159	61	59	113	171
Escorts	8	—	38	83	—	—	—
Submarines	57	77	38	98	?	63	112

* Pre-dreadnoughts.

14

EXPERIMENTS IN THE AIR

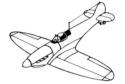

After the 'war to end all wars', governments leave aeronautical progress to a few committed individuals.

World War I had been a shattering experience, and after it the world moved into a new era. Millions had died, and the cost had been all but incalculable; yet perhaps more important still, the Victorian way of life had been demolished, giving way to a new social order and a new manner of thinking.

World War I had been the 'war to end all wars', and so it was inevitable that post-war politicians would not countenance further expenditure on armaments: the world's armed forces would have to make do for the time being with the left-overs of the Great War. This post-war retrenchment was nowhere more apparent than in the air forces of the victorious Allies. A few of the experimental designs produced right at the end of the war were kept in development as test vehicles, but all other development was dropped by the military; electorates, via their governments, would not sanction further expenditure on armaments.

Of necessity this left the immediate future of aeronautical progress to the few enthusiastic manufacturers and pilots prepared to devote themselves to this labour. The next ten years, therefore, were to belong to the experimental, record, and racing aeroplane. The scene was set soon after the war by the first transatlantic flights. The first, from west to east, was achieved by a Curtiss NC-4 flying boat commanded by Lieutenant-Commander A. C. Read of the US Navy. This was an indirect crossing via the Azores, and took 12 days (16–27 May 1919). Far more significant, however, was the first non-stop crossing, by Captain J. Alcock and Lieutenant A. Whitten-Brown in a converted Vickers Vimy bomber. They took off from Newfoundland on 14 June 1919 and crash-landed in Ireland some 16 hours later. It was to be as a result of endeavours such as this that the torch of aeronautical advance was to be kept alight in the lean 1920s. New military aircraft did, of course, make their appearance, but the significant advances were almost exclusively in the field of civil aviation, as we would now call it.

Great strides were made in the field of aircraft structures in the first few years after the end of World War I. One of the most important of these was the gradual swing away from the braced biplane formula to the cantilever monoplane, with its considerable aerodynamic advantages of reduced

drag and simpler maintenance problems. The leaders in this field had emerged in Germany in the closing stages of the war: Reinhold Platz of the Fokker company and Hugo Junkers. The former favoured a high-mounted thick-section cantilever wing of wooden construction and the latter a low-mounted planform, again of thick section, but made of metal and covered with corrugated metal skinning for strength and rigidity. In the long run Junkers's low wing proved superior, but not until a series of high-wing Fokkers had achieved immortality with a succession of stupendous record-breaking flights.

The lean 1920s: designers move towards cantilever monoplane structures and all-metal aircraft.

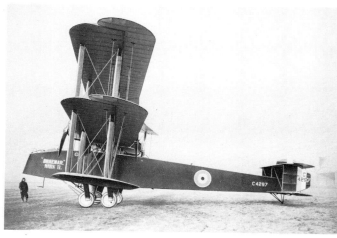

OPPOSITE *The Vickers Vimy, in which Captain Alcock and Lieutenant Whitten-Brown made the first non-stop Atlantic crossing, takes off from Newfoundland on 14 June 1919; the journey to Ireland took them 16 hours.*
TOP *Andrei Tupolev, the Russian designer, in 1923 stands with an arm resting on the side of his ANT-1 aircraft.*
CENTRE *A 1922 photo of the Bristol Bullfinch single seat fighter.*
ABOVE *The Bristol Braemar, a heavy triplane bomber that became ready for service shortly before the 1918 Armistice.*

The main failing of the Junkers idea was not in its basic design philosophy but in the structure, with its corrugated skinning. Although an improvement on the biplane type, the skinning still resulted in a high drag factor; this was recognized by Adolph Rohrbach, who devised a structure based on strong box spars covered with a load-bearing smooth metal skin. In doing so he laid down a pattern that was to recur in most military aircraft up to 1945.

As important as the introduction of the low cantilever wing was the pioneering of all-metal construction and the monocoque fuselage. Metallurgical advances in the 1920s resulted in an ever-increasing number of high-strength alloys, which allowed aeroplane structures in metal that produced both savings in structural weight and general improvements in performance. The monocoque fuselage, in which the more conventional longerons-and-frames structure with a canvas or light metal aerodynamic skinning gave way to a series of frames linked by stringers and covered with a load-bearing skinning, had appeared in the pre-World War I Deperdussin racer. It then found increasing favour in the post-war years, being universally adopted in the 1930s. An important milestone in this direction was the Short Silver Streak of 1920. This was an all-metal biplane with a monocoque fuselage which started the trend in Great Britain towards metal construction.

While all-metal construction and the low monoplane planform were still in the development stage in the 1920s, the pace in the new and fast expanding field of civil transport was set by the early Fokker high-wing monoplanes such as the F-II. This design philosophy reached its culmination in the Lockheed Vega, which first appeared in 1927: of wooden construction, it had a monocoque fuselage and was powered by a 435-hp radial engine, a type that was just about to enter its heyday in the United States. The Vega could carry six passengers up to 900 miles at a speed of nearly 140 mph.

It is worth noting here an apparent divergence between the United States and Europe in the field of power-plants. In the United States the air-cooled radial engine was fast becoming the most important type of power-plant. It was relatively light for its power, mechanically simple, and capable of considerable development. Its main failing, however, was the large frontal area presented to the airflow, and all its attendant drag problems. In time the Americans managed to minimize these problems with the carefully tailored low-drag cowlings that became a special feature.

In Europe there was a greater preference for the liquid-cooled inline engine, although several notable radials were developed by the French Le Rhône and British Bristol companies. The advantage of the inline, to European eyes, was its small frontal area, which allowed for a smooth, low-drag nose.

In the purely military sphere design still tended to lag behind the more advanced civilian types, and fighter aircraft were little more than World War I types updated and fitted with more powerful engines. Classic examples are the British Gloster Gamecock and the Bristol Bulldog, and the American Boeing PW-9 series and the Curtiss Hawks. The mainstays of the bombing forces, despite pressure from the strategic bombing lobby, continued to be types such as the wartime British de Havilland DH-4 and -9, and the American Martin MB-2/Curtiss NBS-1, all of which were large and ponderous biplanes.

As we have noted, it was in the field of racing and record-breaking aircraft that many of the major technical innovations were first introduced. A typical example is the development of the retractable undercarriage, which brought further advances in drag reduction. The idea did not appeal to the military at first, however, because of the complexity and weight of the retraction system. The first retractable undercarriage to appear in the United States was fitted to the Dayton-Wright RB racer of 1920; Great Britain followed in 1922 with the spectacular Bristol mid-wing monoplane racer. But is was not until the arrival of strong light-weight alloys, and incontrovertible proof had been obtained that streamlining requirements at very high speeds made retractable undercarriages necessary, that the military authorities would countenance them.

Most famous of all the air races in the years between the two world wars was the Schneider Trophy series for seaplanes. It is hard to overestimate the importance of this series in Europe and the Pulitzer series in the United States in the way they forced technological progress along, and so kept aviation in the public eye during the austere years of the 1920s.

The two major improvements directly attributable to the Schneider Trophy races are streamlining and the development of powerful inline engines. The 1925 race was the last to be won by a biplane, the beautifully streamlined Curtiss R3C-2 flown by Jimmy Doolittle of the United States. From that date the series hotted up considerably. The Italians won the race in 1926 with a Macchi monoplane, and then the first of the justly celebrated series of monoplane seaplanes designed by a Briton, R. J. Mitchell, entered the scene. In 1927 the race was won by one of Mitchell's Supermarine entries, the S-5, developed from the previous year's unsuccessful S-4. The S-5 was powered by an 800-hp Napier Lion, and won at a speed of 282 mph.

The aircraft were by now taking so long to build that it was decided to hold the races every other year instead of every year, so Mitchell had two years to think about his next

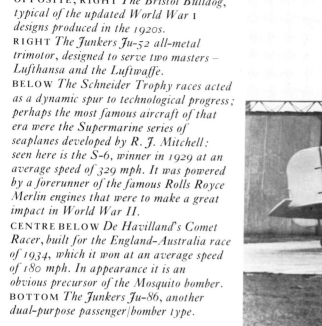

design, the S-6. This was an impressively trim little machine
(powered by the ancestor of the Rolls-Royce Merlin engine
that was to win so much renown in World War II) and it won
the 1929 race at a speed of 329 mph. Later this type pushed
the world air-speed record up to 357·7 mph. The final
Schneider Trophy race was won by Great Britain in 1931
with an improved version of the S-6, the S-6B, which went
on to increase the world speed record to 407 mph.

Meanwhile the military machines of the period were considerably less rapid. In fact the premier fighter of the day,
the British Hawker Fury, introduced in 1930, was the first
military aeroplane in the world to have a top speed of over
200 mph. Comparable military machines of the period were
the French Dewoitine D-27, with a top speed of 194 mph,
and the remarkable Grumman FF-1, an American carrier-
borne design. This was first flown in 1931, had a retractable
undercarriage and a top speed of 201 mph.

The years 1927 and 1928 marked a prolific time for
record-breaking in the sphere of long-distance flying. Quite
apart from spurring on the development of powerful and
reliable engines, such flights were also of special importance
in proving navigation techniques and testing theories of fuel
economy. First came one of the most celebrated flights of all
time – Charles Lindbergh's epic solo non-stop flight from
New York to Paris. He took off in his Ryan Spirit of St Louis
on 20 May 1927 and landed in Paris the next day after a
flight of 3,600 miles.

Then in 1928 a Junkers Bremen flew across the Atlantic
under the command of Captain H. Köhl for the first non-
stop east-to-west crossing – a particularly difficult feat
because the prevailing winds are westerly. In May and June
of the same year, a Fokker monoplane named Southern
Cross was flown across the Pacific in stages from California
to Australia by a crew led by Sir Charles Kingsford-Smith.
These are only the most celebrated flights. At the same time,
pioneers were proving long-range commercial air routes,
and so laying the foundations not only of the present world-

The 1930s: a new generation of military aircraft is born: civilian racers become tomorrow's fighters; Germany builds dual-purpose passenger/bombers.

OPPOSITE *The Boeing 247 transport, a true forerunner of today's low-wing monoplane commercial aircraft; the 247 made its appearance in 1933.*
RIGHT *German Junkers Ju-87 Stukas, or dive-bombers, in the colours of the Condor Legion in the Spanish Civil War (1936-39).*
BELOW *One of the spearheads of Britain's out-of-date air force in the mid-late 1930s was this biplane fighter, the Gloster Gladiator.*
BELOW RIGHT *First of Britain's modern fighter types – the Hawker Hurricane, a low-wing monoplane armed with eight machine guns and capable of 325 mph. Like the Stukas it had an enclosed cockpit.*

The pace in the early 1930s continued to be set by civil developments, both commercial and record-breaking. As we have noted, the Supermarine S-6B won the Schneider Trophy outright for Britain in 1931, and did so with a winning speed of 341 mph. Yet considerably more official effort was devoted in those days to winning a series such as the Schneider than was given to other record-breaking; we can see this by comparing the S-6B's winning speed and the world landplane speed record set up in 1932 by the American Gee Bee 7-11 Super Sportster – a mere 294 mph.

Another classic aeroplane appeared in 1934 in the form of the de Havilland Comet racer, designed for the England–Australia race of that year. The design connection between it and the Mosquito bomber of World War II is unmistakable.

During the early 1930s the leaders in the field of civil transport continued to be the Europeans, with such designs as the Fokker F-XVIII and the Junkers Ju-52/3 trimotors of 1932 and 1931 respectively. Also notable in the early days of this decade was the four-engined Junkers G-38, which paved the way for a forthcoming generation of long-range four-engined airliners, and later bombers. In fact, as Hitler's power in Germany increased, more and more of that country's newer civilian designs bore the clear signs of a dual-purpose philosophy: while there was peace they could serve as airliners, but in war they could be pressed into service as transports and bombers. Typical of this concept were

wide air communications industry, but also of the long-range bomber techniques that were to be so much a part of the next world war. At the end of 1929 the world altitude and distance records stood at 41,794 feet (Junkers W-34) and 4,912 miles (Breguet 19).

Whereas in the 1920s the state of the aeronautical art had rested almost exclusively in the hands of the experimenters and visionaries, in the 1930s there came a universal acceptance of the developments of the previous decade, and a sudden flowering of a new generation of military aircraft. Powerful radials and inline engines of over 1,000-hp output produced speeds of 350 mph; aircraft with fixed undercarriages became oddities, and metal construction and stressed skins were universally adopted.

the Heinkel He-111 and the Junkers Ju-86, which appeared in 1934 in civilian guise. The former was, in particular, to become one of the German Air Force's staple bombers.

But by the middle of the decade the United States had caught up with the Europeans in the development of civil aircraft and had passed them in the military field. Early in 1933 the Boeing company flew the prototype of its 247 airliner, and in the middle of the year Douglas wheeled out the prototype of their rival airliner, the DC-1. These two aeroplanes were the true ancestors of the civil aircraft we know today, with their monoplane, low-wing, monocoque construction, twin engines, retractable undercarriages, flaps on the trailing edges and variable-pitch propellers. It is interesting that the 247's precursor, the Monomail of 1930, also led to the development of two other highly significant types: these were the Boeing B-9 bomber, another all-metal, low-wing monoplane with a retractable undercarriage – and more than a match in performance for most 1931 fighters – and the remarkable Boeing P-26 fighter. The latter was a small single-engined monoplane fighter with a fixed, spatted undercarriage and capable of 235 mph, which was some 30 mph faster than contemporary European fighters in 1931.

Although it was a good design, the Boeing 247 never enjoyed the popularity of its Douglas rival, which was quickly developed via the DC-2 into the 'immortal' DC-3 of 1935. This was basically the same design as the DC-1, and could carry 21 passengers at 170 mph for 500 miles. The emergence of these American designs spurred Europe's designers into fresh activity, but their answers could not match the Americans on commercial grounds. We have already mentioned the Heinkel He-111 and the Junkers Ju-86, and we should also mention their British counterpart, the Bristol 142. Smaller than either of the American airliners, it was later developed into one of the first truly modern light bombers, the Bristol Blenheim.

Although Germany was forbidden by the terms of the Treaty of Versailles, signed in June 1919, to possess military aircraft, the advent of the Nazi regime in 1933 altered that. Hitler was not then ready to declare his intentions openly, but he ordered the clandestine formation of a new air force, the Luftwaffe, from the scattered elements that had kept German air-mindedness alive in the 1920s. He also commanded the nation's aircraft manufacturers to start developing military types for the day when German rearmament would be revealed. This was not an unduly difficult problem as German designers had been operating in other countries, notably Russia, Sweden, Switzerland and Holland, and now it was mostly a question of getting German aircraft factories ready for full-time military production.

Germany's chief advantage in building up her new air force was that she did not have an expensive legacy of old types needing to be used up. As soon as the existence of the new force was revealed in 1935, German manufacturers could start turning out up-to-date machines for immediate adoption. A few older types were produced at first to tide the Luftwaffe over until the new designs could enter widespread service. Such types were the Arado Ar-68 biplane fighter, the Dornier Do-13 bomber, the Heinkel He-51 biplane fighter and the Junkers Ju-52/3 bomber. But more modern designs were already under construction in 1935, and soon the Luftwaffe was the best-equipped air force in the world.

The type selected as the Luftwaffe's standard fighter was the Messerschmitt Bf-109, a clean-lined, low-wing, single-engined monoplane with a retractable undercarriage. Design was started in 1933 and the first prototype flew in the autumn of 1935. The Bf-109B, armed with three 7·9-mm machine guns or two machine guns and one 20-mm cannon, entered service in 1937 and by the following year had proved itself a very formidable fighter in the Spanish Civil War (1936–39).

The Luftwaffe had also developed, in conjunction with the Army, a tactical doctrine of using bombers as 'flying artillery' for the Army, and in this field the Luftwaffe's equivalent of a light bomber, the Junkers Ju-87 Stuka, was

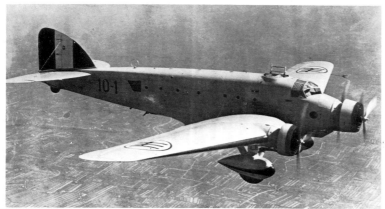

TOP *Andrei Tupolev's ANT-6, a heavy long-range bomber seen here in 1930 mounted on skis; obsolete by the outbreak of war, the type served mostly as a paratroop transport.*

ABOVE *A spectacular view of the Russian ANT-6 on exercise carrying biplane and monoplane fighters.*

ABOVE LEFT *The Italian Savoia-Marchetti SM-81 Pipistrello (Bat) bomber, which flew for the first time in 1935 and ruled the skies in Mussolini's Ethiopian campaign.*

CENTRE LEFT *The Polikarpov I-16, the standard Russian fighter of the 1930s armed with two 20-mm cannon and two machine guns.*

LEFT *An Italian development, the Cant Z-506 seaplane, used in the war for recce work and as a torpedo-bomber. In addition to this and the Pipistrello, above, Italy's other main types were her Fiat CR-32 and -42 biplanes, which gave a good account of themselves in the Spanish Civil War.*

to win great notoriety. Junkers's Swedish office had designed a dive-bomber as early as 1928 (the K-47), but it was the arrival of Ernst Udet, a celebrated World War I ace and flying celebrity, with an American Curtiss adapted for dive-bombing, that decided the Germans that dive-bombing was the optimum method of delivering bombs with great accuracy and with devastating psychological effect. Design of the Stuka began in 1934. It emerged in 1935, a compact and purposeful machine, single-engined, with a low inverted-gull wing and spatted undercarriage. Its bomb-load consisted of either a 550- or 1,100-pound bomb.

Germany had few ideas about strategic bombing after the death of its chief proponent, General Wever, in an accident in 1936, and so her bomber fleet consisted almost exclusively of medium bombers. It was to be a decision that Germany was to regret when she invaded Russia in 1941. The Germans used three main types of bomber in the war: the Heinkel He-111 already mentioned, which entered service in late 1936 (2,200-pound bomb-load); the Dornier Do-17, which entered service in 1937 (2,200-pound bomb-load), and the Junkers Ju-88, which entered service in 1939 (4,000-pound bomb-load) and was one of the most versatile and useful aircraft of the war.

At last recognizing that the threat of war was looming ever closer, the rest of Europe rather belatedly joined the arms race. Great Britain's air force was in the mid-1930s desperately out of date: her fighter mainstay was the 230-mph Gloster Gauntlet biplane, which had an open cockpit and a fixed undercarriage – though the slightly more modern 250-mph Gloster Gladiator, which had an enclosed cockpit, was about to enter service (early in 1937). Aware of the inadequacies of these two fighters, the Royal Air Force set about acquiring more modern types. The first to enter service, in 1937, was the eight-machine-gun, 325-mph Hawker Hurricane, an angular but sturdy low-wing monoplane with an enclosed cockpit and a retractable undercarriage. It was joined in service in 1938 by the superlative eight-gun, 350-

mph Supermarine Spitfire, a descendant of R. J. Mitchell's Schneider Trophy racers.

Britain's bombers were little better than her fighters in the mid-1930s. Her standard light bomber was the Hawker Hart biplane, a two-seater version of the Fury fighter capable of carrying 500 pounds of bombs a distance of 470 miles. The standard heavy bomber was the Handley-Page Heyford biplane, capable of carrying 2,800 pounds of bombs some 920 miles. But in 1937 the Bristol Blenheim entered service. This was capable of carrying 1,000 pounds of bombs at 240 mph up to 1,000 miles, and was for its time a good machine. It was soon joined in service by the new generation of medium and heavy bombers: the Vickers Wellington (4,500 pounds of bombs, 220 mph, 1,100 miles); the Armstrong-Whitworth Whitley (7,000 pounds of bombs, 190 mph, 1,250 miles), and the Handley-Page Hampden (4,000 pounds of bombs, 250 mph, 1,200 miles).

The French started too late for any of their new designs to alter the course of the war in 1940. Their best fighter was the Dewoitine 520, a handy little monoplane armed with four machine guns and a cannon, and capable of 340 mph. And although exciting new designs such as the Amiot 350 series bomber and the Lioré et Olivier LeO-45 bomber had been produced in small numbers, the backbone of the French bomber force was still composed of such obsolete types as the Amiot 143, the Bloch 200 and the Farman 222.

Italy was little better off, having drawn the wrong conclusions from her experiences in both the Spanish Civil War and in Ethiopia. Yet despite their successes the Italians took more than one false direction: even in the first of their monoplane fighters, for example, they went for agility rather than speed, protection and firepower.

Russia had developed the giant Tupolev ANT-6 heavy bomber in the 1930s, then in 1939 her bomber forces were equipped with the excellent Tupolev SB-2 light bomber, which had performed well in Spain, and the equally good Ilyushin DB-3. Russia's standard fighter was still the I-16 monoplane, which had been very advanced on its introduction in 1935, but by 1939 was obsolescent.

Such, then, were the aircraft flown by the major combatant powers when war began in Europe in the autumn of 1939. To summarize the situation: Germany had a modern and powerful tactical air force; Britain had two good fighter types and adequate bombers, but was only just beginning to get into her stride; France had left it too late; Italy had some good aircraft but had not devoted sufficient thought to the needs of the future, and Russia had good bombers but poor fighters, and needed the jolt of her initial defeats – over Finland in 1940 and over her own territory in 1941 – to put her on the right path. Other nations, such as Holland, had some interesting types, but possessed too few of them.

It should be mentioned, too, before we close this chapter, that on 27 August 1939, only five days before Germany invaded Poland, the flight took place of the world's first true jet aeroplane, the Heinkel He-178, powered by a turbojet (Heinkel S-3b) designed by Pabst von Ohain. A new era in aircraft propulsion was not far away.

On the eve of the war, the world air records stood at 469·14 mph (Bf-109R) for speed, 56,046 feet (Caproni 161) for altitude, and 7,148 miles (Vickers Wellesley) for distance.

27 August 1939: the first true jet aircraft flies; current world records for speed, altitude and distance.

PART 4
WORLD WAR II

CHRONOLOGIES OF WORLD WAR II

The War on Land and in the Air

The symbol □ denotes activity over an extended period of time

1939

SEPTEMBER
1   Germans invade Poland in first Blitzkrieg campaign.
3   Britain and France declare war on Germany.
17   Soviet invasion of Poland.
28   Surrender of Warsaw. Russo-German treaty 'partitions' Poland.

OCTOBER
10   First attempt by German U-boats at wolf-pack techniques in Atlantic.
12   First divisions of British Expeditionary Force (BEF) join the Allied line at Lille.
28   First German aircraft brought down on British soil.

NOVEMBER
4   Repeal of US Neutrality Law: materials of war sold to Britain on cash-and-carry basis.
10   US General H. H. Arnold calls for superbomber (later emerges as B-29).
18   Germans start sowing magnetic mines in British waters.
30   Soviet invasion of Finland.

1940

FEBRUARY
1–13 Russian assault on Mannerheim Line launched by tremendous preparatory bombardment. Reduces Finnish morale and facilitates breakthrough.

MARCH
12   Finland capitulates.
14   First British civilian bombing casualties.

APRIL
9   German invasion of Denmark and Norway, supported by massive airborne operations.
10   First Battle of Narvik; Second Battle on 13th.
15   British bombers attack Stavanger in first inland attack of war.

MAY
10   German invasion of France and Low Countries in second major Blitzkrieg operation. Daring airborne attack on Fort Eben-Emael in Belgium.
14   Germans bomb old quarter of Rotterdam, almost totally destroying it.

15   First major RAF bombing raid on Germany hits Ruhr industrial area. Panzers break through on Meuse Front.
16–21 Panzers drive west to secure control of Channel ports.
26   Operation Dynamo begins (evacuation at Dunkirk); completed 4 June.
□   Germans begin up-gunning of Marks III and IV tanks to 50-mm and 70-mm respectively.

JUNE
4   Start of Allied evacuation of Norway, completed on 10th.
10   Italy declares war on the Allies.
11   Malta attacked for first time. RAF bombs targets in Turin.
14   Germans enter Paris; armistice signed on 22nd.

JULY
10   Battle of Britain begins.
16   Hitler orders directive for plan to invade Britain (Operation Sea Lion).
□   Intensification of German raids on airfields and ports in southern Britain.

AUGUST
2   'Adlertag' – date for beginning Battle of Britain – fixed by Goering for 10 August, later postponed to 13th.
15   Heaviest day's aerial fighting in Battle of Britain.
24   First bombs fall on London.

SEPTEMBER
7   Main effort of Luftwaffe switched from airfields to central London; beginning of Blitz.
13   Marshal Graziani's Italian troops invade Egypt.
17   Operation Sea Lion postponed indefinitely after failure of Luftwaffe to defeat RAF.
27   Axis pact signed in Berlin by Germany, Italy and Japan.

OCTOBER
6   First major night raid on London.
28   Italians invade Greece.

NOVEMBER
11   Fleet Air Arm raid on Taranto.
14   Major bombing attack on Coventry.
25   Prototype Mosquito bomber makes first flight.

DECEMBER
9   General O'Connor leads Western Desert Force against Italians in North Africa.

1941

FEBRUARY
6–7 Fall of Benghazi, 20,000 Italians surrender.
10   First raid by British 4-engined bombers (Short Stirlings).
12   General Rommel arrives in Tripoli with advanced elements of Afrika Korps.

THE WAR IN EUROPE 1939-45

▨ AXIS POWERS, AUGUST 1939

━━ LIMIT OF GERMAN ADVANCE ON EASTERN FRONT, 1942

OPPOSITE *Lynx I armoured car, the Canadian version of the Daimler Scout.* BELOW *The German Puma, an eight-wheeled armoured car mounting the short-barrelled 75-mm cannon.*

MARCH

10 Handley-Page Halifax 4-engined bombers make their first raid.
11 Passing of Lend Lease Act by USA.
24 Rommel begins first offensive at El Agheila; Tobruk encircled on 13 April.

APRIL

6 German invasion of Yugoslavia and Greece. Allies begin evacuation of Greece on 22nd.
15 In USA Igor Sikorsky makes first true, controlled helicopter flight.

MAY

10 Last major air-raid on London for three years.
15 Prototype British jet aircraft, Gloster Whittle E/29, flies for first time.
20 Beginning of German airborne invasion of Crete.
26 RAF Catalina flying boat locates German battleship *Bismarck*; she is then crippled and sunk.

JUNE

20 US Army Air Corps becomes US Army Air Forces.
22 Germans invade USSR (Operation Barbarossa). Luftwaffe strikes ahead of advancing armoured columns.

JULY

9 Minsk falls to German armoured pincer. Smolensk is taken on 15th; Germans capture 100,000 Russians.
24 Japan secures 'protection rights' from France over Indo-China.
☐ Lee-Grant M-3 tank goes into quantity production to give Allied armies in North Africa a tank mounting a 75-mm gun.

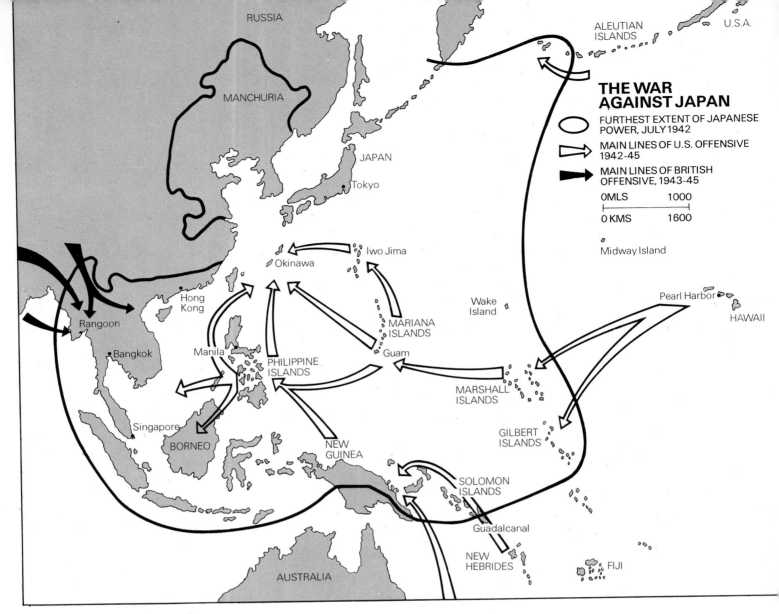

THE WAR AGAINST JAPAN

- ⬭ FURTHEST EXTENT OF JAPANESE POWER, JULY 1942
- ⇨ MAIN LINES OF U.S. OFFENSIVE 1942–45
- ➡ MAIN LINES OF BRITISH OFFENSIVE, 1943–45

0 MLS	1000
0 KMS	1600

Map labels: RUSSIA, MANCHURIA, JAPAN, Tokyo, ALEUTIAN ISLANDS, U.S.A., Midway Island, Iwo Jima, Okinawa, Hong Kong, Rangoon, Bangkok, Manila, PHILIPPINE ISLANDS, Wake Island, MARIANA ISLANDS, Guam, Pearl Harbor, HAWAII, Singapore, BORNEO, NEW GUINEA, MARSHALL ISLANDS, GILBERT ISLANDS, SOLOMON ISLANDS, Guadalcanal, NEW HEBRIDES, FIJI, AUSTRALIA

JULY–AUGUST

☐ Hitler switches main offensive away from Moscow to Ukraine.

SEPTEMBER

8 Leningrad cut off by German tanks.
19 Fall of Kiev.
26 Moscow offensive resumed; advance slowed by autumn rains.

OCTOBER

21 General Zhukov takes command of Moscow's outer defences.

NOVEMBER

☐ RAF gains complete air superiority over Western Desert.
☐ Defence of Moscow and beginning of Russian counter-offensive.
☐ General Auchinleck's desert offensive pushes Rommel back to El Agheila (31 December).

DECEMBER

7 Japanese attack Pearl Harbor, Siam (Thailand) and Malaya.
8 USA declares war on Axis powers.
10 Japan invades Philippines. British capital ships *Prince of Wales* and *Repulse* sunk by Japanese aircraft.
11 Germany and Italy declare war on USA.
28 Heavy Japanese air raids on targets in Philippines.

1942

JANUARY

9 Russian counter-blow reaches Smolensk province.

21 Rommel's second desert offensive drives British back beyond Benghazi.

FEBRUARY

2 German battlecruisers *Scharnhorst* and *Gneisenau* escape to Germany via English Channel despite desperate Fleet Air Arm Swordfish efforts to halt them.
15 Singapore surrenders to Japanese after intensive aerial and artillery bombardment.
☐ Germans stabilize their front in Russia.

MARCH

15–21 Japanese bombardment of Forts Frank and Drum (the 'Concrete Battleship') in Manila Bay.
24 Intensive air and artillery bombardment of US positions on Bataan peninsula demoralizes defenders.

APRIL

5 Japanese aircraft sink HM cruisers *Dorsetshire* and *Cornwall* off Ceylon.
8 Fall of Bataan.
9 Japanese aircraft sink HM carrier *Hermes*.
10 Siege of Corregidor begins; falls on 6 May.
18 Doolittle raid on Tokyo.

MAY

8 Germans launch spring offensive on Eastern Front.
30 RAF make first 1,000 bomber-raid, on Cologne.

JUNE

4–6 Battle of Midway.
7 Operation Sturgeon – German conquest of Crimea. Krupp 80-cm 'Gustav' bombards Sebastopol in largest German artillery concentration of war.
12 USAAF Liberators bomb Ploesti oilfields in Rumania.
14–30 British desert forces (Eighth Army) retreat into Egypt.
24 1,000-bomber raid on Bremen.
28 Germans launch summer offensive in Russia.

JULY

1 First USAAF 8th Air Force B-17s land in Britain.
4 First USAAF air-raid on Occupied Europe.
6 Germans take Voronezh; Hitler orders drive on Stalingrad and Caucasus.
7 US landings on Guadalcanal; island cleared by February 1943.
13 General Montgomery assumes command of Eighth Army, now in El Alamein position.
15 RAF Pathfinder Force formed to help bomber crews.
17 US 8th Air Force B-17s make their first raid.
24 Battle of Stalingrad begins.
31 Battle of Alam Halfa begins. Montgomery deploys tanks in hull-down positions and fends off Rommel, who withdraws on 7 September.

SEPTEMBER
21 Prototype B-29 Superfortress makes maiden flight.
25 Daring raid by RAF Mosquitoes on Gestapo Headquarters in Oslo.
☐ Panzer Tigers receive premature baptism on Leningrad Front.
☐ Japanese offensive in New Guinea halted by Australians.

OCTOBER
1 First American jet aircraft, Bell XP-59A, makes maiden flight.
10 Beginning of last major air offensive on Malta.
23 Battle of El Alamein begins with heavy British artillery concentration. Sherman M-4 tanks supplied for first time to British crews.

NOVEMBER
4 British break through at El Alamein.
8 Anglo-American landings in North Africa (Operation Torch). US forces equipped with bazookas.
19–23 Soviet counter-attack at Stalingrad. German Sixth Army cut off.
20 Siege of Malta lifted.

1943
JANUARY
5 First use of VT (Proximity) Fuses, in shells fired from US cruiser *Helena* against Japanese aircraft.
27 US aircraft raid Germany for first time.
30 First daylight raid on Berlin, by Mosquitoes.

FEBRUARY
2 German Sixth Army surrenders in Stalingrad.
2–20 Russians drive across the Donets.

FEBRUARY–MARCH
☐ General von Manstein organizes German counter-offensive; recaptures Kharkov on 14 March.

MARCH
5 Prototype Gloster Meteor fighter makes maiden flight.

MAY
3–13 Battle of Tunisia ends Axis presence in North Africa.
16 'Dambuster raid' by RAF Lancasters of 617 Squadron.
23 RAF Bomber Command drops its 100,000th ton of bombs on Germany.

JUNE
20 Beginning of RAF shuttle raids, at first over Germany and Italy, starting from Britain and landing in North Africa.
28 Air reconnaissance reveals evidence of German missile work at Peenemunde.
☐ US and British begin combined bomber offensive against Germany.

JULY
4–16 Battle of Kursk – biggest tank battle ever. Russian anti-tank guns destroy 40% of German armoured force, crippling Panzerarmee beyond repair.
10 Allied landings in Sicily – invasion preceded by large-scale airborne landings.
29 Massive raid on Hamburg virtually destroys the city.

AUGUST
1 Heavy raid on Ploesti oilfields in Rumania by USAAF bombers.

17 RAF bombs severely damage Peenemunde experimental station.

AUGUST–NOVEMBER
☐ Russian armour drives Germans beyond Smolensk (25 September) and Kiev (6 November). German Seventeenth Army cut off in Crimea.

SEPTEMBER
3 Allied landings in mainland Italy.
8 Italian armistice, signed on 3rd, becomes effective; Germans begin to disarm and imprison Italian troops.
10 Italian battleship *Roma* sunk by German air-launched guided bomb.

OCTOBER
14 Disastrous USAAF raid on Schweinfurt.

NOVEMBER
1 US landings on Bougainville. Tarawa invaded on 20th using specialized armoured assault vehicles (LVTs).

DECEMBER
5–15 Drive to Rapido River in Italy. Appearance of new American heavy guns gives Allies superiority in heavy artillery for first time in war.
9 Prototype Lockheed XP-80 jet fighter makes maiden flight.
20 Allied landings at Anzio, Italy. 'Anzio Annie' and 'Anzio Express', German 28-cm railway guns, in action; 73% of Allied casualties due to German artillery/mortar fire.

1944
FEBRUARY
15 Monte Cassino Abbey totally destroyed by bombing.
25 Large-scale US raid on Regensburg.

MARCH
4 US bombers, escorted by fighters, raid Berlin.

APRIL
15 Priorities for Allied bombers switched to German transport system.
24 First B-29 bomber for strategic bombing of Japan arrives in China.

MAY–JUNE
☐ Allies break through in Italy and advance on Rome.

JUNE
6 D-Day invasion of France launched (Operation Overlord).
15 Beginning of US strategic raids on Japan from China.
22 Massive Russian assault on German Army Group Centre with 400 guns per mile of front.

JULY
1–24 Allied expansion of Normandy beachhead.
10 Russians begin drive into Poland.
17 Napalm used operationally for first time.
21 US landings on Guam.
25 Massive carpet-bombing raid launched to open way for American ground forces breaking out at Avranches.

AUGUST
1 General Patton's Third Army breaks out of Cherbourg peninsula.
15 Allied landings in south of France.
25 Liberation of Paris.

OCTOBER
21 Allies breach Siegfried Line.

NOVEMBER
12 RAF Lancasters sink battleship *Tirpitz* at her moorings.

DECEMBER
8 Start of US pre-invasion bombardment of Iwo Jima.
16 Germans launch counter-offensive in Ardennes. First land use of VT Fuse against German troops in Battle of Bulge.

1945
JANUARY
1 Last major raid on Britain made by Luftwaffe.

FEBRUARY
13 Beginning of bombing of Dresden: raids over three days result in destruction of city.
16 First US carrier raids on Japan.
25 Largest raid on Tokyo to date causes enormous damage.

MARCH
7 US 9th Armoured Division seizes Remagen Bridge and makes first Allied crossing of the Rhine.

APRIL
1 US landings on Okinawa; cleared by 21 June.
6 Massive Japanese 'Kamikaze' raid on US invasion fleet off Okinawa.
16 Russian guns fire on Berlin.
☐ Allied Pershing and Comet tanks arrive in Europe.

MAY
8 Unconditional German surrender.

AUGUST
6 First atom bomb dropped, on Hiroshima.
8 USSR declares war on Japan.
9 Second atom bomb dropped, on Nagasaki.

SEPTEMBER
2 Japanese instrument of surrender signed aboard US battleship *Missouri* in Tokyo Bay.

BELOW *German Krauss-Maffei half-tracked personnel carrier.*

The War at Sea

The symbol □ denotes activity over an extended period of time

1939

AUGUST
19 German naval units sent to their war stations.
27 German merchant shipping recalled.

SEPTEMBER
1 Germany invades Poland.
3 Britain and France declare war on Germany.
7 First oceanic convoy (Britain to Gibraltar); first transatlantic convoy sails on 15th.
12 US Navy organizes 'neutrality patrols'.
17 HM aircraft carrier *Courageous* sunk in Western Approaches.
25 Deep mining of Straits of Dover; U-boats use north-of-Scotland route from October.

OCTOBER
10 First attempt by Germans to implement wolf-pack tactics.
13 HM battleship *Royal Oak* lost in Scapa Flow.
17 Luftwaffe attacks on Scapa Flow.

NOVEMBER
4 Repeal of US Neutrality Law; materials of war sold to Britain on cash-and-carry basis.

DECEMBER
13 River Plate engagement; *Graf Spee* scuttles herself on 17th.

1940

FEBRUARY
15 Restrictions lifted on German submarine movements.

MARCH
31 First sortie by German auxiliary cruiser.

APRIL
3 Logistic ships sail to support German invasion of Norway.
9 German occupation of Denmark; landings at six cities in Norway.
10 German cruiser *Königsberg* becomes first major unit to be sunk by air action; First Battle of Narvik; Second Battle on 13th.
15 Start of Allied landings in Norway.

MAY
10 German invasion of Benelux countries and France.
26 Start of Dunkirk evacuation (Operation Dynamo); completed on 4 June.

JUNE
4 Start of Allied evacuation from Norway; completed on 10th.
8 HM aircraft carrier *Glorious* sunk by battlecruisers *Scharnhorst* and *Gneisenau*.
10 Italy declares war on Allies.
22 France concludes an armistice.
□ Allied monthly shipping losses pass 500,000 tons for first time.

JULY
3 British attack French fleet at Oran.
16 Hitler issues directive for plan to invade Britain (Operation Sea Lion).
19 US emergency programme authorizes 1,325,000 tons of warship construction.

SEPTEMBER
17 Operation Sea Lion indefinitely postponed after failure of Luftwaffe to defeat RAF.
23 Abortive British assault on French port of Dakar.
27 Axis pact signed in Berlin by Germany, Italy and Japan.

OCTOBER
28 Italians invade Greece.

NOVEMBER
11 Naval aircraft cripple Italian battle fleet in Taranto harbour.

Total Allied shipping losses for 1940 reach 3,991,641 tons.

1941

JANUARY
23 German heavy-ship sortie in Atlantic seen as first stage in build-up of forces in France to threaten North Atlantic trade route.
□ Luftwaffe forces appear for first time in Mediterranean.

MARCH
11 Passing of Lend Lease Act by USA.
30 Battle off Cape Matapan.

APRIL
4 US dockyards authorized to refit British warships.
6 German invasion of Yugoslavia and Greece. Allies begin evacuation of Greece on 22nd.
11 US Defence Zone extended to Longitude 26°W.

MAY
15 US Navy takes over Argentia naval base in Canada.
20 German airborne invasion of Crete.
27 German battleship *Bismarck* sunk after a 9-day sortie during which she sank HM battlecruiser *Hood* (24th). Start of Allied evacuation of Crete; completed on 31st.

JUNE
22 Germany invades USSR (Operation Barbarossa).

JULY
7 US forces relieve British garrison in Iceland; first US convoy sails to Iceland.
24 Japan secures 'protection rights' over Indo-China from France.
26 USA freezes all Japanese assets and institutes oil embargo.

SEPTEMBER
16 US warships form convoy escorts for first time; first clashes with German U-boats. German U-boats diverted to Mediterranean.

NOVEMBER
7 US merchant shipping armed and allowed to enter war zones.
14 HM aircraft carrier *Ark Royal* lost.
25 HM battleship *Barham* lost.

DECEMBER
7 Japanese attack Pearl Harbor, Malaya and Siam (Thailand).
8 USA declares war.
10 Japanese invade Philippines.
11 Germany and Italy declare war on USA.
18 HM battleships *Valiant* and *Queen Elizabeth* sunk in Alexandria harbour by Italian frogmen.

Total Allied shipping losses for 1941: 4,328,558 tons.

1942

JANUARY
11 Japan invades Dutch East Indies: territory capitulates on 8 March.
13 Start of German submarine campaign off east coast of USA.

FEBRUARY
12 Escape from Brest to Germany of *Scharnhorst* and *Gneisenau*.
15 Fall of Singapore to Japanese forces.
27 Battle of Java Sea.

MARCH
28 Normandie Lock at St Nazaire destroyed.
□ Total of 273 Allied merchant ships lost, mostly in Far East.

APRIL
8 Capitulation of Philippines (except Corregidor, 6 May).
18 Doolittle raid on Tokyo.

MAY
4-8 Battle of Coral Sea brings first check to Japanese advance.

JUNE
4-6 Battle of Midway.
□ Highest monthly shipping losses of war – 834,196 tons (including PQ17 disaster).

AUGUST
7 US Landings on Guadalcanal: island not cleared until Japanese evacuations in February 1943.
19 Dieppe Raid.

SEPTEMBER
□ Japanese land offensive in New Guinea halted by Australians.

NOVEMBER
4 Axis forces defeated at El Alamein.
8 Anglo–American landings in North Africa (Operation Torch).
20 Siege of Malta lifted.
27 French fleet at Toulon scuttles itself to prevent German take-over.

DECEMBER
31 Battle of North Cape.

Total Allied shipping losses for 1942: 7,790,321 tons. Japanese iron imports fall to 118,000 tons from 3,000,000 tons in 1940. In USA 119 destroyers are built.

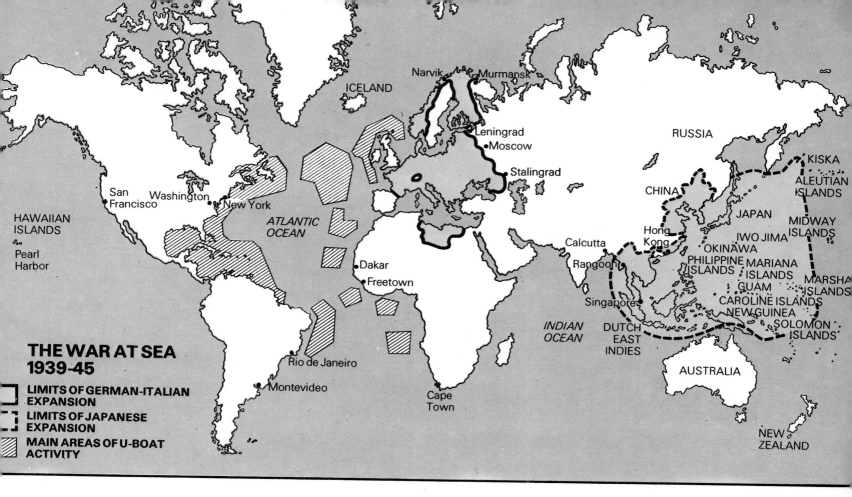

THE WAR AT SEA 1939-45

▭ LIMITS OF GERMAN-ITALIAN EXPANSION
▭ LIMITS OF JAPANESE EXPANSION
▨ MAIN AREAS OF U-BOAT ACTIVITY

1943

MARCH

16-20 Biggest convoy battle of war in North Atlantic.

☐ Air gap in North Atlantic closed; Arctic convoys suspended.

APRIL

7-11 Collapse of Japanese air offensive against Marshall Islands.

☐ Continued heavy fighting in Atlantic; Italians take 60% losses in their attempt to maintain supply route to Tunis.

MAY

13 Fall of Tunis.

☐ Decisive defeat of German U-boats: 37 sunk in North Atlantic.

JUNE

☐ U-boats withdraw from North Atlantic.

30 US landings on New Georgia.

JULY

10 Allied landings in Sicily.

AUGUST

3 Start of German evacuation of Sicily; completed on 17th.

SEPTEMBER

3 Allied landings on mainland Italy.

8 Italian armistice; Italian fleet surrenders on 10th.

OCTOBER

☐ German U-boat offensive resumed and defeated; 26 submarines sunk.

NOVEMBER

1 US landings on Bougainville; Tarawa invaded on 20th.

DECEMBER

26 *Scharnhorst* sunk off North Cape.

Total Allied shipping losses for 1943: 3,220,127 tons.

1944

JANUARY

22 Allied landings at Anzio.

☐ Start of build-up of British Eastern Fleet at Ceylon.

☐ US landings in Marshall Islands.

MAY

☐ Snorkel comes into general use.

JUNE

6 Allied invasion of Normandy.

18-21 Battle of Philippine Sea.

JULY

21 US landings on Guam.

AUGUST

15 Allied landings in south of France.

☐ German surface units give support to Army in Baltic; U-boats withdrawn from French ports and concentrated in Norway.

SEPTEMBER

☐ Start of German submarine campaign in British coastal waters.

OCTOBER

20 US landings at Leyte; first *kamikaze* attacks next day.

24-26 Battle of Leyte Gulf.

NOVEMBER

1 Walcheren assault; Scheldt estuary cleared for Allied use.

12 German battleship *Tirpitz* sunk by RAF Bomber Command.

22 Formation of British Pacific Fleet.

DECEMBER

8 Start of US pre-invasion bombardment of Iwo Jima.

Total Allied shipping losses for 1944: 1,045,629 tons. Japanese losses total 3,892,019 tons (a net loss of 2,157,172 tons); Japan's merchant fleet totals less than 2,750,000 tons by January 1945.

1945

JANUARY

☐ German U-boat *Type XXIII* becomes operational.

9 US landings on Luzon; cleared in June.

FEBRUARY

16 First carrier raids on Japan since 1942 Doolittle Raid.

19 US landings on Iwo Jima; cleared 23 March.

APRIL

☐ German U-boat *Type XXI* becomes operational.

1 US landings on Okinawa; cleared 21 June.

7 Japanese battleship *Yamato* sunk.

MAY

2 British landings at Rangoon.

4 U-boats recalled to Germany.

8 Unconditional German surrender.

JULY

14 First coastal bombardment of Japan.

AUGUST

6 Atomic bombing of Hiroshima.

8 USSR declares war on Japan.

9 Atomic bombing of Nagasaki.

14 Japanese government indicates willingness to surrender.

SEPTEMBER

2 Japanese instrument of surrender signed aboard US battleship *Missouri* in Tokyo Bay.

15

THE NEW
FIGHTING MAN

Influence of improved
firepower and
mobility on
infantry tactics.

During the inter-war years, a period of armed truce prevailed in Europe. The reaction of the victorious armies of the West, the British and the French, was to see their salvation in terms of defensive tactics. In part this reflected a period of economic entrenchment, but in conceptual terms it meant that the casualties of the machine gun were remembered while the victories of the tanks were forgotten by all but a few. Thus at first there was a dearth of innovation by all except the defeated nation, Germany. There the commanders of the new army of the Weimar Republic first digested the lessons they had learned – the most important being that infantry hitting in combination with

armour could restore mobility – and then secretly applied their new set of principles in doctrines which contravened the Treaty of Versailles. The French for their part, with traumatic memories of two German invasions in less than half a century, translated their already bankrupt theories of the all-powerful defensive into the concrete monolith of the Maginot Line. This concept was shattered even before the Line was completed, firstly by the aggressive strategy of the Japanese, who in the 1930s captured vast tracts of territory in China, and nearer home by the Germans' use of the Spanish Civil War as a brutal and calculated dress rehearsal for their painstakingly developed doctrines of the offensive.

Clearly, offensive action was needed to obtain decisive results in infantry combat; and the spirit of attack was still seen in many armies as the prime ingredient of the good fighting soldier. It was widely held that rapid movement on the offensive made it possible to exploit the advantage of firepower. However, the prime need was to avoid the

blunder of the Great War, and so every guile and strategem was employed in the new manuals of infantry tactics to enable an attacking force to seize the objective with the minimum of casualties.

The normal formation in most armies was to hold one unit in reserve (be it company or battalion) while two were used as the spearhead; the same triangular structure was used in defensive configurations. Attacks were rarely frontal in the tradition of the close formations of the 18th and 19th centuries but always sought to slide around enemy strongpoints, either enveloping them from both flanks or concentrating on one flank. The reserve or support unit was used at the appropriate time to drive home the attack on the flank or provide a back-up in the event of a counter-attack. The scenarios for all such tactical innovations envisaged a fluid form of war in which infantry would not fight alone but would be supported by tanks, artillery and tactical strike aircraft in the shape of the new fighter-bombers and dive-bombers. Tactics such as these were honed to new perfection in the shape of Blitzkrieg by the Germans, who emphasized the qualities of the swift dis-organizing attack.

Infantry weapons and tactics were greatly changed by improvements in firepower and mobility. By 1939 tanks were much faster and more powerful than their counter-parts of 1918 while motorized artillery on pneumatic tyres was considerably more mobile than the iron-wheeled horse-drawn gun of World War I. For the infantryman, in particular, the fighting environment was changed out of all recognition by the range and versatility of his own ordnance and the mobility which he received through mass-produced motor transport.

We have seen how in World War I the machine gun had become a highly developed weapon, well suited to the needs of the combat soldier on the ground. At that time, too, the demands of aviation and air combat opened up new con-cepts in automatic weapons, such considerations as weight,

BELOW *German Schmeisser 9-mm submachine guns.*
BELOW LEFT *American M-3 submachine gun with folding wire stock, popularly called the 'Grease Gun'.*
BOTTOM *American Browning automatic rifle on a bipod mount; rate of fire was 550 rounds per minute.*

OPPOSITE, LEFT *German 'Green' policeman of the post-1918 period, armed with a Bergmann submachine gun.*
OPPOSITE, RIGHT *A British soldier demonstrates the all-metal Thompson (Tommy) gun; the drum magazine of this version was later replaced by a vertical type.*

compactness and rate of fire taking on new prominence. By the outbreak of World War II the machine gun had emerged as a reliable, light, compact, rapid-firing automatic weapon, designed to fit the needs of the modern infanteer. The development of a famous British gun is representative of these trends: the gun was called initially the ZB and was first produced in Brno in Czechoslovakia. The British Government acquired the licence to manufacture it before the outbreak of war and it became the standard multi-purpose light machine gun of the British forces. This weapon, which replaced the old and faithful Lewis gun, was manufactured at the Ordnance Factory in Enfield and was called the Bren gun, the name being a contraction of Brno and Enfield. Although the British classed it as a light machine gun, to most other armies it was seen as belonging to the sub-machine gun family, a weapon first developed and used by the Germans (and later the Italians) in the Great War.

A sub-machine gun is a small, light weapon which comes somewhere between an automatic pistol and a rifle. Of simple design, and though usually inaccurate over any real distance, it can deliver a high volume of fire at close quarters; as such it is especially suited to use by shock troops. In the United States the most famous sub-machine gun of all time was patented in 1920 by a retired army officer called John Thompson. It became popularly known as the Tommy gun and its first claim to fame if not notoriety was in the hands of American gangsters and hoodlums in Chicago street battles during Prohibition. It was adopted by the US Army in 1928 and Winston Churchill purchased a quantity for the British forces which stood by to repel the German invasion in 1940. By 1941 the weapon had been simplified by American ordnance experts, constructed completely out of metal and its distinctive drum magazine replaced by a vertical one underneath the bolt. With a .45-inch round it became a highly prized weapon among the infantry of the Allied armies, most of whom considered it better than its British equivalent, the Sten gun. The sub-machine gun, because it is simple and cheap, easily lends itself to the technology of mass production and thus all the armies of World War II had their own versions. The German gun was like the Thompson; an efficient and popular weapon called the Schmeisser, it had a folding stock and weighed under nine pounds.

To meet the need for a powerful infantry weapon to attack armoured vehicles, the British Army in 1939 adopted the Boys anti-tank rifle for the BEF. This was similar in design and appearance to the ordinary bolt-action magazine rifle: it fired a heavy-calibre .55-inch armour-piercing bullet at very high velocity but was only really effective against tanks at dangerously close ranges of less than two hundred yards; it could also deliver a kick like a Missouri mule, and more than one unwary operator suffered a shattered collar bone from its recoil. In effect, this weapon did not solve a need that increased as the war progressed, namely to provide the infantry with its own close-range defence against enemy armoured fighting vehicles. The answer eventually came from the USA, the 'arsenal of the West', when in 1942 the bazooka was introduced in time for the North African landings. This weapon stands out as one of the simplest and most effective developed by either side in World War II.

OPPOSITE *German half-tracked troop carrier; fixed to its side are three projector frames.*
THIS PAGE *The versatile jeep. These all-purpose vehicles had a maximum speed of 65 mph and a range of 285 miles at 19 mpg. Below is a wire-laying version, loaded with drums of cable.*

Half-tracks and field cars of Hitler's army; the Americans produce the jeep.

consequence the bulk of German second-line transport was either horse-drawn or consisted of a hotch-potch of commandeered vehicles, a state of affairs that persisted throughout the war. Nevertheless by 1939 the Wehrmacht was equipped with an excellent little field car which had been developed from the Volkswagen. The new version, the Volkswagen KDF, immediately proved to be a very popular machine especially because of its versatility and the fact that it could negotiate terrain impassable by other wheeled vehicles. The Americans watched this development closely and from it produced their own ubiquitous jeep, a quarter-ton four-wheel-drive utility vehicle. Originally it was seen as a replacement for the motorcycle, to be used by reconnaissance troops, but its light weight and high-powered engine made it unique among military vehicles. It was quickly developed for a variety of tasks: it could haul troops, ammunition or light cargo, tow artillery and with special fittings serve as an ambulance, mobile machine-gun carrier or radio reconnaissance vehicle. No really satisfactory explanation exists for the origin of the word 'jeep', but it is popularly claimed to be a slurring of the initials GP (which stood for General Purpose). The US Army took delivery of its first jeep in 1940 and by the end of the war more than 640,000 had been mass-produced.

To sum up, by 1939, as he moved into a combat environment that had changed out of all recognition, the modern infantryman was better armed and equipped, and more mobile than his counterpart in 1914. His essential role had not changed, however, for he more than any other had the

In terms of mobility, although the Great War had proved the feasibility of motor transport, the truck did not play a decisive role. It was always important, and on occasion critical, an example being the use made of Paris taxis by General Galliéni to carry reinforcements to the Marne in 1914. By 1918 the value of the motor lorry for short haul work, plying between the railhead and the battlefront, was established. For longer journeys of a strategic type the railways were seen as the paramount means of transport. But in the twenty years leading up to World War II the tremendous progress made in motor vehicles, both in terms of design and power, was reflected in the realm of military transport. In the armies of Britain, France and the United States, the horse-drawn vehicle all but disappeared. These improvements were accompanied, in the Western world at least, by innovations in highway construction, the autobahns of Germany, for example, providing an efficient alternative means of moving troops swiftly up to her frontiers. In Germany's case, however, it is ironic that the principal weakness of the Wehrmacht in the period before 1939, and one which it was never able to remedy, was its unduly heavy reliance on horse-drawn transport. This was caused by a variety of factors, many of which were of an economic nature, but also because the High Command showed a distinct preference for half-tracked vehicles, which they saw as more reliable in field operations than all-wheeled vehicles. This belief was borne out by the Polish campaign, and by 1940 most German army motor vehicles were half-tracks.

Despite the High Command's faith, the half-track is neither a simple nor cheap vehicle to mass-produce: in

essential mission of war – to carry the fight to the enemy, and to capture and defeat him. Even so, on the eve of World War II the future for the infantry soldier was much obscured, and the magnitude and extent of infantry combat was unforeseen by the prophets and pundits of the inter-war years.

16

WAR OF THE TANKS

Germany plans to smash the Allied lines in Belgium with tanks massed at selected points.

In May 1940 the British and French armies were as ill-prepared for the German Blitzkrieg as their erstwhile Polish allies had been the previous summer. However, to foreigners in general, and to Englishmen in particular, the French Army was accepted as the most formidable in Europe – even though in reality it was nothing of the kind. It was indifferently armed and tactically out of date, and its morale, which had never really recovered from the shock of the Great War, had since been undermined by political intrigue. In the face of a bold adversary, equipped with novel tactics, willing to take all risks and convinced of its superiority, the French Army was tailormade for disaster.

The whole Blitzkrieg campaign hinged on the employment of armour and was essentially a clash of principles between two rival schools. The Allies outnumbered the Germans in armour but believed in distributing their tanks in fairly even proportions along the entire front; the Panzers, massed in corps formations, were therefore assured of local superiority at the point of impact. The Allies, furthermore, were convinced that the tank could not defeat the anti-tank gun: this, they thought, could only be achieved by the infantry and artillery. But the point was missed that infantry and artillery should be made more mobile. The British Expeditionary Force was the most mobile in Europe but it had only 229 tanks of which 171 were useless light tanks. Neither the British nor the French were capable of deploying adequate air cover for their ground forces and this failure left their armies horribly exposed to the Luftwaffe.

The Allied plan of operations (Plan D), designed to counter a German invasion of France and the Low Countries, gave itself away. It was impossible to launch four Allied armies into Belgium at a moment's notice without providing the German High Command with food for thought. The Germans deduced the likely Allied moves and made their own plans accordingly. After a series of false alarms, when planned offensives were postponed because of bad weather, the Germans drew up their final plan[1] secure in their knowledge of the enemy's; thus the battle of wits was already half won. To achieve the necessary surprise, the Germans simply struck the Allied lines where they were least expected. The French deployed to meet what they thought would be the main blow north of

[1] Initially the Germans intended an armoured sweep in line with General von Schlieffen's invasion plans of 1914, but after much debate they opted for Plan Yellow (see map), sometimes known as the Manstein Variant after its author. With Plan Red, the second phase, the conquest of France would be completed.

General Heinz Guderian, a master of tank strategy, who led the Panzer breakthrough at Sedan.

Namur through the Gembloux Gap; the Germans struck south of Namur and advanced on the Ardennes Forest, which the French considered impenetrable by armour. The Germans proved that it could be penetrated in force and at speed. The Ardennes was undoubtedly a formidable obstacle but like any natural barrier it could be conquered if preparations were sufficiently thorough.

General Gamelin and the French High Command similarly felt that the River Meuse could not be crossed without a lengthy build-up of weapons, supplies and manpower. But the Germans planned this phase of the operation with the same infinite care as they took over the Ardennes. They chose to make their greatest effort on a 50-mile front

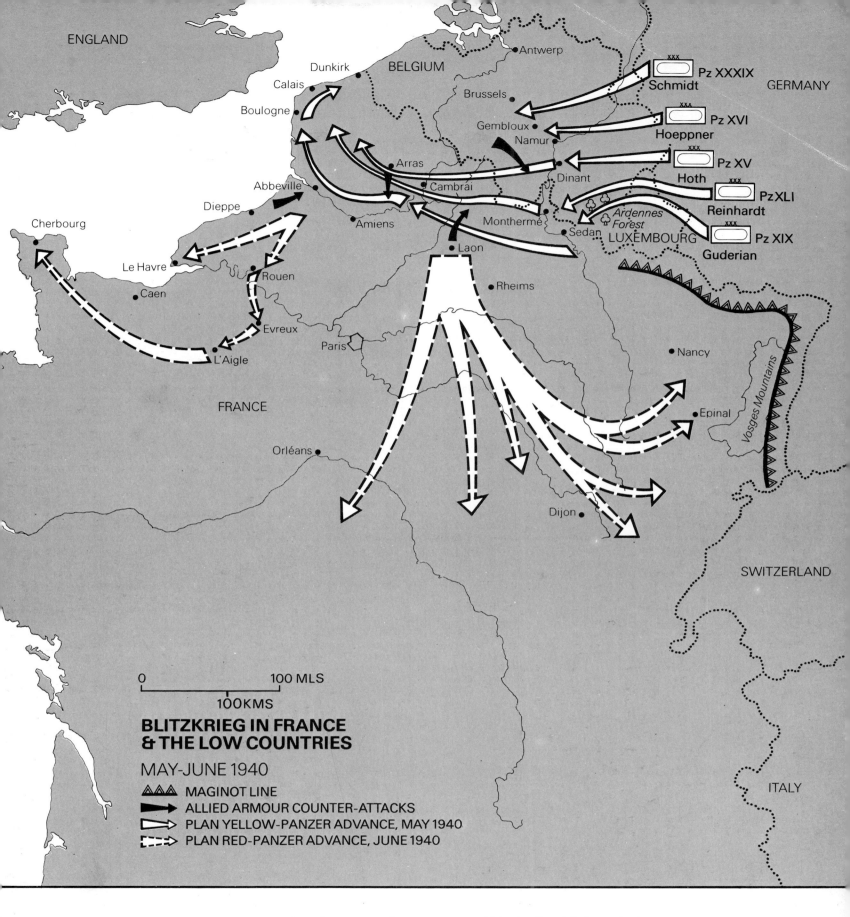

ENGLAND

Dunkirk
Calais
Boulogne

BELGIUM

Antwerp

Brussels

Gembloux
Namur

xxx
Pz XXXIX
Schmidt

GERMANY

xxx
Pz XVI
Hoeppner

Arras
Cambrai

Dinant

xxx
Pz XV
Hoth

Abbeville

Dieppe

Montherme

Ardennes
Forest

xxx
Pz XLI
Reinhardt

Cherbourg

Le Havre

Amiens

Sedan

LUXEMBOURG

xxx
Pz XIX
Guderian

Rouen

Caen

Laon

Rheims

Evreux

Paris

L'Aigle

Nancy

FRANCE

Orléans

Epinal

Dijon

Vosges Mountains

SWITZERLAND

0   100 MLS

100KMS

**BLITZKRIEG IN FRANCE
& THE LOW COUNTRIES**

MAYJUNE 1940

▲▲▲ MAGINOT LINE

► ALLIED ARMOUR COUNTER-ATTACKS

▷ PLAN YELLOW-PANZER ADVANCE, MAY 1940

⇢ PLAN RED-PANZER ADVANCE, JUNE 1940

ITALY

between Houx-Dinant and Sedan against the weak Series
B divisions of the French Ninth and Second Armies;
composed almost entirely of reservists and men over 40
years of age, these were poorly equipped, had little motor
transport and were almost defenceless against either air or
tank assaults.

Within this front the blows fell at Sedan, Monthermé
and Houx, but of these Sedan was the most vital. The city
was pivot to a road and rail network that radiated out to the
coast, towards Paris, and south behind the Maginot Line;

once taken, the opportunities it offered for exploitation were
boundless.

The German advance began on 10 May 1940. While the
Allied armies hurried north-east to cover Brussels and what
they believed to be the main threat, the German Panzers
broke through the thin crust of light mechanized units in
the Ardennes and on 12 May emerged on the east bank of
the Meuse. The decisive part of this operation was en-
trusted to von Kleist's Group, comprising five Panzer and
three motorized divisions further subdivided into two

223

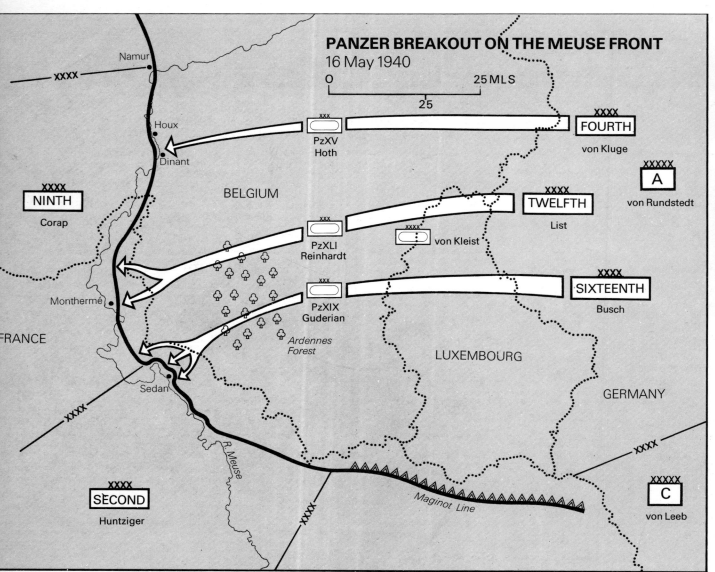

PANZER BREAKOUT ON THE MEUSE FRONT
16 May 1940

0   25 MLS

25

xxx
PzXV
Hoth

XXXX
FOURTH
von Kluge

XXXXX
A
von Rundstedt

Namur

Houx

Dinant

BELGIUM

XXXX
NINTH
Corap

xxx
PzXLI
Reinhardt

XXXX
TWELFTH
List

xxxxx
von Kleist

XXXX
SIXTEENTH
Busch

Monthermé

xxx
PzXIX
Guderian

Ardennes
Forest

LUXEMBOURG

GERMANY

FRANCE

Sedan

R. Meuse

XXXX
SECOND
Huntziger

Maginot Line

XXXXX
C
von Leeb

ABOVE *Charles de Gaulle, who in 1940 commanded the French 4th Armoured Division. De Gaulle's faith in the tank had been a main theme of his controversial book,* The Army of the Future, *published before the war. Escaping to London, de Gaulle made his first resistance broadcast to the French people on 18 June 1940.*

Panzer corps commanded by Reinhardt at Monthermé and Guderian at Sedan. On the morning of 13 May the French infantry was subjected to an air blitz of terrifying proportions while the Panzers deployed off the line of march for the river crossing. At first the French infantry put up a stubborn resistance and three out of the seven crossings attempted by the Germans failed completely; but the other four eventually succeeded after rather shaky starts. Two French armoured divisions were in a position to intervene at that point but there was a terrible muddle in their movement orders with the result that they were never committed to the battle properly and became engulfed in the general chaos and confusion as the front collapsed. (There is, furthermore, no evidence of French GHQ being informed of the nature of the German offensive on the Meuse Front until 16 May.)

After an initial and quite unnecessary halt while the German High Command drew breath, the Panzers fanned out and drove hard for the coast. Their tactics were not new: the Panzers emphasized speed and mobility and simply outflanked or bypassed isolated pockets of resistance in their dash westwards. The French for their part had no general strategic reserve which could deploy against the breakthrough, most of their reserve formations being concentrated behind the Maginot Line.

The bulk of the Panzer divisions was still made up of

Mark I and Mark II tanks, and by the time the forward elements gazed out over the English Channel at Abbeville on 20 May many vehicles had become casualties through mechanical failure. Altogether at this stage the Panzers had lost about 40% of their strength; nevertheless they had executed the greatest of all flanking movements – the encirclement of the Allied armies in Belgium. The French Premier, Paul Reynaud, sacked Gamelin and recalled Weygand from Syria to try and retrieve what was in fact a hopeless situation. Lord Gort, in command of the British Expeditionary Force, now found his line of communications to the base ports of Cherbourg and Le Havre cut and his rear threatened, and ordered a move back to the Channel port of Dunkirk. This began on 19 May when he sent his chief of staff, General Pownall, back to London to begin preparations for an evacuation.

Weygand had no strategic reserve to block the German penetration and so vainly sought to link up with the northern armies, but events had overtaken and paralysed the High Command. De Gaulle and the newly-created 4th Armoured Division counter-attacked at Laon but this was nothing more than a gesture and did little to alter the course of events. The British created two mixed infantry and armoured units and made a determined attempt to relieve the pressure around their main base at Arras on 21 May. At first the lumbering Matildas caused havoc as they caught

Rommel's Panzers in the flank but the Germans quickly retrieved their situation and, from a tactical point of view, the operation failed. On a strategic level, however, its significance was more profound, for the audacity of the Panzers had to a certain extent unnerved the German High Command, which became increasingly concerned with the vulnerability of its over-extended forces and feared a repetition of the Marne reversal of 1914. The result was that the German overreacted to the British counter-attack, ordered the Panzers to halt at Arras and in their present positions on the coast, and forbade any move north-eastwards to Dunkirk. This gave Gort just enough time to garrison the perimeter and thus safeguard his rear areas. Behind this secure defence he was able to organize an orderly evacuation of his beleaguered forces (Operation Dynamo), which took place between 26 May and 4 June.

Much has been written about the failure of the Panzers to complete what many have since regarded as the objective of the operation, the complete destruction of the Allied armies. General Halder, the German Chief of Staff, claimed that it was Hitler who 'prevented the complete destruction of the British Army by withdrawing the German tanks which were already to their rear'. Von Rundstedt, then Colonel-General commanding Army Group A, said after the war that he had wanted three Panzer divisions to complete the operation but this was forbidden by Hitler, an act which he described as an 'incredible blunder'. But the conquest of France was not yet complete and the tanks needed time to refit before they could be ready for their part in Plan Red and the advance southwards across the Somme to Paris and the Mediter-ranean. Moreover Marshal Goering and the Luftwaffe convinced Hitler that they could bombard the Allies into capitulation, while it was Guderian himself who on 28 May made a personal report to Hitler that the terrain around Dunkirk was totally unsuited to tanks. More fundamentally, it is also as well to remember that the German commanders had been weaned on von Clausewitz and the principles of a 'Continental' strategy, and in consequence had failed to anticipate an evacuation by sea.

It was, therefore, German indecision, coupled with the sterling qualities of the British fighting soldier and the magnificent co-operation of the Royal Navy and Air Force, which resulted in more than a third of a million Allied soldiers being evacuated from the beaches and port of Dunkirk. Although the Panzers failed in the last analysis to achieve a decisive victory they had nevertheless demon-strated to the world the true potential of Blitzkrieg when the defence allowed it freedom to operate. Lord Gort in his despatches said:

> The speed with which the enemy exploited his penetration of the French Front, his willingness to accept risks to further his aim, and his exploitation of every success to the uttermost limits emphasized even more fully than in the campaigns of the past the advantage which accrues to the commander who knows how best to use time and make time his servant and not his master.

After Dunkirk there were fewer than 200 battleworthy tanks available for the defence of Britain. Factories were still a long way short of full production and so the old medium tanks had to be brought out of retirement and

May–June 1940: the Panzers encircle the Allied armies but fail to prevent 338,000 men from escaping at Dunkirk.

deployed alongside the A-10 cruisers and the infantry Matildas. New tanks under production compared favour-ably with the Panzers for speed and armour but were already lagging behind in the vital aspect of gunpower. Rough treatment at the hands of the Matilda and Char B had hastened the German conversion to tanks with 50-mm and 75-mm high-velocity guns, while the British had only the now obsolescent 2-pounder (or 40-mm). There was a new British tank gun, the 6-pounder (57-mm), but to have put this into production would have resulted in delays at a time when any gun was better than no gun at all. The neces-sary programmes in research and development were curtailed and untried tanks were rushed into quantity production. In real terms this meant producing obsolete equipment while cutting back on the development of the next generation; thus by sacrificing quality Britain sur-rendered her parity and the chance of ever recovering the lead over the Germans in tank design and construction.

A neutral United States had watched with alarm as events unfurled in Europe and an immediate expansion was ordered in her armed forces. However, in terms of the tank the locust years of the inter-war period had left an indelible mark and the United States was forced merely to emulate others. The new armoured formations were centred on Fort Knox, where the 7th Cavalry formed the nucleus of the 1st Armoured Division, an exact replica of the Panzers in its complement of tanks and infantry. But the only tank in production was the cruiser M-2 A-1, armed with a 37-mm gun; to meet the immediate need for a battle tank the Americans were therefore forced to adapt the experi-mental T-5 E-2, mounting a 75-mm gun in a side sponson.

BELOW *A tank production line at Krupp's, principal supplier of arms to the Wehrmacht.*

Blitzkrieg: the Master Plan

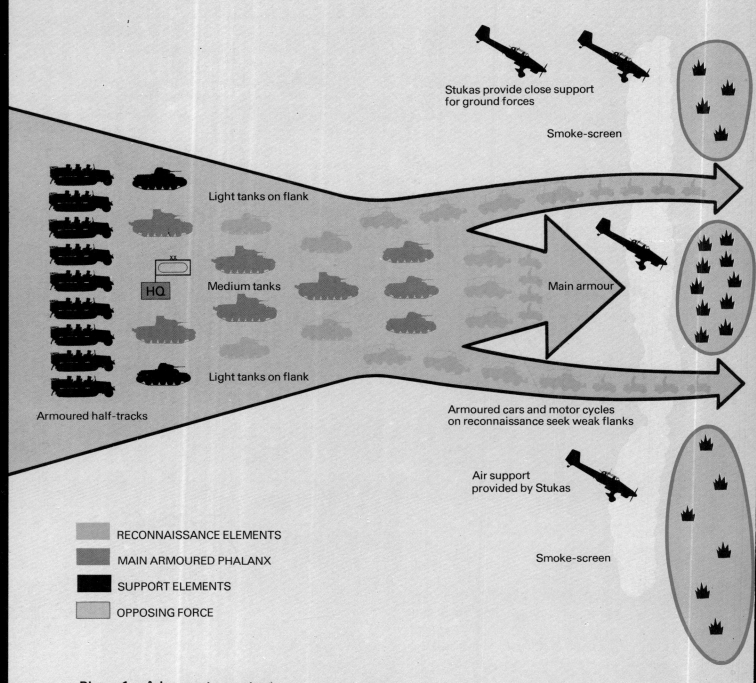

Stukas provide close support
for ground forces

Smoke-screen

Light tanks on flank

Medium tanks

HQ

Light tanks on flank

Armoured half-tracks

Main armour

Armoured cars and motor cycles
on reconnaissance seek weak flanks

Air support
provided by Stukas

Smoke-screen

RECONNAISSANCE ELEMENTS

MAIN ARMOURED PHALANX

SUPPORT ELEMENTS

OPPOSING FORCE

Phase 1 – Advance to contact

*In the opening stage motor cycles and armoured cars
profit from a smoke screen and the close support of their
dive-bombers to surge towards enemy positions, seek out
weaknesses and infiltrate the opposing lines. In their
immediate wake come the Mark II Panzers followed by
the more powerful tanks (Marks III and IV) and the
motorized infantry carried in armoured half-tracks.*

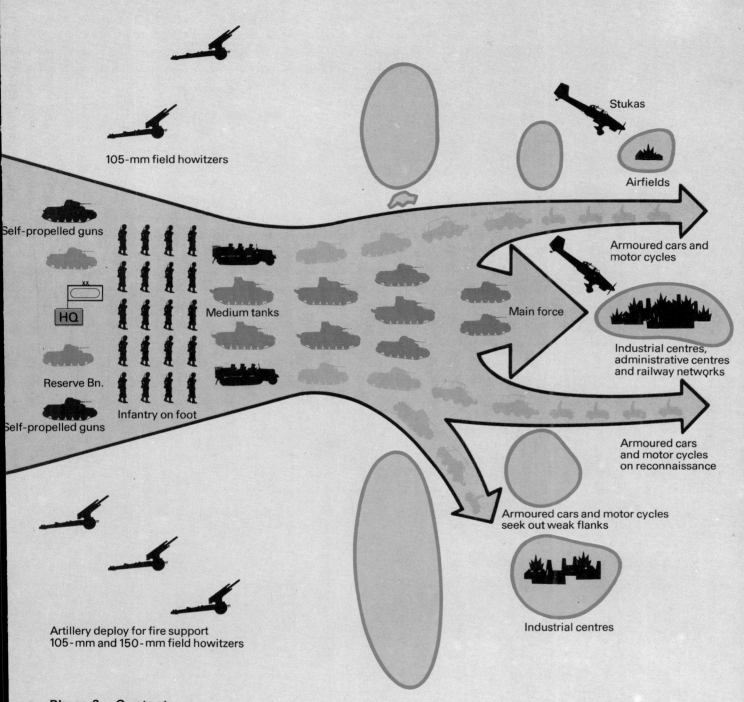

105-mm field howitzers

Self-propelled guns

Medium tanks

HQ

Reserve Bn.

Infantry on foot

Self-propelled guns

Artillery deploy for fire support
105-mm and 150-mm field howitzers

Stukas

Airfields

Armoured cars and
motor cycles

Main force

Industrial centres,
administrative centres
and railway networks

Armoured cars
and motor cycles
on reconnaissance

Armoured cars and motor cycles
seek out weak flanks

Industrial centres

Phase 2 – Contact

*While the outlying enemy forces are being engaged, the
recce units speed on towards the enemy's industrial and
administrative centres, which they again seek to bypass,
isolating them for the main assault, to be delivered by
their infantry and artillery. At the same time Stukas
carry out lightning bombardments, destroying enemy
aircraft on the ground, setting fire to factories and
disrupting communications.*

The Desert War

While the USA watched from the sidelines, the Western Desert of North Africa was already providing the next arena for the clash of armour. The Western Desert region is really one of limestone, with little real desert, and stretches for 1,400 miles between the terminal ports of Tripoli to the west and Alexandria to the east. A German general, von Ravenstein, described it as 'a tactician's paradise and a quartermaster's hell', for there was only one natural defence line between El Agheila and El Alamein and except for the coast road the entire zone was devoid of communications. Thus the farther a force advanced, the more its supply lines were extended and the weaker it became, as well as increasingly vulnerable to counter blows from the opposing side.

The first Western Desert campaign lasted from the autumn of 1940 to February 1941. During this period the Allied Western Desert Force under General O'Connor at first countered a tepid invasion by Marshal Graziani and the Italians and then swung into a brilliantly co-ordinated offensive which carried the British beyond Benghazi. The Italians could find no answer to O'Connor's bold use of tanks as Tobruk and Derna fell and a vast booty was left

the Italian tank was slower than the other two. The Crusader was desperately weak mechanically, however, and its tendency to break down under combat conditions inspired little confidence in it. In contrast the Stuart and the M-13/40 were seeing action after a long period of peacetime development, and although they were adequate at first they too were to fail against the greater protection and hitting power of their later opponents. The high speed and elusive characteristics of the Stuart were no substitute for thicker armour and a bigger gun when action had to be pressed.

For a short while the Matilda infantry tank enjoyed a reputation as a queen of the desert – until it was humbled by the anti-tank guns of the Afrika Korps in the Halfaya Pass. Another British tank was the Valentine: designed by Vickers on St Valentine's Day, 1938, it was a robust tank intended for infantry support but was almost invariably used in the Western Desert in a cruiser role. It was originally armed with the 40-mm gun and was then successfully up-gunned to 57-mm; but by 1943 the Valentine was obsolescent and the chassis were converted for specialized roles and to make self-propelled guns.

After the headlong advance described above and the defeat of large elements of the Italian Army at Beda

behind the retreating Italians. The three principal tanks which featured in these early months were the British Crusader, the American Stuart (or 'Honey', as it was called by its British crews) and the Italian M-13/40. Each represented entirely different design concepts, but superficially there was little to choose between them, except that

Fomm, O'Connor was poised ready to strike further west and capture the last enemy strongholds before Tripoli. However, his commander-in-chief, General Wavell, was ordered by London to send substantial reinforcements to the Balkans, and O'Connor was left holding Cyrenaica with just one infantry division and a raw armoured brigade

OPPOSITE *Italian tank crews stand in front of a group of M-13/40 tanks. The latter was one of the principal types used in North Africa.*
RIGHT *A British Crusader tank, mechanically unreliable but a type that saw considerable service in the early stages of the desert fighting.*

for support. In the circumstances this force seemed capable of containing any Italian initiative, but unbeknown to the British Rommel and the advance elements of his Afrika Korps began to disembark at Tripoli in February 1941.

Within a few short weeks the Germans completed their preparations and launched a major offensive against the unsuspecting British. The British 2nd Armoured Brigade was caught off balance, outmanoeuvred and destroyed;

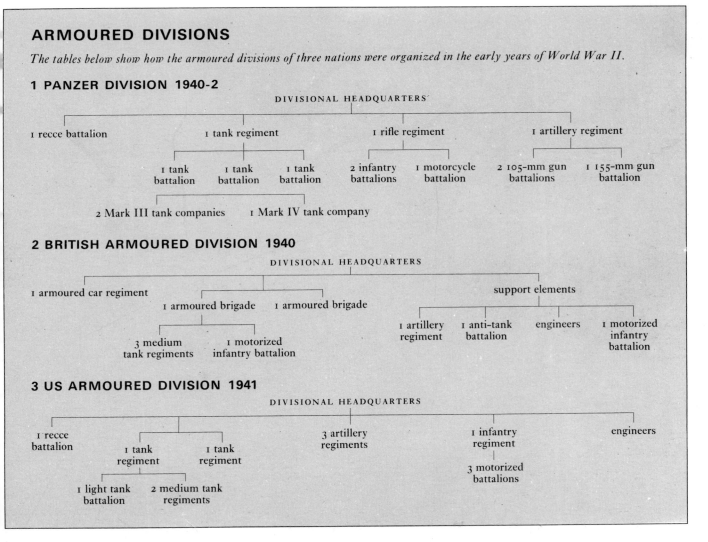

ARMOURED DIVISIONS

The tables below show how the armoured divisions of three nations were organized in the early years of World War II.

1 PANZER DIVISION 1940-2

DIVISIONAL HEADQUARTERS

1 recce battalion — 1 tank regiment — 1 rifle regiment — 1 artillery regiment

1 tank battalion — 1 tank battalion — 1 tank battalion

2 infantry battalions — 1 motorcycle battalion

2 105-mm gun battalions — 1 155-mm gun battalion

2 Mark III tank companies — 1 Mark IV tank company

2 BRITISH ARMOURED DIVISION 1940

DIVISIONAL HEADQUARTERS

1 armoured car regiment — 1 armoured brigade — 1 armoured brigade — support elements

3 medium tank regiments — 1 motorized infantry battalion

1 artillery regiment — 1 anti-tank battalion — engineers — 1 motorized infantry battalion

3 US ARMOURED DIVISION 1941

DIVISIONAL HEADQUARTERS

1 recce battalion — 1 tank regiment — 1 tank regiment — 3 artillery regiments — 1 infantry regiment — engineers

1 light tank battalion — 2 medium tank regiments

3 motorized battalions

ABOVE *Panzers of the Afrika Korps swirl in a haze of dust past a captured British bren-gun carrier. Rommel's superior tactics, using his armour in concentrated units to destroy the British piecemeal, brought him a series of notable victories in 1941–42.*

BELOW *British tanks stand on an Egytian quayside in October 1940, in readiness for General O'Connor's first Allied thrust in the Desert war, which he launched on 9 December. In the background is the cruiser HMS* York.

THE WESTERN DESERT, 1940-43

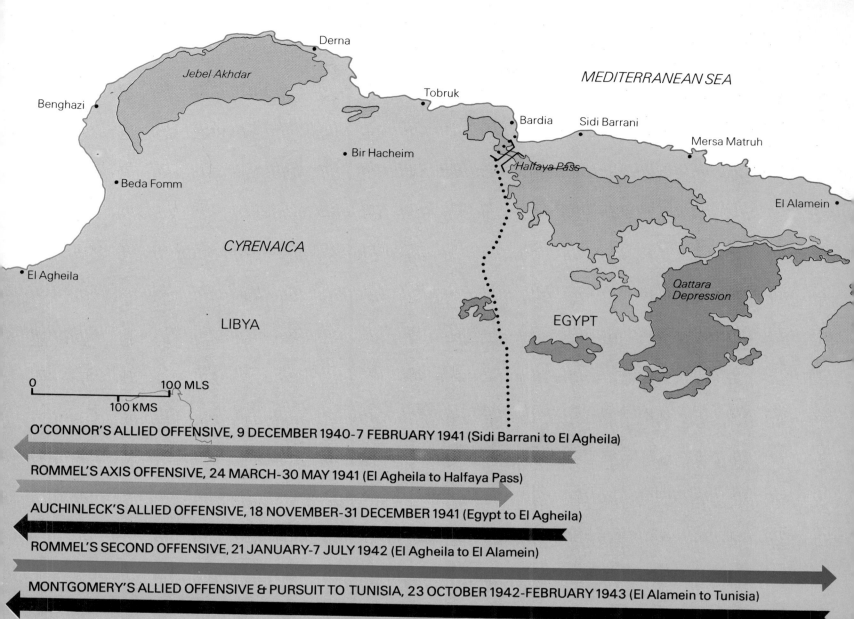

O'CONNOR'S ALLIED OFFENSIVE, 9 DECEMBER 1940-7 FEBRUARY 1941 (Sidi Barrani to El Agheila)

ROMMEL'S AXIS OFFENSIVE, 24 MARCH-30 MAY 1941 (El Agheila to Halfaya Pass)

AUCHINLECK'S ALLIED OFFENSIVE, 18 NOVEMBER-31 DECEMBER 1941 (Egypt to El Agheila)

ROMMEL'S SECOND OFFENSIVE, 21 JANUARY-7 JULY 1942 (El Agheila to El Alamein)

MONTGOMERY'S ALLIED OFFENSIVE & PURSUIT TO TUNISIA, 23 OCTOBER 1942-FEBRUARY 1943 (El Alamein to Tunisia)

the infantry fell back in disarray beyond Benghazi, Tobruk was invested and O'Connor captured.

The Afrika Korps then secured a series of brilliant tactical victories over the British, not through overwhelming strength of superior equipment but because it was a few vital degrees more advanced in its tactics and leadership. In the German view everything centred around the mobility and co-ordination of tanks and artillery. In the open desert unmotorized infantry was powerless unless it was protected by tanks, while even mechanized infantry was obliged to scurry from one area of tank-cleared country to the next.

This type of mobile warfare was never really understood by the succession of infantry-orientated British Army generals who held command in the Western Desert. Such generals had been educated in the halcyon days of the late 1930s, when the Staff Colleges emphasized the necessity of destroying the enemy's main forces as the prime objective on the battlefield. In the Western Desert this was interpreted to mean the destruction of enemy armour first – as a preliminary to the main battle. As a result numerically

superior forces of British tanks scoured the desert in widely scattered groups while Rommel concentrated his Panzers and destroyed the British in batches. On those occasions when the Panzers were outnumbered they would retire behind a screen of cunningly concealed anti-tank guns which in turn would take a heavy toll of the British tanks as they charged headlong into the trap. The British commanders never seemed to learn that an enemy tank force does not present itself as a simple objective in battle; because of its mobility its position is not static like that of infantry, and therefore the only real opportunity to destroy it is indirectly, by drawing it out of cover to retrieve a threatened key point. In conversation with a captured British general, Rommel was recorded as saying: 'What difference does it make if you have two tanks to my one when you spread them out and let me smash them in detail?' He subsequently admitted that it was the British artillery which caused him the most trouble – on the odd occasions when it could deploy in support of armour.

The main armament of all the British tanks – Valentines, Matildas and Crusaders – was still the 2-pounder; while

the new American tank, the Stuart M-3 or Honey, had a 37-mm gun. Although in terms of men there was little to choose between the British and their Axis counterparts, Rommel's greatly superior anti-tank guns gave his side a real advantage. For some time to come the British had to rely on their basic 2-pounder, even though by now it could do little to support its armour or protect its infantry. The gun was mounted on a utility truck which gave it mobility but poor concealment, causing high casualties among crews. In contrast the Germans had the excellent 50-mm Pak (Panzerabwehrkanone) anti-tank gun and the 88-mm artillery piece (though this was not as deadly in the Western Desert as legend would have it).

By the end of 1941 there was a general feeling of inadequacy and disquiet among British tank crews as they bowed before the technical superiority of the Afrika Korps and the mystique which they accorded to Rommel's creative tactical ability. Yet the fundamental feature of such inferiority was the awful inadequacy of British gunpower: the German tanks could kill at 1,000 yards but the British tanks had to close to 800 yards before they could be sure of getting a decisive hit. Against the German anti-tank guns the British tanks had no high explosive, and their position when there was no artillery or mortar support forthcoming from their infantry was little short of hopeless.

Neither side was ever in a position to inflict a major strategic defeat on the other in the Western Desert throughout most of this period. Britain's dependence for supplies on the long and vulnerable Cape Route, coupled with her bankrupt tactical doctrine, meant that she could never hope to achieve a position of superiority over Rommel. On the German side there were fewer problems of supply but the British still barred the narrow Mediterranean sea routes, while Rommel in any case could never be given sufficient forces to defeat the Eighth Army for as long as Hitler concentrated the main German effort on the Eastern Front, against Russia.

OPPOSITE *The British in this early phase of the North African campaign suffered badly from the inadequate gunpower of their tanks. Whereas the German tanks could kill at 1,000 yards, the British had to close to 800 yards; this applied to all three tanks shown here, the American Stuart (top), the Matilda (centre, in convoy) and the Valentine (bottom).*
ABOVE *Rommel, standing in car, and members of his staff inspect a knocked-out Stuart tank in the Western Desert.*
BELOW *The excellent German 50-mm Pak anti-tank gun, which in North Africa served its troops far more effectively than did the corresponding weapon of the Allies, the British 2-pounder.*

Desert Tactics

The tactical superiority of the Africa Korps' armour over its British rivals lasted for much of the desert campaign. One favoured tactic is shown on these pages. It was used when a German patrol, on making contact with British tanks, found itself outnumbered. It would turn and retire, expecting the British to give chase – which they almost invariably did. The retreating Panzers then drew their enemy across the desert and onto the guns of a concealed and conveniently sited anti-tank screen, where the 50-mm Pak 38s extracted their toll from virtually point-blank range.

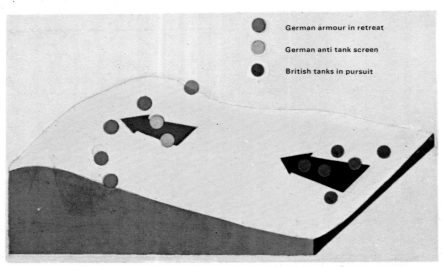

German armour in retreat

German anti tank screen

British tanks in pursuit

Hitler invades
Russia: after five
months the Panzers
arrive at the
outskirts of Moscow.

Operation Barbarossa

Directive No. 21, which laid down the guidelines for Operation Barbarossa and the invasion of Russia in June 1941, laid great emphasis on the tank:

> The bulk of the Russian Army stationed in Western Russia will be destroyed by daring operations led by deeply penetrating armoured spearheads.

Despite the possibly tempting vastness of Russian space, this new German operation in fact had built-in risks which dwarfed the problems earlier confronting the Panzers in France. The main factor in the Panzers' favour was the professionalism and technical excellence of their formations, but their tanks were for the most part the obsolescent Mark III with the short-barrelled 50-mm gun. In relation to the geography of Western Russia the number of Panzers was, moreover, absurdly small (see panel), while their supply formations were to be fatally compromised by the primitive road system. Time, too, was of the very essence since the Panzers, in common with the Wehrmacht in general, were not equipped for winter warfare and in such circumstances the great size of the territory could – and did – tell against them.

The Russians also held a significant advantage that had little to do with geography. This was in the quality of their armour, which produced one of the most startling revelations of the war. The T-34, in particular, rendered obsolete at one stroke all German tank development to date. It was a tank which combined a near-perfect balance between hitting power and self-protection, between long-range mobility and reliability. The broad tracks and low ground-bearing pressure of only 10 pounds per square inch allowed the tank to move across terrain and in weather which immobilized the Panzers. The T-34 was first built in 1939 and was the creation not of any inspirational genius but of the robust common sense of its designer, Mikhail Koshkin, who could envisage the needs of the battlefield with greater clarity than his contemporaries in other countries. In June 1941, as Operation Barbarossa began, there were approximately 1,000 of these tanks available – though initially their value was undermined by the manner in which they were deployed and by the tactical ineptitude

of their crews. (In all some 2,400 vehicles occupied the Russian tank parks on the eve of Barbarossa; many of these were, however, obsolete or in a state of disrepair.)

In previous campaigns the Luftwaffe had always provided invaluable air support for the Panzers, and in Russia it quickly achieved air superiority. Yet its operational efficiency was constantly impaired by the huge proportions of the land battle. This in turn laid a greater burden on the Panzers, and although they drove all before them in their great sweeping drives, Russian resistance from isolated pockets frustrated the eastward advance and bought time for Stalin to reorganize fresh armies for the defence of Moscow.

It will always be debated whether with a different strategy Hitler could have forced a decision in 1941. As it was he temporarily abandoned the drive to Moscow in August and concentrated on the Ukraine, where many Russian armies were encircled and destroyed; by September 1941 the German High Command estimated Russian losses at 2,500,000 men dead, wounded or taken prisoner, and 18,000 tanks and 14,000 aircraft destroyed.

When Hitler returned to the Moscow offensive in the early autumn it was too late: the rains came and choked the Panzer advance in a sea of mud just 40 miles west of the Russian capital. The Wehrmacht had carried out the greatest sustained offensive in military history but at a terrible cost; the infantry had lost 65% of its combat strength while the Panzers, in fighting tanks, were down to a third of their establishment. The forward elements were now being supplied on a hand-to-mouth basis and the Panzer leaders urged that Hitler allow them to adopt a flexible defence. But the German High Command was convinced that Russian resistance was at breaking-point and threw in its last reserves for a final effort.

Heavy snow and sub-zero temperatures thwarted all their efforts and the advance staggered to a halt less than 20 miles from Moscow. Lorries ceased to run; points on rail lines froze solid, as did the lubricants of the tanks, whose tracks required flamethrowers to burn off

OPPOSITE, BELOW *In September 1941, three months after the first German hammer-blows, Russian T-40 reconnaissance tanks are loaded for transportation to the front line. The next two months were critical as the fighting neared Moscow.*

German Armoured Strength
OPERATION BARBAROSSA

The meagre German total of 3,196 tanks ready at the beginning of the Operation was made up as follows:

NUMBER OF TANKS	TYPE OF TANK	TYPE OF GUN
1,893	Mark III	Short-barrelled L-42 50-mm
1,132	Mark IV	High-velocity L-43 75-mm
131	Mark II	37-mm
40	Mark III	Long-barrelled L-60 50-mm

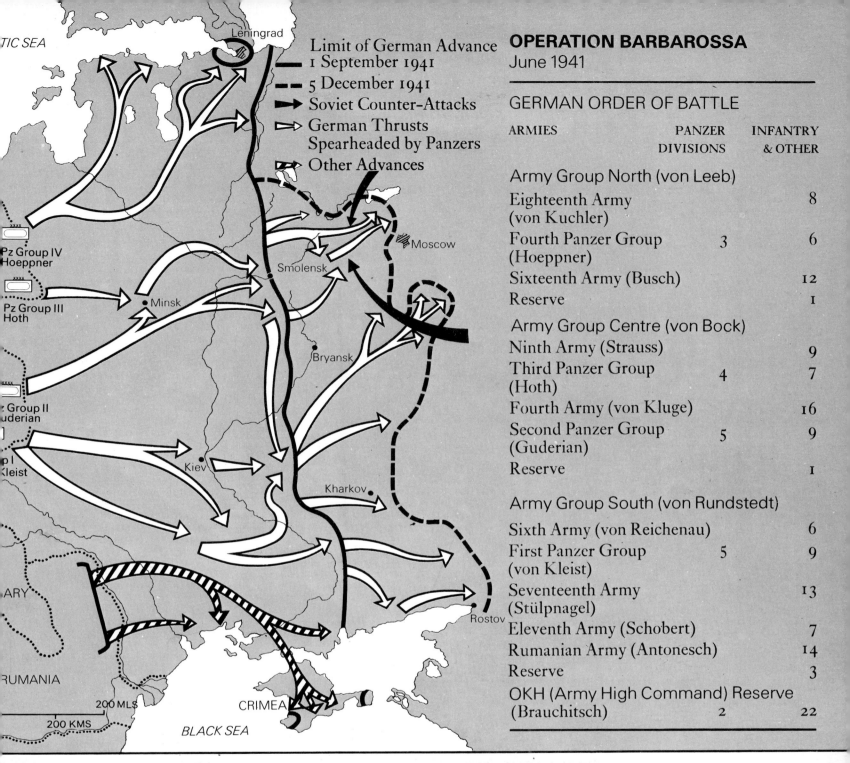

OPERATION BARBAROSSA
June 1941

Limit of German Advance
— 1 September 1941
- - - 5 December 1941
→ Soviet Counter-Attacks
⇒ German Thrusts
Spearheaded by Panzers
⟿ Other Advances

GERMAN ORDER OF BATTLE

ARMIES	PANZER DIVISIONS	INFANTRY & OTHER
Army Group North (von Leeb)		
Eighteenth Army (von Kuchler)		8
Fourth Panzer Group (Hoeppner)	3	6
Sixteenth Army (Busch)		12
Reserve		1
Army Group Centre (von Bock)		
Ninth Army (Strauss)		9
Third Panzer Group (Hoth)	4	7
Fourth Army (von Kluge)		16
Second Panzer Group (Guderian)	5	9
Reserve		1
Army Group South (von Rundstedt)		
Sixth Army (von Reichenau)		6
First Panzer Group (von Kleist)	5	9
Seventeenth Army (Stülpnagel)		13
Eleventh Army (Schobert)		7
Rumanian Army (Antonesch)		14
Reserve		3
OKH (Army High Command) Reserve (Brauchitsch)	2	22

Russian T-34/76 Tank

The T-34 earned its reputation as the greatest tank produced in World War II because it outgunned and outmanoeuvred its opponents on the Eastern Front for longer than any other tank. Deriving originally from the American Christie designs of the early 1930s, and more closely from the later Russian BT series, the T-34 went into production in 1940 and remained in service as the standard Russian medium tank throughout the war. The first main type was armed with a 76-mm gun, and this was gradually superseded from late 1943 by an up-gunned and up-armoured version mounting the 85-mm gun.

METRES

1   2   3

FEET

0   5   10

The T-34 was a robust and finely designed tank, combining to a high degree the essential qualities of firepower, mobility and protection. A predominant feature was the boldly sloped armour, which substantially reduced the penetrative power of enemy shells.

METRES

1   2   3

FEET

0   5   10

Once the crew was inside the tank, and the large turret hatch and the forward driver's hatch were shut, vision was limited to narrow episcopes let into the armour and to the commander's periscope mounted prominently on the turret. Normally, only the company commander's tank carried a radio. The T-34 ran on broad, 19-inch tracks and was able to keep going in soft conditions that often defeated its early German rivals, notably the Pzkw Marks III and IV.

The T-34/76B shown here weighed 27¾ tons, it was 21 feet 7 inches long overall, 9 feet 10 inches wide and 8 feet high. It had a maximum speed of 32 mph and was armed with a long 76.2-mm gun and two machine-guns. Pistols and a box of hand grenades were usually also carried.

5   6

15   20

the hard slush before they could move; telescopic sights frosted over and shattered, and troops died in their hundreds from frostbite. The Russians held firm; and then, in temperatures recording 40° of frost, the Russian field commander, Marshal Zhukov, hurled his Siberian divisions into a frantic counter-attack. Russian armour, now deployed in small battalion units,[2] hit the Germans hard while the Panzers lay immobilized through lack of winter oil. On 5 December Hitler ordered the Panzers to withdraw and refit while the infantry held the line, but as the Russian

[2] A Russian tank brigade now consisted of two battalions each of 25 tanks.

The fighting in Russia was dominated at all times by the urgent needs of both sides for supplies of every kind on a massive scale. For the besieged and starving citizens of Leningrad (opposite) food as well as tanks was a top priority. During the first months of the Great Patriotic War some 1,500 industrial enterprises were evacuated to the east; shown below is a tank factory in the Urals, turning out T-34s. Meanwhile (above and right) the German High Command was directing more and more Panzers to the Eastern Front. Those shown above are Mark IVs, mounting the long-barrelled 75-mm gun fitted with a muzzle brake to control recoil; their hull fronts are protected by extra lengths of track. On the right is a Mark III, armed with the short-barrelled 50-mm gun.

offensive gathered momentum it became impossible for the Panzers to disengage, and tanks and guns were abandoned in the chaos of retreat.

By 10 December the Russian offensive was unleashed along the entire length of the Eastern Front from the Black Sea to the Gulf of Finland, the Germans falling back after Zhukov's tanks had breached their lines at Livny. During December the Russians maintained their momentum, though by now the brunt of the fighting was borne not so much by the T-34s as by specially trained divisions of Cossack cavalry who, ably supported by sledge-drawn artillery, wrought havoc among the German infantry. Behind the ever-fluid front roaming bands of Russian partisans disrupted German supply formations and forced local commanders to divert precious resources to the defence of base areas.

Hitler, taking personal command of the front (by radio from East Prussia), turned his fury on his generals. Von Rundstedt, Guderian and Hoeppner (Fourth Panzer Group) joined the line of officers placed on the retired list for daring to give rather than hold ground. The Russians retained the initiative until the Germans were able to consolidate their defences in February 1942, and although Russian losses must have been enormous, Moscow was saved. The Panzers meanwhile had received their first serious defeat in their short but hitherto untarnished history.

THIS PAGE *German Mark III tanks (above) advance along snow-covered roads towards the Russian capital. When eventually the Germans were halted within 20 miles of Moscow Marshal Zhukov, commanding the city's defences, sent out specially equipped snow-troops with the armour (below) to beat back the enemy; the saving of Moscow marked the Panzers' first major defeat.*
OPPOSITE *A knocked-out Russian T-34 tank is left to burn. The success of the T-34 was such that Guderian called it 'the best tank in any army up to 1943', and General Blumentritt said it 'adversely affected the morale of German infantry'.*

El Alamein to Victory

Throughout 1941, as the pace of the war quickened in Europe and the storm clouds gathered over the Pacific, the United States mobilized her industry for the mass produc-

tion of munitions of war. Even at this stage American tanks were manifestly superior to those of Britain: they were manufactured from robust and well-tested components and were more suited to the rigours of combat than their more complex British counterparts.

The new American medium tank was the Lee-Grant (Medium M-3); it went into quantity production in July 1941 and more than 2,000 were produced in the first six months. The Lee version was produced first and the Grant followed shortly afterwards; the two were broadly similar except that the Grant mounted the square-shaped, British-style turret. Although they were mechanically sound and adequately protected with welded armour, nevertheless their ungainly layout resulted in major tactical disadvantages, for in most positions the tank had to be turned on its tracks before the side-mounted 75-mm gun could fire. The Medium M-3 was intended to fill the void until a more battleworthy medium tank with a turret-mounted 75-mm gun could be produced. This requirement was met in the spring of 1942 by the Sherman, or M-4. Constructed of cast armour and equipped with a high-velocity gun, the Sherman gave the Allies a tank which at last allowed them to engage the Panzers on a more equal footing. The Sherman was fast and highly manoeuvrable even though, like the Grant, it suffered tactically because it was powered by bulky radial engines which made for a high silhouette. Its components were strong on simplicity and ruggedness: features of particular interest were the volute-spring, bogie-type suspension – which gave improved mobility and effectiveness over rough terrain – the highly-developed V-8 engine and the rubber-block, rubber-jointed tracks. A life of 3,000 miles was not unusual for

these tracks, compared for example to about 600 miles for the metal-jointed tracks on the Panzer Mark IV. Altogether 49,234 Shermans were produced, and the large numbers supplied to the Allied armies now made possible the massing of superior tank forces in critical areas, when a major confrontation was imminent.

Initially most of the new American tanks were despatched to the Western Desert to re-equip British armoured divisions, which by the summer of 1942 were in a desperate plight. A continued adherence to dated cavalry tactics was still resulting in enormous casualties at the hands of Rommel and the Panzer Mark IV; while the British infantry had lost the last shreds of any faith in the protective powers of its armoured divisions. Thus a situation close to 'apartheid' had grown up between the two arms.

Rommel's supply position had in the meantime deteriorated but nevertheless by August 1942 he had penetrated deep into Egypt and had pinned the British at El Alamein. Now the Afrika Korps gathered its resources and prepared for the final push for the Suez Canal. Fortunately for the Allies, at this precise moment a commander arrived for the Eighth Army who, though new to desert warfare, was not in the least overawed by the myth of Rommel. By making a few changes to the defence plans of his predecessor, Auchinleck, General Montgomery deployed his new American Grants in hull-down positions along the Alam Halfa ridge; the infantry was secure behind the protection of deep minefields and there was ample artillery support. As the Panzer spearheads wilted before the British defences the Royal Air Force roamed freely in the

OPPOSITE, ABOVE *In the battle smoke of El Alamein a defeated German tank crew surrenders.*
OPPOSITE, BELOW *Cleaning the barrel of a Grant M-3 tank's 75-mm gun; though awkwardly mounted in a side sponson, this gun lent much-needed weight to the Allied armoured strength in North Africa.*
TOP *Once in enemy hands tanks were subjected to much scrutiny and often were remanned and used against their original owners, as was this captured Matilda, repainted in German colours.*
ABOVE *A knocked-out German Mark III; note the spaced turret armour which added an extra protective skin and helped to reduce shock levels.*

The Allied Sherman

The Sherman was the standard Allied medium tank from 1943. As the Lee-Grant's successor it made use of many of the latter's components but its fighting capabilities were much improved by mounting the 75-mm gun in a turret with all-round traverse. The gun, moreover, was hydro-electrically stabilized, which meant that aimed fire could be achieved while the tank was on the move. This was a new development but it was not without its drawbacks in the early years. Introduced in time to join the Eighth Army at El Alamein, the Sherman was then produced in great numbers and at high speed. Altogether 49,234 were built by Ford, Chrysler, General Motors and other enterprises in some twenty different marks. At the peak of its production a finished Sherman could be assembled from pre-fabricated parts in 30 minutes.

METRES

FEET

ABOVE AND BELOW *The 30.2-ton M-4 A-1 (Mark II) Sherman shown here from front and side in its desert livery was 19 feet 7 inches long, 8 feet 9 inches wide and 9 feet 2 inches high. It had rubber block tracks and a maximum speed of 25 mph. It was armed with the 75-mm gun and three machine-guns.*

METRES

FEET

LEFT *In the absence of a US heavy tank in 1944 the Sherman Jumbo was created to fill the gap. Classed as a heavy assault tank it consisted of a standard Sherman to which were added further thicknesses of armour plate on turret and hull. By this time the angular form of hull side had taken over from the rounded type of earlier versions.*

RIGHT *The M-4 A-3, known also as the Mark IV, was up-gunned in later versions to carry the 76-mm gun and had a different suspension system, with horizontal volute springs and return rollers on the hull.*

ABOVE *The M-4 A-4 Firefly. This was the Sherman Mark V armed with the British long 17-pounder (76.2-mm) gun; it was used by all British units equipped with Shermans.*
Numerous other variants of the basic tank included the Sherman DD, a swimming tank (featured on pages 100–101); the BARV (Beach Armoured Recovery Vehicle) which had an armoured superstructure and was water-proofed for deep-wading; the Adder, a flame-thrower; the Crab, a mine-sweeping flail device (also on pages 100–101); and Calliope, which fired rockets in batteries.

5   6

15   20

mounted a cautious and closely-controlled pursuit of the Afrika Korps. Many historians have since criticized his handling of the armour in the pursuit, for indeed, with fewer than 40 combat tanks by that stage, the Germans could have done little to prevent a bold Allied move. However, Montgomery held firmly to his conviction that he had already defeated the Afrika Korps at El Alamein, and consequently there was no need to take extra risks. Although British tank tactics lacked glamour, Montgomery managed to teach Rommel and the Panzers what the French should have taught them in 1940, namely that the tank is a brittle weapon of war. The tank in fact met its true fate in the Western Desert – from the air. The reason for this is that armour needs an elaborate supply and logistical structure which is vulnerable to disruptive air attacks unless a defending air force can produce an umbrella; and in the Western Desert no such umbrella was available to Rommel.

Nevertheless the Desert War dragged on for another six months, and although the Torch Landings in French North Africa in November 1942 sealed the fate of the Afrika Korps, the Panzers were still able to demonstrate new skills in the use of tanks in the defence. In the end, however, neither side learned the right lessons; each saw the desert as a specialized theatre of warfare from which it was impossible to draw conclusions. Each, furthermore, still believed in the idea of an all-powerful armoured torrent, but it was the Germans who were to make the fatal errors. They did so at Stalingrad, soon after the defeat at El Alamein, and later at Kursk in the summer of 1943.

skies above, raining destruction and chaos on the vulnerable Axis supply lines. After a week of bloody fighting Rommel admitted failure and withdrew his battered formations behind their defences to the west of El Alamein.

Montgomery waited six weeks before launching his great offensive against the Afrika Korps. The Battle of El Alamein (23 October – 4 November 1942), with its secure flanks and massive concentrations of infantry and artillery, was closer in character to the Battle of the Somme than any previous desert encounter. Sherman tanks arrived in the theatre in time for British brigades to be equipped with them for the battle; but although he possessed an enormous superiority in tanks, in the event Montgomery allocated the armour a secondary, non-cavalry role.

After the British had broken through the German defences and won the infantry dog-fight, Montgomery

ABOVE *Allied Shermans move up during the Battle of El Alamein.*
BELOW *British infantry take cover behind an abandoned tank.*

The Eastern Front

On the Eastern Front the Panzers spearheaded the great spring offensive of 1942 towards Stalingrad and the Volga. In the main they were equipped at this time with the excellent Mark IV tank which, if it possessed none of the skilfully sloped armour of the T-34, was capable of meeting its opponents on equal terms because of the expertise of the Panzer crews and the hitting power of the high-velocity 75-mm cannon. This tank was destined to give the Panzer divisions good service right up to the end of the war; even so Hitler and his generals had already become obsessed with the need to reassert the technical superiority of their tanks over the Russians. Combat officers at the front, in a counsel of despair, advocated the production of T-34s for their own use since they believed it could not be bettered. But German industry could never have coped with the technicalities of such a project – even if such a decision had been politically acceptable, which it clearly was not.

Instead the High Command flirted with numerous designs for heavy tanks and super-monsters, which wasted valuable industrial capacity while the Panzers at the front had to make do with the Mark III, the Mark IV and indifferent assault guns. Eventually two prototypes went into quantity production: known as the Tiger and the Panther, these tanks were destined to play a major part in Panzer fortunes in the final period of the war. The Tiger weighed 56 tons, had a maximum of 100 mm of frontal armour and was armed with the excellent 88-mm gun; it put the Germans ahead of the Russians and well in advance of the Anglo-Americans. All the same the Tiger had more than its share of teething problems but the Germans,

instead of patiently solving these first, rushed the tank into a premature deployment. It received its baptism of fire in a secondary operation, in unsuitable terrain on the Leningrad Front in September 1942, where the Russians inflicted heavy casualties and the decisive factor of surprise was destroyed. Meanwhile the Panther's designers ran into even greater technical problems in the initial period of that tank's construction, and the delay incurred before it was finally considered ready for combat was to have a major influence on the course of events in 1943.

In the autumn of 1942 the German offensive was forced to a halt, trapped in the claustrophobic arena of Stalingrad – where the Wehrmacht was destined to suffer its greatest single defeat of World War II. The concepts of Blitzkrieg were totally irrelevant in Stalingrad. There the Panzers forfeited all the advantages of their mobile tactics and allowed the Russian infantry to dictate the mode of combat. Marshal Zhukov, the Russian commander, contained the Germans in the city and in November unleashed his new tank armies in a massive counter-attack against indifferent satellite armies fighting on the German flanks. The Russian pincer linked up at Kalatsch on the Don, trapping von Paulus and the 20 divisions that composed his Sixth Army. Hitler refused permission for von Paulus to break out from Stalingrad and instead, in Operation Winter Storm, launched Hoth and the Fourth Panzer Army in a vain attempt to effect a relief. On 2 February 1943 the pathetic remains of the Sixth Army surrendered.

ABOVE *Winter 1942: a German Mark IV is silhouetted against smoke from the fighting around Stalingrad – the battle that isolated and eventually broke the German Sixth Army.*

Besides the enormous losses in manpower the Germans lost 60,000 vehicles and 1,500 tanks – figures that represent the equivalent of six months' production. The shock to the German Army was immense, and it was a blow from which the élite Panzer formations never recovered. The average tank complement in a Panzer division on the Eastern Front was now down to 27 tanks and the only proven vehicle the Germans had was the Mark IV. Behind the front German tank policy was in confusion: the new designs were still nowhere near ready while the artillery wanted the High Command to concentrate on producing a new tank destroyer to replace the vulnerable towed anti-tank gun.

The new weapon, called the Jagdpanzer, was a high-velocity 75-mm gun mounted on a tank chassis. Its form in fact symbolized the change which had come over German thinking about Panzers. For the Jagdpanzer was essentially a *defensive* weapon, best used for ambushes or in semi-fixed positions. Moreover production on a large scale inevitably absorbed part of the German industrial capacity which could otherwise have been devoted to tanks.[1]

After Stalingrad the Soviet tank armies found new strength and vigour. Work began on developing the excellent and by no means obsolescent T-34 to mount the 85-mm high-velocity gun in place of the 76-mm version. Substantial American aid in the form of vehicles and canned foods revolutionized Soviet supply problems and allowed the tank divisions to attempt new dimensions in penetrative power. The Russian generals had learned the lessons of the past and now handled their tank formations with confidence and skill. Their weakness lay in their tendency to

TOP LEFT *German infantry stick closely to the cover of their tanks in the steady advance across the Russian steppes during the spring offensive of* 1942, *directed towards Stalingrad and the Volga River.*
TOP RIGHT *A German Mark III tank armed with the* 50-*mm gun fords a Russian river on its eastward route.*

[1] In October 1942 the monthly production figures for the Mark IV reached the modest total of 100. The highest annual figure in Germany was that for 1944, when 19,000 armoured vehicles were built; in the same period the British produced 30,000, the Russians 30,000, and the Americans 90,000.

ABOVE *A Russian shell bursts a short distance ahead of a German Mark IV pressing with infantry support along a track between maize fields.*
CENTRE RIGHT *A Mark VI Tiger; one of the mid-war breed of German tanks, it made an indifferent début on the Eastern Front but was later to play a significant role in the Panzer effort.*

ABOVE *A train-load of Mark V Panthers, their gun barrels hooded against the harsh weather, moves up to the combat zone on the Eastern Front. A resilient and powerful tank, the Panther weighed 43 tons in its Model D version and mounted a 75-mm gun. Its boldly sloped armour reflected a lesson painfully absorbed by the Wehrmacht after their experiences against the T-34.*

Tank Inferno 1942–43

ABOVE *German tanks regroup before a blazing skyline. By 1943 Panzer divisions had been substantially reorganized, and consisted of four tank battalions, one equipped with Sturmgeschütz assault guns and one with Tiger tanks; there were two rifle regiments to each division, the riflemen being known as Panzer Grenadiers.*

CENTRE *Tanks of General von Kleist's Army Group A surge across the River Don in the Stalingrad campaign.*

BELOW *Russian heavy KV tanks stand in a defensive line. For their defence of Kursk the Russians mustered 3,600 tanks and had an average of 150 guns and mortars per mile of front.*

1942–43: at Stalingrad and Kursk the Russian bear demonstrates the force of his grip.

ABOVE *A German armoured division streams across the Russian steppes in the region of Kursk, where the Panzers were decisively beaten in their attempt to isolate the Russian salient.*

RIGHT *At Kursk, a Panzer Grenadier dashes behind two immobilized Russian vehicles, a heavy BA-32 armoured car fitted with a 45-mm tank gun and a KV-II, the giant vehicle that mounted a 152-mm howitzer.*

BELOW *Russian infantry race forward behind their armour at Kalatsch on the River Don, where in November 1942 the Russians closed a critical pincer, trapping the German Sixth Army under General von Paulus; the Germans retreated into 'Fortress Stalingrad' until their surrender in February 1943.*

253

continue offensives which were unprofitable and resulted in disproportionately heavy casualties. It was this willingness on the part of the Russians to be lavish with their human material, of which they had a great abundance, together with the technical excellence of the Wehrmacht in the defence, that allowed the front to be stabilized and gave the Panzers a chance to recover from the disasters of Stalingrad. In March 1943 von Manstein and his Army Group South recaptured Kharkov in a brilliant armoured operation in which the Tigers were able to demonstrate for the first time their true potential.

Hitler had earlier recalled Germany's greatest tank soldier, Heinz Guderian, from an obscure retirement, and offered him the post of Inspector-General of Armoured Troops. He was given the equivalent powers of an army commander and had control over all Panzer and motorized troops, though not of the artillery Jagdpanzers. The stable front in Russia now attracted Hitler and his closest advisers to the possibilities of securing a decision through a bold use of armour. But Guderian, together with General Model (then commanding the Ninth Army) counselled against any new offensives, saying that the Panzer divisons were in desperate need of a major rest and refit. Guderian had detected a disturbing inflationary situation in his new command, for while the number of divisions had been increased the tank complement per division had shrunk. After much debate Hitler ignored Guderian's and Model's advice in favour of launching a massive tank offensive against the Russian salient around Kursk. Events moved swiftly toward what General von Mellenthin (at that time Chief of Staff to 56th Panzer Corps) was to describe as the *Todesritt*, or death ride, of the Panzers:

> The German Army threw away all its advantages in mobile war and met the Russians on ground of their own choosing ... the German High Command could think of nothing better to do than fling our magnificent Panzers against the strongest fortress in the world.
>
> From *Panzer Battles*, by General F. W. von Mellenthin

The offensive at Kursk was delayed until July 1943 because the new Panthers were not available in sufficient quantity (there were only 100 on the Eastern Front in April) and in the meantime the whole plan of operations had been compromised by the Lucy Ring – an OSS espionage service based in Switzerland. The Russians planned accordingly and met the Panzer thrusts with a

seemingly impregnable network of defences. Rokossovsky's Army, for example, which was deployed to resist the northern thrust by Model's Ninth Army, had prepared 3,000 miles of trenches and 400,000 mines, i.e. 2,400 anti-tank and 2,700 anti-personnel mines per mile of front; on average there were 150 guns and mortars per mile of front. Amidst the maze of trenches and minefields the main Russian stratagem centred on the 'Pak-fronts', which involved groups of 10 anti-tank guns capable of providing concentrated fire through a centralized command.

Hitler was gambling for high stakes at Kursk since the 78 Panzer and Panzer Grenadier divisions deployed there represented nearly all his armour and more than half the line formations available to him on the Eastern Front. However, there could be few less rewarding ways to deploy tanks than at this 'Panzer Verdun'. The basic formation was the Panzer *Keil*, or wedge, a battering-ram technique the spearhead of which was composed of Tigers and lumbering Ferdinands, with the lighter Mark IVs and Panthers deployed on the flanks and mechanized infantry bringing up the rear. The Ferdinands, encountered here for the first time and also known as the Porsche Tiger or 'Elefant', was an enormous self-propelled gun. It weighed 65 tons, had a crew of six, was armed with the 88-mm L-70 gun but had no machine-guns for self-defence. Its frontal armour was 8 inches thick, i.e. more than the British battlecruisers at Jutland in 1916; its top speed was 12 mph and it needed another Ferdinand or Tiger to recover it when it broke down.

The battle began on 4 July 1943, bringing into collision the greatest single assembly of armoured vehicles in military history. The Panzer *Keil* proved to be an immediate failure as the Russians separated the infantry from the armour, peeled away the weaker tanks on the flanks and exposed the heavy Tigers and Ferdinands to overwhelming concentrations of fire. The Panthers, too, did not come up to expectations: they were easily set ablaze because their oil and gasoline feeding systems were inadequately protected, and the crews were insufficiently trained.

The application of Russian bulk against German skill slowed the advance right down and by 12 July it had stalled in the crippling grasp of the minefields. Model in the north had made no headway against Rokossovsky while Hoth in the south after enormous losses had penetrated 20 miles in nine days – a far cry from the heady days of 1940. On 13 July the Fourth Panzer Army had 600 tanks remaining and these Hoth hurled forward in one last desperate attempt to break through; the 'death ride' had begun. Zhukov's Fifth Tank Army blocked the way and 1,500 tanks clashed in close-quarter combat; then, at ranges of often less than 100 yards, the T-34s pressed home the battle. In one day the Wehrmacht lost 400 tanks and more than 10,000 men and the Panzer divisions never recovered from these losses. Zhukov now moved over to a major offensive and pushed the shattered Panzers back beyond Kharkov and the Soviet western frontiers.

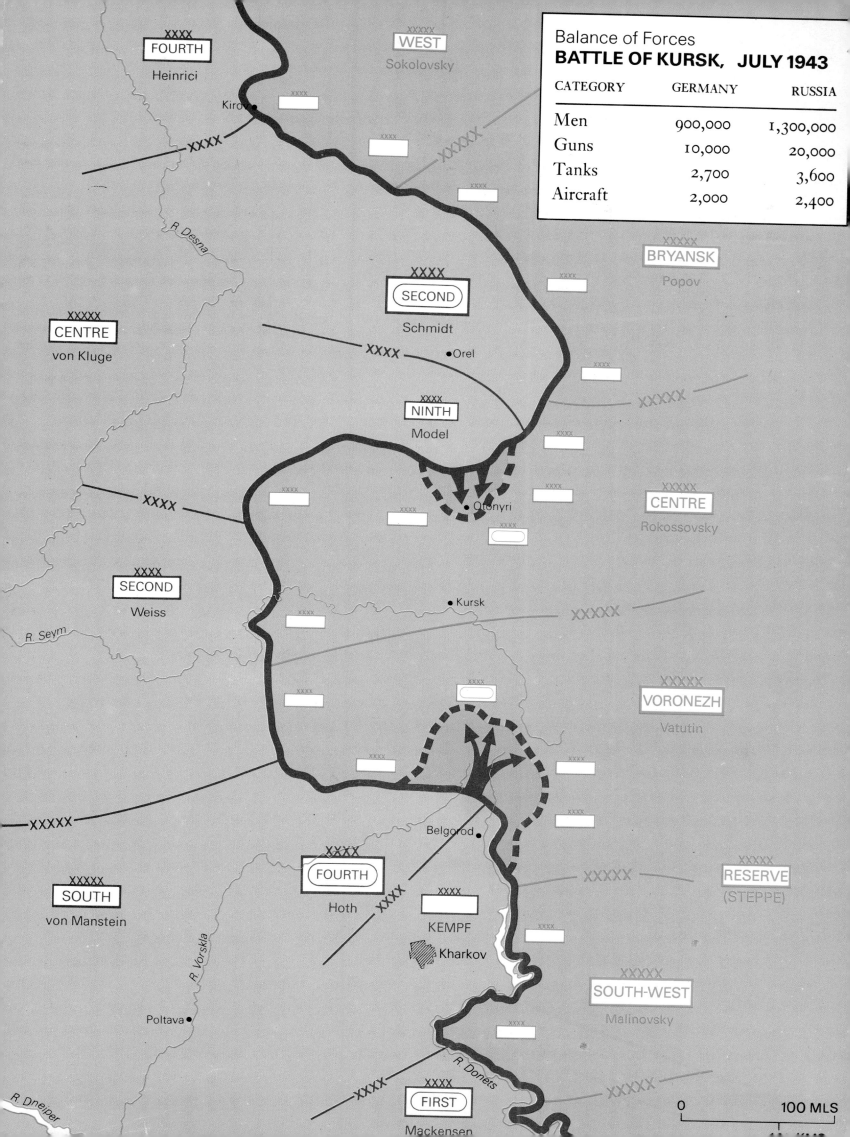

FOURTH
Heinrici

Kirov

WEST
Sokolovsky

Balance of Forces
BATTLE OF KURSK, JULY 1943

CATEGORY	GERMANY	RUSSIA
Men	900,000	1,300,000
Guns	10,000	20,000
Tanks	2,700	3,600
Aircraft	2,000	2,400

R. Desna

BRYANSK
Popov

SECOND
Schmidt

CENTRE
von Kluge

Orel

NINTH
Model

Olonyri

CENTRE
Rokossovsky

SECOND
Weiss

R. Seym

Kursk

VORONEZH
Vatutin

RESERVE
(STEPPE)

SOUTH
von Manstein

R. Vorskla

FOURTH
Hoth

Belgorod

KEMPF

Kharkov

SOUTH-WEST
Malinovsky

Poltava

R. Dnieper

R. Donets

FIRST
Mackensen

0   100 MLS

The Invasion of Europe

The Battle of Kursk was both an illustration and an admission that armour had become fatally inhibited by its enemies on the ground and in the air. Hitler, however, still believed that his armour was a battle-winning force, and as the Western Allies began their invasion of Europe – from the Mediterranean in 1943 and Normandy in 1944 – he sought to use his tanks to exploit imagined schisms in the Western Alliance. German defences in the west were based on a compromise between the fortifications of the Atlantic Wall and the mobile reserves of Panzer Group West, whose better divisions were concentrated to meet what was considered to be the likely Allied avenue of advance through the Pas de Calais.

Rommel was given the task of countering the Allied invasion and his planning was hopelessly wrong. He envisaged the Allied landings as an infantry assault that would create a beachhead into which Allied armour would be deployed. Consequently he moved his tanks close to the coast so that they could destroy the beachheads before the Allied tanks were ashore. But, unfortunately for Rommel, the Allies had developed specialized amphibious and assault armour which moved in with the infantry: these were the tanks of Major-General Hobart's 79th Division, developed from Sherman, Valentine and Churchill chassis. Popularly known as the 'Funnies', they stormed ashore in one of the most brilliant armoured operations of World War II.

These special vehicles included the Sherman DD (Duplex Drive) amphibious tank; the Crab – a flail tank for exploding mines; the Churchill Ark and AVRE, which were gap-crossing combat vehicles, and the Crocodile, which was a flame-thrower. Their contributions to the British landings were invaluable while their absence (except for the Sherman DD) on the American beaches resulted in heavy casualties on D-Day (6 June 1944).

Once they were ashore the Allies' problems centred around the need to break out of the Bocage, where the wooded terrain favoured the defence and inhibited Allied armour. In this close country the Jagdpanzer and the Tiger were supreme; there was no Allied equivalent to these giants for the simple reason that the requirements of sea transport limited tank weights at that time to a maximum of 40 tons, and consequently the Allies had been unable to develop their own heavy battle tanks. The Americans still relied upon Shermans while the British had developed some of their Shermans to mount the new 17-pounder anti-tank gun – the product being known as the Sherman Firefly. But other British tanks such as the infantry Churchill were of little value, in the latter's case because its lack of speed was not compensated for either by extra protection or increased firepower. The latest tank of the cruiser lineage, the Cromwell, also made its début at this time: it had a strange, square turret and though fast and tactically mobile it was no match for the Tigers and Panthers.

For both sides morale was a major factor in the ensuing tank encounters that occurred in Western Europe. The

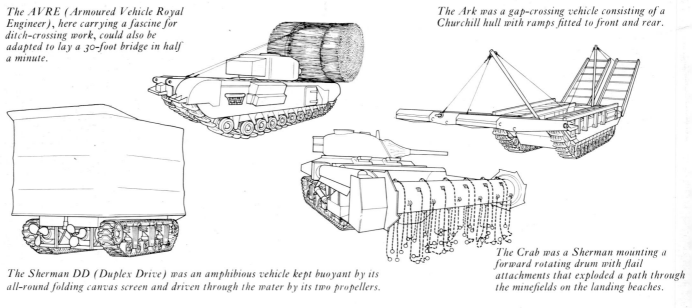

The AVRE (Armoured Vehicle Royal Engineer), here carrying a fascine for ditch-crossing work, could also be adapted to lay a 30-foot bridge in half a minute.

The Ark was a gap-crossing vehicle consisting of a Churchill hull with ramps fitted to front and rear.

The Sherman DD (Duplex Drive) was an amphibious vehicle kept buoyant by its all-round folding canvas screen and driven through the water by its two propellers.

The Crab was a Sherman mounting a forward rotating drum with flail attachments that exploded a path through the minefields on the landing beaches.

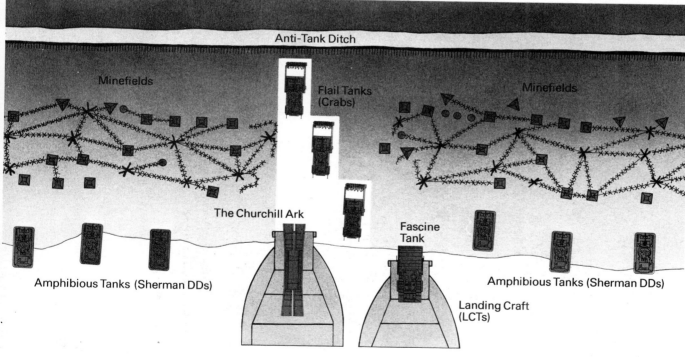

Anti-Tank Ditch

Minefields

Flail Tanks
(Crabs)

Minefields

The Churchill Ark

Fascine
Tank

Amphibious Tanks (Sherman DDs)

Amphibious Tanks (Sherman DDs)

Landing Craft
(LCTs)

OPPOSITE, ABOVE *Specialized armoured vehicles, known as 'Funnies', were developed for the storming of the Normandy beaches. Shown here are four versions; the 'Funnies' were made from the chassis of Sherman, Valentine and Churchill tanks.*

OPPOSITE, BELOW *Rehearsals for the Normandy landings: a bridge-laying AVRE moves up the beach and infantry practise disembarking at speed from landing craft.*

TOP *The first Allied landings in Europe were made in Sicily and southern Italy after the defeat of the Axis powers in North Africa. Here a Sherman lands on Italian soil.*

ABOVE *The diagram shows how various types of 'Funnies' were used on the British beaches on D-Day. (By contrast, the Americans dispensed with specialized armour – except for Sherman DDs – and suffered much higher casualties.) Into this section of beach rolled the flail and gap-crossing tanks (Crabs and Arks) with the aim of clearing a path through the German wire, minefields and anti-tank ditches, dropping fascines into the latter. Behind them amphibious Sherman DDs swam into action from parent craft standing offshore.*

OVERLEAF *Standing by for D-Day – a tank park of Shermans.*

Allies recognized that in order to destroy a Tiger or a Panther they would have to lose a number of tanks before the superior German vehicle could be taken in the flank. Conversely the Panzers fought their tanks in the knowledge that no matter how many Cromwells or Shermans exploded under their fire, eventually they would be overcome by sheer force of numbers. The major advantage for the Allies lay in their total air superiority, while for the Panzers the sky became a source of terror and manoeuvre in daylight was tantamount to suicide. In the Battle of the Bocage, Allied armoured tactics proved suspect and Montgomery learned the hard way – through such costly failures as Operation Goodwood – that material superiority can be neutralized by local conditions. As the British tanks tried to bludgeon a path through to Caen and the open country beyond, German tanks and assault guns, mines and Panzerfausts (infantry rocket launchers) took a fearful toll. In addition Montgomery's task was complicated by the RAF's dropping 2,500 tons of bombs on the town, the streets of which became so blocked that they were easier for the Germans to defend, and the Allies had to call up armoured bulldozers before they could advance further.

Meanwhile, the Americans were poised for the breakout.

General Bradley, once a corps commander under Patton and now elevated to commanding US 12th Army Group, deployed General Patton and his Third Army for a thrust on a three-divisional front west of St Lô. Operation Cobra, as it was called, hit the Wehrmacht at a critical moment, the High Command still reeling from the abortive July plot against Hitler. Those divisions that stood their ground were engulfed in a hailstorm of Blitzkrieg-style fire from the air as well as from the armoured units and infantry. On 18 July General Patton broke free of the Bocage and the American divisions were now able to advance west into Brittany, south to the Loire and then east toward the strategic centre of Le Mans. The British and Canadians took Caen and moved south towards Falaise, trapping the Wehrmacht in a rapidly closing pincer. The Allied formations packed the shoulders of the pocket and destroyed 19 German divisions with artillery and air bombardment. Patton wanted to close the gap with his Shermans but Bradley wisely decided that the Allied tanks would be unable to prevent the Panzers from breaking out. Those Germans who did manage to escape had eventually to swim for their lives across the Seine, and 2,000 tanks and assault guns were either captured or destroyed.

BELOW *On a Normandy beach after D-Day, US infantry keep watch from fox-holes while the beach is cleared.*
OPPOSITE, LEFT *Prior to the breakout at St Lô, American armour advances slowly across the difficult terrain of the Normandy bocage, a prey to German mines, rocket launchers*

and the superior gunpower of the Wehrmacht's Tigers, Panthers and assault guns, now committed to all-out defence.
OPPOSITE, RIGHT *A knocked-out Tiger blocks a shattered street in the Caen-Falaise area. Once the essential breakout from Normandy was made, most of France was quickly liberated.*

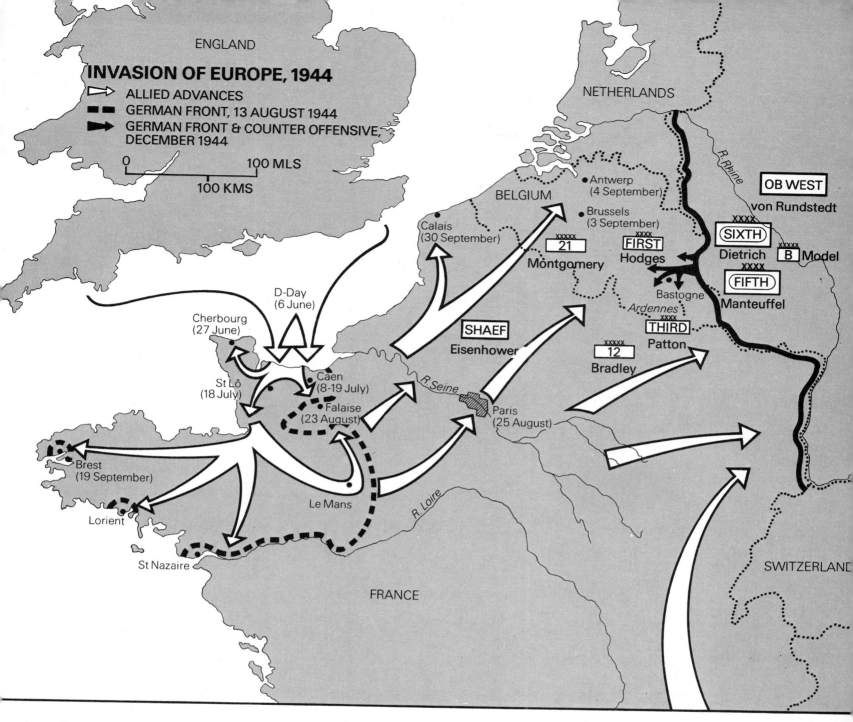

INVASION OF EUROPE, 1944

▷ ALLIED ADVANCES
▬ ▬ GERMAN FRONT, 13 AUGUST 1944
▶ GERMAN FRONT & COUNTER OFFENSIVE, DECEMBER 1944

ENGLAND

0   100 MLS

100 KMS

NETHERLANDS

BELGIUM

Antwerp
(4 September)

Calais
(30 September)

Brussels
(3 September)

OB WEST
von Rundstedt

R. Rhine

XXXXX
21
Montgomery

XXXX
FIRST
Hodges

XXXX
SIXTH
Dietrich

XXXXX
B Model

D-Day
(6 June)

Cherbourg
(27 June)

St Lô
(18 July)

Caen
(8-19 July)

Falaise
(23 August)

Le Mans

R. Seine

SHAEF
Eisenhower

Paris
(25 August)

XXXXX
12
Bradley

Bastogne

Ardennes

XXXX
THIRD
Patton

XXXX
FIFTH
Manteuffel

Brest
(19 September)

Lorient

St Nazaire

R. Loire

FRANCE

SWITZERLAND

Now 20 divisions of Allied armour spearheaded the pursuit of the retreating Wehrmacht through eastern France and the Low Countries to the western frontier of the Third Reich. An armoured division took up 200 miles of road and the logistical problems were intensified as the supply lines became longer and longer, stretching back to their base ports at Cherbourg and Marseilles (liberated on

ABOVE *A shattered German Mark IV tank at Bastogne, Belgium.*
BELOW *A Mark IV in Italy, backed into a farmhouse to serve as an anti-tank gun. Such* improvisations *were common in* 1944, *the Germans being forced increasingly on to the defensive as the Allies swept across France and Belgium and slogged their way more* slowly up through Italy.
OPPOSITE, BELOW *Tanks link up with airborne assault forces beside a glider landing ground, ready for the next push.*

ABOVE *Shermans head for northern Italy after a bitter winter campaign. Far from being a straightforward push through what Churchill called the enemy's 'soft underbelly', it took the Allies 11 months to reach Rome from Sicily.*

28 August). To maintain a controlled advance Eisenhower insisted on adhering to a basic linear strategy – with all armies keeping pace with those on their flanks – though he did sanction Montgomery's attempt in September to secure the bridges over the Waal, Maas and the Rhine through the use of airborne formations. The first and second bridges were taken intact but Allied armour failed to effect a relief of the British airborne troops at Arnhem. By October 1944 the Allies had 70 divisions spread out over 500 miles of front but they were still a long way short of the autumn objective – the Rhine. Despite Montgomery's capture of Antwerp, the Germans still held the Scheldt estuary, with the result that the Allies lacked a major port east of Cherbourg; this, coupled with the early onset of winter and a general exhaustion, resulted in the Allied advance losing momentum just as German resistance stiffened along the western frontiers.

Hitler then attempted one last Panzer gamble. In December he hurled his remaining tanks in a desperate and foolhardy counter-offensive through the Ardennes. The famous Battle of the Bulge which resulted was an attempt to drive a wedge politically and militarily between the British and Americans by recapturing Antwerp. The assault by the Sixth SS Panzer Army and the Fifth Panzer Army caught the Americans by surprise, and with Allied aircraft grounded by bad weather the Germans at first drove all before them. But the Allied reaction after the

initial shock was rapid and decisive. An airborne division held out in Bastogne while the infantry divisions packed the flanks of the breakthrough and denied the vital crossings over the Meuse. Patton moved quickly in a bold drive with his tanks through the Upper Ardennes to relieve Bastogne. On Christmas Eve 1944 the weather cleared and 5,000 tactical aircraft took to the skies and rained havoc and destruction on the exposed Panzers and their supply formations. The German offensive was contained, the Allies regrouped and launched a massive counter-offensive which moved slowly forward through the winter months and so reached the Rhine.

The Fall of Berlin

In their last great offensive of the war the Panzers had bought the Third Reich a few extra weeks of life in the west and had inflicted on the Americans their biggest single defeat in the European war. But the price they paid for this defiant gesture was soon to be felt on the Eastern Front, where, as the Russian army groups deployed along the Oder for the last offensive into Berlin, precious few tanks remained to oppose them. At dawn on 16 April 1945 40,000 guns opened fire on a 250-mile front and 6,000 Soviet tanks began to move along the last 50 miles of road into Berlin. The bulk of the Russian armour consisted of well-tried T-34s supplemented by small numbers of the latest battle tanks, which arrived in time for the final battle. The new tank, the JS III, had been developed from the KV series and its sloping armour and 122-mm gun gave it a powerful battle capability; but firepower and protection had been compromised and it could carry only small reserves of ammunition.

The final march on Berlin was not, as it has often been presented, an impressive armoured punch: indeed the tanks found little freedom to move against the German defences. The Wehrmacht and SS Divisions fought with enormous devotion to a lost cause, no quarter was asked or given and casualties were enormous on both sides. When the Russians eventually encircled Berlin they hurled their tanks with optimistic arrogance into the street battles only to see them destroyed piecemeal by fanatical defenders equipped with the short-range but lethal Panzerfaust.

On 25 April the last barrage of the war on the Eastern Front began as 2,000,000 shells rained down on to the inner suburbs of Berlin. Soviet infantry and armour fought its way forward from street to street until only a few acres round the Reich Chancellery and Hitler's bunker survived. On 30 April, Hitler committed suicide and General Krebs, Chief of Staff of the 56th Panzer Corps, surrendered the remnants of the Berlin garrison to General Vasili Chuikov, commander of the Eighth Guards Army, and the battle was over.

While the battle for Berlin was being fought, Allied armour in the west had crossed the Rhine and moved eastwards to link up with the Russians on the Elbe. Patton and the Third Army swung south into Austria while Montgomery and the British sped across the old Panzer training areas on the Lüneburg Heath to Hamburg. Two new Allied tanks appeared in time to join the final phase of the fighting and these helped somewhat to restore the prestige of Allied armour. The Americans had the Pershing, an excellent tank armed with a 90-mm gun, while the British had the Comet, which exploited the mechanical reliability of the Cromwell and had a new 75-mm gun and sloped armour – factors which combined to make it, belatedly, the best British tank of the war.

OPPOSITE *Russian tank-riders armed with submachine guns ford a stream aboard a column of T-34/85s. The death-rate among the tank-riders, who fought with scant cover from a continually unsteady platform, was extremely high.*
ABOVE *A British Comet tank, a new cruiser type armed with a 75-mm gun that entered service towards the end of the war.*
RIGHT *Russian armour enters the battered streets of Berlin during the final assault on Germany's last stronghold.*
BELOW *Moving up to Berlin – Pershing tanks of the US Ninth Army cross the Rhine.*

Balance of Forces FINAL RUSSIAN OFFENSIVE 16 APRIL - 7 MAY 1945		
CATEGORY	RUSSIA	GERMANY
Divisions	193	85
Men	2,500,000	1,000,000
Guns/mortars	41,000	10,000
Tanks/self-propelled guns	6,250	1,500
Aircraft	7,500	3,300

Tanks in the Far East and Pacific

In the period up to the end of World War II the tank made its most spectacular contributions to the battlefield in the Western world. Yet this account would certainly be incomplete if mention were not made of the role of the tank in the Far East and generally in the war against Japan.

There were only a few isolated instances of tank battles as such, and this was because the Japanese had earlier paid scant attention to the tank; consequently those which they did possess were decidedly inferior to Western types. In these circumstances the Allied tank crews found themselves acting mainly in the role of self-propelled artillery in close support of the infantry. In Burma, the Pacific atolls and New Guinea the tanks engaged Japanese pillboxes and strongpoints at close range and in terrain where air support and conventional, i.e. static, artillery proved less effective.

At first the enormous logistical problems involved made the Allied use lighter tanks than were best suited to these theatres of operation, but the need was soon appreciated for more powerful, better protected and more heavily armed cruiser tanks. In the Pacific this placed a new premium on landing ships and assault craft, while in Burma it required feats of engineering wizardry before the primitive hill roads and jungle trails could support the weight of Grants and Shermans.

The British had the additional problem of training units of their redoubtable Indian soldiery in the technological skills needed to man and maintain sophisticated armour in battle. As early as 1942 pundits in the hierarchy and establishment of the Indian Army had raised considerable opposition to such a scheme, doubting the possibility of training Indian peasants at all for work going beyond the demands of infantry duties. But in the event all the time, effort, sweat and political infighting that went into the creation and deployment in battle of a distinct Indian Armoured Corps paid dividends. In the seemingly impenetrable jungle their Shermans and Grants hurled aside natural obstacles and paved a way to the very mouths of the Japanese bunkers. In so doing, the armoured formations saved countless lives among the infantry, whose task this had formerly been.

This story was repeated on innumerable occasions in the Pacific, where the tanks were present from the first offensive at Guadalcanal (1942–43) to the final amphibious operation at Okinawa in 1945. The Pacific campaign is also important in the present context because of its contribution to the development of amphibious armoured operations. Specialized vehicles known as Landing Vehicles Tracked (LVTs) were originally developed by the US Marine Corps in 1940 as unarmoured supply carriers. Then on Tarawa in 1943 they were employed as armoured assault carriers; these were later joined by turreted gun-carrying versions. Eight Marine and Army LVT battalions led the amphibious assault on Saipan in June 1944 and by the end of the war the Marine Corps alone had 12 LVT battalions deployed in the Pacific theatre.

TOP *A column of Japanese Type 95 light tanks such as saw service in the Malayan and Pacific campaigns. In production from 1935–43, the Type 95 had a light 37-mm gun, was thinly armoured and suffered from a cramped fighting compartment.*
CENTRE *A Type 97, the standard Japanese medium tank at the outbreak of war, capable of the same speed (28 mph) as the Type 95 and armed with a short-barrelled 57-mm gun.*
ABOVE *American Shermans line up at a river crossing in Luzon, Philippines, in June 1945.*

TOP *British tanks manned by the Indian Armoured Corps move up for the final assault on Fort Dufferin, Mandalay, in March* 1945.
CENTRE *A US flamethrower fires on a Japanese strongpoint in the Philippines.*
RIGHT *A Landing Vehicle Tracked (LVT); the importance of these specialized US vehicles grew with the increase in amphibious assault work.*

17

THE GUNS REPLY

Artillery designs of World War II; the race against technological defeat.

World War I had been a fairly straightforward conflict in which the duties of the artillerist had remained for the most part what they had always been. A new form of artillery had been introduced in an attempt to counter aircraft, and crude beginnings had been made towards solving the problem of the tank.

World War II was another matter. All the belligerents were quickly drawn into a deadly race against technological defeat, and both guns and gunners now had to be adaptable to a variety of changing conditions and environments. Understandably, too, the circumstances of individual campaigns rendered some weapons obsolete and thrust others into prominence.

Anti-aircraft and anti-tank guns were developed to near optimum efficiency during the war. Rocket artillery was revived and used extensively for area fire. Mobility was improved through the use of self-propelled mounts and motor traction. And the amount of firepower available to local commanders increased dramatically in two ways; firstly, the use of shaped-charge projectiles, rocket weapons and recoilless guns enabled the infantryman to carry his

own artillery with him; and, secondly, the support of radio and aerial observation enabled the artillery to assist other arms quickly, accurately and decisively. In this way artillery became an important strike element, indeed a force without which no operation would be contemplated.

The artillery of the Great Powers in World War II may be summarized as follows:

I ALLIES

France. The Puteaux '75' was still the standard field gun in 1940. Various modernizations, including 'high-speed' wheels and 'streamline' shells, had improved its cross-country mobility and range. The medium and heavy guns were for the most part late-World War I or immediately post-war models. In keeping with French tactical doctrine, which stressed positional warfare, there was a decided lack of mobility among the larger calibres. The French firms of St Chamond and Schneider had pioneered the development of large-calibre self-propelled (SP) guns during World War I, and many of their models were in action during the Battle of France. These SP guns were not armoured and

French and British gunners at first are gravely impeded by their out-of-date equipment.

OPPOSITE *Before the Fall, 1940: a French 194-mm self-propelled gun lumbers across country. Slow and of basically World War I vintage, the French SP guns were destroyed in droves during the May–June fighting by German dive-bombers and by fast-moving Panzer units.*

ABOVE *Vormarsch! German troops pour at speed through a gap in the French defences; from a painting by Handel-Mazzoti.*

they were slow by World War II standards. Most of them were destroyed by dive-bombers or lost to the rapid movements of the Panzers.

The French artillery was totally unprepared for the task facing it in May 1940. The Germans were struck by the inability of French gunners to cope with the conditions of modern warfare. Field Marshal Erich von Manstein later recorded his 'pleasant surprise' at discovering the weaknesses of French artillery:

Their shooting was not adaptable enough, and their speed in putting down strong concentrations of fire fell far short of the standard required in a war of movement. What was more, they had not developed forward observation technique to anything like the same extent as we had....

(from *Lost Victories*, by Erich von Manstein)

If the effort of the French field artillery was bad, their anti-tank and anti-aircraft measures were worse. The anti-tank guns are covered elsewhere; as for the anti-aircraft defences, the French General A.V. Georges described them as 'non-existent'.

Great Britain. The very advanced 25-pounder gun-howitzer had replaced the World War I vintage 18-pounder field gun and the 4·5-inch howitzer as the standard field

artillery weapon by the time the North African campaign began. The 25-pounder was a remarkable weapon with a number of exceptional features. It could be emplaced in one minute, had a lightweight firing platform which allowed rapid all-round traverse (a valuable asset when fighting tanks) and replaceable tube-liners that could be quickly changed in the field.

The elderly 6-inch howitzer remained the standard British medium howitzer for a time and was used with great effectiveness in the counter-battery role in North Africa (where the Germans had few comparable weapons). But it was obsolete by World War II standards and was in due course replaced by the excellent 5·5-inch gun.

British heavy guns were mostly World War I leftovers. They were notable for their lack of mobility even by pre-war standards, and (fortunately) most had to be left in France following the Dunkirk evacuation. In later campaigns the British relied chiefly on modern heavy guns supplied by the USA.

The British anti-tank effort was similarly handicapped by obsolescent material, but the introduction in 1942 of the 6-pounder AT gun and, a short while later, the 17-pounder, helped to redress the balance. The 3·7-inch AA gun, like the US 90-mm AA gun, was eventually used in many roles and became Britain's best anti-tank gun.

USA. The guns and howitzers of World War I, be they of French or British parentage, were gradually replaced by newer designs following the recommendations of the Westervelt Board of 1919. By the time US participation in World War II seemed likely, US designers had produced a 105-mm howitzer – the famous M-2 – which has remained standard equipment to this day. The older '75s' were gradually replaced by this gun. Corps and army artillery

ABOVE *Gun crew of the US Eleventh Corps Artillery fire an 8-inch howitzer ('Comanche') on pockets of Japanese resistance on Ipo Dam Hill, Luzon, 26 May 1945.*
LEFT AND RIGHT *British 25-pounders operating in the Western Desert, 1942.*
OPPOSITE *A US 240-mm howitzer emplaced near San Vittore, Italy.*

were equipped with the 105-mm and a new 155-mm howitzer M-1.

The long-range guns included the 155-mm M-1 A-1 'Long Tom', the 8-inch gun M-1, the 240-mm howitzer M-1 and the 8-inch howitzer M-1. The 'Long Tom' was a direct descendant of the 155-mm GPF gun of World War I, but had been so improved that it was far superior to other mobile 'heavies' produced during the war. It was ready by 1938 and provided accurate fire to a range of 25,000 yards.

The 8-inch gun used the same carriage as the 240-mm howitzer, which was first used in Italy in 1943. These guns and the 8-inch howitzer greatly increased the strength of Allied heavy artillery. The 8-inch howitzer gained a reputation as the most accurate gun used in the war and was often called upon to deliver destructive pin-point fire on bridges and strongpoints in the enemy's rear that even bombers could not destroy.

The 90-mm 'Baby Long Tom' AA gun was the most prominent of the group of anti-aircraft guns used by US forces during the war. This versatile gun was equally effective as an anti-tank, anti-aircraft or field gun – a facility which earned it the affectionate nickname of 'Triple Threat Gun'. In the Pacific theatre it was used to 'snipe' at

US long-range guns, howitzers and anti-tank weapons; the 'Long Tom' provides accurate fire up to 25,000 yards.

Japanese pill-boxes and bunkers, while in Europe it played a central role in defeating the V-1 raids on London and Antwerp. Of 5,000 V-1s aimed at Antwerp alone, only 211 penetrated the 90-mm AA defences.

The effectiveness of the 90-mm gun was so complete that it was found unnecessary to provide the larger 120-mm AA gun for overseas deployment. The 120-mm AA gun had been built to counter anticipated German high-altitude bombing raids on the USA. It had an effective ceiling of 56,000 feet. Both the 90-mm and 120-mm AA guns were built to receive radar data and had complex electric directors and fire-control equipment.

The USA fielded a representative group of anti-tank guns ranging from the 37-mm M-3 to the 3-inch M-5. The 57-mm M-1, the gun most commonly used in the field, was a light and useful piece but it could not cope with the heavier German armour encountered towards the end of the war. The 90-mm AA gun was frequently found in an anti-tank role during the last campaigns.

USSR. Stalin characterized artillery as the 'god of war', and events on the Eastern Front fully confirmed his

The Soviets envisage artillery as the main strike force, and invest heavily in anti-tank weapons for the defence.

RIGHT *Americans advancing through Normandy in the Battle of the Bocage hit the dirt beside a 57-mm anti-tank gun.*
BELOW *The crew of 'Lottie', a US 105-mm howitzer, receive firing data by telephone from an air spotter.*
BELOW RIGHT *Abandoned Soviet guns at Petroskaja. In the background is a 122-mm field gun M-1937 with its towing tractor. In the foreground is a 76-mm field gun M-1939.*
BOTTOM RIGHT *A Soviet 122-mm howitzer M-1938. This type was widely used both in World War II and in Korea (1950–53). The recoil mechanism is sited in the cradle below the tube and the recuperator is carried above it.*
OPPOSITE *Soviet howitzers in the defence of Moscow. Here, in the winter of 1941, the Germans received a major setback.*

their howitzers, which had little chance of knocking out a tank, were to lay down barrage fire to separate the accompanying infantrymen from their tanks and to harass the tanks with HE shells. After the early setbacks of Operation Barbarossa, when it was driven almost to the gates of Moscow, the Red Army introduced lighter field guns and adopted the concept of in-depth defence first introduced by a German, von Lossberg, in 1917. The most sophisticated defence of this type was created in the Kursk salient in 1943.

2 *In offensive operations, direct fire from masses of guns should be encouraged, and area-fire weapons used extensively.*

The Soviets regarded artillery as the main strike force of any army or 'front' (army group). As in other armies, once the point of main effort had been determined, the artillery was placed well forward to deal with the enemy's guns. The Russians discouraged fire at ranges beyond 6–8 miles. Their artillery preparations were usually either long, rhythmical bombardments or were of the surprise 'drum-fire' type. Soviet insistence on the strike

assertion. Nowhere in World War II was artillery used in such massive concentrations and with such destructive effect as in the titanic battles on the steppes of Russia and Eastern Europe.

The Soviets entered World War II with the beginnings, at least, of a fully modern arsenal, a very advanced tactical doctrine for the artillery, and a great deal of practical experience. The experience had been gained in the Russo-Finnish War (1939–40) and in fighting the Japanese in Manchuria, most notably at the great Battle of Khalkin Gol (1939). There, the need for camouflage and manoeuvrability – skills not easily mastered in peacetime excercises – had been rudely taught by the Japanese aviators.

In 1941, Soviet artillery doctrine was conceptually far in advance of that of the other Great Powers. This doctrine had been promulgated in the mid-1930s. Its chief tenets were:

1 *All defence is primarily anti-tank defence, and all artillery is anti-tank artillery.*

All Russian guns, whatever their formal designation – gun, howitzer or AT gun – had formidable AT capabilities. Insistence on an AT capability had led the Soviets to retain large numbers of field guns in their divisional artillery. They had not whole-heartedly embraced the new 'gun-how' (see page 192). In the Soviet system even

capability of artillery led to the formation of a unique artillery organization beyond divisional and corps levels. This was the artillery reserve of the High Command, a powerful reserve of medium and heavy guns which was used to form artillery 'fists'. Such 'fists' were allocated to important offensive operations which sometimes involved more than 20,000 pieces.

Russian guns and howitzers were of simple design, rugged construction and crude finish. Soviet gunsights and optical equipment were comparatively primitive but were considered to be more accurate than the guns they served. These were factors which may well have contributed to the emphasis on direct fire in Soviet tactical doctrine. Similarly, the poor state of development of Soviet electronic technology did not allow the development of complex electronic directors and computers or radar range-finders for the anti-aircraft artillery, although such devices had been brought to a high state of effectiveness by the Western Allies, in particular by the USA.

2 AXIS

Germany. The superiority of the German Army's organization, training and tactical doctrine carried it to its early victories and sustained it in its darkest hours. Initially, too, the Germans possessed superior weaponry. But as the war progressed, the Allies fielded guns superior to the excellent German pre-war models. By late 1942, German superiority in matériel had been overcome in most areas.

The tendency has been for many commentators to ascribe the early successes of the German Army to its superior weapons. The best example of this phenomenon seems to be the almost mythical aura surrounding the 88-mm AA/AT gun. In reality, however, the reasons for Germany's successes must be sought elsewhere. And, in the context of artillery, a great deal must be attributed to the Germans' advanced tactical thinking.

German tactical doctrine laid great stress on the role of the forward observer. Artillery observers accompanied the infantry in its advance, rode in specially equipped radio tanks with armoured elements, and surveyed the turmoil of the fighting front from Feiseler Storch observation planes. Although most communication was by wire, the radio was used extensively in mobile operations.

Flexibility and co-operation of arms were at the heart of the German system, and unit commanders were taught to be 'artillery minded'–to rely in all instances upon the close-

support fire of their artillery. The close-support function was usually carried out by the divisional artillery's three battalions of 105-mm howitzers (model 1eFH 18); a later model, the 1eFH 44, was a considerable improvement and out-ranged all other light howitzers then in service. Each German artillery division also had a medium battalion equipped with 15-cm howitzers and 15-cm guns. The medium battalion engaged in counter-battery work and general fire support.

The German Army had no corps artillery as such, but if a concentration of guns was required for an operation, groups of guns would be created or assembled from those available. There was a complement of heavy guns available, one of the most famous and most feared being the 17-cm K-18, an excellent long-range piece. Until the appearance of the US 8-inch gun in 1942, this gun outranged all the mobile heavy ordnance of the Allies.

Italy. The standard Italian field gun, the 75/27 (75-mm calibre, or internal diameter/27 calibres long), was quite inadequate by modern standards. It was capable of hurling its 14-pound shell 9,000 yards, which was poor enough in itself, but in order to attain this range (or any range over 6,600 yards) it was necessary to dig a pit for the trail in order to obtain the proper elevation and to use a false angle of sight. Additionally, the shell itself had poor fragmentation capabilities.

Otherwise, Italian guns were unspectacular but generally adequate and remarkably dependable. The most-used piece was the 105/28 gun. This was the standard battalion gun and proved valuable in North Africa. Two howitzers, the 100/17 and the 149/13, were common. These were accurate pieces but, like the 105/28 gun, they were hampered by old carriages and long, unwieldy trails which made them unsuitable for mobile warfare.

The most-feared Italian gun was the Ansaldo 75/46 AA gun, a mobile, rapid-fire piece which could be adapted to a number of field roles. Allied tankmen particularly disliked this gun, whose low silhouette, combined with the Italian practice of camouflaging their guns with light grey and dirty white colours, made it virtually invisible at 500 yards.

Japan. The artillery tradition of the Imperial Japanese Army is confined wholly to the modern era, and for that reason Japanese gunners in World War II were not hamstrung, as others undoubtedly were, by conservative attitudes inherited from old wars. This, however, allied to a general lack of experience, had its drawbacks as well as its benefits. For example, Japanese forces in the field were often weak in armour, but on the other hand their anti-tank defences, based upon the indiscriminate use of any guns available, were usually formidable. In fact, the only weapon the Japanese developed specifically for anti-tank work was the Type 1 (1941) 47-mm gun, which was a copy of a German design; where this gun was not in use, it was not uncommon for Allied tanks to encounter field guns sited to cover tank obstacles.

If the Japanese were somewhat unconventional in their use of artillery, they were also quite inept at first. Years of fighting in China against an enemy without adequate artillery had induced among Japanese gunners a naïve lack

Artillery doctrine of the Axis powers; the Germans' advanced tactical thinking gives them the upper hand until late 1942.

German 88-mm Flak Gun

The famous German '88' was developed from designs worked out under a co-operative arrangement between the firms of Krupp and Bofors in the 1920s, and was first produced under Hitler (who became Führer in 1934). The gun first saw action in the Spanish Civil War, and its World War II career is well known.

The '88' type was comparatively advanced when it was first introduced, but gradually other nations produced guns which were its equivalent if not better. Among these were the US 90-mm AA gun and the British 3·7-inch AA gun.

ABOVE *The '88' as it was used by German forces in North Africa to destroy the tanks of the Allies. The gun also served with distinction on the Eastern Front against the Russian armour.*

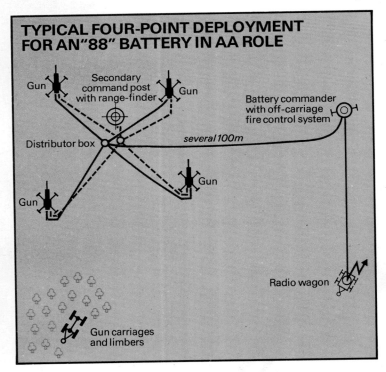

TYPICAL FOUR-POINT DEPLOYMENT FOR AN "88" BATTERY IN AA ROLE

Gun

Gun

Secondary command post with range-finder

Battery commander with off-carriage fire control system

Distributor box

several 100m

Gun

Gun

Radio wagon

Gun carriages and limbers

Much of the 88-mm gun's fame rests not on its performance as a flak, or anti-aircraft, gun but rather on its use as an anti-tank weapon. Its potency in this role was first noticed in Spain, where, although deployed as an AA weapon, it was often called upon to deal with tanks that had broken into front-line positions. During World War II, in North Africa and Russia, the '88' was more often than not employed primarily in the AT role. This was especially true in Russia during the period of Operation Barbarossa when it was found that the '88' was the only German gun capable of dealing with the new Russian T-34 and KV tanks.

SPECIFICATIONS

Calibre	88 mm
Range	35,700 feet (maximum vertical)
	34,770 feet (effective ceiling)
	16,600 yards (maximum horizontal)
Weight in action	4·9 tons
Weight in draught	7·1 tons
Length of barrel	56 calibres (16 feet 1·8 inches)
Elevation	−3 to +85 degrees
Traverse	2 × 360 degrees
Muzzle velocity	2,755 fps
Rate of fire	25 rpm (theoretical)
	12−15 rpm (practical)
Weight of projectile	20·1 pounds or 20·3 pounds (HE)
	21 pounds (AP)
Weight of complete round	31·7 pounds or 32 pounds (HE)
	33 pounds (AP)

LEFT *The '88' seen in the role for which it was originally built – as a Flak or anti-aircraft gun.*

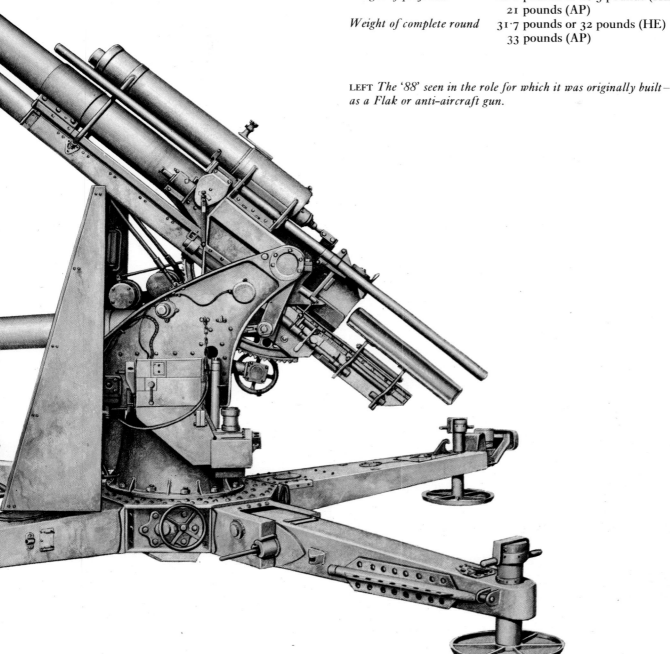

Heavy guns from the Axis armoury — for anti-aircraft, anti-tank and anti-personnel duties.

ABOVE *A Japanese 47-mm anti-tank gun M-1.*

OPPOSITE, ABOVE *Italian mobile AA gun in North Africa, 1942.*
OPPOSITE, BELOW *German recoilless rifle; sketch by Arens.*
CENTRE, ABOVE *German Krauss-Maffei troop carrier in the Western Desert; beside it is a Kubelwagen staff car.*
ABOVE *Afrika Korps heavy-gun crew in action, January 1943.*
ABOVE RIGHT *A battery of Japanese 105-mm guns in China.*

of concern for customary precautions. Thus in the early actions in the Philippines they fought their guns in the open with a total disregard for concealment, dispersion and camouflage. Their counter-battery work was equally poor. In due course, however, exposure to devastating concentrations from US guns brought about a remarkable improvement, and a few months later they seemed to have reacquired their old skills.

A favourite Japanese tactic seems to have been to add a fifth, 'ranging' gun to each battery. While the guns of the battery were firing on their target, this gun would obtain data for the next target by firing ranging shots.

After their early successes, the Japanese became plagued by chronic ammunition shortages. While these shortages certainly reduced the overall effectiveness of Japanese artillery, the Allies could not afford to disregard it. In a situation where every shot counted, the Japanese would often obtain range data in a leisurely fashion, creating the impression that they were engaging in harassing fire, and then deluge the target with a brief concentration.

Japanese guns were, for the most part, modern, tractor-towed types. They included the Type 90 (1930) 75-mm field gun, an excellent long-barrelled weapon with a slotted muzzle-brake and an extreme range of 16,350 yards, and the Type 95 (1935) 75-mm gun, which had been designed to replace the venerable Type 38 (1905) 75-mm gun in the divisional artillery. The older types were still prevalent in quiet areas. The training manual of the Type 31 (1898) 75-mm mountain gun was still being printed as late as

The Japanese are quick to master new techniques of concentrated fire; in later campaigns they suffer from severe shortages of ammunition.

1938; this antique gun served on many Pacific islands.

Heavier guns included the Type 92 (1932) 105-mm gun, easily recognized by its massive wooden wheels and solid rubber tyres, and the Type 89 (1929) 150-mm gun, a useful model frequently encountered in cave positions. The Type 89 could be broken down into two loads for transport. Among the howitzers were the Type 91 (1931) 105-mm light divisional howitzer, and the Type 96 (1936) 150-mm howitzer, a very modern design.

If there was an area in which the Japanese were weak, it was in their anti-aircraft defence. Their fire-direction and ranging equipment was crude, and their anti-aircraft guns little better. They were usually equipped with light anti-aircraft guns mostly of naval origin–captured or copied Bofors guns and Oerlikon 20-mm aircraft guns. Medium and heavy anti-aircraft fire was provided by an array of naval guns and the Type 88 (1928) 75-mm AA gun, a mobile piece with unimpressive capabilities.

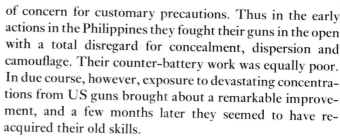

German 15-cm Nebelwerfer 41

SPECIFICATIONS

Weight	1,191 pounds (firing position)
Range	7,723 yards (HE)
	7,546 yards (smoke)
Elevation	+ 5 to + 45 degrees
Traverse	27 degrees
Projectile	15-cm spin-stabilized rocket
Weight of projectile	70 pounds (HE)
	79 pounds (smoke)
Velocity	1,120 fps
Firing mechanism	electrical hand-generator

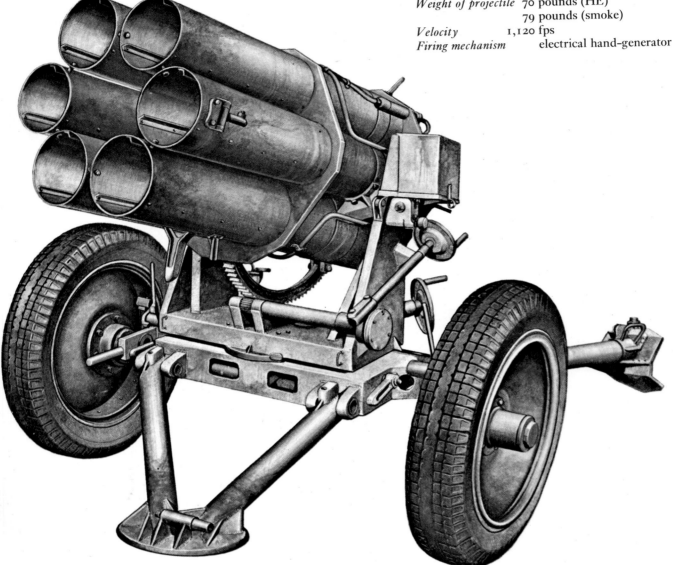

Rocket artillery is probably as old as gunpowder, and rockets were first used on European battlefields as early as 1232. The British Army formed rocket batteries equipped with Sir William Congreve's rockets during the Napoleonic Wars and used them with great success. The United States formed a rocket battery for use in the Mexican War, and by 1860 there were rocket batteries in the British, French, Russian and Austrian armies. Thereafter, rockets fell out of favour with professional military men, probably because of their inaccuracy; according to General Lallemand, a Frenchman, they were 'at best fit to frighten horses'. No rockets were used in World War I, but the experiments of various scientists, notably Dr Robert H. Goddard, coupled with improvements in high explosives, had seemed to point to a day when rockets would once again be extensively used.

During the 1930s extensive experimentation with war rockets and launchers was carried out in Russia and Germany. The Russians developed the Katyusha mobile rocket battery and an air-to-surface AT rocket. German development was extensive in the surface-to-surface category, leading to potent area-fire weapons of the Nebelwerfer type. German self-propelled rocket batteries were usually mounted on half-tracks.

The Nebelwerfer 41 was widely used by the Wehrmacht, beginning in 1942. It could saturate an area with HE, smoke or chemical shells (the latter were not used in combat) and its volume of fire was greatly feared. Nebelwerfers were difficult to conceal in action because, like all rocket weapons, they gave off a heavy back-blast, and each rocket left long, smoky trails along its trajectory.

Anti-Tank Guns in Europe 1940–42

The 'phoney war' on the Western Front ended on 10 May 1940 when the Panzer divisions rolled into France and the Low Countries. In the French campaign German anti-tank gunners played a limited but crucial role. The Flak gunners attached to the Panzer divisions were especially important to the German effort as few German tanks were capable of challenging heavily armoured Allied tanks like the British Matilda or the French Somua.

The story of the German Flakartillerie (Flak=*Flugabwehrkanone* or anti-aircraft gun) intrudes on our narrative about anti-tank guns because the Wehrmacht, partly by design and partly as a matter of expediency, employed AA guns in AT roles. Indeed, the standard heavy AA gun of the Flakartillerie–the '88', or 8·8-cm Flak 18 (also 36 and 38)– is primarily remembered as a tank-killer.

The German experience in the 'rehearsal' provided by the Spanish Civil War (1936–39) had shown that the Flak guns, while engaging in their primary AA role, were frequently called upon for AT work. Thereafter the most-used German AA guns were specifically designed for a dual AA/AT role, and it was a common practice for fully motorized Luftwaffe Flak units to be attached to army units in the field.

The French campaign further reinforced the conviction that the Flak units should play a dual role, for it was in France that the '88' began engaging Allied armour that the under-gunned Panzers could not handle. The Wehrmacht's standard anti-tank gun in 1940, the 37-mm Pak 35/36, was, like nearly every other AT gun then available, ineffective at ranges beyond 500 yards.

On the other hand the Allied anti-tank effort in France is best described in the words of a young French officer, written just before his suicide: 'One cannot send men to fight tanks with rifles'. This was no exaggeration. Most French units were 33–50% below establishment in AT weapons. The British Expeditionary Force was equipped with a superbly designed 2-pounder anti-tank gun, but, like its German counterpart, this gun was not effective beyond short ranges. The best anti-tank gun available to the Allies was the venerable French 75-mm field gun which, of course, was not designed for AT work and was vulnerable to German field artillery when employed in the AT role.

As Allied resistance in France crumbled, General Maxime Weygand ordered the French armies to form a defence in depth on a system resembling a checkerboard. The idea behind Weygand's *quadrillage* defence system was to blunt, contain and ultimately destroy the Panzer divisions. The order came too late to have an appreciable effect on operations in France, but the Germans would encounter a sophisticated variation of the *quadrillage* system at Kursk in Russia, where Soviet AT guns would take an incredible toll of German armour.

The Germans solve the AT-gun problem ahead of the Allies – by using their AA guns in a dual role.

RIGHT *A Soviet 76-mm anti-tank gun M-1942. This light and mobile weapon was the standard divisional AT gun of the Soviet armies. Using high-velocity armour-piercing ammunition it had an exceptional muzzle velocity of 3,167 fps. The gun weighed one ton and had a maximum range of 14,545 yards.*
BELOW *On the Eastern Front the crew of a German Pak 40 AT gun brings light-machine-gun fire to bear on a group of Russian farm huts and outbuildings.*

British 2-pounder, combined with the inability of the British field artillery–good though it was–to act in co-operation with its tank forces, made North Africa a graveyard for Allied tanks.

Throughout those years the gun-armour race ground on. Eventually, even bigger guns and more powerful projectiles with greater armour-piercing capabilities were introduced. Anti-tank guns were especially critical on the Eastern Front. The Russians found that their 76-mm divisional gun M-1942 was unable to deal with heavy German tanks and they eventually settled on the 100-mm M-1944 for this role. The Germans progressed from the 75-mm Pak 40 (introduced for service in late 1942) to the 128-mm Pak 44. The biggest British anti-tank gun was the 17-pounder Mark 1. This gun arrived in Tunisia just in time to deal with the new German heavy tank, the Tiger.

The Anti-Tank War Phase 2

The story of the anti-tank gun inevitably leads from the gun-armour race to the development of sophisticated systems of anti-tank defences. Although there had been little optimism among military men at the ability of guns to stop tanks, far-sighted theorists like Generals J. F. C. Fuller and S. L. A. Marshall had advocated the construction of elaborate, co-operative defence systems, and Rommel had given substance to their theories with his tank-proof localities in the Western Desert.

The most complex application of this principle was the defence system created by the Russian armies in the Kursk salient in 1943. At Kursk the Russians held a mammoth salient projecting into the lines of von Kluge's Army Group Centre. Against it the Germans prepared a strike force of their finest Panzer and infantry divisions. But because of the activities of the Swiss master-spy 'Lucy', the Russians were well aware of the Germans' intentions and had adequately prepared to meet the attack.

Along the perimeter of the salient the Russians constructed several parallel lines of defence. These lines were protected by massive minefield belts which were arranged with the additional object of channelling the Panzers towards innumerable clusters of anti-tank guns. The anti-tank guns were formed in groups of 10 guns (called 'Pak-fronts' by the Germans), which were instructed to hold their fire until the target presented a flank shot. The idea was to allow penetration of the front lines and then, by a process of peeling away the enemy's flank armour, break up the impetus of the attack. The reserve consisted of artillery and Koniev's Fifth Tank Army. Altogether, the Kursk salient held 20,000 guns (6,000 in the Pak-fronts) and 920 Katyusha rocket-launchers.

The German plan of attack called for a pincer movement against the northern and southern flanks of the salient. Model's Ninth Army would strike the northern face from the direction of Orel, while Hoth's Fourth Panzer Army would strike the southern face. The build-up for the attack took months to complete and eventually involved drawing the bulk of German armour on the Eastern Front into the

In the North African campaign of 1940–43 the overall German superiority in weaponry, so evident in Poland and France, had begun to wear thin by 1942. The Germans managed to retain superiority only in the quality of their anti-tank guns. Indeed, the startling string of successes put together by General Erwin Rommel's Afrika Korps (DAK) may be attributed in large measure to Rommel's skilful use of anti-tank guns. At the very heart of Rommel's technique lay the German *Einheit* (unit) system of organization and co-operation of arms. As General von Mellenthin described it:

> A German Panzer division was a highly flexible formation of all arms, which always relied on artillery in attack or defence. In contrast, the British regarded the anti-tank gun as a defensive weapon.
>
> (from *Panzer Battles*, by General F. W. von Mellenthin)

The Panzers were, quite literally, never alone. The artillery attached to a Panzer division kept pace with it even on sustained offensives. The British cruiser tanks, on the other hand, operated somewhat like the heavy cavalry brigades of the Napoleonic Wars. They would charge forward, far outstripping their artillery and infantry supports. In the face of this charge, the Panzers would withdraw, luring the British tanks forward to be smashed by the waiting Flak and AT guns.

The British were further handicapped in North Africa because the 2-pounder was the only anti-tank gun they systematically used until the introduction in 1942 of the 6-pounder (57-mm) AT gun. A conservative obstinacy concerning the proper role of the 3·7-inch AA gun, a weapon superior to the German '88' in almost every respect, prevented its use in the AT role.

The standard German anti-tank gun in North Africa was the 50-mm Pak 38. This weapon had replaced the obsolete Pak 35/36 very early in the campaign. In 1942 large numbers of captured Russian field guns, mostly converted 76-mm Pak 36s, began to appear in the anti-tank armoury of the DAK. The superiority of these weapons to the

RIGHT *A German 75/55-mm AT gun with tapered bore. The last AT gun put into service by the German Army in World War II, it employed the highly successful Gerlich or coned-bore principle. The bore tapered from 75 mm at the breech to 55 mm at the muzzle. An extremely high muzzle velocity of 4,000 fps (estimated) could be attained with this coned bore and a flanged tungsten carbide projectile. The shot could penetrate 5 inches of armour at 1,500 yards.*

ABOVE *A battery of German Nebelwerfer rockets deployed in racks of four. The Nebelwerfer were used as area-fire weapons, to blanket a chosen zone with HE or smoke; this type of launcher was often attached to the sides of half-tracked vehicles, forming mobile rocket batteries.*

BELOW *Action on the Eastern Front: a German 21-cm gun fires on the Russian defences.*

German Sd Kfz 138 Marder III

This German SP (self-propelled) gun is typical of the SP guns of World War II. A tank chassis (in this case the Czech 38t Praga) was utilized as a weapons carrier, and a thinly armoured superstructure, incorporating the fighting compartment, was built over it. These were stop-gap measures, designed to meet demand.

Such guns, in co-operation with motorized infantry (Panzergrenadiers in the German Army) acted with armoured divisions in wide-ranging operations, providing the fire support and staying power that armour lacked. Some, like the vehicle shown here, were Panzerjägers (tank-hunters) and fulfilled the same role in the motorized unit as the anti-tank gun in conventional units.

The Marder III began to appear in March 1942. The first production models were equipped with the Russian 76·2-mm field gun, but one year later a much-improved version with the 75-mm Pak 40/3 was put into production. The one great fault of the Marder III was its open fighting compartment which exposed the crew to blast and splinters from enemy HE fire. By May 1944 production of the Marder was terminated, and the Jagdpanzer 38 Hetzer, which had a fully enclosed fighting compartment, began to take its place in front-line units.

SPECIFICATIONS

Length	15 feet 6 inches
Width	7 feet 10 inches
Height	8 feet 4 inches
Weight	10·8 tons
Speed	28 mph
Range	112 miles
Armament	1 × 75-mm Pak 40/3 with 38 rounds
	1 × MG 34 with 600 rounds
Armour	15 mm (front)
	11 mm (glacis)
	10 mm (fighting compartment)
	10 mm (flanks)
	10 mm (rear)
Crew	4

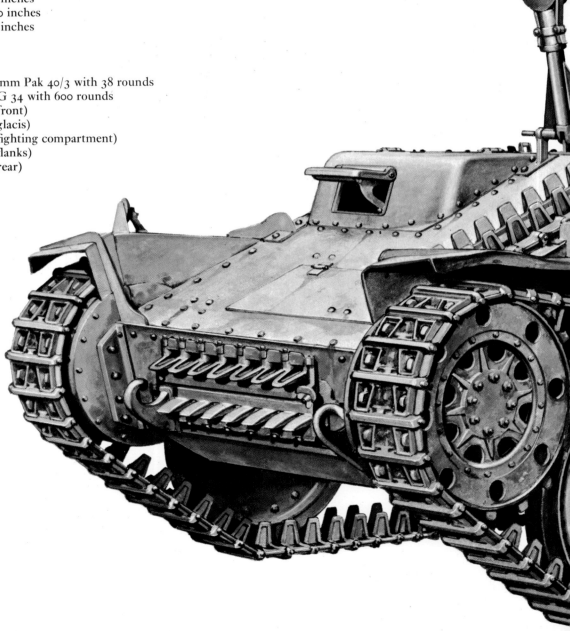

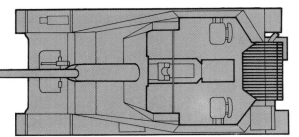

LEFT *This top view of the Marder III highlights its chief drawback as a combat vehicle, namely the lack of protection for the crew in the gun's fighting compartment. This shortcoming was rectified in the later SP guns of World War II.*
BELOW *The large view shows the two basic elements of the Marder III – the Czech 38t tank chassis and the armoured superstructure housing the main armament that was built onto it. Note also the spare sections of track fixed to the vehicle.*

area around Kursk (75% of the strength of the entire German Army was then in Russia). The concentration of guns and tanks on the attack fronts was dense even by German standards. Model's front, the strongest, averaged 60–80 tanks and 110–130 guns per mile of front.

Tactically, the Germans formed their tanks in arrowhead-like formations known as the Panzer *Keil*, or wedge. In this formation heavily armoured tanks and assault guns such as the Tiger and the Ferdinand took the lead, while medium tanks, mostly Panthers and Mark IVs, followed in echelon behind.

On 5 July 1943 the Battle of Kursk opened. What followed has been described as the greatest tank battle in history, but that familiar and laconic description should not be allowed to obscure the fact that Kursk was won largely by the gunners of the Russian Pak-fronts. At first there was no stopping the mammoth Ferdinands, which soon outstripped the smaller tanks, but the Russian anti-tank guns slowed, stopped or disorganized most of the German thrusts, and then flamethrower crews dealt one by one with the isolated Ferdinands. On 12 July Koniev's tanks struck the flank of the floundering German advance near Prokhorovka, and the outcome was settled.

Kursk was one of the truly decisive battles in world history. German losses were immense and irreplaceable. Of the total of some 2,700 tanks Model and Hoth had hurled against the salient, over 90 per cent were left on the field of battle. The effort broke the back of Hitler's Panzer armies, and the Russians took charge in the Ukraine.

From there the war on the Eastern Front became, from the German side, an almost continuous rearguard action lasting nearly two years as the Russians pushed westwards through Poland to the outskirts of Berlin. On 25 April 1945 they opened up on the inner suburbs with a barrage of 2,000,000 shells. Within a fortnight the war in the West was over.

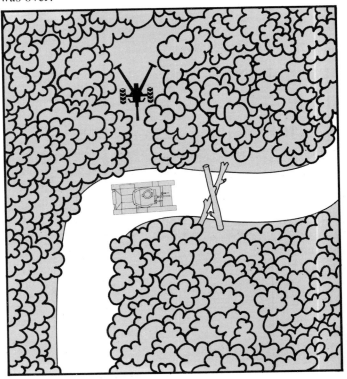

The Allies launch a double assault from east and west on Germany's dwindling territories.

OPPOSITE, ABOVE *Scenario for a tank ambush: the tank turns the bend in the road and is halted by the road block of trees; in this position it presents a maximum (broadside) target to the camouflaged enemy gun.*

OPPOSITE, BELOW *A Soviet fully tracked carriage with a 203-mm howitzer M-1931. This was the standard heavy howitzer in service with the Russian armies, the tracks proving especially useful in difficult terrain. It had a range of 19,700 yards.*

THIS PAGE *Allied mobile rocket launchers on the Eastern and Western Fronts. Above is a Sherman M-4 tank fitted with a double-banked launcher. Calliope, as this version of the tank was called, had tubes for 60 rockets; elevation of the frame was made through the gun barrel, to which it was clamped.*

BELOW *Russian Katyusha rocket teams load up during the final assault on Berlin. The truck-mounted rockets were fired electrically from the driving cab.*

'Gustav' at Sebastopol

The largest guns ever built were two 80-cm rail guns made by Krupp to bombard the Maginot Line. These Brobdingnagian pieces were nicknamed 'Gustav' and 'Dora'. Only Gustav saw action, being used at Sebastopol in 1942 and at Warsaw in 1944. Field Marshal Erich von Manstein, who commanded the German Eleventh Army in the operations against Sebastopol, described Gustav as:

A miracle of technical achievement. The barrel must have been 90 feet long and the carriage as high as a two-storey house. Sixty trains had been required to bring it into position along a railway specially laid for the purpose. Two anti-aircraft regiments had to be constantly in attendance.

(from *Lost Victories*, by Erich von Manstein)

Gustav's capabilities were equally impressive. One of its seven-ton concrete-piercing shells crashed through 90 feet of hard rock and destroyed a Russian ammunition dump near Severnaya Bay. But, despite its awesome credentials, Gustav was something of a white elephant. As von Manstein expressed it: 'The effectiveness of the cannon bore no real relation to all the effort and expense that had gone into making it? Not that it was a lone performer.

Joining Gustav in the task of battering Sebastopol into submission were two mammoth 60-cm 'Karl' SP howitzers and numerous other heavy guns. Altogether, von Manstein's Eleventh Army marshalled 208 batteries along a 22-mile front. This was the greatest German artillery concentration of the war. Much of the credit for the German conquest of the Crimea in 1942 must in fact be given to the artillery, for von Manstein's army was operating almost the whole time without armour. (In the air, though, it was a different story: for the duration of the siege the Luftwaffe were able to provide 600 aircraft, to which the Russians had little answer.)

On the ground, the defenders mustered some 3,600 strongpoints, arrayed in considerable depth, among them the Maxim Gorky fort, a mighty turreted battery housing four 305-mm guns. The siege lasted three weeks, in which time the Germans fired an estimated total of 47,000 tons of shells into the Russian defences. In 1944 Gustav was in action outside Warsaw, then disappeared, presumably falling into Russian hands.

ABOVE *'Gustav', the giant 80-cm rail gun originally built by Krupp to bombard the Maginot Line. It had a 100-foot barrel, weighed 1,350 tons in the firing position, and discharged its seven-ton shells at up to three an hour.*

LEFT AND OPPOSITE *Two more German mammoths in the 22-mile artillery front assembled by von Manstein to bombard Sebastopol.*

Self-Propelled Guns

There are two main types of self-propelled (SP) guns: firstly, there are the heavily armoured assault guns and tank destroyers; secondly, the lightly armoured support guns. SP guns fulfil the same functions as their horse- and tractor-drawn counterparts but, of course, enjoy the advantages of independent mobility.

SP guns saw limited action during World War I. Early models were slow and, for the most part, lacked armour protection for their crews. During World War II the SP gun really came of age. Each of the belligerents fielded great numbers of them, most notably Germany, which by the end of the war had more Panzerjägers (self-propelled anti-tank guns, literally 'tank-hunters') than tanks.

Another type of SP gun appeared during the war. This was the assault gun. The first assault guns used in battle were a small number of German Sturmgeschütz IIIs armed with the short 75-mm Stu.K L/24; these were used in the Ardennes sector during the invasion of France in 1940. The experiment was a success, and the Germans eventually built over 10,500 Sturmgeschütz-type assault guns during the war, while their Italian allies produced an excellent version, the Semovente M-40 and M-41 mounting the DA 75/18 gun. Another group of assault guns was built specifically for attacking fortifications or for use in street fighting. These,

of course, were larger and more heavily armoured and they mounted bigger guns. Among them were the box-like Brummbär (Growler) assault howitzer and the Sturmtiger, which mounted the 38-cm RW-61 rocket mortar.

The Soviet Union built its first unarmoured SP gun in 1932, and during World War II developed an entire family of SP assault and support guns built around the chassis of their successful T-34 medium and JS heavy tanks. The SU-76 support gun mounted the 76-mm M-1942 divisional gun and was originally developed as a tank destroyer; but it was unsuccessful in that role and finished the war as the standard Soviet SP support gun. The first heavily armoured Soviet assault gun was the SU-85, which appeared in the battles in the Ukraine in 1944. It mounted the 85-mm AA gun on the T-34 chassis. The SU-85 was followed by the SU-100, which mounted the powerful 100-mm M-1944 field gun; the JSU-122 mounting the 122-mm gun A-195; and the JSU-152 (152-mm gun-howitzer M-1937).

During the great Soviet offensives of 1944–45 the assault guns were well to the front. Each assault-gun battery had orders to follow the infantry or armour it was supporting by no more than 400 yards. Their fire was used to engage enemy tanks and artillery and to destroy strongpoints. Most of these assault guns remained in service in the decade following the war, not only with Soviet and Eastern European armies but also in the Middle East.

The Russians build a family of SP guns around the chassis of their T-34 and JS tanks.

LEFT *During the takeover of Berlin, a column of Soviet JSU-152a assault guns parks at the side of the road.*

ABOVE *An American M-10 tank destroyer in action against a German pillbox near Echternach, Luxembourg, during the Allied drive in 1945. M-10s were thinly armoured on the sides but had heavy frontal protection; American versions at first mounted the 76-mm gun, then the 90-mm, while British M-10s had a 76.2-mm gun.*

RIGHT *A German Sturmgeschütz assault gun advances with infantry support on Russian positions near Voronezh in 1943.*

BELOW *An Italian Ansaldo 90/53 SP gun M-1941 captured in Sicily.*

The appearance of seemingly unlimited numbers of Russian tanks and assault guns in the last years of the war forced the Germans to resort to the cheap expedient of the Panzerjäger. Early German tank-hunters had been built with open fighting compartments, but there were obvious drawbacks associated with this mode of construction. Usually they had to wait for the enemy to come to them and, after their first shots, were then subjected to massive retaliatory fire. The second generation of tank-hunters was therefore built with a closed and heavily armoured fighting compartment to protect the crew. Among the vehicles in this class were the Hetzer, the Jagdpanther, the Jagdtiger and the redoubtable Ferdinand.

Assault guns and tank-hunters were the most prevalent form of SP artillery on the Eastern Front, but the Western Allies favoured the SP support gun. The need for SP support guns had become evident in North Africa. At first, the Lee-Grant tank was used in this role, firing its short 75-mm sponson gun from hull- and turret-down positions. Later, the appearance of the M-7 Priest gave the Allies an

TOP *A German Jagdpanther; this was one of the second generation of German tank-hunters developed in wartime. This vehicle was knocked out in March 1945 by a US tank destroyer.*
ABOVE *Also out of action – a 70-ton Sturmtiger; a massive assault vehicle designed partly for a street-fighting role. Its main armament was the RW-61 rocket launcher; the rocket's exhaust gases escaped through the circular vents at the muzzle.*

excellent SP gun comparable to the German Wespe, which mounted the 10·5-cm L/28. Another favoured type was the M-10 tank destroyer. The first British SP field-gun was the Sexton, which mounted the 25-pounder. The Sexton was not a successful type, however, since its high silhouette made concealment difficult.

Anti-Aircraft Guns

ABOVE *A Bofors gun crew at action stations on one of the island forts sited off the coast of Britain.*

Anti-aircraft artillery had performed in a satisfactory, albeit clumsy, manner in World War I, and for some years after 1918 there seemed to be little need to improve on the capabilities of existing AA guns. Suddenly, in the mid-1930s, aircraft development accelerated, and by the time of the Spanish Civil War (1936–39) it was clear that aircraft would take a major role in any future conflict.

Following the war in Spain ordnance experts in the United States and Great Britain worked to develop AA guns and complex new detection and aiming devices capable of putting up a strong defence against fast attack aircraft and high-flying bombers. Top priority was given to the development of a light, Quick-Firing AA gun with sufficient hitting power to bring down dive-bombers and ground-attack fighters such as the German Stukas. Initial attempts to develop light cannon for this role did not meet with much success. The US Army, for example, adapted its 37-mm AT gun for this purpose, but the gun was found to be inaccurate, weak in hitting power, in fact totally unsuited for the role the experts had thrust upon it. Eventually, nearly all the major combatant nations in World War II settled on the Bofors 40-mm AA gun (or copies or derivatives of it) as their standard light flak weapon.

The Bofors 40-mm gun was developed in Sweden in the early 1930s. It first proved its worth against low-level attacks in the Battle of Britain and eventually also it was useful as an assault gun against ground targets. What made the Bofors especially deadly in either role was its high cyclic rate of fire. It was capable of firing two rounds per second over a slant range of four miles. The shells were fed into the loading tray in four-round clips and automatically rammed into the firing chamber.

Anti-aircraft defence against high-flying bombers was a much simpler proposition. In this category, at least, there was no need for the ordnance experts to adapt or develop in haste. Guns capable of bringing down a strategic bomber had been in existence since World War I; even so, such guns were becoming outmoded by 1939 even if they were not quite obsolescent.

The German 88-mm Flak 18, which made its début in the Spanish Civil War, was the first of a new generation of heavy AA guns. The appearance of the '88' caused quite a stir, because it was far superior to the older mobile AA guns. Soon, however, other nations produced AA guns comparable to the '88' in service performance. Great Britain's 3·7-inch Mark I was ready for service in 1939 but was not used extensively until the North African campaign. Until then the 3-inch 20-cwt gun, of World War I vintage, was used by British and Commonwealth units. The last development of the 3·7-inch gun, the Mark 6, was in service at the war's end; this was a very superior piece which remained standard until it was replaced by surface-to-air missiles. A US gun, the 90-mm M-2, was introduced for service in 1942; it could fire 20–25 rounds per minute to a height of nine miles. All these new-generation guns were also effective in the anti-tank role, although the British and American guns were used less often for this purpose.

The heaviest mobile AA gun produced during the war was the US 120-mm M-1. This weapon, known as the 'Stratosphere Gun', was designed specifically to counter an anticipated high-level German bombing raid on the USA. It had a vertical range of 12 miles (20,000 feet higher than any other mobile AA gun).

Notable improvements were made during the pre-war

Advances in fire-control apparatus and radar early-warning systems; birth of the VT Proximity Fuse.

years in AA fire-control systems and in the use of radio (radar) directors. The first electrical fire-control systems were developed after World War I, but truly efficient systems were not produced before the 1930s. These systems rapidly supplanted plotting boards and mechanical fire-control equipment, which were slow, cumbersome and, of course, plagued by the element of human error.

The new electrical fire-control apparatus collected data from the tracker and range-finder and transmitted it continuously to a computer which instantly calculated the proper setting for the shell's time fuse and the correct direction and elevation for gun-laying. The computer also made instantaneous corrections for wind, weather and barometric conditions. The data was then transmitted to the gun and fuse-setter; a great deal of time was saved and the possibility of human error was eliminated from that part of the operation.

The next important improvement was in the field of radar directors. The British and Americans developed radar 'early-warning' systems almost simultaneously in 1936; within a year, the US Army successfully demonstrated a radar detector and director system at the Signal Corps laboratories in Fort Monmouth, New Jersey. When radar detection and direction systems were combined with electrical fire-control and (later) the VT fuse, AA guns became very efficient indeed. In the course of World War II the USA, Great Britain and Germany all used sophisticated detection and direction systems for their AA guns.

VT Fuse

On 16 December 1944 the German counter-offensive (the Battle of the Bulge) was in full stride in the Ardennes. Harsh weather, fog and surprise had aided the advance. Suddenly, German troops were caught in the open by an intense, surprisingly lethal artillery concentration. Road columns of infantry and highway intersections were engulfed in flame and shell fragments. Each shell burst above the ground at precisely the height from which its fragments would do the most damage. There had been no ranging shots and, therefore, no warning. The fog, traditionally a shield behind which troops could be moved in some safety, had been no protection. As confusion and consternation spread among the German troops, their great counter-offensive ground to a halt.

This was the first instance of the use of a truly revolutionary ordnance development– the VT fuse–against a ground target. Its use was credited with stopping the Germans in the Ardennes and, ultimately, helping to win the Battle of the Bulge. General Patton later commented: 'The new shell with the "funny fuse" is devastating. . . . I think that when all armies get this fuse, we will have to devise some new method of warfare'.

The VT fuse had been developed by a team of American researchers led by Dr Vannevar Bush. Each VT fuse incorporated a tiny radio receiving and transmitting set. The fuse could detonate the shell at any height or distance from the target based upon the radar impulses the fuse received during the flight of the shell. As opposed to conventional time fuses, which were pre-set before firing, the VT fuse responded to the proximity of the target, detonating its shell when it detected that it was within lethal distance.

The devastating potential of the new fuse was well understood. At first, its use was limited to AA work, where there was no possibility of the enemy recovering a 'dud' and copying the fuse. Its effectiveness was established beyond question in the Pacific and in countering the V-1 rocket attacks on London. Shells fitted with VT fuses hit 79% of the rockets launched against London.

Later, as we have seen, the VT fuse was issued for land use, and is credited with increasing the effectiveness of artillery by a factor of 10 times over shells fitted with conventional time fuses.

The Germans failed to produce a satisfactory proximity fuse in time, although they were working at it up to the end of the war. This is revealed, for example, by the fact that their air-to-air rockets were equipped with recesses to take the fuse as and when it became available.

OPPOSITE, ABOVE *On a Normandy beachhead on D-Day the crew of a US 90-mm AA gun blast enemy targets.*
OPPOSITE, BELOW *A flying bomb is near, and British crews race to man their Bofors AA guns.*
ABOVE *Demonstrating the VT Fuse. Note the dust rising where shell splinters have penetrated the roofs.*
BELOW *German AA gunners manning a 37-mm Flak 36 AA gun in the Caucasus. As the Russians began to achieve air superiority, the Flakartillerie's role became critical.*

US 75-mm Recoilless Rifle M-20

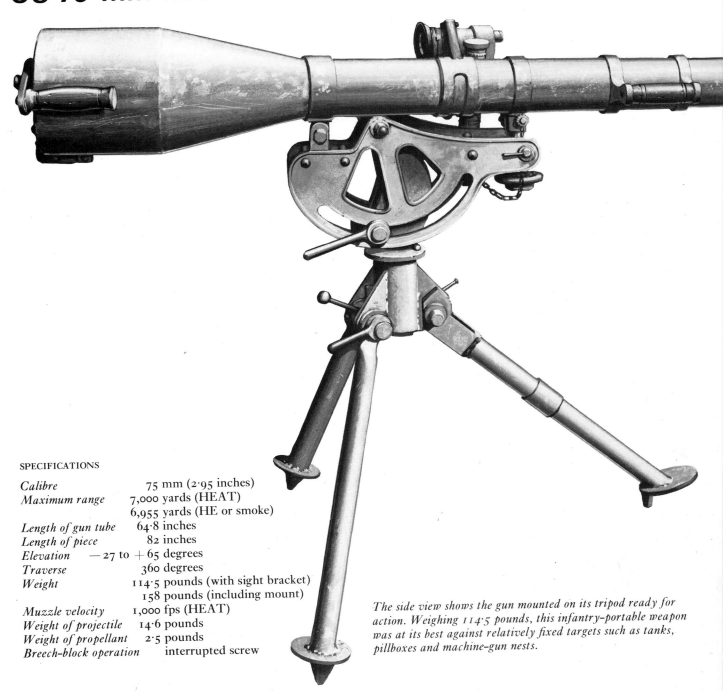

SPECIFICATIONS

Calibre	75 mm (2·95 inches)
Maximum range	7,000 yards (HEAT)
	6,955 yards (HE or smoke)
Length of gun tube	64·8 inches
Length of piece	82 inches
Elevation	−27 to +65 degrees
Traverse	360 degrees
Weight	114·5 pounds (with sight bracket)
	158 pounds (including mount)
Muzzle velocity	1,000 fps (HEAT)
Weight of projectile	14·6 pounds
Weight of propellant	2·5 pounds
Breech-block operation	interrupted screw

The side view shows the gun mounted on its tripod ready for action. Weighing 114·5 pounds, this infantry-portable weapon was at its best against relatively fixed targets such as tanks, pillboxes and machine-gun nests.

The first recoilless (RCL) gun was the Davis Gun (*c*. 1910). This gun, which was employed to a limited extent in World War I, utilized a principle of physics to do away with the problem of recoil. The Davis Gun had two diametrically opposing barrels sharing a common powder chamber. Two projectiles of equal weight were loaded into the gun. When the gun was fired there was no recoil as the two projectiles moved down the opposing barrels at equal speed and exerted equal but opposite recoil stress on the gun. The 'second' projectile, or countershot, consisted of a mixture of grease and small shot and was dispersed on leaving the rear barrel.

Although the advantages of the Davis Gun were manifest, the end of the war also brought an end to its brief career. The next stage was to use, in place of the latter's countershot, a stream of high-velocity gas. During World War II the Germans were the first to field recoilless guns, followed closely by British and US models.

The US recoilless rifles of the Kromuskit family are fairly typical of modern recoilless weapons. Named after their inventors, Kroger and Musser, two such rifles were developed during World War II – a 57-mm model and one of 75-mm – and both were used with great success in the Pacific and European theatres as light infantry-support weapons. The 75-mm recoilless rifle was especially valuable to infantry and airborne units advancing without artillery support who were held up by enemy strongpoints. The gun's light weight enabled it to accompany

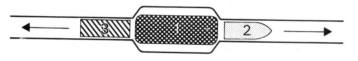

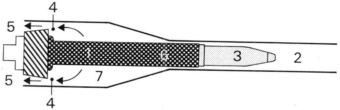

Davis Gun – the RCL pioneer

The first recoilless gun featured two opposite-facing barrels sharing a common powder chamber. The projectile occupied one barrel and a countershot of equal weight the other. On firing, they exerted an equal recoil stress and so cancelled each other out.

1 Cartridge
2 Projectile
3 Countershot

Cross-section of RCL

This cross-section through a hypothetical recoilless rifle illustrates the following key principles and components:

1 Many recoilless rifles fire fixed ammunition with a perforated cartridge case. The case is so designed to allow gases to escape to the rear of the piece through a venturi 'throat' after a low pressure has been reached.

2 Rifled bore. The size of the bore is equal to the size of the throats.

3 Standard projectile. This has a pre-engraved rifled band and a standard fuse.

4 Throat, the passage through which gases escape to the rear of the gun.

5 Venturi, the rear opening characteristic of recoilless guns.

6 Charge. Recoilless guns are low-efficiency weapons. Their powder charge has to be comparatively large to achieve a muzzle velocity comparable, though lower, to that of howitzers of the same calibre.

7 Powder chamber. This is abnormally large in weapons of the Kromuskit family.

infantry in the advance, and its accuracy gained it a considerable reputation as a tank-killer.

RCL weapons have certain important disadvantages, however. The foremost is the pronounced back-blast which can endanger a careless crew (the crews of German 7·5-cm RCLs had to wear specially designed ear protectors) and makes concealing the weapon from enemy observation difficult.

Since World War II the Kromuskit RCLs have been replaced by weapons with larger calibres. Today's RCLs have ·50-calibre spotting rifles attached to the tube: these fire tracer bullets for ranging. RCLs were particularly helpful in Korea, where difficult terrain often prevented the artillery from fighting in the front lines.

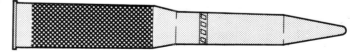

Above is a complete round of HEAT (High Explosive Anti-Tank) ammunition for the 75-mm recoilless rifle; rounds were made with perforated cases to permit propellant gases to escape through the exhaust ports at the rear of the piece.

The War in the Pacific

Operations in the Pacific theatre against the Japanese presented Allied gunners with an altogether different set of problems to those facing their comrades in Europe and Africa. This was largely because Japan was weak industrially and in resources. Two important consequences were that Japanese tanks never became a decisive factor and Allied air supremacy was never seriously challenged (anti-tank and anti-aircraft actions were in fact comparatively rare). Also, in the jungle warfare which characterized most of the campaigns in East Asia and the Pacific, the Japanese were usually on the defensive and almost invariably without air, naval or armoured support. Under these circumstances, artillery became a major element in their defensive systems.

The problems usually associated with campaigning in the Pacific and East Asia created hardships on both sides, but the Allies were better prepared to meet them. Firstly, there was the environment itself, which was generally forbidding and inhospitable; then there were numerous logistical problems, compounded by long distances and the undeveloped nature of the terrain, which further hampered operations. Nevertheless, Allied artillerymen were usually well supplied with whatever they needed and could afford to expend ammunition lavishly, whereas their Japanese counterparts were significantly less well supplied and had to make every shot count. Another basic problem for the Japanese was their severe shortage of raw industrial chemicals, especially aromatics such as toluene (a basic ingredient of TNT), while the coal-tar industry of the Home Islands was wholly inadequate. As a result Japan could never produce enough explosives to supply her forces in the field.

Following the attack on Pearl Harbor in December 1941, the Japanese struck quickly at the great bases of the Allies in East Asia and the Philippines. The battles fought at Singapore and in the Manila Bay area were the last instances in the war in which the Japanese massed their guns to achieve artillery superiority. Singapore fell to General Yamashita's daring amphibious assault backed by 440 guns. The assault came at night, and British Empire artillery which might have stopped it failed to do so largely because of poor communications.

In the Manila Bay area there were titanic artillery duels between the guns of the island forts (Corregidor and Forts Frank, Hughes and Drum) and Japanese guns on the mainland at Cavite and Bataan. The duels began on 6 February 1942 after the Japanese had secured suitable positions on the Cavite shore. Eventually, the Japanese managed to emplace over 800 guns, including some of 240-mm calibre, and the bombardment rose to peaks of almost incredible intensity.

On 29 April the Japanese commemorated the Emperor's birthday with a tremendous day-long bombardment. Over 10,000 shells devastated Corregidor. Then, on 4 May, over 16,000 shells were directed at 'The Rock', destroying the few guns which remained capable of reply. On the same day Fort Drum, the 'concrete battleship', took 1,000 hits.

Two days later the island forts surrendered before the incessant artillery bombardment. During the siege US counter-battery fire had been fierce but generally in-effective. The gunners had been impeded by the fact that the Manila Bay forts, like the fortress at Singapore, had been designed to repel a hostile fleet, and were vulnerable to land or air attack. Most of the ammunition for the big guns and mortars was armour-piercing, and the fuses were mostly of the impact-delay type usually associated with deck-piercing ammunition. This ammunition was quite useless for anti-personnel or counter-battery work. Also, most of the guns were emplaced in open concrete pits and so were easy victims of plunging fire and strafing. The few AA guns at the defence's disposal were obsolete.

So Corregidor and the Manila Bay forts fell, like Singapore, to Japanese armies which were inferior in numbers but superior in artillery. These victories, however, signalled the end of the great days of the Japanese artillery. Never again would the Imperial Japanese Army bring together masses of guns as at Singapore or Manila Bay. The early successes of the IJA in fact contributed to its demise, leading in terms of its artillery to a too-thin dispersal of contingents in 'penny-packet' garrisons throughout the Pacific and East Asia, which were subsequently dealt with piecemeal by the Allies.

Artillery also played a little-known but vital role in supporting amphibious assaults during the Allied island-hopping campaigns in the Pacific. Whenever geography allowed, as at Okinawa, small islands off the coast of the primary objective were seized and converted into fire bases for heavy guns like the 155-mm Long Toms. Tiny airstrips were built, from which observers in spotter planes could range over the objective reporting targets and directing their guns.

Whenever such arrangements could be made, the task of the assault force was made much easier. Naval bombardment was comforting but was never an adequate substitute for the support fire of land-based guns. This is because naval guns are high-velocity, flat-trajectory weapons, incapable of hitting targets behind hills and in defiles. Land-based guns, on the other hand, can hit 'hidden' targets by means of their searching type of fire.

In amphibious operations the assault force is usually at its most vulnerable while the landings are actually being made. Support fire from naval vessels is usually lifted during this period, and the landing group is without artillery. But this was not the case whenever land-based guns were firing from positions on islets off the coast of the objective. In a variation on the same theme, British artillery firing across the Strait of Messina from Sicily very effectively covered landings at Calabria on the Italian mainland.

In the jungle the Japanese, usually plagued by inferior artillery, would go to extremes to disguise the positions of their guns and so preserve them from the powerful artillery of the Allies. For example, in operations in Northern Luzon (9 January–30 June 1945), US troops took fire from a 30-cm naval howitzer emplaced in a timber pit and covered by a native hut mounted on rails which was slid aside when the gun was to be fired. To complete the deception, all signs of military activity were removed, and the ground about the hut was planted as a garden. Other gun positions were in caves and tunnels (see also overleaf).

Allied artillery played important offensive and defensive roles in the Asian operations. It was especially useful against pill-boxes, bunkers and tunnel positions. Destroying a bunker was like destroying an enormously strong, but immobile, tank. Once the bunker had been located, its cover of brush, undergrowth and other 'soft' material had to be peeled away. Howitzer fire or a thermite grenade usually sufficed for this operation. Then the bunker could be penetrated or destroyed by a sniper gun. Only high-velocity AA or AT guns could be employed for this purpose – the bigger the better. Two of the guns commonly used to snipe at bunkers were the British 2-pounder AT gun and the US 90-mm AA gun. Once the bunker had been penetrated by an AP shell, it was ready to be finished off by flame-throwers.

In general, any gun that could be dismantled for pack transport or towed along a bulldozed track had its uses in the jungle. Once the gunners had learned to co-operate closely with the infantry, artillery fire could be as devastating in the jungle as it was in other environments.

ABOVE *A Japanese M-90 self-propelled gun; these vehicles used the chassis of the M-97 medium tank and were equipped with a 75-mm gun.*
RIGHT *A Japanese 37-mm Type II (1922) infantry pack howitzer fitted with a tripod – a handy weapon for service in difficult terrain.*
BELOW *A battery of British 25-pounder gun-howitzers mounted on a 'Z' craft in Burma. These barge mountings gave valuable mobility in jungle areas.*

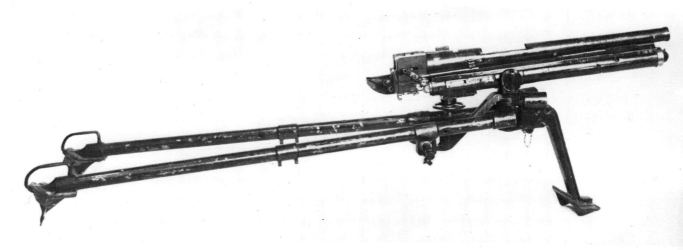

Japanese Island Defences

In their struggle to retain the Pacific islands which they had themselves taken with little difficulty, the Japanese showed all the near-inhuman hardness characteristic of the Emperor's do-or-die army. On the defensive almost unceasingly for the last three years of the war, the island garrisons emplaced and concealed their artillery with immense thoroughness. They planted new trees and gardens and even built dummy huts mounted on rails to disguise the presence of their larger cannon. For the soldiers manning these gun sites retreat was unthinkable, and the invading Allies had to destroy each position with grenades, guns and flamethrowers.

The beach diagram shows a typical Japanese defensive layout. As they approached the beach, invading forces were shelled and machine-gunned from emplacements at the back of the beach (in the slit trenches shown) and from others higher up in the jungle beyond. Under this steady fire the men in the landing craft had to negotiate a further deadly blend of natural and man-made hazards. These began with the jagged banks of coral surrounding the island. Once inside the lagoon, the invaders' way was strewn with posts and other obstacles; anti-boat mines lay near the shore-line. Lastly came the box mines, concealed with their sensitive trip wires beneath the sand.

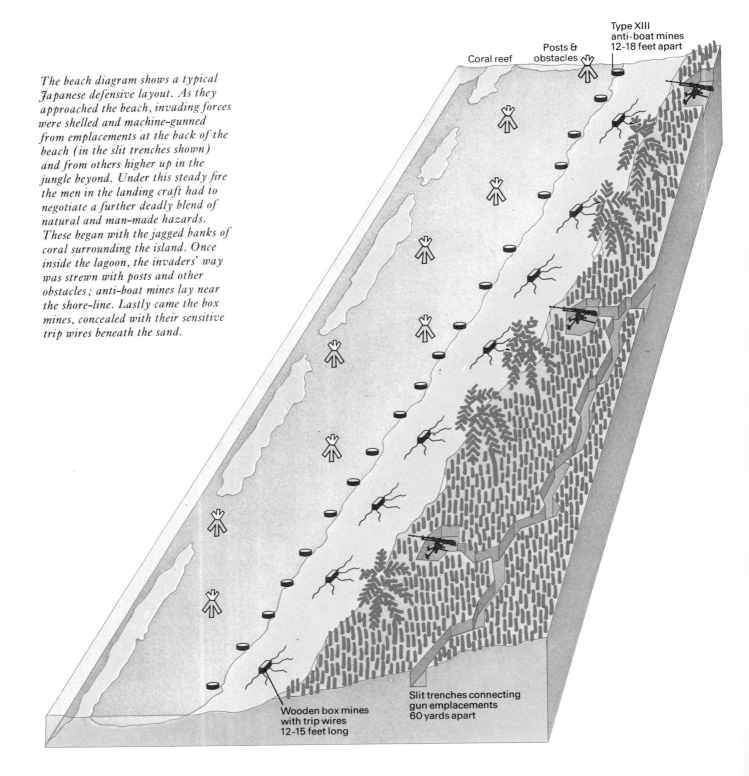

Coral reef

Posts & obstacles

Type XIII anti-boat mines 12-18 feet apart

Wooden box mines with trip wires 12-15 feet long

Slit trenches connecting gun emplacements 60 yards apart

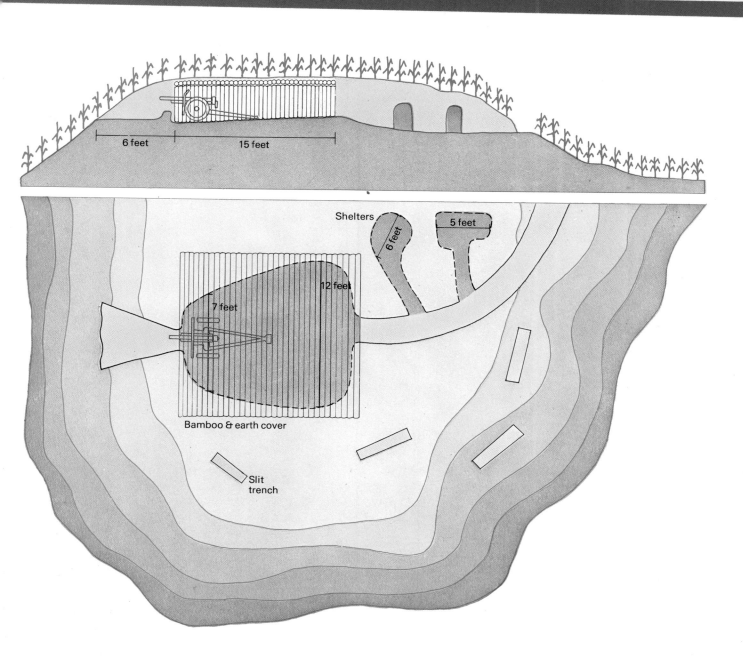

6 feet

15 feet

Shelters

6 feet

5 feet

12 feet

7 feet

Bamboo & earth cover

Slit
trench

ABOVE *Featured here is a typical Japanese hill emplacement. The gun is sited in a hollowed-out cave some 7 feet wide at the front broadening to 12 feet at the rear. The roof consists of bamboo logs and earth; above it a thick cover of trees makes the position virtually undetectable from the air. To the rear of the gun an exit passage with sleeping bays opens onto the reverse slope of the hill. The site is hedged about with slit trenches from which the infantry can bring small-arms fire to bear on the enemy.*

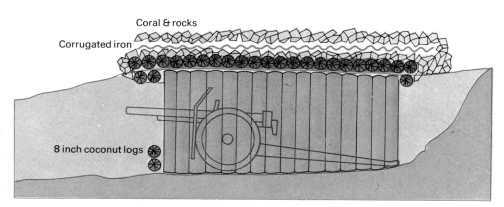

Coral & rocks

Corrugated iron

8 inch coconut logs

LEFT *In the smaller illustration the gun has been concealed in a dug-out of the kind usually found in the vicinity of a beach. Here the local coral is used together with a sheet of corrugated iron and a row of coconut logs to give cover and concealment from the air. (The logs forming the roof rest on ledges not shown in this view.) The side walls of the dug-out are also made of coconut logs.*

18

SURVIVAL AT SEA

Battleships still appear supreme, but the offensive power of aircraft is fast outstripping their ability to defend themselves.

This war marked the eclipse of two institutions whose supremacy had been constant factors for over two centuries. Between 1941 and 1945 the US Navy, backed by almost unlimited resources, finally relegated the Royal Navy to a position of inferiority; this, but for the Washington Treaty, would have happened earlier. Also during this period, the battleship lost its place as queen of the seas and arbiter of naval conflict.

From early in the war, in Norway and at Dunkirk, it became obvious that surface vessels could not operate in waters controlled by enemy aircraft, yet only gradually did changes of attitude occur concerning the relative balance between gun and aircraft. In 1939 the battleship was still supreme, the aircraft merely an extension of its guns. The aircraft was for reconnaissance: it was to spot for the guns, provide air defence and make attacks on a fleeing enemy with the object of delivering prey to a pursuing battle fleet.

To the British, faced with enemies who lacked carriers, such concepts were both sensible and successful. At Oran, in 1940, aircraft spotted for the guns of the battle fleet and carried out torpedo attacks on the French fleet; in 1941 enemies in retreat were destroyed by surface units after having been crippled by air strikes – at the battle off Cape Matapan and in the chasing of the *Bismarck*. Yet all the while the power of the aircraft, in terms both of endurance and detecting ability, and also the power of its torpedoes were growing at rates faster than the battleship's defensive power, which had reached its zenith.

Designers improved the defensive power of battleships: beam size increased, bulkheading grew in intricacy and there was a massive increase in anti-aircraft firepower; but such innovations did not save the battleship. When commissioned, the monster Japanese battleship *Yamato* carried a secondary armament of 12 (4 × 3) 6·1-inch guns and an anti-aircraft defence of 12 (6 × 2) 5-inch guns, 24 (8 × 3) 25-mm and 4 (2 × 2) 13-mm guns. When she sailed on her last mission, her main armament was equipped with a special AA shell which contained 6,000 rounds of 25-mm bullets fired on a time fuse, like a shotgun, to a maximum range of 30,000 yards. Half her 6·1-inch guns had been suppressed; instead she carried 24 (12 × 2) 5-inch and 146 (40 × 3 and 26 × 1) 25-mm anti-aircraft guns. Such defences, however, proved inadequate. Intercepted by US naval aircraft on a one-way sortie to help relieve Okinawa in April 1945, she was quickly sunk; her banks of AA guns failed to make up for a lack of air cover.

British and American capital ships also increased their anti-aircraft armament, but never to the extent of the Japanese. The *Duke of York*, for example, in addition to her original armament of 16 (8 × 2) 5·25-inch dual-purpose guns (which had a rate of fire of 18 rounds per minute) and 48 (6 × 8) 2-pounder AA guns, was given another 40 (2 × 8 and 6 × 4) 2-pounder, 8 (2 × 4) 40-mm and 16 (8 × 2) 20-mm anti-aircraft guns. Yet the survival of battleships could not be guaranteed by their own guns and powers of resistance. At Taranto and Pearl Harbor, aircraft unmistakeably showed their ability to sink capital ships; and on 10 December 1941 HMS *Repulse* became the first capital ship to be sunk by aircraft whilst on the

In World War II aircraft held the key to mobility at sea. OPPOSITE, ABOVE *In May 1940 German bombs fall around the British troopship* Mashobra *in Harstadt harbour, Norway.* RIGHT *The Japanese attack on Pearl Harbor, 7 December 1941. In the centre, surrounded by a huge cloud of smoke, is the* Arizona, *which was sunk. To the left are the* West Virginia *and the* Tennessee, *both of which suffered severe damage.*

The assaults at Taranto and Pearl Harbor prove that capital ships can be sunk from the air.

open sea. If gunned capital ships were still to operate, they now had to do so only after air supremacy was assured or they had to be accompanied by carriers that were prepared to fight for and secure command of the air.

Thus during the war the battleship was relegated to secondary duties: pre-invasion bombardment, convoy protection, the provision of anti-aircraft defence for carriers and to act as their last line of defence in the event of a surface attack. Battleships were also used for special operations such as the movement of gold and key personnel. The carrier took over as the major strike weapon. In the Pacific, it did so immediately after Pearl Harbor, when the Americans were bereft of serviceable battleships; to make up for this deficiency, the concept of the Fast Carrier Force was devised. (For a demonstration of how rapidly the use of carriers came to dominate warfare at sea, turn to the map/diagram on pages 326–7, which follows the course of the Battle of the Philippine Sea. The result of this battle, fought in June 1944 across a huge span of the Pacific theatre, made Japan's defeat inevitable.)

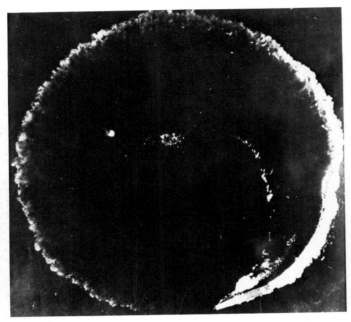

The War in the Pacific

In the six months after Pearl Harbor the Imperial Japanese armed forces ran amok in the Pacific, seizing Malaya, the Philippines and the Dutch East Indies. Their gains were immense; even so, behind the conquests there was neither the manpower, the industrial resources, the merchant fleet nor the fighting ships that the Japanese needed to implement their policy. This was to build defence lines on which the enemy would expend his strength until he tired of war and accepted a negotiated peace.

Japanese policy depended entirely on the survival of the Imperial battle fleet, which was to operate on internal lines of communication and there meet and defeat American counter-attacks. But in the Battle of Midway (June 1942) the Japanese lost four of the six large carriers with which they had started the war. During 1942 American losses were equally severe, but there was one important difference: the Japanese could not replace their lost pilots, aircraft and carriers at the same rate as the Americans and therefore

ABOVE LEFT *The Japanese carrier* Soryu *circles as she tries to avoid the bombs of American B-17s at the Battle of Midway, June 1942.*
ABOVE AND OPPOSITE, ABOVE *A Japanese destroyer*

is singled out and blown up by an American B-25 bomber at Ormoc Bay.
BELOW *HMS* Repulse *sails from Singapore on her last voyage, on 8 December 1941. Two days later she fell*

victim to a Japanese
air attack – the first
capital ship to be sunk by
aircraft on the open seas.
RIGHT *A 20-mm Quad
anti-aircraft gun in operation
aboard the German ship*

Prinz Eugen.
BELOW *The 15-inch guns of
HMS Valiant. In the
background are the* Barham
and the Warspite, *'steaming'
in line-ahead formation as they
discharge their guns.*

1943: the Americans introduce the first of their *Essex* class carriers in the struggle for command of the Pacific.

had to contend, as time went by, with a growing inferiority.

In 1943 the Americans replaced their losses from the year before with the first of the *Essex* class carriers. These ships displaced 27,000 tons and could steam at 32 knots. For defence they carried 12 5-inch and up to 68 40-mm AA guns. An extreme beam of 147½ feet incorporated for the first time an outboard lift and an overhanging flight-deck to port; ships of this class could carry 100 aircraft. Unlike British carriers, the American ships at this time did not have armoured flight-decks and hangars. They were, nevertheless, extremely rugged and although many were hit and some extensively damaged, none was sunk.

In time the Americans also came to appreciate the value of defensive armour. The *Midway* class, built during the war but commissioned too late for active service against Japan, had an armoured flight-deck; this was not, moreover, included at the expense of speed or offensive power. These ships, displacing 45,000 tons, could carry 137 aircraft. Increased displacement was in fact central to the *Midway* class's great carrying ability, and it was also favoured by the British, who were working from the other end of the equation; their ships already had a strong defensive arrangement but needed greater striking power. In October 1942 the first of the new *Audacious* class was

laid down and it was anticipated that these 36,000-ton ships would be the Royal Navy's first carriers to operate 100 aircraft; this however, turned out to be an unrealized dream.

In the war in the Pacific it was the *Essex* class carriers that spearheaded the American victory. Using radar and improved aircraft that gave them a considerable material advantage over the Japanese, these carriers quickly eliminated enemy air and sea strength in the South Pacific. Thrusting through the Carolines and Marianas, the US Navy provoked the Japanese to fight and lose the Battle of the Philippine Sea in July 1944 – the first carrier battle for two years. In this engagement the Japanese lost three carriers and most of their aircraft and crews. Thus devoid of cover, the Philippines were invaded and conquered despite a despairing sortie by the Imperial Japanese Navy, which was crushed in the Battle of Leyte Gulf. Ranging over the Philippines, the Ryukus, Indo-China, the Chinese coast, Formosa and finally the Japanese homeland itself, the carrier aircraft cleared the seas of the enemy merchant and fighting ships that remained; and provided air defence for the battleships when they started their bombardment of the Japanese coast in July 1945.

By the time that the atomic bombs were dropped, Japan

US carrier aircraft and submarines combine to destroy Japan's vulnerable supply lines.

ABOVE *An American LSM (Landing Ship Medium) softens Japanese opposition with a battery of rockets.*
BELOW *A panoramic view of the chaos at Pearl Harbor. Around the black cloud in the centre, emanating chiefly from the stricken USS* Arizona, *are smaller black puffs of smoke from the American AA guns which accounted for 28 Japanese aircraft. The smaller clouds to the left mark where the* Shaw *and a floating dock were hit.*
BOTTOM *The art of naval camouflage. The USS* New Orleans *lies concealed beneath netting and foliage at Tulagi in 1942.*
OPPOSITE *Naval pilots under instruction in the USA learn flying skills in a Link Trainer.*

was at the end of her tether. Her Navy had virtually ceased to exist and her Army had been defeated in most theatres. Economically, too, her position was desperate: her people were on the brink of starvation and her factories were drastically under-supplied. The vital supply lines that brought food and raw materials to Japan and took troops and supplies to the theatres of war had been severed; the Japanese merchant fleet had been all but annihilated. In 1941 Japan had needed 10,000,000 tons of shipping a year to maintain herself, of which her own fleet could carry only six millions, the balance having to be carried in foreign-owned ships. Yet, excluding any that she could capture, four million tons of foreign shipping was lost to Japan as soon as she went to war.

In December 1941, with no other means of taking the fight to the enemy, the Americans launched unrestricted submarine warfare. Operating mainly from Hawaii until early 1945, when the submarine base was moved to Guam, US submarines sank 1,153 merchant ships totalling 4,889,000 tons at a cost of 52 of their own number. Japan was able to sustain her losses until November 1943. After that date she was compelled, in her efforts to reinforce island garrisons under attack, to send merchant ships into waters controlled by US air and naval forces; there the

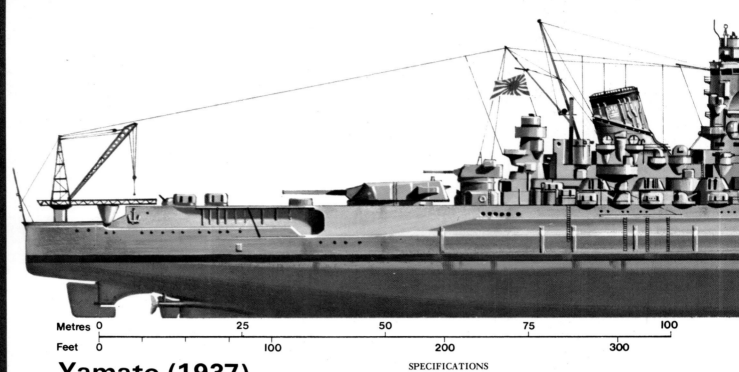

| Metres | 0 | | 25 | | 50 | | 75 | | 100 |
| Feet | 0 | | 100 | | 200 | | 300 | | |

Yamato (1937)

In World War II the Imperial Japanese Navy acquired two monster battleships, the *Yamato* and her sister ship *Musashi*. They were the largest battleships ever built. On these pages the *Yamato* is seen at different stages in her development; in her brief career her anti-aircraft armament was progressively strengthened from 24 25-mm machine guns to a final total of 146. She entered service in February 1942 and served in the Pacific theatre until she was caught, on 6 April 1945, in a massed attack by carrier-borne aircraft. Although immensely strong she was unable to withstand a bombardment that in the space of two hours registered seven bomb and 12 torpedo hits, and she blew up and sank.

SPECIFICATIONS

Displacement	64,000 tons
Length	863 feet
Beam	127 feet
Draught	35 feet
Armament	9 18-inch guns
(when completed)	12 6·1-inch guns
	12 5-inch guns
	24 25-mm AA guns
	4 13-mm guns
	6 aircraft
Armour	16 inch belt
Engines	150,000 hp; steam turbines
Speed	27 knots

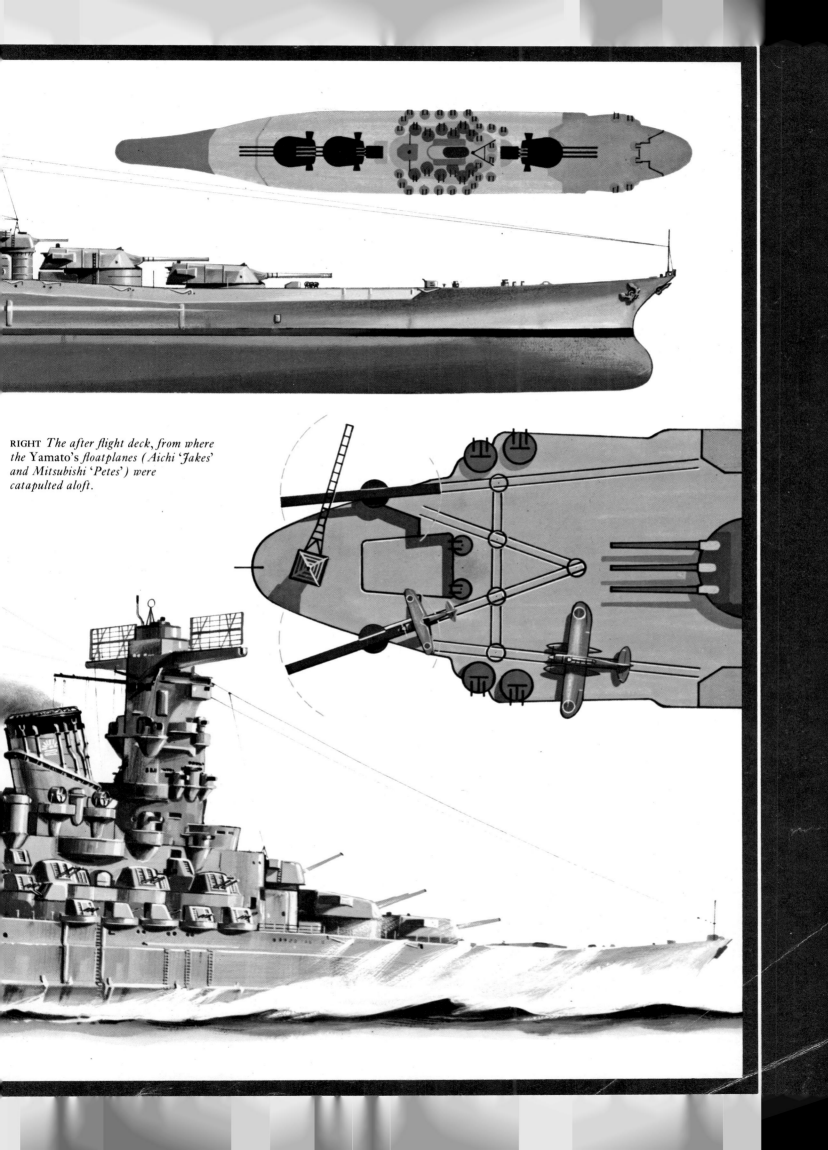

RIGHT *The after flight deck, from where the* Yamato's *floatplanes (Aichi 'Jakes' and Mitsubishi 'Petes') were catapulted aloft.*

American industry outbuilds the Japanese, ensuring victory in the battle of the sea lanes.

merchant ships took losses on a scale far greater than Japan's limited construction facilities could ever hope to keep pace with.

Many of the reasons for this state of affairs lay in the technical inferiority of Japanese equipment as compared to that of the USA. Whereas, for example, Japanese aircraft showed relatively little improvement during the course of the war, American aircraft improved out of all recognition and ultimately outclassed the Japanese. And while, in the submarine war, Japanese units lacked radar, throughout 1943 American submarines were being equipped with the new and very effective SJ sets. The Japanese also lacked a means of locating the High Frequency voice radios used by the submarines. Nor, in the strategic field, did they aid their own cause by their attitude towards convoys: initially reluctant to adopt the system at all, when they finally did so their escorts were fatally weak. Instead they preferred to mount offensive patrols just as the British had done in the Great War – and with an equal lack of success. These weaknesses in numbers and in the quality of their equipment were critical deficiencies that cost Japan the battle of the sea lanes. In nature, however, they were not dissimilar to weaknesses experienced by the British and Americans in the Atlantic, but which those powers managed to remedy before this struggle reached its climax in the spring of 1943.

BELOW *US Navy landing craft bring essential supplies to back up the troops engaged in the struggle for Iwo Jima in 1945. To drive the tenacious Japanese from this tiny volcanic island, 4¾ miles by 2¼, took the Marines over five weeks, during which time they hit the Japanese strongpoints with a preliminary naval bombardment, air strikes and a ferocious battery from 700* heavy guns and howitzers, mortars, rocket launchers, anti-tank guns and 22 tanks. Of the Japanese garrison of 21,000, only 216 survived.

ABOVE *Japanese seamen take to the water from the sides of their fast-sinking destroyer, shattered in a raid by the American 345th Bomber Group.*

1940–41: Britain's merchant losses in the Atlantic run at twice the replacement capacity; convoy techniques are slowly improved.

The Battle of the Atlantic

In the European context the war at sea was, in the absence of a strong German surface fleet and a determined Italian navy, a struggle conducted along the sea lanes by German submarines against Britain's trade. Initially, the German submarines operated under two handicaps. Firstly, war had come too early, at a time when only 57 craft were available instead of the 300 that in the Germans' estimation was the number needed if they were to bring Britain to her knees; and, secondly, even that small number was restricted in its operations. On the other hand Britain, with 20,000,000 tons of shipping, offered many weakly defended targets: indeed, she went to war with a mere 87 escort vessels of which only 26 were in the Western Approaches. Furthermore, most of these escorts lacked the range to protect merchantmen more than a few hundred miles west of Ireland. This was so because the British had neglected to build up between the wars a fleet train that could replenish ships at sea.

In the early days convoys were protected not by ships that had been trained to work together but by those that were available at the time; in such a situation numbers were more important than teamwork, technique and training. The consequences were entirely predictable. In 1940 the Germans lost 23 U-boats, in 1941 35 and in 1942 87. But against these figures must be put those of a strenuous building programme: in the last quarter of 1941 alone 69 new submarines were commissioned and in January 1942 U-boat strength stood at 249, of which 90 were operational. Britain's merchant shipping losses in 1940 and 1941 were about 4,000,000 tons in each year – more than twice the replacement capacity.

However, losses were considerably reduced in the North Atlantic between July and December 1941, when the monthly average was only about 100,000 tons. The principal reason for this drop lay in the improved defences of the convoys; and, partly as a result of the tightening-up by the British, U-boats began to be moved away from the area. British corvettes with a transatlantic capability were increasing in numbers, and sloops of the *Black Swan* class were diverted from other theatres to the North Atlantic. A further improvement was that the new escorts were being trained as groups – in the hope, of course, that they would be kept together and not be squandered piecemeal. In addition, U-boats were losing their invulnerability. The increasingly widespread use of radar now gave escorts the opportunity to counter-attack a surfaced U-boat as it moved in on a convoy; in other words the escorts took up the offensive before, and not after, the enemy could claim any victims.

By an unfortunate chain of consequences, the entry of the United States into the war was initially disastrous for the Allied cause. Following the fall of France, the United States had adopted an increasingly hostile position *vis-à-vis* Germany; in material ways this attitude was demonstrated through the provision of escorts for British convoys and through the declaration of Neutrality Zones off the east coast of America, in which shipping could move without danger. But when the Axis Powers declared war on the United States, the hitherto protected ships lost their invulnerability. The result was a slaughter of American shipping in the first six months of 1942. In that year 1,006 ships were sunk in the North Atlantic and submarines accounted for 1,160 Allied ships in all theatres. The total Allied losses, from all causes and in all theatres, was a

Essex Class Carriers

The fleet carriers of the *Essex* class were a decisive force in the Pacific theatre. Arriving in 1943, they spearheaded the US offensive through the Carolinas and Marianas, their commanders using their technological superiority in terms both of the ships themselves and of their more powerful aircraft to batter a path to within reach of the Japanese homeland. The *Essex* carriers were tough ships, even though, unlike their British counterparts, their flight-decks and hangars were not armoured. They were big ships, too, with room for 100 aircraft; and their design included an outboard elevator.

FAR LEFT AND BELOW The representative ship
on these pages is the *Essex*, first of the new
class. She was laid down in April 1941 and
completed in December the following year.
Dimensions, etc., vary among the 20 ships of
the class that were built in wartime, but those
of the *Essex* were as follows:

Displacement	27,000 tons
Length	820 feet
Beam (extreme)	147 feet 6 inches
Draught	20 feet
Armament	12 × 5 inch guns
	40 × 40 mm AA guns
	50 × 20 mm guns (quadruple mounts)
Armour (max.)	2-3 inches (side amidships)
Engines	150,000 hp; geared turbines
Carrier capacity	100 aircraft
Speed	32 knots

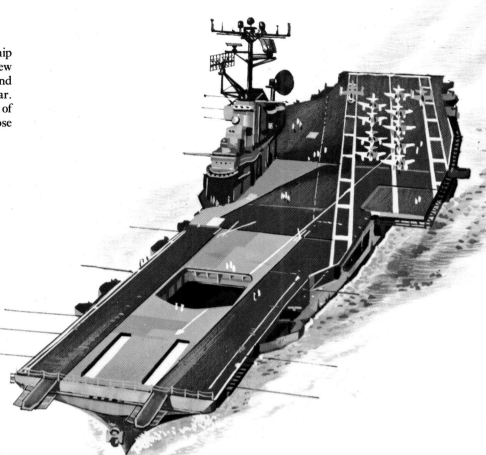

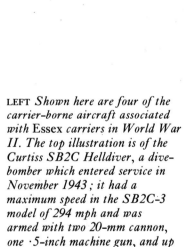

LEFT *Shown here are four of the
carrier-borne aircraft associated
with Essex carriers in World War
II. The top illustration is of the
Curtiss SB2C Helldiver, a dive-
bomber which entered service in
November 1943; it had a
maximum speed in the SB2C-3
model of 294 mph and was
armed with two 20-mm cannon,
one ·5-inch machine gun, and up
to 1,000 pounds of bombs or one*
*torpedo carried internally;
maximum range was 1,925 miles.
Second is the Grumman TBM
Avenger, one of the war's most
successful torpedo bombers. It had
a speed of 270 mph and a range of
1,020 miles; armament consisted
of five machine guns and up to
2,000 pounds of bombs, one 1,920-
pound torpedo or eight rockets.
The third aircraft shown is a
Chance Vought F4U-1D*
*Corsair fighter bomber, a variant
in the powerful Corsair series of
naval fighters; in the F4U-4
version these aircraft could
achieve a maximum speed of 446
mph. The bottom aircraft is a
Grumman F6F-3 Hellcat fighter;
these were a scaled-up and more
powerful version of the earlier
Wildcat; armament was six ·5-
inch machine guns, top speed 375
mph and range 1,090 miles.*

ABOVE *The USS* Intrepid,
*an Essex class carrier laid
down in December 1941,
here seen after major
conversion work completed
in 1957 had given her an
angled flight deck, steam
catapult and an enclosed
bow.*

staggering 1,664 ships totalling 7,800,000 tons. The winter months brought some relief to the Allies but in March 1943, despite increasing escort strength, the U-boats achieved their third highest total of monthly sinkings in the war (627,377 tons), and it seemed that Britain might be defeated despite the convoy system and American resources.

However, in the summer of 1943 the submarine challenge was not simply beaten back but decisively defeated. Despite the high rate of sinkings in March, the Germans were now failing to destroy ships faster than the Allies could build replacements. Mainly because of the mass production techniques of the American yards, construction was running at 8,800,000 tons a year in the last quarter of 1942; a year later the rate of building had almost doubled (16,400,000 tons). In the first quarter of 1943 building exceeded losses for the first time since 1939, and the Germans were subsequently unable to reverse this trend.

Nor were they able to maintain their high rate of sinkings. Better convoy protection ensured more safe arrivals: in August 1943 only two ships were lost in the North Atlantic and between June 1943 and May 1944 only 442,684 tons were lost in that theatre. The submarines were forced to more distant and less lucrative waters, away from the vital USA–UK supply route. Increased convoy protection also produced greater success against the U-boats. In the first six months of 1943, 96 submarines were sunk, and 237 in the whole year. At the height of the battle, in May, 41 U-boats failed to return to their pens. Increasing strength, better weapons, and effective co-ordination and teamwork were the simple but indispensable factors behind the Allied success.

Air cover for the convoys was of the utmost importance in the Battle of the Atlantic. In the early years of the war,

vast areas of the ocean had been safe for the submarines, but gradually the air gap – the area between Britain and the American continent not covered by air patrols – was cut down. In July 1941, RAF Coastal Command had only one squadron of nine Very Long Range aircraft; two years later there were 105 aircraft in nine squadrons. Long Range aircraft and flying boats similarly increased in numbers. For the first time there were no safe areas for the U-boats to run to on the surface and recharge their batteries. From the middle of 1942 onwards, convoys had their own air cover on an ever-growing scale, and the escort carrier began to appear in force. By October 1943 the British had 25 such ships, nearly all American-built. These redoubtable craft doubled, when necessary, for fleet carriers and assault carriers during invasions, but their greatest service was in searching for and hunting down submarines in the vicinity of convoys. They displaced about 12,000 tons and carried up to 18 aircraft.

Equally as important as the increasing number of aircraft was their improved equipment. In the summer of 1942 a new 1·5-metre radar set was introduced; this was followed early the next year by the 10-cm set. The latter, to which the Germans failed to find a counter in the critical phase of the battle, allowed aircraft to make contact in extremely bad weather conditions and at night. Combined with new, shallow-pattern depth-charges, which were introduced to aircraft in mid-1942, this equipment was so effective that in 1943 aircraft accounted for 116 submarines.

Surface escorts also increased in numbers and hitting power. New depth-charges with a 500-foot capability were introduced, and a mortar that could throw 24 contact bombs some 250 yards forwards of the ship entered service at the start of 1943. This mortar was extremely useful because it enabled an attack to be made without losing

contact with the submarine, whereas in a depth-charge attack the Asdic lost contact as the range was closed. (Forward-throwing and fast-sinking depth-charges appeared later, towards the end of the war.) In addition, detection devices for locating signalling U-boats began to appear in growing numbers during 1942. All these weapons and detection devices substantially contributed to victory, though in the end the critical factors were the strength and training of the escorts. In October 1943 the Royal Navy disposed of 288 destroyers and escort destroyers and 325 sloops, frigates and corvettes. By the end of the war 257 destroyers (of both types), 50 sloops, 235 frigates and 257 corvettes flew the White Ensign.

Most of this anti-submarine strength was concentrated against the 400 U-boats that remained to Germany at the end of the war; the results of this confrontation were such that, in April 1945, for example, 15 U-boats were sunk in the waters around the British Isles. Interestingly though, all these losses were of submarines of a standard design; no losses were taken by the new types of submarine that were then becoming available. The latter craft in fact enjoyed a remarkable immunity from detection, and hence from destruction.

Germany had been denied submarines until 1935, and the majority of the U-boats with which she went to war were of the *Type I* and *II* varieties, which were quickly relegated to training duties. There were, however, 18 *Type VII* and seven *Type IX* submarines; these were the forerunners of the most common types of U-boat built by Germany in the course of the war.

The Germans planned to use submarines in packs that could search for convoys and swamp the escort ships. Since, too, the intention was to use submarines in surface night attacks, the emphasis in their design was placed on

U-boat detection devices improve, and convoy escort strengths multiply.

OPPOSITE *Depth charges from a US Army B-25 explode around a U-boat in the Atlantic.*
ABOVE *Foredeck and 3·5-inch gun of a German Type VII-C U-boat in the Arctic Sea north of Norway.*
BELOW LEFT *The map shows how the air gap narrowed, progressively inhibiting the activities of the U-boats.*
BELOW *A U-boat construction yard in wartime.*

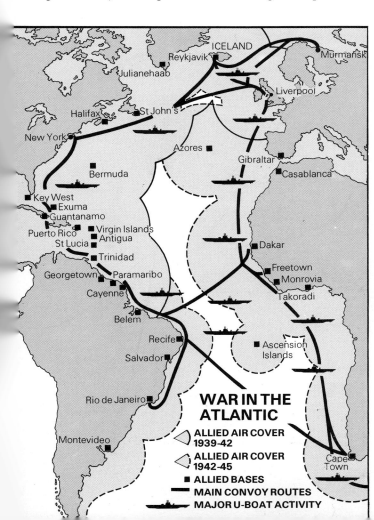

WAR IN THE ATLANTIC

◁ ALLIED AIR COVER 1939-42
◁ ALLIED AIR COVER 1942-45
■ ALLIED BASES
— MAIN CONVOY ROUTES
⊂ MAJOR U-BOAT ACTIVITY

ICELAND
Reykjavik
Murmansk
Julianehaab
Liverpool
Halifax
St John's
New York
Azores
Gibraltar
Bermuda
Casablanca
Key West
Exuma
Guantanamo
Puerto Rico
Virgin Islands
Antigua
St Lucia
Dakar
Trinidad
Georgetown
Paramaribo
Freetown
Monrovia
Cayenne
Takoradi
Belem
Recife
Ascension Islands
Salvador
Rio de Janeiro
Montevideo
Cape Town

torpedoes – not gunfire – and on speed and surface performance. Thus the *Type VII-B*, though only 753 tons, could make 17·25 knots on the surface (which was faster than a corvette of the *Flower* class). This class of submarine, which was virtually the same as Germany's most common type of submarine, the *Type VII-C*, had a 6,500-mile range and an armament of 12 torpedoes.

Another class of U-boat, the type *IX-A*, had a range of 8,100 miles, displaced 1,032 tons and carried 22 torpedoes. Subsequently the Germans developed the rather remarkable *Type IX-D2*, which, on a displacement of only 1,616 tons, carried 24 torpedoes and had a range of 23,700 miles at 12 knots; its maximum surface speed was 20 knots. However, only 30 of these craft were built.

German submarines proved satisfactory until the use of radar became widespread in British and American escorts. Until that time submarines enjoyed the advantage of near-invisibility during a night attack. But radar forced the Germans to resort to a vessel capable of operating and attacking from beneath the surface. The first solution to their problems was the snorkel, which had been developed by the Dutch Navy before the war. This was a breathing device that drew in fresh air and expelled fumes and so allowed the diesel engines to run when the submarine was submerged. The snorkel also provided greater security, since it was difficult for enemy radar to make contact with

Early U-boats, designed for surface night attacks, prove inadequate as the Allies step up their use of radar.

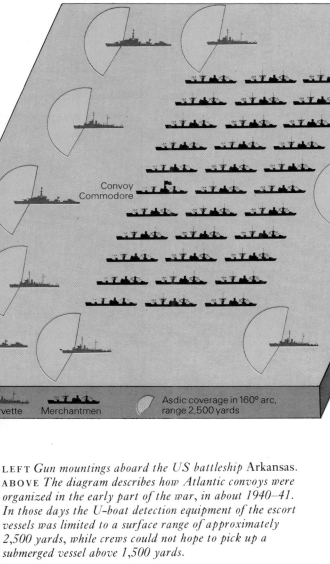

Convoy Commodore

Destroyer Corvette Merchantmen Asdic coverage in 160° arc, range 2,500 yards

LEFT *Gun mountings aboard the US battleship* Arkansas. ABOVE *The diagram describes how Atlantic convoys were organized in the early part of the war, in about 1940–41. In those days the U-boat detection equipment of the escort vessels was limited to a surface range of approximately 2,500 yards, while crews could not hope to pick up a submerged vessel above 1,500 yards.*

Germany's new generation of U-boats have a high underwater performance and are much harder to detect.

such a small and otherwise invisible target (though the 3-cm radar introduced in 1945 enjoyed reasonable success). However, the new security was achieved at the cost of mobility. Maximum speed fell to 6 knots, which was insufficient for concentration against a convoy or for escape from the escorts.

To solve this problem the Germans broke away from the accepted concept of the submarine – that of a surface craft that could dive. Priority was now given to underwater performance, which meant high submerged speeds and an improved battery capacity. These requirements produced the 1,621-ton *Type XXI* for ocean work, and the *Type*

XXIII (232 tons) for coastal work. Whereas earlier submarines had a maximum submerged speed of eight knots for one hour, the *Type XXI* had a maximum speed of 17 knots for one hour – enough to out-run most escorts and their depth-charges. The new submarine could also make five knots on silent electrical motors for three days. But, for all their technical efficiency, only 123 *Type XXI*s and 59 *Type XXIII*s were ready by the end of the war.

Both the new types of submarine were considerable technical successes and major advances over earlier types. Also at this time the Germans were building a *Type XXVI*, of which four were completed before the war. These were

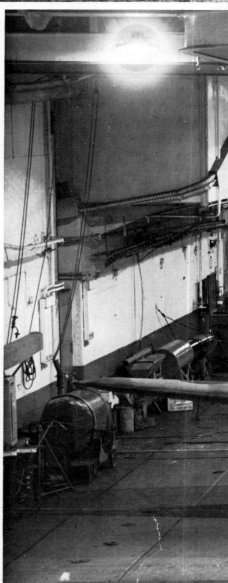

OPPOSITE, BELOW *The* Tirpitz *in Narvik-Bogen Fjord in July 1942, surrounded by anti-torpedo netting.*
BELOW *A sequence of four photographs that shows the sinking, in June 1941, of the SS* Kemmendine, *hit by a German torpedo.*
BOTTOM *Mechanics at work in the hangar of HMS* Argus. *Of 1917 vintage, the* Argus *underwent various modifications before serving in World War II as an escort carrier and ferry transporting aircraft into the combat zones.*

the Walther boats, whose high speed was obtained through a dangerous and expensive fuel, Ingolin, which was the energy source for a gas-driven, closed-circuit turbine. Exhausts dissolved in the sea and left no trace, while the closed circuit did not use up the submarine's air. The system gave high speed for long periods, but fuel consumption was high and the submarine needed diesel/electrical propulsion to reach the patrol areas. This meant that the submarine had three different sets of machinery. Its snorkelling performance, though poor, was offset by the development of improved hydrophones that enabled accurate salvoes of torpedoes to be fired at a depth of 150 feet.

The Germans' last and most deadly submarines of the war, the Walther boats, can fire torpedoes at depths of up to 150 feet.

Surface Actions

During World War II there were no major fleet actions in the European theatre. The Germans lacked a balanced fleet and usually sought to avoid action when opposed by units of the Royal Navy. Because of this, many convoys were saved from the attentions of German surface raiders.

Several engagements were fought out to a finish: the pocket battleship *Graf Spee* was hounded to an ignominious end by British cruisers in the River Plate in December 1939; the battleship *Bismarck*, crippled by air strikes as she made for Brest, was hammered into scrap by the guns of the Home Fleet, and the *Scharnhorst*, often a lucky ship, was sunk off the North Cape on 26 December 1943 in the last engagement in European waters between gunned capital ships. Only at Narvik, during the Norwegian campaign, did several actions take place. Most were fleeting and inconclusive, but at the Second Battle of Narvik the battleship *Warspite*, screened by nine destroyers, entered

OPPOSITE *In the Mediterranean the Fleet Air Arm staged a successful raid on Taranto, sinking the battleship* Littorio *(left) and crippling two others. The aerial view shows the harbour after the attack.*
BELOW *The German pocket battleship* Graf Spee *in flames off Montevideo after the River Plate engagement that gave a lift to British morale in the first winter of the war.*

TOP LEFT *The* Ark Royal *shortly before she sank off Gibraltar in November 1941.*

TOP RIGHT *The* Barham *explodes, 25 November 1941.*

OPPOSITE AND ABOVE *The sinking of the US carrier* Lexington *at the Battle of the Coral Sea, May 1942. While a destroyer takes off the sick and wounded, others of the crew slide down ropes to be picked up by small boats.*

the fjord and sank eight German destroyers. Revenge was extracted when Germany's two battlecruisers cornered and sank the aircraft carrier *Glorious* and her two destroyer escorts; this was the only action of the war in which a fleet carrier was sunk by gunned capital ships.

In the Mediterranean there was a similar lack of decisive action despite the presence of four fleets: the French, the Italian, and two British forces at Gibraltar and Alexandria. The first major action was Operation Catapult, the unfortunate attack on the French fleet at its anchorage at Oran. One battleship, the *Bretagne*, was sunk and two more crippled by the combined attentions of the *Hood, Valiant* and *Resolution*. Most of the actions in the Mediterranean were between aircraft, and submarines, against British surface units. In their efforts to keep Malta supplied, the British suffered very heavy losses, especially during Operation Pedestal in August 1942. Out of 14 merchant ships that set sail only four reached Malta, while one carrier was sunk and another crippled in their defence. Greece and Crete also cost the British heavy losses: at Crete three cruisers and six destroyers were lost and seven other ships, including two battleships and a carrier, were damaged beyond local repair. But losses were not all one way. A night attack by the Fleet Air Arm sunk one Italian

TOP *The type II-B; one of the early, coastal types in service at the beginning of the war, survivors were later kept on for training duties. These U-boats were armed with three 21-inch torpedo tubes and carried six torpedoes or eight mines.*

The U-Boats

On these pages are four of the principal types of U-boat used against Allied shipping in the Atlantic. The campaign opened with dramatic successes for the U-boats and huge losses for the Allies until they learnt successfully to apply the convoy system. The decisive years were 1942–43: in '42 1,006 ships were sunk in the North Atlantic and submarines accounted for 1,160 Allied ships in all theatres; total tonnage lost that year amounted to 7,800,000 tons. But by the end of the year production in the American shipyards was booming, and convoy techniques were being tightened up, with tangible results. In the first quarter of 1943 the rate of Allied building exceeded losses for the first time since 1939. The U-boats were never to recover their supremacy; instead their own losses mounted, thanks to the greater strength of the Allied convoys, their improved weapons, co-ordination and increasingly effective air cover.

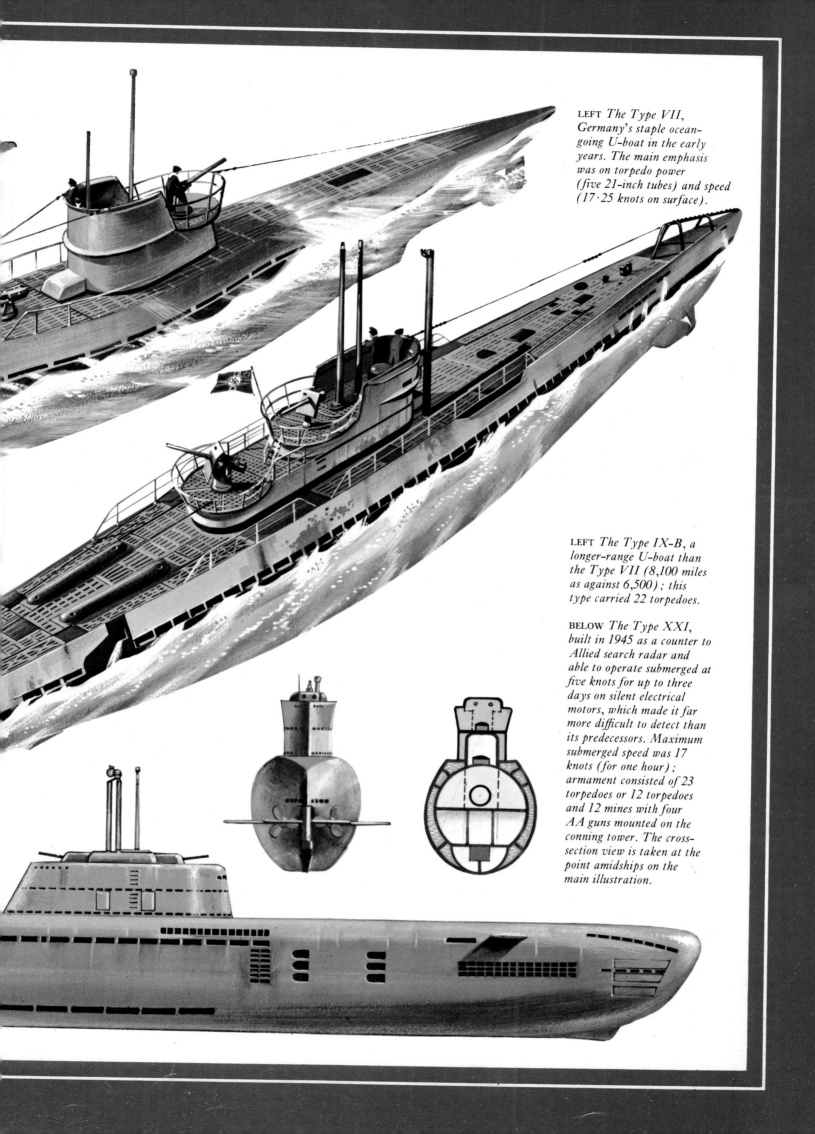

LEFT *The Type VII,
Germany's staple ocean-
going U-boat in the early
years. The main emphasis
was on torpedo power
(five 21-inch tubes) and speed
(17·25 knots on surface).*

LEFT *The Type IX-B, a
longer-range U-boat than
the Type VII (8,100 miles
as against 6,500); this
type carried 22 torpedoes.*

BELOW *The Type XXI,
built in 1945 as a counter to
Allied search radar and
able to operate submerged at
five knots for up to three
days on silent electrical
motors, which made it far
more difficult to detect than
its predecessors. Maximum
submerged speed was 17
knots (for one hour);
armament consisted of 23
torpedoes or 12 torpedoes
and 12 mines with four
AA guns mounted on the
conning tower. The cross-
section view is taken at the
point amidships on the
main illustration.*

battleship and crippled two more at Taranto; and three heavy cruisers and two destroyers were accounted for in a night action with the British battle fleet off Cape Matapan.

In the Pacific, fleet actions were more common, for in this theatre were two fleets that needed command of the seas and were prepared to fight for it. In an attempt to secure an overwhelming initial advantage, the Japanese attacked the US fleet at Pearl Harbor. Four American battleships were sunk in this pre-emptive attack (though two were subsequently recovered). Unfortunately for the Japanese, the oil installations, dockyard facilities and the carriers were not destroyed and Japan was forced to turn her attention to completing this task within six months of the outbreak of war. In the meantime, however, several battles had been fought. At the Battle of the Java Sea a mixed force of American, Dutch, British and Australian cruisers and destroyers was crushed, and on 9 April 1942 the British

lost a carrier and two cruisers in the Indian Ocean to Japan's carrier aircraft. Between 4 and 8 May, however, the unbroken run of Japanese successes was halted at the Battle of the Coral Sea. In this, the first naval battle to be fought entirely by aircraft, the Japanese lost the carrier *Shoho* and in return sank the *Lexington* and crippled the *Yorktown*. Thus although the balance of losses superficially favoured Japan, she could not in fact afford the loss of a single carrier at a time when American building was getting into its stride.

In an effort to bring about the destruction of the American carriers, the Japanese tried to make the Americans give battle by invading Midway Island. Aided by a knowledge of Japanese dispositions and intentions, the Americans fought a defensive battle which smashed Japan's main carrier force. Four Japanese carriers were sunk for the loss of the hastily-repaired *Yorktown*.

ABOVE *Japanese strike aircraft attack and sink the USS* Hornet *at the Battle of Santa Cruz, 26 October 1942, in the face of scant anti-aircraft fire.*

BELOW *An aerial view of the Japanese heavy cruiser* Mikuma *burning during the Battle of Midway, June 1942. In this battle the Japanese lost four carriers.*

OPPOSITE *During the fierce Battle of Cape Engano, 25 October 1944, the Japanese carrier* Zuiho *is attacked by aircraft from USS* Enterprise.

Midway ushered in a period of balance: neither side was powerful enough to seize the initiative and force its will upon the enemy. The Americans were strong enough, however, to contest Japanese activity in the Solomons. American landings on Guadalcanal on 7 August sparked off a series of actions which drained Japanese strength more severely than it depleted the US Navy. On 9 August one Australian and three American cruisers were sunk in the Battle of Savo Island as the Japanese sought to contest the landings. On 23–24 August, in the Battle of the Eastern Solomons, a Japanese attempt to supply its garrison resulted in the loss of the carrier *Ryuko* and, on the opposing side, the severe battering of the American carrier *Enterprise*. The fierce actions continued: Japanese submarines caused heavy damage to the carrier *Saratoga* on 31 August and sank the *Wasp* on 15 September. The Battle of Cape Esperance (11–12 October) was indecisive with

to be their last major effort at Guadalcanal. The American losses (two cruisers and eight destroyers) were a heavy price to pay but they could be accepted in view of American resources. In the last major action in these waters, the Japanese sank one cruiser and damaged three more at the Battle of Tassafaronga on 30 November. Japanese resistance on Guadalcanal ceased on 9 February 1943.

Thereafter the Americans were able to undertake an increasingly dynamic offensive. For most of 1943 action was mainly centred on the Solomons, as the Americans slowly drove up the island chain until in November the first landings were made in the Gilberts and Marshalls. The landings on Saipan the following June resulted in the Battle of the Philippine Sea, where the Japanese, giving battle for the first time for nearly two years, lost three carriers and over 400 aircraft in the last carrier battle of the war. The result of this battle effectively sealed the fate

After Midway comes a spell of stalemate, then the balance tilts towards the USA as their forces drive through the Pacific island chain.

losses approximately equal. The Battle of Santa Cruz, fought two weeks later, saw the virtual elimination of the carrier forces of both sides. The Americans lost the *Hornet*, and the *Enterprise* was again badly mauled. In return the *Zuiho* and *Shokaku* were severely damaged. Thereafter it was the turn of the battleships. In a series of night actions between 12 and 15 November the Japanese lost two battleships, a cruiser and three destroyers in what turned out

of Japan and her Navy. An attempt, in October, to counter the American landings at Leyte not only resulted in the last action between battleships (fought in the Surigao Strait) but in the annihilation of the Japanese fleet. Three battleships, four carriers, 10 cruisers and nine destroyers were sunk for the cost of one carrier, two escort carriers and three destroyers. From that point the Americans had little more to do than mop up the remainder.

Battle of the Philippine Sea, 18–21 June 194

The massive clashes in this battle between carrier-borne aircraft were characteristic of the new brand of long-range naval warfare. Thus Vice-Admiral Ozawa could plan a major assault on the US Fifth Fleet while keeping his own ships some 400 miles from the enemy's position until hours before the attack was launched. On the Allied side, Admiral Spruance knew that the outcome hinged on successfully exploiting his 2-1 superiority in naval aircraft.

The Airborne Forces
Spruance's deadly blend of 891 fighters, torpedo-bombers and dive-bombers eventually crushed the Japanese force of 430, of which barely 30 survived.

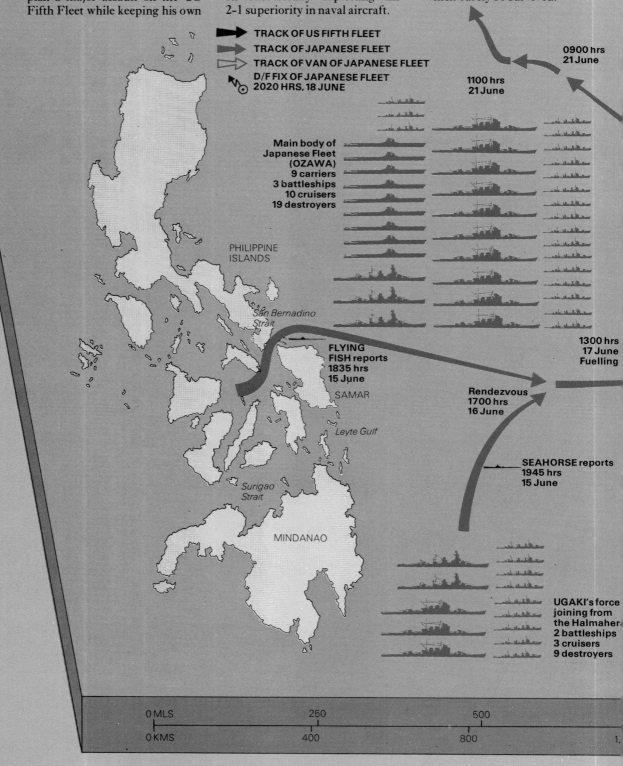

TRACK OF US FIFTH FLEET
TRACK OF JAPANESE FLEET
TRACK OF VAN OF JAPANESE FLEET
D/F FIX OF JAPANESE FLEET
2020 HRS, 18 JUNE

Main body of Japanese Fleet (OZAWA)
9 carriers
3 battleships
10 cruisers
19 destroyers

PHILIPPINE ISLANDS

San Bernadino Strait

FLYING FISH reports
1835 hrs
15 June

SAMAR

Leyte Gulf

Surigao Strait

MINDANAO

0900 hrs
21 June

1100 hrs
21 June

1300 hrs
17 June
Fuelling

Rendezvous
1700 hrs
16 June

SEAHORSE reports
1945 hrs
15 June

UGAKI's force
joining from
the Halmahera
2 battleships
3 cruisers
9 destroyers

0 MLS		250		500
0 KMS		400		800

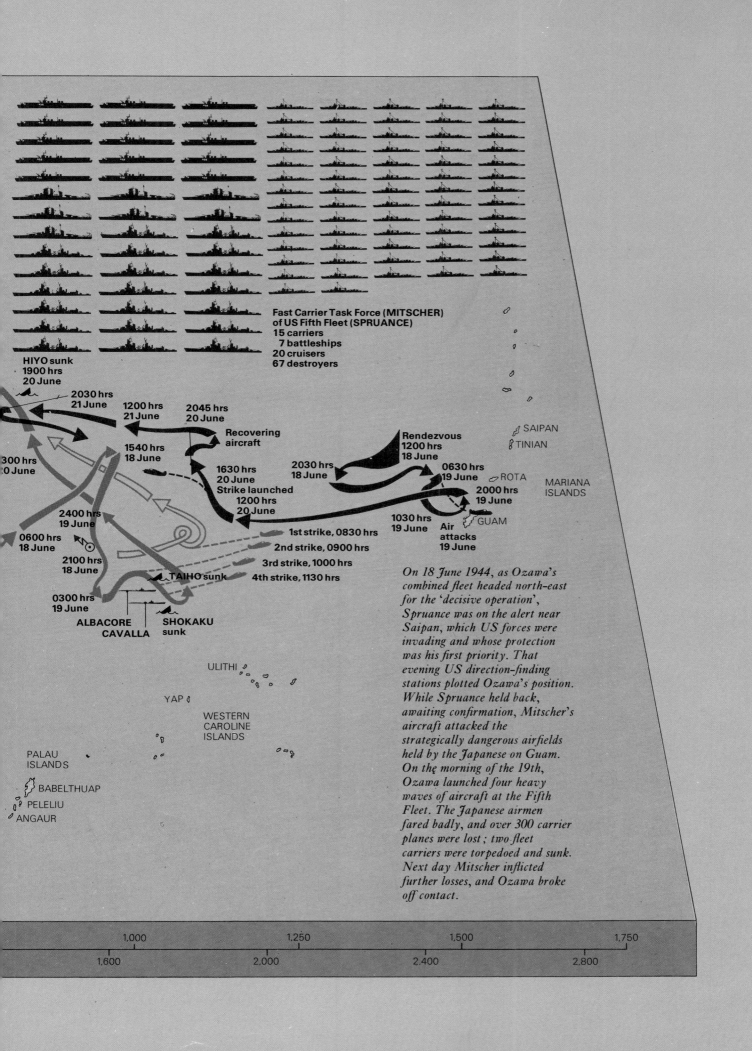

Fast Carrier Task Force (MITSCHER)
of US Fifth Fleet (SPRUANCE)
15 carriers
7 battleships
20 cruisers
67 destroyers

HIYO sunk
1900 hrs
20 June

2030 hrs
21 June

1200 hrs
21 June

2045 hrs
20 June

Recovering
aircraft

1540 hrs
18 June

300 hrs
0 June

1630 hrs
20 June
Strike launched
1200 hrs
20 June

2030 hrs
18 June

Rendezvous
1200 hrs
18 June

0630 hrs
19 June

2000 hrs
19 June

ROTA

SAIPAN
TINIAN

MARIANA
ISLANDS

2400 hrs
19 June

0600 hrs
18 June

2100 hrs
18 June

0300 hrs
19 June

1030 hrs
19 June

Air
attacks
19 June

GUAM

1st strike, 0830 hrs
2nd strike, 0900 hrs
3rd strike, 1000 hrs
4th strike, 1130 hrs

TAIHO sunk

ALBACORE
CAVALLA

SHOKAKU
sunk

ULITHI

YAP

WESTERN
CAROLINE
ISLANDS

PALAU
ISLANDS

BABELTHUAP

PELELIU

ANGAUR

On 18 June 1944, as Ozawa's combined fleet headed north-east for the 'decisive operation', Spruance was on the alert near Saipan, which US forces were invading and whose protection was his first priority. That evening US direction-finding stations plotted Ozawa's position. While Spruance held back, awaiting confirmation, Mitscher's aircraft attacked the strategically dangerous airfields held by the Japanese on Guam. On the morning of the 19th, Ozawa launched four heavy waves of aircraft at the Fifth Fleet. The Japanese airmen fared badly, and over 300 carrier planes were lost; two fleet carriers were torpedoed and sunk. Next day Mitscher inflicted further losses, and Ozawa broke off contact.

1,000   1,250   1,500   1,750

1,600   2,000   2,400   2,800

An American destroyer speeds into action as, in the background, the USS Intrepid lists heavily after being hit by a Japanese suicide plane; this photograph was taken from the USS Alaska.

INSET *An American LCT-5 (Landing Craft Tank) on manoeuvres in Chesapeake Bay in 1943.*

19
FROM BLITZ TO A-BOMB

September 1939: the Stukas triumph in the Polish Blitzkrieg, smashing a path for the Panzers.

The pattern of air operations on the German side became apparent as early as the invasion of Poland. The PZL P-11 fighters of the Polish Air Force, which with their shoulder-mounted gull wing and cannon armament had been in the forefront of fighter development when they were introduced in 1932, were obsolete compared with the Bf-109s of the Luftwaffe; consequently, for all the gallantry of their pilots, they were soon knocked out of the way. This allowed the German bombers to roam the skies virtually unmolested, destroying the Polish rear areas and breaking all Polish rail and telephone communications. At the front itself, close-support aircraft such as the Henschel Hs-126 and the Stukas blasted the way open for the German armoured and infantry formations.

In the winter of 1939, air operations on the Western Front were as sporadic as the ground operations of the 'phoney war', and there were few means of assessing the relative merits of the men and matériel on each side. It was not until the German offensive of May 1940 that the Allies were to learn how under-equipped their air forces still were.

One fact did become apparent in the first few months of the war, however: that the defensive armament of British bombers was wholly inadequate. On 18 December 1939, 24 Wellington bombers set off to raid the German fleet in Wilhelmshaven. Each was armed defensively with six ·303-inch machine guns, and it was hoped that by flying in a tight 'box' the various aircraft would be able to cover each other. The formation was intercepted off Heligoland by Messerschmitt Bf-109 and -110 fighters.[1] Ten of the Wellingtons were shot down and three others severely damaged

---

[1] The Bf-110 was a twin-engined 'destroyer', designed to intercept bombers, at which it proved excellent, and not as a long-range escort fighter, the role that was later pressed on it and in which it proved a failure.

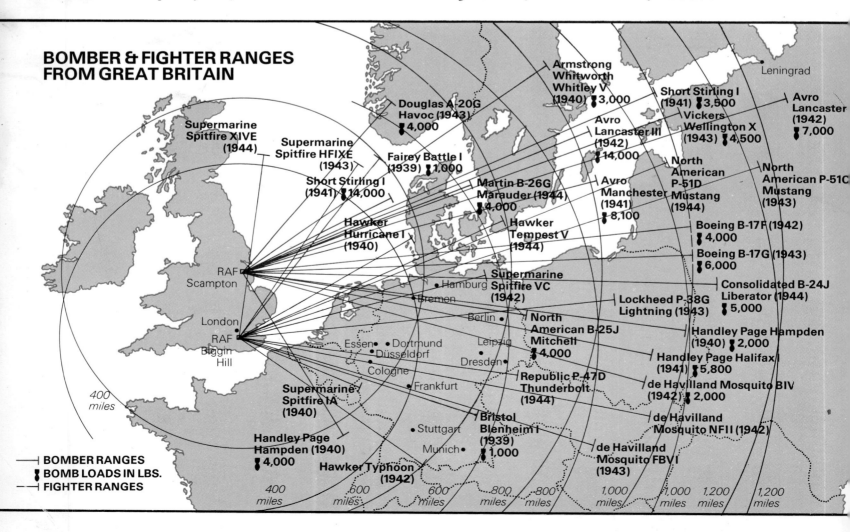

BOMBER & FIGHTER RANGES FROM GREAT BRITAIN

Supermarine Spitfire XIVE (1944)

Supermarine Spitfire HFIXE (1943)

Douglas A-20G Havoc (1943) 4,000

Armstrong Whitworth Whitley V (1940) 3,000

Short Stirling I (1941) 3,500

Vickers Wellington X (1943) 4,500

Avro Lancaster (1942) 7,000

Leningrad

Fairey Battle I (1939) 1,000

Short Stirling I (1941) 14,000

Martin B-26G Marauder (1944) 4,000

Avro Lancaster III (1942) 14,000

North American P-51D Mustang (1944)

North American P-51C Mustang (1943)

Hawker Hurricane I (1940)

Hawker Tempest V (1944)

Avro Manchester (1941) 8,100

Boeing B-17F (1942) 4,000

Boeing B-17G (1943) 6,000

RAF Scampton

Hamburg

Supermarine Spitfire VC (1942)

Bremen

Berlin

Lockheed P-38G Lightning (1943)

Consolidated B-24J Liberator (1944) 5,000

London

RAF Biggin Hill

Essen • Dortmund • Düsseldorf

Leipzig

Dresden

North American B-25J Mitchell 4,000

Handley Page Hampden (1940) 2,000

Cologne

Frankfurt

Republic P-47D Thunderbolt (1944)

Handley Page Halifax I (1941) 5,800

de Havilland Mosquito BIV (1942) 2,000

Supermarine Spitfire IA (1940)

400 miles

Stuttgart

Bristol Blenheim I (1939) 1,000

de Havilland Mosquito NFII (1942)

Munich

Handley Page Hampden (1940) 4,000

Hawker Typhoon (1942)

de Havilland Mosquito FBVI (1943)

BOMBER RANGES
BOMB LOADS IN LBS.
FIGHTER RANGES

400 miles   600 miles   600 miles   800 miles   800 miles   1,000 miles   1,000 miles   1,200 miles   1,200 miles

ABOVE *The RAF Hurricane used in World War II by Group Captain Douglas Bader, the legless ace who claimed 23 victims before he was shot down in 1941 and captured.*

BELOW *A torpedo-armed Fairey Swordfish stands by with wings folded. Nicknamed 'Stringbag', this remarkably sturdy machine served as a torpedo bomber and as a convoy escort.*

in broadside attacks by the German fighters. It was experiences such as these that convinced the Royal Air Force that there was no future in daylight raids, and that night operations would result in lower, more acceptable casualties.

In April 1940 the Germans sprang a major surprise on the Allies by invading Denmark and Norway. As well as the more conventional seaborne invasion, there was an unconventional airborne assault; German paratroops were dropped ahead of the main forces to secure airfields and other strategic points, and were quickly backed up by what we would now call air-portable troops, *i.e.* light infantry flown in by transport aircraft. By the daring use of such forces the Germans were able to secure their objectives at the cost of considerably fewer casualties than they would otherwise have done. As it was, the losses to the 'conventional' forces, in particular the naval units, were heavy.

Then came the German onslaught into Holland, Belgium and France. And here there was another surprise: gliderborne troops landed on the top of the key Belgian fortress of Eben-Emael and neutralized its defences. Otherwise the German invasion, following the pattern of the attack on Poland, consisted chiefly of deep thrusts by the armoured columns while the Luftwaffe's fighters held off the Allied bombers and the Stukas blew a way open for the tanks. It was a carefully thought-out and rehearsed example of how best to use tactical air power. The Allies, with no combat experience that might have helped the pilots – or at least shown up the shortcomings of their aircraft – suffered heavily. A classic example was the slaughter of all the Fairey

Battle light bombers sent to destroy the Maastricht bridges on 10 May 1940. These aircraft were totally obsolete and stood no chance against the experienced German defences. On the 20th of the same month, the situation was so desperate that 71 Battles were sent to attack German pontoon bridges over the Meuse at Sedan. Forty were shot down.

The Battle of France merely confirmed that as yet the Germans were not to be mastered in the use of tactical air power. Their bombers were fast and carried an ample bombload for the tasks allotted them; the Stukas could operate to devastating effect when they had air superiority, and the Messerschmitt fighters, with their heavy-cannon armament and armour protection, were equal to the British Hurricanes and the French Dewoitines and Bloch 151s and 152s that were sent against them.

But the summer of 1940 exposed failings in Germany's pre-war planning. If Britain were to be invaded, the Luftwaffe must first neutralize her aerial defences. This was a

strategic not a tactical operation, and the Germans simply did not possess the aircraft for it. The Messerschmitts carried only enough fuel for 20 minutes of combat over southern England; consequently the bombers could not rely on being escorted much beyond Kent, Sussex and Hampshire, and without an escort they, in particular the Stukas, were easy meat for RAF Fighter Command's Hurricanes. Moreover, the Bf-109, even in the E or Emil model by then in service, found a worthy opponent in the Supermarine Spitfire, especially once the latter had been fitted with a constant-speed propeller to take full advantage of the power available from its Rolls-Royce Merlin engine at all operating altitudes.[2] The British had also learned the tactical lessons of their defeat in France: no longer did they fly in rigid formations, but rather in easy-to-maintain and tactically superior pairs or groups of pairs.

The Battle of Britain was a major turning point for both sides: it showed the Germans that they could not undertake

OPPOSITE, BELOW *A Henschel Hs-126; this close-support type helped clear a path for the German armour in Poland.*
OPPOSITE, ABOVE *A versatile Junkers Ju-88 fighter-bomber.*
BELOW *A British Wellington bomber; in 1939 these suffered heavy losses in daylight raids over Germany.*

gradually phased into a new career as a heavily-armed (four 20- or two 40-mm cannon and bombs or rockets) ground-attack and anti-tank machine. And in an effort to match the new model of the Bf-109, the F mark, the Mark V Spitfire (the next major version to see widespread service) was fitted with two 20-mm cannon and four machine guns, plus an improved engine that now gave it a speed of 375 mph at 13,000 feet. Still later models were given provision for an armament of four 20-mm cannon, or two cannon and four machine guns, or two cannon and two ·5-inch machine guns, plus up to 2,000 pounds of bombs. And with ever increased engine power, first with the Merlin, and then with a development of the Merlin, the Griffon, speed rose to 404 mph in the Mark LF IX, to 448 mph in the Mark XIV and to 454 mph in the Mark 24. At the same time combat range was increased from an initial 500 miles in the role of a pure interceptor to, late in the war, nearly 1,000 miles (with drop tanks) when the Spitfire served as a fighter-bomber.

Similar changes were made to the Bf-109. Armament on the Bf-109E was two 20-mm cannon and two 7·9-mm machine guns plus up to 550 pounds of bombs, rising by the end of the war, on the Bf-109G-6, to a variable combination of 30- and 20-mm cannon, 12·7-mm machine guns and bombs. Performance was also raised by fitting more

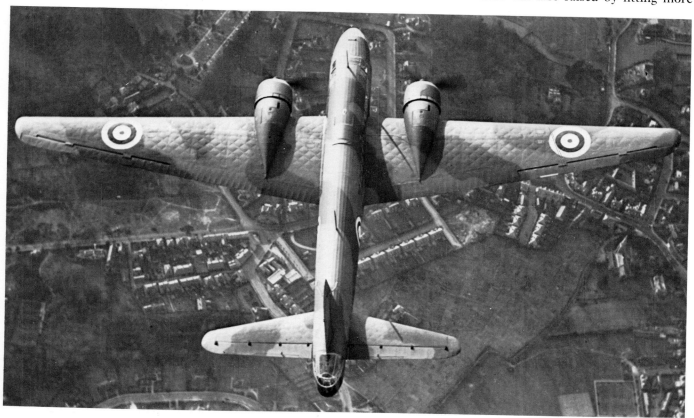

a strategic role with the aircraft they then had; and it showed the British that they could take on and beat the nation that had overrun most of northern Europe. Of course, the British had also learned other lessons. In particular, it was apparent that the Hurricane was nearing the end of its usefulness as a first-line interceptor, and that the eight-gun armament of the Spitfire left much to be desired. So the Hurricane was

powerful Daimler-Benz 601 engines and then the newer 605. Speed rose from 354 mph at 12,300 feet on the E-1 to 390 mph at 22,000 feet on the F-3 and to 452 mph at 19,685 feet on the K-4, one of the last variants to be produced in the war. All in all the Spitfire and Bf-109 had closely parallel careers, each being updated mark by mark in an effort to win a qualitative superiority over the other side, finally ending the war as vastly improved fighter-bomber versions of the original interceptors.

With the failure of the Luftwaffe to crush the Royal Air Force in the Battle of Britain, and the failure of the Blitz to

---

[2] The constant-speed propeller was developed to obtain maximum benefit from the ever-increasing power of piston engines. It automatically adjusted itself to make the best use of engine revolutions at varying altitudes. This was of special benefit to interceptor fighters as they climbed to engage the enemy.

Blitzkrieg Tactics

The combined land/air *Blitzkrieg* (lightning war) tactics that made so great a contribution to the German successes early in the war were the logical conclusion of the storm troop tactics developed by General Hutier for the German Army's last offensives in 1918, as Wilhelm II's *Reich* made its last attempts at victory in World War I. Hutier's tactics envisaged a first wave of storm troops who advanced as quickly as possible, bypassing major obstacles, towards the enemy's gun line and communications. Once these had been reached and captured, the slower troops following up in the rear could take their time in reducing

the obstacles that had been left by the first wave and mopping up any other opposition. The *Blitzkrieg* was essentially similar.

The tactics were carefully thought out, and the individual components thoroughly tested, in the Spanish Civil War. Instead of infantry storm troopers, the first wave was now to be composed of armoured fighting vehicles, with armoured cars reconnoitring at the very spearhead and tanks forming the main striking power of the initial thrust. Carefully controlled artillery, which had provided the best means of removing obstacles in World War I, was now supplemented and almost totally replaced by tactical air power. Aircraft opened the way for the armoured spearhead and prevented enemy reinforcements from moving up, while the conventional forces moving up in the rear

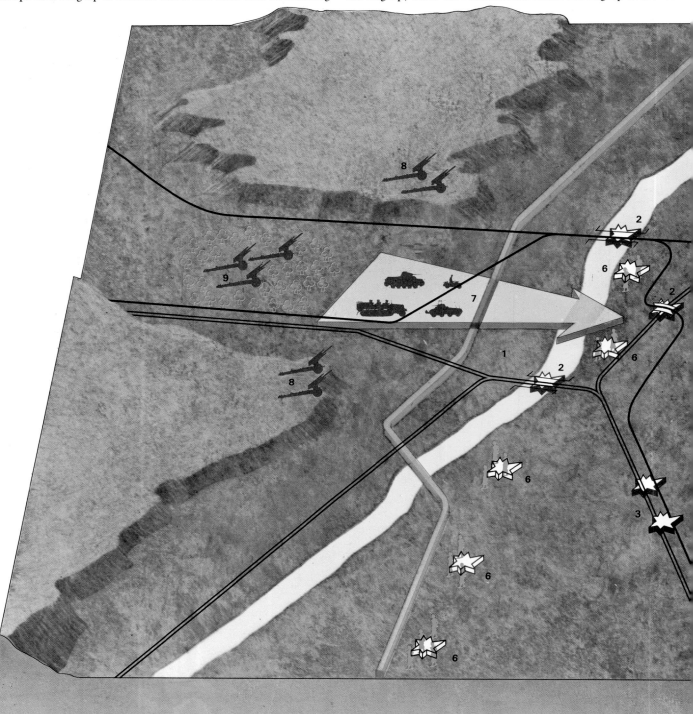

mopped up and consolidated as quickly as they could. The armour meanwhile pressed on as far as it could.

The key to the successful combination of armoured and air power was the forward controller (1), who was in constant touch with the aircraft supporting his ground forces and passed on the requirements of the ground commander, and in turn passed back the fruits of any reconnaissance in front of the ground forces. As well as pressing on as fast as they could, the Germans also wished to cut off all the enemy forces they could, and to this effect Junkers Ju-87 Stukas would be called in to dive-bomb and destroy bridges in the enemy's rear (2), to prevent them from escaping. At the same time, Heinkel He-111 and Dornier Do-17 medium bombers, perhaps aided by Stukas, would cut

the road and rail links to the front (3), both to prevent enemy reinforcements and *matériel* reaching the front and to halt any large-scale evacuation of front line forces. Any reserves would also be attacked by the bombers, and also by Messerschmitt Bf-109 and Henschel Hs-123 fighters and ground-attack aircraft (4). Major towns and any marshalling yards behind the front would also be bombed (5). When the actual assault was sent in, fighters and ground-attack aircraft would harass the front line opposition (6) to soften it up for the assault (7). German anti-aircraft guns on the high ground would prevent enemy aircraft hampering the German thrust (8), and further guns concealed in woods protected the German communications (9), the enemy's AA guns having been knocked out by Stukas (10).

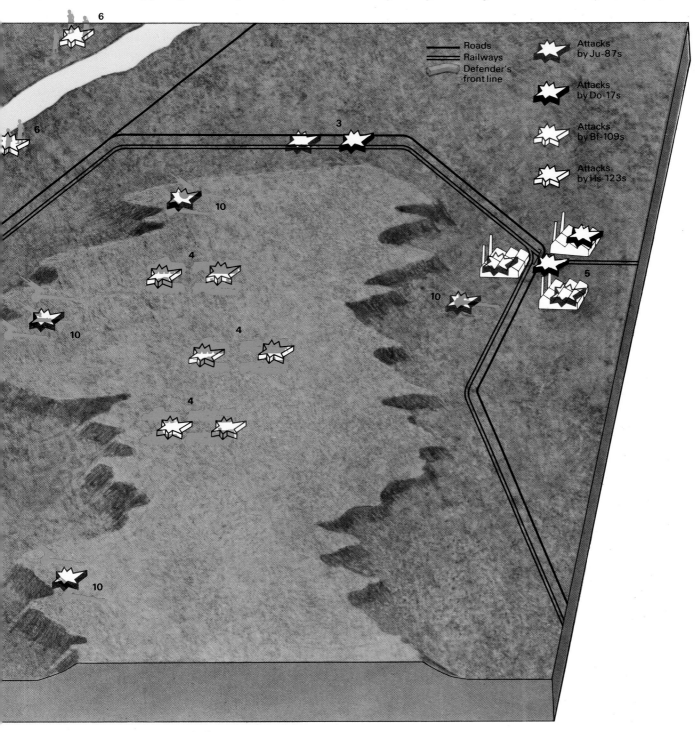

crush civilian morale and British industry, new and vital decisions could be taken about the future conduct of the war. One such was the implementation of a plan to attack the Axis forces on the ground, and to do so not in Europe – this was recognized as impossible after the all-too-recent debacles in France, Norway and elsewhere – but in North Africa, where the opposition was seen to be weaker.

The air side of the North African campaign opened in a somewhat haphazard fashion, yet by 1943 this theatre had taken over the lead in the development of aerial tactics. In the beginning, in late 1940, the theatre was the repository of Britain's obsolete aircraft and Italy's front-line but obsolescent types. The war was initially spasmodic, then built up in intensity and in the quality of the aircraft available to both sides, particularly after February 1941 as Rommel and his Afrika Korps made their appearance. Soon an intensive air campaign was being waged – and one that was remarkable for World War II in that it was almost purely military (there being few worthwhile civilian targets).

But perhaps a still more significant aspect of the North African campaign was that it provided a trial ground for the evolution of the close-support tactics that characterized Allied air operations both in the final stages of the desert war, in Tunisia in 1943, and in the later invasion and conquest of north-western Europe.

Gradually, too, as the pressure on the homeland was eased, the Royal Air Force moved over to the offensive, and the night bombing of Germany began to gather momentum. This was by no means achieved through a mere change of policy. Navigation, for example, at first threatened to be an insuperable problem, and only a minute percentage of the bomb tonnage dropped by the RAF in 1942 and 1943 fell within five miles of its target. However, with the gradual introduction of electronic aids such as H2S, Gee, and Oboe, plus the arrival of the first Pathfinder crews to mark the targets, bombing accuracy improved. From that time, too,

TOP *In the Western Desert campaign a flight of Fairey Albacore bombers passes above the Libyan coast. Albacores were designed as successors to the Swordfish (though they did not outlive them) and fought with distinction in the Battle of Cape Matapan in 1941.*
ABOVE *A Dornier Do-17 bomber photographed over London during the Blitz. With a maximum bomb-load of 2,200 pounds, the Do-17s or 'Flying Pencils' were prominent in the Luftwaffe's raids over England.*
OPPOSITE, ABOVE *British troops examine a Messerschmitt Bf-109F fighter shot down in the desert.*
OPPOSITE, BELOW *A Fairey Swordfish drops her torpedo; these obsolete yet tough aircraft did notable work in the long struggle against the U-boats.*

the area bombing of targets such as Hamburg, Essen, Cologne and other German industrial centres became a major factor in the RAF's calculations.

H2S was a radar system that scanned the area underneath an aircraft, and thus produced a radar map of the land over which the bomber was flying. Using this device, bomber crews stood a good chance of finding their targets.

Gee was a device using three ground transmitters to lay a grid of varied pulses over Europe. The navigator of a bomber fitted with the correct Gee receiver could measure the pulses and work out from his special map where he was. The device was accurate to six miles at a distance of 400 miles from the farthest receiver.

Oboe was a far more sophisticated device, using the ground radar transmitters and a receiver in the aircraft. By plotting the aircraft's position accurately the first transmitter station, at Dover, could control the aircraft along a circular path towards its destination. The second station, at Cromer, could plot this path and, when the bomber passed over the target, radio instructions to drop the bomb. Range was up to 270 miles.

The Pathfinders were a force of specially selected and trained aircrews under Air Vice-Marshal D. C. T. Bennett. The force was raised, against considerable Bomber Command opposition, to fly ahead of the main bomber force on raids and mark final turning points and the target area. This the crews did with special coloured markers and bombs. Thus the inability of the average bomber crew to find its target with any accuracy at night was to some extent overcome.

But even if the bombing operations of 1942 had been accurate, the aircraft available to RAF Bomber Command were not capable of carrying a sufficient bomb-load far enough into Germany. What was needed was a new sort of machine – a true heavy bomber.

The first to arrive on the scene was the four-engined Short Stirling, which was introduced in August 1940. But,

with a bomb-load of 14,000 pounds, a range of only 590 miles and a ceiling of only 19,000 feet, the Stirling was only moderately successful. Even so, its existence ensured that much was learned about operational techniques. Next was the Handley-Page Halifax, the first of which entered service in November 1940. Maximum bomb-load was 13,000 pounds, and with a 5,800-pound load the range was 1,860 miles, a considerable improvement on the Stirling. Defensive armament on both types consisted of eight ·303-inch machine guns – still inadequate against the ever-improving armament of the German night fighters.

Next in the RAF's heavy-bomber inventory came the unsuccessful twin-engined Avro Manchester, which entered service in November 1940 but was soon phased out because its Rolls-Royce Vulture engines were found to be unreliable. Re-engined with four Merlins it became the celebrated Lancaster, which first became available early in 1942. Again, this type had an insufficient defensive armament – eight small machine guns – but offensively it could

Vickers Supermarine Spitfire I

SPECIFICATION

Type		single-seat interceptor fighter
Engine		Rolls-Royce Merlin III 12-cylinder Vee liquid-cooled inline, 1,030-hp at take-off
Armament		eight ·303-inch Browning machine guns with 300 rounds per gun
Speed	362	mph at 19,000 feet
Initial climb rate	2,500	feet per minute
Climb	9	minutes 24 seconds to 20,000 feet
Ceiling	31,900	feet
Range	395	miles
Weight	4,810	pounds (empty)
	6,200	pounds (loaded)
Span	32	feet 10 inches
Length	29	feet 11 inches
Height	12	feet 3 inches

The Supermarine Spitfire I illustrated was a machine of No. 19 Squadron, RAF Fighter Command, operating from Duxford in Cambridgeshire. QV were the unit code letters of 19 Squadron from the beginning to the end of World War II. The first service Spitfires were allocated to this squadron in 1938, when its code was WZ.

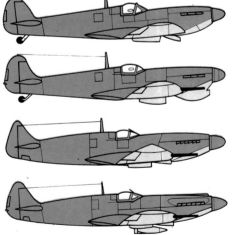

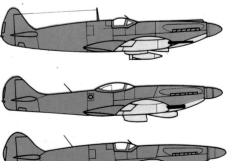

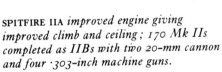

SPITFIRE IIA *improved engine giving improved climb and ceiling; 170 Mk IIs completed as IIBs with two 20-mm cannon and four ·303-inch machine guns.*

SPITFIRE VC *introduced in March 1941 with more powerful engine giving better performance; could carry bombs and was used as a fighter-bomber.*

SPITFIRE VII *extended wings for high altitude work and two-stage Merlin to give a speed of over 400 mph at 25,000 feet; ceiling 43,000 feet.*

SPITFIRE XII *first Griffon-engined model; fighter-bomber that could climb to 20,000 feet in 6 minutes 42 seconds; ceiling 40,000 feet; introduced spring 1943.*

SPITFIRE XIVE *cut-down fuselage and all-round vision bubble canopy; speed 448 mph, range 850 miles and ceiling 44,500 feet; introduced January 1944.*

SPITFIRE 21 *introduced February 1944; features stronger wing; speed 454 mph, armament four 20-mm cannon and up to 1,000 pounds of bombs.*

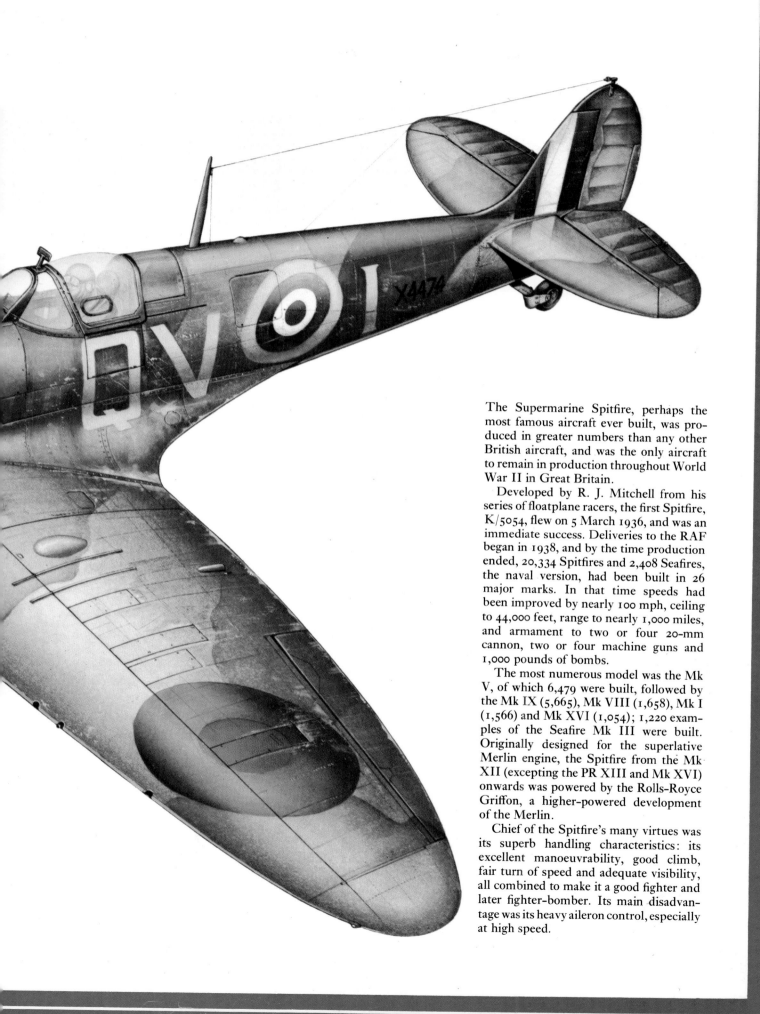

The Supermarine Spitfire, perhaps the most famous aircraft ever built, was produced in greater numbers than any other British aircraft, and was the only aircraft to remain in production throughout World War II in Great Britain.

Developed by R. J. Mitchell from his series of floatplane racers, the first Spitfire, K/5054, flew on 5 March 1936, and was an immediate success. Deliveries to the RAF began in 1938, and by the time production ended, 20,334 Spitfires and 2,408 Seafires, the naval version, had been built in 26 major marks. In that time speeds had been improved by nearly 100 mph, ceiling to 44,000 feet, range to nearly 1,000 miles, and armament to two or four 20-mm cannon, two or four machine guns and 1,000 pounds of bombs.

The most numerous model was the Mk V, of which 6,479 were built, followed by the Mk IX (5,665), Mk VIII (1,658), Mk I (1,566) and Mk XVI (1,054); 1,220 examples of the Seafire Mk III were built. Originally designed for the superlative Merlin engine, the Spitfire from the Mk XII (excepting the PR XIII and Mk XVI) onwards was powered by the Rolls-Royce Griffon, a higher-powered development of the Merlin.

Chief of the Spitfire's many virtues was its superb handling characteristics: its excellent manoeuvrability, good climb, fair turn of speed and adequate visibility, all combined to make it a good fighter and later fighter-bomber. Its main disadvantage was its heavy aileron control, especially at high speed.

carry loads up to the massive 22,000-pound Grand Slam 'earthquake' bomb, or a more usual 14,000 pounds over a range of 1,660 miles. The top speeds of the Stirling, Halifax and Lancaster were 270, 285 and 287 mph.

To counter the British night-bomber offensive, the Germans built up a massive night-fighter and anti-aircraft force, the former centred around adapted Bf-110 and Ju-88 aircraft, and the latter around the famous 88-mm gun. Typical of the highly successful Bf-110 night fighters was the G-4, which had an armament of four 20-mm cannon

BELOW *The Short Stirling, first of the new British heavy bombers; it could carry 14,000 pounds of bombs but range was only 590 miles.*
ABOVE, RIGHT *Next was the Handley-Page Halifax, with a range of 1,860 miles carrying 5,800 pounds of bombs; maximum load was 13,000 pounds.*
OPPOSITE, TOP RIGHT *The short-lived Avro Manchester.*
ABOVE *The famous Lancaster, capable of carrying 14,000 pounds of bombs for 1,660 miles or, on special missions, a single 22,000-pounder (known as the Grand Slam bomb).*
OPPOSITE, CENTRE *The versatile de Havilland Mosquito.*
OPPOSITE, BELOW *A Heinkel He-219 Uhu night fighter.*

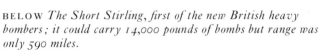

Focke-Wulf Fw 190A-3

The Focke-Wulf F2 190 fighter and fighter-bomber was Germany's best such aircraft of World War II, the other contender for this position being the Messerschmitt Bf 109. The latter, however, was an older design and reached the end of its development potential before the end of the war, unlike the Fw 190. The Focke-Wulf design was intended as a back-up in the event of the failure of the Messerschmitt fighter, and the first prototype flew on 1 July 1939. Despite initial reservations about its air-cooled radial engine, the design soon showed itself to be an excellent one and and the type was ordered into service.

The aircraft illustrated is a Focke-Wulf Fw 190-3 of 8/JG2 'Richthofen', that is an aircraft of the 8th Staffel or squadron, which was part of the 3rd Gruppe or wing, which was in turn part of the Luftwaffe's 2nd Jagdgeschwader (JG) or fighter group, named 'Richthofen' in honour of the great World War I ace. The vertical bar on the rear fuselage marked all III Gruppe

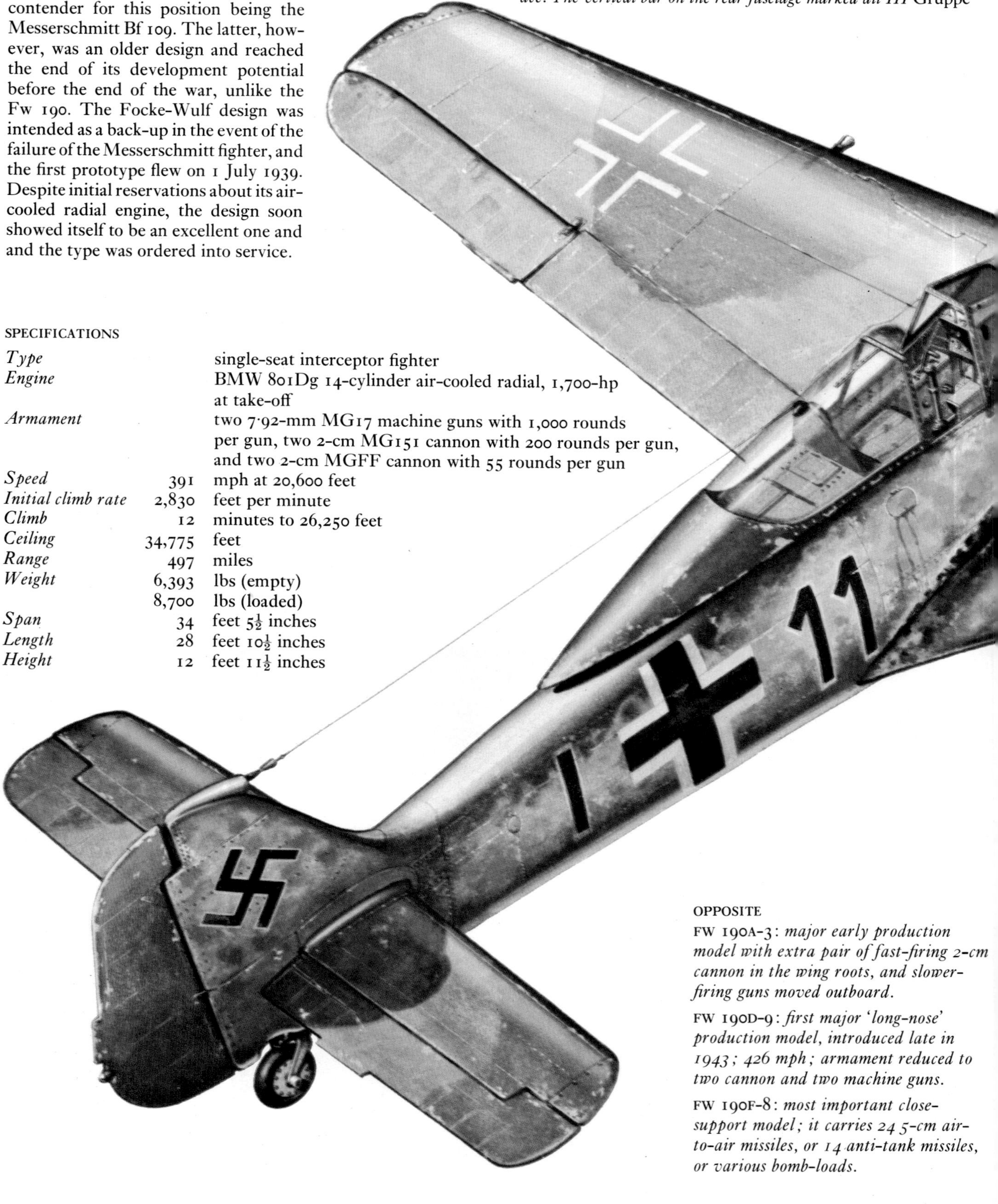

SPECIFICATIONS

Type		single-seat interceptor fighter
Engine		BMW 801Dg 14-cylinder air-cooled radial, 1,700-hp at take-off
Armament		two 7·92-mm MG17 machine guns with 1,000 rounds per gun, two 2-cm MG151 cannon with 200 rounds per gun, and two 2-cm MGFF cannon with 55 rounds per gun
Speed	391	mph at 20,600 feet
Initial climb rate	2,830	feet per minute
Climb	12	minutes to 26,250 feet
Ceiling	34,775	feet
Range	497	miles
Weight	6,393	lbs (empty)
	8,700	lbs (loaded)
Span	34	feet 5½ inches
Length	28	feet 10½ inches
Height	12	feet 11½ inches

OPPOSITE

FW 190A-3: *major early production model with extra pair of fast-firing 2-cm cannon in the wing roots, and slower-firing guns moved outboard.*

FW 190D-9: *first major 'long-nose' production model, introduced late in 1943; 426 mph; armament reduced to two cannon and two machine guns.*

FW 190F-8: *most important close-support model; it carries 24 5-cm air-to-air missiles, or 14 anti-tank missiles, or various bomb-loads.*

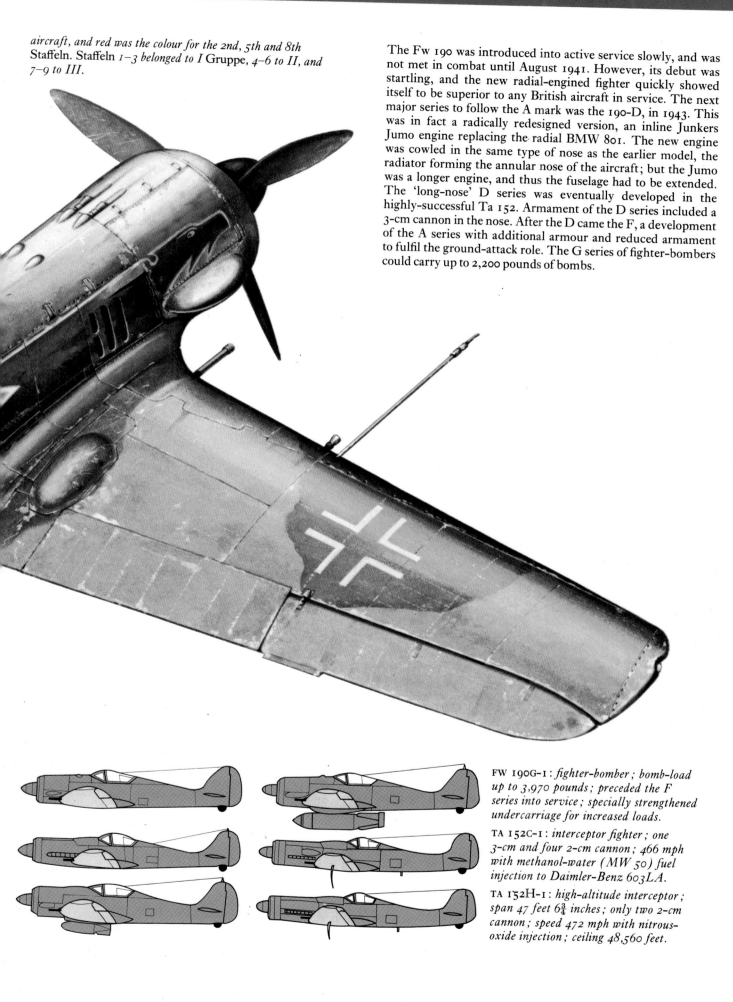

aircraft, and red was the colour for the 2nd, 5th and 8th Staffeln. Staffeln 1–3 belonged to I Gruppe, 4–6 to II, and 7–9 to III.

The Fw 190 was introduced into active service slowly, and was not met in combat until August 1941. However, its debut was startling, and the new radial-engined fighter quickly showed itself to be superior to any British aircraft in service. The next major series to follow the A mark was the 190-D, in 1943. This was in fact a radically redesigned version, an inline Junkers Jumo engine replacing the radial BMW 801. The new engine was cowled in the same type of nose as the earlier model, the radiator forming the annular nose of the aircraft; but the Jumo was a longer engine, and thus the fuselage had to be extended. The 'long-nose' D series was eventually developed in the highly-successful Ta 152. Armament of the D series included a 3-cm cannon in the nose. After the D came the F, a development of the A series with additional armour and reduced armament to fulfil the ground-attack role. The G series of fighter-bombers could carry up to 2,200 pounds of bombs.

FW 190G-1: fighter-bomber; bomb-load up to 3,970 pounds; preceded the F series into service; specially strengthened undercarriage for increased loads.

TA 152C-1: interceptor fighter; one 3-cm and four 2-cm cannon; 466 mph with methanol-water (MW 50) fuel injection to Daimler-Benz 603LA.

TA 152H-1: high-altitude interceptor; span 47 feet 6¾ inches; only two 2-cm cannon; speed 472 mph with nitrous-oxide injection; ceiling 48,560 feet.

Night fighters of Germany and the Allies; versatile aircraft appear, designed for strike-fighter, bombing and recce work.

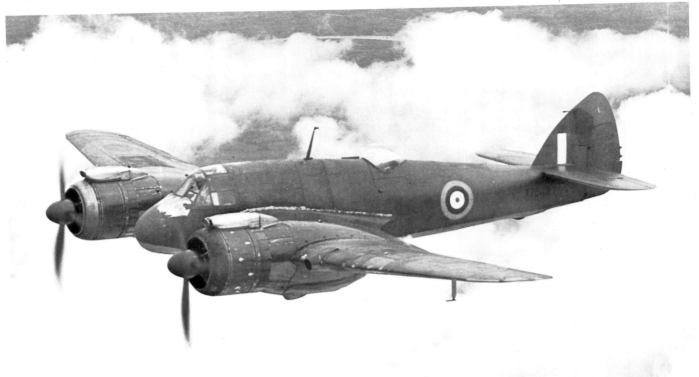

ABOVE *The Bristol Beaufighter, a successful night-fighting machine that performed equally well as an anti-shipping strike fighter.*
LEFT *The powerful Henschel Hs-129, primarily a ground-attack aircraft, armed with a 75-mm anti-tank gun protruding from a specially designed central gondola.*
OPPOSITE *Victim of a Hawker Typhoon – a German Fw-190 is hit and explodes in a ball of flame and smoke.*

and four 7·9-mm machine guns, a top speed of 342 mph and a range of 1,300 miles. It was equipped with Lichtenstein SN-2 radar. An eminent example of the Ju-88 night fighters was the G-7, which had three 20-mm cannon, three 7·9-mm machine guns and one 13-mm machine gun, a top speed of 389 mph and a range of 1,380 miles. The German night-fighter arm was very efficient, and took a heavy toll of the British night-bomber fleet throughout the campaign.

The best night fighter produced in the war was in all probability the Heinkel 219 Uhu, which entered service in 1943. The A-7 version had an armament of two 30-mm and four 20-mm cannon, a top speed of 416 mph and a range of 1,240 miles. Other notable night fighters of the war were the British Bristol Beaufighter, with an armament of four 20-mm cannon and six ·303-inch machine guns and a top speed of 323 mph; the de Havilland Mosquito NF Mark XII, armed with four 20-mm cannon and four ·303-inch machine guns and with a top speed of 370 mph and a range of 1,860 miles; and the American Northrop P-61 Black Widow, having four 20-mm cannon and four machine guns, a top speed of 430 mph and a range of 1,415 miles.

The Beaufighter and the Mosquito also served in other roles. The Beaufighter found its greatest fame as an anti-shipping strike fighter, where its armament of cannon, torpedo and eight rockets gave it phenomenal firepower. The Mosquito, like the Ju-88, was a design of almost limitless possibilities. It was of wooden construction, and served from autumn 1941 as an unarmed bomber, a reconnaissance machine, a fighter-bomber, a night fighter, and as a strike fighter. As a bomber it could outfly almost any German fighter other than the Focke-Wulf Fw-190, even when carrying a 4,000-pound bomb-load, and in its other roles it showed extreme manoeuvrability, considerable load-carrying capacity, and great ruggedness. Powered by two Merlin inlines, the slowest version, the NF Mark II, was still capable of 370 mph, and the fastest, the Bomber Mark XVI, could achieve 415 mph. Truly the Mosquito was one of the world's great aircraft.

With the gradual switch from the strategic defensive of 1940–42 to the offensive of late 1943–44, the RAF needed to develop new types to support land operations. In the field of strike aircraft, two magnificent types were produced,

1

2

3

4

the Hawker Typhoon and the Hawker Tempest. Both were powered by massive inline engines and were very heavy machines. The Typhoon had a troublesome entry into service as a result of certain structural weaknesses in the tail, and although it failed in its intended role as an interceptor, it proved a very useful ground-attack machine with its four 20-mm cannon and eight 60-pound rockets or two 1,000-pound bombs. It entered service in 1942, and was later joined by the Tempest, which carried the same armament but had a top speed 15 mph higher at 427 mph and a range 550 miles greater at 1,530 miles.

The Germans also produced some good ground-attack aircraft, notably the Henschel Hs-129, armed with a powerful 75-mm anti-tank gun but underpowered, and the G-1 model of the Ju-87, which featured two 37-mm cannon. There were also ground-attack versions of the Ju-88, the

P-1 and P-2, mounting a 75-mm gun or two 37-mm cannon respectively. The ubiquitous Focke Wulf Fw-190 could also operate very effectively as a ground-attack machine, but it was in its true element as a fighter. Introduced in late 1940, the Fw-190 soon acquired a formidable reputation and was in all probability the best conventional fighter produced by the Germans. Early models had four 7·9-mm machine guns, but two of these were soon changed to 20-mm cannon, and then an additional pair of 20-mm cannon was added. Later models had a 30-mm cannon firing through the propeller boss or could carry a single 4,000-pound bomb in the fighter-bomber role. The early A-2 version was capable of 389 mph, but later models reached 426 mph with an inline engine replacing the original radials; the last model, the Ta-152H-1, was capable of 472 mph with nitrous oxide injection.

The Eastern Front

In the field of tactical air power, it was the Russians who ruled supreme at the end of the war. Their Air Force was for the most part obsolescent when Germany invaded the Soviet Union on 22 June 1941 (Operation Barbarossa), and the Russians lost almost all their front-line aircraft. In the short term this was a disastrous blow, but in the long run it had its uses since the Russians could then turn their whole attention to producing the best possible designs for the specific job of supporting the armies on the ground. In the course of the war Russia produced some excellent fighters, such as the Lavochkin LaGG-3, the La-5 and -7, and the Yakovlev Yak-3, -7 and -9. Both series were simple, rugged designs, unsophisticated by Western standards but more than adequate to the task in hand (their German counterparts were the Bf-109 and Fw-190).

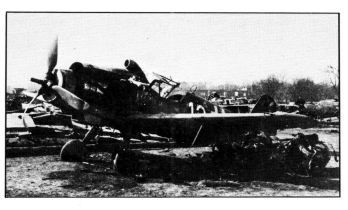

OPPOSITE *A Russian Yak-3 fighter and ground attack plane, armed with one 20-mm cannon and two machine guns.*
ABOVE *The LaGG-3; a rugged, all-wood design, she carried one cannon, three machine guns and up to 484 pounds of bombs.*

ABOVE *German aircraft wrecked on a forward airfield near Minsk on the 2nd Byelorussian Front in 1944.*
BELOW *Russian Il-2 assault planes bank towards the target area; agility at low altitudes was a feature of most Soviet fighters.*

Russia leads the way in developing cannon and rockets for aircraft use.

The basic design philosophy of the Russians was to update designs as necessary, disturbing production as little as possible. This explains the basic similarities retained in particular series. The La-7 appeared in 1943, and had a top speed of 425 mph. Armament comprised three 20-mm cannon, which proved equal to their task in the type's first battle, fought above the great tank action around Kursk in 1943. The Yak-9 was brought into service in 1945 and had an armament of one 20-mm cannon and two 12·7-mm machine guns, with a top speed of 415 mph in the 7-P variant and a range of 900 miles.

In the ground-attack field, the Russians had the superlative Ilyushin Il-2m3. This was a massive two-seater, the central portion of the machine actually being built of armour plate which rendered it all but immune from ground fire. (Germany's Henschel Hs-129 was designed to a similar requirement but it was underpowered and generally

not a success.) Armed with two 20-mm cannon, three smaller cannon, eight 83-mm rockets and up to 1,325 pounds of bombs, the Il-2m3 could deliver devastating attacks at very low levels. Top speed was 264 mph and range only 372 miles, but the type was designed to absorb punishment and could operate from airfields close up behind the line. It provided invaluable service in the major battles from Stalingrad to Kursk and then during the Russians' two-year drive to Berlin.

Although the use of both cannon and rockets as aircraft armament had been pioneered by the French in World War I, it was the Russians who had led the way in developing these two types of weapon as standard equipment during the 1930s. Thus, in addition to their two major ground-attack rockets of 82- and 132-mm calibre, the Russians in

World War II had a wide variety of aircraft cannon, in calibres between 20- and 37-mm, available for use. As well as producing a range of cannon of different calibres, the Russians also developed two major types of cannon. These were high-velocity weapons for air-combat use, and extra high-velocity weapons for use against armoured fighting vehicles.

Best of the Russian bombers was the Petlyakov Pe-2, a sturdy and agile machine that performed remarkably well in a variety of roles: first and foremost it operated as a conventional light bomber, but it also did valuable duty in the reconnaissance and ground-attack roles. The Pe-2's stablemate in the bitter combat that raged over and beyond the Russian and German front lines was the Tupolev SB-2, a veteran of the Spanish Civil War which was nevertheless

Bombers on the Eastern Front — the Russian preference for light-medium types.

fast, handy and could carry a sizeable bomb-load (up to 2,200 pounds). The SB-2 was primarily used as a light/medium bomber on a virtually non-stop programme of raids on enemy positions.

The only heavy bomber used by the Russians in World War II, though in limited numbers, was the excellent high-performance Petlyakov Pe-8, a four-engined machine with a maximum range of 2,320 miles, which first flew in November 1936.

The chief German counterparts of these two machines were the Heinkel He-111, the highly versatile Junkers Ju-88 and the Dornier Do-17 (the 'Flying Pencil'). All of these were of mid-late 1930s vintage, but their reliability at a time when the German war industry found itself under extreme pressure kept them in service for almost the entire war.

OPPOSITE *The urgent scramble to outbuild the enemy, seen at a wartime Russian aircraft factory. After the German invasion of 1941, many munitions factories were evacuated and re-established as far to the east as the Urals.*
TOP *The ANT-42, forerunner of the Petlyakov Pe-8 heavy bomber.*
ABOVE *Petlyakov Pe-2 light bombers, armed with five machine guns and up to 2,200 pounds of bombs.*

Ilyushin Il-2m3

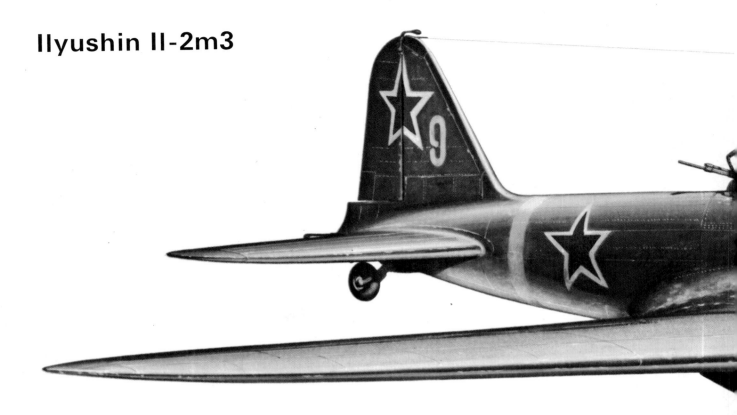

The Ilyushin Il-2 was the Red Air Force's most successful and most celebrated aircraft of World War II. In all, some 35,000 examples of the type were built, making it the most widely produced aircraft of all time. To the world in general the Il-2 is known as the *Shturmovik*, but to the combatants of the Eastern Front it was known differently: *Ilyusha* to the Russians, and *Schwarz Tod* (Black Death) to the Germans.

The task envisaged in the 1930s for the Red Air Force in any future war was that of tactical support for the army, hence the need for a fast, rugged, self-sufficient ground-attack aircraft capable of dealing knock-out blows to enemy tanks, pillboxes and infantry. Several designers produced unsuccessful prototypes, and then in late 1939 Sergei V. Ilyushin completed his CKB-57. The type proved successful after it was given a more powerful engine (1,680-hp AM-38) in place of the original 1,370-hp AM-35, and it was ordered into production as the Il-2 in March 1941. The most notable features of the Il-2 were the raised cockpit enclosure for the pilot and the armoured 'bath' which formed the front part of the fuselage. This was made of armour plate between 5 and 12 mm thick, and protected the engine and cockpit: examination of shot-down *Shturmoviki* usually revealed that this armour bath was intact although the rest of the machine might have been almost totally destroyed.

This first production proved moderately successful in combat, but certain defects were soon brought to the notice of the designers by combat pilots. Chief amongst these were the lack of a second crew member, a gunner, to provide rear defence, and lack of adequate armament to deal with the newer German armoured vehicles. The new requirements were finalized in spring 1942, and soon the Il-2m3 (model 3) appeared. This had a lengthened cockpit enclosure (with the armour bath lengthened also to protect it) to accommodate the rear gunner, and 23-mm VJa cannon in place of the earlier 20-mm Shvak weapons,

the muzzle velocity of which had been found to be too low.

In 1943 the VJa cannon were in turn replaced by 37-mm N-37 (or 11-P-37) cannon, which had far superior armour-piercing capabilities. So armed, the aircraft now became the Il-2m3 (Modified), entering service just in time to render invaluable service against German armour in the Battle of Kursk in July 1943. By this time the Russians were also using 132-mm rockets to replace the earlier 82-mm weapons for attacks on fixed emplacements. These large rockets could carry a hollow-charge warhead that proved absolutely devastating. Other modifications allowed the Il-2 to carry a 21-inch torpedo below the fuselage or a reconnaissance camera in the fuselage behind the gunner. The final development of the basic design was in fact a considerable redesign, and appeared too late to see service in World War II. It was produced as the Il-10.

The Il-2 was at its most effective at low altitude. and many missions were flown at heights of below 200 feet. This meant that Il-2 pilots were often able to obtain complete surprise and attack German armour and emplacements with horizontal fire, very close to right angles with the armour plate—the most effective angle. The best tactic employed by Il-2 pilots was the co-called 'circle of death', in which the aircraft crossed the front to one side of the target and then attacked from the rear, then circled round again, allowing the aircraft behind it in the circle to launch its attack. A dozen aircraft could keep up this tactic of continuous attack for about 30 minutes until all their ammunition was expended. At Kursk 20 minutes of this tactic cost the 9th Panzer Division 70 tanks; another spell of 120 minutes reduced the 3rd Panzer Division by 270 tanks and a further attack lasting 240 minutes destroyed 240 tanks out of the 17th Panzer Division's total of 300. Undoubtedly the Ilyushin Il-2 was a magnificent fighting aircraft. It was also the Red Air Force's safest combat type of World War II.

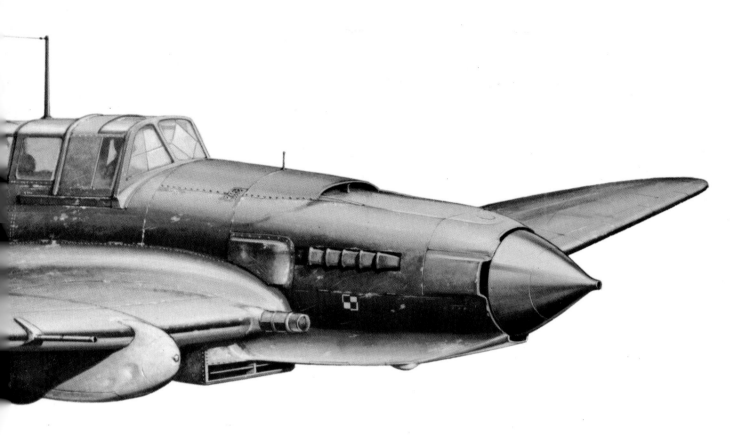

SPECIFICATIONS

Type — two-seat ground-attack aircraft

Engine — Mikulin AM-38F 12-cylinder Vee liquid-cooled inline, 1,770-hp at take-off

Armament — two 23-mm VJa cannon, two 7·62-mm Shkas machine guns, and one 12·7-mm BS machine gun, plus one DAG 10 grenade launcher and eight 83-mm RS 82 or 132-mm RS 132 rockets, or 1,325 pounds of bombs

Speed	251	mph at 6,560 feet
Ceiling	19,500	feet
Range	372	miles
Weight	9,604	lbs (empty)
	12,136	lbs (loaded)
Span	48	feet 0½ inch
Length	38	feet 0½ inch
Height	11	feet 1½ inches

The Ilyushin Il-2m3 illustrated was a machine of the Assault Regiment of the 1st Polish Mixed Air Division in 1945.

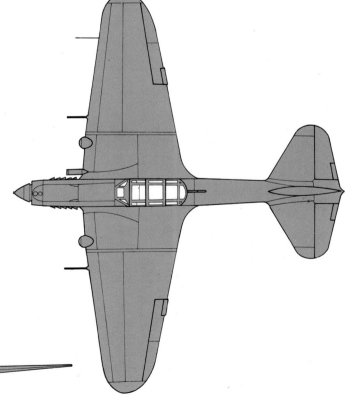

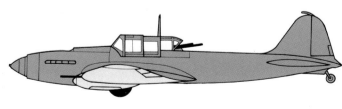

American strategic bombers lead the world; heavy defensive armament is carried for protection on daylight precision raids.

America's War

The country that turned out more aircraft than any other in World War II was the United States. Luckily for them, and for the Allied effort, the Americans did not enter the war in 1939 but in December 1941, after the Japanese attack on Pearl Harbor. This in effect gave them time to improve the the state of their Air Force, which had previously been as unprepared as those of her principal allies.

The US had long been proponents of the theory of strategic bombing, and produced the progenitor of all World War II's heavy four-engined bombers in the Boeing Model-299 bomber of 1935, which was accepted into service by the Americans in 1939 as the B-17 Flying Fortress. This large machine was designed to operate in fleets, delivering massive knock-out blows in daylight precision raids. The heavy defensive armament of each bomber would, it was confidently expected, interlock to prevent any enemy fighter breaking into the bomber box. As a result of combat experience with the Royal Air Force, the 17E of 1941 became the first really definitive combat model: it introduced a tail turret, a ventral 'ball' turret, increased armour and fuel-tank protection, and the fitting

of a uniform machine-gun armament throughout (all ·5-inch guns). This still proved insufficient however, and an additional twin-gun 'chin' turret was added on the final model, the 17G (as the name suggests, it was sited beneath and slightly to the rear of the nose). The B-17's useful bomb-load was somewhere in the region of 8,000 pounds for long-range missions. All production models were powered by variants of the Wright R-1830 Cyclone radial, and the top speed of the early B-17B (291 mph) gradually crept up to the 323 mph of the 17C and then down again to 287 mph on the heavily loaded 17G. Range for these three models was 2,400, 2,000 and 2,000 miles respectively, with ceilings at 36,000, 37,000 and 35,600 feet.

The other main heavy bomber of the B-17's vintage was the Consolidated B-24 Liberator, a large and heavy four-engined machine. Deliveries to the USAAF began early in 1941, though earlier consignments had gone to the Royal Air Force. The type went through many modifications, culminating in the B-24J model. This had a defensive armament of ten ·5-inch machine guns, an offensive load of 12,800 pounds, a top speed of 290 mph and a range of 2,100 miles. It performed sterling service in Europe but was really at its best in the Pacific, where its reliability and

OPPOSITE *A B-24D Liberator bomber flying low over the English coast on the 'Biscay Beat' patrol.* LEFT *B-17 Flying Fortresses over Germany during a mission to bomb Nazi fighter factories in Brunswick.* BELOW *A Chinese sentry stands guard under the wing of a B-25 Mitchell medium bomber.*

New fighters take over from the Curtiss P-40 series — the Thunderbolt, Mustang and Lightning.

the services of the automatic pilot were keenly valued.

The third of the United States' heavy bombers was the Boeing B-29 Superfortress, which was used only in the Pacific theatre. Deliveries of this super-bomber began in July 1943 and it proved a remarkably successful design, with exceptional load and range characteristics. Aircraft of this type dropped the atomic bombs on Hiroshima and Nagasaki to end the war against Japan. Powered by four Wright R-3350 radials, the B-29 had a top speed of 358 mph at 25,000 feet, a range of 3,250 miles and a ceiling of 31,850 feet. Stripped of most of its defensive armament, it could carry up to 20,000 pounds of bombs.

The USA also had several very useful medium bombers: the North American B-25 Mitchell, the Martin B-26 Marauder and the Douglas Boston, or Havoc, which was normally used in the attack role under the designation A-20. The B-25 was a really outstanding design, which entered service in the second half of 1940. The various models carried up to fourteen ·5-inch machine guns and 3,000 pounds of bombs at speeds of about 280 mph over ranges of 1,500 miles. The B-26 entered service in 1941 and was armed with up to eleven ·5-inch machine guns and 4,000 pounds of bombs or a torpedo. Top speed was 283 mph in

the G model, and range was 1,100 miles. The A-20 proved eminently suited to the attack role, and had a top speed of 339 mph in the G model, and a range of 1,100 miles.

As far as fighters were concerned, the US Army's main fighter in 1941 was the Curtiss P-40 series. This was an adequate design when it first appeared, but it was obsolescent by the time the US entered the war. It suffered very badly at the hands of the Japanese, its only advantages being its strength and high diving speed. However, three new fighters soon appeared to take over from the P-40: the Republic P-47 Thunderbolt, the North American P-51 Mustang, and the Lockheed P-38 Lightning.

The P-47 was the biggest single-engined fighter to see service in the war, and was a huge radial-engined monoplane derived from the earlier P-43 Lancer. It was armed with six or eight ·5-inch machine guns, and was later given provision for a massive load of bombs and rockets. Top speed rose from the 412 mph of the B version to the 467 mph of the N, with ranges of over 1,000 miles available with drop tanks. One experimental model even topped 500 mph.

The P-51 was a classic design. Originally suggested by a British mission visiting the United States to buy aircraft, the first P-51 flew in 1940. Powered by an Allison inline, it

ABOVE *An American P-38 Lightning, a twin-boom long-range fighter and fighter-bomber.*

LEFT *The P-51 Mustang, a classic high-performance fighter-bomber and escort machine.*

OPPOSITE, TOP *P-47 Thunderbolts of the 10th USAAF fly over mountainous country in northern Burma on a mission against Japanese installations.*

OPPOSITE, CENTRE *The aggressive if portly shape of the US Navy's Grumman F4F Wildcat fighter; unequal to the Japanese Zeros, it was in time superseded by the Hellcat.*

OPPOSITE, BELOW *Barracudas and Corsairs on the deck of HMS* Illustrious.

American and Japanese opponents in the Pacific air battle; other important maritime aircraft of the war.

ABOVE *A US Devastator torpedo-bomber spreads its wings in readiness for take-off. These machines formed an important element of the US Navy's carrier strike force during the early part of the Pacific war.*
LEFT *The versatile SBD Dauntless dive-bomber, bomber and recce machine, here seen in action in the Pacific. In that theatre the Dauntless had the lowest loss rate of all the US carrier aircraft. Production continued until July 1944, a total of 5,936 being built.*

did not at first prove very successful, but when re-engined with the Packard-built Merlin its performance was phenomenal: speed rose from 390 mph in the A model to 439 mph in the C, and to 487 mph in the final H model. At the same time range was increased from 450 miles to well over 1,000 with the use of drop tanks. Ceiling also increased from 31,350 feet to 41,900, and then to 42,000 feet. Armament comprised six ·5-inch machine guns plus two 1,000-pound bombs or racks of rockets. Apart from its performance, the P-51 also had superb handling character-istics, and provided the USAAF with its first escort fighter capable of taking Flying Fortresses to Berlin and back.

The third of the USAAF's main fighters was the Lock-heed P-38 Lightning, a clean-lined twin-boom design intro-duced into service in the middle of 1941. Armament com-prised four machine guns and one cannon, plus bombs and rockets on later models. The P-38G had a top speed of 400 mph and a range with drop tanks well in excess of 1,000 miles.

The US Navy has its own air force, and its machines need to be discussed separately, in particular because they formed the backbone of American air power in the Pacific. Whereas the USAAF's aircraft, with the exception of the Superfortress, served in both Western and Eastern theatres, the bulk of the US Navy's forces was deployed against Japan in an all-out effort to eliminate Japanese air and sea power.

At the beginning of the war, the main carrier-borne fighter in service was the portly Grumman F4F Wildcat, which entered service in 1940. Although armed with only four ·5-inch machine guns, the Wildcat was reasonably fast, at 330 mph, and had a good range of some 845 miles; added

equipment in the definitive F4F-4 reduced these figures to 318 mph and 770 miles. The type was not quite a match for the Zero of the Imperial Japanese Navy, however, and in late 1942 the Grumman F6F Hellcat began to enter service. This was basically a scaled-up and more powerful version of the Wildcat, and it proved very successful. Armament was six ·5-inch machine guns, top speed 375 mph and range 1,090 miles.

The US Navy started the war with the Douglas TBD-1 Devastator as its standard torpedo bomber, but this was quickly replaced by the more modern Grumman TBF Avenger, which entered service in January 1942. This type turned out to be a robust design, well able to take care of itself in the air. The TBF-1 had a top speed of 271 mph and a range of 1,215 miles.

Also serving in large numbers on US and Allied carriers was the Douglas SBD Dauntless, a tough and accurate dive-bomber which did much to redress the early imbalance of naval forces in favour of the United States. Offensive armament was a 1,000-pound bomb, top speed 262 mph (in the SBD-6 version) and range 1,230 miles.

Finally, in this brief review of the aircraft of the US Navy, we must mention the great Vought F4U Corsair. Armed with six ·5-inch machine guns and 2,000 pounds of bombs or eight rockets, the Corsair was indubitably the best carrier-borne machine of the war, either as a fighter or as a strike aircraft. Capable of 446 mph in the F4U-4 version, it could outfly any Japanese aircraft put up against it.

Other significant maritime aircraft were the Consoli-dated PBY Catalina flying boat, the Consolidated PB2Y Coronado flying boat, the British Short Sunderland flying boat, and the totally obsolete yet very useful Fairey Sword-

ABOVE *The two-seat Aichi D3A Val dive-bomber; this picture was taken from Japanese film captured in wartime.*
RIGHT *A Kamikaze suicide plane crashes on the flight deck of HMS* Illustrious.
BELOW *One of the famous Mitsubishi A6M Zeros in flight. These remarkable aircraft served in a multiplicity of roles as carrier- and land-based fighters, fighter-bombers, dive-bombers and suicide planes.*
BOTTOM *A Kawasaki Ki-61 Hien (Swallow) fighter and fighter-bomber, nicknamed Tony by the Allies. It first went into service in summer 1942.*

fish torpedo and reconnaissance aircraft. These did much to defeat the U-boat menace during the war, and even if their part was not necessarily a glamorous one, it was one whose importance can hardly be overestimated.

Inevitably, in turning to Japanese aircraft, we must think of the Mitsubishi A6M Zero, or Zeke. This carrier-borne fighter raised the art of the naval aircraft designer to new heights. It was capable at the height of its importance of besting most of its land-based opponents, and it remained a formidable opponent, although obsolescent, right to the end of the war. Armed with two 20-mm cannon and two 7·7-mm machine guns, it had considerable firepower – though its

Wartime turbo-jets herald new departures in aircraft design.

protection was inadequate and by the end of the war even small bursts of concentrated ·5-inch machine-gun fire were sufficient to knock it down. The Aichi D3A Val dive-bomber and Nakajima B5N torpedo bomber were worthy companions for the Zero in the opening months of the Pacific war.

On land, the Japanese had several notable designs, including the Kawasaki Ki-61 Hien fighter, the Mitsubishi G-4M bomber, the Nakajima Ki-43 Hayabusa fighter and the Nakajima Ki-84 Hayate fighter. But demands by Japanese pilots before the war that manoeuvrability should be preferred over protection of fuel tanks and pilots, and over high performance as well, coupled with the High Command's constant requirement of very long ranges (because the Japanese forces would be operating from island bases far from the enemy), meant that Japanese aircraft were light and fairly flimsy. One result was that, later in the war, they could not stand up to American firepower. What was more, Japanese design always lagged a little behind the Americans, and this, combined with lack of fuel, severely limited Japanese air activity from the middle of 1943 onwards.

A New Era

Among the machines of World War II were types that presaged a new era in aircraft design – the turbojets. Only three of these saw service in the war: the Messerschmitt Me-262 twin-jet fighter, the Arado Ar-234 Blitz bomber, and the Gloster Meteor fighter.

Research into jet propulsion had been going on since before the war (Germany's first jet aircraft, the Heinkel He-178, had flown before the outbreak of hostilities) but both Germany and Britain placed higher priority on more conventional types until late in the war. The United States was also developing jet aircraft by the end of the war, but in common with British types these were little more than machines based on the piston-engined design philosophy and adapted for jet engines.

The Germans, however, had made very considerable advances in the field of aerodynamics, and this led them to adopt the slightly swept wing of the Me-262, while further types, still on the drawing board at the end of the war, were even more advanced. This design material, captured by the Americans and the Russians in 1945, was to prove a revelation, as will be seen in the next chapter. Meanwhile, of the three types actually to see active service, none had a profound effect on the outcome of the war. Also of note was

First age of the turbojets – and a new rocket type.
TOP *The swept-wing Messerschmitt Me-262 Sturmvogel twin-jet fighter.*
ABOVE *The Arado Ar-234 Blitz bomber; the projection visible above the cockpit is a fairing for the periscope bomb sight and gun sight.*
RIGHT *The British Gloster Meteor fighter.*
BELOW *Messerschmitt's Me-163B Komet, a single-seat rocket-propelled interceptor fighter powered by the dangerous Walther bi-fuel liquid rocket unit.*

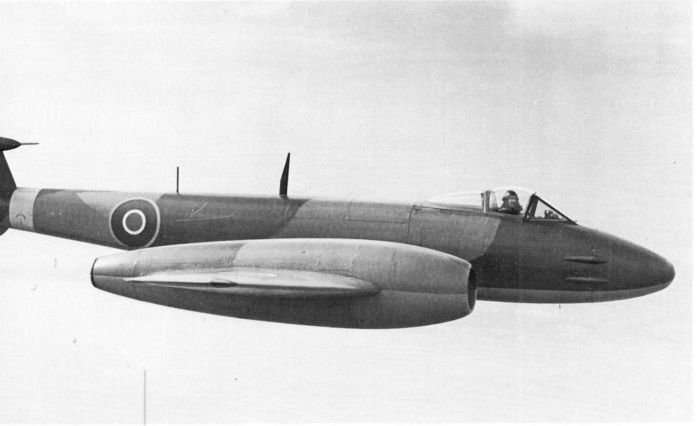

the Messerschmitt Me-163, a swept delta-winged design powered by a highly dangerous rocket engine.

Among the types under test at the end of the war were several interesting designs. The Germans, by 1945 desperate to introduce superior types in a last effort to halt the Allies, had rushed into development the fascinating Heinkel He-162 Salamander, a lightweight design with a tricycle undercarriage whose engine, mounted in a pod above the fuselage, exhausted between the twin vertical tail surfaces.

The British were forging ahead with the de Havilland Vampire, a dainty fighter design with the empennage mounted on twin booms to permit the engine placed in the central fuselage to exhaust through the shortest ducting possible. The Americans were more conventional in their approach, with the twin-engined Bell P-59 Airacomet and Lockheed P-80 Shooting Star single-engined fighters undergoing advanced testing. They were also experimenting with mixed powerplants to obtain greater range than was possible with jet engines alone, such as on the Ryan FR-1 Fireball. Clearly the piston-engined era was fast approaching its end.

PART 5
THE POST-WAR
YEARS

20

WARRIORS AND POLICEMEN

Specialist infantry become more elusive, mobile and aggressive than ever before.

For the first decade in the post-war period there was little significant change in infantry tactics or formations, despite the fact that in theory at least the heralding of the atomic age had rendered obsolete most hitherto known forms of warfare. Infantry units in all armies broadly maintained the triangular structure which had been found to work well in the many and varied theatres of combat during World War II. The increasing tendency of infantry to specialize was also maintained and carried foward by the peacetime armies. Thus, airborne units were to be found in most major armies, as were armoured infantry formations, first developed by the Germans in the shape of the Panzer Grenadiers and then adopted by the Allied armies. Such formations fought from their own armoured personnel carriers, these being low-silhouette tracked vehicles with passenger compartments. At first these were hybrid affairs fashioned from the materials at hand, i.e. in most instances from obsolescent tank chassis.

World War II also saw the development of special infantry units which adopted the basic traditions and tactics of guerrilla formations. The Russians were the first to use such forces on a major scale with partisan units operating deep behind German lines (in a more limited way the Wehrmacht had already produced its own élite formation, the Brandenburghers). The British and Americans evolved their specialized infantry in the form of the Commandos, Rangers and Raiders. These élite fighting formations were used in desert, mountain and jungle terrain, and excelled at spearheading amphibious assaults in the van of invading armies. Units such as these survived into the modern period despite the fact that their traditional role has become increasingly anachronistic in the nuclear age. Instead, armies have employed them as trouble-shooters in wars where political sensitivities have required rapid action to resolve the situation. In every campaign these special units have been equipped to meet the needs of particular tasks; in consequence infantry has become specialized to a degree that could never have been anticipated before 1939.

One thing that has not changed is that the infantry remains the arm of decision; no matter what the degree of specialization, it is still the infanteer who carries the war to the enemy. Nevertheless, the inexorable increase in firepower, a process which began in earnest during World War II and has continued with unabated energy ever since, has meant that the infanteer has had to advance against an ever-mounting weight of destructive fire. To some

extent this has been neutralized by the introduction, also initiated in World War II, of more effective fire support for the infantry, characterized by the rocket launcher and the recoilless rifle. In his essential role, therefore, the infanteer continues to seek survival through the use of cover and concealment while retaining his powers of offensive action. Technological improvements have also ensured that in the post-war period he has become more elusive, more mobile and more aggressive than ever before.

The irony of the first major conflict of the nuclear age, the Korean War (1950–53), was that, more than ever, it was an infantry war. On the one hand the United Nations forces enjoyed a range of support and comfort hitherto unparalleled in the annals of warfare. A wounded man could be airlifted by helicopter out of combat and within a very few minutes be receiving first-class surgery in a hospital equipped with the latest aids and amenities; while a battalion cut off and stranded behind the enemy line could receive, through highly sophisticated airdrop techniques, goods that had been pre-packed in Japan for this very purpose.

The converse was that Allied infantry was overstretched as never before and, given the peculiar nature of the rocky terrain, Korea rapidly emerged as an infantry war with an amazingly high incidence of hand-to-hand combat. The Communist armies (from North Korea and China) placed little reliance on artillery, air power or armour, but in all their operations made prodigious use of ground protection and night cover. Using human porters to carry forward their combat supplies, they infiltrated the defences of the road-bound Allied armies or attacked en masse, depending heavily on machine guns and hand-held weapons, many of Russian origin. After an initial period of movement, of heady advances and humiliating retreats, the war congealed into a stagnant form where infantry tactics reverted to a bygone age, reminiscent of the trenches of the Great War. Patrols and ambushes became the familiar techniques of opposing forces trying to dominate the no-man's land and disrupt offences; and contrary to general opinion, which had envisaged a computerized war of missiles, combat instead reverted to small-scale infantry actions at the levels of platoon and company.

There was one major tactical innovation in the Korean War, namely the revival of body armour for combat

OPPOSITE, ABOVE *A conventionally equipped South Vietnamese infantryman in action in 1975.*
OPPOSITE, BELOW *A fighting hovercraft, one of the new patrol and transport vehicles introduced during the war in Vietnam.*

infantry. After an interval of several centuries, the miracle of 20th-century plastics made it possible for the fighting soldier to be equipped with what was to be popularly called the bullet-proof vest. This device had in fact made a limited appearance towards the latter stages of World War II, and by the time of the truce in Korea virtually all American infantry were equipped with the new vest. Nylon pads and thin wedges of fibreglass were combined in a sleeveless garment which weighed less than nine pounds; its light weight and singlet shape allowed the soldier to negotiate difficult terrain and fight in close combat without it impeding his movements. It considerably reduced casualties from small-arms fire, shapnel and grenade fragments, but its real value lay in the fact that troops *believed* in its protective powers; this greatly boosted morale, especially in offensive actions.

In terms of personal weapons the infantry in Korea still used the same weapons that had seen their formations through the major campaigns of World War II. For the American infantry the basic weapon was still the Garand or M-1 which the US forces had first adopted in 1936; this, together with the M-1 Carbine and Thompson, was not replaced until the new NATO standardized weapons appeared in the late 1950s.

American military involvement in Asia continued with a long-drawn-out and ultimately tragic war in Vietnam. Her thirty years in Indo-China caused the United States more than 50,000 casualties; despite all the sophistication of the world's most advanced technology, US forces failed in the long run to overcome the hardened professional veterans from the Communist North. The United States, partly in an attempt to reduce infantry casualties and partly in a vain attempt to impose an artificial 20th-century battle environment on an Asian society, sought to prove that the answer to insurgency lay in firepower. The American forces in this war numbered at their maximum more than 600,000

The bullet-proof vest: the old concept of body armour for the infantry is reapplied, and morale much improved.

OPPOSITE *A British infantryman trains in protective clothing and a respirator designed to safeguard him against nuclear, biological and chemical hazards.*
ABOVE *The 'Wheelbarrow', a mobile trolley used for examining suspect objects; if necessary it can detonate a terrorist's bomb while its operator remains at a safe distance. In this photograph the Wheelbarrow's window-breaking attachment is seen at work. Full title of the machine is the Remote Handling Equipment (Tracked) Explosive Ordnance Disposal.*
BELOW *British paratroopers make an arrest in Londonderry, dragging their captive at speed to an armoured 'Pig'.*

men, of whom less than a quarter were actively employed in close combat with the enemy, who greatly complicated matters by being continually elusive. While Marines and line infantry fought from a new generation of armoured personnel carriers which spouted multiple cannon and rocketry, a new type of infantry was developed to overcome the problems of mobility in an inhospitable terrain. Airborne infantry carried in literally hundreds of helicopters and protected by numerous helicopter gunships comprised the new formations of air cavalry; but even they with all their sophisticated techniques failed to bring the enemy to a decisive engagement on a strategic scale. Vietnam was an infantry war of strange contrasts, for while sophisticated surveillance and hitherto undreamed-of firepower lent new dimensions to combat, the demands of 'bodycounts', and other forms of statistical proof of enemy casualties, introduced a naked disregard for human life and produced a most savage and total war on the ground.

The wars in Southern Asia, the Middle East and elsewhere provoked a revolution in infantry combat, albeit within the conventional confines of modern warfare, and stimulated a fresh wave of new theories about the role of infantry in a tactical nuclear land battle. The modern infanteer moves into the combat zone in APCs which are guaranteed to afford protection against the effects of nuclear and chemical (and biological) weapons. Further protected by attendant squadrons of armour and with indigenous artillery on self-propelled chassis, infantry formations advance to contact in dispersed groups before concentrating at the last possible moment to fight a war of movement of a kind inconceivable to the infanteer of World War II. When fighting dismounted from their armoured vehicles, the infantry now possess a sophisticated array of man-portable weapon systems, and, as the Yom Kippur War of 1973 revealed, are by themselves capable of neutralizing an opponent's armour and air support.

LEFT *US National Guardsmen practise the arts of public confrontation.*
ABOVE *On the side of law and order – Paris riot police stand behind a street barricade of paving stones thrown up during the students' rebellion of May 1968. At that time the troubled French establishment had resort to a variety of anti-riot formations. In addition to the conventional* agent, *the truncheon-carrying policemen, there were Paris's own anti-riot 'intervention companies'; the CRS, a 14,000-strong national force, armed with round shields and truncheons, and, for real emergencies, the rifle-armed* gendarmerie, *which in 1968 had 16,000 men.*

While at the present time the Superpowers continue to pump their latest devices into their respective clients of the Third World, war has nevertheless become both more costly and burdensome for small nations incapable of sustaining campaigns aimed at attrition. In this situation the infantry have retained their position as the dominant force on the battlefield. The foot soldier is still required to hold ground and to advance against an ever more impressive spectrum of weapon systems. To give a further example of the latter, a traditional weapon such as the minefield, where technology reached new heights of horror in World War II, has become even more refined with the introduction of electronics into warfare.

Finally, as the divisions between war and peace grow increasingly indistinct, it is important to note that the infanteer has also made a return to one of his traditional roles. The regular soldier throughout history has been called upon to act as aid to the civil powers, and in recent years civil-military relations have assumed major significance in a succession of bloody encounters fought at street-level in Northern Ireland, Portugal, Lebanon and elsewhere. The soldier-turned-policeman has had to relearn old skills and develop even more fortitude and resilience as he becomes subjected to all the tests and ingenuities of the urban guerrilla. In some parts of the world, particularly in the United States and Latin America, this has also resulted in the police forces taking on a para-military complexion; at the same time the armaments industries have found a ready market on a worldwide scale for riot-control weapons which range from the sophisticated sniper rifle to the simple wooden truncheon. In Northern Ireland and other centres of urban insurrection the infanteer is protected by body armour, helmet and shield. Except that these are lighter, more durable and made of plastic compounds, it might seem to the impartial observer that the clock, started in the wars of prehistory, has turned full-circle.

21

THE PROGRESS OF ARMOUR

Theories about the role of armour in a nuclear setting are brought rudely to earth by the World War II-style clashes of the Korean War.

The danger in studying the history and performance of a weapon system in isolation is that its contribution on the battlefield may be exaggerated. The history of the tank is one of an attempt to transform a siege-breaking machine into the armoured horse of mechanized cavalry. The late Sir Basil Liddell-Hart contended, along with other writers of military history, that ever since the Napoleonic era the weapons of the defence have gained a growing material superiority over those of the offence. Certainly the tank never became the invincible armoured horse; and its one phase of superiority, achieved by Guderian and his Panzers in 1940, was in essence an aberration caused by the French High Command's crass neglect of the principles of defence in battle.

In the decisive battles of World War II – Stalingrad, El Alamein, and the D-Day Landings – the tank was not the decisive or even the predominant weapon. Kursk, though rightly claimed as the greatest tank encounter in history, was a massive battle of attrition nearer to the concept of Haig than Liddell-Hart or Guderian. In the context of armour World War II unfolds as warfare with tanks rather than as tank warfare.

The introduction of any new weapon system is to a considerable degree a self-defeating process: in the case of the tank, its arrival sponsored the development of the anti-tank guns, mines, bazookas and tactical aircraft whose job was to produce a more hostile environment for it. Some pundits have even seen in this sequence a form of progression to a point at which the tank could become so vulnerable that it would cease to have any valid role at all. However, while it is true that the weapons introduced to counter the tank have all succeeded in showing that its armoured skin could be penetrated, a still more important factor to bear in mind is that armoured protection has never really been considered the tank's principal asset. This, first and foremost, has been its ability to provide a high degree of tactical mobility to heavy, crew-operated, direct-fire weapons; at the same time its armoured skin has afforded it protection from a significant number of battlefield weapons. It is this combination which accounted for the survival of

Any analysis of tanks developed since 1917 will show only a small proportion whose primary aim was to provide their crews with maximum protection through virtually impenetrable armour. Tank designers have always been divided into two groups, those who see protection in terms of the armoured skin and those who see it being provided through high speed. The tactical mobility of tanks depends

OPPOSITE *Principal opponents in the Korean War (1950–53) were the Soviet-built T-34/85 (top), which were used to great effect early on by the North Koreans, and the American Patton and British* Centurion (centre and bottom) with which the United Nations force eventually responded after the relative failure in the initial phase of its Pershings and Comets of World War II vintage.* BELOW *A UN Sherman operating beside a burning farmhouse in Korea in 1950.* ABOVE *A present-day tank position manned by South Korean soldiers and guarding the south bank of the Imjin River.*

on the successful combination of firepower, protection and speed. This ensured not just its survival but its validity as a battlefield weapon during World War II – and its continued development in the post-war period.

At first the fortunes of the tank in Western armies suffered a decline. In the atmosphere of general euphoria at the end of the war, to which was joined a mystical belief in the power of the nuclear weapon, armoured divisions were disbanded at an alarming rate. However, the Western Alliance was shaken out of its complacency when Soviet T-34/85s, deployed by only moderately skilled North Koreans, wrought havoc among the infantry units of South Korea and the United States in June 1950. The mobile phase of the Korean War lasted until the summer of 1951 and the United Nations was forced to deploy tanks of World War II vintage, the American Pershing and the British Comet. It is ironic, too, that when the new tanks – Pattons and Centurions – did reach the theatre they were deployed in support of infantry in the slogging trench warfare that lasted until the ceasefire of June 1953. Yet the Korean War is an important episode in the story of the tank because it reawakened an interest in armour in the Western Alliance and accelerated the gun and armour race with the Soviet Union. This confrontation has, furthermore, taken place on a global scale with both sides liberally distributing their latest tanks to client and satellite powers which in turn have used them to fight their own wars in Asia and the Middle East.

The Arab-Israeli Wars

The almost permanent nature of the quarrel between Arab and Jew has provided a ready-made testing ground for the tank and other armoured fighting vehicles. The Sinai campaign of 1956 offered little of value since the outmoded machines and old-fashioned tactics that were used did little to change the art of tank warfare. The 1967 campaign, however, was far more important since it provided the arena for the first large-scale collision of Western and Soviet tanks of modern design.

In four days of fast-moving desert combat Israeli armour inflicted a decisive defeat on the numerically superior Egyptian tank formations. The Israeli Air Force in a pre-emptive strike gained mastery of the skies above Sinai and this allowed the armoured divisions great freedom of movement. But even more conclusive was the manifest superiority of the Israeli armour. The Army had re-equipped with new tanks, mostly Pattons and Centurions, and at first experienced many difficulties in handling their complex machines. In border clashes with Syria in 1965 the Arab Panzer Mark IVs proved more than a match for the Israelis and this resulted in a crisis of confidence in the Israeli Armoured Corps.

General Tal was appointed chief of the armoured forces and immediately carried through a major reform of his units. By 1967 the armoured divisions had been completely reformed and their popular image of a 'civilianized' bunch of freedom fighters was far removed from reality. The tank formations were an élite corps of well-drilled, disciplined troopers with a standard training programme, and although they were still largely composed of militia Tal had ensured that there was also a strong base of long-term regulars.

The tank campaign in Sinai was essentially a clash between the classic Soviet concepts of defence and the Israeli version of Guderian's Blitzkrieg. The Tal armoured divisions shocked the Egyptians into flight and then kept them on the run until they were exhausted; once through the first line of defences the Israeli tanks deployed to meet the main force of Egyptian armour. If the Arabs had fought with more resolution within their fortified positions, or if their Air Force had not been so effectively neutralized, then the cavalry charge by the Israeli tanks might well have stalled on the Egyptian wire. There were some very good combat units in the Egyptian Army, but they were the exception; in general the Egyptians' Russian instructors had had scant success in training their pupils in the complexities of a European-style tank war.

There is little documented evidence available on this lightning campaign: the Arabs are understandably reticent while Israeli information tends to mislead rather than inform. But although the details of this campaign remain obscure it appears that the Israelis attacked with three armoured divisions and achieved a major rupture of the Egyptian positions within the first 24 hours. During this first phase some of the heaviest fighting occurred, and the

BELOW *An Israeli Sherman on the Northern Front advances into Syria during the 1967 campaign.*

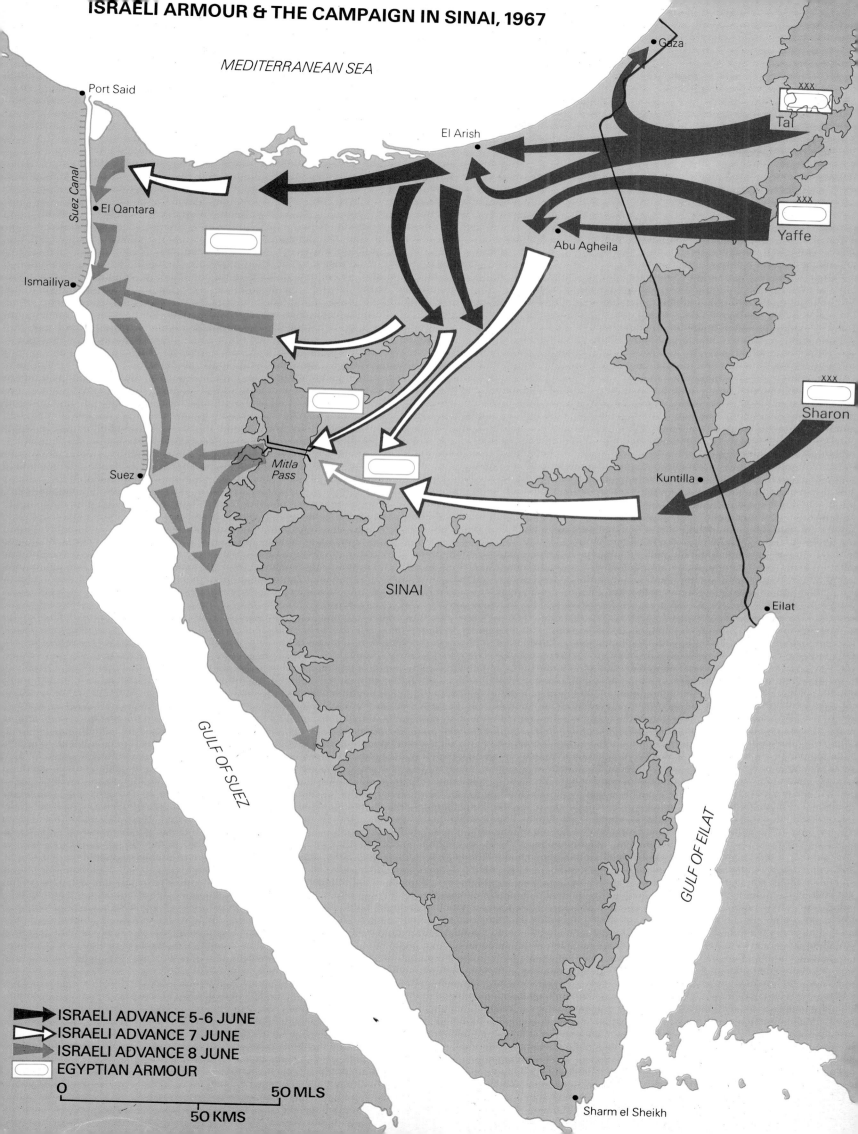

ISRAELI ARMOUR & THE CAMPAIGN IN SINAI, 1967

MEDITERRANEAN SEA

Port Said

Suez Canal

El Qantara

El Arish

Gaza

Tal

Yaffe

Abu Agheila

Ismailiya

Suez

Mitla
Pass

Sharon

Kuntilla

SINAI

Eilat

GULF OF SUEZ

GULF OF EILAT

➤ ISRAELI ADVANCE 5-6 JUNE
➤ ISRAELI ADVANCE 7 JUNE
➤ ISRAELI ADVANCE 8 JUNE
▭ EGYPTIAN ARMOUR

O   50 MLS

50 KMS

Sharm el Sheikh

Israeli tank units, though hit by supply problems in the desert, outmanoeuvre and destroy their Egyptian opponents.

Egyptian minefields and artillery took a heavy toll of the advancing tanks. In the north General Tal 'pinched off' the Gaza Strip but then became embroiled in a large-scale fire-fight against the main Egyptian position astride the Ismalia Road. These forces were saved from further punishment when General Yaffe, who had struck largely unnoticed in the centre, was able to sweep northwards to rescue his leader. General Sharon and his division in the south had a tough battle against well-entrenched Egyptian units at Abu Aghelia, but a daring night assault through the minefields cleared the last of the defences and he moved south and west without pause for re-supply. The crucial tank encounters occurred on a wide front throughout the second and third days, when the Egyptian T-54s and T-55s proved no match for the technically superior Israeli tanks. The Arab tank formations were either out-flanked or destroyed piecemeal as the Israeli armour raced for the vital Mitla Pass and the road to the Suez Canal.

The great levelling factor in previous campaigns involving fast-moving armour had been the problem of supply, and in the present case war broke out before General Tal had been able to effect any genuine reform of the supply echelons of his tank formations. Hastily impressed lorries and their undisciplined drivers created massive traffic jams on the roads into Sinai and this self-inflicted strangulation meant that very few tanks were able to deploy in the Mitla Pass. Tanks with any fuel in store towed others which were bone-dry into blocking positions and so they were able to deny the pass to the retreating Egyptians until relief came. Air strikes also played a major role in the desert battle in the last three days of combat, and although the use of napalm by the Israelis meant that pinpoint accuracy was no longer required, very few Egyptian tanks were in fact 'killed' by air strikes. The real impact of the Israeli Air Force was felt in the massive destruction of supply echelons that took place as the Egyptian convoys tried to run for cover.

Much has been written about this campaign and the equally impressive operations against the Jordanians and Syrians, and some pundits of air power and the tank have performed incredible feats of academic gymnastics in trying to demonstrate new lessons. But the plain fact is that nothing new came out of that last cavalry ride to glory

LEFT *An Israeli tank tows another on the Northern Front in 1973; by the side of the road is a knocked-out Syrian tank of Russian origin.*
ABOVE *The French light AMX-13 tank, armed with the 75-mm gun, with which Egyptian armoured units were equipped in the 1967 war.*

Balance of Forces
ARAB/ISRAELI WAR JUNE 1967

CATEGORY	ISRAEL	EGYPT
1 Total armed forces	71,000 regulars (275,000 including reservists)	190,000 regulars (310,000 including reservists/ national guard)
2 Army	60,000 regulars (204,000 including reservists) Equipped with: 600 front-line tanks 200 Shermans 250 self-propelled guns	160,000 regulars plus reservists Equipped with: 1,200 tanks and self-propelled guns, the former consisting mainly of T-34/85, T-54, T-55, Centurion and AMX-13 tanks
3 Air Force	350 combat aircraft, including the Mirage IIIC, Super Mystère and Vautour	550 combat aircraft, including MiG-15, -19 and -21 interceptors

in a campaign which simply transported us back 25 years. The battle was won by a disciplined, technologically skilled nation that was able to defeat a well-equipped but badly-led army which apparently lacked the educational and social framework to fight a machine-age war.

In October 1973 the desert wastes of Sinai, still littered with the rusting hulks of the June 1967 war, witnessed a new clash of armour that took a different course. The war in fact began on two fronts: while élite Egyptian mechanized forces stormed the Bar-Lev Line on the east bank of the Suez canal, to the north Syrian tanks in massed formations advanced against complacent, and thinly held, Israeli outposts along the Golan Heights.

For 20 days the armoured units of both sides fought a series of bloody tank battles in a classic style: only on this occasion there was no Israeli Blitzkrieg to shock the Arab armies into premature flight. Instead it was the turn of the Arabs to confound the pundits as their tank regiments and supporting infantry fought with great skill and professionalism.

The Israelis' strategy soon became clear. This was to give priority to the Northern Front and so quell the danger there before counter-attacking in the south. But in the field their tactics were compromised by an overriding need to keep casualties to an acceptable minimum. In late October, with the Northern Front stabilized into an artillery duel and the Syrian forces pushed back to their start lines, an Israeli tank force burst through the Egyptian lines in the south and seized a bridgehead on the west bank of the Canal. Although the Israelis were able to expand their bridgehead and encircle the Egyptian Third Corps in and around the town of Suez, they were eventually stopped by a ceasefire, brought about by concerted pressure from the Great Powers and the UN, from completing the operation.

Throughout the campaign the Egyptians used new tactics. In the air the Israeli tactical strike aircraft found themselves inhibited by the accuracy of the Egyptians' surface-to-air missiles (mostly of the SAM-6 type), while on the ground the Egyptians matched their infantry against Israeli tanks and their own armour against Israeli infantry. That they were able to do so was in part due to the large stocks of wire-guided Sagger anti-tank missiles available to the infantry.

In this war more tanks were apparently destroyed than in any of the previous encounters, and this once again, predictably enough, resulted in experts forecasting the end of the battle tank. But the casualties, though high, were suffered primarily because both sides used tanks on such a large scale; the figures nevertheless also underline the effectiveness of tank cannon in the hands of confident and skilled crewmen.

TOP *Israeli troops in armoured personnel carriers move across the Sinai Desert in 1967.*
ABOVE *Now a museum piece – a Russian-built SU-100 assault gun with its Egyptian markings preserved.*
RIGHT *In between wars – Israeli tank reservists on exercise.*

LEFT *An Israeli tank crew on the alert in the precarious peace between* 1967 *and* 1973.
OPPOSITE AND BELOW *The debris of war – knocked-out Russian tanks formerly part of the Arabs' armoured strength in* 1967.

The Indo-Pakistan Wars

A pattern similar to that of the Arab-Israeli wars emerged when the Pakistanis and Indians clashed in 1965 and again in 1971. The western border war in 1965 provided the experts with a unique opportunity to assess the respective qualities of one Western tank against another as Pakistani Pattons tangled with Indian Centurions. But sterile tactics on both sides blunted this contest and produced a short, savage war of attrition in which neither side possessed the resilience to pursue matters beyond an indefinite conclusion. The advanced weapon systems that were used cancelled one another out very quickly, and if the Centurion emerged with its reputation more intact than the Patton, this was probably because it was far less sophisticated and much easier to handle.

The unsatisfactory truce achieved through Russian arbitration at Tashkent resulted in an uneasy lull, and open conflict, this time on a wider scale, erupted in 1971. The main centre of interest was focused on the eastern frontiers as both sides became embroiled in the birth pangs of secessionist Bangladesh. Little documentary evidence has emerged from this recent campaign but the accepted Indian version of events relates how within a brief period of twelve days their armoured columns executed one of the most decisive campaigns of liberation in military history. The largely infantry-orientated Pakistani forces in the east based their defences on a number of seemingly impregnable strategically located strongholds covering the lines of best

approach. Indian armour moved across ground hitherto considered inaccessible to tanks and outwitted an already demoralized enemy by swift outflanking movements.

The success of the Indian armour during this campaign confounded the image that experts in the Western world had formed of the Indian Army. But the construction under licence in India of a modified version of the Vickers battle tank (renamed the Vijayanta), added to their existing aircraft industry, made the Indians surprisingly self-sufficient for a developing nation. The London *Sunday Times*, in an article published on 19 December 1971, said:

> It took only twelve days for the Indian Army to smash its way to Dacca, an achievement reminiscent of the German Blitzkrieg across France in 1940. The strategy was the same, speed, ferocity and flexibility.

On the western frontiers the Pakistanis launched major offensives to try and divert Indian forces from the major operations in the east. This stratagem failed and though the fighting in the west proved less decisive the Indians made some territorial gains by straightening out salients which had been created in 1965. Heavy fighting in this sector lasted until 17 December. The biggest tank battle occurred in the Shakargarh salient where Indian Army Centurions of the Poona Horse clashed with the Pakistani 6th Armour Division's Pattons, which contained elements of Hobson's Horse and Skinner's Horse. As the names themselves suggest, the irony of this particular encounter was that all these regiments had once been eminent cavalry formations in the British Indian Army.

Balance of Forces
INDO/PAKISTANI WAR DECEMBER 1971

CATEGORY	INDIA	PAKISTAN
1 Total armed forces	960,000 men	395,000 men
2 Army	840,000	278,000

[a] *Armoured formations*	2 armoured divisions
	3 independent armoured brigades
	Equipped with:
	   200 Centurions (Mks 5/7)
	   250 Shermans
	   450 T-54s, T-55s
	   300 Vijayantas
	   150 PT-76s
	   140 AMX-13s
		2 armoured divisions
		1 independent armoured brigade
		Equipped with:
		   135 M-47 Pattons
		   65 M-48 Pattons
		   50 T-55s
		   200 T-59s
		   200 light tanks

[b] *Infantry formations*	13 infantry divisions 10 mountain divisions 6 independent infantry brigades 2 parachute brigades	10 infantry divisions
3 Air Force	650 combat aircraft	Not available

Pakistan's infantry-dominated forces in the east are no match for the armoured thrusts of the Indians.

OPPOSITE *The Vickers Main Battle Tank, built under licence in India as the Vijayanta (Freedom), was a key element in the 1971 war. Carrying a 105-mm gun in the main armament and with a road speed of 35 mph, the Vijayantas of the Indian Army rapidly forced a path through to Dacca.*

BELOW LEFT *Three Pakistani soldiers pose for the world's press with an Indian tank captured in the Kashmir.*
BELOW *A display of arms, ammunition and documents seized from Pakistani troops during the Indians' drive towards the Bangladeshi homelands.*

LEFT *Although helicopters are dealt with more fully in the final chapter, and in particular between pages 430 and 433, it is appropriate here to include some examples of the fighting helicopter, which since the Vietnam War has been seen in some quarters as a parallel weapon system to the tank. Shown here are the US Huey Cobra (above), fitted with rockets, grenades and machine-guns, and the British Scout firing an anti-tank missile.*

BELOW *An American Patton tank fires on a suspected Vietcong infiltration route; in Vietnam night firing was carried out with the limited aim of restricting the Communist guerrillas in their movements.*

OPPOSITE *Russian tanks demonstrate their strength during the overrunning of Prague in 1968.*

Armour Today

The contribution of armour to the fighting in Vietnam is difficult to assess as a whole but it does seem that many valuable lessons have been learned, some of which have already been applied to the European theatre. For a number of years the Americans, their allies and clients have made good use of armoured personnel carriers – vehicles which have fulfilled the role of the light tank, whose virtues were so mistakenly espoused by Liddell-Hart and the British in the period from 1918 to 1939. The main battle tank made its appearance in the theatre only in the final phase of the war after 1968.

The Armoured Branch of the US Army advocated the use of tanks in the first instance because it believed that future tank development would be jeopardized unless the tank could draw at least some of the limelight away from the infantry. But, aside from this partisan motive, the tank was also needed by the Army Command to provide support for the infantry during this latter period of large-scale combat, when casualties were at their highest. Yet in a counter-insurgency operation the use of armour can have little value since the guerrilla is too elusive an objective for the tank and a sophisticated armoured thrust is hardly the most appropriate way to attack his primitive lines of communication, which can be easily reassembled.

The war in Vietnam caused a reformation in the research and development of conventional weapon systems – activities which had lain dormant in Europe since the end of World War II. In the context of armour the weapon which

has aroused the greatest interest and controversy is the helicopter. In Vietnam helicopters performed a variety of tasks but they were at their most spectacular as a weapons carrier: on many occasions their ability to pour plunging fire of great density and little discrimination caused havoc among those caught in open country or confined in a village street. In terms of Europe it is this aspect of the helicopter, especially when converted to the role of tank killer, that has aroused the most interest and speculation; and there are some experts who predict the demise of the battle tank because of its vulnerability to the helicopter. The modern helicopter can carry a lethal missile that can be fired at a range of four kilometres – well beyond the range of any tank's defending fire. The great speed and manoeuvrability of the helicopter mean that it is also able rapidly to bring reinforcement to a situation of crisis on a modern battle-field; it is this factor above all which many observers find so attractive.

There is no doubt that the helicopter is a weapon system of great potency and potential, but it is much open to doubt whether it can usurp the place previously held by the battle tank. The essential quality which the tank has displayed in the past – and which is needed just as much today – is its high degree of tactical mobility in terms of cross-country performance and armour protection from a significant number of hostile weapon systems. In Vietnam helicopter casualties were high despite the fact that operations were carried out in a secure air environment; probably only the wealthiest of armies could afford such losses. There is, moreover, no helicopter yet in service which can carry the

Tank doctrines of the Soviet bloc and Western Alliance; the nuclear factor and attitudes provoked by it.

Balance of Forces
NATO/WARSAW PACT 1975

CATEGORY	NORTH AND CENTRAL EUROPE			SOUTHERN EUROPE		
	NATO	WARSAW PACT	(OF WHICH USSR)	NATO	WARSAW PACT	(OF WHICH USSR)
1 Armoured divisions	12	31	19	6	7	3
1a Main battle tanks (in peacetime deployment)	7,000	19,000	11,500	3,500	7,250	2,250
2 Infantry (mechanized, airborne divisions)	15	37	21	33	24	5

most efficient anti-tank weapon of all – the high-velocity, large-calibre cannon; the helicopter's operational capability is also affected by poor weather and at night, while in terms of Europe there are few areas where a killing range of four kilometres is at all practical.

The Soviet and Warsaw Pact forces have deployed a large number of helicopters, but the major emphasis is still placed on the proven qualities of the tank. A new battle tank is rumoured to be in quantity production in the Soviet Union while the satellite armies are being re-equipped with the T-62 to replace their obsolescent T-54s and T-55s. In the present conventional phase of warfare, published Soviet doctrine places great stress on the deployment of tank and mechanized divisions: the tank is also given an equally vital role in the nuclear scenario. In addition to the tank's substantial firepower, speed and manoeuvrability, the Russians seem to value it for the protection it provides against the effects of nuclear blast. In 1968 Chief Marshal of Tanks Rotmistrov wrote:

Under conditions of a missile and nuclear war, the armour of a modern tank protects the crew from the light radiation of the nuclear blast and significantly weakens the penetrating radiation. Because of its weight it easily withstands the impact of the shock wave which arises at the moment of blast and also serves as a protection against shell and bullet fragments. In essence the tank is not only a powerful offensive weapon, it is also a mobile shelter, protecting against the harmful elements of the nuclear blast and standard weapons fire.

The Western Alliance for its part remains sceptical of such Soviet claims for an armoured offensive moving through contaminated zones, and undoubtedly this stereotyped Soviet account of how such an offensive would be waged displays a high degree of optimism. Even without the use of nuclear weapons it is difficult to avoid the conclusion that the reality would be rather different. To counter what sanguine Western observers believe would be a two-to-one superiority on the Central Front by the Warsaw Pact, the North Atlantic Alliance is defensively orientated and equipped to offer a flexible response by means of area-defence weapons, close-range anti-tank missiles and its own main battle tanks.

The main battle tank deployed by the Americans is the M-60 A-1, which is armed with a 105-mm high-velocity gun of British origin; this tank has been in service for some years and there are no immediate plans to introduce a successor. It is supplemented by the lighter, air-portable Sheridan M-551, equipped with the versatile 152-mm gun-launcher. In theory the gun and missile launcher combine the advantages of both weapons in a single system but in practice it is regarded by many as an ineffective compromise. The West German Bundeswehr has the Leopard, a battle tank with a spectacular cross-country performance; it too is armed with the British 105-mm gun. The British Army has completed its re-equipment programme and all its tank regiments now have the Chieftain instead of the redoubtable Centurion. The Chieftain is generally acknowledged to be the best battle tank in Europe: its design emphasizes armour protection and simplicity, and it has a 120-mm cannon of unparalleled power and accuracy. The French Army has equipped its armoured divisions with the AMX-30 mounting a 105-mm gun in an oscillating turret; this tank replaces the older and lighter AMX-13.

In the future few changes are likely in the shape and design of armoured formations within the Western Alliance. The Americans and the West Germans cancelled their joint project, called the MBT-70, because of rapidly escalating costs. The Americans for a while flirted with a tank project of advanced design known as the XM-803 but have now abandoned this in favour of a more modest project. The West Germans plan to improve on the Leopard while at the same time co-operating with Britain on a joint project for a battle tank that is scheduled at the time of writing to replace existing equipment by 1980.

Two other countries outside the main Alliance have recently developed main battle tanks. One of these, Sweden, has the S tank, built by Bofors; this vehicle is of a revolutionary design and shape but is regarded by many purists as a super-self-propelled gun, rather than a tank. The other country, Japan, showed only slight interest in armour during World War II, but now, in modest quantities, she possesses a battle tank called the Type 61. This tank, however, shares so many similarities with the American Patton that one wonders why the Japanese bothered to build their own.

At the present time the emphasis placed on tanks by the major armies of the world reflects the continuing validity of armoured vehicles to the modern battlefield despite the accelerating development of anti-tank weapons. However, in a European context the tank can no longer be deployed as cavalry; armoured divisions will never again lie massed in reserve to exploit a fractured battle front. The tactical nuclear weapon has shrunk the battlefield, inhibited the mobility of the tank, and placed a fresh emphasis on the need for systematic destruction through the use of over-whelming firepower. In 1971 *The Economist* (London) said:

> The tank for a long period has been the king of European warfare – indeed for most people it has become the symbol of armed might and coercion; now it looks as if it has been dethroned from supreme power.

THIS PAGE *Soviet armoured units spearheaded by tanks and amphibious PT-76s display their present capabilities in a variety of land and waterborne operations. In the foreground below is a BTR-60P armoured personnel carrier.*

ABOVE *A British Chieftain tank emerges through the orange cloud of a smoke grenade while on exercise and, in the larger picture, demonstrates the sweep of its 120-mm gun. The 51-ton Chieftain is the most powerful battle tank in Europe; it is protected also against NBC (nuclear, biological and chemical) weapons by a ventilation system that keeps it fully sealed for up to 48 hours.*

RIGHT *The British Scorpion armoured recce vehicle, armed with a 76-mm gun, is the basic member of a family of armoured vehicles: others include the Spartan (personnel carrier), the Samaritan (ambulance) and the Striker (for guided anti-tank missiles).*

The future of tanks has been questioned many times and for the most part the conclusions reached have suggested that their end was at hand. In the past tanks have been written off because of the development of new armour-piercing weapons. This happened in the 1930s with the arrival of small-calibre anti-tank guns and again in World War II when experts pointed to the destructive capabilities of the rocket-firing Stuka aircraft and to the infantry bazooka. And in the present-day period guided heli-borne missiles are seen by many as the instruments most likely to determine the fate of the tank. At the same time the rapid acquisition of tanks by the emergent armies of the Third World confirms that armour will continue to find a ready market for years to come. Iran now has a larger force of Chieftains than the British Army of the Rhine, while the Socialist Republic of Somalia, supplied by Russia, is the most heavily armoured force in Black Africa.

Certainly, the panic response that greeted the apparent reversal of tanks in Sinai in 1973 has subsided. Tanks, it is now remembered, have never been immune to hostile fire. They remain a potent force on the battlefield.

Thus all conclusions that tanks are liable to be made obsolete by new anti-tank weapons are logical – but are derived from a false premise. For the principal asset of the tank is, as we stated earlier, its ability to provide a high degree of tactical mobility to heavy, direct-fire weapons. This simple fact accounts for the tank's survival despite its increasing vulnerability – and also explains why it is likely to continue to be developed for many years ahead.

Continuing battlefield relevance of the tank; its acquisition by armies in the Third World.

A brief guide to the armoured philosophies of four nations.

TOP The MBT-70, a US–West German co-venture that was recently cancelled because of excessively mounting costs.

ABOVE The AMX-30, the French main battle tank mounting a 105-mm gun; it has infra-red driving and fire-control equipment and can be fitted with a snorkel for deep wading. Variants include a bridgelayer and a missile carrier.

BELOW The Leopard, a 40-mph West German medium tank armed with a 105-mm gun. Among its variants are armoured recovery and anti-aircraft vehicles.

OPPOSITE, ABOVE The US M-60, in effect a diesel-engined M-48 (the Mark III Patton) mounting the British-designed 105-mm gun; the A-1 E-1 version mounts the Shillelagh gun/guided missile.

OPPOSITE, BELOW A three-quarter view of the remarkable Swedish 'S' or Stridsvagn tank, built by Bofors. Its revolutionary design, with ultra-low profile, places great emphasis on the fixed main armament, a 105-mm gun; to fire it, the whole vehicle has to be swung hydraulically onto the target; rate of fire is 10–15 rounds per minute.

OPPOSITE *A captured 85-mm AA gun of Russian origin seen near Pyongyang, Korea.* LEFT *A North Korean (ex-Russian) SU-76 SP gun captured during the drive towards the Naktong River, September 1950.* BELOW *British gunners prepare their 25-pounder for firing on the Han River Front in March 1951.*

The relatively low rate of fire of the Red gunners, mentioned above, was more the product of poor logistics than lack of training. Nevertheless, their mortars caused a great number of casualties. Some 35% of UN troops killed and 75% of those wounded were victims of artillery fire.

Moreover, the CCF and North Korean AA artillery, equipped chiefly with light 37-mm and Soviet medium 85-mm AA guns, accounted for 87% of all UN aircraft lost. This record is all the more remarkable considering the absence of anything approaching modern fire-control systems in the Red armies.

The artillery used by UN forces in Korea consisted almost wholly of US and British guns of World War II vintage. The hardest-used guns were the US 105-mm and 155-mm howitzers; a total of 900,000 tons of 105-mm and 155-mm howitzer ammunition was expended in the course of the war. This was almost as much ammunition as had been fired in the Mediterranean and Pacific theatres during World War II.

The protective barrage of World War I was revived in the form of intense 'flash fires', which could be called in to cover the front of any beleaguered position with an impassable screen of HE. Fire-direction techniques had become so advanced, and the response to calls for fire missions so instantaneous, that enemy movement within the range of UN guns was severely hampered. The best example of this was the famous 'Wonjou Shoot' of February 1951, which took place during a series of limited-objective attacks launched by General Ridgeway with the aim of driving slowly northwards. Wonjou is situated in the

centre of the country, slightly to the south of Seoul. The action was launched by UN air reconnaissance spotting several North Korean infantry divisions moving in the open. They immediately called for artillery fire on the target. It was provided, and to such effect that after some three hours of intensive bombardment 3,500 North Koreans lay dead near Wonjou, their divisions utterly destroyed.

A persistent problem for UN gunners in Korea was deciding where to place the guns. Much of Korea is either hill, mountain or paddy, little of which is suitable for the deployment of artillery. This made the need for SP mounts acute (and in due course significantly more SP guns were designed and built as a result of the Korean experience). Also, Communist infiltration tactics forced artillerists on many occasions to defend their guns in hand-to-hand combat. Such actions usually involved firing HE and WP (white phosphorous) shells into enemy infantry at very short range and eventually led to the revival of case shot as an artillery round.

Because of the special terrain problems in Korea, the most indispensable artillery pieces were mortars and recoilless rifles. These were infantry weapons, easily transported over rough terrain and quite effective in the close-support role. Two SP types of AA battery were found invaluable in this role: one was the Quad-50, mounting four ·50-calibre Browning heavy machine guns; the other was the M-19 motor carriage, mounting two 40-mm Bofors guns.

ABOVE *American 155-mm 'Long Toms' of World War II vintage release a barrage against a Communist position a few miles south of Seoul in May 1951.*

BELOW *US Marines look on as an artillery team fires its 8-inch howitzer, here seen in full recoil; this piece could fire a 200-pound shell to a range of 18,500 yards.*

Ordeal of Dien Bien Phu

The biggest and most decisive battle of the Indo–China War (1946–54) was the 55-day siege of the French fortress at Dien Bien Phu. The French had purposely placed a small army of paratroopers and men of the Foreign Legion in the valley round the village of Dien Bien Phu in the hope that they could lure a large force of Ho Chi Minh's Vietminh rebels into a set-piece battle and there annihilate them.

The position of the French Union force was highly vulnerable. They occupied a valley surrounded by precipitous hills covered with thick jungle growth. Normally an army in such a position, entirely surrounded by enemy forces, would consider its situation perilous. But the French had the utmost contempt for the Vietminh. They knew that the rebel army had 105-mm howitzers and 75-mm pack howitzers, captured from American forces in Korea. However, they not only thought the Vietminh gunners incompetent, they also decided that they would not be able to transport their guns through the mountains to within range of Dien Bien Phu. As the French saw the coming battle, the Vietminh would be decimated as they attacked the forts by a deadly combination of artillery fire and napalm bombs.

But, though the French were baiting the trap, it was to be the Vietminh who would spring it. Chinese instructors had trained the gunners of General Vu Hien's 351st Heavy Division to a high degree of proficiency. Furthermore, by the most extraordinary labour, all the guns of this division had been dismantled and transported through hundreds of miles of forbidding jungle terrain to Dien Bien Phu.

Throughout January and February 1954, the Vietminh

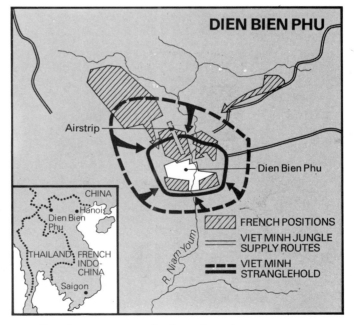

TOP *French troops occupy the doomed garrison.*

carefully emplaced their guns and mortars. In March they began to bombard the French positions in earnest.

Much depended upon the control of Dien Bien Phu's airstrip. If the Communist artillery came close enough to dispute its use, the fortress's only link with the outside would be severed. The French artillery commander, Colonel Piroth, had vowed to destroy any Vietminh gun careless enough to reveal its position by firing. He had also refused adequately to fortify the position of his 155-mm howitzers, dismissing the suggestion with the pithy answer:

French insouciance turns to despair; the rebels take the fortress by storm.

'Who could hit them?' But the Vietminh were not rank amateurs in the matter of camouflage and concealment, and they soon rendered the airstrip useless by their fire. Piroth was unable to locate many of the Vietminh guns. He committed suicide with a grenade on 14 March. By then the French were having to resort to air drops to supply the fortress.

Soon even the air drops became dangerous and haphazard. The Vietminh were employing about 20 Russian Bofors-type 37-mm AA guns to create a 'flak envelope' around the French positions in the valley. Consequently, the transport planes involved in the air drops were forced to release their cargoes from altitudes of over 8,000 feet in order to avoid the fire of the Vietminh guns. Naturally there was a great wastage of essential supplies, and the rebel position grew correspondingly stronger.

French attempts to interdict the supply trails of the Vietminh by aerial bombardment were met by flak concentrations comparable to that encountered during World War II by Allied bombers over the Ruhr.

On 7 May Dien Bien Phu was taken by storm. In the course of the siege the Vietminh artillery had fired 100,000 shells. The French, in planning the operation, had overlooked the possibility of the Vietminh seriously challenging their air and artillery supremacy. This was a grievous error. In the end the Vietminh gunners broke the back of the defence, turned the supply effort into a shambles and prevented the French from disrupting their own supply lines. Their efforts thus made a significant contribution to one of the decisive battles of our era.

Tube Artillery since World War II

Conventional artillery has undoubtedly forfeited some of its functions to rockets and missiles, but it is clear from recent experience that missile weapons have by no means superseded guns. In fact, conventional artillery seems to have experienced something of a resurgence in recent years, while missiles have become less faddish. This trend is strongly indicated in several ways. One has been the continuing emphasis on conventional guns in the armed forces of the Soviet Union. It is now estimated that one-third of the Soviet ground army consists of artillery, and most of the weapons of this arm are conventional tube artillery. Another pointer was provided by the vast programme for modernizing its conventional weapons that was carried out by the US Army during the Kennedy administration. A major target of this programme, which cost $1,800,000,000, was the artillery.

This revival of conventional artillery must not be seen as indicative of a retreat from technology. It is, rather, an admission that, if we are all to survive, some way must be found to meet a variety of threats to world peace. The Communist Bloc, for example, has maintained large conventionally equipped ground forces at peak efficiency

BELOW LEFT *An early parachute drop falls inside the perimeter.*
BOTTOM LEFT *Jungle fires burn beside the vulnerable airstrip.*
BELOW *Tending the wounded in the garrison; their commander, comprehensively outmanoeuvred, had already committed suicide.*

throughout the post-war decades. In 1961, at the height of the Berlin crisis, it was discovered that the AP (armour-piercing) ammunition issued to American units was not capable of penetrating the armour of the newer Soviet tanks. Had the Soviets made a thrust into central Europe at that time, there would have been no way of stopping them short of using nuclear weapons—a move which would undoubtedly have plunged the world into the nightmare of total war. As a consequence of this scare, the USA modernized its conventional ground forces; in 1962 the ROAD Division, an infantry division with significantly more conventional firepower, was created as the basic operational unit of the US Army.

The Korean War was fought mainly with conventional artillery of World War II vintage, which was not suited to the requirements of modern warfare. Soon after the Korean War the NATO nations began to produce radically advanced SP support guns. Most of these new weapons have fully enclosed fighting compartments with all-round traverse. Some of them incorporate defence systems against ABC (atomic, bacteriological and chemical) weapons. Such systems will allow the crew to operate the gun in relative safety on the 'deserted battlefields' of the future. NATO

ABOVE *North Vietnamese coastal batteries point seawards, manned by soldiers of the People's Army.*
LEFT *A US Marine at Conthien fires an 81-mm mortar on a North Vietnamese position.*

SP guns, with the exception of the German Jagdpanzer 90-mm tank-hunter, follow the traditional emphasis of the Western Allies on the support, rather than the assault, role.

The Soviets have never really strayed very far from conventional artillery, even in more recent times. In fact, the development and production of new conventional guns to replace the USSR's elderly World War II armoury was proceeding as that war ended, and was to continue for at least a decade. The first objectives of the renewal programme were the anti-tank and anti-aircraft guns. Two very powerful anti-tank guns had been developed too late to see much

BELOW AND OPPOSITE *Vietnam – the men and the guns of Fire Base Carroll bombard the unseen foe.*

action in the war. These were the M-1944 100-mm field gun, which was used as a heavy AT gun at corps level, and the D-44 85-mm divisional gun. The D-44 remained the standard divisional piece until 1955, but the M-1945 85-mm AT gun soon replaced it as the divisional AT gun. The M-1945 85-mm AT gun was a very advanced design with an auxiliary engine and a trail-mounted castor wheel which allowed it to move under its own power when un-limbered. The new AA guns were the M-1949 100-mm AA gun, which replaced the 85-mm AA gun of World War II, and the M-1955 122-mm AA gun. With these guns, the Soviets began to use off-carriage radar and directors, thus serving notice on the other Powers that their technology was much improved. Indeed, there is evidence that the Soviet-built 37-mm light flak guns used by the Vietminh at Dien Bien Phu incorporated radar range-finders.

In 1955 the Soviets further renewed their artillery with advanced models of several familiar calibres. The M-1955 203-mm gun-howitzer was the first modern Soviet heavy gun since 1940. It replaced several obsolescent pieces, including the M-1935 152-mm gun, the M-1931 203-mm howitzer and the M-1939 280-mm howitzer. The new gun was similar to the US 8-inch howitzer and was thought to have an atomic-shell capability.

In the design of their new guns, the Soviets have incor-porated all the virtues of their wartime family of guns—mobility, firepower, simplicity and standardization. The artillery doctrine of World War II seems also to have been retained to a large extent, and artillery is still regarded as the main strike force. Anti-tank and assault guns remain the most prominent battlefield types, although lately the USSR has been building more SP support guns.

This new emphasis on SP support guns may indicate that the Soviets are trying to close the gap between their artillery and that of the Western Powers. Soviet heavy artillery—unlike the other types we have looked at—has never been very mobile or very flexible. This was of very little consequence in World War II because, from 1943 anyway, the Soviet Air Force controlled the air space above the guns and prevented destructive strikes by the Luftwaffe.

The Arab-Israeli War of 1967 revealed, however, the flaw in Soviet doctrine. The Army of the UAR was equipped with Soviet tanks and guns and followed Soviet tactical doctrine. The Israeli Army was equipped with American, British and French tanks and guns. Most Israeli guns were SP support guns, including some heavy types on Israeli-designed mounts. These guns acted in support of Israeli armour but did not operate directly behind the tanks. The technique used was one developed by the British during the fighting in the Western Desert in World War II. The SPs followed the tanks but stayed beyond the range of the enemy's tank and anti-tank guns. Thus, they could operate in relative safety and, by using indirect fire, provide artillery support for the armour. With this method, too, the limited traverse of SP artillery may be utilized to best advantage. Arab heavy artillery, on the other hand, was towed to a fixed position and, more often than not, remained there after Israeli armour had bypassed it or the Israeli Air Force had bombed and strafed the position. It was soon evident that Soviet-built heavy guns simply could not function effectively on a modern battlefield.

Rocket Artillery

Rocket artillery became very fashionable after World War II. Strong precedents had been set by Germany's success with the Nebelwerfer series of area-fire weapons and Maultier SP rocket launchers; by Russia's use of powerful batteries of Katyusha multiple-tube launchers, and by the devastating effect of Allied rocket bombardments in amphibious operations. The development of area-fire batteries continued after the war, and a relatively new type of rocket weapon, the guided missile, was intensively developed for a variety of field and long-range bombard-ment roles. The main types produced for land warfare are as follows:

Surface-to-surface. This is a comprehensive category which includes rocket weapons as diverse as mammoth ICBMs (intercontinental ballistic missiles) and the Davy Crockett, a diminutive rocket which can deliver a low-yield atomic shell over a distance of two miles yet may be launched from a tripod or light vehicle.

Free rockets (unguided) fired from multiple-tube rocket launchers continued to be the most prevalent form of rocket artillery in the Soviet Army during the post-war years. The M-13 Katyusha was replaced by a variety of similar weapons from the M13-14 140-mm rocket launcher to the M-31 300-mm launcher. These area-fire weapons were considered adequate for Soviet needs at the time but they had certain inherent limitations which would probably preclude their appearance on any modern battlefield—although the Katyusha was used by Communist forces in Korea and Indo-China. They were simple, mobile batteries with very little recoil, but they gave off a prominent back-

blast when fired and had to be used in masses, since the rockets were inaccurate and erratic in flight.

By 1960 the Soviets had developed the FROG (free rocket over-ground) series which corresponded roughly to the first generation of US tactical rockets. In this area the Soviets (still limited by primitive technology) were far behind the Americans, who had developed operational tactical missiles, both guided and free, by the early 1950s.

US guided missile research in World War II was exten-sive. Two simple operational missiles, the Bat air-to-ship missile and the Azon air-to-ground guided bomb, were developed and used successfully in combat. These missiles were the ancestors of the 'smart bombs' used in Vietnam. Their guidance systems and control apparatuses have sub-sequently been refined, and these and other projects formed

TITAN II LAUNCH

OPPOSITE *A V-1 flying bomb, ancestor of today's rocket artillery, photographed immediately after being launched.*
ABOVE *A US tactical rocket, Honest John (range 24 miles), is fired during manoeuvres in West Germany in 1955.*
LEFT *The Titan II, a US two-stage Inter Continental Ballistic Missile (ICBM), maximum range 6,300 miles, rears from its launch pad at the USAF Missile Test Center at Cape Kennedy.*

the basis for continuing programmes of post-war research.

The US Army's first combat-ready guided missile for ground support was the Corporal (1953). The Corporal was soon followed by a series of tactical and strategic rockets. The Davy Crockett, mentioned above, was a close-support rocket with a range of two miles, comparable to that of the 81-mm and 4·2-inch mortars. Little John (range 12½ miles) and Honest John (range 24 miles) were conceived as tactical rockets roughly comparable in range to the divisional and heavy artillery then in service. The first US long-range (strategic) missile was the experimental Redstone, which was a copy of the German V-2 of World

Wire-guided and
infra-red missiles
for anti-tank work;
anti-aircraft
rockets since World
War II.

War II (as was the Soviet T-1). The operational strategic missiles included the Serjeant (range 75+ miles) and the Pershing (range 400+ miles).

Any one of these rockets can deliver a heavier and more destructive conventional projectile than comparable tube artillery weapons, while there is of course no gun with a range even close to that attained by the Pershing's warhead. But these missiles are something less than accurate; nevertheless, nuclear shells fired from conventional artillery, though lighter, are sufficiently powerful more than to offset the disparity in weight of the projectiles.

Anti-tank rockets. A great variety of anti-tank rockets has been developed in recent years. Simple infantry projectors, like the Panzerfaust and its derivatives, or the bazooka, are not strictly speaking artillery, but both they and the larger AT missiles utilize a HEAT shaped-charge projectile to 'kill' a tank (HEAT=high explosive anti-tank). These projectiles are best delivered by smooth-bore guns or rockets, since the spin imparted by a gun's rifling tends to dissipate the effect of the jet by dispersing it upon impact.

Anti-tank rockets are quite deadly – one hit usually puts a tank out of action – but they suffer from the usual rocket-weapon handicaps, including low velocity and low acceleration, both of which allow the target time to manoeuvre and so reduce the chances of scoring a hit.

Most AT missiles are wire-guided, that is, controlled by the gunner after firing by means of electronic impulses sent along fine wires played out by the rocket in flight. In effect, the gunner 'steers' the rocket onto the target. This is by no means a foolproof system, and there are ongoing experiments with infra-red, laser and computer guidance systems. The best recent developments are the 152-mm Shillelagh 'sure-kill' missile, which follows an infra-red beam to its target, and the TOW (a tube-launched, optically tracked, wire-guided AT missile). The TOW missile will hit its target so long as the gunner keeps the launching tube's telescopic sight focused on it.

Anti-aircraft rockets. The British made some limited use of AA rockets during World War II, and the Germans were in production with their Luftfaust, a multiple-tube hand-held rocket-launcher, at the war's end. These early AA missiles were in fact relatively unsophisticated barrage-fire weapons.

Modern AA missiles utilize various types of guidance systems. Nearly all have electronic 'brains' and 'eyes' which perform a variety of functions. The earliest sophisticated AA missiles, like the Nike (operational in 1954), were 'beam riders' which followed a radar beam to their targets. Nike, and its successors, Nike Ajax and Nike-B, intercept at twice the speed of sound and have a slant range of 18–23 miles. These missiles were designed to intercept high-flying strategic bombers and have been installed in permanent

Missiles for defence
against high-flying
strategic bombers
and low-flying
tactical aircraft.

emplacements near US cities and industrial areas. But today ICBMs and IRBMs (intermediate-range ballistic missiles) constitute the most important long-range bombardment threat. Nike cannot intercept these missiles. Surface-to-air missile research today concentrates on developing an ABM (anti-ballistic missile) which could intercept an ICBM.

Nike has proved adequate for defence against strategic bombers, but other SAMs are needed to intercept tactical aircraft. Most missiles used against low-flying aircraft have homing devices which react to signals sent out by the target aircraft. The sensor device is usually a radar set or a photo-electric eye sensitive to heat. Some of the US missiles in this category are Hawk and Chaparral. In the Arab-Israeli War of 1973, the Egyptians took a heavy initial toll of Israeli aircraft with their Russian-built SAMs, mostly of the SAM-6 variety; these seriously inhibited the Israelis' tactical strike effort until the missile sites were overrun.

strike effort until such time as the missile sites were overrun and the danger removed.

From this brief account it will be evident that rocket development has already reached a point at which there are rockets capable of fulfilling all the functions of conventional tube artillery. This has led some to predict that missile artillery will eventually replace conventional forms. The school of experience, however, has taught the necessity of maintaining a balance in the field, and the predicted obsolescence of cannon has so far not come to pass.

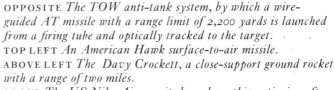

OPPOSITE *The TOW anti-tank system, by which a wire-guided AT missile with a range limit of 2,200 yards is launched from a firing tube and optically tracked to the target.*
TOP LEFT *An American Hawk surface-to-air missile.*
ABOVE LEFT *The Davy Crockett, a close-support ground rocket with a range of two miles.*
ABOVE *The US Nike Ajax on its launcher; this anti-aircraft rocket, now superseded by the Nike Hercules, was designed to intercept high-flying strategic bombers.*

399

23

NEW FIGHTING SHIPS

After 1945 the US Navy ranks as the world's largest naval force.

At the end of World War II there were, in effect, only two navies – those of the United States and Great Britain and her Empire. The navies of their enemies had, for the most part, ceased to exist and those of other nations were of little account. The Soviet Navy was quite strong on paper, for it disposed of one battleship, a couple of cruisers, some 20 destroyers and over 100 submarines. But in fact it was very weak. Its performance during the war had not been impressive, its training was of a low standard and its equipment obsolescent. Much of its manpower had been lost in the course of the land fighting on the Eastern Front. Added to this was the fact that the fleet had to be divided among all the seas that wash the Soviet Union.

The US Navy emerged from the war as the world's largest naval force. The Royal Navy was dwarfed in comparison yet it it was the only navy that could be realistically assessed against the American fleets. With over 3,600 named vessels, of which 23 were battleships, 20 were fleet carriers, eight were light carriers and 71 were escort carriers, the US Navy was more powerful than all the other navies of the world combined. In addition to this already overwhelming strength, American yards were building a further 21 carriers, all but two of which were fleet carriers. US naval aviation boasted 40,000 aircraft with more than 60,000 qualified pilots. By comparison, the Royal Navy possessed seven fleet carriers, five light carriers, 38 escort carriers and over 1,300 aircraft – still an extremely powerful force but one that now had to face the harsh realities of peacetime. One unpalatable truth was that an impoverished Britain, committed to a much-needed programme of post-war reform and reconstruction, could no longer afford to build and maintain a powerful fleet. Another arose from the simple fact that 34 escort carriers and over two-thirds of the aircraft – including most of the high-performance aircraft – had been supplied by and had to be returned to the United States.

Immediately after the war the American and the British fleets entered a period of decline. The immediate reduction of government spending was bound to affect the Navies and for a time new construction was halted and ships were paid off. Neither the onset of the Cold War nor the build-up of the Soviet Navy redeemed the fortunes of the Western navies, for at the time there was no real naval threat from the Soviet Union. The US Navy also failed to secure for itself a nuclear role. It wanted to have nuclear weapons for its carriers, but it lost its case to the newly-formed US Air Force, which in the B-36 had an effective long-range bomber that could penetrate Soviet air space. After the war, with no other nation possessing the atomic bomb and the United States in possession of a massive strategic bombing force, there was no real need for the Americans to have several different means of delivering the deterrent. It is therefore hardly surprising that the US Navy failed

OPPOSITE *The US guided-missile cruiser* Albany *fires three surface-to-air test missiles simultaneously from forward, aft and one side of the ship.*
BELOW *After the Bomb – the USS* New York *is hosed down after the second atomic bomb test at Bikini, September 1946. This was done to wash away radio-active material before an inspection party was sent aboard to test how the ship had withstood the blast.*

Russia begins her
naval build-up as
the Cold War
sets in.

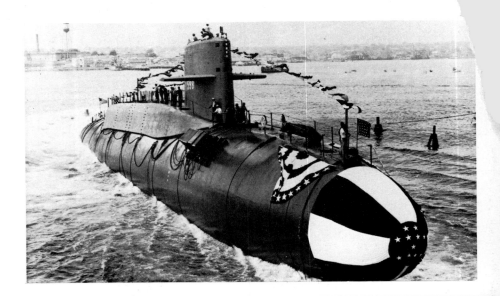

OPPOSITE *A Polaris missile breaks the ocean surface after being fired from the submerged HMS* Revenge.
BELOW RIGHT *HMS* Revenge, *seen on exercise in 1970.*
RIGHT *The launching of the George Washington, which in 1960 became the first submarine to fire a missile from beneath the surface of the sea. At that period she was armed with 16 Polaris missiles: these had a single warhead and range of 1,500 miles. Since then the Poseidon missile has entered service: each of these contains ten 50-kiloton warheads. Accuracy has been improved and range increased to 2,875 miles.*

Seen here is a cutaway of the USS George Washington (1959) the first submarine to fire a missile from beneath the surface of the sea.

1 Engine room	*13 Crew's mess*
2 Reactor room	*14 Officers' wardroom*
3 Missile room	*15 Forward torpedo room*
4 Missile control centre	
5 Navigation room	
6 Gyro room	
7 Stores	
8 Batteries	
9 Bridge	
10 Periscope room	
11 Control room	
12 Crew's quarters	

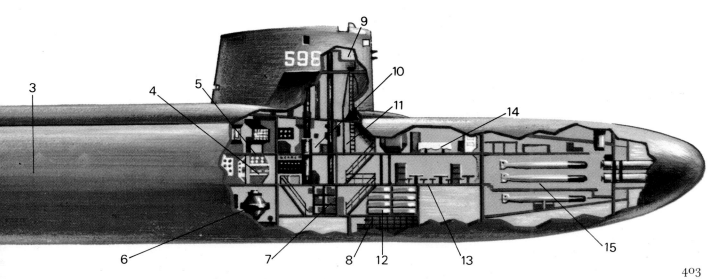

Demonstrations of US naval
striking power.
LEFT *The USS* Forrestal, *seen on
manoeuvres with the Sixth Fleet.
The broad white line running
diagonally across the flight deck is
used by the pilots of landing aircraft
to correct their angle of approach.
Both take-offs and landings can be
handled simultaneously from the
Forrestal's massive flight deck;
overall length of the ship is
1,039 feet.*
TOP *A salvo from the 16-inch guns
of the USS* Missouri, *in action at
Chong Jin, Korea.*

ABOVE *The US nuclear fleet
displays Einstein's famous equation
during Exercise Sea Orbit. The
ships are the carrier* Enterprise, *the*
Long Beach *and the* Bainbridge.

to win the argument. Later, by 1950, the US Navy had been reduced in strength to seven fleet carriers.

The outbreak of the Korean War in 1950 restored the fortunes of the US Navy. The need for naval strength in helping to fight 'limited wars' and the great flexibility bestowed by carriers were clearly shown. By the end of the war the US Navy had 18 carriers in commission of which 11 saw action. The air strength they provided was extremely important in securing air supremacy, supporting land operations and maintaining a blockade of the North Korean coast. Battleships and cruisers, fitted with radar-controlled guns, also played a vital part in giving gun support and covering invasions and evacuations. The possibility of further Koreas ensured that after the war the US Navy would not have her conventional forces run down as they had been after 1945. On the other hand, by 1953 the Soviet Union had obtained a thermo-nuclear capability and was improving her air defences. The

Americans now saw, despite the impending arrival of highly advanced B-52 bomber to replace the B-36, there was a need for more delivery systems. Thus US Navy was ensured a nuclear role through its carrie and its new submarines.

The new carriers that were built owed much to Britis development, for the Royal Navy was not deficient in technique, only in numbers. In 1952 trials were conducted with an angled flight-deck on HMS *Triumph*. This arrangement allowed the storage of aircraft on the flight-deck and the landing and dispatching of aircraft to be conducted at the same time; this had been impossible with

OPPOSITE *A Soviet-built Egyptian submarine of the W class.*
BELOW *The scene on the flight deck of the commando carrier HMS* Albion. *Helicopters have a growing role to play as reconnaissance machines and as interceptors armed with air-to-ship missiles. With the advent of more sophisticated 'listening' devices, the helicopter is also an effective submarine hunter/killer.*

The US Navy's nuclear role; its new generation of carriers and submarines.

the ordinary flight-deck because of the danger of a landing aircraft overshooting. At the same time, too, the standard hydro-pneumatic catapults were replaced by more powerful steam versions, and flight-deck mirrors were incorporated to aid landings (a system first proposed by the Japanese in the 1920s). These British-developed features were worked into USS *Forrestal*, which Congress authorized in 1951. This ship, displacing over 60,000 tons, was the first American ship too large to use the Panama Canal. The longer landings and take-offs needed by jets, as compared to earlier aircraft, meant that she was over 1,000 feet long; her maximum beam, 152 feet, incorporated deck-edge lifts and an overhanging bridge.

The *Forrestal* was followed by the *Enterprise*, the first, and to date the only nuclear-powered carrier in commission. Research and development costs incurred during her construction left the American taxpayer with a bill for $451,000,000; and the increasing costs of reactors, materials and labour mean that the nuclear carriers being built in the USA at the present time will cost much more. The *Nimitz* (CVAN-68) will cost about $540,000,000 and the *Eisenhower* (CVAN-69) about $510,000,000; the unnamed CVAN-70, due to be started in 1974, is likely to cost more than $1,000,000,000 and her aircraft more than the *Nimitz* herself.

The *Enterprise* has proved a considerable technical and

operational success. The lack of a funnel eliminated corrosion and turbulence whilst her unique power source gives her immense flexibility and virtually unlimited high-speed endurance. On her original uranium cores she steamed more than 200,000 miles; on one cruise, Exercise Sea Orbit, she steamed 30,565 miles in 65 days without resupply of any kind. She made five Vietnam tours; during one tour, in December 1965, a record number of air strikes in a single day (165) flew from her decks. Her immunity from attack contrasted strongly with the vulnerability of aircraft in bases in the south to Vietcong and North Vietnamese Army rocket attack.

Nuclear power was incorporated into American submarines slightly before it was used in the *Enterprise*. It was used not in the weapons but in the power source; thus the first application of nuclear power was aimed at improving the submarine's performance (rather than changing its role). The result was more or less the true submarine – a craft designed to operate completely submerged for an indefinite period. The first nuclear submarine, USS *Nautilus*, was commissioned in January 1955. Displacing 3,180 tons, she had a submerged speed of 20 knots and auxiliary electric motors. She was armed with conventional

torpedoes but the following year the first submarine designed to carry nuclear missiles, the *Halibut*, was laid down. She was equipped with three Regulus missiles that could be fired only when the submarine was surfaced. This weakness was remedied in July 1960 when the *George Washington*, which was armed with 16 Polaris missiles,

OPPOSITE *The first launching of a Polaris missile from a surfaced vessel, the US nuclear-powered submarine* Henry Clay. *The debris is from the launch adaptors, which automatically detach themselves on launching. The slight list of the submarine is intentional, being a standard part of surfaced launch procedure.*
RIGHT *Soviet rendezvous during naval manoeuvres between a submarine and a helicopter.*
BELOW *A Russian submarine taking part in a naval parade; this vessel is equipped to fire underwater-to-surface and surface-to-surface missiles.*
BOTTOM *Soviet J-class submarine.*

became the first submarine to fire a missile from beneath the surface of the sea.

The early Polaris missiles carried a single warhead and had a 1,500-mile range; since then both power and range have been increased. In 1964 the UGM-27C missile was first deployed. This missile carried a single 1-megaton warhead over 2,800 miles; subsequently the payload was converted into three smaller warheads. In 1971 the Poseidon UGM-73A missile entered service. This missile has a MIRV[1] capability with ten 50 kiloton warheads per missile – an arrangement that, combined with improvements in target accuracy, makes the Poseidon submarine many times more powerful than the Polaris craft. The US Navy has programmes for 31 Poseidon-carrying submarines with a total of 4,960 warheads.

After World War II the Soviet Union built up a numerically powerful fleet. The emphasis was placed on submarines and coastal craft to protect the flanks of the Red Army and to counter any Western amphibious attack. (The fleet's independent long-range capacity was limited – just a few cruisers, designed for commerce-raiding.) Soviet submarine strength probably rose to a peak of about 400; from that point Soviet policy seems to have concentrated on replacing older types by new, long-range submarines.

The development of a nuclear-powered submarine armed with nuclear missiles gave the Soviet Union the opportunity to possess for the first time a credible deterrent against the United States. Whereas the Americans saw the submarine as an alternative delivery system to their aircraft and land-based missiles, the Soviets in the late 1950s and early '60s saw the submarine as *the* means of delivery, for at that time they lacked long-range bombers and their missiles could only be effective against Western Europe.

[1] The abbreviation MIRV stands for multiple independently-targetable re-entry vehicle(s).

Submarine weaponry
The diagram illustrates, in ideal form, how versatile submarines could become in the near future. The operational system shown here was devised by Vickers Ltd, and revolves around the SLAM (Submarine Launched Airflight Missile); a photograph of the missile system is at far right. The six Blowpipe missiles have a range of two miles.

The submarine, by carrying the short-ranged missiles to within range of the American coasts, provided the first means of striking at the United States homeland. Since 1958 the Soviets have deployed submarines carrying nuclear weapons, but initially these were conventional diesel craft that had to surface to fire their few, short-

...ed missiles. These *G* and *H* class submarines, 24 of ...ch are still operational, carried the SSN-4 Sark and ...N-5 Serb missiles in threes. During the 1960s the Soviets ...veloped the SSN-6 Sawfly missile, which had a 1-mega-...n warhead and a 1,750-mile range; they also built ...uclear-powered submarines carrying 16 missiles.

Thus the two Superpowers have built up through their nuclear submarines powerful deterrents that are reasonably cheap, extremely flexible and, for the moment, invulnerable. The importance of the submarine has increased and the power of the bomber, even when equipped with stand-off weapons, has declined as air-defence systems have improved. Up to the present time the submarine has been able to keep ahead of anti-submarine techniques; moreover, submarines and missiles of greatly improved capability are being developed. This is being done partly through fear that some anti-submarine breakthrough may also be achieved in the near future, and partly as a means of trying to keep ahead of the enemy, if only to provide diplomatic 'chips' for future arms limitation talks.

At the moment only small parts of the world's oceans are suited to a nuclear submarine on patrol, for the submarine is limited by the range of its missiles and the depth to which it can dive. It is possible, too, that detection could

Submarines remain one jump ahead of anti-submarine devices, but are limited by their diving capability and the range of their missiles.

LEFT *Shown here is a Sea Cat missile on demonstration in the Baltic with the Swedish ship* Sodermanland. *The British-built Sea Cat is in service with more than a dozen navies; it has a range of 2·2 miles. In an anti-aircraft role these missiles can be deployed in seconds against low flying fighters.*

At the heart of this submarine is a computerized data system that displays the tactical picture to the onboard command. Decisions can then be taken whether or not to fire:
1 *Anti-ship or anti-submarine torpedoes.*
2 *Blowpipe missiles from the SLAM system, for short-range use against hostile ships or helicopters.*
3 *USGWs, for use against enemy warships.*

ABOVE *The British destroyer HMS* Devonshire *fires a Sea Slug missile on trials off the Scottish coast. The Sea Slug is 20 feet long and can be used against both surface and air targets.*

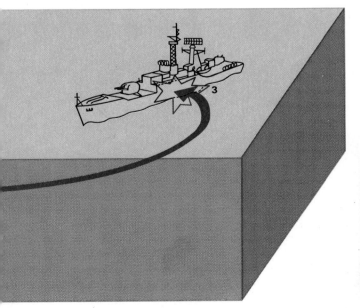

New weapons for conventional submarines: the Under Surface Guided Weapon (USGW), M-48 torpedo, and Submarine Launched Airflight Missile (SLAM).

reach a point at which submarines could be tracked through such measures as sonar positioned on the seabed or dipped from surface craft. For the time being this seems either unlikely or at least a long-term prospect. However, deeper-diving submarines armed with longer-ranged missiles would make the task of tracking much harder. In response to this notion the Soviet Union has developed new missiles with ranges of up to 3,500 miles, which will be carried in the latest Y class submarine. The US Navy's plans include a new submarine and new missiles. The new missile is the Trident-1 (C-4) which is a boosted Poseidon with a 4,350-mile range; this should be deployed in 1978. The subsequent Trident-2 is to have a 6,000-mile range. From their base at Bangor, Washington State, submarines carrying this missile would be within range of any worthwhile target anywhere in China and the USSR without even leaving harbour. The submarines would displace at least 12,000 tons and would carry a minimum of 20, perhaps as many as 24 missiles. The cost per submarine would be in the region of $1,300,000,000 – a price thought excessive by some observers given the Americans' other means of delivery.

It is hardly surprising that, with so much emphasis and money placed on the nuclear submarine and its missiles, the conventional submarine and its armament should to some extent have been neglected. That the latter have become the Cinderellas of their fleets is demonstrated, for example, by the fact that the Royal Navy's submarines are still equipped with a torpedo designed before 1939. But in the last few years developments have considerably increased the power of the conventional submarine. Possibly the most important, certainly the most spectacular of these is the Under Surface Guided Weapon (USGW). This weapon will allow the submarine to attack a searching enemy warship beyond the increasing range of anti-submarine weapon systems. Able to operate from 21-inch torpedo tubes, the USGW breaks the surface and, travelling through the air, homes on the enemy ship. It may also be possible for future USGWs to re-enter the water to attack a submarine.

Another major development is the M-48 torpedo that entered service with the US Navy in February 1972. This weapon, which has a half-hour range at 50 knots, is designed for action against either surface or submerged craft. Its maximum depth is 3,000 feet and it can be wire-guided until its own homing device picks up its target. Finally, there is the Submarine Launched Airflight Missile (SLAM), which is being developed by the Royal Navy; trials were carried out in 1972. The system features an armament of six Blowpipe missiles built around a camera and infra-red sensor. The Blowpipe, which is a thumb-operated, one-man anti-aircraft missile originally built for land forces, has a range of two miles and a five-pound warhead. Such a weapon could be extremely useful in counter-attacking an enemy helicopter.

The increasing sophistication of weapons and the growing cost of ships has led in the last ten years to the navies of the lesser powers being all but priced out of existence. In the present climate of rising costs and increasing complexity, only the Soviet Union and the United States can afford new weapon systems – and even

OPPOSITE *An aerial view of the flight deck of HMS* Ark Royal.
TOP *Trials in 1970 of the British Harrier V/Stol (Vertical take-off and landing) aircraft.*
ABOVE *Crew members of the* Forrestal *transfer a Navy Skyhawk jet to the flight deck via the deck-edge elevator.*
BELOW *An artist's impression of the Royal Navy's latest ship type, the Through Deck Cruiser; she will act as a small-scale carrier, equipped with Sea King helicopters and a version of the Harrier.*

The Soviets build their first carriers; Western navies invest in smaller specialized ships; the gun/missile balance.

these nations are beginning to feel the strain. At the present moment the US Navy still retains a considerable superiority over the Soviet Navy. The former can always have more nuclear submarines on station at any one time and can use them to better effect than the Soviets, who lack overseas bases and are still handicapped by their long tail of old submarines and missiles. Moreover, American carrier strength, usually decried by the Soviets as obsolescent, gives the West an overwhelming advantage over the Soviets, who lack an integrated naval air defence.

To try to offset American air supremacy, the Soviets are working on their first carriers. No details have been announced but space surveillance suggests that the first will be about 40,000 tons and over 900 feet long. Although she will have an angled flight-deck, it seems unlikely that she will carry either catapults or a full-length flight-deck; the forecastle will carry missiles and AA guns. It seems probable that she will be equipped with fixed-wing aircraft – but she could conceivably be a commando carrier, equipped to carry amphibious troops.

The building of a carrier by the USSR has coincided with the decline of the carrier in the British Navy. Rising costs and the increasing problem of manning the fleet since the abolition of national service have resulted in the passing of all the fleet carriers but one. She, the *Ark Royal*, was also to have been phased out by 1972, but a change of government brought about a stay of execution. This, however, can be no more than a temporary measure.

To replace her the Royal Navy has ordered HMS *Invincible*, the first of what should be a new type of ship, the Through Deck Cruiser. This ship is designed to be a command and control unit as much as a ship that can give an integrated recce, strike and air-defence capability. In essence the cruisers will be mini-carriers that displace about 20,000 tons. Sea Dart missiles will provide a surface-to-surface and a surface-to-air capability with Sea King helicopters, equipped with their own sonar and weapons, acting in an anti-submarine role. It is believed, indeed there would be little point in building such ships unless it were so, that the Through Deck Carrier will carry a version of the Harrier V/STOL (Vertical/short take-off and landing). The ship, 630 feet long, should have a top speed of about 30 knots with gas turbines and would cost about £30,000,000. Obviously more than one needs to be built if such ships are to play any important role in the fleet.

The reliance of the Western navies upon the aircraft for attack purposes, combined with the high cost of ships and armaments, has led over the last 20 years to specialization on the part of the smaller ships. Ships have tended to concentrate primarily on either an ASW or an AA role, almost to the exclusion of the other capability.

It seems likely that in future ships will have to carry, either internally or through a helicopter, an anti-ship weapons system. In 1967 the Israeli destroyer *Eilat* was sunk by a Soviet-built fast patrol boat that never left harbour. The heavily gunned destroyer, taken by surprise, was sunk by SSN-2 Styx missiles. This event intensified a search for equivalent weapons in the Western navies. At the moment Norway, Sweden, Israel and the United States have ship-to-ship missiles in service whilst the French are developing the Exocet missile by themselves and the Otomat missile in conjunction with the Italians. The latter has a 40-mile range and will need a relay if it is to be used to its full potential, i.e. against targets beyond the horizon line.

The helicopter offers a means of intercepting an attacking patrol boat before it closes to decisive range. The Royal Navy has developed the CI-834 missile for use in the Anglo–French Lynx helicopter in order to achieve this. The Italians have also developed an air-to-ship missile, the Airtos. This weapon has a 7-mile range at a speed of up to Mach 2; target acquisition – the point at which the weapon sees and locks on to a target – is at 10 miles. The weapon is supposed to be effective against targets moving at speeds of up to 90 knots – a performance that will probably be needed if interceptions are to be made against future hydrofoils and fast patrol boats.

The British have several missiles with a ship-to-ship capability but, for the most part, these weapons are primarily ship-to-air missiles. The Italians have, for their anti-aircraft protection, modifications of either the Indigo or the Albatros missiles. The Indigo was originally land-based and has a ceiling of 6,000 metres and a slant range of 6·25 miles. The Albatros uses air-to-air missiles against missiles and aircraft.

The rapid development of missiles has not, to date, led to the suppression of the gun. Indeed, the majority of ships in service still retain guns and it is likely that this situation will persist for some time. The gun still has several very important advantages over the missile, not least its cheapness. In addition, its robustness, its high rate of fire and its ability to engage air, sea and land targets at horizon range (approx. 16 miles) still make it an extremely attractive weapon. The largest naval guns are the nine 16-inch guns of the battleship *New Jersey*, which were used in coastal operations off South Vietnam (the cost of recommissioning this ship for active service was approximately $21,000,000). The latest French gun, the 100-mm, is fully automatic and can fire 60 rounds a minute. Smaller anti-aircraft weapons are used for close-range defence.

The shift in the balance between missile and gun since the end of World War II has been matched by a shift in the overall balance of power, the most obvious features of which have been the relative decline of the European powers and the emergence of the Soviet Navy as an oceanic force capable of securing local command of the sea and also of contesting the West's general superiority. Nevertheless, even without the United States NATO outnumbers those naval forces that the Soviets could deploy against it, while the level of serviceability maintained by the European powers is generally higher than that of the Soviets and Americans.

The West's margin of naval superiority, so overwhelming in 1945, remains undisputed in one vital respect – the integrated air arm of the US Navy; and this is likely to remain the case for some time. In other fields the Soviet challenge has been more strongly made; the results of this can clearly be seen in our concluding table.

OPPOSITE *A Russian fast patrol boat, one of a compact class of vessels used to deliver anti-ship missiles of the SSN-2 Styx type, which have a range of 29 miles.*

The Balance of Naval Power 1973–74

Although the seven nations listed differ in the way they interpret the functions of their ships, most of the major differences are accounted for in the footnotes. In addition, American strengths do not include the US Marine Corps, while Soviet figures include the Naval Air Force and Naval Infantry. Air strengths, where appropriate, embrace all types of aircraft, including helicopters. The US Navy's reserve strength is given in parentheses.

The high Soviet and Chinese totals for coastal defence craft, etc., and landing ships and craft are reached partly through including ships of small size not incorporated in Western naval lists. China has one submarine with missile tubes, but it is not known whether it has any missiles. The US Navy possesses many more mine warfare ships than the 92 major units indicated.

CATEGORY	USA	USSR	GB	FRANCE	CHINA	S VIETNAM	JAPAN
Manpower in 000s	564 (131)	475	81	69	180	45	41
Surface ships in commission	221 (54)	212	78	47	n/a	n/a	n/a
Nuclear submarines of all types	60	65	8	4	1 (?)	—	—
Other submarines	24 (8)	220	22	19	48	—	13
Aircraft (S=squadrons, AT=all types, CA=combat aircraft)	163 (70)S	1,160AT	17S	15S	n/a	n/a	110CA
Battleships	(4)	—	—	—	—	—	—
Attack aircraft carriers	15 (6)	—	1	2	—	—	—
Other aircraft carriers	—	—	2	1[g]	—	—	—
SAM cruisers	8 (2)	—	2	2[h]	—	—	—
Other types of cruiser	1 (12)	32[a]	—	—	—	—	—
SAM frigates	28	—	—	—	—	—	—
Other types of frigates	(2)	—	62[f]	25	—	9	—
SAM destroyers	29	32[b]	9	6	—	—	1
Other types of destroyer	71 (43)	44[c]	—	11	6[i]	—	28
SAM destroyer-escorts	6	—	—	—	—	—	—
Other destroyer escorts	62 (33)	269[d]	—	—	9	—	14
Amphibious warfare ships inc. landing ships and craft	65 (74)	233	2	20	570[j]	40	53
Various types of mine warfare craft	10 (82)	295	44	46	72	2	45
Logistics and operations support craft	150 (75)	n/a	56	12	n/a	n/a	n/a
Coastal defence, Fast Patrol Boats and torpedo boats	n/a	327[e]	11	14	596	55	5
Riverine craft	—	—	—	—	—	800	—
Diesel junks	—	—	—	—	—	250	—

Australia, India, Argentina and Brazil are the only other nations to have aircraft carriers, that of Brazil being ASW. All are ex-British Navy carriers (that of Argentina reaching her via the Royal Netherlands Navy), and are of less than 20,000 tons fully laden with no more than 20 aircraft. Like the British carriers listed, all were laid down during World War II and must now be approaching the end of their active lives.

[a] Of which 2 ASW helicopter, 14 gunned and 16 with SSM and SAM capabilities. [b] Four have SSM also. [c] Of which 7 have SSM. [d] Oceanic and coastal. [e] Of which 187 carry Styx SSM. [f] Of which 20 ASW. [g] Helicopter carrier. [h] Including 1 helicopter cruiser. [i] All SSM. [j] Of which 25 carry Styx SSM.

Key to Abbreviations

SAM	Surface-to-air missiles
ASW	Anti-submarine warfare
SSM	Surface-to-surface missiles

24

AIR POWER TODAY

Early jet types; influence of German wartime research on post-war designs.

In the aftermath of World War II, the world's aeronautical manufacturers suffered many of the afflictions that had plagued their predecessors after the end of World War I. The state of the art was advancing rapidly, but post-war economic retrenchment meant that governments had to spend the resources available to them on general re-building, rather than on re-equipping their armed forces.

So radical, however, were the possibilities opened up by the development of the turbojet engine as a means of propulsion, that most of the victorious nations thought that research into jet engines should continue at a high level of priority. The British were the only Allies to have had an operational jet aeroplane in the war, but the Americans had also designed several types; meanwhile, too, with the aid of captured German technical personnel and wartime information from her Allies, the Russians were soon in the race.

she had three types in the air – the wartime Meteor fighter, the new de Havilland Vampire fighter and the English Electric Canberra bomber. Then the Americans' vast aeronautics industry began to catch up with Britain, and although her earliest jets did not prove successful, with the exception of the Lockheed F-80 Shooting Star, by the end of 1946 the first of a new generation, the Republic F-84 Thunderjet, had flown.

It was notable in all these designs that the new jet aircraft were little more advanced than contemporary piston-engined machines: they were, in effect, the piston-engined concept powered by the new jets. But all this began to alter as the results of German wartime research into high-speed aerodynamics, captured in large quantities by the Allies at the end of the war, began to filter through into the latest designs. Most important among the Germans' researches

And the French, somewhat more slowly, built up the theoretical and experimental background that has made their aerospace industry one of the most formidable in the world today.

As we have noted, Great Britain had an initial advantage in jet aircraft over the United States, and soon after the war

had been the work into the problem of compressibility and how the worst effects of this might be avoided or overcome.

This problem is basically a simple one: as the aircraft approaches the speed of sound, the air displaced by the aircraft is compressed into a series of high-pressure waves that stream back in a cone from the nose of the machine.

As these hit the wing, they cause the airflow over that part of the aircraft to break up, resulting in an increase of drag; they also set up extreme buffeting conditions, with harmful effects to the structure of the wing. The Germans found that if they swept back the wing, this delayed the onset of compressibility problems and allowed higher subsonic speeds to be attained. Soon the results of their findings had been checked and assimilated into American design philosophy, and a new batch of swept-wing aircraft began to take shape on the drawing boards.

Despite these advances, the mainstays of most of the world's air forces in the period up to the beginning of the

OPPOSITE *The USAF's Lockheed F-80 Shooting Star, America's first successful jet fighter.*
ABOVE *A Yak-15, officially the first Soviet jet fighter, seen in 1946.*
LEFT *A British jet of the post-war period, the English Electric P-1 Canberra bomber.*
BELOW *The British Vampire fighter, a World War II design still much in evidence in the Korean War (1950–53).*

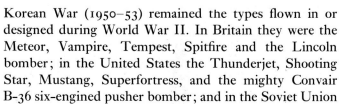

Korean War (1950–53) remained the types flown in or designed during World War II. In Britain they were the Meteor, Vampire, Tempest, Spitfire and the Lincoln bomber; in the United States the Thunderjet, Shooting Star, Mustang, Superfortress, and the mighty Convair B-36 six-engined pusher bomber; and in the Soviet Union

there was an assortment of wartime types with a hybrid mixture of machines boosted by jets or rockets.

The Korean War itself acted as a great spur to progress. After some initial reverses the Americans (under the aegis of the United Nations) fought back with great vigour and were soon thinking that they would be able to end the war

without much further delay. How mistaken they were, for the Communist Chinese (who had latterly ousted the last of Chiang Kai-shek's Nationalists from mainland China) and the Russians started to aid the North Koreans. Here not the least of the Americans' worries was the appearance of some fast and well-armed Russian jet fighters – the Mikoyan-Gurevich MiG-15s. The Russians had produced the type in great secrecy, and the Western Alliance was considerably dismayed to see how much progress they had made in terms of swept-wing design. But the antidote was not long in arriving.

This was the superlative North American F-86 Sabre, a clean-lined, sturdy, swept-wing fighter that was to prove one of the classic combat aircraft of all time. Derived directly from German researches, it was in every way superior to the MiG-15, although it was still armed only with six ·5-inch machine guns. At much the same time, the F-84 underwent major surgery and emerged as the F-84F Thunderstreak, with swept wings and an excellent all-round performance in both the fighter and fighter-bomber roles. A later version, the RF-84F Thunderflash reconnaissance machine, was equally successful and was sold in considerable numbers to America's NATO allies, as were the earlier models.

But the Russians had not been standing still, and in 1953 an updated version of the MiG-15, the MiG-17, appeared. This was similar to the earlier MiG-15, with some aerodynamic refinements. Also flown in the same year was the prototype MiG-19: this was to enter service as the Soviet Union's first supersonic fighter, having a top speed of Mach 1·3. The Americans, working on the same principle, had in the meantime redesigned the Sabre with an increased sweep on the wings and improved aerodynamics to produce their first supersonic fighter, the F-100 Super Sabre.

While the traditional American fighter manufacturers were continuing to press ahead with their chosen types, the major US bomber manufacturer, Boeing, had also turned to jet aircraft. First to appear was the B-47 Stratojet, a clean design with the unusual feature of a bicycle-type undercarriage under the fuselage and outriggers under the inboard engine nacelles to provide added balance. Speed was over 600 mph and range in the order of 4,000 miles, and the type began to enter service in 1951. Soon after this another new Boeing design, the B-52 Stratofortress, appeared. This was similar to the B-47 in appearance but considerably larger,

having a span of 185 feet compared with 116 feet, and powered by eight engines instead of six. Deliveries to the US Air Force started in 1955, and since that time the huge B-52 has been the most important type in America's strategic bomber fleet. Needless to say, considerable development has taken place, and although performance remains

The F-84F Thunderstreak fighter and fighter-bomber, in effect the F-84 Thunderjet transformed with a swept-wing layout.

Now a museum piece: a Soviet MiG-15 jet fighter on display at the Monino Aeronautical Museum.

unaltered (600+ mph and a range in excess of 10,000 miles), its bomb-load has been increased to up to 75,000 pounds, and a considerable array of missiles can be carried for decoy purposes or stand-off bombing. The B-52's multi-purpose electronic equipment has also been refined virtually beyond recognition.

In Europe, the aircraft designed in the early 1950s were not as ambitious as the American machines. Britain's standard fighters, the Meteor and Vampire, were gradually phased out in favour of the newer Hawker Hunter, which soon showed itself to be an excellent and versatile machine in the fighter, ground-attack and reconnaissance roles. The

America's jet bombers culminate in the mighty B-52 Stratofortress.

A partner to the famous MiG-15 in the early days of the jet fighter—the Soviet La-15.

TOP *The giant Convair B-36 bomber, a six-engined pusher type in service in the early 1950s.*
ABOVE *The North American F-86A Sabre fighter, a strong swept-wing machine that was built as a counter to the Russian MiG designs.*

Hunter entered service in 1954, and is still used in large numbers by several European, Middle Eastern and South American countries. At the same time, the first of Britain's nuclear bombers, the Vickers Valiant, was about to enter service. In lieu of an atomic weapon, a maximum of 10,000 pounds of bombs could be carried, a paltry amount compared with the wartime Lancaster (up to 22,000 pounds), let alone the B-52. The Valiant was joined in 1956 by the Avro Vulcan, a massive delta-wing design, which could carry 21,000 pounds of bombs at a high subsonic speed. The third of Britain's 'V' bombers, the Handley-Page Victor, entered service in 1958. This last was notable for its crescent-shaped wing planform and a design that permitted it to be pushed through the sound barrier in a shallow dive.

By the mid-1950s the French aeronautical industry had recovered from its hard wartime years, and several good designs were either on the drawing boards or already in the air. The post-war Dassault Ouragan fighter was in service and proving a useful machine, and soon after this an updated version, the Mystère, entered production. At much the same time the allweather Sud-Ouest Vautour made its appearance. With the exception of the Mystère, which was transonic, these French aircraft were subsonic, but soon a remarkable supersonic type was to enter upon the scene. This was the Dassault Mirage, which first appeared in 1955 and soon exceeded the speed of sound. One of the most successful military machines in history, it remains in service today in considerable numbers throughout the world. More important from a design point of view, the Mirage has proved so successful that it has appeared in swept-wing, delta and variable-geometry forms, and also in a scaled-up version, the Mirage IV, which is a nuclear bomber rather than a fighter – as the Mirage was originally conceived.

Britain started development of a supersonic fighter in the 1940s. This was the English Electric Lightning, a squat and powerful design that entered service in 1960 after a protracted development period. The type has since proved successful, and is being exported for service in the interceptor and ground-attack roles.

In Russia, considerable experimental work was under-

TOP LEFT *The B-47 Stratojet, first American jet bomber.*
TOP AND TOP RIGHT *Two F-100 Super Sabres, the USA's first supersonic fighter, and a Super Sabre pilot equipped for the pressures and g-forces of flying faster than sound.*
ABOVE RIGHT *The Vickers Valiant, first of Britain's nuclear bombers, whose maximum bomb capacity in lieu of an atomic weapon was a mere 10,000 pounds.*
ABOVE *No. 2 of Britain's 'V' bombers, the huge delta-wing Avro Vulcan, which entered service in 1956.*

British, French and Russian supersonic fighters of the mid-late 1950s.

taken in the 1950s, but the types to enter service were relatively few. The Sukhoi Su-7 and -9 entered service in the late 1950s and are close-support and fighter types respectively. Taking over from the MiG-19 in the late 1950s, the MiG-21 fighter appeared for the first time in 1956, and has been exported extensively within the Warsaw Pact and to Russia's allies in the Middle East and in India.

At present the Mach 3 MiG-23 is entering service. This is faster than any of the American machines at present in combat service.

One of the most heated controversies to have occurred in air circles since the end of World War II is the question of the manned strategic bomber. With the development first of the A-bomb, and then of the H-bomb, air power at last

Boeing B-52H Stratofortress

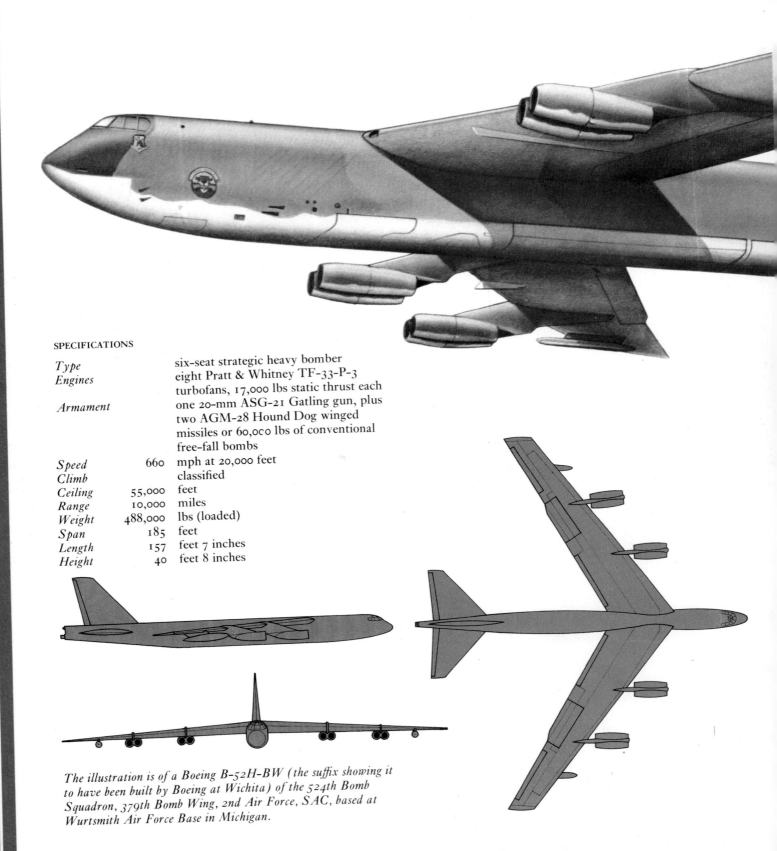

SPECIFICATIONS

Type		six-seat strategic heavy bomber
Engines		eight Pratt & Whitney TF-33-P-3 turbofans, 17,000 lbs static thrust each
Armament		one 20-mm ASG-21 Gatling gun, plus two AGM-28 Hound Dog winged missiles or 60,000 lbs of conventional free-fall bombs
Speed	660	mph at 20,000 feet
Climb		classified
Ceiling	55,000	feet
Range	10,000	miles
Weight	488,000	lbs (loaded)
Span	185	feet
Length	157	feet 7 inches
Height	40	feet 8 inches

The illustration is of a Boeing B-52H-BW (the suffix showing it to have been built by Boeing at Wichita) of the 524th Bomb Squadron, 379th Bomb Wing, 2nd Air Force, SAC, based at Wurtsmith Air Force Base in Michigan.

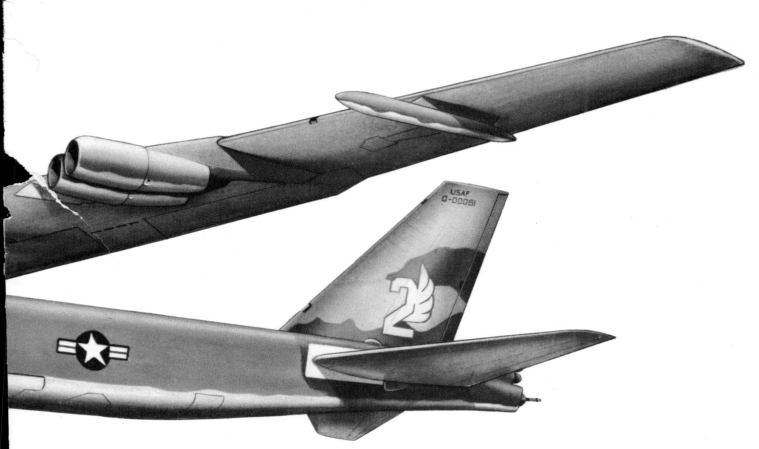

Contrary to popular belief, the Boeing B-52 Stratofortress is not a scaled-up version of the same company's B-47 Stratojet. The design is in fact derived from April 1945 studies for a turboprop-powered long-range bomber to be produced at the same time as the B-47. This originally had straight wings, but soon a 20° sweep was adopted. In July 1948 the USAF ordered two prototype XB-52 aircraft, with turboprop engines, but in an effort to procure a better machine, the turboprop concept was abandoned at the end of the year in favour of a pure jet with eight engines in four underwing pods and wings with 35° of sweep. Although the XB-52 was completed in November 1951, it did not fly until October 1952. It was preceded into the air by the pre-production YB-52 in April.

One of the chief features of the B-52 design is the thin, flexible wing that droops when the aircraft is on the ground, but shows marked dihedral when it is supporting the bomber in the air. As in the B-47, the two main undercarriage members are in the fuselage, outriggers under the wings balancing the aircraft on the ground.

The B-52 was ordered into production in February 1951, and the first production B-52A flew in August 1954. This differed from the XB and YB-52 principally in having the two pilots seated side-by-side in a new cockpit instead of in tandem as in the original design. Development work meant that the first bomber was not delivered to the Strategic Air Command (SAC) until the end of 1957. Better operational equipment was introduced on the B-52B and RB-52B, a reconnaissance version, which first flew in January 1955, deliveries to SAC commencing in June of the same year. On 21 May 1956 a B-52 dropped the first air-dropped hydrogen bomb over Bikini atoll in the Pacific.

The B-52C, which had the same multi-mission capability as the B-52B, flew for the first time in March 1956. This version had larger underwing fuel tanks and increased gross weights. Deliveries began in June 1956. At the same time, the B-52D was in production. The first of these had in fact flown ten days

before the prototype B-52C, but deliveries began only in December. The B-52D was intended only for long-range bombing, and 170 in all were built.

The first example of the next model, the B-52E, flew in October 1957, and had improved bombing, navigation and electronics systems. Deliveries of the 100 produced began in July 1957. The B-52F, which had more powerful engines, first flew in May 1958, and the first of 89 was delivered in June 1958.

The B-52G marked a fairly radical departure from earlier models: fuel tanks in the wing were introduced, the tail gunner was moved up the fuselage to a position near the electronics countermeasures operator, and the fin and rudder were shortened and widened in chord. The first flew in October 1958, and deliveries of the 193 built commenced in February 1959. The B-52G also had the capability of carrying two Hound Dog stand-off missiles, one under each wing.

Final version of the B-52 design is the B-52H, which is powered by turbofan engines, and has improved range and all-up weights. The quadruple ·5-inch rear gun armament is replaced by a single 20-mm multi-barrel 'Gatling gun' fixture. The first B-52H flew in March 1961, and the last of the 102 built was delivered in October 1963.

A total of 744 B-52s was built, the last two versions being able to carry ADM-20 Quail decoy missiles and AGM-69A short-range attack missiles. Up to 20 of these Mach 3 missiles can be carried by the B-52H, six on each of two underwing pylons and eight in a rotary launcher in the bomb bay.

B-52 bombers have not been sold by the United States to any other nations, and have been used in combat only over Indo-China. In this theatre the USAF has used the Stratofortress extensively over Vietnam and Cambodia as a conventional weapons launcher, operating from major bases in Thailand and Guam and bombing from altitude using special ground-scanning radar. The question of a B-52 successor is at present under close scrutiny in the United States.

OPPOSITE, ABOVE *The American F-106 Delta Dart interceptor, one of the USA's supersonic fighters introduced in the 1960s.*
OPPOSITE, BELOW *Two French fighters, the post-war Dassault Ouragan, left, and the remarkable supersonic Dassault Mirage. The latter made its appearance in 1955 and remains in service today in many* parts of the world, having been produced in a variety of delta, swept-wing and variable-geometry forms.
LEFT *The Soviet Union's first supersonic fighter, the MiG-19.*
ABOVE *Russian MiG-23 interceptors, not only supersonic but capable of Mach 3.*
BELOW *The English Electric Lightning.*

McDonnell Douglas F-4 Phantom II

SPECIFICATIONS (F-4B)

Type		two-seat interceptor and attack aircraft
Engines		two General Electric J79-GE-8 turbojets, 17,000 lbs thrust each with afterburning
Armament		six Raytheon Sparrow III, or 4 Sparrow III and 4 General Electric Sidewinder I air-to-air missiles, plus up to 16,000 lbs of external stores. These can be made up of a mixture of 250-, 500-, 750-, or 1,000-lb bombs, nuclear weapons, rocket launchers, landmines, napalm bombs, chemical warfare bombs, leaflet bombs, and sometimes GAM-83A Bullpup missiles and 20-mm Vulpod or 7·62-mm Minipod gun packs
Speed	1,548	mph at 48,000 feet (Mach 2·4)
Initial climb rate	28,000	feet per minute
Ceiling	71,000	feet
Combat radius	900	miles
Ferry range	2,300	miles
Weight	28,000	lbs (empty)
	56,000	lbs (loaded)
Span	38	feet $4\frac{7}{8}$ inches
Length	58	feet $3\frac{1}{8}$ inches
Height	16	feet 3 inches

F-4 PHANTOM II MARKS

F-4A: 23 prototypes and 24 training aircraft for US Navy.
F-4B: production ship-board fighter and attack aircraft for the US Navy and US Marine Corps.
RF-4B: unarmed reconnaissance variant for US Marine Corps.
F-4C: air superiority and close support fighter for the USAF.
RF-4C: unarmed reconnaissance variant for USAF.
F-4D: USAF fighter with improved weapons system. Also ordered by Iran.
F-4E: USAF fighter with integral cannon armament. Also ordered by Japan and Israel.
RF-4E: reconnaissance variant of F-4E. Ordered by the West German Air Force or Luftwaffe.
F-4G: experimental adaptation of F-4B for automatic deck-landing trials.
F-4J: improved US Navy and Marine Corps combat type.
F-4K: Spey-engined version of F-4J for Royal Navy.
F-4M: RAF fighter-bomber/reconnaissance version of F-4K.

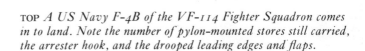

TOP *A US Navy F-4B of the VF-114 Fighter Squadron comes in to land. Note the number of pylon-mounted stores still carried, the arrester hook, and the drooped leading edges and flaps.*

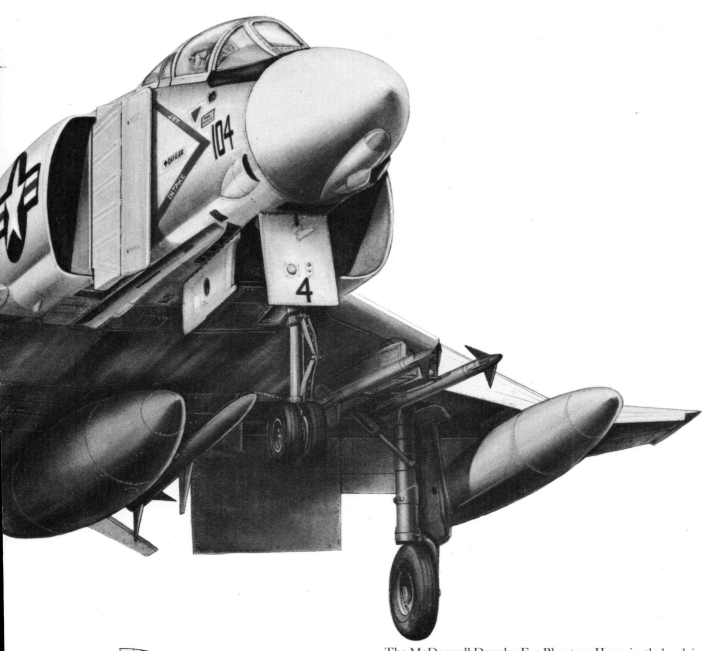

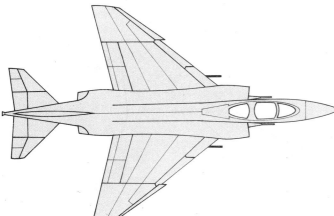

ABOVE AND LEFT *Three views of the Phantom. Note the massive fuselage, 'droop snoot' nose, anhedral tailplane and dihedral only on the outer panels of the wings.*

The McDonnell Douglas F-4 Phantom II can justly be claimed to be the best combat aircraft to have served with the air forces of the Western world since 1945. Although more advanced types will gradually replace the Phantom from 1975 onwards, this versatile machine will still continue to contribute greatly to the attack and defence capability of the West for some time to come.

The Phantom I of 1946 was the US Navy's first operational jet aircraft, and the development of the Phantom II can be traced from its earlier namesake via the F-2H Banshee, the F-3H Demon, and the USAF's F-101 Voodoo. On their own initiative, McDonnell started design work on a new carrier-borne fighter in 1953. By the end of 1954 the Navy had decided that it needed a larger, faster type than had originally been envisaged, and McDonnell redesigned their F-3H-G idea so that by August 1956 construction of the XF-4H-1 prototype Phantom II could begin; it was completed in April 1958 and proved immediately successful. Squadron service began in February 1961.

had a weapon of truly grand strategic capabilities. Initially, only manned bombers could deliver these weapons, and so there was little dissension when the B-36, B-47 and B-52 bombers were built. But the advent of the guided ballistic missile seemed to presage a complete change: delivery systems such as the Atlas, Titan, Minuteman, and submarine-launched Polaris and Poseidon were thought to be capable of supplanting the bomb entirely. However, the development of anti-missile systems has once again put the bomber back into court. For the bomber, unlike the missile, can alter course radically in the light of tactical developments; it can bomb from high and low altitudes, both subsonically and supersonically, and it can bomb a different target if the last-minute situation warrants it. And so it seems likely that a new generation of heavy bombers will be developed by both the Superpowers.

Certainly Russia has become increasingly conscious since 1945 of her lack of an effective strategic bomber force, and several enormous machines have been produced. Principal amongst these are the Myasishchev Mya-4, which is capable of delivering a 10,000-pound bomb-load over a range of 7,000 miles, the Tupolev Tu-16 medium bomber, the Tu-20 turboprop-driven heavy bomber and long-range reconnaissance machine, the Mach 1·5 Tu-22 and the later In the mid-1970s Soviet Russia is in the process of introducing a new generation of manned strategic bombers in the form of the Mach 2.5 Tupolev 'Backfire', an advanced variable-goemetry design.

In the 1960s the United States produced a variety of supersonic types, ranging from the not-very-successful Convair B-58 Hustler supersonic bomber and the General Dynamics F-111 variable-geometry fighter and long-range supersonic bomber via the US Air Force's Lockheed F-104 Starfighter, its Convair F-106 Delta Dart interceptors and Republic F-105 fighter and fighter-bomber to the magnificent McDonnell F-4 Phantom series. This is probably the most successful aircraft ever built for the military, and it has served in the fighter, fighter-bomber, reconnaissance and bomber roles, as well as being able to undertake strike and ground-attack missions. In the Arab-Israeli War of 1973 it was through her Phantoms that Israel eventually achieved air superiority – though she suffered considerable losses from Egypt's Russian-built surface-to-air missiles in the process. The United States' counterpart of the 'Backfire' is the Rockwell B-1, which has a top speed in the order of Mach 2, but is considerably larger (and probably has a larger payload) than the 'Backfire'. The B-1 also has variable geometry.

The states of Western Europe, no longer able to match either of the Superpowers, have in recent years opted for the all-purpose, internationally designed and produced aircraft. This has led to the development of such types as the SEPECAT Jaguar trainer, fighter and strike aircraft, and the Multi-Role Combat Aircraft design (MRCA) which is currently being built under the joint control of a European consortium.

LEFT *Close-up of an Egyptian SAM-2 missile captured by Israeli forces on the west bank of the Suez Canal. These surface-to-air missiles accounted for a high proportion of Israeli aircraft in 1973.*
RIGHT *Two American Inter-Continental Ballistic Missiles (ICBMs), the Titan and Minuteman.*
BELOW *A US Minuteman prototype on its transporter. Despite the power of the ICBMs, the bomber seems likely to hold its own for many years to come, largely because it is more flexible and can react quickly to changes in the tactical situation.*
BOTTOM *A British Lightning alongside a Soviet Bear long-range interceptor.*

LEFT *A Chinook helicopter brings supplies and reinforcements to US troops under fire on a hill in South Vietnam.*
ABOVE *The Autogyro, a forerunner of the helicopter idea that was finally perfected by Juan de la Cierva, a Spaniard, and the Russian designer Igor Sikorsky.*
TOP *A British Army Sioux helicopter.*

Helicopters

The helicopter emerged as a practicable military vehicle in the closing stages of World War II, and has grown to a considerable, if disputed, prominence in the last 25 years. Its first widespread use in war occurred in the Korean conflict, where the Americans made considerable use of its then unique vertical take-off and landing and hovering characteristics for observation and casualty evacuation purposes. Since then the type has continued to give valuable service in these two roles, and also as a commando carrier. In this role the Israelis have been the helicopter's chief exponents, using it profitably in 1956, 1967 and 1973.

The Americans, however, have attempted to turn the helicopter into a fighting machine, fitting it with rockets, flexible machine guns and even machine-gun turrets. The most notable of these machines is the Bell Huey Cobra, of which more than 16,000 have been built. But it seems that such a machine can only operate within a tolerable loss limit when the user has complete air superiority, and when the ground forces attacked have no sophsticated anti-aircraft defences. In fact, the American helicopter forces suffered very heavy casualties to ground fire in Vietnam. Thus the future of the helicopter as a strike aircraft is now much in doubt, although poorer countries may be attracted to the idea by the relative cheapness of the helicopter compared with even the least sophisticated conventional aircraft.

431

Despite this, both the Superpowers and the more technologically advanced Western nations are continuing to experiment with strike helicopters, especially in the anti-tank role. In this capacity they are normally armed with guided missiles, and often have laser ranging or guidance equipment.

Also of considerable importance, especially for land operations in poor terrain, are developments in the field of heavy 'flying crane' helicopters. In this area the USA and the USSR predominate. The former uses the Sikorsky CH-54B, which can lift some 12½ tons, and the latter the mighty Mil Mi-12, which can carry upwards of 35 tons. Both countries also use helicopters in the assault transport role, examples being the Sikorsky S-65 and the Mil Mi-6 and 8.

Strike helicopters in the anti-tank role; heavy helicopters used as 'flying cranes'.

OPPOSITE, ABOVE *Royal Navy helicopters on display at the Farnborough Air Show. This is one aspect—the 'passive' side—of the helicopter's military potential, i.e. as a troop and supplies carrier and as a battlefield observer.*
OPPOSITE, BELOW *A Russian Mil Mi-6, designed for assault transport duties.*
BELOW *The British missile-armed Scout helicopter.*
BOTTOM *The US Bell Huey Cobra, which embodies the helicopter-gunship concept; over 16,000 have been built.*

The Years Ahead

What can the future be expected to bring? Will the Super-powers continue to build considerable numbers of sophisticated and basically one-purpose aircraft, or will they too be forced by the sheer economics of special metals and expensive electronics to turn to the European idea of multi-purpose machines like the MRCA or the cheaper but nonetheless efficient types such as the radical Hawker Siddeley Harrier vertical take-off and landing aircraft?

It is a difficult, if not impossible, question to answer. It is clear, however, that the missile, in aircraft use, is not altogether invincible, and that for some time to come great reliance will still have to be placed on manned aircraft and helicopters armed with guns as well as missiles, and capable of outflying as well as out-thinking their opponents' onboard computers. Changes in the next decades are thus likely to be gradual, not revolutionary.

TOP *Harriers on exercise in Germany. As one machine makes a vertical landing, another is towed to a camouflaged position.* ABOVE *First of the MRCA prototypes; the versatility of this low-cost aircraft is described in the diagram opposite.*

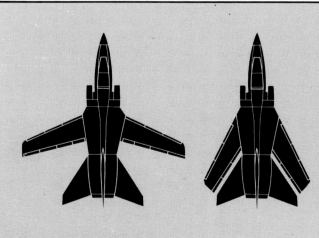

The European MRCA (Multi Role Combat Aircraft) is designed to fulfil five major roles: close air support; interdictor and naval strike; reconnaissance; air superiority, and interception. The MRCA's variable-geometry wing makes it especially versatile: the swept wing ensures a low gust response, giving high speed at low levels during the weapons delivery phase; while the extended wing is used for V/STOL. Some 800 aircraft are planned for service with Britain, Italy and West Germany.

435

PART 6
THE WEAPONS
OF WAR:
DATA SECTION

Anatomy of a Tank

These illustrations are intended to show the principal components of a main battle tank. The shape and performance of tanks has undergone many radical changes since the first of the breed went into action on the Somme in 1916. Even so, the principle of a gunned and armoured obstacle-crossing vehicle has remained more or less constant. As our representative tank we feature the German Pzkw Mark VI Tiger 1, first used on active service in September 1942 on the Leningrad front.

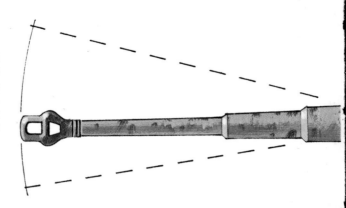

RIGHT *This front view demonstrates the all-round traversing capabilities of the turret and main gun, and the arc within which the muzzle could be elevated or depressed. Also shown are the driver's vision slit, and the hull machine-gun.*

TURRET
1 *Main armament*
2 *Rifled barrel*
3 *Commander's position*
4 *Gunner's position*
5 *Loader's position*
6 *Smoke dischargers*
7 *Turret bustle*

HULL
8 *Driver's position*
9 *Hull machine-gunner's position*
10 *Glacis plate*
11 *Road wheel*
12 *Linked track*
13 *Engine compartment*
14 *Spare containers*
15 *Armour plate (here coated with anti-magnetic plaster finish)*
16 *Exhausts*

KEY TO SYMBOLS USED IN MAPS

SYMBOL	MEANING	SPECIFIC MEANING OF EXAMPLE

1 Infantry Formations

X	Brigade or regiment	
XX	Division	
XXX IV — Fr	Corps	French Fourth Corps
XXXX THIRD — US — Patton	Army	US Third Army commanded by General Patton
XXXXX 21 — Montgomery	Army Group	Twenty-first Army Group commanded by General Montgomery

2 Armoured Formations

X	Brigade or regiment	
XX	Division	
XXX Pz XV — Hoth	Corps	Fifteenth Panzer Corps commanded by General Hoth
XXXX Pz Group II — Guderian	Panzer Group	Second Panzer Group commanded by General Guderian
XXXX SIXTH — Dietrich	Army	Sixth Panzer Army commanded by General Dietrich

3 Boundaries

— xxx —	Corps boundary
— xxxx —	Army boundary
– xxxxx –	Army group boundary

4 Commands

SHAEF — Eisenhower	Supreme Command	Supreme Head-quarters Allied Expeditionary Forces commanded by General Eisenhower
OB WEST — von Rundstedt	High Command	Hitler's Western High Command led by Field-Marshal von Rundstedt

1

DETAILS OF IMPORTANT TANKS

Table 1 : Details of important tanks

The statistical information in this table has been gathered from many sources, among which variations occur. The figures given here are those which seemed to the author and the editors most likely to be accurate. The category 'length (overall)' includes any part of the main gun overhanging the front of the tank.

'Range' refers to the longest distance a tank can cover on level road on one filling of fuel; in cross-country movement a tank's range is always considerably reduced, usually by 20-30 per cent., though the precise amount varies according to the vehicle and the conditions in which it operates.

World War I

MARK I Male
(Britain) 1916

Length	32 feet 6 inches (with tail)
Width	13 feet 9 inches
Height	8 feet 0 inches
Weight	28 tons
Speed	3·7 mph (max.)
Range	23·6 miles
Armament	2 × 57-mm (6-pounder) guns with 332 rounds 4 machine-guns with 6,272 rounds
Armour	10 mm (max. thickness)
Crew	8

MARK V Male
(Britain) 1918

Length	26 feet 5 inches (overall)
Width	12 feet 9 inches
Height	8 feet 8 inches
Weight	29 tons
Speed	4·6 mph (max.)
Range	45 miles
Armament	2 × 57-mm (6-pounder) guns with 207 rounds 4 machine-guns with 5,700 rounds
Armour	12 mm (max. thickness)
Crew	8

ST CHAMOND Char d'assaut
(France) 1916

Length	26 feet 6 inches (overall)
Width	8 feet 11 inches
Height	7 feet 10 inches
Weight	23 tons
Speed	5 mph (max.)
Range	37 miles
Armament	1 × 75-mm gun with 106 rounds 4 × 7·92-mm machine-guns with 7,488 rounds
Armour	17 mm (max. thickness)
Crew	8

RENAULT FT
(France) 1917

Length	16 feet 6 inches (overall)
Width	5 feet 10 inches
Height	7 feet 2 inches
Weight	6·5 tons
Speed	5 mph (max.)
Range	37 miles
Armament	1 × 37-mm gun with 240 rounds *or* 1 × 7·92-mm machine-gun with 4,800 rounds
Armour	22 mm (max. thickness)
Crew	2

MEDIUM A WHIPPET
(Britain) 1918

Length	20 feet 0 inches (overall)	*Range*	80 miles
Width	8 feet 7 inches	*Armament*	4 machine-guns with 5,400 rounds
Height	9 feet 0 inches		
Weight	14 tons	*Armour*	14 mm (max. thickness)
Speed	8·3 mph (max.)	*Crew*	3

Inter-War Period

VICKERS MEDIUM MARK II
(Britain) 1927

Length	17 feet 6 inches (overall)
Width	9 feet 2 inches
Height	9 feet 3 inches
Weight	12·5 tons
Speed	15 mph (max.)
Range	150 miles
Armament	1 × 47-mm (3-pounder) gun
	6 × ·303-inch machine-guns
Armour	8 mm (max. thickness)
Crew	5

PZKW MARK IA
(Germany) 1934

Length	13 feet 2 inches (overall)
Width	6 feet 10 inches
Height	5 feet 8 inches
Weight	5·4 tons
Speed	22 mph (max.)
Range	90 miles
Armament	2 × 7·92-mm machine-guns with 3,050 rounds
Armour	13 mm (max. thickness)
Crew	2

AR B
(France) 1931

Length	21 feet 9 inches (overall)
Width	8 feet 3 inches
Height	9 feet 4 inches
Weight	31 tons
Speed	17 mph (max.)
Range	125 miles
Armament	1 × 75-mm howitzer with 74 rounds
	1 × 37-mm gun with 75 rounds
	2 × 7·5-mm machine-guns with 5,100 rounds
Armour	60 mm (max. thickness)
Crew	4

VICKERS LIGHT MARK VI
(Britain) 1935

Length	13 feet 2 inches (overall)
Width	6 feet 9 inches
Height	7 feet 3 inches
Weight	5·2 tons
Speed	29 mph (max.)
Range	125 miles
Armament	1 × ·303-inch machine-gun with 2,500 rounds
	1 × ·5-inch machine-gun with 400 rounds
Armour	14 mm (max. thickness)
Crew	3

BT-5
(USSR) 1933

Length	18 feet 2 inches (overall)
Width	7 feet 2 inches
Height	7 feet 8 inches
Weight	11·5 tons
Speed	38 mph (max.)
Range	112 miles
Armament	1 × 45-mm gun with 115 rounds
	1 × 7·62-mm machine-gun with 2,500 rounds
Armour	13 mm (max. thickness)
Crew	3

A-10 CRUISER MARK IIA
(Britain) 1935

Length	18 feet 1 inch (overall)
Width	8 feet 3 inches
Height	8 feet 6 inches
Weight	14 tons
Speed	15 mph (max.)
Range	100 miles
Armament	1 × 40-mm (2-pounder) gun
	2 × 7·92-mm machine-guns
Armour	30 mm (max. thickness)
Crew	5

MATILDA INFANTRY MARK II
(Britain) 1938

Length	18 feet 5 inches (overall)
Width	8 feet 3 inches
Height	7 feet 10 inches
Weight	26 tons
Speed	15 mph (max.)
Range	60 miles
Armament	1 × 40-mm (2-pounder) gun
	1 × 7·92-mm machine-gun
Armour	80 mm (max. thickness)
Crew	4

KV-I
(USSR) 1939

Length	22 feet 6 inches (overall)
Width	11 feet 0 inches
Height	9 feet 0 inches
Weight	43·5 tons
Speed	25 mph (max.)
Range	210 miles
Armament	1 × 76·2-mm gun with 111 rounds
	3 × 7·62-mm machine-guns with 3,000 rounds
Armour	90 mm (max. thickness)
Crew	5

PZKW MARK IIIA
(Germany) 1938

Length	18 feet 11 inches (overall)
Width	9 feet 4 inches
Height	7 feet 9 inches
Weight	15 tons
Speed	20 mph (max.)
Range	100 miles
Armament	1 × 37-mm gun with 150 rounds
	3 × 7·92-mm machine-guns with 4,500 rounds
Armour	14·5 mm (max. thickness)
Crew	5

T-34/76A
(USSR) 1939

Length	21 feet 7 inches (overall)
Width	9 feet 10 inches
Height	8 feet 0 inches
Weight	28 tons
Speed	32 mph (max.)
Range	190 miles
Armament	1 × 76·2-mm gun with 76 rounds
	2 × 7·62-mm machine-guns with 2,900 rounds
Armour	45 mm (max. thickness)
Crew	4

World War II

GRANT MEDIUM M-3
(USA) 1941

Length	18 feet 6 inches (overall)
Width	8 feet 11 inches
Height	10 feet 4 inches
Weight	29 tons
Speed	26 mph (max.)
Range	160 miles
Armament	1 × 75-mm gun with 46 rounds
	1 × 37-mm gun with 178 rounds
	4 × ·3-inch machine-guns with 9,200 rounds
Armour	57 mm (max. thickness)
Crew	6

PZKW MARK IVE
(Germany) 1941

Length	19 feet 8½ inches (overall)
Width	9 feet 6½ inches
Height	8 feet 11 inches
Weight	21 tons
Speed	27 mph (max.)
Range	125 miles
Armament	1 × 75-mm gun with 87 rounds
	2 × 7·92-mm machine-guns with 2,700 rounds
Armour	60 mm (max. thickness)
Crew	5

CRUSADER CRUISER MARK I
(Britain) 1939

Length	19 feet 7 inches (overall)
Width	9 feet 1 inch
Height	7 feet 4 inches
Weight	18·5 tons
Speed	27 mph (max.)
Range	200 miles
Armament	1 × 40-mm (2-pounder) gun with 110 rounds
	2 × 7·92-mm machine-guns with 4,500 rounds
Armour	40 mm (max. thickness)
Crew	5

STUART M-3 MARK I
(USA) 1940

Length	14 feet 10 inches (overall)
Width	7 feet 4 inches
Height	8 feet 3 inches
Weight	12·25 tons
Speed	37 mph (max.)
Range	100 miles
Armament	1 × 37-mm gun with 103 rounds
	3 machine-guns
Armour	38 mm (max. thickness)
Crew	4

M-13/40
(Italy) 1940

Length	16 feet 2 inches
Width	7 feet 3 inches
Height	7 feet 4 inches
Weight	14 tons
Speed	20 mph (max.)
Range	125 miles
Armament	1 × 47-mm gun
	3 machine-guns
Armour	40 mm (max. thickness)
Crew	4

SHERMAN MARK V
(USA) 1942

Length	21 feet 6 inches (overall)
Width	8 feet 9 inches
Height	9 feet 5 inches
Weight	33 tons
Speed	25 mph (max.)
Range	100 miles
Armament	1 × 75-mm gun
	2 machine-guns
Armour	85 mm (max. thickness)
Crew	5

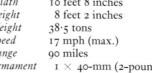

CHURCHILL MARK II
(Britain) 1942

Length	24 feet 5 inches (overall)
Width	10 feet 8 inches
Height	8 feet 2 inches
Weight	38·5 tons
Speed	17 mph (max.)
Range	90 miles
Armament	1 × 40-mm (2-pounder) gun
	2 × 7·92-mm machine-guns
Armour	102 mm (max. thickness)
Crew	5

PANTHER D
(Germany) 1942

Length	29 feet 6 inches (overall)
Width	11 feet 5 inches
Height	9 feet 10 inches
Weight	43 tons
Speed	28 mph (max.)
Range	105 miles
Armament	1 × 75-mm gun with 79 rounds
	1 × 7·92-mm machine-gun
	with 4,200 rounds
Armour	80 mm (max. thickness)
Crew	5

TIGER MARK IE
(Germany) 1942

Length	27 feet 5 inches (overall)
Width	12 feet 6 inches
Height	9 feet 6 inches
Weight	56 tons
Speed	24 mph (max.)
Range	62 miles
Armament	1 × 88-mm gun with 92 rounds
	2 × 7·92-mm machine-guns
	with 3,920 rounds
Armour	100 mm (max. thickness)
Crew	5

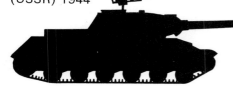

T-34/85
(USSR) 1942

Length	24 feet 9 inches (overall)
Width	9 feet 10 inches
Height	7 feet 11 inches
Weight	32 tons
Speed	32 mph (max.)
Range	190 miles
Armament	1 × 85-mm gun with 55 rounds
	2 × 7·62-mm machine-guns
	with 2,745 rounds
Armour	75 mm (max. thickness)
Crew	5

CROMWELL MARK IV
(Britain) 1944

Length	20 feet 10 inches (overall)
Width	9 feet 7 inches
Height	8 feet 3 inches
Weight	28 tons
Speed	38 mph (max.)
Range	165 miles
Armament	1 × 75-mm gun with 64 rounds
	2 × 7·92-mm machine-guns
	with 4,950 rounds
Armour	76 mm (max. thickness)
Crew	5

JS-III
(USSR) 1944

Length	32 feet 9 inches (overall)		*Armament*	1 × 122-mm gun with 28 rounds
Width	10 feet 6 inches			2 × 7·62-mm machine-guns
Height	8 feet 10 inches			1 × 12·7-mm machine-gun
Weight	46 tons		*Armour*	230 mm (max. thickness)
Speed	23 mph (max.)		*Crew*	4
Range	130 miles			

PERSHING M-26
(USA) 1945

COMET
(Britain) 1945

Length	28 feet 10 inches (overall)
Width	11 feet 8 inches
Height	9 feet 3 inches
Weight	42 tons
Speed	30 mph (max.)
Range	100 miles
Armament	1 × 90-mm gun
	2 × ·30-inch machine-guns
Armour	102 mm (max. thickness)
Crew	5

Length	25 feet 2 inches (overall)
Width	10 feet 0 inches
Height	8 feet 9 inches
Weight	33 tons
Speed	29 mph (max.)
Range	120 miles
Armament	1 × 77-mm gun with 61 rounds
	2 × 7·92-mm machine-guns
	with 5,175 rounds
Armour	101 mm (max. thickness)
Crew	5

Post-1945 Period

CENTURION MARK 3
(Britain) 1948

Length	32 feet 3 inches (overall)
Width	11 feet 1 inch
Height	9 feet 8 inches
Weight	49 tons
Speed	22 mph (max.)
Range	85 miles
Armament	1 × 83·4-mm (20-pounder) gun with 65 rounds
	1 × 7·92-mm machine-gun with 3,600 rounds
Armour	152 mm (max. thickness)
Crew	4

AMX-13
(France) 1949

Length	20 feet 9 inches (overall)
Width	8 feet 3 inches
Height	7 feet 4 inches
Weight	14·7 tons
Speed	40 mph (max.)
Range	205 miles
Armament	1 × 75-mm gun with 40 rounds
	1 × 7·5-mm machine-gun with 3,000 rounds
Armour	40 mm (max. thickness)
Crew	3

PATTON M-47
(USA) 1949

Length	27 feet 9 inches (overall)
Width	11 feet 6 inches
Height	9 feet 8 inches
Weight	44 tons
Speed	35 mph (max.)
Range	75 miles
Armament	1 × 90-mm gun with 71 rounds
	2 × 12·7-mm machine-guns
	1 × 7·62-mm machine-gun
Armour	115 mm (max. thickness)
Crew	4

LEOPARD
(West Germany) 1965

Length	31 feet 0 inches (overall)
Width	10 feet 7 inches
Height	7 feet 10 inches
Weight	40 tons
Speed	42 mph (max.)
Range	310 miles
Armament	1 × 105-mm gun with 60 rounds
	2 × 7·62-mm machine-guns
Armour	–
Crew	4

T-54A
(USSR) 1954

Length	29 feet 6 inches (overall)
Width	10 feet 9 inches
Height	7 feet 10 inches
Weight	36 tons
Speed	34 mph (max.)
Range	210 miles
Armament	1 × 100-mm gun with 42 rounds
	1 × 12·7-mm machine-gun with 500 rounds
	2 × 7·62-mm machine-guns with 3,000 rounds
Armour	105 mm (max. thickness)
Crew	4

AMX-30
(France) 1966

Length	30 feet 9 inches (overall)
Width	10 feet 3 inches
Height	8 feet 2 inches
Weight	34 tons
Speed	40 mph (max.)
Range	350 miles
Armament	1 × 105-mm gun with 56 rounds
	1 × 12·7-mm machine-gun with 600 rounds
	1 × 7·62-mm machine-gun with 1,600 rounds
Armour	–
Crew	4

T-62
(USSR) 1963

Length	31 feet 0 inches (overall)
Width	11 feet 0 inches
Height	7 feet 4 inches
Weight	37 tons
Speed	34 mph (max.)
Range	190 miles
Armament	1 × 115-mm gun with 45 rounds
	1 × 7·62-mm machine-gun with 2,200 rounds
Armour	100 mm (max. thickness)
Crew	4

M-60 A-1
(USA) 1961

Length	30 feet 11 inches (overall)
Width	11 feet 11 inches
Height	10 feet 4 inches
Weight	46 tons
Speed	35 mph (max.)
Range	300 miles
Armament	1 × 105-mm gun with 63 rounds
	3 machine-guns
Armour	110 mm (est. max. thickness)
Crew	4

TYPE 61
(Japan) 1962

Length	27 feet 8 inches (overall)
Width	9 feet 8 inches
Height	7 feet 4 inches
Weight	34 tons
Speed	28 mph (max.)
Range	125 miles
Armament	1 × 90-mm gun
	1 × 12·7-mm machine-gun
	1 × 7·7-mm machine-gun
Armour	–
Crew	4

S-TANK
(Sweden) 1967

Length	29 feet 4 inches (overall)
Width	10 feet 11 inches
Height	7 feet 0 inches
Weight	37 tons
Speed	30 mph (max.)
Range	200 miles
Armament	1 × 105-mm gun with 50 rounds
	2 × 7·62-mm machine-gun with 2,650 rounds
Armour	–
Crew	3

CHIEFTAIN MARK 2
(Britain) 1965

Length	35 feet 2 inches (overall)
Width	11 feet 6 inches
Height	9 feet 3 inches
Weight	51 tons
Speed	25 mph (max.)
Range	250 miles
Armament	1 × 120-mm gun with 53 rounds
	1 × 12·7-mm machine-gun with 600 rounds
	2 × 7·62-mm machine-guns with 6,000 rounds
Armour	–
Crew	4

2

DETAILS OF IMPORTANT GUNS

World War I

French 75-mm field gun M-1897

The first modern Quick-Firing field gun. In service by 1898, it became the standard field gun of both the French Army and the American Expeditionary Force.

Calibre	75 mm
Range	7,500 yards
Elevation	− 10 to + 19 degrees
Traverse	6 degrees
Weight	2,513 pounds
Muzzle velocity	2,047 feet per second
Rate of fire	12 rounds per minute

Austrian Skoda 30·5-cm field mortar M-1911

Nicknamed 'Schlanke (slim) Emma'; used in the attack on the Liège forts in 1914. A very mobile heavy field mortar.

Calibre	305 mm
Range	10,500 yards
Elevation	+ 45 to + 75 degrees
Weight	24 tons
Rate of fire	1 round per 6 minutes
Weight of shell	838 pounds

German 77-mm field gun C96 n/A

Standard German field gun in World War I until replaced by the FK-16 beginning in 1916; remained especially effective in the anti-tank role.

Calibre	77 mm
Range	9,186 yards
Elevation	− 12 to + 16 degrees
Traverse	8 degrees
Weight	1,930 pounds
Muzzle velocity	1,525 fps

German 77-mm field gun FK-16

Improved 77-mm field gun; replaced the C 96 n/A from 1916 onwards.

Calibre	77 mm
Range	11,264 yards
Elevation	− 9·5 to + 35 degrees
Traverse	4 degrees
Weight	2,750 pounds
Muzzle velocity	1,968 fps

German 105-mm light field howitzer 98/09

The 105-mm was the standard German field howitzer in World War I.

Calibre	105 mm
Range	7,655 yards
Elevation	− 13 to + 40 degrees
Traverse	4 degrees
Weight	2,250 pounds
Muzzle velocity	991 fps

British 6-inch howitzer

The standard British medium howitzer in
World War I. Used also in early World War
II campaigns.

Calibre	152·4 mm
Range	11,400 yards
Elevation	0 to + 45 degrees
Traverse	8 degrees
Weight	9,318 pounds
	(travelling position)
Muzzle velocity	1,352 fps
Rate of fire	2 rpm

World War II and after

Soviet 122-mm howitzer M-1938

This gun used the same carriage as the
152-mm (D-1) M-1943 howitzer. It could be
fired without spreading the trails but had a
traverse of only 1·5 degrees if fired in this
manner.

Calibre	122 mm
Range	13,000 yards
Elevation	— 3 to + 63·5 degrees
Traverse	49 degrees
Weight	5,510 pounds
	(travelling position)
Muzzle velocity	1,700 fps
Rate of fire	5 — 6 rpm
Penetration	7·87 inches at 0 degrees

Swedish Bofors 40-mm AA gun

This Bofors 1936 model was adopted by the
USA, Britain and Russia as their standard
medium AA gun. Some were also used by the
Japanese and Germans in World War II.

Calibre	40 mm
Range	23,200 feet (vertical)
	16,200 feet (effective ceiling)
	12,300 yards (horizontal)
Elevation	— 5 to + 90 degrees
Traverse	360 degrees
Weight	4,234 pounds
Muzzle velocity	2,950 fps
Rate of fire	80 — 120 rpm

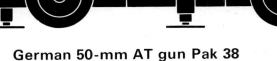

German 50-mm AT gun Pak 38

Standard German anti-tank gun in North
Africa; subsequently replaced by 75-mm
Pak 40.

Calibre	50 mm
Range	3,000 yards
Elevation	— 13 to + 22·5 degrees
Traverse	60 degrees
Weight	2,016 pounds
Muzzle velocity	2,953 — 3,280 fps
Rate of fire	16 rpm
Penetration	71 mm at 30
	degrees at
	600 yards

German 75-mm AT gun Pak 40

A product of the gun-armour race, this
anti-tank gun took over from the 50-mm
Pak 38 beginning in late 1942 and remained in
service for the rest of the war.

Calibre	75 mm
Range	8,750 yards
Elevation	— 5 to + 22 degrees
Traverse	60 degrees
Weight	3,350 pounds
Muzzle velocity	3,070 fps
Rate of fire	12 — 15 rpm
Penetration	3·43 inches at 30 degrees at
	1,000 yards

US 75-mm M-1 A-1 pack howitzer

A low-velocity howitzer well-suited to both
mule and air transport.

Calibre	75 mm
Range	9,600 yards
Elevation	− 5 to + 45 degrees
Traverse	6 degrees
Weight	1,442 pounds
Muzzle velocity	1,250 fps
Rate of fire	6 rpm

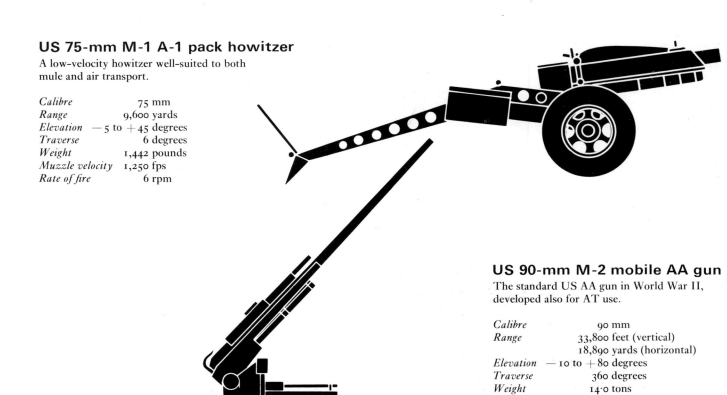

US 90-mm M-2 mobile AA gun

The standard US AA gun in World War II,
developed also for AT use.

Calibre	90 mm
Range	33,800 feet (vertical)
	18,890 yards (horizontal)
Elevation	− 10 to + 80 degrees
Traverse	360 degrees
Weight	14·0 tons
Muzzle velocity	2,700 fps
Rate of fire	20−30 rpm
Time to emplace	7 minutes

US 37-mm AT gun M-3 A-1

This gun closely resembles and was modelled
on the German Rheinmetall 37-mm Pak
35/36.

Calibre	37 mm
Range	13,000 yards
Elevation	− 10 to + 15 degrees
Traverse	60 degrees
Weight	912 pounds
Muzzle velocity	2,640 fps
Rate of fire	25 rpm
Penetration	2·4 inches at 20 degrees
	at 520 yards

Soviet 57-mm AT gun M-1943

This gun was based on the successful 57-mm
AT gun M-1941 but utilized a modern tubular
split trail instead of a box section trail. It
used the same carriage as the 76-mm gun
M-1942.

Calibre	57 mm
Range	9,200 yards
Elevation	− 5 to + 25 degrees
Traverse	56 degrees
Weight	2,535 pounds
Muzzle velocity	4,200 fps
Rate of fire	20−25 rpm
Penetration	5·5 inches at 0 degrees at
	550 yards

British 25-pounder gun-howitzer Mark 2

By the beginning of the Western Desert
campaign this gun had replaced the
18-pounder field gun and the 4·5-inch
howitzer as the standard British field
artillery weapon.

Calibre	87·6 mm
Range	13,400 yards
Elevation	− 5 to + 40 degrees
Traverse	8 degrees (without
	travelling field
	platform)
Weight	7,335 pounds
Muzzle velocity	1,485 fps
Rate of fire	5 rpm
Penetration	2·52 inches at 30 degrees at
	1,000 yards

US 155-mm M-1 mount M-4 gun M-1918

This was a self-propelled gun created by
wedding the World War I vintage 155-mm
GPF gun and the M-3 medium tank chassis.
It was also the first American SP gun to
incorporate the large rear-end recoil spade as a
design feature.

Calibre	155 mm
Range	18,700 yards
Elevation	— 5 to + 30 degrees
Traverse	28 degrees
Weight	25·9 tons
Muzzle velocity	2,410 fps
Rate of fire	4 rpm

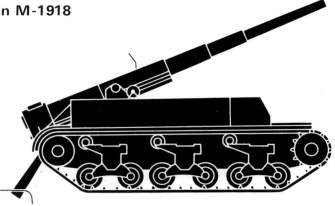

German quad 20-mm AA gun (2-cm Flakvierling 38)

Standard German light Flak in World War II,
it consisted of four 20-mm Flak 38 guns on a
quadruple mount. The magazines of two
guns could be changed while the remaining
two fired. Sometimes mounted on tank
chassis or half-tracks.

Calibre	20 mm
Range	12,465 feet (vertical)
	7,215 feet (effective ceiling)
	5,230 yards (horizontal)
Elevation	— 10 to + 100 degrees
Traverse	360 degrees
Weight	2,979 pounds
Muzzle velocity	2,950 fps (HE)
	2,720 fps (AP)
Rate of fire	700—800 rpm

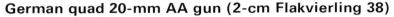

US 155-mm M-1 and M-1 A-1 gun

The famous 'Long Tom'. This gun replaced
the 155-mm M-1 GPF gun M-1918 of
World War I vintage as the principal long-
range heavy artillery piece in the US arsenal.

Calibre	155 mm
Range	25,395 yards
Elevation	— 1 to + 63 degrees
Traverse	60 degrees
Weight	13·3 tons
Muzzle velocity	2,800 fps
Rate of fire	1 rpm
Time to emplace	30 minutes

US 8-inch M-1 howitzer

This was the workhorse of the Allied Artillery
effort in World War II.

Calibre	203·2 mm
Range	18,510 yards
Elevation	— 2 to + 65 degrees
Traverse	60 degrees
Weight	12·5 tons
Muzzle velocity	1,950 pounds
Rate of fire	1 rpm
Time to emplace	30—60 minutes

US 120-mm AA gun M-1

An excellent heavy anti-aircraft gun. Though
not the largest AA gun produced during
World War II, it out-performed all others.

Calibre	120 mm
Range	47,400 feet (vertical)
	27,100 yards (horizontal)
Elevation	— 5 to + 80 degrees
Traverse	360 degrees continuous
Weight	21·8 tons
Muzzle velocity	3,100 fps
Rate of fire	12 rpm
Time to emplace	40 minutes

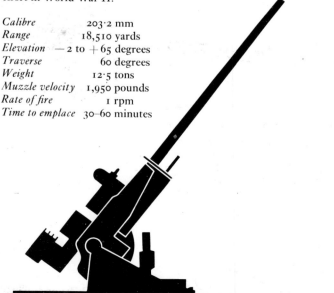

US 3-inch AT gun M-5

This was the largest pure anti-tank gun built by the United States during World War II.

Calibre	81 mm
Range	16,100 yards
Elevation	—5 to +30 degrees
Traverse	45 degrees
Weight	4,785 pounds
Muzzle velocity	2,800 fps
Rate of fire	20 rpm

3
TYPES OF SHELLS

Gas shell: for French 75-mm field gun M-1897

This French shell was the prototype of all successful gas shells used in World War I. The bursting charge was just strong enough to crack the shell open. Too large a charge would have dispersed the gas over a wide area, rendering it ineffective. Gas was not used in World War II.

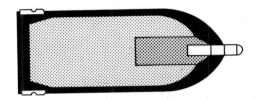

World War I Shell: Shrapnel

This is modern shrapnel, not to be confused with spherical case or early shrapnel, a type of shell invented by Lieutenant Henry Shrapnel and first used in 1804. Modern shrapnel was developed in the 1880s and was used extensively in World War I. It might best be described as an airborne canister round. Shrapnel was of little use against field works or dispersed infantry and was soon discarded.

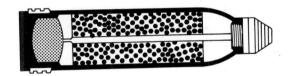

HE: High explosive

The standard projectile for use against personnel or 'soft targets'. This shell depends primarily upon blast for effect, but the shower of fine steel splinters from its casing will kill infantry in the open.

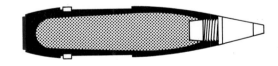

HVAP: Hyper velocity armour-piercing

This is a modern composite rigid armour-piercing shot considered to be about 50% more effective than standard AP, although about 60% lighter because of the aluminium sheath. It is really a sabot-type round in which the sheath (sabot) disintegrates when the projectile strikes the target. Only the hard tungsten carbide core penetrates. HVAP was the standard AP round for Gerlich AT guns.

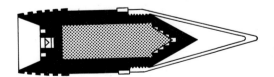

HEAT: High explosive anti-tank

This shell utilizes a physical principle to penetrate armour that was discovered by the American engineer Monroe (the Monroe effect). When the shell strikes the target the shaped charge is detonated by the base fuse and becomes a very hot flame which, because of the shape of the charge, will burst forward in a thin jet and literally sear its way through armour.

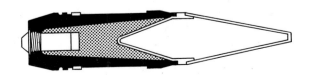

4
DETAILS OF IMPORTANT WARSHIPS

Battleship MAJESTIC

(Britain) 1894

Class	Majestic
Displacement	14,900 tons
Length	390 feet
Beam	75 feet
Draught	26 feet 6 inches
Armament	4 × 12 inch guns
	12 × 6 inch guns
	16 × 12 pounders
	12 × 3 pounders
	5 × 18 inch torpedo tubes (1 stern mounted, 4 submerged)
Main armour	9 inch belt
Engines	10,000 hp; triple expansion
Speed	16 knots

First of a new class of battleship using Harvey steel armour (which allowed a 50% reduction in thickness for the same protection) and the new wire-wound 12-inch gun.

Armoured Frigate WARRIOR

(Britain) 1859

Displacement	9,210 tons
Length	380 feet
Beam	58 feet 6 inches
Draught	26 feet
Armament (first)	26 × 68 pounder muzzle-loaders
	14 × 110 pounder breech-loaders
	4 × 70 pounder breech-loaders
Main armour	4·5 inch belt
Engines	5,500 hp; trunk
Speed	14 knots (steam)
	10 knots (sail)

The world's first iron warship; subsequently re-armed solely with 68-pounders.

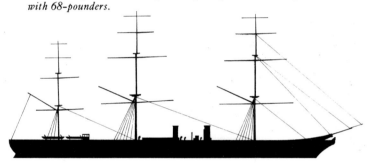

Armoured turretship MONARCH

(Britain) 1866

Displacement	8,300 tons
Length	330 feet
Beam	57 feet
Draught	26 feet
Armament (first)	4 × 12 inch rifled muzzle-loaders
	3 × 7 inch rifled muzzle-loaders
Main armour	7·5 to 4·5 inch sides
	4·5 inch bulkheads
	10 to 8 inch turrets
Engines	7,840 hp; return connecting-rod
Speed	14 knots (steam)
	13 knots (sail)

The first ocean-going ship equipped with turrets (2), which carried the main armament.

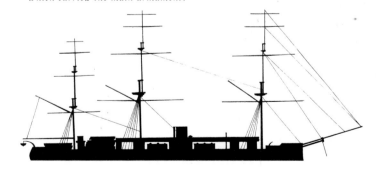

Battleship DUILIO

(Italy) 1872

Displacement	11,200 tons
Length	340 feet
Beam	64 feet
Draught	26 feet 9 inches
Armament	4 × 17·7 inch guns
	4 × 10 inch guns
	7 × 6·1 inch guns
	5 × 4·7 inch guns
	16 × 57 mm guns
	2 × 37 mm guns
Max. armour	22 inches (sides)
Engines	7,700 hp
Speed	11 knots

A world-leader in the race to produce a monster-gunned battleship.

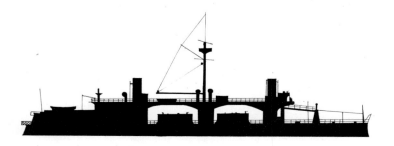

Battleship KENTUCKY

(USA) 1896

Class	Kearsarge (2 built)
Displacement	11,540 tons
Length	375 feet 4 inches
Beam	72 feet 3 inches
Draught	23 feet 6 inches
Armament	4 × 13 inch guns
	4 × 8 inch guns
	14 × 5 inch guns
	20 × 6 pounder guns
	4 × 18 inch torpedo tubes
Main armour	17 to 9 inch belt
Engines	10,000 hp; reciprocating
Speed	16 knots

US battleship featuring three gun-types in the main armament (13-inch, 8-inch and 5-inch).

Battleship KING EDWARD VII

(Britain) 1902

Class	King Edward VII (8 built)
Displacement	16,350 tons
Length	453 feet 9 inches
Beam	78 feet
Draught	25 feet
Armament	4 × 12 inch guns
	4 × 9·2 inch guns
	10 × 6 inch guns
	14 × 12 pounders
	14 × 3 pounders
	4 × 18 inch torpedo tubes
Main armour	9 to 4 inch belt
Engines	18,000 hp; triple expansion
Speed	18·5 knots

One of a new class of more heavily armed British battleships built to keep pace with developments overseas.

Battleship DREADNOUGHT

(Britain) 1906

Class	Dreadnought
Displacement	17,900 tons
Length	527 feet
Beam	82 feet
Draught	26 feet 6 inches
Armament	10 × 12 inch guns
	27 × 12 pounders
	5 × 18 inch torpedo tubes
Main armour	11 to 4 inch belt
Engines	23,000 hp; turbines
Speed	21 knots

A revolutionary design centred round a uniform heavy armament; the name became a universal description for ships of her type.

Battleship SOUTH CAROLINA

(USA) 1906

Class	South Carolina (2 built)
Displacement	16,000 tons
Length	452 feet 9 inches
Beam	80 feet 3 inches
Draught	24 feet 6 inches
Armament	8 × 12 inch guns
	22 × 3 inch guns
	2 × 21 inch torpedo tubes
Main armour	12 to 9 inch belt
Engines	16,500 hp; reciprocating
Speed	18·5 knots

One of the first American dreadnoughts; her superimposed gun arrangement was a major design innovation later adopted by all nations.

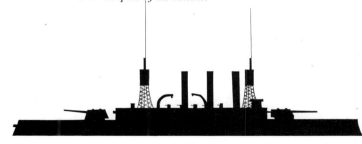

Battleship FUSO

(Japan) 1912

Displacement	29,330 tons
Length	630 feet
Beam	94 feet
Draught	28 feet 4 inches
Armament	12 × 14 inch guns
	16 × 6 inch guns
	4 × 3 inch AA guns
	6 × 21 inch torpedo tubes
Main armour	12 to 4 inch belt
Engines	40,000 hp; turbines
Speed	23 knots

With this ship the Japanese increased the heavy armament of their dreadnoughts to 14-inch guns.

Battlecruiser INVINCIBLE

(Britain) 1906

Class	Invincible (3 built)
Displacement	17,250 tons
Length	567 feet
Beam	78 feet 6 inches
Draught	25 feet 6 inches
Armament	8 × 12 inch guns
	16 × 4 inch guns
	1 × 3 inch gun
	5 × 18 inch torpedo tubes
Main armour	6 to 4 inch belt
Engines	41,000 hp; turbines
Speed	28 knots

First of a new type of warship designed to act independently in fast battle-squadrons and to scout for and support the battleships.

Battlecruiser VON DER TANN

(Germany) 1907

Displacement	21,000 tons
Length	561 feet (overall)
Beam	85 feet
Draught	27 feet
Armament	8 × 11 inch guns
	10 × 6 inch guns
	16 × 24 pounder guns
	4 × 18 inch torpedo tubes
Main armour	9·75 to 7 inch belt
Engines	50,000 hp; turbines
Speed	25 knots

Germany's first battlecruiser, better equipped defensively than her British rivals.

Torpedo-boat destroyers TRIBAL

(Britain) 1906–8

Class	Tribal (12 built)
Displacement	850 to 1,045 tons
Length	250 to 280 feet
Beam	25 to 27 feet
Draught	15 to 17 feet
Armament (first)	3 × 12 pounders
	2 × 18 inch torpedo tubes
Engines	21,000 to 27,000 hp; turbines
Speed	33 knots

First class of British destroyers to have turbines; also first to burn oil in place of coal. Later ships of this class were armed with two 4-inch 25-pounder guns.

Torpedo boat LIGHTNING

(Britain) 1877

Displacement	40 tons
Length	90 feet
Engines	2,850 hp; triple expansion
Speed	19 knots

First of a new generation of enlarged British torpedo boats, built for the high seas.

Cruiser IRIS

(Britain) 1878

Displacement	3,730 tons
Length	331 feet 6 inches
Beam	46 feet
Draught	22 feet
Armament (first)	10 × 64 pounder muzzle-loaders
	4 torpedo tubes
Engines	6,000 hp; compound
Speed	18·6 knots

This fast ship (still equipped with auxiliary sail to save coal stocks) was the first steel cruiser; she was designed to scout for the battle fleet and to protect and prey on commercial shipping.

Cruiser TAKACHIKO

(Japan) 1884

Displacement	3,650 tons
Length	300 feet
Beam	46 feet
Draught	18 feet 6 inches
Armament	2 × 10·3 inch guns
	6 × 5·9 inch guns
	2 × 6 pounder guns
	10 × 1 pounder guns
	4 × 14 inch torpedo tubes
Engines	7,000 hp; reciprocating
Speed	18·5 knots

Typical of the next generation of protected cruisers, she combined high speed with greater fighting power.

Cruiser DUPUY DE LOME
(France) 1888

Displacement	6,300 tons
Length	352 feet
Beam	46 feet 8 inches
Draught	18 feet 10 inches
Armament	2 × 7·6 inch guns
	6 × 6·4 inch guns
	6 × 5·5 inch guns
Main armour	4 inch belt
Speed	20 knots

A fast, well armed and protected cruiser built to give the French a more powerful type of commerce-raider.

Cruiser MINOTAUR
(Britain) 1905

Class	Minotaur (3 built)
Displacement	14,600 tons
Length	519 feet
Beam	74 feet 6 inches
Draught	26 feet
Armament	4 × 9·2 inch guns
	10 × 7·5 inch guns
	16 × 12 pounders
	5 × 18 inch torpedo tubes
Main armour	6 to 3 inch belt
Engines	27,000 hp; triple expansion
Speed	23 knots

Typical of British armoured cruisers in the first decade of the 20th century, when increasing emphasis was given to offensive power.

Light cruiser BREMEN
(Germany) 1903

Displacement	3,250 tons (normal)
Length	341 feet (waterline)
Beam	43 feet 6 inches
Draught	17 feet 6 inches
Armament	10 × 4·1 inch guns
	10 × 1 pounder guns
	4 × 18 inch torpedo tubes
Engines	11,000 hp; triple expansion
Speed	23 knots

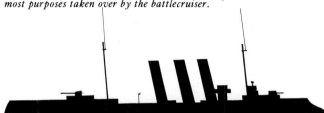

First of a new type of cruiser built for reconnaissance work; the offensive role of armoured cruisers was for most purposes taken over by the battlecruiser.

Submarine A-1
(Britain) 1904

Displacement	165 tons (surface)
Length	99 feet
Beam	12 feet 9 inches
Armament	2 × 18 inch torpedo tubes
Motive power	450/80 hp; petrol (surface)
	electric (diving)
Speed	11 knots (surface)
	7 knots (submerged)

First British version of the American Holland submarine; the latter was the prototype for most of the world's navies.

Seaplane carrier LE FOUDRE
(France) 1892

Displacement	6,086 tons
Length	374 feet
Beam	52 feet
Draught	25 feet
Armament	8 × 4 inch guns
	4 × 9 pounder guns
	2 × 3 pounder guns
Engines	11,930 hp
Speed	19·6 knots

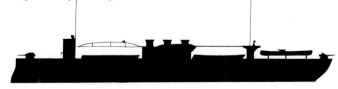

A converted depot ship, in 1912 she became the first seaplane carrier to be commissioned and so meet the need for a vessel capable of operating aircraft. In World War I landings on the surface of the sea remained the only means of recovery.

Aircraft carrier ARGUS
(Britain) 1917

Displacement	14,000 tons
Length	560 feet
Beam	68 feet
Draught	21 feet
Armament (first)	6 × 4 inch guns
Carrier capacity	20 aircraft
Engines	20,000 hp; triple expansion
Speed	20 knots

The prototype aircraft carrier with a continuous free deck; completed too late for action in World War I.

Battleship NAGATO

(Japan) 1917

Displacement	32,720 tons (standard)
Length	661 feet
Beam	95 feet
Draught	30 feet
Armament	8 × 16 inch guns
	20 × 5·5 inch guns
	4 × 3 inch guns
	8 × 21 inch torpedo tubes
Main armour	12 to 4 inch belt
Engines	80,000 hp; turbines
Speed	27 knots

Most powerful ship in the world when completed in 1920; later refitted in 1924 and rebuilt between 1934 and 1936.

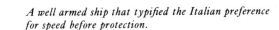

Battlecruiser HOOD

(Britain) 1916

Displacement	41,200 tons
Length	860 feet
Beam	104 feet
Draught	28 feet 6 inches
Armament	8 × 15 inch guns
	12 × 5·5 inch guns
	4 × 4 inch AA guns
	4 × 3 pounders
	6 × 21 inch torpedo tubes
Main armour	12 to 5 inch belt
Engines	144,000 hp; turbines
Speed	31 knots

World's heaviest warship for most of her active lifetime (1920–41), she nevertheless suffered from inadequate armour protection.

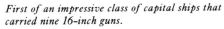

Battlecruiser VITTORIO VENETO

(Italy) 1937

Displacement	35,000 tons (standard)
Length	754 feet
Beam	106 feet 6 inches
Draught	30 feet 6 inches
Armament	9 × 15 inch guns
	12 × 6 inch guns
	12 × 3·5 inch AA guns
	3 aircraft
Main armour	12 to 9 inch belt
Engines	130,000 hp; geared turbines
Speed	30 knots

A well armed ship that typified the Italian preference for speed before protection.

Battleship WASHINGTON

(USA) 1938

Class	Washington (6 built)
Displacement	35,000 tons
Length	729 feet
Beam	108 feet
Draught	26 feet 8 inches
Armament	9 × 16 inch guns
	20 × 5 inch DP guns
	3 aircraft (with 2 catapults)
Main armour	16 inch belt
Engines	121,000 hp; geared turbines
Speed	27 knots

First of an impressive class of capital ships that carried nine 16-inch guns.

Battleship YAMATO

(Japan) 1937

Displacement	64,000 tons
Length	863 feet
Beam	127 feet
Draught	35 feet
Armament (first)	9 × 18·1 inch guns
	12 × 6·1 inch guns
	12 × 5 inch AA guns
	24 × 25 mm AA guns
	4 × 13 mm guns
	6 aircraft
Main armour	16 inch belt
Engines	150,000 hp; steam turbines
Speed	27 knots

This ship and her sister, the Musashi, were the greatest battleships ever built. Completed after Pearl Harbor (December 1941), they were, however, already obsolescent, made thus by the carrier and its aircraft.

Aircraft carrier LEXINGTON

(USA) 1921

Displacement	36,000 tons
Length	888 feet
Beam	105 feet
Draught	24 feet
Armament	8 × 8 inch guns
	12 × 5 inch AA guns
	4 × 6 pounder guns
Carrier capacity	72 aircraft (later 90)
Engines	180,000 hp; turbines
Speed	34 knots

Originally laid down as battlecruisers, she and the Saratoga were converted and became the world's largest carriers.

Fleet carrier WASP

(USA) 1936

Class	Essex
Displacement	27,100 tons
Length	820 feet
Beam	147 feet 6 inches
Draught	20 feet
Armament	12 × 5 inch guns
	40 × 40 mm AA guns
Carrier capacity	100 aircraft
Engines	turbines
Speed	32 knots

One of the Essex class ships that became the standard US fleet carrier of World War II.

Cruiser ASHIGARA

(Japan) 1925

Class	Ashigara (4 built)
Displacement	10,900 tons
Length	631 feet
Beam	57 feet
Draught	19 feet
Armament	10 × 7·9 inch guns
	6 × 4·7 inch guns
	12 torpedo tubes
	2 aircraft
Main armour	4 inch belt
Engines	130,000 hp; turbines
Speed	35 knots

First class of Japanese cruisers designed from the beginning to exceed Washington Treaty limitations (set at 10,000 tons for cruisers).

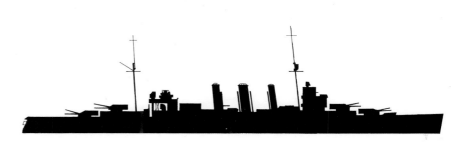

Cruiser KENT

(Britain) 1926

Class	County (11 built)
Displacement	9,750 tons
Length	630 feet
Beam	68 feet
Draught	16 feet
Armament	8 × 8 inch guns
	8 × 4 inch AA guns
	8 × 2 pounder AA guns
	8 × 21 inch torpedo tubes
Main armour	5 to 3 inch belt
Engines	80,000 hp; turbines
Speed	32 knots

County class cruiser built to maximum Washington Treaty limits and equipped with 8-inch guns.

Cruiser BOISE

(USA) 1936

Class	Brooklyn (9 built)
Displacement	10,000 tons
Length	608 feet
Beam	62 feet
Draught	19 feet 6 inches
Armament	15 × 6 inch guns
	8 × 5 inch AA guns
	4 × 3 pounders
	5 × 1 pounders
	4 aircraft
Main armour	4 to 1½ inch sides
Engines	100,000 hp; geared turbines
Speed	33 knots

A Brooklyn class cruiser with seaplane catapult placed in the stern.

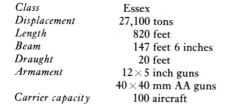

Cruiser LEIPZIG

(Germany) 1929 (launch date)

Displacement	6,000 tons
Length	544 feet
Beam	53 feet 6 inches
Draught	15 feet 9 inches
Armament	9 × 5·9 inch guns
	6 × 3·5 inch AA guns
	8 × 37 mm AA guns
	12 × 21 inch torpedo tubes
	2 aircraft (with catapult)
Main armour	4 to 3 inch sides
Engines	60,000 hp; geared turbines
Speed	32 knots

A powerful commerce-raider equipped with 5·9 inch guns – which were within the limits imposed by the 1919 Treaty of Versailles.

Pocket battleship DEUTSCHLAND

(Germany) 1929

Displacement	11,700 tons
Length	609 feet (overall)
Beam	67 feet 6 inches
Draught	21 feet 9 inches
Armament	6 × 11 inch guns
	8 × 5·9 inch guns
	6 × 4·1 inch AA guns
	8 × 37 mm AA guns
	8 × 21 inch torpedo tubes
	2 aircraft (with catapult)
Main armour	4 inch belt
Engines	54,000 hp; diesel
Speed	27 knots

First of a new type of cruiser, which exceeded Treaty limits and belonged properly in the capital ship class.

10 × 20 mm AA guns

Destroyer LAFOREY

(Britain) 1940

Class	L class (8 built)
Displacement	1,935 tons
Length	362 feet 6 inches
Beam	36 feet 6 inches
Draught	10 feet
Armament	6 × 4·7 inch DP guns
	16 inch belt
	4 × 2 pounder AA guns
	8 × 21 inch torpedo tubes
Engines	48,000 hp; geared turbines
Speed	36 knots

British L class destroyer, first to be fitted with dual purpose (DP) guns.

10 × 20 mm AA guns

Destroyer CRAVEN

(USA) 1937 (launch date)

Class	Gridley (10 built, plus 12 of related Benham class)
Displacement	2,350 tons
Length	341 feet
Beam	35 feet
Draught	9 feet 9 inches
Armament	
	4 × 1·1 inch AA guns
	16 × 21 inch torpedo tubes
Engines	50,000 hp; geared turbines
Speed	40 knots

Long-range American destroyer of the Gridley class, the first to be able to refuel at sea.

Destroyer AKITSUKI

(Japan) 1940

Displacement	2,700 tons
Length	413 feet 6 inches
Beam	38 feet
Draught	13 feet 6 inches
Armament (first)	8 × 3·9 inch DP guns
	4 × 25 mm guns
	4 × 24 inch torpedo tubes
Engines	52,000 hp; turbines
Speed	33 knots

One of the Type B class of large destroyers which had the powerful 3·9-inch DP gun which outranged the contemporary US 5-inch gun.

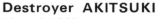

Sloop BLACK SWAN
(Britain) 1939

Class	Black Swan (9 built, plus 22 modified versions)
Displacement	1,250 tons
Length	299 feet 6 inches
Beam	37 feet 6 inches
Draught	8 feet 6 inches
Armament	6×4 inch AA guns
	4×2 pounder AA guns
	4×0·5 inch AA guns
Engines	3,600 hp; turbines
Speed	19 knots

First of a class of sloops which carried out vital escort work in the North Atlantic.

Submarine TYPE VII-B
(Germany)

Displacement	753 tons
Length	218 feet
Beam	20 feet
Draught	15 feet 6 inches
Armament	1×3·5 inch gun
	1×20 mm AA gun
	5×21 inch torpedo tubes with 12 torpedoes
	or 14 mines
Speed	17·25 knots (surface)
	8 knots (submerged)

Staple German submarine in the early part of the Battle of the Atlantic.

Submarine I 400
(Japan) 1943

Displacement	6,550 tons
Length	380 feet
Beam	39 feet
Draught	23 feet
Armament	1×5·5 inch gun
	10×25 mm guns
	8×21 inch torpedo tubes
	3 seaplanes
Engines	7,700/2,400 hp; diesel/electric
Speed	18·75 knots (surface)
	6·5 knots (submerged)

One of the Type STO submarines – the largest conventionally powered submarines ever built.

Landing craft infantry LCI-1
(USA)

Displacement	216 tons
Length	154 feet
Beam	23 feet
Engines	1,600 hp; diesel
Speed	15 knots

A new type of ship designed for amphibious operations in World War II.

Fast patrol boat OSA
(USSR) c.1959

Class	Osa (approx. 125 built)
Displacement	165 tons
Length	128 feet
Beam	25 feet
Draught	6 feet
Armament	Styx missiles
	4×30 mm guns
Engines	13,000 hp; diesel
Speed	32 knots

Soviet class of light missile-armed ship, one of which sank the Israeli destroyer Eilat with a Styx missile in the 1967 war.

Submarine GEORGE WASHINGTON
(USA) 1959

Class	George Washington (5 built to date)
Displacement	5,900 tons
Length	382 feet
Beam	33 feet
Draught	29 feet
Armament	16 Polaris missiles
	6×21 inch torpedo tubes
Main machinery	1 nuclear reactor
	1 geared turbine (15,000 hp)

First submarine to fire a nuclear missile from beneath the surface of the sea.

Aircraft carrier FORRESTAL
(USA) 1952

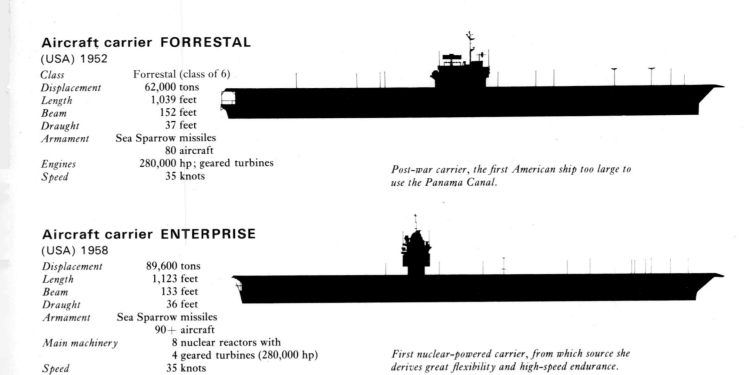

Class	Forrestal (class of 6)
Displacement	62,000 tons
Length	1,039 feet
Beam	152 feet
Draught	37 feet
Armament	Sea Sparrow missiles
	80 aircraft
Engines	280,000 hp; geared turbines
Speed	35 knots

Post-war carrier, the first American ship too large to use the Panama Canal.

Aircraft carrier ENTERPRISE
(USA) 1958

Displacement	89,600 tons
Length	1,123 feet
Beam	133 feet
Draught	36 feet
Armament	Sea Sparrow missiles
	90+ aircraft
Main machinery	8 nuclear reactors with
	4 geared turbines (280,000 hp)
Speed	35 knots

First nuclear-powered carrier, from which source she derives great flexibility and high-speed endurance.

5

MISSILES OF THE WORLD'S NAVIES

Group 1 Strategic Missiles

POLARIS
(USA) 1960

Underwater-to-surface or surface-to-surface ballistic missile. In service of USA.

Length	31 feet 0 inches
Diameter	4 feet 6 inches
Weight	35,000 pounds
Speed	6,600 mph
Range	2,875 miles
Warhead	thermonuclear

SSN-4 SARK
(USSR) c.1961

Underwater-to-surface or surface-to-surface missile. In service of USSR.

Length	48 feet 0 inches
Diameter	5 feet 9 inches
Weight and performance	not known
Warhead	nuclear

POSEIDON
(USA) 1970

Underwater-to-surface or surface-to-surface ballistic missile. In service of USA.

Length	34 feet 0 inches
Diameter	6 feet 2 inches
Weight	65,000 pounds
Range	2,875 miles
Warhead	thermonuclear

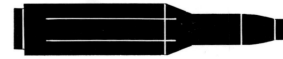

SSN-5 SERB
(USSR) c.1963

Underwater-to-surface or surface-to-surface missile. In service of USSR.

Length	35 feet 1 inch
Diameter	4 feet 10 inches
Weight and speed	not known
Range	750 miles
Warhead	nuclear or thermonuclear

SSN-6 SAWFLY

(USSR) c.1970

Underwater-to-surface or surface-to-surface missile.
In service of USSR.

Length	42 feet 0 inches
Diameter	5 feet 6 inches
Weight and speed	not known
Range	1,750 miles
Warhead	nuclear or thermonuclear

MSBS

(France)

Submarine-launched ballistic missile. In service of
France.

Length	34 feet 2 inches
Diameter	5 feet 0 inches
Weight	39,700 pounds
Range and speed	secret
Warhead	nuclear (500 kilotons)

Group 2 Surface-to-Surface Guided Weapons (SSGW)

EXOCET

(France) 1971

Surface-to-surface tactical missile. In service of
France, Peru, Britain.

Length	16 feet 9 inches
Diameter	1 foot 3 inches
Weight	1,550 pounds
Speed	Mach 1
Range	23 miles
Warhead	high explosive (220 pounds)

OTOMAT

(Italy) 1970

Surface-to-surface tactical missile. In service of Italy.

Length	15 foot 8 inches
Diameter	1 foot 5 inches
Weight	1,530 pounds
Speed	Mach 0·8
Range	40 miles
Warhead	semi-armour-piercing (450 pounds)

GABRIEL

(Israel) 1970

Surface-to-surface missile. In service of Israel.

Length	11 feet 0 inches
Diameter	1 foot 0 inches
Weight	880 pounds
Speed	Mach 0·7
Range	12 miles
Warhead	high explosive (330 pounds)

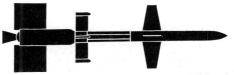

VOLCANO

(Italy) 1969

Surface-to-surface missile, also known as Sea Killer
Mark 2. In service of Italy.

Length	15 feet 4 inches
Diameter	8 inches
Weight	530 pounds
Speed	Mach 1
Range	5·6 miles
Warhead	semi-armour-piercing high explosive

PENGUIN

(Norway) 1970

Surface-to-surface tactical missile. In service of
Norway.

Length	10 feet 0 inches
Diameter	1 foot 0 inches
Weight	72 pounds
Speed	Mach 0·7
Range	18 miles
Warhead	high explosive (275 pounds)

RBO8A

(Sweden) 1968

Surface-to-surface missile. In service of Sweden.

Length	18 feet 9 inches
Diameter	2 feet 2 inches
Weight	1,985 pounds
Speed and range	secret
Warhead	high explosive

SS-12
(France) 1965

Surface-to-air tactical missile. In service of France.

Length	6 feet 3 inches
Diameter	7 inches
Weight	165 pounds
Speed	425 mph
Range	19,650 feet (3·7 miles)
Warhead	armour-piercing

STANDARD RIM-66A
(USA) 1970

Supersonic surface-to-air missile. In service of USA.

Length	15 feet 3 inches
Diameter	1 foot 0 inches
Weight	1,300 pounds
Speed	Mach 1+
Range	15 miles
Warhead	high explosive

Group 3 Cruise Missiles

SSN-3 SHADDOCK
(USSR) 1970

Surface-to-surface cruise missile. In service of USSR.

Length	36 feet 0 inches (approx.)
Diameter and weight	not known
Speed	600 mph (approx.)
Range	400 miles (approx.)
Warhead	nuclear or conventional

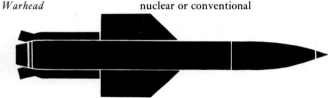

GOA
(USSR) 1970

Surface-to-air short-range missile. In service of USSR.

Length	19 feet 5 inches
Diameter	1 foot 8 inches
Weight and speed	not known
Range	15 miles (approx.)
Warhead	high explosive

Group 4 Surface-to-Air Guided Weapons (SAGW)

SEA CAT
(Britain) 1962

Surface-to-air and surface-to-surface missile for short-range work. In service of Britain, Australia, New Zealand, Sweden, Netherlands, and some South American countries.

Length	4 feet 11 inches
Diameter	7 inches
Weight	150 pounds
Speed	secret
Range	2·2 miles
Warhead	high explosive

SLAM
(Britain) 1970

Ship-launched missile system still under development and consisting of a cluster of six Blowpipe missiles launched from a common mounting. The details for the Blowpipe missile are:

Length	.4 feet 6 inches
Diameter	4 inches
Weight and speed	secret
Range	·2 miles
Warhead	high explosive (5 pounds)

SEA SLUG
(Britain) 1967

Surface-to-air and surface-to-surface missile. In service of Britain.

Length	20 feet 0 inches
Diameter	1 foot 10 inches
Weight and performance	secret
Warhead	high explosive

SEA DART
(Britain) 1965

Surface-to-air and surface-to-surface missile. In service of Britain, Argentina.

Length	14 feet 3 inches
Diameter	1 foot 5 inches
Weight	1,210 pounds
Speed	secret
Range	20 miles
Warhead	high explosive

6

DETAILS OF IMPORTANT AIRCRAFT

US Wright Flyer A (1908)

Type		two-seat reconnaissance machine
Engine		Wright 4-cylinder water-cooled inline, 30-hp
Armament		none
Speed	44	mph
Climb	?	
Ceiling	?	
Range	90	miles
Weight	740	lbs (empty)
	1,200	lbs (loaded)
Span	36	feet 6 inches
Length	28	feet 11 inches
Height	8	feet 1 inch

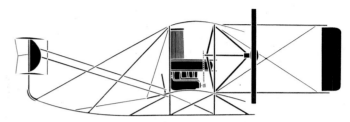

The Military Flyer tested in 1908 and 1909 was an adaptation of the basic Flyer A, and after acceptance became Signal Corps No. 1. Data are for this machine.

French Morane-Saulnier Type N (1913)

Type		single-seat fighter
Engine		Le Rhône 9C 9-cylinder air-cooled rotary, 80-hp
Armament		one fixed 8-mm Hotchkiss machine gun
Speed	90	mph at sea level
Climb	10	minutes to 6,560 feet
Ceiling	13,125	feet
Endurance	1½	hours
Weight	633	lbs (empty)
	976	lbs (loaded)
Span	26	feet 8¾ inches
Length	19	feet 1½ inches
Height	7	feet 4½ inches

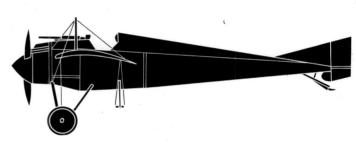

The Morane-Saulnier N, a pleasing and well-streamlined monoplane, entered service with the French air force in 1914.

British Royal Aircraft Factory BE 2b (1913)

Type		two-seat reconnaissance machine
Engine		Renault 8-cylinder water-cooled inline, 70-hp
Armament		miscellaneous small arms
Speed	70	mph at sea level
Climb	35	minutes to 7,000 feet
Ceiling	10,000	feet
Endurance	3	hours
Weight	1,274	lbs (empty)
	1,600	lbs (loaded)
Span	35	feet 0½ inch
Length	29	feet 6½ inches
Height	10	feet 2 inches

The BE 2b was the first British type to enter quantity production for the RFC.

German Fokker E-III (1915)

Type		single-seat fighter
Engine		Iberursel U-I 9-cylinder air-cooled rotary, 100-hp
Armament		one fixed 7·92-mm Spandau machine gun
Speed	87½	mph at sea level
Climb	30	minutes to 9,840 feet
Ceiling	11,500	feet
Endurance	1½	hours
Weight	878	lbs (empty)
	1,342	lbs (loaded)
Span	31	feet 2¾ inches
Length	23	feet 7½ inches
Height	7	feet 10½ inches

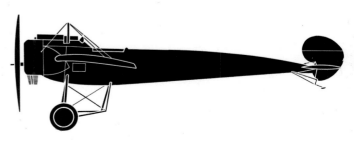

The Fokker E-III was the major production variant of the Fokker *Eindekker* type, the world's first true fighter.

British Handley Page 0/100 (1915)

Type		three-seat heavy bomber
Engines		two Rolls-Royce Eagle II 8-cylinder water-cooled inlines, 266-hp each
Armament		three to five flexible ·303-inch Lewis guns, plus up to 2,000 lbs of bombs
Speed	85	mph at sea level
Climb	15+	minutes to 5,000 feet
Ceiling	7,000	feet
Range	700	miles
Weight	8,300	lbs (empty)
	14,000	lbs (loaded)
Span	100	feet
Length	62	feet 10¼ inches
Height	22	feet

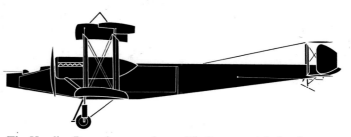

The Handley Page 0/100 was the world's first true night bomber, and originated from an Admiralty request for a 'bloody paralyser' of a bomber. Only 46 examples of the type were built before production was switched to the improved 0/400 with better engines.

German Albatros D-III (1916)

Type		single-seat fighter
Engine		Mercedes D-IIIa 6-cylinder water-cooled inline, 160-hp
Armament		two fixed 7·92-mm Spandau machine guns
Speed	109	mph at sea level
Climb	12	minutes 1 second to 9,840 feet
Ceiling	18,050	feet
Endurance	2	hours
Weight	1,454	lbs (empty)
	1,949	lbs (loaded)
Span	29	feet 8¼ inches
Length	24	feet 0¾inch
Height	9	feet 9¼ inches

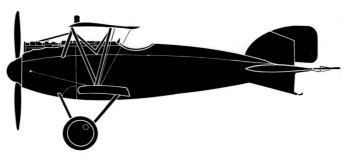

The Albatros D-III was primarily responsible for German air superiority in the early months of 1917.

French Breguet 14B.2 (1916)

Type		two-seat bomber and reconnaissance machine
Engine		Renault 12Fcx 12-cylinder water-cooled inline, 300-hp
Armament		one fixed ·303-inch Vickers gun and two or three flexible ·303-inch Lewis guns, plus up to 560 lbs of bombs
Speed	110	mph at 6,560 feet
Climb	16	minutes 30 seconds to 9,840 feet
Ceiling	19,000	feet
Endurance	2¾	hours
Weight	2,283	lbs (empty)
	3,892	lbs (loaded)
Span	47	feet 1¼ inches
Length	29	feet 1¼ inches
Height	10	feet 10 inches

The Breguet 14 was undoubtedly France's best light bomber of World War I, and began to enter service in September 1917. It had an excellent defensive armament.

British de Havilland 4 (1916)

Type		two-seat bomber
Engine		Rolls-Royce Eagle VIII 8-cylinder water-cooled inline, 375-hp
Armament		one or two fixed ·303-inch Vickers guns and one or two ·303-inch flexible Lewis guns, plus up to 460 lbs of bombs
Speed	143	mph at sea level
Climb	9	minutes to 10,000 feet
Ceiling	22,000	feet
Range	435	miles
Weight	2,387	lbs (empty)
	3,472	lbs (loaded)
Span	42	feet 4¾ inches
Length	30	feet 8 inches
Height	10	feet

The de Havilland 4 was the best light bomber of the war, and served with the American as well as the British air force. Its one failing was the separation of the pilot and the observer, a fault rectified in the otherwise inferior de Havilland 9.

French Nieuport 17 (1916)

Type		single-seat fighter
Engine		Le Rhône 9-cylinder air-cooled rotary, 110-hp
Armament		one .303-inch Vickers or Lewis machine gun
Speed	110	mph at 6,560 feet
Climb	9	minutes to 10,000 feet
Ceiling	17,400	feet
Endurance	2	hours
Weight	825	lbs (empty)
	1,246	lbs (loaded)
Span	26	feet 11¾ inches
Length	18	feet 10 inches
Height	7	feet 7¾ inches

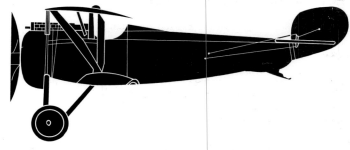

The Nieuport 17 was the best of the company's sesquiplane fighters.

French Spad S.7 (1916)

Type		single-seat fighter
Engine		Hispano-Suiza 8Ac 8-cylinder water-cooled inline, 175-hp
Armament		one fixed ·303-inch Vickers gun
Speed	119	mph at 6,560 feet
Climb	11	minutes 30 seconds to 9,840 feet
Ceiling	18,000	feet
Endurance	2¼	hours
Weight	1,100	lbs (empty)
	1,550	lbs (loaded)
Span	25	feet 8 inches
Length	20	feet 3½ inches
Height	7	feet

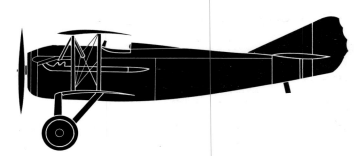

The Spad S.7 was a fast and very sturdy fighter, and was an excellent gun platform.

Italian Ansaldo SVA-5 (1917)

Type		single-seat reconnaissance and bomber machine
Engine		SPA Type 6A 6-cylinder water-cooled inline, 220-hp
Armament		two fixed ·303-inch Vickers guns
Speed	143	mph at sea level
Climb	10	minutes to 9,840 feet
Ceiling	22,000	feet
Endurance	4	hours
Weight	1,507	lbs (empty)
	2,090	lbs (loaded)
Span	29	feet 10¼ inches
Length	26	feet 7 inches
Height	10	feet 6 inches

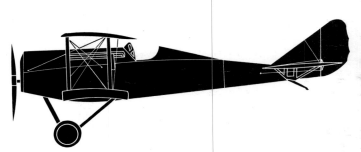

The Ansaldo SVA-5, although designed as a fighter, lacked the manoeuvrability vital for this function in World War I, and found its *métier* as a long-range strategic reconnaissance machine.

German Fokker D-VII (1917)

Type		single-seat fighter
Engine		BMW IIIa 6-cylinder water-cooled inline, 185 hp
Armament		two fixed 7·92-mm Spandau machine guns
Speed	124	mph at sea level
Climb	8	minutes 30 seconds to 9,840 feet
Ceiling	22,900	feet
Endurance	1½	hours
Weight	1,513	lbs (empty)
	1,993	lbs (loaded)
Span	29	feet 3⅓ inches
Length	22	feet 9¾ inches
Height	9	feet 2 inches

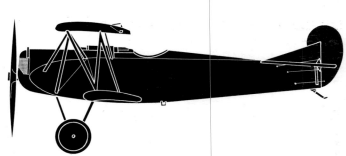

The Fokker D-VII was undoubtedly Germany's best fighter of World War I, and may have been the equal of the British Sopwith Camel.

German Hannover CL-IIIa (1917)

Type		two-seat escort and ground-attack fighter
Engine		Argus As-III 6-cylinder water-cooled inline, 180-hp
Armament		one fixed 7·92-mm Spandau machine gun and one flexible 7·92-mm Parabellum machine gun
Speed	103	mph at 16,400 feet
Climb	5	minutes 18 seconds to 3,280 feet
Ceiling	24,600	feet
Endurance	3	hours
Weight	1,577	lbs (empty)
	2,378	lbs (loaded)
Span	38	feet 4⅔ inches
Length	24	feet 10½ inches
Height	9	feet 2¼ inches

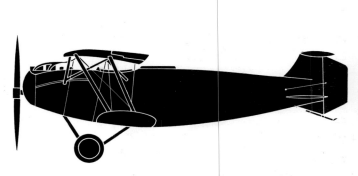

The Hannover CL-IIIa was one of Germany's best aircraft in World War I, and although it was a two-seater its manoeuvrability compared favourably with single-seaters'.

British Hawker Hart (1928)

Type		two-seat bomber
Engine		Rolls-Royce Kestrel IB 12-cylinder liquid-cooled inline, 525-hp
Armament		one fixed ·303-inch Vickers gun and one flexible ·303-inch Lewis gun, plus up to 500 lbs of bombs
Speed	184	mph at 5,000 feet
Climb	8	minutes 20 seconds to 10,000 feet
Ceiling	21,000	feet
Range	470	miles
Weight	2,530	lbs (empty)
	4,554	lbs (loaded)
Span	37	feet 3 inches
Length	29	feet 4 inches
Height	10	feet 5 inches

The Hawker Hart was an extremely versatile two-seat biplane, originally designed as a light day bomber but subsequently adapted for several other roles. Nearly 1,000 were built, and many of these were exported.

British Handley Page Heyford (1930)

Type		four-seat heavy bomber
Engines		two Rolls-Royce Kestrel IIIS 12-cylinder liquid-cooled inlines, 575-hp each at 11,500 feet
Armament		three flexible ·303-inch Lewis guns and up to 3,500 lbs of bombs
Speed	142	mph at 12,500 feet
Ceiling	21,000	feet
Range	920	miles with 1,598-lb bomb-load
Weight	10,080	lbs (empty)
	16,750	lbs (loaded)
Span	75	feet
Length	58	feet
Height	20	feet 6 inches

The Handley Page Heyford was a very unusual machine: its fuselage was mounted under the top wing, the bomb-load was carried in the thickened centre section of the lower wing.

US Boeing P-26 (1932)

Type		single-seat fighter
Engine		Pratt & Whitney R-1340-27 9-cylinder air-cooled radial, 500-hp
Armament		two fixed ·3-inch or one ·3-inch and one ·5-inch machine gun, plus up to 200 lbs of bombs
Speed	234	mph at 7,500 feet
Climb	2,360	feet per minute initially
Ceiling	27,400	feet
Range	360	miles
Weight	2,197	lbs (empty)
	2,955	lbs (loaded)
Span	27	feet 11½ inches
Length	23	feet 7¼ inches
Height	10	feet 0½ inch

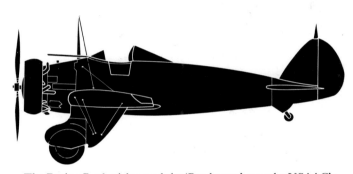

The Boeing P-26, nicknamed the 'Peashooter', was the USAAC's first all-metal, low-wing monoplane fighter.

US Curtiss F11C Goshawk (1932)

Type		single-seat carrier fighter-bomber
Engine		Wright R-1820-04 9-cylinder air-cooled radial, 700-hp
Armament		two fixed ·3-inch Browning machine guns, plus up to 474 lbs of bombs
Speed	225	mph at 8,000 feet
Climb	2	minutes 36 seconds to 5,000 feet
Ceiling	27,000	feet
Range	797	miles
Weight	3,329	lbs (empty)
	5,086	lbs (loaded)
Span	31	feet 6 inches
Length	23	feet
Height	10	feet 10 inches

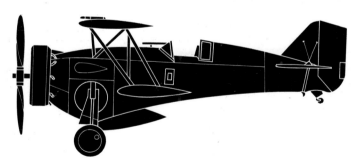

The Curtiss F11C, a versatile US Navy bomber-fighter, was chiefly remarkable for being a biplane with a retractable undercarriage.

British Gloster Gladiator (1934)

Type		single-seat fighter
Engine		Bristol Mercury IXS 9-cylinder air-cooled radial, 840-hp
Armament		four fixed ·303-inch Browning guns
Speed	253	mph at 14,500 feet
Climb	4	minutes 40 seconds to 10,000 feet
Ceiling	33,000	feet
Range	428	miles
Weight	3,217	lbs (empty)
	4,592	lbs (loaded)
Span	32	feet 3 inches
Length	27	feet 5 inches
Height	11	feet 9 inches

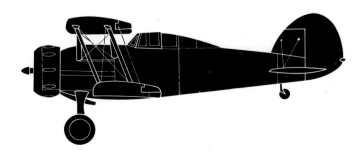

The Gloster Gladiator was the last biplane fighter to serve with British forces.

Russian Polikarpov I-16 (1934)

Type		single-seat fighter-bomber
Engine		Shvetsov M-62 9-cylinder air-cooled radial, 1,000-hp
Armament		two 20-mm ShVAK cannon, two 7·62-mm ShKAS machine guns, plus six 82-mm RS-82 rockets or two VAP-6M or ZAP-6 chemical containers
Speed	326	mph at sea level
Climb	4	minutes 48 seconds to 16,400 feet
Ceiling	29,530	feet
Range	435	miles
Weight	3,285	lbs (empty)
	4,520	lbs (loaded)
Span	29	feet 6½ inches
Length	20	feet 1¼ inches
Height	8	feet 5 inches

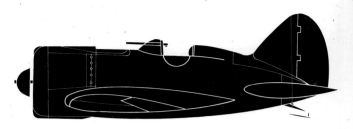

The Polikarpov I-16 was the first all-metal, low-wing, cantilever monoplane fighter in the world to be fitted with a retractable undercarriage, and performed sterling service with the Russian and Spanish Republican air forces before being relegated to training duties in the early months of 1943.

US Boeing B-17 Flying Fortress (1935)

Type		nine-seat heavy bomber
Engines		four Wright GR-1820-39 9-cylinder air-cooled radials, 930-hp each
Armament		five flexible ·3-inch Browning machine guns, plus up to 10,496 lbs of bombs
Speed	292	mph at 25,000 feet
Climb	6	minutes 30 seconds to 10,000 feet
Ceiling	36,000	feet
Range	2,400	miles
Weight	25,500	lbs (empty)
	47,920	lbs (loaded)
Span	103	feet 9 inches
Length	67	feet 11 inches
Height	15	feet 5 inches

The Boeing B-17 was the United States' most celebrated bomber of World War II, and bore the brunt of the daylight offensive waged against Germany. The final mark, the 17G, differed quite considerably from the earlier prewar models, being very much better armed, and far less liable to catch fire when hit, the besetting problem of the first marks.

British Hawker Hurricane (1935)

Type		single-seat fighter-bomber
Engine		Rolls-Royce Merlin XX 12-cylinder liquid-cooled inline, 1,460-hp at take-off
Armament		four 20-mm Oerlikon cannon and up to 1,000 lbs of bombs
Speed	342	mph at 22,000 feet
Climb	9	minutes 6 seconds to 20,000 feet
Ceiling	35,600	feet
Range	970	miles
Weight	5,800	lbs (empty)
	7,800	lbs (loaded)
Span	40	feet
Length	32	feet 2½ inches
Height	8	feet 9 inches

The Hawker Hurricane was the first British fighter to be fitted with an armament of eight machine guns, and was the Spitfire's chief companion in the Battle of Britain. During this battle, Hurricanes shot down more German aircraft than all the other types combined. In its obsolescence it was transformed into an excellent fighter-bomber and tank-busting aircraft.

German Junkers Ju 87 (1935)

Type		two-seat dive-bomber and close support machine
Engine		Junkers Jumo 211J-1 12-cylinder liquid-cooled inline, 1,400-hp at take-off
Armament		two fixed 7·92-mm MG17 and one flexible 7·92-mm twin-barrelled MG8Iz machine gun, plus up to 3,968 lbs of bombs, or two pods containing six MG17 machine guns or two 2-cm MGFF cannon each, or two packs of 92 4·4-lb anti-personnel bombs
Speed	255	mph at 13,500 feet
Climb	19	minutes 48 seconds to 16,400 feet
Ceiling	23,905	feet
Range	954	miles
Weight	8,600	lbs (empty)
	14,550	lbs (loaded)
Span	45	feet 3⅓ inches
Length	37	feet 8¾ inches
Height	12	feet 9¼ inches

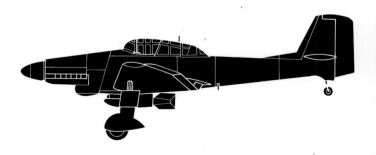

The Junkers Ju 87, more commonly known as the 'Stuka', was not an especially good machine, but performed very creditably in World War II with the aid of its devastating psychological impact.

468

German Messerschmitt Bf 109 (1935)

Type		single-seat fighter
Engine		Daimler-Benz 601E-1 12-cylinder liquid-cooled inline, 1,350-hp at take-off
Armament		one 2-cm MG151 cannon and two 7·92-mm MG17 machine guns
Speed	388	mph at 21,325 feet
Climb	2	minutes 36 seconds to 9,840 feet
Ceiling	39,370	feet
Range	528	miles
Weight	5,269	lbs (empty)
	6,872	lbs (loaded)
Span	32	feet 5¾ inches
Length	29	feet 0⅛ inch
Height	8	feet 6 inches

The Messerschmitt Bf 109, Germany's most celebrated fighter of the World War II era, was tested in combat in Spain, and much of real value was learned there, as regards both the aircraft and the tactics that suited it. It was built in greater numbers than any other German machine, but the need for heavier armament and more engine power at the end of the war detracted greatly from the type's flying characteristics, which peaked in the F of 1942.

Italian Savoia-Marchetti 81 *Pipistrello* (1935)

Type		six-seat bomber and transport machine
Engines		three Piaggio P.IX RC 40 9-cylinder air-cooled radials, 680-hp each
Armament		six flexible 7·7-mm machine guns and up to 2,205 lbs of bombs
Speed	205	mph at 13,120 feet
Ceiling	22,965	feet
Range	932	miles
Weight	14,300	lbs (empty)
	22,220	lbs (loaded)
Span	78	feet 8¾ inches
Length	58	feet 4¾ inches
Height	14	feet 7¼ inches

The Savoia-Marchetti 81 was for its time an excellent medium bomber, and proved very useful to the Italians in the conquest of Abyssinia and in the Spanish Civil War. The type was derived from a civilian airliner, and had a good performance coupled with a strong defensive armament of six machine guns. The *Pipistrello* (Bat) was obsolescent by World War II.

German Junkers Ju 88 (1936)

Type		three-seat bomber
Engines		two BMW 801G-2 14-cylinder air-cooled radials, 1,730-hp each at 5,000 feet
Armament		one flexible 13-mm MG131 machine gun, plus up to 4,410 lbs of bombs
Speed	340	mph at 26,250 feet
Ceiling	38,000	feet
Range	1,660	miles
Weight	18,250	lbs (empty)
	30,400	lbs (loaded)
Span	65	feet 7½ inches
Length	48	feet 2⅝ inches
Height	15	feet 8½ inches

The Junkers Ju 88 was the most versatile aircraft produced by Germany in World War II, serving as a bomber, fighter, ground-attack, reconnaissance, anti-shipping, and night fighter. It was even pressed into service as the main component of a 'piggy-back' assault weapon, the nose being replaced by a large shaped charge.

British Short Sunderland (1937)

Type		13-seat maritime patrol and reconnaissance machine
Engines		four Pratt & Whitney R-1830-90B 14-cylinder air-cooled radials, 1,200-hp each
Armament		two ·5-inch and between eight and twelve ·303-inch Browning machine guns, plus up to 2,000 lbs of bombs
Speed	213	mph at 5,000 feet
Climb	840	feet per minute initially
Ceiling	17,900	feet
Range	2,980	miles
Weight	37,000	lbs (empty)
	60,000	lbs (loaded)
Span	112	feet 9½ inches
Length	85	fee 4 inches
Height	32	feet 10½ inches

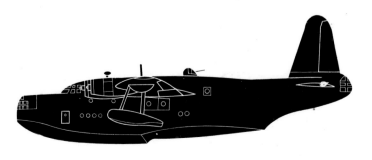

The Short Sunderland was designed to replace Britain's biplane patrol flying boats, and proved a remarkably successful machine, effective against U-boats and German long-range fighters.

British Bristol Beaufighter (1939)

Type		two-seat anti-shipping strike fighter
Engines		two Bristol Hercules XVII 14-cylinder air-cooled radials, 1,770-hp each
Armament		four 20-mm Hispano cannon, six ·303-inch Browning machine guns, one ·303-inch Vickers K gun, plus one 1,650-lb or 2,127-lb torpedo, or eight 90-lb rockets and two 250-lb bombs
Speed	303	mph at 1,300 feet
Ceiling	15,000	feet
Range	1,470	miles
Weight	15,600	lbs (empty)
	25,200	lbs (loaded)
Span	57	feet 10 inches
Length	41	feet 8 inches
Height	15	feet 10 inches

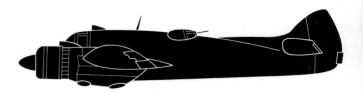

The Bristol Beaufighter was evolved from the Beaufort torpedo-bomber, but soon showed itself to be a far superior machine. It was a massive and sturdy machine, but possessed of considerable speed, range, and firepower. The Beaufighter was at its best as a heavily-armed, radar-equipped night fighter, or as an anti-shipping strike fighter with an armament of bombs, rockets, or an 18- or 21-inch torpedo.

Japanese Mitsubishi A6M *Zero-sen* (1939)

Type		single-seat carrier fighter
Engine		Nakajima NK1F Sakae 21 14-cylinder air-cooled radial, 1,130-hp at take-off
Armament		two 20-mm Type 99 cannon and two 7·7-mm Type 97 machine guns
Speed	338	mph at 19,685 feet
Climb	7	minutes 19 seconds to 19,685 feet
Ceiling	36,250	feet
Range	1,477	miles
Weight	3,984	lbs (empty)
	5,609	lbs (loaded)
Span	36	feet 1 inch
Length	29	feet 8¾ inches
Height	11	feet 6 inches

The Mitsubishi A6M, most commonly known as the Zero, was a landmark in naval fighter design, as it was the first such aircraft to be able to best its land-based counterparts. The capabilities of the Zero came as a rude shock to the Allies at the beginning of the Pacific war, and it was not until 1943 that a satisfactory counter was introduced. The Zero had excellent manoeuvrability and range, but lacked strength against heavy battle damage.

British de Havilland Mosquito (1940)

Type		two-seater bomber
Engines		two Rolls-Royce Merlin 21 12-cylinder liquid-cooled inlines, 1,460-hp each at 6,250 feet
Armament		up to 4,000 lbs of bombs
Speed	385	mph at 13,000 feet
Climb	2,500	feet per minute initially
Ceiling	34,000	feet
Range	2,040	miles
Weight	13,400	lbs (empty)
	22,570	lbs (loaded)
Span	54	feet 2 inches
Length	40	feet 9½ inches
Height	17	feet 5 inches

The de Havilland Mosquito was the British equivalent of the Junkers 88, and was first conceived as a bomber with speed sufficient to enable it to outrun German fighters, thus obviating the need for defensive armament. Performance was so spectacular, however, that the Mosquito was soon adapted as a fighter, night fighter, fighter bomber, reconnaissance machine, and anti-shipping strike fighter.

US North American B-25 Mitchell (1940)

Type		six-seat bomber
Engines		two Wright R-2600-92 14-cylinder air-cooled radials, 1,700-hp each
Armament		twelve ·5-inch Browning machine guns, plus eight 5-inch rockets and up to 3,000 lbs of bombs
Speed	272	mph at 12,000 feet
Ceiling	24,200	feet
Range	1,350	miles
Weight	19,480	lbs (empty)
	35,000	lbs (loaded)
Span	67	feet 7 inches
Length	52	feet 11 inches
Height	16	feet 4 inches

The North American Mitchell was one of the most important aircraft in the inventories of the Allies, being used by Russia, Britain, Holland, Brazil, and Canada as well as the United States. The B-25G and H models were exceptionally heavily armed ground-attack variants, being armed with a 75-mm gun in addition to 14 .5-inch machine guns, plus a torpedo or 3,200 lbs of bombs. The last model, the 25J, reverted to the conventional bomber design.

US North American P-51 Mustang (1940)

Type		single-seat escort fighter and fighter-bomber
Engine		Packard V-1650-7 Merlin 12-cylinder liquid-cooled inline, 1,694-hp
Armament		six ·5-inch Browning MG 53-2 machine guns, plus 2,000 lbs of bombs or six 5-inch rockets
Speed	437	mph at 25,000 feet
Climb	7	minutes 18 seconds to 20,000 feet
Ceiling	41,900	feet
Range	2,080	miles
Weight	7,125	lbs (empty)
	12,100	lbs (loaded)
Span	37	feet 0¼ inch
Length	32	feet 3 inches
Height	8	feet 8 inches

The North American Mustang, designed to a British specification, was undoubtedly the best fighter of World War II. The first mark, powered by an American Allison inline, performed creditably at low altitudes, but the marriage of the P-51 to the British Rolls-Royce Merlin in the P-51B paved the way for the development of the Mustang's remarkable abilities as a fighter and fighter-bomber.

US Vought F4U Corsair (1940)

Type		single-seat carrier fighter
Engine		Pratt & Whitney R-2800-8W 18-cylinder air-cooled radial, 2,250-hp
Armament		six ·5-inch Browning MG 53-2 machine guns, plus 2,000 lbs of bombs or eight 5-inch rockets
Speed	425	mph at 20,000 feet
Climb	3,120	feet per minute initially
Ceiling	37,000	feet
Range	1,562	miles
Weight	8,694	lbs (empty)
	13,120	lbs (loaded)
Span	40	feet 11 inches
Length	33	feet 4 inches
Height	15	feet 1 inch

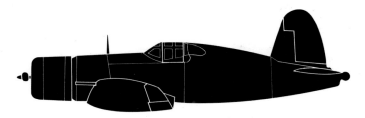

The Vought Corsair naval fighter and fighter-bomber was the best such machine of World War II, and proved to be an extremely potent machine, shooting down over 2,000 aircraft and providing fast, devastating support with guns, rockets, and bombs for US invasion forces in the Pacific theatre.

British Avro Lancaster (1941)

Type		seven-seat heavy bomber
Engines		four Rolls-Royce Merlin 24 12-cylinder liquid-cooled inlines, 1,640-hp each
Armament		ten flexible ·303-inch machine guns, plus up to 22,000 lbs of bombs
Speed	287	mph at 11,500 feet
Ceiling	24,500	feet
Range	1,660	miles
Weight	36,900	lbs (empty)
	70,000	lbs (loaded)
Span	102	feet
Length	69	feet 2 inches
Height	20	feet

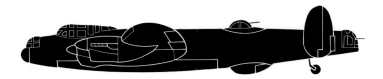

The Avro Lancaster was the best British bomber of World War II, and was a four-engined derivative of the ill-starred two-engined Manchester of 1939. Special adaptation enabled the Lancaster to carry the 22,000-lb 'Grand Slam', the largest bomb of the war, and another modification allowed the cylindrical 'dambuster' bomb to be used. The Lancaster was a sturdy and efficient machine, and bore the brunt of Bomber Command's night offensive against Germany.

US Grumman TBF Avenger (1941)

Type		three-seat carrier torpedo-bomber
Engine		Wright R-2600-8 14-cylinder air-cooled radial, 1,700-hp
Armament		one fixed ·3-inch, one flexible ·3-inch and one flexible ·5-inch Browning machine gun, plus 1,600 lbs of bombs or one 21-inch torpedo
Speed	271	mph at 12,000 feet
Climb	1,430	feet per minute initially
Ceiling	22,400	feet
Range	1,215	miles
Weight	10,080	lbs (empty)
	15,905	lbs (loaded)
Span	54	feet 2 inches
Length	40	feet
Height	16	feet 5 inches

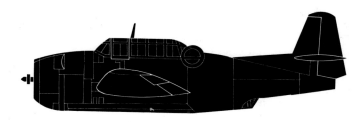

The Grumman Avenger was the US Navy's best torpedo-bomber of World War II, and was also able to pack a heavy punch with bombs and rockets. Nearly 1,000 of these versatile machines were supplied to the British Fleet Air Arm, with which they also had a distinguished career.

US Republic P-47 Thunderbolt (1941)

Type		single-seat escort fighter
Engine		Pratt & Whitney R-2800-59 18-cylinder air-cooled radial, 2,300-hp
Armament		eight ·5-inch Browning machine guns
Speed	433	mph at 30,000 feet
Climb	7	minutes 12 seconds to 15,000 feet
Ceiling	42,000	feet
Range	1,250	miles
Weight	9,900	lbs (empty)
	14,925	lbs (loaded)
Span	40	feet 9¾ inches
Length	35	feet 3¼ inches
Height	14	feet 1¾ inches

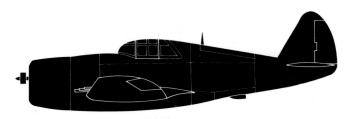

The magnificent Republic Thunderbolt was at the time of its introduction the largest and heaviest single-seat fighter in the world, and with eight .5-inch machine guns was very heavily armed. The all-round vision bubble canopy was introduced on the 47D. The type was also a formidable fighter-bomber.

US Boeing B-29 Superfortress (1942)

Type		ten-seat heavy bomber
Engines		four Wright R-3350 18-cylinder air-cooled radials, 2,200-hp each
Armament		eleven flexible ·5-inch Browning machine guns, plus up to 20,000 lbs of bombs
Speed	358	mph at 25,000 feet
Climb	38	minutes to 20,000 feet
Ceiling	31,850	feet
Range	3,250	miles
Weight	70,140	lbs (empty)
	124,000	lbs (loaded)
Span	141	feet 3 inches
Length	99	feet
Height	29	feet 7 inches

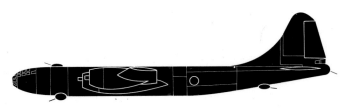

The Boeing Superfortress was designed to a USAAF requirement for a well-armed strategic bomber with excellent range. The design was exceptionally clean, with the engines closely cowled and conventional turrets, except that in the tail, replaced by remotely-controlled barbettes. With the elimination of Japanese air power, all defensive armament but the rear turret was often removed.

US Grumman F6F Hellcat (1942)

Type		single-seat carrier fighter and fighter-bomber
Engine		Pratt & Whitney R-2800-10W 18-cylinder air-cooled radial, 2,000-hp
Armament		six ·5-inch Browning machine guns, plus up to 2,000 lbs of bombs or six 5-inch rockets
Speed	386	mph at 17,300 feet
Climb	3,410	feet per minute initially
Ceiling	37,300	feet
Range	1,530	miles
Weight	9,153	lbs (empty)
	15,413	lbs (loaded)
Span	42	feet 10 inches
Length	33	feet 7 inches
Height	13	feet 1 inch

The Grumman Hellcat was a tubby naval fighter derived from the F4F Wildcat, and when it entered service in 1943, proved to be the first US aircraft in the Pacific capable of operating against the redoubtable Zero on anything like equal terms. Later models featured wing-mounted radar for night fighting, or provision for bombs or rockets for the fighter-bomber role. A further derivative, the F8F Bearcat, was about to enter service when war ended.

British Hawker Tempest (1942)

Type		single-seat fighter and fighter-bomber
Engine		Napier Sabre IIC 24-cylinder liquid-cooled inline, 2,180-hp
Armament		four 20-mm Hispano MK V cannon, plus 2,000 lbs of bombs or eight 60-lb rockets
Speed	426	mph at 18,500 feet
Climb	5	minutes to 15,000 feet
Ceiling	36,500	feet
Range	1,530	miles
Weight	9,000	lbs (empty)
	13,540	lbs (loaded)
Span	41	feet
Length	33	feet 8 inches
Height	16	feet 1 inch

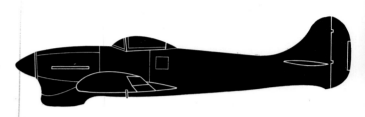

The Hawker Tempest, the culmination of Britain's land-based piston engined fighters, was built in two major marks: the Mark V with an inline engine, and the Mark II with a radial engine. The latter was too late to see wartime service. The Tempest V performed very ably in both the interceptor and ground-attack roles, in the latter proving a worthy successor to the Typhoon.

German Messerschmitt Me 262 (1942)

Type		single-seat fighter
Engines		two Junkers Jumo 004B-1 turbojets, 1,980-lbs static thrust each
Armament		four 3-cm MK108 cannon
Speed	˙540	mph at 19,685 feet
Climb	6	minutes 48 seconds to 19,685 feet
Ceiling	37,565	feet
Range	652	miles
Weight	8,378	lbs (empty)
	14,101	lbs (loaded)
Span	40	feet 11½ inches
Length	34	feet 9½ inches
Height	12	feet 7 inches

The Messerschmitt 262 was the world's first jet-powered operational fighter, and marked the beginning of a new era in fighter design. Although the Allies produced jet fighters of their own, they were essentially piston-engined in concept, while the swept wings of the Me 262 showed the true road ahead.

Russian Lavochkin La-7 (1943)

Type		single-seat fighter and fighter-bomber
Engine		Shvetsov ASh-82FNU 14-cylinder air-cooled radial, 1,775-hp
Armament		three 20-mm ShVAK cannon, plus up to 330 lbs of bombs
Speed	425	mph at 18,372 feet
Climb	4	minutes 27 seconds to 16,400 feet
Ceiling	34,448	feet
Range	394	miles
Weight	?	(empty)
	7,495	lbs (loaded)
Span	32	feet 2 inches
Length	27	feet 10½ inches
Height	9	feet 3 inches

The Lavochkin 7 exemplified all the salient features of Russian fighter design: careful development from earlier models (in this case the La-5), simple but clean aerodynamics, a powerful engine, good armament, and lack of unnecessary sophistication. This last meant that serviceability was high, and maintenance simple on the poor airfields the Russians had to use. Moreover, Russian fighters were the equal of most German and Allied machines.

Russian Mikoyan-Gurevich MiG-15 (1947)

Type		single-seat fighter
Engine		VK-1A turbojet, 6,990-lbs thrust with water injection
Armament		one 30-mm N and two 23-mm NS cannon, plus up to 1,100 lbs of bombs or rockets
Speed	746	mph at 10,000 feet
Climb	10,400	feet per minute initially
Ceiling	51,000	feet
Range	560	miles
Weight	11,085	lbs (loaded)
Span	33	feet 1 inch
Length	36	feet 3¼ inches
Height	11	feet 1¾ inches

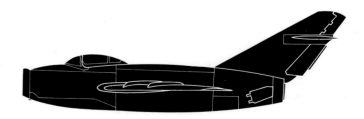

The MiG-15 was the Sabre's best opponent over Korea, and served in great numbers both with the Red Air Force and with the air forces of the Russian satellites. It had a better rate of climb and ceiling than the Sabre, as well as a tighter turn and superior speed.

British English Electric Canberra (1949)

Type		two-seater night interdictor or high-altitude bomber
Engines		two Rolls-Royce Avon Mark 109 turbojets, 7,400-lbs static thrust each
Armament		four 20-mm Hispano cannon and 3,000 lbs of bombs, or 6,000 lbs of bombs
Speed	541	mph at 40,000 feet
Ceiling	48,000	feet
Range	3,630	miles
Weight	56,250	lbs (loaded)
Span	63	feet 11½ inches
Length	65	feet 6 inches
Height	15	feet 8 inches
Climb	3,800	feet per minute initially

The English Electric Canberra was the first jet bomber to serve with the Royal Air Force, established several world records, and was the only British aircraft to have been built under licence in the United States since World War II until the Harrier. Many have also been exported to countries all over the world. The Canberra is a very clean design and has excellent manoeuvrability, sufficient to warrant one version, the B(I) Mark 8 and its derivatives, being fitted with a cannon armament for use in the interdiction role.

US North American F-86 Sabre (1947)

Type		single-seat fighter and fighter-bomber
Engine		General Electric J47-GE-13 turbojet, 5,200-lbs static thrust
Armament		six ·5-inch Browning machine guns, plus 2,000 lbs of bombs or sixteen 5-inch rockets
Speed	675	mph at 2,500 feet
Climb	7,630	feet per minute initially
Ceiling	48,300	feet
Range	785	miles
Weight	10,495	lbs (empty)
	16,357	lbs (loaded)
Span	37	feet 1 inch
Length	37	feet 6 inches
Height	14	feet 8 inches

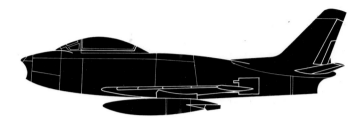

The North American Sabre was a classic postwar first-generation jet fighter, and proved its worth in the air over Korea in the early 1950s. By European and Russian standards, however, it was lacking in weight of armament, having only machine guns instead of cannon.

British Hawker Hunter (1951)

Type		single-seat fighter and ground attack aircraft
Engine		Rolls-Royce Avon Mk 203 turbojet, 10,000-lbs static thrust
Armament		four 30-mm Aden cannon, plus up to 2,000 lbs of bombs and various combinations of rockets
Speed	Mach 0·95	at 36,000 feet
Climb	7	minutes 30 seconds to 45,000 feet
Ceiling	51,500	feet
Range	1,650	miles
Weight	12,760	lbs (empty)
	24,000	lbs (loaded)
Span	33	feet 8 inches
Length	45	feet 10½ inches
Height	13	feet 2 inches

The Hawker Hunter was one of the classic jet aircraft designed after World War II, and proved the most successful subsonic jet fighter exported by Great Britain—over 400 in all, with another 460 built under licence. Early marks were intended as pure fighters, but later marks, developed as the basic design began to grow obsolescent, had dual capabilities as fighters and ground-attack machines.

US Lockheed F-104 Starfighter (1954)

Type		single-seat fighter-bomber
Engine		General Electric J79-GE-7 turbojet, 10,000-lbs static thrust (15,800-lbs with afterburning)
Armament		one 20-mm six-barrel Vulcan cannon, plus 2,000 lbs of bombs or two or four Sidewinder missiles
Speed	1,450	mph at 40,000 feet
Climb	40,000	feet per minute initially
Ceiling	55,000+	feet
Range	1,000+	miles
Weight	14,300	lbs (empty)
	23,590	lbs (loaded)
Span	21	feet 11 inches
Length	54	feet 9 inches
Height	13	feet 6 inches

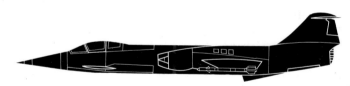

The Lockheed Starfighter was designed as a very high performance day interceptor fighter, and as such was built in limited numbers for use by the US Air Force. However, the design attracted much foreign interest, and the Starfighter has since been adapted to several other missions, the most important being ground-attack. Most of these later developments have been built under licence by manufacturers in Canada, Germany, Italy, Holland, Belgium, and Holland. It is also used by Pakistan, Turkey, Norway, and others.

Russian Mikoyan-Gurevich MiG-21 (1955)

Type		single-seat fighter
Engine		Tumansky RD-11 F300 turbojet, 13,000-lbs static thrust with afterburning
Armament		one 30-mm cannon, plus two K-13 AAMs or two pods with 16 55-mm rockets
Speed	Mach 2	at 45,000+ feet
Climb	30,000	feet per minute initially
Ceiling	65,000+	feet
Range	700	miles
Weight	12,100	lbs (empty)
	17,000	lbs (loaded)
Span	23	feet 5½ inches
Length	51	feet 8½ inches (including nose boom)
Height	14	feet 9 inches

The MiG-21 has been the standard fighter of the Soviet Union, its satellites, and allies throughout the 1960s and early 1970s, and is built under licence in Czechoslovakia and India. Main armament consists of two cannon and two air-to-air missiles, but other stores can be carried on a pylon under the fuselage. Several improved versions of the basic design have been produced, as well as an experimental STOL version with lift engines in the fuselage. It is supplemented at present by the Mach 3 MiG-23 fighter.

INDEX

INDEX

462

ACKNOWLEDGEMENTS

The publishers would like to thank the following individuals and organizations for their kind permission to reproduce the photographs in this book:

Army Air Corps 378 centre; *Army Aviation Centre* 433 above; *Army Public Relations Office* 365 below; *Associated Press* 187 below, 188 above, 372 above left, 378 below; *Chris Barker* 170–171; *Barnaby's Picture Library* 430–431; *Barratts Photo Press Ltd.* 267 above; *A. B. Bofors* 385 below; *BPC Picture Library* 186 below; *British Aircraft Corporation* 434–435 above; *British Museum (Fotomas Index)* 10 above; *Camera Press* back jacket, front jacket, 200, 200–201, 258–259, 313 below right, 369 above, 373 below right, 374–375, 377 below left, 391 above, 392 above left, 392 below left, 392 right, 393 above, 393 below, 394–395, 395 above; *Central Office of Information* 271 below left, 364, 382–383 above, 382 left; *Daily Telegraph Colour Library* 370, 374 above, 375 above; *William Gordon Davis* 81 below, 82 below, 83 right, 83 below, 84 above, 85 above left, 86 below, 87 centre right, 152, 164–165, 202, 203 centre, 203 below; *C. M. Dixon* 14 above right, 14 below right; *Mary Evans Picture Library* 16, 79; *Flight International* 86 above, 87 above, 87 below, 88 above right, 89 above, 153 above left, 153 centre right, 153 below, 156 above left, 158 above, 158 below right, 160 above, 160 below, 204 left, 204 right, 205 above, 205 above centre, 205 below centre, 206 left, 206 below right, 207, 333, 337 below, 340 above, 340 below, 340–341, 341 above, 341 centre, 344 above, 345 below, 358–359 below, 417 centre, 417 below, 420 below, 420–421, 421 above, 421 below, 431 below; *Fox Photos* 122 above, 412 centre; *General Dynamics* 402 above; *Heeresgeschichtles Museum, Vienna* 38–39; *John Hillelson Agency* 378 above; *Michael Holford* 14 left, 63 below, 409 above, 409 centre; *Anne Horton* 37 below, 49 centre, 56 below, 57, 60 above, 60 below left, 61 above, 61 below; *Robert Hunt Library* 2–3, 20 below, 128, 133 below, 134 below, 135 below, 136 below, 138, 139 below, 142, 184, 185 below, 188 below, 189 below, 194–195, 197 right, 201, 206–207 above, 208 below, 222, 228, 229, 230 above, 230 below, 232 above, 232 centre, 232 below, 233 above, 233 below, 240 above left, 241, 242 above, 242 below, 243, 245 above, 245 below, 248 above, 249, 250, 250–251, 251 above, 251 centre, 251 below, 252 above, 252 centre, 252 below, 253 above, 253 centre, 256 below, 257 above, 261 below left, 261 below right, 262 above, 262 below,

263 above, 263 below, 264, 265 centre right, 265 below right, 266 above, 267 centre, 270–271, 285 above, 289 centre, 302 above right, 303 above, 303 below right, 305 below, 308–309 above, 312, 313 above, 319 above left, 319 above right, 321 above, 324 above, 324 below, 325, 328–329, 357 above left, 357 above right, 357 centre, 357 below; *Illustrated London News* 59 centre right; *Imperial War Museum* front endpapers, 13 above, 13 below, 16 below, 22 above, 22 below, 24, 56 above, 63 above, 68 above, 72–73, 73 above, 74 above, 74 below, 75, 76, 77, 88–89, 92, 94, 95, 97 above left, 97 above right, 97 below, 102 below left, 136 above left, 140–141, 141 above, 141 below right, 143 above, 143 centre right, 144 centre, 144–145 above, 145 above right, 145 below, 148 above left, 149 above, 149 below, 150–151 above, 151 below right, 154 above, 155, 159 above left, 159 below, 162–163, 164 inset, 165 inset, 168 centre, 168 below, 169 above, 172, 173 above, 173 centre, 173 below, 176 left, 176 below right, 176–177, 192, 196 left, 196–197 above, 196–197 below, 198 above, 198 below, 205 below, 208 above centre, 212, 213, 215, 218 left, 218 right, 219 left, 219 above right, 219 below right, 220, 221 left, 221 right, 248 below, 270, 276 above, 277 below left, 286 above, 291, 292–293 below, 300–301 below, 302 below right, 303 below left, 305 centre, 316 below left, 316–317 below, 318–319, 320 above, 332 above, 336 above, 336 below, 337 above, 341 below, 345, 352–353, 353 above, 353 below, 354–355 above, 355 above, 355 centre, 356 above, 356 below, 358–359 above, 358 above, 358 below, 396; *Imperial War Museum/ BPC Picture Library* 240 above right; *Imperial War Museum/Robert Hunt Library* 125 below right, 137 below; *Imperial War Museum/Roxby Press* 436–437; *Keystone Press Agency* 180–181, 189 above, 199, 265 above, 308 below, 369 below, 377 below right, 390 above, 400–401, 404–405, 408, 410–411, 412 above; *Michael Leitch* 15, 64 above, 66–67 below; *Library of Congress* 11 above, 20–21, 25 above, 25 below, 29 above, 29 below, 32, 33 centre left, 33 above right, 39 below, 45 centre right, 47 below, 101, 102 above, 103 inset, 108 below, 117 above, 120–121 below, 120 above, 121 above, 193, 272 centre right, 272 below right, 273, 277 above left, 279 above, 281 centre, 284 below, 285 below, 293 below; *Mansell Collection* 16 above, 52 above right, 52–53 below, 72 above left, 80, 81 above, 82 above; *Ministry of Defence* 365 above, 409 below, 411 below, 412 below, 413, 429 below 434–435 below; *Ministry of Defence/Royal Navy* 402 centre, 403 above; *Musée de l'Air*

84–85, 85 above right, 154 below, 158 below left, 159 above right, 160–161, 168 above, 169 below, 424 below left, 424 below right; *National Army Museum* 20 above, 44–45, 45 above; *National Gallery (Michael Holford)* 54–55; *National Maritime Museum* 50–51, 50 below, 51 below left, 52 above left, 53 above, 55 above, 64–65, 68 centre, 68–69, 69 above, 304, 355 below; *National Maritime Museum (Michael Holford)* 62; *Novosti Press Agency* 17 above, 68 below, 185 above, 187 above, 203 above, 208 above, 208 below centre, 208–209, 237 below, 240 below, 253 below, 254, 305 above, 346–347 below, 346 above, 347 above left, 347 above right, 348 left, 348–349 above, 348–349 below, 381 above, 381 centre left, 381 centre right, 381 below, 415 below, 417 above, 418 below right, 419 below left, 425 above left, 425 above right, 432 below; *Pattern Room Collection, Enfield/ Chris Barker* 10 below, 11 below; *Pennsylvania Academy of Fine Arts* 30–31 above; *Sir Isaac Pitman & Sons Ltd.* 87 centre left, 88 above left; *Popperfoto* 6, 93, 135 above, 146–147, 150–151 below, 210–211, 225, 260, 301 above, 314–315, 316 above left, 316 above right, 317 above left, 317 above right, 320 below, 321 below, 363 above, 363 below, 366–367, 367 right, 405 above, 411 above, back endpapers; *R.A.C. Tank Museum, Bovington* 124, 129 above, 129 centre, 129 below, 180, 181 above, 186 above left, 186 centre, 266 centre, 266 below, 267 below, 368 above, 368 centre, 368 below, 372 above right, 373 below left, 384 above, 384 centre, 384 below, 385 above; *Radio Times Hulton Picture Library* 37 above, 38 below; *Rex Features* 428–429; *Ronan Picture Library* 78 left, 78 above right, 78 below right; *Science Museum* 48–49, 49 above, 51 below right; *Signal Magazine* 287; *Soldier Magazine* 382–383 below; *Spectrum* 331 above, 331 below, 354 below, 405–407, 407 above, 418 below left, 424–425, 431 above, 432; *Staatsbibliothek, Berlin* 17 below; *State of Israel Press Office* 373 above; *Syndication International* 379; *J. W. R. Taylor* 156–157 above, 156–157 below; *Ullstein Verlag* 286 below, 332 below; *U.S. Airforce* 397 below, 416–417, 418–419, 419 below right, 420 above, 424 above, 429 above centre, 429 above right, 433 below; *U.S. Army* 33 below, 41 below, 44 above, 103, 191 above, 191 centre, 269, 271 centre right, 276 below, 277 right, 289 above, 289 below, 290 above, 293 above, 297 below, 386–387, 387 above, 388, 389 above, 389 below, 390 below, 398, 399 below left; *U.S. National Archives* 8–9, 19 above, 19 below, 28, 33 above left, 40 above, 40 below,

40–41 above, 40–41 below, 41 above, 42 left, 42 right, 43, 46 above, 46 below, 47 above, 58–59 above, 66 above, 67 above, 100, 104 above, 104 centre, 104 below, 105 above, 105 below, 108 above left, 108 above right, 108–109 above, 109 below, 113 above, 113 below left, 113 below right, 116–117, 118–119 below, 119 above, 122 below, 190, 191 below, 268, 272 above left, 272 above right, 277 centre left, 280, 281 above, 281 below, 288–289 below, 290 below, 292 above, 297 above, 297 centre, 302 left, 397 above, 399 above left, 399 right, 429 above left; *U.S. Navy* 58–59 below, 195 above, 328 inset, 401 above, 405 below; *Valentine Museum* 30 below, 31 below; *Vickers Ltd.* 186 above right, 376; *H. Roger Viollet* 125 above, 125 below left, 130 above, 130 below, 131 above, 131 below right, 133 above, 134 above, 224 right; *Derrick E. Witty* 12 left, 12–13 right, 60 below right.